THE ROUTLEDGE HANDBOOK OF RELIGIONS AND GLOBAL DEVELOPMENT

This *Handbook* provides a cutting-edge survey of the state of research on religions and global development. Part 1 highlights critical debates that have emerged within research on religions and development, particularly with respect to theoretical, conceptual and methodological considerations, from the perspective of development studies and its associated disciplines. Parts 2 to 6 look at different regional and national development contexts and the place of religion within these. These parts integrate and examine the critical debates raised in Part 1 within empirical case studies from a range of religions and regions. Different religions are situated within actual locations and case studies, thus allowing a detailed and contextual understanding of their relationships to development to emerge. Part 7 examines the links between some important areas within development policy and practice where religion is now being considered, including:

- faith-based organizations and development
- public health, religion and development
- human rights, religion and development
- global institutions and religious engagement in development
- sustainable development, climate change and religion
- economic development and religion
- religion, development and fragile states
- development and faith-based education.

Taking a global approach, the *Handbook* covers Africa, Latin America, South Asia, East and South–East Asia, and the Middle East. It is essential reading for students and researchers in development studies and religious studies, and is highly relevant to those working in area studies, as well as a range of disciplines, from theology, anthropology and economics to geography, international relations, politics and sociology.

Emma Tomalin is the Director of the Centre for Religion and Public Life and a Senior Lecturer in Religious Studies at the University of Leeds, UK.

"Comprehensive, clear and cutting-edge, this volume offers the first truly global survey of the intertwining of religions with development. All the contributions are authoritative, up-to-date and firmly rooted in command of theoretical ideas and case studies. It should be essential reading for researchers, policy makers and practitioners concerned with development." – *James A. Beckford, University of Warwick, UK*

"This new Handbook is the first to present an extensive overview of an important emerging subject – religion in development. Combining an interdisciplinary approach with case studies from all parts of the world, this volume makes a unique contribution to our scholarly knowledge. I recommend it to academics and practitioners alike." – *Gerrie ter Haar, Erasmus University Rotterdam, The Netherlands*

"This book represents a remarkable achievement. It not only offers a wide and comprehensive introduction to religion and development in theory and practice, it also propels the study of religion into a more truly global frame of reference. It will be read with great profit by students, academics, practitioners and policymakers alike." – *Linda Woodhead, Lancaster University, UK*

"A valuable and comprehensive overview of what has become a mature field of study. Twenty-nine carefully researched chapters demonstrate that religion can no longer be pushed to the margins in analyses of economic development. The case studies in this volume will define the field and inspire future research." – *Erica Bornstein, University of Wisconsin-Milwaukee, USA*

THE ROUTLEDGE HANDBOOK OF RELIGIONS AND GLOBAL DEVELOPMENT

Edited by Emma Tomalin

Routledge
Taylor & Francis Group

LONDON AND NEW YORK

First published 2015 by Routledge

2 Park Square, Milton Park, Abingdon, Oxon OX14 4RN
711 Third Avenue, New York, NY 10017, USA

Routledge is an imprint of the Taylor & Francis Group, an informa business

First issued in paperback 2017

British Library Cataloguing-in-Publication Data
A catalogue record for this book is available from the British Library

Library of Congress Cataloging-in-Publication Data
The Routledge handbook of religions and global development/edited by Emma Tomalin.
pages cm.
Includes bibliographical references and index.
1. Economic development—Religious aspects. 2. Economic development—Religious aspects—Case studies. 3. Sustainable development—Religious aspects.
4. Sustainable development—Religious aspects—Case studies. I. Tomalin, Emma, editor of compilation. II. Title: Handbook of religions and global development.
HD75.R68 2015
338.9—dc23
2014026988

ISBN: 978-0-415-83636-4 (hbk)
ISBN: 978-1-138-07075-2 (pbk)

Typeset in Bembo
by Swales & Willis Ltd, Exeter, Devon, UK

CONTENTS

Contents

Contents

FIGURES

TABLES

CONTRIBUTORS

Sigurd Bergmann is Professor in Religious Studies at the Department of Philosophy and Religious Studies at the Norwegian University of Science and Technology in Trondheim. Ongoing projects investigate the relation of space or place and religion and 'religion in climatic change'.

Barbara Bompani is Senior Lecturer in African Development, Centre of African Studies, School of Social and Political Science, the University of Edinburgh. Her work has focused on the intersection between religion, politics and development in South Africa.

Tamsin Bradley is Reader in International Development Studies at the University of Portsmouth. She has published extensively on religion, gender and violence against women.

Ezra Chitando is Theology Consultant on HIV and AIDS for the World Council of Churches Ecumenical HIV and AIDS Initiative in Africa and Professor of History and Phenomenology of Religion at the University of Zimbabwe.

Gregory Deacon is a British Academy Postdoctoral Research Fellow in African Studies at the University of Oxford and a Junior Research Fellow of St Antony's College. His work focuses on Kenyan, Pentecostal and Evangelical Christianity, looking at its socioeconomic role, political evolution, and significance for national identity and citizenship.

Jill DeTemple is Associate Professor of Religious Studies at Southern Methodist University in Dallas, Texas. Her research interests include theory and method in the study of religion, international development, and Latin America.

Monica Lindberg Falk is Associate Professor of Social Anthropology and Vice-Director at the Centre for East and South-East Asian Studies at Lund University, Sweden. Her research interests include gender, Buddhism, anthropology of disaster, and social change in South-East Asia. Her scholarship includes extensive fieldwork in Thailand.

Philip Fountain is a Senior Research Fellow at the Asia Research Institute, National University of Singapore. He received his doctorate in anthropology from the Australian National University. His current research includes work on Christian development actors, religion and disaster relief, and political theologies of development.

Dena Freeman is a Visiting Fellow in the Department of Anthropology at the London School of Economics. She is a specialist on Southern Ethiopia and her research interests are the dynamics of cultural transformation, Pentecostalism and development, and wellbeing.

Paul Freston is a sociologist of religion. He is the CIGI Chair in Religion and Politics in Global Context at the Balsillie School of International Affairs and Wilfrid Laurier University, Canada. He is also Professor Colaborador on the post-graduate programme in sociology at the Universidade Federal de São Carlos, Brazil. He has worked mainly on religion and politics, the growth of Evangelicalism in the global South, and questions of religion and globalization.

Tara Hefferan is Visiting Assistant Professor, Anthropology Department, Grand Valley State University, Michigan, USA and an applied cultural anthropologist with interests in faith-based organizations, midwifery, and power and knowledge.

Rana Jawad is a Lecturer in Social Policy at the University of Bath. She has extensive research experience on the social and development policies of the MENA region, with particular focus on the role of religion. She is the founder and current convener of the MENA Social Policy Network.

Marie Juul Petersen is a Researcher at the Danish Institute for Human Rights, focusing on topics related to development, human rights and religion.

Seth D. Kaplan is a Professorial Lecturer in the Paul H. Nitze School of Advanced International Studies (SAIS) at Johns Hopkins University and an adviser to organizations working on transitions, governance, Middle East issues, and poverty reduction. He runs the Fragile States website.

Kirsteen Kim is Professor of Theology and World Christianity at Leeds Trinity University. She has been a consultant to the World Council of Churches (2004–13) and to the University of Birmingham project on Religions and Development (2006–07), among others. She was a member of the council of the British Association for Korean Studies in 2007–12 and is a contributing editor to the *Journal of Korean Religions*.

Nida Kirmani is Assistant Professor of Sociology at the Lahore University of Management Sciences. Her research interests include the intersections between religion, gender and development, with a particular focus on the gendered impacts of urban conflicts in South Asia.

André Laliberté is Full Professor at the School of Political Studies, University of Ottawa, and a Research Fellow at Purdue University's Center for Religion and Chinese Society, and at the Groupe Sociétés, Religions et Laïcités in Paris. He has written on religious issues and politics in Taiwan and China. He received his doctoral degree from the University of British Columbia in 1999.

Katherine Marshall is Senior Fellow at Georgetown University's Berkley Center for Religion, Peace and World Affairs, and Visiting Professor in the School of Foreign Service. She spent 35 years at the World Bank as an operational manager in several regions and then as counsellor to the Bank's president on ethics, values, and faith in development.

Amin Mohseni-Cheraghlou is an Assistant Professor of Economics at American University, Washington, DC. His research and teaching interests are development macroeconomics, Islamic economics and finance, social economics, and political economy of the Middle East and North Africa. He is also part of the core team of World Bank staff working on the *Global Financial Development Report*, a fairly new annual report published by the World Bank Group.

David Mosse is Professor of Social Anthropology at SOAS, University of London. He worked for Oxfam as Representative for South India in Bangalore, as a social development adviser and consultant for DFID, and other international development organizations.

Laurie A. Occhipinti is Professor of Anthropology at Clarion University of Pennsylvania. Her research interests include faith-based organizations, economic development, indigenous peoples, and religion in Latin America.

Jill Olivier is based at the University of Cape Town in the Health Policy and Systems Division. She is the Research Director for the International Religious Health Assets Programme, lectures on health systems, and coordinates related research projects. Prior to this she was based in Washington, DC as a consultant for the World Bank with a focus on faith-based health service delivery and community response to HIV/AIDS. She has a background in the social sciences, and her current publication focus is on health systems research, the interface of religion and public health, community engagement, interdisciplinary research and multisectoral collaboration.

Stephen Plant is Dean and Runcie Fellow at Trinity Hall, Cambridge, and Affiliated Lecturer in the Cambridge University Faculty of Divinity. In 2008 he was Visiting Professor at the Freie Universität in Berlin, in 2010 Visiting Professor at Flensburg Universität, and in 2014 Northey Lecturer at the Centre for Theology and Ministry in the Melbourne University of Divinity.

Carole Rakodi is Emeritus Professor in the International Development Department at Birmingham University. She was the Director of the DFID-funded Religions and Development Research Programme (2005–10).

Daromir Rudnyckyj is an Associate Professor in the Department of Anthropology at the University of Victoria, Canada. His current research examines the globalization of Islamic finance and analyses efforts to make Kuala Lumpur the 'New York of the Muslim World'.

Amy Stambach is Professor of Education at the University of Oxford. Her research and teaching interests focus on theoretical and methodological issues in comparative and international education, theories of social and educational change, and the anthropological study of education.

Mariz Tadros is a Fellow at the Institute of Development Studies, University of Sussex, specializing in the politics and human development of the Middle East. Areas of focus include democratization, Islamist politics, gender, sectarianism, human security, and religion and development.

Emma Tomalin is a Senior Lecturer in Religious Studies at the University of Leeds and is the Director of the Centre for Religion and Public Life. Generally her research interests are focused in the areas of gender and religion, religion and development, and religion and environmentalism. She is co-editor of the Routledge Research in Religion and Development series.

Juan Marco Vaggione is Researcher at the National Research Council (CONICET) and Professor in Sociology at the Faculty of Law and Social Sciences, National University of Cordoba, Argentina. His background is in law (doctorate, National University of Córdoba) and sociology (Ph.D., New School for Social Research).

Adriaan van Klinken is Lecturer in African Christianity at the University of Leeds. His research focuses on issues of religion, gender and sexuality in contemporary Africa, particularly focusing on Pentecostalism. He currently works on a project examining public religion and the politicization of homosexuality in Zambia.

Daniel H. Weiss is the Polonsky–Coexist Lecturer in Jewish Studies in the Faculty of Divinity at the University of Cambridge. His research examines the intersection between philosophical thought and classical Jewish texts. He is actively involved in various forms of inter-faith dialogue and research via the Cambridge Interfaith Programme and the practice of Scriptural Reasoning.

ACKNOWLEDGEMENTS

Editing this volume has been tremendously rewarding as well as challenging. First of all I would like to acknowledge the hard work of each of the contributors in producing chapters of such high quality about topics of global significance to both the academic and non-academic worlds. I am also tremendously grateful to each of the anonymous reviewers of the chapters for providing helpful, detailed and timely feedback that has sharpened and deepened the contributions within this volume. Particular thanks also need to be extended to Professors Carole Rakodi and Katherine Marshall, who constituted my editorial board for this publication. Both of them gave much of their time to discussing the volume with me and reading and commenting on drafts. Finally, I must acknowledge the quiet support of my husband Andy and my three sons – Reuben, Toby and Theo – who have been more or less patient with my extended writing absences in the final month of editing.

1

INTRODUCTION

Emma Tomalin

Introduction: why 'religions and global development'?

Significant research on the topic of 'religions and global development' has begun to emerge only relatively recently. Over the past decade or so there has been a noticeable shift within some areas of international development policy, practice and research to include religion as a relevant factor. For instance, the views of religious leaders have been invited on key initiatives such as the implementation of the United Nations Millennium Development Goals, development partners such as DFID and USAID seem more open to engaging with and funding faith-based organizations (FBOs), development studies journals are witnessing an upturn in the publication of research articles that deal with the relationships between religions and international development, and a good number of monographs and edited volumes on the topic have been published (e.g. Tyndale 2006; Haynes 2007; Clarke and Jennings 2008; Deneulin 2009; ter Haar 2011; Barnett and Stein 2012; Carbonnier 2013; Tomalin 2013). However, this interest needs a broader context. Beyond examining how western development organizations have engaged with religion, research on 'religions and global development' needs to take into account how governments of nations in the Global South as well as communities within those nations engage with the nexus between religion and development in ways that reflect their own socio-political context. It is important not to view 'development' purely in the light of conceptions advanced by the 'global aid business'.

While religious actors have made significant contributions to various sorts of 'development' work in practice, until very recently this was largely ignored by major international development players, as well as by the academic disciplines that contribute to development studies. This can be partially explained by the assumption held by many that religion is largely opposed to economic development and that, as societies modernize, they will become less religious (and thus religion will deserve less priority). However, such simplistic theories of modernization and secularization have been critiqued and indeed thoroughly debunked. Rather than disappearing or completely diminishing in significance, it is now widely recognized that the significant and continuing role of religion in public life (as well as in people's private lives), whether it is increasing or simply recognized, demands that the relationship between religion and society, even if it is both complex and controversial, needs to be taken seriously. It must be recognized from the outset that the relationships are both positive and negative: although religious traditions have

1

contributed greatly to humanitarian, relief and development work for many centuries, they are also implicated in sustaining different sorts of injustice, from violence to gender discrimination. Whichever the case they are vitally important.

The first major global initiative in this area – bringing together development actors, faith groups and academics – was an initiative by former World Bank president James Wolfensohn and former Archbishop of Canterbury Lord Carey of Clifton. They organized a series of conferences of senior development institution executives and faith leaders (in London in 1998, Washington, DC in 1999, Canterbury, England in 2002, and Dublin in 2005) (Clarke 2008: 2). Wolfensohn and Carey created a dedicated organization to support the effort, the World Faiths Development Dialogue (WFDD), in 1998, which was to respond to 'the opportunities and concerns of many faith leaders and development practitioners who saw untapped potential for partnerships' (Development Dialogue on Values and Ethics, n.d.). After both had retired, a further meeting was held in Accra in 2009, but the high-level support for the effort faltered thereafter. In the early 2000s WFDD was a UK charity but was reorganized as a US non-governmental organization in 2006, and currently operates in Washington, DC, based at the Berkley Center for Religion, Peace and World Affairs at Georgetown University. In the early years WFDD worked closely with a World Bank unit, the (now defunct) Development Dialogue on Values and Ethics (DDVE), which led both policy analysis and research from within the World Bank (publications include Marshall and Marsh 2003; Marshall and Keough 2004; Marshall and Van Saanen 2007; Osorio and Wodon 2014; Wodon 2014).

Several other international organizations have also drawn attention to the importance of understanding religion and engaging with religious actors around development goals. The UNFPA, for instance, now has decades of experience working with faith-based organizations and in 2009 produced 'Guidelines for Engaging Faith-Based Organizations as Cultural Agents of Change'. Beyond this, it has a number of publications that explore the role of religion and culture in its work (2005, 2007, 2008). The UNFPA also organized a network of faith organizations and a UN inter-agency working group. More recently, a Joint Learning Initiative on Faith and Local Communities aims to bring together academics, development practitioners and faith groups around the goal of working to 'increase the quality and quantity of robust, practical evidence on the pervasive, but poorly understood and uncharted, role of local faith communities (LFCs) in community health and development' (Joint Learning Initiative on Faith and Local Communities, n.d.).

A good number of chapters in this *Handbook* examine the engagement at the level of governments with religion and development. Laliberté, for instance, in Chapter 16, looks at religion and development in China, where, contrary to the earlier avoidance of religion, a policy and legal 'opinion' was issued in February 2012, 'by a number of Party and state organs, about the desirability for religious organizations to deliver social services and serve the public interest' (p. 239). At the level of Northern governments the engagement between religion and development has also attracted interest. In the USA, as well as a number of European settings, the role of religion in 'development cooperation' is beginning to be taken more seriously. In the US the rise of the 'religious right' since the 1980s and reactions after 9/11 have both contributed to a greater focus on the role of 'faith' in society, including increased funding for FBOs. In 2001 the Center for Faith-Based and Community Initiatives (CFBCI) was established at USAID 'to create a level playing field for faith and community based organizations to compete for USAID programs' (USAID, n.d.; see the treatment of this in Stambach, Chapter 29). In Europe also, a shift towards taking religion more seriously in government agendas as well as academic research is noticeable. Over the past decade development partners have increasingly chosen to support the work of FBOs. The USA has gone furthest, with George W. Bush, during his presidency, almost doubling funding to 'faith-based' groups, from 10.5 per cent of aid in 2001 to 19.9 per cent in 2005 (James 2009: 5). In the UK, the Department for International Development (DFID)'s 2009 White Paper promised to double funding to FBOs (2009: 5), reflecting 'recognition' of the 'unique contribution that they can make in both delivering development on the ground, and connecting with communities here and abroad' (DFID 2009: 134). More recently, DFID has launched a new 'Principles Paper' to guide its collaboration with faith groups, underscoring the key principles of the partnership between faith groups and DFID as transparency, mutual respect and understanding (DFID 2012; Williams 2012).

While many in the global development community are more likely these days to think about religion as a topic that is relevant to their work, reflecting broader social, cultural and political shifts that have thrust religion back into the public sphere, decades (even centuries) of neglect of religion in public life in policy arenas, coupled with a fear of and even negative feelings about religion, have meant that many development policy makers and practitioners are poorly equipped to deal with religion when they encounter it. Certainly levels of religious literacy are low, both in terms of knowledge about the beliefs and practices embodied within different religious traditions and also in terms of how 'religion' is manifested in different settings in ways that do not match the western Christianized view of what a religion should be (this is discussed below). Others have been critical that in bringing religion and development together there is a pernicious instrumentalism, where development policy makers and agencies are guilty of picking and choosing which types of religion to engage with (Deneulin 2009). For instance, development donors are seen to be more likely to seek engagement with organizations that express their faith 'passively' than those that obviously combine their development work with activities that aim to gain converts (Clarke 2008).

Thus, while many welcome this 'turn to religion', others are more cautious, especially where engagement with religious leaders or organizations may risk undermining progressive development goals such as gender equality (Pearson and Tomalin 2008; Tadros 2011; Tomalin 2011). The 'resurgence of religion' in recent decades has had a marked impact on women's rights globally, and this is something that the international development community needs to be acutely attuned to (Bayes and Tohidi 2001). So this is not only a new field of academic study but also one that deals with controversial and contested issues and debates.

In response to such shifts, a new and exciting teaching and research agenda has emerged in recent years, which is concerned with the interactions between 'religions and global development'. This topic has attracted funding from major bodies (e.g. DFID in the UK and the Henry R. Luce Foundation in the USA). In the UK, between 2005 and 2010, DFID funded a large £3.5 million research programme based at the University of Birmingham (Religions and Development Research Programme n.d.; Stambach 2005; Clarke 2007). In Switzerland (Holenstein 2005), Scandinavia and the Netherlands, such reflection is also under way. In the Netherlands, for instance, The Knowledge Centre Religion and Development was established by the Oikos Foundation, Interchurch Organization for Development Cooperation (ICCO) and Institute for Social Studies in the Hague, and the Ministry of Foreign Affairs has also shown marked interest in faith and development (Knowledge Centre Religion and Development, n.d.).

The discussion so far has established that the topic of 'religions and global development' is of increasing salience for development studies, policy and practice. In the next section of this chapter I will also argue that this is an important and emerging area for the study of religion that builds on existing critical approaches and theories. I will introduce some important conceptual and theoretical debates relevant to this area of research, including those that examine the impact of modernization and globalization on religion in contemporary societies and the implications of the post-secular for how we view the relationships between religions and global development. In the final section I will give an outline of the book's structure and an overview of the content of the individual sections and chapters.

From modernization to globalization: religion and development in a post-secular era

As Rakodi discusses in Chapter 2, modernization theory underpinned the 'belief that development would (and should) take the form of a unilinear path towards a commonly accepted and desired future' (p. 17) but also that secularization would occur as an inevitable part of the modernizing development processes that were set in place after the Second World War. The beginnings of this modern development project signalled a positive and some would say even evangelical spirit (see Fountain, Chapter 6) about the benefits that modernization could bring to the poor and marginalized across the world, as well as the central role that western governments would play in bringing this about. Truman's famous Inaugural Address in 1949 expresses such a global vision, where 'we must embark on a bold new program for making the benefits of our scientific advances and industrial progress available for the improvement and growth of underdeveloped areas' (Rist 2002: 71). Roosevelt's 'Four Freedoms Speech' (the 1941 State of the Union Address) also captured this mood in proposing the four freedoms that everyone should enjoy: freedom of speech; freedom of worship; freedom from want; and freedom from fear. Subsequent reflections suggest that freedom of religion as Roosevelt saw it at the time, while an important principle, focused on the privatized religion that was compatible with the First Amendment to the Constitution, and not the public styles of religiosity found across the globe, which modernization theory suggested were likely to get in the way of progress and development.

This focus on secularization – as an inevitable part of the modernizing development process – has been critiqued not only for reflecting a western normative position but also for going against the evidence. Bompani, in Chapter 7, highlights two assumptions regarding the role of religion in people's lives in Africa and other parts of the Global South: first, that 'religion will wither and die as Africa develops' and, second, that 'religion is antithetical to development and progress' (p. 101). However, rather than withering away, religion seems to be growing in strength in some parts of the globe, both rich and poor, and theories of secularization now appear to be simplistic and limited in their ability to account for the perseverance or even resurgence of religion. Nor can religion be so easily associated with forces that work against economic development. For example, as Freeman (Chapter 8) and Freston (Chapter 10) both point out, Pentecostalism and its prosperity gospel suggest a significant role for religion in Africa and Latin America in boosting economic success.

Debates about the 'global resurgence of religion' have been building momentum since the 1980s, if not earlier (Thomas 2005), and of particular interest for foreign policy and development actors has been the wave of religio-political movements that have sprung up, many apparently threatening secular liberal democratic values, including human rights. In the wake of the Iranian Islamic revolution of 1979, the following decades have witnessed many examples of religiously inspired social and political action across the globe – from the rise of nationalist Hindu politics in India and of Islamic political parties in Pakistan (see Tomalin, Chapter 13) to the watershed event of 9/11 (Thomas 2005). However, in addition to such particularistic and conservative styles of religiously based politics, religious actors have also responded in ways that are ecumenical and liberal (Beyer 1994). These actors have formed or joined movements based on freedom, tolerance, individualism and other globalized values, such as gender, environmental or human rights. Examples in this volume include liberation theology (see Plant and Weiss, Chapter 4), rights-based approaches to development (see Juul Petersen, Chapter 24) and the modern environmental movement (see Bergmann, Chapter 26).

Thus, globalization has given rise to the emergence of diverse styles of religiosity that were not predicted by modernization theory. While classical modernization theory can be seen as unilinear and ethnocentric, Beyer (2007) suggests that we look to theories of globalization ('both the compression of the world and the intensification of consciousness of the world' (Robertson 1992: 8)) to describe and explain these contemporary religious expressions (see also Freston, Chapter 10):

> Modernization temporalized its universalism: eventually all would/could become modern. Globalization spatializes it: the local has to come to terms with the global. It (re)constitutes itself in the way that it does this. The reverse side of this mutual relation is that the global cannot be global except as plural versions of the local. Hence globalization is always also glocalization (Robertson 1995), the global expressed in the local and the local as the particularization of the global.
>
> (Beyer 2007: 98)

Rather than the modernist ways of thinking about religion (i.e. in terms of secularization or privatization) becoming completely irrelevant, Beyer (2007) argues that these are subordinated by the presence of religious diversity. As demonstrated throughout this *Handbook*, in modern global societies we find religion that is traditional and conservative as well as that which is modern and liberal, religion that is institutionalized as well as that which is not, religion that is publicly influential as well as that which is privatized, and 'religion that is specifically enacted as religion' and other social forms that may have religious functions (Beyer 2007: 100). Thus, globalization has allowed diverse manifestations of religions to flourish rather than dwindle, as it was presumed they would under the influence of the spread of western secular values.

Globalization is a recent concept, only arising in academic circles in the 1980s, and referring specifically to the rapid changes that occurred during the twentieth century as a result of technological advances in travel and communications. Despite precedents in the so-called 'age of discovery' and the colonization of territories in Africa and Asia by European nations since the seventeenth century, which led to a rapid increase in knowledge about other parts of the globe and diverse cultures and religions, there are important differences between the earlier imperialist projects of the colonial period and contemporary processes of globalization. Apart from being more rapid and deeply penetrating across localities, whereas imperialist projects are characterized by the domination by a more powerful actor of a less powerful one (where the weaker actor has less impact on the stronger), globalization cannot be viewed as a one-way process – it is multidirectional, with the travel of ideas and products no longer being dominated by a North–South vector, and instead South–North and South–South influences are increasingly salient. Stambach draws attention to this in Chapter 29 with respect to the role that neo-Confucian ethics play in motivating Chinese development policy in Africa.

There has nonetheless been much debate about whether or not globalization is good or bad for development, and whether it is likely to stimulate greater equality and democracy or instead fragmentation and the growth of inequality. The truth is that it works in both directions. Thus, while globalization has brought many benefits to poorer regions of the globe, including a widening of opportunities through education and vastly improved health care systems, as well as the possibility of realizing human rights and democracy, this is not uniform. 'Economic globalization' – the 'increasing interdependence of world economies as a result of the growing scale of cross-border trade of commodities and services, flow of international capital and wide and rapid spread of technologies' (Shangquan 2010: 1) – is a good example of the way that globalization pulls in both directions. While as more countries are brought into global markets overall their economies have grown, the impact on the poorest is mixed and, as Huwart and Verdier point out, 'in the last 20 years, rapid globalization has occurred alongside a worldwide decrease in extreme poverty. . . . These numbers owe a lot to China's good results. . . . Some world regions have become poorer. Comparatively speaking, the poorest country in 2011 was poorer than the poorest country in 1980' (2013; see also Piketty 2014).

While the effects of globalization are uneven and unpredictable, what we can say is that it is not leading to a more unified global culture and, as Eisenstadt has argued, 'the actual developments in modern societies have refuted the homogenizing and hegemonic assumptions of this Western program of modernity' (2000: 1). Instead he proposed the idea of 'multiple modernities', 'a story of continual constitution and reconstitution of a multiplicity of cultural programs' (2000: 2). Thus, what is meant by 'modern' or 'modernity' now has to be viewed apart from the western European version, and what exactly we mean by 'modern' as opposed to 'contemporary' for instance can be difficult to ascertain. As Rakodi points out in Chapter 2, 'critics problematize the tendency to take modern to mean contemporary, meaning that everything is modern and the concept loses its analytical value' (p. 29). However, specifically in using the word 'modern' – in the sense of 'modernization' – we imply a process of becoming better and improving upon how things were in the past but not necessarily along the lines of the classical western version of the theory. For our purposes the significant point is that the view that a particular style of modernization is inevitable as societies 'develop' and that a marker of this will be the decline of religion as a public force is no longer taken for granted in the way that it once was. As Thomas writes, 'what if the global resurgence of religion can no longer be interpreted within the traditional categories of social theory?' (2005: 44), and he suggests instead that we need to adopt a 'postmodern' frame of reference:

> What a postmodern perspective opens up is the possibility that there may be other ways of being 'modern', making 'progress', or being 'developed'. Although postmodernity can mean a lot of things, in this sense it suggests that rather than there only being one path to modernity – Westernization, there may be multiple paths, 'multiple modernities', or multiple ways of being modern appropriate to the different cultural and religious traditions in the modern developing world.
>
> (2005: 45)

However, as Freston warns in Chapter 10, this should not be 'a postmodern celebration of diversity which argues that any normative truth claims are to be censured as divisive' but, in order to take religious pluralism seriously (and to find ways of integrating it meaningfully into social and economic programmes), there is a need to accept that 'real pluralism includes clashing normative claims' (p. 142). The failure of traditional categories of social theory to accommodate religious pluralism has given rise to calls for a 'new paradigm' in the sociology of religion (Warner 1993; Berger 2014). Whereas the 'old paradigm' considered that religious pluralism would eventually lead to the demise of religion as there was no longer one overarching 'sacred canopy', the 'new paradigm' deals with two types of pluralism: the existence of different religious discourses and of secular discourses alongside religious discourses (Berger 2014).

Another way of viewing this is in terms of the existence of 'multiple modernities' within which 'religions are usually considered one element that can account for different pathways to modernity' (Rosati and Stoeckl 2012: 2). Thus, we cannot necessarily delink becoming 'modern' and being religious in the way that early theories of modernization insisted that we should. Although a number of chapters in this volume demonstrate the ways in which religions can hold people back from development and progress, others demonstrate that religions can play a crucial and determining role. Rudnyckyj, in Chapter 27, for instance, examines how Islam plays a role in simulating economic development within a Javanese steel company. And Mohseni-Cheraghlou demonstrates in Chapter 20 how people in the MENA region are less likely to be 'financially included' (i.e. have bank accounts) if there are no Islamic banking facilities available to them.

Widespread religious diversity, in both the global North and the global South, has also led to the idea that we are now living in a 'post-secular' age. However, debates about the 'post-secular' go beyond a descriptive proposition about the fact that 'religion continues to assert itself' (Habermas 2006: 258), but, as Rosati and Stoeckl (2012) argue, these debates also have a normative dimension where 'there is a need . . . to find more just ways of accommodating religious claims in liberal institutions' (2012: 3). Habermas advocates a 'complementary learning process, [where] both sides can . . . then take seriously each other's contributions to controversial themes in the public sphere' (2006: 258). While for this to happen there needs to be a reflexivity and a will for dialogue on both sides, which is not always a given, the crucial point here is that in a post-secular society we are not facing 'de-secularization' but instead (resonating with Berger's 'new paradigm') a situation where 'the secular and the religious are part of the same field' and 'interact dialectically' (Rosati and Stoeckl 2012: 4).

This debate about the post-secular is also relevant to thinking about the relationships between religions and global development. Deneulin and Bano, for instance, are critical of the way in which secular development actors have engaged with religion instrumentally and on their terms (2009). Instead they suggest that because religions are holistic – they encompass the whole lives of the believer – then the international development community should deal with them with holistically rather than picking and choosing which parts they like and which they do not. Exactly how development actors are to negotiate this terrain, however, is far from clear, but dialogue and Habermas's idea of a 'complementary learning process' could do much to mitigate some of the tensions that currently exist and that arise as a result of rigid views existing across the religious–secular divide. However, what does the relationship between religion and development in a post-secular age look like? In order to answer this question we first need to look at how understandings of religion and the secular have been shaped by particular historical processes that are now being challenged by thinking about multiple modernities and post-secularism.

Religion and development in a post-secular age

The idea of a distinction between the religious and the secular is a marked feature of a secular age, where religion is essentially relegated to the private sphere. This conceptual split between the secular and the religious can be traced to the era of the Protestant Reformation in the sixteenth century, which removed the all-encompassing role of the Catholic Church. Religion did not disappear but became reconfigured as it was divorced from the state. This was also an era of colonial expansion and missionary activity, and being able to identify religions in new locations became crucial. As Asad writes, it is at this point that we find 'the earliest systematic attempts at producing a universal definition of religion . . . in terms of beliefs (about a supreme power), practices (its ordered worship), and ethics (a code of conduct based on rewards and punishments after this life) – said to exist in all societies' (1993: 40). This emphasis on belief was also a sign of the times, where increasingly it was important that 'religion could be conceived as a set of propositions to which believers gave assent, and which could therefore be judged and compared as between different religions and as against natural science' (Asad 1993: 41).

Scholars since the 1960s have questioned the idea of the existence of discrete 'world religions' that are differentiated from one another according to the beliefs they promote. As Wilfred Cantwell Smith famously wrote:

> The term 'Hinduism' is, in my judgment, a particularly false conceptualisation, one that is conspicuously incompatible with any adequate understanding of the religious outlook of Hindus. . . . [T]he classical Hindus were inhibited by no lack of sophistication or self-consciousness. They thought about what we call religious questions profusely and with critical analysis. . . . [T]hey could not think of Hinduism because that is the name we give to a totality whatever it might be that they thought, or did, or thought worth doing.
>
> (1991 [1962]: 61)

While the term 'Hinduism' is used today, Smith and others have argued that prior to the late 1700s there was no such thing as a 'world religion' called 'Hinduism'. This is not to imply that a new religion as such was formed, but instead to draw attention to the ways in which the colonial 'orientalist' scholars, missionaries and administrators gave a name ('Hinduism') to the totality of diverse practices found in India followed by the majority of the population (and that were not perceived to be associated with other religions). Similar processes can also be demonstrated for Sikhism and Buddhism (Almond 1988; Oberoi 1994). Moreover, in defining 'Hinduism', the beliefs and practices associated with the priestly Brahmin caste (e.g. the elite Sanskrit tradition) were focused upon rather than the colloquial village or popular 'religion' that most people actually engaged in. Popular religion was generally regarded as an aberration, a corruption of an authentic religious tradition that reflected a golden age of human civilization (e.g. the religion of the Aryan authors of the Vedas, the most ancient 'Hindu' texts). Thus, it has been argued that Hinduism was 'invented' by outsiders and then defined (i.e. in terms of focusing on texts and belief) in a manner that did not reflect its actual lived reality but rather reflected the Christian idea of what a religion should look like.

Therefore, when we attempt to define what a religion is in terms of substantive cross-cultural attributes in order to be able to distinguish religion from other social phenomena – particularly belief in a transcendental reality and/or (a) spiritual being(s), religiosity (which is signified by the beliefs held and practices of adherents) and affiliation to a religious organization – we reinforce particular western views of what a religion *should* be (see Hefferan, Chapter 3 for a discussion of definitions of religion). As Asad argues, 'there cannot be a universal definition of religion, not only because its constituent elements and relationships are historically specific, but because that definition is itself the historical product of discursive processes' (1993: 29).

Nonetheless, colonialism and globalization have prompted efforts to view religion in terms of discrete traditions that can be differentiated in terms of belief. Such visions also colour how people think about their own religions. It is not, however, the case that this globalized religious category is completely universalized, and indeed other ways of 'doing' religion co-exist in a post-secular age that have not been flattened by the world religions paradigm. These present a number of challenges for studying the relationships between religions and global development in a post-secular age and require reflexivity in the application of the familiar tools and concepts that we bring to the study of religion. I will briefly discuss three areas which are important in developing skills in 'religious literacy', understood not just in terms of the beliefs and practices embodied within different religious traditions but also with respect to how 'religion' is manifested in different settings in ways that do not match the western Christianized view of what a religion should be:

1   According to the 'world religions paradigm', 'world religions' tend to demand exclusivity and, while conversion is normally a possibility, people are not permitted to 'belong' to more than one religion at a time. However, the existence of styles of 'religious syncretism' or 'hybridity' in many parts of the globe, where the boundaries between different religious traditions are less clear cut, points to limitations within the 'world religions paradigm'. For instance, we find syncretism within religions in India, including Hinduism, Islam, Sikhism and Christianity, which not only overlap with each other but also often include elements of indigenous (*adivasi*) religion. It is also the case in Africa, where people often practise African traditional religions (ATR) alongside Christianity or Islam.

2   Whereas the idea of 'right belief' is central to Christianity, a distinction is sometimes drawn between those religions that focus on 'orthodoxy' (right belief) and those that focus on 'orthopraxy' (right action). The latter type includes Asian traditions, such as Hinduism or Confucianism, where there is more emphasis upon correct religious practice and one's social role vis-à-vis the conventions of that religion than upon believing in particular doctrines or teachings. Thus, definitions of religion that emphasize belief and doctrine may be unable to capture the relative unimportance of these within some traditions outside the Abrahamic religions (i.e. Christianity, Islam and Judaism). However, in focusing on religion as concerned with 'orthodoxy', scholars are more likely to prioritize 'official' versions as codified in texts and propounded by religious leaders, rather than the lived religion actually practised by people. If we look for religion only in the obvious places, for example in the form of religious leaders, institutions or texts, then we are unlikely to get a full picture of patterns of religiosity.

3   While another premise of the world religious paradigm is the distinction between the religious and the secular, in practice it is often not possible to separate clearly the religious from the secular in the way that western models of religion demand. In highly religious contexts, people may not think about what they do or what influences them as being 'religious'. Neither may apparently religious organizations be clearly labelled as 'faith-based' (see Tomalin, Chapter 13; Occhipinti, Chapter 22; Marshall, Chapter 25). Moreover, the secularization theories underpinning understandings of development and modernization have proved to be particularly flawed in non-western settings where religion has not diminished or disappeared to the private sphere. In fact the differentiation of public–private does not seem to fit the way that people live out their religion in many settings.

Thus, over the past few decades those involved in the study of religion have developed critiques of modernist ways of viewing the nature and future of religious traditions globally. Straightforward theories of secularization as well as the desirability or inevitability of the spread of secularism have been debunked, and instead theories about contemporary religion point towards the emergence of a 'new paradigm' where there are multiple modernities co-existing within post-secular societies. What this is also pointing towards is a disruption of the notion that 'secular reason can provide a neutral stance from which to interpret religion' (Thomas 2005: 21), and instead we need to develop new frameworks to interpret religious pluralism.

The aim of this book is to provide a rich description and analysis of the roles that religion plays in global development and to add to the instruments and frameworks necessary to interpret them. It provides a survey of the current state of research on 'religions and global development' and points towards the research agenda for the coming years. The salience of religion for global development in a post-secular age is clear, but in order to understand it in a way that can lead to positive outcomes there is a need to approach the topic in ways that are reflexive and do not just replicate modernist ideas about what a religion should be, including the view that it is likely to disappear.

Structure of the book

The book is divided into seven parts and has 29 chapters. The aim of Part 1, 'Critical debates for religions and global development' (which includes six chapters), is to highlight debates that have emerged within research on 'religions and global development', particularly with respect to theoretical, conceptual and methodological considerations. In Chapter 2, 'Development, religion and modernity', Carole Rakodi examines the antecedents of contemporary development ideas and policies and how 'religion' fits into them, including ideas about progress, modernity, religion and secularization. In Chapter 3, 'Researching religions and development', Tara Hefferan explores methodological issues associated with the social scientific study of religions and global development, and in Chapter 4, 'Theology and development: Christian and Jewish approaches', Stephen Plant and Daniel H. Weiss examine this from the perspective of 'doing theology'. Whereas the social scientific study of religion is an 'outsider' approach, theologies present a way of thinking about religions and global development from an 'insider' perspective.

The final chapters in Part 1 move on to explore a different set of critical considerations around the historical antecedents of development, arguably shaped by religious forces, and the apparent 'amnesia' of modern of development policy to acknowledge its religious roots. In Chapter 5, 'A history of faith-based aid and development', Gregory Deacon and Emma Tomalin examine the Christian missionary roots of modern development and the renewed engagement with religion by development actors since the early 2000s. In Chapter 6, 'Proselytizing development', Philip Fountain explores the ways in which proselytization has become a problem for development such that it is frequently regarded as illegitimate, coercive and dangerous. Yet the historical roots of development lie in missionary endeavours, and contemporary missionary actors continue to have a significant impact on development processes.

In Parts 2 to 6 of the volume, the focus is upon 'religions and regions'. The aim here is to look at different regional and national development contexts and the place of religion within them. Rather than dealing with each religious tradition in turn and looking at how development issues might be viewed from within them, different religious traditions are located within particular development contexts. Given the heterogeneous and contested nature of religious traditions, it is impossible to establish fixed 'religious' approaches to development issues, and viewing them in context enables a better understanding of their relationships to development processes and outcomes.

Each of Parts 2 to 6 begins with a broad, regionally focused chapter that looks at links between religion and development processes and outcomes, both historically and currently, in the particular region. The second chapter in each part addresses themes of relevance to the particular region, and in each case the focus is different. While this of course leaves out much that could be considered to be relevant within particular regions, the work presented is at the cutting edge of religion and development debates within the particular region. The final chapter in each part focuses upon gender relations, including masculinities and sexuality.

Part 2 focuses on Sub-Saharan Africa. In Chapter 7, Bompani provides an overview of religion and development in Sub-Saharan Africa, which is then followed by Freeman's Chapter 8 on Pentecostalism and economic development. Part 2 concludes with van Klinken and Chitando, who in Chapter 9 examine the HIV epidemic in Africa as a gendered phenomenon and the role of religion in shaping a gender-based response that deals with questions of masculinity.

Part 3 focuses on Latin America, and in Chapter 10 Paul Freston opens with a discussion on development and religious change in Latin America, concentrating on Pentecostalism 'as the engine of religious change in Latin America' (p. 141). Jill DeTemple, in Chapter 11, takes Ecuador 'as an ideal case study for the many ways that religion and development interact in Latin America' (p. 156), and examines the fluctuating role government institutions, ideologies and policies have had in creating, controlling and resisting this combination. Finally, Juan Marco Vaggione, in Chapter 12, looks at the role of the Catholic Church in contemporary sexual politics and development in Latin America.

Part 4 focuses on South Asia and begins with a chapter by Emma Tomalin that explores religion and development in Pakistan and India, the most salient states politically and economically in the region. David Mosse, in Chapter 14, then examines religion and development in India through the lens of caste and the severely marginalized Dalit communities in India. The part ends with Chapter 15, where Tamsin Bradley and Nida Kirmani discuss the links between religion, gender and development in Pakistan and India, where in both settings the women's movements have been secular yet may engage with religious actors strategically.

Part 5 focuses on East and South-East Asia and begins with Chapter 16, where André Laliberté looks at religion and development in China, distinguishing between China as a civilization (hence including a number of other societies, such as Taiwan and Hong Kong) and China as a polity (i.e. the PRC). Kirsteen Kim, in Chapter 17, then examines the role that Christianity in particular played in the development of South Korea post-1945. Finally, Monica Lindberg Falk, in Chapter 18, provides a discussion of the role of religion in shaping attitudes towards gender and sexuality in South-East Asia, one of the most culturally and religiously heterogeneous areas in the world, but one where it is often alleged that women enjoy a higher status than those in neighbouring countries, particularly India, Pakistan and China.

Part 6 focuses on the Middle East and North Africa (MENA) and begins with Chapter 19, where Rana Jawad discusses the extent to which religion and development in the MENA region focus on poverty relief or social transformation. Then in Chapter 20 Amin Mohseni-Cheraghlou analyses data which reveal that people in MENA are more likely to remain 'unbanked' for religious reasons. Providing evidence that suggests financial inclusion is a means to poverty reduction and development, he argues that this points towards the importance of Islamic banking for poverty reduction in MENA. Finally, Mariz Tadros, in Chapter 21, looks at the way in which gender and religion interacted in Arab Spring uprisings and their aftermath, highlighting how 'Islamist movements, though varying in agenda and across time and space, spearheaded processes of regulating women's sexuality' (p. 326).

Finally, Part 7 includes eight chapters that each examine a particular facet of the engagement between mainstream development policy and practice and religious actors. In Chapter 22 Laurie A. Occhipinti addresses the complex issues around faith-based organizations and development, providing a helpful discussion about definitions of the term 'FBO', as well as offering some typologies that can assist in researching and evaluating FBOs. In Chapter 23, Jill Olivier takes up the issues of public health, development and religious organizations and argues for a health policy and systems research (HPSR) approach as a suitable tool for navigating this complex practice-research environment. In Chapter 24, Marie Juul Petersen looks at the ways human rights discourses increasingly influence the ways in which development organizations conduct their work, often under the heading of a 'rights-based approach', and the different ways in which a group of Muslim aid organizations engage with the nexus between human rights, religion and development.

In Chapter 25, Katherine Marshall provides a framework consisting of types of religious institution that are all important providers of welfare and development services as well as being relevant sites for engagement with development institutions.

In Chapter 26, Sigurd Bergmann examines the ways in which contemporary climate science and policy could benefit from engaging with the religious world views of those affected by climate change. In Chapter 27, Daromir Rudnyckyj argues that economic development cannot be fully understood without attention to religion, from the classical accounts presented by Marx and Weber, to contemporary examples from Indonesia and Malaysia of the introduction of religious practice into corporate workplaces and the attempt to create a financial system concordant with religious principles. In Chapter 28, Seth D. Kaplan examines the relationships between religion and development in fragile states, arguing that religion can be both a blessing and a curse. Religion can be a mechanism to sow social divisions, but shared religious values also can be a way to bridge differences. Finally, in Chapter 29, Amy Stambach discusses links between education, development and religion and examines international agencies' support for faith-based education policies and programmes.

References

Almond, Philip C. (1988) *The British Discovery of Buddhism*, Cambridge: Cambridge University Press.

Asad, Talal (1993) *Genealogies of Religion: Discipline and Reasons of Power in Christianity and Islam*, Baltimore, MD: Johns Hopkins University Press.

Barnett, Michael and Stein, Janice (eds) (2012) *Sacred Aid: Faith and Humanitarianism*, Oxford: Oxford University Press.

Bayes, Jane and Tohidi, Nayereh (2001) *Globalization, Gender and Religion: The Politics of Women's Rights in Catholic and Muslim Contexts*, Basingstoke: Palgrave Macmillan.

Berger, Peter (2014) *The Many Altars of Modernity: Toward a Paradigm for Religion in a Pluralist Age*, Boston, MA: De Gruyter.

Beyer, Peter (1994) *Religion and Globalization*, London: Sage.

Beyer, Peter (2007) 'Globalization and Glocalization', in James A. Beckford and N. Jay Demerath (eds), *The Sage Handbook of the Sociology of Religion*, London: Sage, pp. 98–117.

Carbonnier, Gilles (ed.) (2013) *International Development Policy: Religion and Development*, Basingstoke: Palgrave Macmillan.

Clarke, Gerard (2007) 'Agents of Transformation? Donors, Faith-Based Organisations and International Development', *Third World Quarterly*, 28 (1), 77–96.

Clarke, Gerard (2008) 'Faith-Based Organizations and International Development: An Overview', in Gerard Clarke and Michael Jennings (eds), *Development, Civil Society and Faith-Based Organizations*, Basingstoke: Palgrave, pp. 17–45.

Clarke, Gerard and Jennings, Michael (2008) 'Introduction', in G. Clarke and M. Jennings (eds), *Development, Civil Society and Faith-Based Organizations: Bridging the Sacred and the Secular*, Basingstoke: Palgrave Macmillan, pp. 1–16.

Deneulin, Séverine with Bano, Masooda (2009) *Religion in Development: Rewriting the Secular Script*, London: Zed Books.

Development Dialogue on Values and Ethics (n.d.) *World Faiths Development Dialogue*, http://web.world-bank.org/WBSITE/EXTERNAL/EXTABOUTUS/PARTNERS/EXTDEVDIALOGUE/0,,con tentMDK:21955861~menuPK:5555051~pagePK:64192523~piPK:64192458~theSitePK:537298,00. html (accessed 1 July 2014).

DFID (2009) *Eliminating World Poverty: Building Our Common Future*, White Paper, London: Department for International Development.

DFID (2012) *Faith Partnership Principles: Working Effectively with Faith Groups to Fight Global Poverty*, London: Department for International Development, https://www.gov.uk/government/uploads/system/uploads/attachment_data/file/67352/faith-partnership-principles.pdf (accessed 8 June 2014).

Eisenstadt, S. N. (2000) 'Multiple Modernities', *Daedalus*, 129 (1), 1–29.

Habermas, Jürgen (2006) 'Multiple Modernities and Postsecular Societies', in Hent de Vries and Lawrence E. Sullivan (eds), *Political Theologies: Public Religions in a Post-Secular World*, New York: Fordham University Press.

Haynes, Jeffery (2007) *Religion and Development: Conflict or Cooperation?*, Basingstoke: Palgrave Macmillan.

Holenstein, Anne-Marie (2005) *Role and Significance of Religion and Spirituality in Development Co-operation*, Bern: Swiss Agency for Development and Cooperation.

Huwart, Jean-Yves and Verdier, Loïc (2013) 'Does Globalisation Promote Development?', in *Economic Globalisation: Origins and Consequences*, Paris: OECD Publishing, http://dx.doi.org/10.1787/9789264111905-6-en (accessed 8 June 2014).

James, Rick (2009) *Handle with Care: Engaging with Faith-Based Organisations in Development*, http://www.intrac.org/data/files/resources/625/Handle-With-Care-Engaging-with-faith-based-organisations.pdf (accessed 8 June 2014).

Joint Learning Initiative on Faith and Local Communities (n.d.) 'Welcome to the Joint Learning Initiative on Faith and Local Communities Website', http://www.jliflc.com (accessed 1 July 2014).

Knowledge Centre Religion and Development (n.d.) Home page, http://www.religion-and-development.nl/home (accessed 1 July 2014).

Marshall, Katherine and Keough, Lucy (eds) (2004) *Mind, Heart and Soul in the Fight against Poverty*, Washington, DC: World Bank Publications.

Marshall, Katherine and Marsh, Richard (eds) (2003) *Millennium Challenges for Development and Faith Institutions*, Washington, DC: World Bank Publications.

Marshall, Katherine and Van Saanen, Marisa (2007) *Development and Faith: Where Mind, Heart, and Soul Work Together*, Washington, DC: World Bank Publications.

Oberoi, H. (1994) *The Construction of Religious Boundaries: Culture, Identity and Diversity in the Sikh Tradition*, Delhi: Oxford University Press.

Osorio, Juan Carlos Parra and Wodon, Quentin (2014) *Faith-Based Schools in Latin America: Case Studies on Fe Y Alegria*, Washington, DC: World Bank, https://openknowledge.worldbank.org/handle/10986/16375 (accessed 8 June 2014).

Pearson, Ruth and Tomalin, Emma (2008) 'Intelligent Design? A Gender Sensitive Interrogation of Religion and Development', in Gerard Clarke and Michael Jennings (eds), *Development, Civil Society and Faith-Based Organizations*, Basingstoke: Palgrave, pp. 46–71.

Piketty, Thomas (2014) *Capital in the Twenty-First Century*, Cambridge, MA: Harvard University Press.

Religions and Development Research Programme (n.d.) Home page, http://www.religionsanddevelopment.org/ (accessed 1 July 2014).

Rist, Gilbert (2002) *The History of Development: From Western Origins to a Global Faith*, London: Zed Books.

Robertson, Roland (1992) *Globalization: Social Theory and Global Culture*, London: Sage.

Robertson, Roland (1995) 'Glocalization: Time–Space and Homogeneity–Heterogeneity', in Mike Featherstone, Scott Lash and Roland Robertson (eds), *Global Modernities*, London: Sage, pp. 25–44.

Rosati, Massimo and Stoeckl, Kristina (2012) *Multiple Modernities and Postsecular Societies*, Farnham: Ashgate.

Shangquan, Gao (2010) *Economic Globalization: Trends, Risks and Risk Prevention*, CDP Background Paper no. 1, New York: United Nations, Development Policy and Analysis Division, Department of Economic and Social Affairs.

Smith, Wilfred Cantwell (1991 [1962]) *The Meaning and End of Religion*, Minneapolis, MN: Fortress Press.

Stambach, Amy (2005) 'Rallying the Armies or Bridging the Gulf: Questioning the Significance of Faith-Based Educational Initiatives in a Global Age', *Indiana Journal of Global Legal Studies*, 12 (1), 205–26.

Tadros, Mariz (2011) 'Introduction: Gender, Rights and Religion at the Crossroads', *IDS Bulletin*, 42 (1), 1–9.

ter Haar, Gerrie (ed.) (2011) *Religion and Development: Ways of Transforming the World*, London: C. Hurst & Co.

Thomas, Scott M. (2005) *The Global Resurgence of Religion and the Transformation of International Relations: The Struggle for the Soul of the Twenty-First Century*, Basingstoke: Palgrave Macmillan.

Tomalin, Emma (2011) *Gender, Faith and Development*, Oxford: Oxfam, and Rugby: Practical Action Publishing.

Tomalin, Emma (2013) *Religions and Development*, Abingdon: Routledge.

Tyndale, Wendy (ed.) (2006) *Visions of Development: Faith-Based Initiatives*, Aldershot: Ashgate.

UNFPA (2005) *Culture Matters: Working with Communities and Faith-Based Organizations: Case Studies from Country Programmes*, New York: UNFPA, http://www.unfpa.org/public/publications/pid/1430 (accessed 8 June 2014).

UNFPA (2007) *Engaging Faith-Based Organizations in HIV Prevention*, New York: UNFPA, http://www.unfpa.org/public/global/pid/398 (accessed 8 June 2014).

UNFPA (2008) *Culture Matters: Lessons from a Legacy of Engaging Faith-Based Organizations*, New York: UNFPA, http://www.unfpa.org/public/pid/1353 (accessed 8 June 2014).

USAID (n.d.) 'Center for Faith-Based and Community Initiatives: History', http://www.usaid.gov/faith-based-and-community-initiatives/history (accessed 1 July 2014).

Warner, R. Stephen (1993) 'Work in Progress toward a New Paradigm for the Sociological Study of Religion in the United States', *American Journal of Sociology*, 98 (5), 1044–93.

Williams, Rowan (2012) 'Faith, Poverty and Justice', Lambeth Palace Inter-Faith Event with DFID, 26 June, http://rowanwilliams.archbishopofcanterbury.org/articles.php/2539/faith-poverty-and-justice-lambeth-palace-inter-faith-event-with-dfid (accessed 1 July 2014).

Wodon, Quentin (2014) *Education in Sub-Saharan Africa: Comparing Faith-Inspired, Private Secular, and Public Schools*, World Bank Studies, Washington, DC: World Bank Publications.

PART 1

Critical debates for religions and global development

2

DEVELOPMENT, RELIGION AND MODERNITY

Carole Rakodi

Introduction

The idea of 'development', as it emerged in the post–Second World War era of de-colonization and American hegemony, embodied notions of 'progress' and 'modernity'. Many development theorists have discussed how it came to have these connotations and produced a set of remarkably uniform discourses and practices, which influenced the economic, political and social policies adopted by both poorer countries and multi- and bilateral development agencies. The body of ideas and practices espoused by 'mainstream' development policy has been sustained by geopolitical dynamics, the aspirations of post-colonial governments, the interests vested in the 'aid business' and the emergence of development studies as a multidisciplinary field of study. This is not to say that specific development objectives, the organizational arrangements for regulating relationships between 'developed' and 'developing' countries, and development policies and practices have not changed since the 1950s. As the ex-colonies have become more economically differentiated, authoritarian and democratic regimes have come and gone, alternative theoretical ideas about 'development' and 'underdevelopment' have asserted their greater explanatory power, and policies have changed in the light of experience, the early certainties have been challenged.

In the mid-twentieth century, modernization, based on the belief that development would (and should) take the form of a unilinear path towards a commonly accepted and desired future, was the dominant development paradigm. However, theories based on the expectation that developing countries would follow the path followed by developed countries were soon challenged, initially by Neo-Marxist analysts and then by critics of the development approaches adopted in the 1950s and 1960s. Some of the latter rejected mainstream development thinking and the prevailing development model, but more influential was a strong neoliberal turn in economic and political thinking. One result of the discrediting of modernization approaches was the disappearance of the term 'modernity' from mainstream development discourse. However, it did not disappear from other discourses, including postmodernism and post-colonialism, or from the aspirations of many in developing countries.

To appreciate the place of religion in countries' visions of their future and its influence on the political and legal arrangements adopted, it is necessary to understand how European and North American political and academic thought and experience influenced both thinking about how economic transformation might be achieved and also understanding of the relations between states and religious traditions. Post-colonial and subsequent constitutional settlements were almost all secular, while assumptions about the nature and role of religion led to its neglect in development theory and policy. Nevertheless, in many countries in the South, levels of religiosity remain high, new religious movements have proliferated, and religion has had a continuing and sometimes increased influence on politics at both the domestic and international levels.

In this chapter, the origins of some of the key ideas underpinning development studies and policy will be examined, noting how 'religion' fits into them.[1] First, the key tenets of the dominant theory of development of the twentieth century, modernization theory, will be outlined. Some of the main challenges to modernization theory will then be discussed and the divergent approaches to development analysis, policy and practice that emerged in the later twentieth century identified. In both sections, the discussion will focus on the place of ideas about modernity, religion and secularization.

The emergence of mainstream development theory and policy

The contemporary idea of 'development' and the analyses, policies and practices with which it is associated are generally traced to the period after the Second World War, with the establishment of the Bretton Woods institutions and the first of a new wave of de-colonizations in Africa, Asia and the Caribbean. It had, of course, antecedents. While analysts' views on its origins and history vary (see, for example, Preston 1986; Watts 1993; Cowen and Shenton 1996; Gardner and Lewis 1996; Simon 1998; Mehmet 1999; Kothari 2002; Edelman and Haugerud 2005; Rist 2008; Hart 2009; Nederveen Pieterse 2010), there is general agreement that 'development' can be defined as 'organized intervention in collective affairs according to a standard of improvement' (Nederveen Pieterse 2010: 3).

Intellectual debts and historical influences

In the eighteenth and nineteenth centuries, feudalism was undermined by a series of radical social and political struggles, accompanied by the emergence of thinking that stressed tolerance and reason, and by the rise of science and technology. These changes were heralded as ushering in a new age of rationality and enlightenment, rather than ignorance and superstition. Influenced by Darwin's *Origin of Species* (1859), evolutionary ideas were applied to human societies (for example, by Durkheim). Amongst the key antecedents of development, therefore, were the concepts of 'progress' and 'modernity'. Unlike earlier ideas based on observation of natural cycles (recurrent sequences of expansion and decay), 'progress' implies a historical process of social transformation based on a conviction that the future will be an improvement on the past (Cowen and Shenton 1996; see also Asad 1993). This future was to be 'modern', generally interpreted as based on the universal values of rationality, reason and democracy, although there was much discussion of the concept and its origins (Mohan 1994; Haynes 2008). While, 'in popular usage, "modern" usually means contemporary or recent . . . in academic parlance it is defined by two key referents: the Enlightenment project and (nineteenth and early twentieth century) industrial capitalism' (Simon 1998: 227; see also King 1995; Therborn 1995; Cooper 2005). The former refers to the eighteenth-century Age of Enlightenment, in which tradition and religion as the ultimate source of truth were challenged and thinking based on knowledge and reason promoted, and the idea that nature could be harnessed and controlled gained purchase. The construction of 'religion' was part of the modern project, and it figured largely in the founding fathers' theories of social change (see Tomalin, Chapter 1). However, while acknowledging its power to shape worldviews and the role of religious movements in enabling people to shape new public identities, potentially challenge marginalization and develop new forms of social organization, modernists expected it to disappear (or at least to change) (Zavos 2010). To simplify a complex analysis, Weber, for example, identified the emergence of Protestantism as key to explaining the development of capitalism in Western Europe, because it fostered rational thinking and made available religious sanctions that encouraged discipline and hard work, although ultimately he expected that it would be displaced by reason and knowledge derived from scientific methods (Preston 1986; Corbridge 1993; Furseth and Repstad 2006).

In parallel with the emergence of Enlightenment thinking and capitalism, it was recognized that economic growth, industrialization and urbanization had given rise to disorder and social crisis. Initially, the role of development was seen as being to tackle these problems. Although modernity and industrial capitalism emerged in Western Europe and spread to the US, it was believed that the vision, the values and the underlying institutions (such as bureaucratic modes of administration) were universally valid. In some cases, for example Japan, modernity was induced by external threats (Therborn 1995). Between the mid-nineteenth and mid-twentieth centuries, it was also imposed by colonization. Notions of enlightenment and progress were important in colonial discourses, with the 'natives' constructed as backward and the colonizers as the rational agents of progress (Said 1995 [1978]: 40). Earlier, in Europe, the model of governance that could solve problems of disorder and backwardness was conceived of as 'trusteeship', in which governance is exercised by those with the capacity to utilize land, labour and capital, namely capitalists (Cowen and Shenton 1996). Colonial thinking was similar: modernity was held up as a model for colonized people, based on a belief that, if the necessary values and institutions were instilled, societies would be able to evolve along similar paths to a similar future, while external political power was exercised in the name of 'trusteeship' (Therborn 1995; Cooper 2005). The necessary changes were for the most part to be achieved through the establishment of new political and bureaucratic systems, the introduction of European-style education and the spread of Christianity. However, the relationship between colonialism and religion was complex: it was aided by religion, especially the Christian missions, led to the construction of other systems of belief and practice as 'religions' (for example Hinduism), and affected colonized territories and their societies and existing religious traditions; and the contact with other religious traditions also had an influence on the religion of the colonizers (Woodhead 2001; Zavos 2010).

By the twentieth century, earlier conceptions of development as dealing with the disorderly side effects of capitalist growth were superseded by the idea that it involves deliberate efforts aimed at progress (A. Thomas 1992). Colonization had produced impoverished countries lacking viable economies and political infrastructures. In addition to its palliative role, therefore, 'development' came to offer a vision of an improved future for these countries and, supposedly, a means of achieving it. It was believed that not only their governments, but also their previous colonizers, and wealthy countries in general, should bear responsibility for assisting them to achieve their development objectives. The US, in particular, which had itself experienced a transition from a settler society to an economically developed democracy, started to finance development studies and projects, although its motives were, of course, not purely altruistic – its interest was also related to Cold War competition with the USSR, especially in Latin America (Ish-Shalom 2006; Rist 2008; Schuurman 2009; Nederveen Pieterse 2010).

Given that the laws of development were thought to be the same for all, it was assumed that what had happened in Europe (and later the US) must be reproduced elsewhere (Rist 2008). In the post-war period, therefore, development was commonly understood as being based on two key principles: difference (the Third World is different, so a separate field of study is needed) and similarity (it is the job of development policy to make 'them' more like 'us') (Corbridge 2007;

see also Mehmet 1999). The central thesis of what might be called 'developmentalism' was that socio-economic change occurs according to a pre-established pattern, the logic and direction of which are known. Although there was little explicit consideration of where the values on which development was to be based and against which outcomes would be evaluated should come from, typically they were those adopted by European and North American states: prosperity, freedom to choose, self-esteem and equality. It was assumed that those furthest along the developmental path had not only privileged knowledge, but also a template which had enabled them to manage their colonies and could now be used to assist ex-colonies to navigate the stages through which it was assumed they would evolve.

The knowledge base for this approach was derived from European thinking, in particular the sciences, both natural and social, as they gradually split into defined disciplines with their own ontological viewpoints and epistemological approaches. Development studies emerged out of these established disciplines as an interdisciplinary field of study, a net importer of theory from the social sciences, for example economics and anthropology, the influence of which will be discussed below (Nederveen Pieterse 2010).

In the eighteenth and nineteenth centuries, economists sought to explain industrialization and the emergence of capitalism. Influenced by the natural sciences, neo-classical theory came to dominate economic thinking, and was still dominant in the mid-twentieth century. The assumptions on which it is based are both rationalist and reductionist: that economics is value-free, the playing field for those involved in economic transactions is level, alternatives to self-interested utility maximization are irrational, market forces determine resource allocation and distribute rewards according to productivity, human relations can be reduced to market relations, a positivist approach based on methodological individualism is the most appropriate, and universal laws resembling those in natural science apply to economic transactions and the evolution of markets (Preston 1986; Mehmet 1999; Fine 2006; Rist 2008). Culture and religion had no place in this schema. With de-colonization and the growth in international development assistance, funding and institutional positions became available for economists with the expertise considered necessary to transform the economies of newly independent countries. Their influence grew, and a specialist branch of development economics emerged (Ferguson 2005).

Social anthropology, which had different origins, emerged as a discipline during the nineteenth century. Although less powerful than economics, it nevertheless influenced colonial and post-colonial development thinking. Initially based on the idea of social evolution ('civilized men' had evolved out of 'savages'), anthropology aimed to study societies apparently unaffected by economic and social change, in order to understand 'primitive' human society and how new and higher stages of society might emerge out of older and simpler ones (Lewis 2009). Using a distinctive ethnographic methodology, anthropologists compared (mostly rural) societies and cultures conceived of as separate units, but were also (along with sociologists, geographers and political scientists) called upon to provide useful information to colonial governments to enable them to understand and thereby control the behaviour of the 'natives' (Asad 1993; Gardner and Lewis 1996; Corbridge 2007; Nederveen Pieterse 2010). Unlike economists, because of anthropologists' concern with social organization and culture, the 'study of religion has been central to [the discipline] since its inception' (Bowie 2006: 3). Because of anthropologists' interest in 'traditional' societies, this meant religions other than Christianity, for example Hinduism or 'folk religion', although some also studied the impact of Christian missions. Often, they identified apparent incompatibilities between groups' religio-cultural practices (for example their experience of reality in terms of personalized spiritual powers such as witches and demons) and the expectations and demands of 'modern' (colonial and post-colonial) society, which appeared to be compatible with the supernatural elements of Christianity (Bowie 2006). Criticisms of traditional practices were expressed, for example, in the Hindu reform movements of colonial India, which sought to outlaw practices such as *sati* (self-immolation by widows). As with economics, following the growth of the aid industry in the mid-twentieth century and recognition that development is more than economic growth, demand for anthropological insights (for example in agrarian studies) grew, leading to the emergence of the sub-field of development anthropology. Although the influence of sociologists and anthropologists on mainstream development theory and policy waxed and waned over time, and many post-independence governments were suspicious of it because of its association with colonialism (Asad 1993; Edelman and Haugerud 2005), it nevertheless influenced mainstream development theory and policy.[2]

Modernization theory

Emerging out of these historical and intellectual currents, the two theoretical perspectives that most strongly influenced post-colonial development ideas were economic, especially Rostow's 'stages of growth' theory (Rostow 1960), and sociological/anthropological – modernization theory. An American economic historian, Rostow put forward a historical and normative model, which placed all societies in one of five categories which purported to describe Euro-American economic evolution, as well as providing an indication of what developing countries might expect and a guide to what policies might be needed:

- traditional societies, which are in a natural state of 'underdevelopment', owing to their ignorance of the modern technology that allows nature to be exploited, their fatalistic ethos, and the strong family and kin ties that limit investment and circumscribe economically rational decision making;
- the preconditions for take-off, during which traditional institutions and values start to break down and nation states with new elites emerge, helped by colonialism and independence;
- take-off, when the blocks to economic growth are overcome, investment increases, agriculture is commercialized, new industries using modern technology are established, countries are dominated by a ruling class that is eager to modernize, and growth becomes normal;
- the drive to maturity, when technology, the entrepreneurial spirit and major investment make it possible to overcome the values and institutions of traditional society;
- the age of high mass consumption, when productivity gains are distributed to workers to increase consumption (as in the US) or are used to create a welfare state (as in Western Europe), and communism would, according to Rostow, wither.

For developing countries the central issue was to achieve 'take-off', which it was thought could be achieved through increased domestic investment, industrialization and modifications to the political and social framework in order to exploit economic opportunities. Despite its rather slim evidence base, Rostow's book, *The Stages of Economic Growth* (1960), was popular and widely read (Ish-Shalom 2006; Nederveen Pieterse 2010). In addition, he was appointed to senior posts in the Kennedy and Johnson administrations and influenced US foreign policy in Latin America, including the establishment of the Inter-American Development Bank and a grant for the Social Progress Trust Fund (an investment and development fund) (Ish-Shalom 2006). Like others influenced by their experience of the 1930s depression and the war, for example John Maynard Keynes, the British delegate to the Bretton Woods conference, Rostow advocated some restrictions on unfettered capitalism and the institutionalization of national economic planning to promote growth. The nation state was seen as the geographical or political space in which progress would be made, and so bore the ultimate responsibility for taking the necessary actions – interventionist economic policies and the provision of infrastructure and services, assisted by the UN and the newly established international financial institutions (IFIs) (Edelman and Haugerud 2005).

However, economic growth and transformation turned out to be elusive. Rather than attributing the problems to economic and political relations between developing countries and the rich world (see below), they were linked to social and cultural features of developing countries themselves. Two elements of sociological thought were particularly influential. First was the view of society as a system made up of a set of interdependent parts, including social structures, cultural beliefs, legal and political institutions, and economic and technological organization. If one of these parts becomes out of step with the others, it was thought, the social equilibrium would be upset, while, if change in one part is considered desirable, others would need to adapt – in this instance, if transformation of a country's economic structure is to occur, social, cultural and political institutions would also need to be transformed. The second influential element of sociological thought was the notion that role relationships in society and therefore social structure could be explained by ascertaining the particular combinations of value orientations characteristic of that society. These were simplified (for example by Hoselitz 1960) by holding one set of values to characterize 'traditional' and the other 'modern' societies. Modernization could, therefore, be achieved not only by replacing traditional social, cultural and institutional features by modern ones, but also by instilling modern values and beliefs by means of, for example, the educational system and the media. For example, peasants might be induced to behave in a more economically rational profit-oriented way, while rewarding achievement rather than allocating roles according to inheritance or tradition would, it was thought, foster the emergence of entrepreneurial and managerial elites. Influenced in particular by Weberian and Parsonian sociology, individual societies were examined to identify the aspects of their 'traditional' social and cultural features that posed obstacles to 'modernization', meaning the values and social practices conducive to economic rationality and capitalist growth. Talcott Parsons's pattern variables, for example, defined modernization in terms of a movement from particularism to universalism, ascription to achievement, functional diffuseness to functional specificity, and affective rules to affective neutrality (Preston 1986; Nederveen Pieterse 2010). A famous example is the anthropologist Clifford Geertz's work in Indonesia (cited in Edelman and Haugerud 2005: 15). He

> compared a Javanese and Balinese town, dominated respectively by Islamic and Hindu elites, with a view to explaining contrasting patterns of economic activity and attitudes towards accumulation. The traders in the Javanese bazaar were, according to Geertz, heirs to an early-twentieth-century reform movement in Islam that created 'a genuinely bourgeois ethic', akin to the Protestant ethic that Weber saw as propelling the rise of European capitalism ([Geertz] 1963: 49). The largely agrarian Hindu aristocrats in Bali, on the other hand, eschewed the individualism of the Javanese bazaar merchants in favour of employing non-economic, cross-class ties to mobilize labour and intra-class ties to amass capital in large, firm-like enterprises.

Modernization theory was particularly influential on development thinking in the US, where the first development studies journal, *Economic Development and Cultural Change*, launched in 1952, provided an outlet for sociological and anthropological studies of developing countries. It was never quite so dominant in Europe, where the trajectories from feudalism to capitalism had been more complex and varied (Cooper 2005).

A dimension of modernization theory that is particularly relevant to the concerns of this volume is its perception of the role of religion in society. Berger, in *The Sacred Canopy* (1967), argued that religion is an over-arching canopy that created meaning and order in pre-modern societies. During the Enlightenment in Western Europe and the US, however, not only did Christianity become more plural, with each denomination making its own truth claims, but the new thinking urged that religion as a source of truth would and should be ousted by knowledge and reason. Modernity and capitalist development were expected, therefore, to be accompanied by the secularization of society. This implied that 'religion' would decrease in importance, as obligations based on religious values were replaced by a utilitarian rationale for individual choices and actions; religion would have fewer social functions and less influence over economic and social life; it would no longer be used to legitimate political power or legislation; it would have less influence over cultural life; and it would be replaced by scientific explanations for human life, nature and society (Casanova 1994; Beckford 2003; Furseth and Repstad 2006; Kapoor 2008; Nederveen Pieterse 2010). The notion of religion in this analysis was essentially Christian (monotheistic, expansionist, patriarchal, hierarchically organized and engaged in the provision of education and health services), and it was this conception that traders, colonial officials and missionaries carried with them and that provided the lens through which they interpreted the unfamiliar societies to which they travelled.

In the development context, which was also the mission context, as noted above, 'traditional' aspects of society were considered to be obstacles to development. These included the values, beliefs and practices associated with pre-existing religious and cultural traditions, including Hinduism, Islam, Buddhism and folk religions.[3] Like other aspects of modernization, secularization was therefore regarded initially as an inevitable dimension of the social changes associated with modernity and capitalism, and then promoted to a necessary precondition for both increased prosperity (based on a liberal economic model) and government capable of achieving development goals (a liberal political model). The expectation that newly independent countries would be best served by formal representative democracy was based not only on political theory but also on the models that had evolved over many centuries in developed countries, where the European history of wars in which religion had been implicated had led to a determination to keep religion and politics separate – the doctrine of secularism (S. M. Thomas 2005). As noted above, therefore, most post-colonial constitutional arrangements were secular.

Initially, for the most part, the Eurocentrism of development studies and policy was taken for granted, and the baggage of assumptions, ideas, ideology and experience embedded in development thinking was often implicit rather than explicit. For a couple of decades in the mid-twentieth century, the approaches to development discussed above were dominant, influencing the thinking and actions of Southern and Northern governments and aid agencies alike.[4] However, the selective perspectives that they embodied and the shortcomings of the theories and policies were soon evident, leading to a series of challenges.

Challenges to mainstream development theory and policy: beyond 'stages of growth' and modernization

Dependency and underdevelopment

The first set of challenges to the dominant development theories and models of the 1950s and 1960s arose out of the experience of Latin American countries, which had gained independence much earlier but whose prosperity had increased less than expected, and Marxist theory and analysis, itself based on a stages view of history. In contrast to the dominant theory, which regarded countries as autonomous entities and considered the obstacles to economic growth to be internal, theories of dependency diagnosed the barriers as being mainly external.

Dependency theorists attributed underdevelopment to the adverse terms on which countries were, during both the colonial and the US-dominated post-war periods, integrated into the world economy, which ensured that 'the potential surplus which would otherwise be available for domestic investment was drained to the North' (Cowen and Shenton 1996: 62; see also Preston 1986; Gardner and Lewis 1996; Edelman and Haugerud 2005; Haynes 2008; Kapoor 2008; Kelly 2008; Rist 2008). Latin American scholars such as Frank, Baran and Prebisch concluded that development was not possible because states were constrained by these unfavourable terms of trade.

However, dependency theory was soon criticized, first for implying that the development of the centre was entirely dependent on the underdevelopment of the periphery, when North–North trade and endogenous economic growth were clearly important (Rist 2008), and second for attributing underdevelopment solely to external factors. Cardoso and Faletto (1969), for example, pointed out that external forces interact with local conditions, so that the outcomes vary between contexts (cited in Cowen and Shenton 1996), and Marxist analysts such as Frank (1967) came to the conclusion that Latin American bourgeoisies were not prepared to ally with the working class to overthrow the landed oligarchies. Although the power and role of the Roman Catholic Church was discussed in some of these analyses, the Marxian rejection of a positive role for religion reinforced views of it as an obstacle to progress and development. Neither theory produced much in the way of guidance on the way forward, other than completely disengaging from the world economy or ousting the capitalist class by revolutionary struggle. While the ideas of dependency theory continue to be influential, the failure of Marxist analysis to produce workable alternative strategies led by the end of the 1970s to an 'impasse' (Booth 1985; Schuurman 1993a; Kiely 1995; Corbridge 1998). Its influence waned and its fate was eventually sealed by the collapse of the communist economic model and the disintegration of the USSR.

The appeal of modernization theory was also undermined by reduced US hegemony, the end of the post-war economic boom, mounting criticism of functionalism and Parsonian sociology and the experience of developing countries (Nederveen Pieterse 2010). The standard economic growth prescription was undermined by the experience of the latter, in which, even if economic growth had been achieved through resource exploitation or industrialization, the benefits were unevenly distributed both geographically between regions within countries and amongst population groups, with few trickling down to the poorest localities and people (Rist 2008). Disillusion with both the dominant model and dependency and underdevelopment theories led some to challenge the entire development model. This challenge came from an eclectic range of perspectives that can be grouped under the label 'post-development'.

Post-development thinking: postmodernism, post-colonialism and alternative development models

Post-development ideas were influenced by wider intellectual trends, including the constructivist turn in the social sciences, postmodernism, post-colonialism and populism.[5] The central premise in all these strands is that the 'idea of development is founded upon the European tradition of knowing, a tradition which creates its own grounds for logically dominating, and thereby forcibly eliminating, non-European forms of knowledge. It is the culture of the West, and the movement of this culture, "Westernisation", which is . . . taken to mean development' (Marglin *et al.*, cited in Cowen and Shenton 1996: 457). This view is criticized for undermining the authentic values of indigenous culture and ignoring other sources of knowledge (for example, Islamic scholarship – Mehmet (1999) notes the failure of European scholars to acknowledge the work of Ibn Khaldun, a Muslim scholar who had developed most of Adam Smith's ideas three centuries before).

Postmodernism refers to a movement in art, architecture and literature which sought to deconstruct modernism by stressing the ambiguous, individualist and consumerist characteristics of contemporary European and North American culture (Simon 1998; Beckford 2003; Nederveen Pieterse 2010).[6] It involved the rejection of unitary theories of progress and belief in scientific reality in favour of the view that everyone experiences reality differently, so that there can be no single account of it (Gardner and Lewis 1996). Postmodernists therefore reject both modernity and the belief that positivism provides 'an objective, universal and ideology-free foundation' for scientific knowledge (Ish-Shalom 2006: 289). To capture subjects' own interpretation of reality, constructivist methodologies grew in popularity and importance, enabling postmodernism to claim that it provides a way of recovering lost and asserting new hybrid identities and experiences (Simon 1998). Its influence spread to cultural studies in general, with religious studies scholars emphasizing the constructed and contingent nature of the category of religion.

While postmodernism was largely concerned with European and North American culture and had only limited influence elsewhere, a parallel and more influential strand of scholarship that also emerged from literary studies was post-colonialism, in particular with the publication of Edward Said's book *Orientalism* in 1978 (Corbridge 1993, 2007; Watts 1993; Simon 1998; Kothari 2002; Mercer *et al.* 2003; Kapoor 2008). Referring particularly to India, Said linked Western imperialism and Western culture, arguing that together they had produced a 'systematic "body of theory and practice" that constructs or represents the Orient' (1995 [1978]: 6), sociologically, militarily, scientifically and imaginatively. By 'theory' he meant the Western imperial 'episteme' – its cultural and intellectual production, including ideas, writing and images – while 'practice' referred to the accompanying socio-cultural institutions and structures, such as colonial administration, education and the media. The monolithic Orientalist discourse that emerged during the imperial and colonial periods, he asserted, played a key role in the exercise of power, although he later acknowledged that it would be more accurate to portray it as discontinuous, hybrid and ambivalent than all-powerful. While Said popularized Orientalist critiques, his analysis was rooted in other traditions of work in India, for example subaltern studies. Rooted in Marxism as well as post-colonial analysis, subaltern studies sought to show how the complexities of Indian politics, society and culture explain why the 'fully Western' forms of modernity so marked in the discourses of Nehru and Ambedkar have not been (and cannot be) realized in post-colonial India, where concepts such as civil society and participation have little meaning for people's everyday lives (Corbridge 1993, 2007; see also Watts 1993; Connell 2006; Kapoor 2008). Among other things, these and other studies sought to show how colonial constructions of Hinduism (and caste) and Islam were driven by colonial administrative needs and influenced by the Christian concept of religion (Dirks 2001; Bloch *et al.* 2010). Even though the extent to which Hinduism is (1) a religion and (2) purely a colonial construct continues to be hotly debated (see, for example, the chapters in Bloch *et al.* 2010), it is accepted that these constructions have contributed to new ways of imagining the Hindu and Muslim faith traditions as 'communities', reinforced by separate laws and administrative practices. Not only did these processes result in the emergence of more stable religious identities than before, but many contemporary Indians continue as a result to think about their identities through religious ideas and practices (Corbridge and Harriss 2000).

As well as revealing some of the assumptions underlying the colonial project, post-colonialist analysis has increased awareness of the neo-colonial practices that may be embodied in common development terms, concepts and institutions. It shares territory with dependency theory in that it is based on:

a suspicion of Western liberal modernity, a historical-global analysis and a critical politics. . . . [However, d]ependency chooses a structuralist and socioeconomic perspective, seeing imperialism as tied to the unfolding of capitalism, whereas postcolonial theory favours a poststructuralist and cultural perspective, linking imperialism and agency to discourse and the politics of representation. Dependency's politics is premised on state and class control of capitalist development; postcolonial theory's on the subaltern subversion of orientalist discourses.

(Kapoor 2008: 3)

Such subversion, Said and others assert, occurs not only because post-colonialist analysis enables a significant critique of mainstream development practices, but also because it provides scope for agency amongst the colonized.

Influenced by postmodernism and post-colonialism, a similar critique emerged within development studies (Nederveen Pieterse 2010). Part of a more general shift in the social sciences from structuralist, materialist and reductionist approaches to constructivist, multidimensional and holistic views, this signified a shift from 'an account of social realities as determined and patterned by macro-structures, to an account of social realities as being socially constructed' (Nederveen Pieterse 2010). It rejected conventional development theory, criticizing modernization theory for its over-simple dichotomy between traditional and modern and failure to recognize the complexity of tradition's relationship with modernity, as well as the continued political significance of so-called traditional phenomena (for example clientelism, religion and ethnicity) (Haynes 2008). Instead, it stressed the importance of recognizing diversity, respecting indigenous institutions and understanding local actors' views.[7] For example, in *Encountering Development* (1995), Escobar argued that the development discourse that had emerged in the mid-twentieth century, which required the 'othering' and homogenization of the Third World, had led to the exploitation, control and perversion of local culture, grassroots interests and perceptions (Nederveen Pieterse 2010). Instead, Escobar and others asserted, culture is 'contested, flexible, fragmentary . . . and contingent' (Edelman and Haugerud 2005: 30). Thus difference and hybridity should be celebrated and spaces of empowerment carved out in which people can define the lives they want, in accordance with their own values and culture. Rather than traditional communities being obstacles to development, such analysts assert, they reflect deeply embedded and widely accepted local values, are the primary source of local or indigenous knowledge and are arenas in which new hybrid identities can emerge in response to wider socio-economic trends and influences (Simon 1998; Edelman and Haugerud 2005).

Not content with critiquing mainstream models, and influenced by post-colonial, post-development and populist thinking, some advocated 'another development', positing a model that is local, self-reliant and egalitarian (Rist 2008; Nederveen Pieterse 2010). In practice, the alternative development models of the 1970s were not influential because of the extreme position they adopted, their anti-state bias, lack of institutional connections, political naivety and impracticality (Sanyal 1994). The faith traditions may provide another source of alternative models, because they provide guidance about values, behaviour and right social ordering, as well as examples through their engagement in charitable, welfare and development work. Sometimes these approaches authorize individual reason and experience and are consonant with modern cultural values such as dignity and equality, but, because of the threat such values pose to religious authority and solidarity, they may also be resisted, leading to the advocacy of literalist, fundamentalist and socially conservative alternatives (Woodhead 2001). Universal human rights, for example, continue to be contested by many religious groups, because they are seen to challenge the primary importance of religious guides to behaviour, and to prioritize individuals over social groups and rights over responsibilities (Haynes 2008; Kapoor 2008; see Juul Petersen, Chapter 24). The alternative models advanced within different faith traditions cannot be discussed here, but examples include liberation theology within the Catholic Church, especially in Latin America (see also Plant 2009), engaged Buddhism (Tomalin 2007) and Islamic economics (see Zaman 2008 for an overview; also Sardar 1996), while the significance and potential value of their practical contribution has been recognized by some governments and development agencies.

A critique of post-development thinking: revisiting development and modernity

Post-colonial and post-development critiques of modernity and mainstream development models are timely, acute and correct in many respects (Gidwani and Sivaramakrishnan 2003). Corbridge (1993, 1998) welcomes their attempts to challenge the idea that there can be a single site of representation, celebrate a plurality of voices, encourage marginalized people to put forward their own accounts of their conditions and aspirations, and recognize a multiplicity of local practices of resistance.

However, they are also widely criticized. They are said to portray modernity and development 'as monolithic, depoliticizing processes, everywhere the same and always tainted beyond redemption by their progressivist European provenance' (Gidwani and Sivaramakrishnan 2003: 202; see also Cooper 2005). Often, modernity is equated with 'Western', as if all other cultures are homogeneously non-Western, none value reason, science and bureaucracy, and the rationalizing processes within economy and society that are associated with modernity have not occurred at different times and places autonomous of European influence, for example in pre-colonial India, where incipient capitalist relations in the economy and state institutions were often adapted rather than supplanted by colonialism (Gidwani and Sivaramakrishnan 2003). Similarly, development is portrayed as a homogeneous approach based on a few simple axioms, ignoring both the ways in which policy has evolved in response to experience and some of the good results that have been achieved (Corbridge 1993, 1998, 2007; Rist 2008). Moreover, post-development thinking and models, it is claimed, reflect 'a kind of anti-modernist romanticism or a dangerous cultural relativism' (Rist 2008: 259; see also Simon 1998). In privileging the local, communities, culture and indigenous knowledge, such analyses fail to acknowledge the ways in which local culture has been and continues to be influenced by migration, trade, mission and colonialism, is contradictory and contested, and may be associated with socially conservative attitudes that undermine universal human rights (Amin 1998; Kiely 1999; Edelman and Haugerud 2005).

Mainstream development policies have co-opted elements of alternative development, including respect for cultural diversity and religious traditions, concern for local development, and recognition of the importance of local and grassroots agency (Muller 2006). However, like many 'alternative development' models, these efforts are criticized for simplifying culture (and religion) into discrete and sometimes static traits (Edelman and Haugerud 2005) and instrumentalizing it (termed 'add culture and stir' by Nederveen Pieterse 2010). More is needed, it is pointed out, than tools such as participation (Kothari 2002). Localism is critiqued for failing to acknowledge the difficulty of de-linking, tackle the structural issues that create and sustain inequality and poverty, and challenge the predominant development model (Kothari 2002). Not only does the idea of local empowerment downplay power relationships and inequalities, but relying on communities and NGOs (including religious organizations) as the central development actors overrates their capacity and undermines the state.

The critics conclude that rejecting development as impossible or undesirable and advocating idealized 'alternatives to development' contribute little to the ongoing debate, while being for or against modernity is far too simple. More useful than the perception of development as a single dominant model, it is asserted, is a perception of it 'as a system of hegemonic ideas . . . that is perforated rather than saturating, whose legitimacy must constantly be reproduced and which, as such, is potentially open to contestation' (Gidwani and Sivaramakrishnan 2003: 202). With respect to modernity, moreover, Amin (1998), for example, argues that there has been progress in material production, scientific knowledge, social and ethical advance, and democratization, so there is no reason in his view to abandon modernity in favour of 'tradition', while Schuurman (1993b: 27) notes that 'Social movements (old and new) in the Third World are not expressions of resistance against modernity, rather they are demands for access to it.' Rejection of development and modernity ignores and devalues the widespread desire for both, as demonstrated in many contemporary national development plans, for example the *Uganda Vision 2040* produced in 2013, which aims to transform Uganda into 'a modern and prosperous country within 30 years', Vietnam's *Socio-Economic Development Strategy for 2011–2020*, which intends that Vietnam will 'become a modern industrialized country by 2020', Romania's *National Sustainable Development Strategy 2013–2020–2030*, which aspires to 'modern, sustainable development' and Bangladesh's *Rio + 20: National Report on Sustainable Development*, whose vision for Bangladesh is a 'modern democratic society' with modern land administration, infrastructure, policing and education.[8] However, paralleling the need for mainstream development theory and policy to learn from post-development thinking, to avoid a purely Eurocentric idea of modernity we need to examine how 'ideals, practices and institutional forms of Eurowestern modernity have travelled via colonialism and neo-colonialism, and articulate with regional polities and practices to produce distinctive "regional modernities"' (Gidwani and Sivaramakrishnan 2003: 188) in different times and places, including those in which the vast majority of people are religious (see also Eisenstadt 2000). Examples include the news, opinion, lifestyle, business and sports website in Ghana with the address www.modernghana.com, which has a section on religion, and Goodale's study in Bolivia, which 'shows how marginalized *campesinos* [in Bolivia] appropriate and vernacularize expectations of modernity' – they not merely are conscripted into this episteme, but link it on the one hand to their own historical and political experience and on the other to human rights discourse (cited in Hart 2009: 136). Corbridge and Harriss (2000) use the term 'fractured modernities' to convey the contested views on modernity's desirability held by elites, business communities, the middle classes and Hindu nationalists, in contrast to the state arrogating to itself the capacity to define a singular modernity for the nation state in India.

Religious traditions have responded to economic opportunities, social change and modernity in diverse and at times contradictory ways (Zaidi 2006). According to Tibi (2009), religion should not be equated with reluctance to engage in market capitalism and nor should modernity be seen as the preserve of the European Enlightenment – its cultural roots (reason and the pursuit of scientific knowledge), he argues, existed in Islamic thought until they were undermined by the Salafist *fiqh* orthodoxy. Similarly, Therborn notes that, 'Though the forces of all religions have formed major battalions of anti-modernity, cultural modernity should not be equated with anti-clericalism, atheism or religious indifference' (1995: 136). Moreover, although so-called fundamentalists in all the religious traditions seek to return to what they see as 'authentic' interpretation and practice, they usually accept and exploit science and technology, participate in market activities, use the media, are global in their reach and practice, and subscribe to some 'modern' values, such as working hard or the positive value of education, if not others, such as individual autonomy, permissive morality and perhaps political secularism (Beckford 2003; see also Rosander 1997; Moaddel 1998; Eisenstadt 2000; Cooper 2005; S. M. Thomas 2005;

Tibi 2005; Furseth and Repstad 2006). Within Islam, for example, '"modernist" Muslims may be said to seek to modernize Islam while more radical reforms . . . seek to Islamize modernity' (Waines 2001: 250).[9]

The idea of multiple modernities is, therefore, both descriptive and normative. It implies that modernity can and should be separated from Westernization and secularization, that the violent colonial imposition of ideas such as democracy, equality, justice and secularism does not mean that they are invalid, and that the languages and practices of modernity (and development) can be contested or appropriated by subordinate groups, enabling the emergence of new practices. These may or may not have positive results. For example, Gidwani and Sivaramakrishnan (2003) note, contemporary circular migration in India can have emancipatory potential for groups subordinated by 'tradition' in rural India, by allowing the transformation of place-based identity and relations of subjugation. In contrast, there is a danger that the view of the modern as desirable can be used by one group to denigrate another (for example the attribution of Muslim disadvantage in India by advocates of Hindutva to supposedly unmodern aspects of Islam) (Corbridge and Harriss 2000). Debates about multiple modernities have undoubtedly generated new insights. Nevertheless, critics problematize the tendency to take modern to mean contemporary, meaning that everything is modern and the concept loses its analytical value (Cooper 2005).

Challenges to mainstream economic development theory and policy: neoliberalism and beyond

To a considerable extent unaffected by the debates associated with post-colonialism, post-development and modernity, mainstream economic development policy evolved along its own track. In particular, a liberal counter-revolution in the 1980s resumed the tradition of liberalism after the limits of the state-led economic development approaches adopted in the 1950s and 1960s had become clear. The confluence of debt, recession and monetarism gave rise, under the influence of the International Monetary Fund and the World Bank, to a package of neoliberal policies based on market principles (stabilization through devaluation, financial and price reform, and adjustment by state shrinkage and deregulation) – the Washington consensus. These were imposed on countries in economic difficulty because of the impact of oil price increases, indebtedness and poorly designed policies. The uncertain economic recovery that followed and the devastating side effects of the overnight imposition of these policies are well known, and they were soon challenged in terms of both theory and practice.

The most influential theoretical challenge probably came from Amartya Sen (1999), who argued that what enables people to convert the commodities they command into well-being are their entitlements. The aim of development should therefore be to increase people's ability to make choices, through a potential set of functionings to do or to be, thereby enhancing their capabilities. Along with renewed attention to the 'redistribution with growth' ideas of the 1970s, his ideas influenced the UNDP, which responded by advocating 'human development', focusing on human security and poverty reduction. While these ideas are consonant with liberalism, they are based on different values to the Washington consensus (Gore 2000; Nederveen Pieterse 2010). Important challenges to the neoliberal orthodoxy also came from the East Asian experience of state-led development and the mixed outcomes of stabilization and structural adjustment policies, which resulted in renewed economic growth in some countries but not all, widespread increases in poverty and inequality, and deficiencies in service provision as alternative providers (private enterprises, NGOs, religious organizations and community-based organizations) failed to take up the slack created by state divestment.

Modifications to mainstream economic development policy were introduced in the 1990s to deal with these side effects, for example the Highly Indebted Poor Countries (HIPC) Initiative, renewed attention to market regulation, adoption of Keynesian macro-economic policies and the restoration or introduction of social protection policies (sometimes termed the post-Washington consensus, reflecting the continued ability of the IFIs to dictate policies). However, it is clear that the role of the state still needs considerable rethinking (Fine 2006; Kelly 2008), and there is significant resistance to change, which Rist (2008) attributes to vested interests in the 'development industry' seeking to maintain and reproduce themselves. Views differ on whether current thinking has radically undermined the Washington consensus (Colclough 1993; Watts 1994; Gore 2000; Edelman and Haugerud 2005; Van Waeyenberge 2006; Hart 2009; Stewart 2009). Fine (2002), for example, argues that it merely indicates a new phase of economics imperialism, in which, although the new institutional economics seeks to understand how real markets work, it still operates within the frame of methodological individualism and utility maximization. However, Schuurman (2009) suggests that the 2008 financial and economic crisis has led economic thinking to lose much of its triumphalism. In contrast to the parallel debates in post-colonialism and post-development, the dominance of economics and the pre-eminent role in the development industry of Western governments which are resolutely secularist (whatever the role and significance of religion in their own societies) mean that, although discussions about the concept of modernity and the role of religion in development, as well as a willingness to explore ways of working with religious organizations, have become somewhat more common, these continue to be largely absent from mainstream development discourse and practice.

Conclusion

In this chapter, some of the ideas that underlie or challenge the concept of 'development' as it has evolved since the mid-twentieth century have been explored, in particular ideas about modernity and the role of religion in society. The immediate aim was to clarify some of the key assumptions on which dominant development theories and policies are based, but it also seeks to aid understanding of the aspirations and actions of developing country governments and citizens on the one hand and the actors that constitute the 'development industry' on the other.

Development can be 'characterized as "hope", in that it carries ideas about shaping a better future, as "administration" in that it has since the 1950s amassed a range of agencies and technologies designed to produce it, and as "critical understanding" because it constitutes a site of knowledge about the world' (Quarles van Ufford *et al.*, cited in Lewis 2009: 37). It can therefore best be understood as 'sets of social practices, or technologies of rule, the organization and effects of which need to be . . . contested and subjected to political and scholarly review' (Corbridge 2007: 179), while development studies is a 'discursive field' which embodies 'a cartography of power and knowledge' at both the local and global levels (Watts 1993). Once theories enter the world of practice, Ish-Shalom suggests, 'they are bound to fail because of the immanent contrast between their parsimonious epistemology and the complex ontology of reality. . . . [They] try to explain reality, and at the same time have some mark on it' (2006: 305). So it is with development theory.

The post-war model of development was seductive, both in the North, where it justified policies that emphasized domestic economic growth in poor countries and the positive role of foreign aid, and in the South, where newly independent countries aspired to a more prosperous future. Ideas central to the dominant development theories and models of the 1950s and 1960s can be traced to the intellectual evolution and political and religious history of Europe and North America – progress, modernity, secularization and secularism. Modernization theory has been discredited, its rise and fall demonstrating 'the consequences of theoretical pretentiousness coupled with a lack of humility' (Ish-Shalom 2006: 307), although economic theory still tends to claim superiority. Nevertheless, for the most part people continue to desire 'development' if its excesses and adverse effects can be avoided, and many of the assumptions of modernization theory (the traditional/modern binary, supposed cultural obstacles to change[10]) are alive and well in contemporary language and development practice, because they seem to resonate with people's aspirations and experience of the world (Gardner and Lewis 1996; Edelman and Haugerud 2005). The same is true of ideas about modernity. Thus in discarding modernization theory, Woolcock asserts, 'development studies have also largely discarded a focus on the processes of modernity as historical fact and contemporary reality, and with it a clear eye for understanding modernity's capacities for both fulfilling and undermining development' (2009: 5).

Similarly, ideas about the secularization of society that was expected to accompany modernity, together with the 'secular' political systems adopted by European and North American governments and assertions of the superiority of economic rationality, led mainstream development theory, policies and agencies to neglect religion and its continuing role in societies and states throughout the South. This occurred even though secularization has been shown to be an inadequate reading of European history (Cooper 2005), misleading where high levels of religiosity persist (most countries outside Europe, with the exception of some ex-communist countries), unhelpful where religion has been intertwined with politics from the outset and particularly inappropriate in the light of religion's increasing visibility and salience in the public sphere (Casanova 1994; An-Na'im 1999; Berger 1999; S. M. Thomas 2005; Riesebrodt 2006). Movements within Islam, for example, are seeking to 're-enchant' modernity, not only through the Islamicization of knowledge, often justified with respect to a simplified view of Western positivist approaches, but also by the promotion of political Islam, in part in reaction to perceived state failure (An-Na'im 1999; Tibi 2005). However, the harnessing of religion for political ends is by no means confined to Islam, as attested by the rise of Hindutva in India (Ram-Prasad 2003) or increased political engagement of the Christian churches in response to Muslim assertiveness in Nigeria.

Without abandoning some of the key elements of the early models, such as the important role of the state, development thinking and policies have changed in response to the problematic outcomes they have produced, often resulting in more appropriate policies and better results. However, more recently, mainstream development analysis seems, rather unproductively, to have bifurcated into two broad streams – one inspired by neoliberal economics, which has had most influence on the IFIs and many bilateral donors, and the other an interpretive stream that seeks to deconstruct development and unpack its claims and discourse, sometimes repudiates development as an external intervention and form of discipline, but has had only limited influence on mainstream development practice. Rather than equating modernity with Westernization or appropriate development with endogenous development and localism, development studies and policy need to reconsider in the following ways. First, they need to recognize the ways in which linkages between processes and structures at the local, national and global levels explain inequality and enable or constrain the achievement of development goals; second, they need to recognize and take account of the persistence, complexity and variability of ideas about modernity; third, improved levels of religious literacy are required in order to increase understanding of the ways in which religious ideas, practices and organizations interact with aspirations for development and modernity and determine the roles religion plays in the public and private spheres; and, lastly, a better understanding is needed of the development process, not as progress towards a single defined end but as learning processes, analysed in terms of the historical trajectories of ideas, organizations and interventions in particular contexts.

31

Notes

1 Space precludes a detailed discussion of the nature of 'religion' here, but see, for example, Asad (1993), Woodhead (2001), Segal (2005), Furseth and Repstad (2006), Riesebrodt (2006) and Saler (2008).
2 This was not invariably the case. For example, Asad (1993) notes that anthropology's knowledge of minority or tribal communities in India led to its institutionalization in government.
3 Although these views were sometimes accepted in developing countries, especially where traditional beliefs and practices had been eroded during the colonial period, in other cases they were resisted (for example, by Syed Hussein Alatas in Malaysia, 1977).
4 This is not to say that they were uniform and monolithic. Alternative policy orientations were suggested from within the paradigm. For example, the failure of 'trickle-down' led in the 1970s to advocacy of 'redistribution with growth' by the World Bank and economists based at the Institute for Development Studies in England and a basic needs approach by the ILO and some at the World Bank.
5 A parallel alternative perspective was put forward by feminists, who challenged the masculinist bias of much development theory (Kapoor 2008).
6 King (1995) points out that, like postmodernism, modernist movements in the arts, literature and architecture between 1890 and 1940 mainly occurred in Europe and North America. In religious terms, postmodern characteristics (pastiche, hybridity, bricolage of beliefs and practices) are most evident in the New Age Movement, although this also has modernist characteristics (Beckford 2003).
7 The many strands of post-development analysis include detailed studies of development agencies, programmes and projects, which challenged the technocratic depoliticized approaches of the aid industry (for example Ferguson 1990; Mosse 2004; Scott 2004) and studies of the institutions governing social and economic systems, especially those needed for markets or governments to operate effectively, although oddly the role of religious institutions has rarely been considered (for example Platteau 1994a, 1994b).
8 http://www.jlos.go.ug/index.php/document-centre/document-centre/cat_view/121-government-of-uganda-planning-strategies; www.un.org.vn/en/about-viet-nam/overview.html; www.un.org.ezproxy.bham.ac.uk/esa/dsd/dsd_aofwni/nipdfs/NationalReports/romania/Romania.pdf; and http://sustainabledevelopment.un.org/content/documents/981bangladesh.pdf (accessed 7 March 2014).
9 The papers in Woodhead *et al.* (2001) discuss how religions in different parts of the world have interacted with modernity, although this is defined very generally as 'processes, dynamics and societal characteristics' that produce profound social changes.
10 This is brought out in Nederveen Pieterse's (2010) review of the 2004 UNDP Human Development Report *Cultural Liberty in Today's Diverse World*, which claims that human development can be held back by the defence of tradition. By posing cultural liberty as the framework for analysing culture and development, the report, he argues, views developing countries through the lens of Western values and the ideological base of liberalism and freedom.

References

Alatas, Syed Hussein (1977) *The Myth of the Lazy Native: A Study of the Image of Malays, Filipinos and Javanese from the 16th Century to the 20th Century and Its Function in the Ideology of Colonial Capitalism*, London: Frank Cass.
Amin, S. (1998) *Spectres of Capitalism: A Critique of Current Intellectual Fashions*, New York: Monthly Review Press.
An-Na'im, A. A. (1999) 'Political Islam in National Politics and International Relations', in P. L. Berger (ed.), *The Desecularization of the World: Resurgent Religion in World Politics*, Grand Rapids, MI: Eerdmans, pp. 103–21.
Asad, T. (1993) *Genealogies of Religion*, Baltimore, MD: Johns Hopkins University Press.
Beckford, J. (2003) *Social Theory and Religion*, Cambridge: Cambridge University Press.
Berger, P. (1967) *The Sacred Canopy: Elements of a Sociological Theory of Religion*, New York: Doubleday.
Berger, P. L. (1999) 'The Desecularization of the World: A Global Overview', in P. L. Berger (ed.), *The Desecularization of the World: Resurgent Religion in World Politics*, Grand Rapids, MI: Eerdmans, pp. 1–18.
Bloch, E., Keppens, M. and Hegde, M. (eds) (2010) *Rethinking Religion in India: The Colonial Construction of Hinduism*, London: Routledge.
Booth, D. (1985) 'Marxism and Development Sociology: Interpreting the Impasse', *World Development*, 13, 761–87.

Bowie, F. (2006) *The Anthropology of Religion*, Oxford: Blackwell.

Cardoso, F. H. and Faletto, E. (1969) *Dependencia y Desarrollo en América Latina: Ensayo de Interpretación Sociológica*, Mexico City: Siglo XXI.

Casanova, J. (1994) *Public Religions in the Modern World*, Chicago: University of Chicago Press.

Colclough, C. (1993) 'Structuralism vs Neo-Liberalism: An Introduction', in C. Colclough and J. Manor (eds), *States or Markets? Neo-Liberalism and the Development Policy Debate*, Oxford: Clarendon, pp. 1–25.

Connell, R. (2006) *Southern Theory*, Cambridge: Polity Press.

Cooper, F. (2005) *Colonialism in Question: Theory, Knowledge, History*, Los Angeles: University of California Press.

Corbridge, S. (1993) 'Marxisms, Modernities, and Moralities: Development Praxis and the Claims of Distant Strangers', *Society and Space*, 11 (4), 449–72.

Corbridge, S. (1998) '"Beneath the Pavement Only Soil": The Poverty of Post-Development', *Journal of Development Studies*, 34 (6), 138–48.

Corbridge, S. (2007) 'The (Im)possibility of Development Studies', *Economy and Society*, 36 (2), 179–211.

Corbridge, S. and Harriss, J. (2000) *Reinventing India: Liberalization, Hindu Nationalism and Popular Democracy*, Cambridge: Polity Press.

Cowen, M. P. and Shenton, R. W. (1996) *Doctrines of Development*, London: Routledge.

Dirks, N. B. (2001) *Castes of Mind: Colonialism and the Making of Modern India*, Princeton, NJ: Princeton University Press.

Edelman, M. and Haugerud, A. (2005) 'Introduction: The Anthropology of Development and Globalization', in M. Edelman and A. Haugerud (eds), *The Anthropology of Development and Globalization*, Oxford: Blackwell, pp. 1–52.

Eisenstadt, S. N. (2000) 'Multiple Modernities', *Daedalus*, 129 (1), 1–29.

Escobar, A. (1995) *Encountering Development*, Princeton, NJ: Princeton University Press.

Ferguson, J. (1990) *The Anti-Politics Machine: Development, Depoliticization and Bureaucratic Power in the Third World*, Cambridge: Cambridge University Press.

Ferguson, J. (2005) 'Anthropology and Its Evil Twin: "Development" in the Constitution of a Discipline', in M. Edelman and A. Haugerud (eds), *The Anthropology of Development and Globalization*, Oxford: Blackwell, pp. 140–53.

Fine, B. (2002) 'Economics Imperialism and the New Development Economics as a Kuhnian Paradigm Shift?', *World Development*, 30 (12), 2057–70.

Fine, B. (2006) 'The Developmental State and the Political Economy of Development', in B. Fine and K. S. Jomo (eds), *The New Development Economics: After the Washington Consensus*, Delhi: Tulika, and London: Zed Books, pp. 101–22.

Frank, A. G. (1967) *Capitalism and Underdevelopment in Latin America*, New York: Monthly Review Press.

Furseth, I. and Repstad, P. (2006) *An Introduction to the Sociology of Religion: Classical and Contemporary Perspectives*, Aldershot: Ashgate.

Gardner, K. and Lewis, D. (1996) *Anthropology, Development and the Post-Modern Challenge*, London: Pluto Press.

Geertz, C. (1963) *Peddlers and Princes: Social Change and Economic Modernization in Two Indonesian Towns*, Chicago: University of Chicago Press.

Gidwani, V. and Sivaramakrishnan, K. (2003) 'Circular Migration and the Spaces of Cultural Assertion', *Annals of the American Association of Geographers*, 93 (1), 186–213.

Gore, C. (2000) 'The Rise and Fall of the Washington Consensus as a Paradigm for Developing Countries', *World Development*, 28 (5), 789–804.

Hart, G. (2009) 'D/developments after the Meltdown', *Antipode*, 41, 117–41.

Haynes, J. (2008) *Development Studies*, Cambridge: Polity Press.

Hoselitz, B. E. (1960) *Sociological Aspects of Economic Growth*, Glencoe, IL: Free Press.

Ish-Shalom, P. (2006) 'Theory Gets Real, and the Case for a Normative Ethic: Rostow, Modernization Theory, and the Alliance for Progress', *International Studies Quarterly*, 50, 287–311.

Kapoor, I. (2008) *The Postcolonial Politics of Development*, London: Routledge.

Kelly, R. E. (2008) 'No "Return to the State": Dependency and Developmentalism against Neo-Liberalism', *Development in Practice*, 18 (3), 319–32.

Kiely, R. (1995) *Sociology and Development: The Impasse and Beyond*, London: UCL Press.

Kiely, R. (1999) 'The Last Refuge of the Noble Savage? A Critical Assessment of Post-Development Theory', *European Journal of Development Research*, 11 (1), 30–55.

King, A. D. (1995) 'The Times and Spaces of Modernity (or Who Needs Postmodernism?)', in M. Featherstone, S. Lash and R. Robertson (eds), *Global Modernities*, London: Sage, pp. 108–23.

Kothari, U. (2002) 'Feminist and Postcolonial Challenges to Development', in U. Kothari and M. Minogue (eds), *Development Theory and Practice: Critical Perspectives*, Basingstoke: Palgrave, pp. 35–51.

Lewis, D. (2009) 'International Development and the "Perpetual Present": Anthropological Approaches to the Re-Historicization of Policy', *European Journal of Development Research*, 21 (1), 32–46.

Mehmet, O. (1999) *Westernizing the Third World: The Eurocentricity of Economic Development Theories*, 2nd edn, London: Routledge.

Mercer, C., Mohan, G. and Power, M. (2003) 'Towards a Critical Political Economy of African Development', *Geoforum*, 34, 419–36.

Moaddel, M. (1998) 'Diversities and Discontinuities in the Islamic Response to Modernity', in M. Cousineau (ed.), *Religion in a Changing World: Comparative Studies in Sociology*, Westport, CT: Praeger, pp. 159–66.

Mohan, G. (1994) 'Manufacturing Consensus: (Geo)political Knowledge and Policy-Based Lending', *Review of African Political Economy*, 62, 525–38.

Mosse, D. (2004) *Cultivating Development: An Ethnography of Aid Policy and Practice*, London: Pluto.

Muller, M. (2006) 'Discourses of Postmodern Epistemology: Radical Impetus Lost?', *Progress in Development Studies*, 6 (1), 306–20.

Nederveen Pieterse, J. (2010) *Development Theory*, 2nd edn, Los Angeles: Sage.

Plant, S. J. (2009) 'International Development and Belief in Progress', *Journal of International Development*, 21, 844–55.

Platteau, J.-P. (1994a) 'Behind the Market Stage Where Real Societies Exist, Part I', *Journal of Development Studies*, 30 (3), 533–77.

Platteau, J.-P. (1994b) 'Behind the Market Stage Where Real Societies Exist, Part II', *Journal of Development Studies*, 30 (4), 753–817.

Preston, P. W. (1986) *Making Sense of Development: An Introduction to Classical and Contemporary Theories of Development and Their Application to South East Asia*, London: Routledge & Kegan Paul.

Ram-Prasad, C. (2003) 'Contemporary Political Hinduism', in G. Flood (ed.), *Blackwell Companion to Hinduism*, Oxford: Blackwell, pp. 526–50.

Riesebrodt, M. (2006) 'Religion in Global Perspective', in M. Juergensmeyer (ed.), *The Oxford Handbook of Global Religions*, Oxford: Oxford University Press, pp. 597–609.

Rist, G. (2008) *The History of Development: From Western Origins to Global Faith*, 3rd edn, London: Zed Books (first written in 1996, translated in 1997).

Rosander, E. E. (1997) 'The Islamicization of "Tradition" and "Modernity"', in D. Westerlund and E. E. Rosander (eds), *African Islam and Islam in Africa: Encounters between Sufis and Islamists*, London: Hurst & Co., pp. 1–27.

Rostow, W. W. (1960) *The Stages of Economic Growth: A Non-Communist Manifesto*, Cambridge: Cambridge University Press.

Said, E. (1995 [1978]) *Orientalism: Western Conceptions of the Orient*, 2nd edn, Harmondsworth: Penguin Books.

Saler, B. (2008) 'Conceptualising Religion: Some Recent Reflections', *Religion*, 38, 219–25.

Sanyal, B. (1994) 'Ideas and Institutions: Why the Alternative Development Paradigm Withered Away', *Regional Development Dialogue*, 15 (1), 23–35.

Sardar, Z. (1996) 'Beyond Development: An Islamic Perspective', *European Journal of Development Research*, 8 (2), 36–55.

Schuurman, F. (ed.) (1993a) *Beyond the Impasse: New Directions in Development Theory*, London: Zed Books.

Schuurman, F. (1993b) 'Introduction: Development Theory in the 1990s', in F. Schuurman (ed.), *Beyond the Impasse: New Directions in Development Theory*, London: Zed Books, pp. 1–48.

Schuurman, F. J. (2009) 'Critical Development Theory: Moving Out of the Twilight Zone', *Third World Quarterly*, 30 (5), 831–48.

Scott, J. D. (2004) *Seeing like a State: How Certain Schemes to Improve the Human Condition Have Failed*, New Haven, CT: Yale University Press.

Segal, R. A. (2005) 'Theories of Religion', in J. R. Hinnell (ed.), *The Routledge Companion to the Study of Religion*, London: Routledge, pp. 49–60.

Sen, A. K. (1999) *Development as Freedom*, Oxford: Oxford University Press.

Simon, D. (1998) 'Rethinking (Post)modernism, Postcolonialism, and Posttraditionalism: South–North Perspectives', *Society and Space*, 16 (2), 219–45.

Stewart, F. (2009) 'Relaxing the Shackles: The Invisible Pendulum', *Journal of International Development*, 21, 765–71.

Therborn, G. (1995) 'Routes to/through Modernity', in M. Featherstone, S. Lash and R. Robertson (eds), *Global Modernities*, London: Sage, pp. 124–39.

Thomas, A. (1992) 'Introduction', in T. Allen and A. Thomas (eds), *Poverty and Development in the 1990s*, Oxford: Oxford University Press.

Thomas, S. M. (2005) *The Global Resurgence of Religion and the Transformation of International Relations: The Struggle for the Soul of the Twenty-First Century*, Basingstoke: Palgrave Macmillan.

Tibi, B. (2005) *Islam between Culture and Politics*, 2nd edn, Basingstoke: Palgrave Macmillan.

Tibi, B. (2009) *Islam's Predicament with Modernity: Religion, Reform and Cultural Change*, London: Routledge.

Tomalin, E. (2007) *Buddhism and Development: A Background Paper*, Religions and Development Research Programme, Working Paper 18, Birmingham: Religions and Development.

Van Waeyenberge, E. (2006) 'From Washington to Post-Washington Consensus: Illusions of Development', in B. Fine and K. S. Jomo (eds), *The New Development Economics: After the Washington Consensus*, Delhi: Tulika, and London: Zed Books, pp. 21–45.

Waines, D. (2001) 'Islam', in L. Woodhead, H. Kawanami and C. Partridge (eds), *Religions in the Modern World: Traditions and Transformations*, 2nd edn, London: Routledge, pp. 237–64.

Watts, M. J. (1993) 'Development I: Power, Knowledge, Discursive Practice', *Progress in Human Geography*, 17 (2), 257–72.

Watts, M. J. (1994) 'Development II: The Privatization of Everything?', *Progress in Human Geography*, 18 (3), 371–84.

Woodhead, L. (2001) 'Introduction: Modern Contexts of Religion', in L. Woodhead, H. Kawanami and C. Partridge (eds), *Religions in the Modern World: Traditions and Transformations*, 2nd edn, London: Routledge, pp. 1–12.

Woodhead, L., Kawanami, H. and Partridge, C. (eds) (2001) *Religions in the Modern World: Traditions and Transformations*, 2nd edn, London: Routledge.

Woolcock, M. (2009) 'The Next 10 Years in Development Studies: From Modernization to Multiple Modernities in Theory and Practice', *European Journal of Development Studies*, 21 (1), 4–9.

Zaidi, A. H. (2006) 'Muslim Reconstructions of Knowledge and the Re-Enchantment of Modernity', *Theory, Culture and Society*, 23 (5), 69–91.

Zaman, A. (2008) *Islamic Economics: A Survey of the Literature*, Religions and Development Research Programme, Working Paper 22, Birmingham: Religions and Development.

Zavos, J. (2010) 'Representing Religion in Colonial India', in E. Bloch, M. Keppens and R. Hegde (eds), *Rethinking Religion in India*, London: Routledge.

3

RESEARCHING RELIGIONS AND DEVELOPMENT

Tara Hefferan

Introduction

Drawing together examples of empirical research and theoretical discussion found in the wide-ranging religions and development literature, the task of this chapter is explore the various methodologies[1] scholars employ in the study of religions and development. The focus here is on the ways that scholars have approached the study of religions and development, with an eye toward identifying competing perspectives on the best way for research to proceed. The chapter also explores various 'types' of methods used in the study of religions and development, with a focus on specific techniques that religions and development researchers employ. Through detailed discussion of examples found in the religions and development literature, the chapter intends to leave readers with a clearer understanding of the multiple ways to research the links between religions and development.

Is there a methodology distinctly associated with religions and development? A scan of the literature suggests that there is not. Rather, as an interdisciplinary field of inquiry, the religions and development literature draws from existing frameworks found within anthropology, economics, history, political science, religious studies, and sociology, among others.[2] The methodological diversity inherent within and across these disciplines is mirrored within the religions and development literature. Thus the chapter will explore some of the 'fault lines' that divide religions and development research – and social science research more generally. The chapter also will consider some of the issues associated with the study of religions and development, including conceptual concerns surrounding religion, development, faith, and culture. Finally, the chapter turns to examples of various methods in action, looking at both the strengths and the weaknesses of different methods, including surveys, participant-observation, and various types of interviews.

Fault lines

Positivist versus interpretivist

Across the social sciences, and indeed within certain disciplines, considerable debate exists among scholars about the 'best' ways to go about studying the world. Certain debates emerge from epistemology, theories of knowledge, or 'how we know things' (Bernard 1995: 1). Competing epistemologies within the social sciences centre on the utility of positivism. Positivism is an orientation built around the scientific method, where the attempt is to be objective, logical, and systematic (Bernard 1995: 3). Positivism intends to locate and identify patterns or 'social laws' that are generalizable across time and place. It does this through the 'direct observations or measurements of phenomena' (Krauss 2005: 760). For the study of religions and development, positivism often is associated with the 'statistical recording of relations between [religious] data and variables' (Berzano and Riis 2012: vii). For example, Barro and McCleary (2003: 36) draw on data collected in six international surveys to 'construct a set of instrumental variables to . . . estimate the effects of religion on economic growth'. Through this analysis, they find that, for select countries and religions, increases in church attendance tend to reduce economic growth while certain religious beliefs – including those in heaven and hell – tend to increase economic growth (2003: 36).

In opposition to the positivist approach, interpretivism (also known as humanism, constructivism, and hermeneutics) argues that objectivity is an illusion. Rather, 'knowledge is established through the meanings attached to the phenomena studied. Researchers interact with subjects of study to obtain data; inquiry changes both researcher and subject; and knowledge is context and time dependent' (Krauss 2005: 759). Interpretivists, for example, believe that specific context is so central to any set of beliefs, values, or practices that insights from one context cannot be extrapolated to another. Berzano and Riis (2012: viii) suggest that interpretivism – which they formulate as hermeneutics – 'has attributed importance to the comprehension of the subjective and symbolic structures on the basis of which individuals organize and interpret their relationships with others'. For the study of religions and development, interpretivism is associated with the quest for meaning. For example, how do religiously motivated development professionals conceptualize their work, its purpose, and its goals? What are the competing understandings of development that might exist among the staff of a particular faith-based organization?

Positivist versus interpretivist approaches represent 'objective' versus 'subjective' ways of knowing. Translated into practice, does the study intend to capture some sort of external truth about the reality of the world through observation or does it search for the internal reality created by people as they seek to make sense of the world (Krauss 2005)? For positivists, there is one objective reality that can be captured through rigorous scientific study. For interpretivists, there are multiple realities, which are ever shifting and context dependent.

Emma Tomalin (2013) suggests that these two competing paradigms exist alongside a third option in the study of religions and development: phenomenology. Arising from religious studies, which was founded in the 1960s, phenomenology is a distinct methodology focused on empathy, whereby the researcher 'bracket[s] his or her own interpretation of religious phenomena and instead endeavour[s] to enter into empathy with the believer in order to describe and understand their religious beliefs and actions' (Tomalin 2013: 1622). In so doing, researchers attempt to 'get behind' what has been 'experienced' in order find its 'essence' (Riis 2012: 98). This requires that researchers suspend judgement and, to the degree possible, do not impose 'alien categories' on to the study of religious phenomena but rather 'bring out what religious acts mean to the actors' (Smart in Tomalin 2013: 1640). The intention, then, for phenomenologists is to 'produce convincing descriptions of what they experience rather than provide explanations and causes' (Bernard 1995: 15).

These different approaches will be further explicated below.

Qualitative versus quantitative orientations

Epistemological orientation is important, for it directs researchers toward asking particular kinds of questions and designing specific methodologies. The result is that positivist research often generates hypotheses that are tested through the collection and analysis of quantitative data, while interpretivist and phenomenological research searches for meaning through qualitative data collection and analysis. Despite this, however, many positivists collect qualitative data, while interpretivists may collect quantitative data (see Bernard 1995). And Guma and Lincoln note 'both qualitative and quantitative methods may be used appropriately with any research paradigm', whether positivist, interpretivist or something else (1994: 105). Indeed, there has been in recent years recognition of the value of 'mixed method' approaches, discussed below.

That said, there is a pattern that can be discerned across the positivist/interpretivist fault line that roughly corresponds to two distinct orientations in the religions and development field: quantitative and qualitative. Quantitative studies rely on mathematical measurement, whereby relevant variables are identified, with dependent variables measured 'by categories, ranks, or scores' and independent variables 'measured, controlled, or randomized' (Brink 1995: 467). Analysing data through descriptive and inferential statistical methods, quantitative researchers attempt to understand relationships between variables in mathematical terms.

Conversely, qualitative approaches are word based, open ended, and typically in depth. They often attempt to understand phenomena and behaviour from the perspective of research subjects, through interpretation of words, texts, art, context, and the like. Consistency and coherence are important criteria for interpretation (Riis 2012: 93). Ole Riis identifies a variety of qualitative approaches, including grounded theory, ethnography, case study research, and phenomenology. Often focusing on one to a few case studies 'based on observation of humans in their "natural environment"', qualitative research uses techniques like life histories, in-depth interviews, diaries, and content analysis (Riis 2012: 93).

While the research universe has these two poles – quantitative at one end, qualitative at the other – the reality is that many social scientists now appreciate the blending of methods and so situate their research somewhere in the middle. Indeed, social scientists increasingly are drawing upon 'mixed methods', relying solely neither on quantitative nor on qualitative approaches, but instead combining elements of both. This combination might reflect one approach more than the other, or it can be an equal pairing of quantitative and qualitative techniques (Riis 2012). The combinations might be concurrent, with both quantitative and qualitative techniques deployed simultaneously, or sequential, with the findings of one approach informing the development of another (Riis 2012).

As framed by Brink (1995: 463), the qualitative versus quantitative debate can be understood as one between richness and precision, as scholars debate the relative merits of each. While quantitative approaches often yield broad insights based on objective analysis, qualitative approaches typically are narrow and deep, yielding rich narrative descriptions of subjective experience and meaning. But, 'since the accuracy of descriptions requires precision and their adequacy requires richness, both poles are essential'. This is to say, 'a complete description of human experience' requires both qualitative and quantitative data (Brink 1995: 463).

Macro- versus micro-level analysis

The religions and development literature can be sorted by its level of analysis. Does a work attempt to understand and analyse religion and development from the macro-, meso-, or micro-level? By macro-level, social scientists tend to mean nationally or globally. By micro-level, scholars refer to face-to-face or local-level interactions or individual understandings. The meso-level is sandwiched in between, with the term often used to refer to specific organizations, institutions, or segments of society. When thinking about types of religions and development research, scholars begin by identifying the 'level' they are targeting for investigation, as each level has methods better suited to it. What's the unit of analysis? Is it a specific local organization? A coalition of organizations? A multilateral development agency? Or is it the beneficiaries of a project? The pastors who are assembling medical missions? The activist blogging about her development work?

Clearly, level of analysis links with the above discussion, in that those interested in micro-level subjective experiences are more likely to be qualitatively oriented and interpretive in their approaches. Meanwhile, those interested in understanding regional characteristics of faith-based social services delivery, for example, would probably be more oriented toward positivism and quantitative methods. Assessing the religions and development literature as a whole, Ben Jones and Marie Juul Petersen (2011) suggest that much of the emerging literature tends to be situated at the meso- and macro-levels, as scholars attempt to make sense of how religion informs and is deployed by organizations. One example of this can been seen in the work of Laurie Occhipinti (2005, 2009), who explores the ways two Catholic development organizations working in Argentina challenge conventional notions of neoliberal, capitalist development paradigms.

Methodological considerations

Having located themselves according to the considerations above, scholars face the practical question of how to go about studying religion and development. As in all fields of scholarly inquiry, a literature review is essential. The review allows scholars to see what research already has been completed on their specific topic. While no single database exists to compile all relevant religions and development scholarship, there are many electronic databases, typically available through university libraries, that are useful. Some especially relevant to the study of religions and development include: Abstracts in Anthropology, AnthroSource, ATLA Religion Database, EconLit, First Search, JSTOR, the Online Computer Library Center (OCLC), PAIS International, Political Science Abstracts, ProQuest Sociology, Social Sciences Citation Index, Sociological Abstracts, and WorldCat. Many relevant publications are also freely available through the Internet. For example, the website for the Religions and Development Research Programme, housed from 2005 to 2011 at the University of Birmingham, England, contains full-text working papers, research summaries, policy briefs, and other publications on religions and development topics.

What gets studied by religions and development scholars?

In their review and critique of recent works on religions and development, Ben Jones and Marie Juul Petersen (2011) suggest the literature is characterized by three (problematic) trends. First, it is focused on the positive contributions that religion might make to development – 'can religious organisations or religious knowledge inform development thinking or make development practice more effective?' (1296). Much of the literature suggests that religion does have a positive impact on development practice. Second, the literature tends to be characterized by a focus on Christian faith-based organizations (FBOs), 'at the expense of other types of religious actors, religious expressions or forms' (1297). Third, the literature is 'normative'. It assumes that religious practices and FBOs stand apart from – and provide alternative visions to – secular development. These are sound critiques of the emerging literature, though exceptions to these three trends are reflected both in the discussions below and elsewhere. For example, a more inclusive stance is put forth by Carole Rakodi (2012: 635), whose work demonstrates that 'religion and development are not separate spheres of life – they are intertwined and each influences the other', a point expanded below.

Emma Tomalin (2007, 2013) identifies another trend within religions and development scholarship: the lack of attention to gender considerations. While the broader development studies literature has built in recent decades a solid gender focus, gender analysis has yet to be fully applied to the religious dimensions of development theory and practice (as exceptions, cf. Hoodfar 2007; Pearson and Tomalin 2007; Bradley 2011; Adamu and Para-Mallam 2012; Bradley and Saigol 2012; DeTemple 2013). As Tomalin (2007, 2013) and others (e.g. Bradley 2011) have noted, this lack of attention to gender can produce a simplified version of reality, whereby religion in its 'ideal' form becomes divorced from religion as it is lived and practised. The ideal version is the dominant view, often expressed publicly by male leaders within a tradition, to the exclusion of women. But what people actually do on a day-to-day basis, how they live their lives and make sense of the world around them, can be very different from what a distant set of supposed 'rules' requires that they do (Ortner 1984; Abu-Lughod 2008).

Moreover, the ideal version suggests that religion is monolithic, with adherents interpreting teachings in the same ways, holding neatly defined beliefs and values, and behaving within a clearly bounded field of possibilities. The reality is that religion, like all dimensions of social life, is far messier than this simplified version allows. Such a misrepresentation of actual lived religion is further compounded by tendencies amongst researchers and religious actors to identify religion with official received teachings, which are typically promulgated by male religious leaders (the 'official' representatives of religious traditions). By contrast, in attempting to understand what religion is and its significance within different settings, including questions about the links between religion and development, it is important to be attuned to the distinction between 'official' and 'popular' religion, and received religious teachings and 'lived religion', and to select locations for research that reflect these observations.

What is religion?

While at the surface it seems self-evident, there is little agreement surrounding the content or character of 'religion' (see Tomalin, Chapter 1). This is owing, in part, to the great diversity of religions in the world, which makes it difficult – if not impossible – to distil all religions into a set of discrete traits or characteristics. Moreover, the very notion of 'religion' itself might be problematic. As Rakodi notes, '"religion" and the English words to talk about it, such as faith or belief, do not translate directly into other religious traditions and languages' (2012: 640). This raises the question of whether the concept is even meaningful cross-culturally or beyond Christianity (Rakodi 2012).

In trying to locate religion, some scholars discuss the distinction between 'substantive' and 'functional' definitions (e.g. Deneulin and Rakodi 2011; Rakodi 2012; Tomalin 2013). A substantive definition focuses on 'what religion is, particularly, belief in a transcendental reality or spiritual being, the sacred' (Rakodi 2012: 638). A functionalist definition focuses on what religion 'does' for society or a group (Tomalin 2013: 1483). For example, sociologists examine the role of religion in blessing the norms of a society, providing explanations for the otherwise inexplicable, or in promoting social cohesion and sense of belonging. Functionalist scholars sometimes draw on the classic understandings of anthropologist Clifford Geertz (1993: 90–91), who frames religion as a 'system of symbols' that establishes 'powerful, pervasive, and long-lasting moods and motivations' for people, by creating understandings of a 'general order of existence' that seems true. Geertz here is suggesting that religion draws people together in systems of meaning making and belonging, and that these are seated deep within individuals and communities.

What is faith?

Some scholars and religious actors distinguish 'faith' from 'religion'. They offer that 'religion' is associated with established traditions, characterized by a supreme being and codified in sacred texts, for example Christianity/Bible, Islam/Qur'an, and Hinduism/Bhagavad Gita (Clarke and Jennings 2008; Carbonnier 2013). By contrast, 'faith' 'attempts to capture the dimension of religions that extend beyond the codification of values, rules and social practices within particular traditions' (Tomalin 2013: 11). In this way, religion is formal and organized, while faith is more nebulous and expansive. But not all scholars and religious actors make a distinction between faith and religion, suggesting instead that this division is largely political, emerging from the 1996 'Charitable Choice' provision that encouraged faith-based organizations in the USA to apply for federal funding to support welfare projects. Moreover, some suggest that the term 'faith' does not have relevance outside Western Christian contexts. Jeavons, for instance, suggests that the term relates 'more closely with the religious tradition(s) of Christianity and distances it from others – like Islam or Hinduism – in which, in fact, faith is not a particularly meaningful concept or term' (2004: 141).

What is the relationship between culture and religion?

There are competing views surrounding the relationship between culture and religion. One perspective – dominant in anthropology and sociology – suggests that religion is part of the larger culture within which it is found. That is, culture is the umbrella concept, under which various institutions, traditions, identities, and customs – including religion – are brought together. Here, culture is holistic, in the sense that each dimension of culture is dependent upon, shaped by, and influences all the other dimensions. To fully understand a people's religion, then, necessitates understanding the broader context in which it is lived and experienced, and how it 'fits' with other dimensions of the culture.

Religious studies shares a similar orientation. Jill DeTemple (2013: 111) describes the religious studies view as one that understands religion as a 'flexible force woven throughout the fabric of society'. This force is at once dynamic and pervasive, and 'not only shapes morality and worldviews' but informs how adherents 'negotiate everything from immigration to sexuality' (DeTemple 2013: 111). Here again, the relationship between culture and religion is dense and entangled, suggesting the difficulty of trying to pick apart where religion starts and where it ends within a society.

Emma Tomalin (2013) identifies another view, one put forth by religious practitioners cautious about 'reducing religion to culture'. Here, boundaries between religion and culture might be drawn as a way of bringing attention to – and distancing from – beliefs and practices that are thought to fall outside the religious tradition, and yet which are carried forth in the name of that religion. Tomalin points to female genital mutilation (FGM) as an example, where arguments are made that FGM is a 'cultural' rather than an Islamic 'religious' practice. Moreover, by rejecting the idea that religion is culture, practitioners avoid the implication that their religion was created or influenced by human agency rather than it being timeless or divinely inspired.

Another view of the relationship between religion and culture comes from within the field of international development, where religion is sometimes framed as a cultural 'thing' to be manipulated, deployed, or extinguished. This view can cut both ways, with religion variously understood to signal a cultural 'backwardness' that needs to be overcome in the push to modernize or as a valuable tool that can be put to use in meeting development goals. For example, Heather Marquette (2012) examines the ways that religion has been highlighted by economists, religious leaders, and others as a way to combat corruption. The more religious a country, the less corruption it will have, and with less corruption comes higher income levels, say some scholars (Nussbaum 2006 in Marquette 2012). Hence, transforming religious values might allow a country to become more prosperous. Marquette's article takes issue with this perspective, however, by showing the multiple situational factors that mediate how values are (or are not) translated into behaviour.

What is religiosity?

Religiosity is 'how people are religious', as well as 'how religious people are' (Rakodi 2012: 641). Religiosity has been conceptualized by Helen Rose Ebaugh *et al.* (2006: 2259) as 'religious commitment' manifested through ritual practice, ideology or belief, experience, and knowledge of religious matters. Applying this idea of religious commitment to faith-based organizations, Ebaugh *et al.* suggest there are three dimensions in which faith-based organizations often demonstrate religiosity: service religiosity, in terms of FBO–client interactions; staff religiosity, in hiring and staff interactions; and organizational religiosity, in how the organization manages its public impression.

What is a faith-based organization?

Discussed in more detail elsewhere in this *Handbook* (see Occhipinti, Chapter 22), Gerard Clarke and Michael Jennings (2008: 6) have defined a 'faith-based organization' as one that 'derives inspiration and guidance for its activities from the teaching and principles of the faith or from a particular interpretation of the faith'. Jones and Juul Petersen (2012: 1298) contend that the religions and development literature has taken the term 'faith-based organization' to be a 'relatively unproblematic category'. The issue is that the label 'faith-based organization' is so broad – capturing such a vast array of different types of organizations – that defining what precisely an FBO is proves difficult.

One way this complexity has been managed is through the production of 'typologies' of faith-based organizations. While typologies are critiqued for oversimplifying reality, they – by flagging particular dimensions of an organization for greater scrutiny – nonetheless help researchers to make sense of the religious and secular dimensions of an organization. Moreover, typologies can help to facilitate discussion among researchers who are working in diverse settings, with a variety of organization forms.

For example, Tara Hefferan, Laurie Occhipinti and Julie Adkins (2009) modified a typology put forth by Sider and Unruh – a typology focused on the US context – to consider what role 'faith' plays in FBOs working in Latin America and the Caribbean. By identifying several key areas for examining faith, the typology allows researchers to consider how 'faith and religion are manifested in goals, mission, programming, and funding' along six different faith axes, ranging from 'secular' to 'faith-saturated' (Hefferan *et al.* 2009: 9).

What is development?

'Development' is a contentious term, understood in a variety of ways across both scholarly and applied realms (see also Rakodi, Chapter 2). One dominant view suggests that development is both an ideology and a set of practices that arose in the post-Second World War era as a way to socially engineer progress, modernity, and economic growth in the global South. From this perspective – and drawing inspiration from US President Truman's (1997 [1949]) Four Point Address – the world is divided into centres of economic and scientific progress and areas of poverty and 'backwardness'. Those who have achieved progress have both the ability and an obligation to share their economic expertise and technological know-how with those in poverty.

Exemplifying this kind of thinking, W. W. Rostow's (1960) modernization theory – which is discussed in more detail in Chapter 2 – was based in an evolutionary framework that located countries according to their stage of development. At one end were pre-modern societies, hampered by traditional beliefs and values that stood in the way of technological progress and industrialization. At the other end were advanced industrialized countries, with high economic growth and high living standards. While modernization occurred first in the West, Rostow believed that all countries could progress to become high-growth societies. But changing cultural values and attitudes that stymied belief in progress and discouraged individual achievement was a necessary prerequisite. Education was one way this transformation could occur.

Drawing from some of Rostow's ideas, a growth-focused development agenda became entrenched in the 1980s, with a focus on advancing productivity, trade, and economic growth. Yoked with neoliberal policy prescriptions, this agenda was formalized as the 'Washington Consensus' and came to dominate development institutions like the World Bank, USAID, and others (Williamson 1993).

While growth-oriented development continues to occupy a privileged spot in development thinking and practice, there are simultaneously a number of competing approaches that emphasize micro-level processes or personhood and/or that critique capitalism. For example, 'basic needs' approaches in the 1970s emphasized that development should attend first to the primary material needs of those living in poverty (Gardner and Lewis 1996). Similarly, human development approaches have gained traction since the 1990s. These emphasize that development should lead to an expanding of people's capabilities, enlarging their choices, and allowing them to lead full lives and to meet their potential (Sen 1999, 2009; Nussbaum 2000). These sentiments have been formulated as the UN Millennium Development Goals.

Moreover, there is 'post-development', a set of critiques expressed most prominently by Wolfgang Sachs (1992), Arturo Escobar (1995, 2000), and others (e.g. Ferguson 1994; Crush 1995; Rahnema and Bawtree 1997; Rist 1997). These scholars actively oppose the continuation of development thinking and practice, calling instead for its 'death'. From this perspective, development has been a destructive force, replacing overt colonial management with the seemingly more benign development regime. But development ultimately is an 'anti-politics' machine, turning exploitation, suffering, resource imbalances, and the like into apolitical problems that can be addressed through technical solutions that reproduce and consolidate existing power structures (Ferguson 1994). That is, development is not really intended to promote social change or social justice; rather, it serves to keep the current system intact, to the overall benefit of those doing the developing.

While the approaches to development just discussed vary significantly in terms of focus and goals, they share a tendency to neglect or dismiss religion. Indeed, until fairly recently, development studies has been largely silent on issues related to faith and religion. But, for reasons traced elsewhere in the *Handbook*, religion is now on the development studies agenda, as evidenced by the World Bank's 'Development Dialogue on Values and Ethics', the institutionalization of religion and development research programmes – including programmes at Georgetown University in the US and at Birmingham University in the UK – and the creation of a burgeoning literature, referenced both in this chapter and throughout the *Handbook*.

What problems might be presented?

Religions and development fieldwork – whereby researchers visit development organizations, study projects on the ground, engage in participant-observation, and the like – can be complicated by issues of access. Sometimes researchers have difficulty gaining permission to study people, organizations, or communities. Laura Reese (2000: 378), for example, discusses this difficulty within congregational settings, writing that 'Several forces converge to almost ensure that clergy in congregations most active in economic development will be least willing to be interviewed, simply due to lack of time and scheduling conflict.' Even when formal access to organizations is granted, the reality of actually having to interact with – and allocate time and resources to – researchers can lead an organization to be less cooperative than anticipated. Erica Bornstein (2005) recounts how she had 'seven letters' of invitation in hand, each indicating an NGO's willingness to work with her. But their ability to host her sometimes ran up against time and labour constraints. Interviews, for example, can take hours to complete, and, when there is other work to do and deadlines to meet, organizations understandably prioritize their own goals over those of the researcher.

'Lack of comfort with or suspicion of the research process' can also limit research access, particularly when the benefits of the research are not immediately clear to participants (Reese 2000: 378). This was certainly true of my on-the-ground research tracing financial flows between churches in the US and Haiti. With the flow of money from North to South, US churches were particularly keen to account for how and where the money they sent was spent. By contrast, Haitian churches were reluctant to discuss with any degree of detail how money was being dispersed or who specifically was benefiting. And, given the power imbalances separating US and Haitian parishes, such suspicions of the research process are certainly understandable and perhaps self-protective (Hefferan 2007).

Methods in action: some examples and lessons

Social scientists increasingly have turned their attention to understanding the intersections between religions and development. Yet many of the works now emerging are void of explicit or detailed discussion of methodology (as exceptions, see Deneulin and Rakodi 2011; Rakodi 2011, 2012; Tomalin 2013). Perhaps this is owing to the general trajectory of the literature, which Jones and Juul Petersen (2011) suggest has largely been donor initiated, focusing on questions that have practical relevance to organizations and sponsors. Or it might stem from a bias in the literature, one that assumes that religion has a positive contribution to make to development.

The dearth of methodologically oriented articles is not unique to the study of religions and development, however. Berzano and Riis report that in their searching of the 2010 *Social Compass*, 'among the many hundreds of articles [examining the sociology of religion], three addressed general methodological problems' (2012: x). In their review of literature on faith-based organizations, Bielefeld and Cleveland (2013) found 611 US-focused books and peer-reviewed publications, dating from 1912. Of these, 64 focused on methods (2013: 44–45).

Thus the religions and development literature's minor attention to methodology is not unusual within the broader framework of studying religion. That said, available discussion suggests at least three broad approaches in the study of religions and development: quantitative, case study, and ethnographic.

As discussed earlier, quantitative approaches gather 'numerical data that are analysed using mathematically based models (in particular statistics)' (Aliaga and Gunderson in Muijs 2011: 1). The aim is to understand the relationship between variables. While case study research is good for generating hypotheses, a point made below, quantitative approaches are particularly suited to testing hypotheses. For example, religions and development scholars might be interested in exploring whether there is a relationship between religious orientation and income levels in

Haiti. After reviewing the existing literature, perhaps they might generate a hypothesis that Catholics have higher income levels than others in Haiti. This could then be tested through the collection and analysis of quantitative data.

Case studies focus on a single unit for analysis, for example an individual, group, organization, or the like, during an identifiable point in time (Gerring 2007). As an inductive approach, case studies are beneficial as 'first line of evidence' research, when a topic has not yet been well studied or when it is being approached in a new way (Gerring 2007). They allow for deep understanding of the phenomenon under investigation, though such understanding cannot be generalized to other cases. Case study research can proceed in a number of directions, from single observations to multiple observations, or it might not include face-to-face interactions at all, while it can be either quantitatively or qualitatively oriented.

Ethnographic approaches bring researchers into prolonged face-to-face contact with research subjects. Through immersion with the group or in the culture being studied, researchers gain a grounded and deep understanding of the goings-on of a culture, in a particular place, at a particular moment in time. Ethnography relies heavily on observation, often participant-observation, discussed below. One benefit of ethnography is that it can locate the actual behaviours of individuals and groups. This is important, for as already mentioned there often is a gap between what people say they do and what they actually do in practice. Ethnography allows researchers to witness and record the lived dimensions of religion and development.

Each of these three approaches has strengths and weaknesses, which must be balanced against the objectives of the research and the researcher's epistemological stance. After mining the available secondary data, researchers formulate a research question or hypothesis, and then decide which methodology is most appropriate to the aims and objectives of the study. That is, the research question drives the specific approach used. From there, the specific techniques, tools, or methods of data collection can be designed.

What follows below is a collection of different techniques 'in action', organized by method to illustrate how scholars have employed – or might employ – various techniques in their studies of religions and development. The discussion begins with techniques more closely associated with quantitative approaches and ends with those more closely aligned with ethnography.

Survey research

Economics, political science, and some branches of sociology rely heavily on survey methods, using structured questionnaires to gather data about religiosity, demographic characteristics, income levels, and more. Survey questionnaires are typically standardized so that each respondent is presented with an equivalent – if not identical – set of questions. This technique has advantages. First, in many contexts, survey questionnaires can be self-administered via mail, telephone, or Internet relatively quickly and inexpensively, meaning interviewers need not be hired and trained. Interviewers are typically necessary when surveying illiterate populations, however. Second, because their identity remains confidential, respondents might report on sensitive research topics that cannot be pursued openly. Third, survey research allows for the drawing of representative samples, from which generalizations about the wider population might be drawn.

The World Values Survey (WVS) (http://www.worldvaluessurvey.org/) is 'a global network of social scientists who are analyzing the basic values and beliefs of people throughout the world'. In collaboration with the European Values Survey, the WVS reports carrying out nationally representative surveys in over 100 countries, containing 90 per cent of the world's population. While the WVS has completed six 'waves' of surveys to track changes in values and culture over time, secondary researchers have taken the existing data to run their own analyses, producing more than 4,000 WVS-related publications.

For example, Stephanie Seguino (2010: 1317) has drawn data from waves 2–5 of the World Values Survey to analyse how religiosity impacts gender attitudes. Seguino (2010: 1309–10) uses WVS questions that measure the intensity of religious beliefs (e.g. 'How important is religion to your life?' 'Do you belong to a religious denomination?') and religious participation ('Apart from weddings, funerals, and christenings, about how often do you attend religious services these days?'), as well as questions that capture gender attitudes around women's roles (e.g. 'A woman needs children to be fulfilled. Agree?') and gender hierarchies (e.g. 'When jobs are scarce, men should have more right to a job than women. Agree?'). Using multivariate regression techniques, Seguino (2010: 1317) is able to demonstrate that 'the gender attitudes index has a negative and significant effect on all measures of gender equality and well-being'. Another example of macro-level research drawing from survey research comes from Ambe J. Njoh and Fenda A. Akiwumi (2012), who assess the role of religion on women's empowerment in Africa. First, they used the CIA *World Factbook* to determine the religious affiliations of Africans in 47 African countries. The UNESCO Institute Data Center website was used for data on education and literacy levels (UNESCO Online). Women's political participation levels were gathered from Inter-Parliamentary Union website. The International Labour Organization (ILO) was the data source on women's participation in the labour force. Finally, the World Bank's World Development Indicators online data were used to compile development information. Njoh and Akiwumi looked at eight variables, with religious affiliation as the independent variable and women's education, labour force participation, political participation, and empowerment as dependent variables. Through statistical analysis, they identified significant positive associations between predictor variables and women's empowerment, measured as improvements in women's rates of participation in schooling, non-agricultural labour, and government, as well as increased literacy levels. Indigenous religion, for example, links with women's participation in the formal labour force. Christianity positively impacts women's literacy and labour force participation, which they note runs counter to assumptions put forth by Mama (1996) and Sudarkasa (1986) about Christianity in Africa as disempowering for women. But Njoh and Akiwumi suggest the 'most important revelation of the study' is that 'religion [religious beliefs] explains a statistically significant portion (22%) of the variability in women empowerment as a Millennium Development Goal (MDG). This suggests that any meaningful effort to empower women especially as an MDG must pay more than passing attention to the influences of religion' (2012: 16).

Quantitative studies of this kind are sometimes critiqued for being methodologically 'insufficient for proving – one way or another – a causal relationship' (Marquette 2010: 4). The fault lines identified above, between positivism and interpretivism, qualitative and quantitative, and macro and micro, are in evidence here. Indeed, the critique that Marquette and others (cf. Deneulin and Rakodi 2011) make concerns the quality of country-level data, and how such data fail to capture micro-level attitudes, beliefs, or practices. 'The [religions and development] literature is largely quantitative, with a dearth of empirical, fieldwork-based evidence. The results are often contradictory, depending on which international dataset has been used' (Marquette 2010: 4). Moreover, such surveys often 'detach' religion from the broader socio-historical and cultural frames within which it is seated (Deneulin and Rakodi 2011: 50) and can lack validity, as the self-reporting of religiosity is notoriously problematic. The reasons for this might include respondents' desire to appear more religious than they actually are by over-reporting their attendance in worship services, for example, or conversely their attempts to appear unaffiliated with a politically marginalized religion by under-reporting their religious activities or disavowing unpopular religious views.

Interviews

For many religions and development scholars, particularly those working from an interpretivist orientation, in-depth interviews serve as a primary data collection technique. Interview techniques can range from highly structured – where an interview schedule is strictly followed, with each respondent answering the same questions, in the same order, without deviation, as with survey questionnaires discussed above – to largely informal, perhaps consisting of chats with informants or conversations with those with knowledge the researcher seeks to understand. Many researchers prefer a semi-structured protocol, where a list of questions is used to guide research, but researchers have the flexibility of following new directions in the midst of the interview, should the occasion arise.

Gerard Clarke (2007) relied on face-to-face and telephone interviews in his research into why governments and donors have turned toward faith-based organizations in recent years. This question is subjective, asking respondents about their interpretation of history. Looking at the United Kingdom's Department for International Development (DFID)'s engagement with faith-based organizations, Clarke interviewed 21 staff members at DFID headquarters. Additionally, Clarke interviewed 15 FBO representatives and representatives of three donor agencies.

Through the interviews, as well as archival research of DFID and FBO publications and documents, and an email survey to 36 DFID offices, Clarke identified policy shifts at the World Bank, changes at the political level, for example US Charitable Choice legislation or more civil society focus within DFID, and activist movements, such as Jubilee 2000 and Make Poverty History, that contributed to FBO interest among government and donors.

Distinctions can be drawn between individual interviews and group – or focus group – interviews, as well. Group interviews bring together a relatively homogeneous group of individuals with the goal of collectively exploring a topic or set of topics. Group interviews can have advantages over individual interviews when time constraints exist, since several people can be interviewed simultaneously. Moreover, because focus groups tend to be conversational, they create space for respondents to engage with one another, jointly reconstructing key events. They might also permit more open exploration of sensitive topics, given that participants can talk 'in general' about such topics rather than identifying controversial viewpoints as their own.

Free-listing

Cultural domains are those areas of culture that respondents are able to list (Bernard 1995). Free-listing is a technique that researchers can use to study a particular domain. 'In free-listing, you tell informants: "Please list all the X you know about" or ask them "What kinds of X are there?"' (Bernard 1995: 240). For example, in my research on Catholic parish twinning, partnerships that link parishes in the US and Haiti in economic and religious relationships, I was interested in the ways lay Catholics in Michigan, USA understood economic development. To get at this, I gave informants a piece of paper, divided into three columns. I asked them 'When you think about development, about what it means to be developed, what sort of things come to mind?' I asked that they list, as quickly as possible, their answers in column one. After a few minutes, I then asked respondents to rank-order their responses according to importance in the middle column. Finally, I asked respondents to use the right column to explain the ordering of their lists (Hefferan 2007: 123). From this exercise, I was able to identify the development 'domain' and – combining this exercise with in-depth interviews and participant-observation – compare the degree to which lay conceptualizations of development among respondents reflected or challenged more conventional, professional understandings.

This type of free-listing exercise works best in contexts where respondents are literate, though a modified version could be crafted for other contexts, perhaps using drawings, pictures, or other visual sources.

Life histories

In micro-level, qualitative research like ethnography, life histories provide an in-depth and subjective accounting of the ways individuals experience their worlds. Typically, life histories are 'retrospective' accounts of respondents' lives, or a dimension of their lives, relayed in their own words (Plummer 2001: 19; Lewis 2008: 560). Indeed, life histories might be thought of as 'case studies' of individual lives, where the intersections between biography and history are illuminated through the telling of one's own personal stories (Sokolovsky 1996: 282; Mills 2000).

While much of the religions and development literature has been focused on either macro-level religious indicators or meso-level religious organizations, Nanlai Cao (2007) looks at individual Christian entrepreneurs in post-Mao China. The research uses both participant-observation and life history interviews to explore 'embodied systems of beliefs and processes of meaning making in daily life' (2007: 48). Cao traces the contours of the lives of Wenzhou 'bosses' to discover the ways that individual Chinese Christians negotiate the meaning of the market and Christianity. For example, 'Brother Liu' requires that his managerial staff attend weekly bible study meetings to learn the 'culture of Christianity'. Combining business development with evangelization, Wenzhou Christian entrepreneurs are creating 'a Christianity-based enterprise culture that they perceive as modern, progressive, and productive' (Cao 2007: 57).

Participant-observation

Ethnographers – particularly those situated within anthropology and sociology – draw on participant-observation as a primary research technique. Participant-observation entails spending time 'in the field' in order to get 'close to people and mak[e] them feel comfortable enough with your presence so that you can observe and record information about their lives' (Bernard 1995: 136). As the label implies, researchers are at once participating in the life of the community while also observing and recording the goings-on around them. Indeed, researchers often spend a year or more 'in the field' participating in and recording daily life.

Erica Bornstein (2005) writes about the joys and challenges of doing participant-observation among Christian NGOs in Zimbabwe. Working as an intern at Christian Care and World Vision, Bornstein also interviewed and 'hung around' with workers from several other local NGOs. Working in NGO offices, going to church services with development workers, and attending community meetings, Bornstein honestly discusses the methodological challenges of studying evangelical Christians, with whom she is at once friend, colleague, and potential convert. 'The first time someone tried to convert me and I actually considered it, I was sitting in church in Harare with a friend', she writes (2005: 30). As a 'cultural Jew', Bornstein found immersing herself in the worlds of evangelical Christians led to unexpected existential crises. She says she became hyper-attuned to a world of good versus evil. 'Perhaps

being surrounded by so much "goodness", I came to embody its opposite: transgression'
(2005: 36), she writes, while reflecting on a sudden and unprecedented urge to steal during
fieldwork.

Conclusion

This chapter has suggested that researching religions and development is a complex and diverse
endeavour, as scholars work across positivist/interpretivist, qualitative/quantitative, and macro/
micro fault lines. The lessons to take away from this discussion are these. First, as a field of inquiry,
religions and development scholarship requires researchers to be conversant across such fault
lines. Research situated firmly in any one camp will be critiqued by members of the other as
partial and incomplete. To understand why this is the case requires that scholars working in different traditions take seriously the insights of those situated within other frameworks. Second,
religions and development scholarship can inform the broader social scientific debates surrounding these fault lines. As a field of inquiry that at once attempts to delineate the development
enterprise while also understanding how individuals construct and make meaning relative to
it, religions and development has at its centre a mixed methods imperative – if not within any
single study, then through broader discussions and analyses of individual, local, national, regional,
and topical concerns.

For scholars interested in entering this field of inquiry, the question is how to identify what
constitutes 'religions and development' and then how best to study it. The methodological and
practical suggestions contained herein offer preliminary answers. Listed in the 'Online resources'
below are some additional resources that might prove useful to the novice (and more experienced) religions and development scholar.

Notes

1 This chapter draws on the distinction between methodology, as a 'theory and analysis for how research
   should proceed', and method, as 'techniques for gathering evidence' (Harding 1987: 2).
2 Here, the focus is on social scientific versus theological or philosophical approaches to religions and
   development. While social scientific approaches often come from 'outside' the religious tradition being
   examined, 'insider scholarship' is situated from within and often is an attempt to interpret and communicate religious thinking to adherents of the religion. Debate exists about whether a researcher should
   be an insider to the religious tradition being researched. Some argue that only those inside a religion
   have the ability to understand it fully. By contrast, others suggest that objectivity and perspective can be
   compromised when studying within one's own tradition. Moreover, an outsider's perspective allows one
   to see the taken-for-granted assumptions that might be naturalized by adherents.

Online resources

Afrobarometer: http://www.afrobarometer.org/
Association of Religious Data Archives: http://www.thearda.com/rcms2010/rcms_notes.asp
Association of Statisticians of American Religious Bodies: http://www.asarb.org/
Center for Faith-Based and Community Initiatives: http://www.usaid.gov/who-we-are/organisation/
    independent-offices/office-faith-based-and-community-initiatives
Center for Religion and Civic Culture: http://crcc.usc.edu/research/expertise/scholarly-resource-
    development.html
Luce Project on Religion and Global Civil Society: http://www.global.ucsb.edu/luceproject/
Oslo Center, Religion and Development: http://www.oslocenter.no/en/2012/09/religion-and-
    development/
Pew Religion and Public Life Project: http://religions.pewforum.org/

Religions and Development Research Programme: http://www.religionsanddevelopment.org/
World Faiths Development Dialogue: http://berkleycenter.georgetown.edu/wfdd
World Values Survey, Center for Political Studies, University of Michigan: http://www.isr.umich.edu/
cps/project_wvs.html

References

Abu-Lughod, Lia (2008) *Writing Women's Worlds: Bedouin Stories*, 15th anniversary edn, Berkeley: University of California Press.

Adamu, Fatima L. and Para-Mallam, Oluwafunmilayo J. (2012) 'The Role of Women's Campaigns for Legal Reform in Nigeria', *Development in Practice*, 22 (5–6), 803–18.

Barro, Robert J. and McCleary, Rachel M. (2003) 'Religion and Economic Growth across Countries', *American Sociological Review*, 68 (5), 760–81.

Bernard, H. Russell (1995) *Research Methods in Anthropology*, 2nd edn, Walnut Creek, CA: AltaMira Press.

Berzano, Luigi and Riis, Ole (2012) *Annual Review of Sociology of Religion*, Vol. 3: *New Methods in the Sociology of Religion*, Leiden: Brill.

Bielefeld, Wolfgang and Cleveland, William Suhs (2013) 'Defining Faith-Based Organizations and Understanding Them through Research', *Nonprofit and Voluntary Sector Quarterly*, 42 (3), 442–67.

Bornstein, Erica (2005) *In the Spirit of Development: Protestant NGOs, Morality, and Economics in Zimbabwe*, Stanford, CA: Stanford University Press.

Bradley, Tamsin (2011) *Religion and Gender in the Developing World: Faith-Based Organizations and Feminism in India*, London: I. B. Tauris.

Bradley, Tamsin and Saigol, Rubina (2012) 'Religious Values and Beliefs and Education for Women in Pakistan', *Development in Practice*, 22 (5–6), 675–88.

Brink, T. L. (1995) 'Quantitative and/or Qualitative Methods in the Scientific Study of Religion', *Zygon*, 30 (3), 461–75.

Cao, Nanlai (2007) 'Christian Entrepreneurs and the Post-Mao State: An Ethnographic Account of Church–State Relations in China's Economic Transition', *Sociology of Religion*, 68 (1), 45–66.

Carbonnier, Gilles (2013) *International Development Policy: Religion and Development*, Basingstoke: Palgrave Macmillan.

Clarke, Gerard (2007) 'Agents of Transformation? Donors, Faith-Based Organizations and International Development', *Third World Quarterly*, 28 (1), 77–96.

Clarke, Gerard and Jennings, Michael (2008) 'Introduction', in G. Clarke and M. Jennings (eds), *Development, Civil Society, and Faith-Based Organizations: Bridging the Sacred and Secular*, Basingstoke: Palgrave Macmillan, pp. 1–16.

Crush, Jonathan (1995) *Power of Development*, London: Routledge.

Deneulin, Séverine and Rakodi, Carole (2011) 'Revisiting Religion and Development 30 Years On', *World Development*, 39 (1), 45–54.

DeTemple, Jill (2013) 'Imagining Development: Religious Studies in the Context of International Economic Development', *Journal of the American Academy of Religion*, 81 (1), 107–29.

Ebaugh, H. R., Chafetz, J. S. and Pipes, P. F. (2006) 'Where's the Faith in Faith-Based Organizations? Measures and Correlates of Religiosity in Faith-Based Social Service Coalitions', *Social Forces*, 84, 2259–72.

Escobar, Arturo (1995) *The Making and Unmaking of the Third World*, Princeton, NJ: Princeton University Press.

Escobar, Arturo (2000) 'Beyond the Search for a Paradigm? Post-Development and Beyond', *Development*, 43 (4), 11–15.

Ferguson, James (1994) *The Anti-Politics Machine: 'Development', Depoliticization, and Bureaucratic Power in Lesotho*, Minneapolis: University of Minnesota Press.

Gardner, Katy and Lewis, David (1996) *Anthropology, Development and the Post-Modern Challenge*, Chicago: Pluto Press.

Geertz, Clifford (1993) 'Religion as a Cultural System', in *The Interpretation of Cultures: Selected Essays*, Waukegan, IL: Fontana Press, pp. 87–125.

Gerring, John (2007) *Case Study Research*, Cambridge: Cambridge University Press.

Guma, Egon G. and Lincoln, Yvonna S. (1994) 'Competing Paradigms in Qualitative Research', *Handbook of Qualitative Research*, Thousand Oaks, CA: Sage, pp. 105–17.

Harding, Sandra (1987) 'Introduction: Is There a Feminist Method?', in Sandra Harding (ed.), *Feminism and Methodology: Social Sciences Issues*, Bloomington: Indiana University Press, pp. 1–14.

Hefferan, Tara (2007) *Twinning Faith and Development: Catholic Parish Partnering in the US and Haiti*, West Hartford, CT: Kumarian Press.

Hefferan, Tara, Occhipinti, Laurie and Adkins, Julie (2009) 'Faith-Based Organizations, Neoliberalism, and Development: An Introduction', in T. Hefferan, J. Adkins and L. Occhipinti (eds), *Bridging the Gaps: Faith-Based Organizations, Neoliberalism, and Development*, Lanham, MD: Lexington Books, pp. 1–34.

Hoodfar, Homa (2007) 'Women, Religion and the "Afghan Education Movement" in Iran', *Journal of Development Studies*, 43 (2), 265–93.

Jeavons, Thomas H. (2004) 'Religious and Faith-Based Organizations: Do We Know One When We See One?', *Nonprofit and Voluntary Sector Quarterly*, 33 (1), 140–45.

Jones, Ben and Juul Petersen, Marie (2011) 'Instrumental, Narrow, Normative? Reviewing Recent Work on Religion and Development', *Third World Quarterly*, 32 (7), 1291–1306.

Krauss, Steven Eric (2005) 'Research Paradigms and Meaning Making: A Primer', *Qualitative Report*, 10 (4), 758–70.

Lewis, David (2008) 'Using Life Histories in Social Policy Research: The Case of Third Sector/Public Sector Boundary Crossing', *International Social Policy*, 37 (4), 559–78.

Mama, Amina (1996) *Women's Studies and Studies of Women in Africa during the 1990s*, Working Paper Series 5/96, Dakar: CODESRIA.

Marquette, Heather (2010) *Corruption, Religion and Moral Development*, Religions and Development Research Programme, Working Paper 42, Birmingham: Religions and Development.

Marquette, Heather (2012) '"Finding God" or "Moral Disengagement" in the Fight against Corruption in Developing Countries? Evidence from India and Nigeria', *Public Administration and Development*, 32, 11–26.

Mills, C. Wright (2000) *The Sociological Imagination*, 40th anniversary edn, New York: Oxford University Press.

Muijs, Daniel (2011) *Doing Quantitative Research in Education with SPSS*, Thousand Oaks, CA: Sage.

Njoh, Ambe J. and Akiwumi, Fenda A. (2012) 'The Impact of Religion on Women Empowerment as a Millennium Development Goal in Africa', *Social Indicator Research*, 107, 1–18.

Nussbaum, David (2006) 'Money vs. Morality: Is Corruption Just a Matter of Misaligned Incentives?', STICERD and DESTIN Public Lecture, London, 18 October.

Nussbaum, Martha (2000) *Women and Human Development: The Capabilities Approach*, Cambridge: Cambridge University Press.

Occhipinti, Laurie (2005) *Acting on Faith: Religious Development Organizations in Northwestern Argentina*, Lanham, MD: Lexington Books.

Occhipinti, Laurie (2009) 'Faith, Hope, Charity: Catholic Development Organizations in Argentina', in T. Hefferan, J. Adkins and L. Occhipinti (eds), *Bridging the Gaps: Faith-Based Organizations, Neoliberalism, and Development*, Lanham, MD: Lexington Books, pp. 197–212.

Ortner, Sherry (1984) 'Theory in Anthropology since the Sixties', *Comparative Studies in Society and History*, 26 (1), 126–66.

Pearson, Ruth and Tomalin, Emma (2007) 'Intelligent Design? A Gender Sensitive Interrogation of Religion and Development', in G. Clarke, M. Jennings and T. Shaw (eds), *Development, Civil Society, and Faith-Based Organizations*, Basingstoke: Palgrave, pp. 46–71.

Plummer, Ken (2001) *Documents of Life 2: An Invitation to Critical Humanism*, Thousand Oaks, CA: Sage.

Rahnema, Majid and Bawtree, Victoria (eds) (1997) *The Post-Development Reader*, Cape Town: David Philip.

Rakodi, Carole (2011) *A Guide to Analyzing the Relationships between Religion and Development*, Religions and Development Research Programme, Working Paper 67, Birmingham: Religions and Development.

Rakodi, Carole (2012) 'A Framework for Analysing the Links between Religion and Development', *Development in Practice*, 22 (5), 634–50.

Reese, Laura A. (2000) 'Should the Government Regulate Prophets? Methodological Problems with the Study of Faith-Based Organizations', *Economic Development Quarterly*, 14, 376–83.

Riis, Ole (2012) 'Combining Quantitative and Qualitative Methods in the Sociology of Religion', in Luigi Berzano and Ole Riis, *Annual Review of Sociology of Religion*, Vol. 3: *New Methods in the Sociology of Religion*, Leiden: Brill, pp. 91–115.

Rist, Gilbert (1997) *The History of Development: From Western Origins to Global Faith*, London: Zed Books.

Rostow, Walt Whitman (1960) *Stages of Economic Growth: A Noncommunist Manifesto*, Cambridge: Cambridge University Press.

Sachs, Wolfgang (ed.) (1992) *The Development Dictionary: A Guide to Knowledge as Power*, London: Zed Books.

Seguino, Stephanie (2010) 'Help or Hindrance? Religion's Impact on Gender Inequality in Attitudes and Outcomes', *World Development*, 39 (8), 1308–21.

Sen, Amartya (1999) *Development as Freedom*, Oxford: Oxford University Press.

Sen, Amartya (2009) *The Idea of Justice*, London: Allen Lane.

Sokolovsky, Matvey (1996) 'Case Study as a Research Method to Study Life Histories of Elderly People: Some Ideas and a Case Study of a Case Study', *Journal of Aging Studies*, 10 (4), 281–94.

Sudarkasa, Niara (1986) '"The Status of Women" in Indigenous African Societies', *Feminist Studies*, 12 (1), 91–103.

Tomalin, Emma (2007) *Gender Studies Approaches to the Relationship between Religion and Development*, Religions and Development Research Programme, Working Paper 8, Birmingham: Religions and Development.

Tomalin, Emma (2013) *Religions and Development*, London: Routledge.

Truman, H. S. (1997 [1949]) 'President Truman's Point Four Message', in G. Rist, *The History of Development: From Western Origins to Global Faith*, New York: Zed Books.

Williamson, J. (1993) 'Democracy and the "Washington Consensus"', *World Development*, 21 (8), 1329–36.

4

THEOLOGY AND DEVELOPMENT

Christian and Jewish approaches

Stephen Plant and Daniel H. Weiss

Introduction

In this chapter we explore how theological thinking informs the relationship between two faith communities and global development. Following a discussion of Christian and Jewish understandings of what 'theology' is, we then aim to outline distinctive methodological features of theological approaches when compared to social science approaches. This will be followed by an examination of some of the ways in which Christian and Jewish theologians have thought about and responded to poverty, and we will then explore some of the challenges and questions raised for these faith traditions by post-war theories and practices of development. In conclusion we make several constructive proposals about directions future theological thinking might take.

At the outset it is important to note the intention behind joint authorship of such a short contribution. In our view, there is no such thing as 'theology' abstracted from the beliefs and practices of particular faith communities. One may speak of Hindu theology or Theravada Buddhist theology,[1] and it may even be possible to identify some common features of these practices, but one should not *assume* there to be similarities without very careful analysis. Nowhere is such collapsing of one distinctive faith tradition into another more obvious than in the term 'Judaeo-Christian', with its suggestion that Judaism and Christianity are essentially alike or that Judaism is merely a historical precursor of Christianity. (It is to disrupt such assumptions that the title of this chapter, and the order in which the discussion unfolds, takes Christianity first, though it is commonly viewed as the 'younger' faith tradition.) There are exceptional circumstances in which a member of one faith tradition, or an agnostic or an atheist, may make a significant contribution to the theology of another faith tradition: one thinks, for example, of the impact on Christian and Jewish thought of the robust criticism of Friedrich Nietzsche, who was an atheist. But usually theology is a practice undertaken by confessionally committed members of particular faith traditions, which raises both methodological and epistemological questions.

Further questions surround the term 'development'. In the period following the Second World War, the term 'development' has attached loosely and metaphorically to economic, social and political processes, to the efforts of Western nations to bring about development in 'underdeveloped' countries, and to one or more ideologies, including colonial and neo-liberal (Tomalin 2013: 16–49). In the same period, and in some cases somewhat earlier (Cowen and Shenton 1996: 60–115), theologians have engaged in similar definitional and ideological debates

53

about 'development' without coming any closer to a consensus than social scientists have done. Later in this chapter we will 'sample' some of these theological debates; for now, we are working with a deliberately loose and neutral definition of 'development' that allows for all three possible understandings.

What is 'theology'? A Christian view

Before we can consider some of the issues a theologian might consider in relation to global development we need to pause on the vexed question of what theology is. The word 'theology' is constructed from two Greek words. The first, *theos*, means 'god'; the second, *logos*, has several possible meanings, some with long and rich histories in classical thought, including 'word', 'talk', 'speech' or – rather more complexly – 'the inward thought' or 'reason itself'. This etymological complexity is reflected in the variety of ways the term 'theology' is used, including at its broadest any kind of statement about 'god'. 'Theology' can, however, have a narrower, more technical sense, as a descriptor of the practice of reasoned reflection on God, and on creation in light of the knowledge of God. One classic way to define theology in this second sense is the description of theology by Anselm of Canterbury (1033–1109) as faith seeking understanding. In a passage addressed to God in his *Proslogion*, Anselm writes that 'I do desire to understand Your truth a little, that truth that my heart believes and loves. For I do not seek to understand so that I may believe; but I believe so that I may understand' (Anselm 2008: 87). This short and widely used definition of theology suggests three features of the theological task from a Christian perspective. First, theology is not 'God-talk' in the abstract. Theology is reasoned reflection that arises out of the practices and experience of a particular faith community; in turn theology tests and is itself tested by the faith practices and experience of the community it has arisen from. Secondly, theology is a practice of human *reasoning* that is obliged to follow the normal rules of disciplined conversation; it must be coherent, be clearly expressed and take account of norms, primarily the Bible and secondarily natural human reason and Church tradition. It is, in short, a pursuit of understanding. Thirdly, theology is a practice of *human* reasoning and, as such, while a theologian may ask God to point out the beginning, direct the progress and help in completion of his or her work, theology can never transcend the limits of human understanding.

What is 'theology'? A Jewish view

Any discussion of 'Jewish theology' must address the fact that, in the modern period, many have questioned whether such a notion even makes sense. Such doubts often stem from the notable observation that the Jewish tradition, in comparison to the Christian tradition, has historically produced fewer instances of *systematic* theology, and has generally not viewed the achievement of formal doctrinal systematicity as an important religious goal. Thus there are certain senses of 'theology', as employed by Christian thinkers, that may very well *not* apply to the tradition of Jewish thought and intellectual reflection. Nevertheless, the disjunction should not be overstated, and in many regards a Jewish understanding of 'theology' can have much in common with the Christian understanding detailed in the section above. In particular, the features of reasoned reflection on God and God's creation, carried out by human beings in the context of a specific community and its practices, can be identified as central to many historical Jewish texts and sources, from classical rabbinic literature, through medieval Jewish philosophical, legal and mystical traditions, down to the reflections of a wide range of Jewish thinkers in the modern period. Thus the Jewish tradition can indeed be said to contain many examples of theological reflection that may prove relevant to contemporary efforts at engaging with questions of poverty, need and development.

In addition to the aforementioned features, a key element that characterizes much of Jewish theological reflection is a strong hermeneutical drive: not simply reasoned reflection, but reasoning *from out of* earlier Jewish textual sources. While not standing in absolute contrast to the Christian tradition, the tendency to reason from texts, rather than from doctrinal or creedal propositions, has marked a notable difference in emphasis in the Jewish theological tradition. In this regard, the title and project of Hermann Cohen's monumental 1919 work *Religion of Reason out of the Sources of Judaism* illustrate this tendency clearly. Accordingly, Jewish theology involves a reflection on earlier core texts – particularly biblical and classical rabbinic literature – in a manner that seeks faithfully to be informed by past textual tradition but which leaves room for reapplication and reinterpretation of older texts in the new context of present concerns, questions and sufferings (Ochs and Levene 2002). In this sense, Jewish theology engages with past reflections on God and God's creation, in light of present problems, for the sake of future reparation and healing, and by means of reasoned reflection carried out anew.

Methodological considerations: theological approaches in comparison to social scientific approaches

Although there can be numerous areas of overlap between theological approaches and social scientific approaches to the study of religions and development, a key distinguishing methodological feature of theological approaches is their inherently *normative* quality. Social scientific approaches, broadly speaking, seek to determine 'what is the case' in relation to the data presented by a complex social environment, through the application of sociological, anthropological, historical or psychological methods. By contrast, theological approaches seek to assess 'what should be the case': how we ought to understand a particular present-day topic or phenomenon (such as international development) in light of previous reflection within a particular theological tradition. In other words, the theologian is called upon to integrate two sets of data: *past* reflection from within the historical tradition, on the one hand, and *present* social phenomena and concerns, on the other hand. From these two data sets, the theologian endeavours to construct a theological account that remains faithful to the contours of previous tradition while also extrapolating in new ways to expand understanding to the topic under consideration.

Accordingly, it is possible that two different theologians from different streams of tradition might approach the very same present phenomena and data, but might arrive at two very different theological accounts, because their respective analyses are shaped by different sets of normative commitments arising from differing inherited traditions of thought. While different social scientists might also sometimes arrive at different conclusions with regard to the same data, the theological approach is differentiated by an explicit affirmation that past tradition and reflection *ought* to affect the conclusions to which one comes: in the context of theological approaches, being influenced in one's present observation by 'previous results' is not an error to avoid, but rather a goal towards which to strive. By incorporating the conceptual richness of past tradition in this manner, theological approaches can enrich our understanding of modern phenomena in ways that extend beyond, while complementing, the perspectives provided by social scientific approaches alone.

To be sure, past tradition does not absolutely determine present theological accounts, as the theologian must employ her reason and judgement in evaluating which elements of previous tradition should be emphasized, and how they should be applied to topics that, in some cases, have not previously received sustained treatment within the tradition. The topic of development is a case in point, as the phenomenon itself has only risen to prominence in recent decades. The theologian must therefore draw upon past reflection on related, but not identical, topics that *have* been treated in the tradition (such as basic themes of poverty and justice), and must attempt to propose ways in which that specific theological tradition can be extended to these new questions of global development. Although the underdetermined nature of this endeavour means two theologians from the same tradition may end up extrapolating in different ways, careful consideration of the conceptual commitments that have come before should still provide a common grounding for those extrapolations. Thus, we examine below different ways in which the Christian and Jewish traditions, respectively, have engaged with questions of poverty and justice, in order to highlight the types of existing commitments that should shape attempts to engage theologically with the more recent phenomenon of development. In this manner, theological approaches, with their awareness of inherited conceptual commitments and of the rich particularity of previous tradition, can highlight elements of both dissonance and resonance that might be expected to arise from the encounter of existing religious traditions with contemporary social phenomena.

Christian engagements with poverty and justice – a very brief history

Before development there was charity, and though earlier Christian thinking and practice do not necessarily *determine* what comes later it is uncontroversial that they *shape* it in important ways. The oldest parts of the New Testament are the letters of Paul, the earliest of which was written in the late 40s AD. Paul's concern for social and economic relationships in the early Christian communities is evident in several letters. For example, Paul chides the church at Corinth because at community meals remembering Jesus's Last Supper – the early form of the sacrament of the Eucharist – he observed that wealthier people ate and drank well while poorer church members went hungry (I Corinthians 11: 17–22). Similarly, when the church in Jerusalem faced famine Paul was involved in collecting money from Gentile Christians in Greece and Asia Minor to help (see Acts 11: 27–30; Romans 15: 25–8; 1 Corinthians 16: 1–4; 2 Corinthians 8: 1–7). Two things are immediately noticeable about Paul's response to material need. Firstly, Paul's concern is sharing resources between Christians and not for any wider relief effort. Secondly, Paul attributed *theological* significance to such giving as an expression of the unity of each local Christian community and of the unity of the Church as a whole in which his collection was not merely intended to relieve suffering, but to help heal tensions between Jewish and Gentile Christian communities.

Jesus's view of how his followers should respond to those in need is evident in two examples in the Gospels. In Matthew 25: 31–45 a description is given of the last judgment by the Son of Man, who is typically identified with Jesus himself in Christian commentary on the story. In the parable people are set apart according to how they have lived their lives. The Son of Man tells them that they will inherit God's kingdom because 'I was hungry and you gave me food, I was thirsty and you gave me something to drink, I was a stranger and you welcomed me, I was naked and you gave me clothing, I was sick and you took care of me, I was in prison and you visited me' (Matthew 25: 35–7). The righteous express surprise at this judgment and receive the reply that 'just as you did it to one of the least of these who are members of my family you did it to me' (Matthew 25: 40). As with Paul's letters, here too 'these who are members of my family' means Christians. The suggestion that to help those in need is to help Jesus himself has worried some modern commentators, who argue it makes those in need a means to the end of loving Christ. But a 'plain sense' reading suggests little more than that serving those in need is the highest form of the Christian life.

An equally well-known passage concerned with charity is the parable of the Good Samaritan in the Gospel of Luke (Luke 10: 25–37). In the story a traveller is beaten, robbed and left by the roadside to die. A priest and a temple official pass the man by. The injured man is helped by a Samaritan, who was an outsider from the perspective of Jesus's first-century Jewish audience. The meaning of the story is spelled out in its conclusion: the injured man's neighbour is 'the one who showed him mercy' and Jesus concludes simply that one should 'go and do likewise' (Luke 10: 37).

In spite of the emphasis on charity, addressing the *causes* of poverty does not seem to have been on the mind of the writers of the New Testament. Poverty was accepted as a fact of life. According to Géza Alföldy, nearly 90 per cent of the total population of the Roman Empire lived on or from the land (1985: 98), making them highly susceptible to periodic food shortages caused by natural events such as bad weather. Justin Meggitt concludes that 'the non-élite, over 99% of the Empire's population, could expect little more from life than abject poverty' (Meggitt 1998: 50).

The general view held by the New Testament writers that governing authorities could do little about poverty helps explain their political stance. Paul held the view that 'there is no [governing] authority except from God, and those authorities that exist have been instituted by God' (Romans 13: 1). Jesus's relation to the governing authorities is similarly complex, as may be seen in the notoriously difficult saying 'give to Caesar that which is Caesar's and to God that which is God's'. This is at once an acknowledgement of Imperial authority and an expression of the view that earthly political authority is not total. In contrast, the closing book of the New Testament, the book of Revelation, takes a more radical view of political authority, describing earthly Imperial powers in lurid terms.

The Church grew slowly until the third century, after which it expanded rapidly in the cities of the Roman Empire. One of the distinctive features of Christianity, relative to the many other religions of the classical Mediterranean world, was the Church's charitable activity. The classical world was characterized by patronage: the wealthy gave generously, for example to public building projects or religious festivals, but this was always in expectation of enhancing their prestige. 'In general', as Gary B. Ferngren shows:

> it may be said that philanthropy among the Greeks did not take the form of private charity or of a personal concern for those in need, such as orphans, widows or the sick. There was no religious or ethical impulse for almsgiving; nor was pity recognized either as a desirable emotional response to need and suffering or as a motive for charity.
>
> (2009: 87)

Early Christian authors actively encouraged charitable works. By the late fourth century, Christians were pioneering quite a new kind of institution where hospitality was offered to those in need and where treatments by physicians were often part of the overall picture. There had been infirmaries before, but mainly for soldiers or for slaves, who were valuable 'assets'. Hospitals that treated all in need on the basis of a charitable motivation were in large measure Christian innovations. As the Church grew, its institutional organization of benevolent work grew with it – a process with which the growth, from the fourth century onwards, of monastic communities became increasingly tied up.

It is possible to produce a plausible narrative of the history of Christian charity in Britain that proceeds in an orderly way from charity for personal salvation from the Middle Ages, to charity as social responsibility from the early seventeenth century, to charity as moral responsibility from the nineteenth century, to the formation of the welfare state in the twentieth century (e.g. Alvey 1995). What such a narrative fails to account for, however, is local variation, exceptions to the rule and the stubborn resistance of the historical evidence to attempts to order it. Links, for example, between economic fluctuations and charitable trends prove to be unpredictable: sometimes famine has led to increased charitable giving and at other times to a decrease. In the early modern period, patterns of support by Christian individuals and institutions remained complex. However, the ongoing use of Christian rhetoric and the continued role played by Christian beliefs and values in shaping the varied motives and forms of charity remain discernible at least until the twentieth century (Ben-Amos 2008).

Until the Spanish and Portuguese began colonization of the New World from 1492, Christianity was largely – though by no means entirely – confined to Europe, Asia Minor and North Africa. From the seventeenth century, first the development of trading companies in, for example, the Indian subcontinent and later Dutch, French and British imperial expansion resulted in the formation of Christian missionary societies that sought to bring Christianity to Asia and Africa along with the manufactured goods of trade. Historical assessments of the missionary enterprise have swung from undiluted Christian admiration to undiluted post-colonial criticism: a more measured assessment capable of seeing positive and negative aspects of Christian missions may now be in order (see Deacon and Tomalin, Chapter 5). In many regions whole educational and medical infrastructures were built up and maintained by the churches.

The shift from charity to development that emerged during and after the Second World War, like all social change, has taken time to percolate through to the churches. However, from the outset individual Christians were instrumental in founding international relief and development agencies, such as the UK NGOs Oxfam (1942) and VSO (1958). In the same period Christian agencies were also established, including Christian Aid (1945), CAFOD (1962) and Tearfund (1973), which represent the full spectrum of Christian life in Britain from mainstream Protestantism, through Roman Catholicism to Protestant evangelicalism. It seems more than likely that a post-colonial crisis in confidence within European churches about *mission* in developing countries has meant a redistribution of commitment and resources to development agencies, which undertake much of the same work once undertaken by missionaries. This would account for the steady downsizing of leading mission agencies such as the Anglican USPG and CMS and the Baptist BMS since the Second World War and the steady growth of Cafod, Christian Aid and Tearfund. The Missionary Society once occupied the whole of what is now Methodist Church House in London, for example, but now occupies a part of one floor. This historical summary of the Christian practice of charity is important background if we are to grasp what Christian theology contributes to reflection on development.

Jewish engagements with poverty and justice – a very brief history

The Hebrew Bible, particularly its legal sections, repeatedly emphasizes God's command to address and respond to the needs of the poor and to establish a social order predicated on the enactment of justice and righteousness. These commandments include both specific stipulations – from the obligation to leave the corners of one's field for the poor to glean (Lev. 19: 9–10), to the prohibition against taking a widow's garment as a pledge for a loan (Deut. 24: 17), to the restoration of property in the Jubilee year (Lev. 25: 10) – and more general exhortations to support those who have fallen into impoverishment (Lev. 25: 35), to protect the widow and the orphan (Ex. 22: 21–3) and to provide for the needs of the stranger on the basis of God's love for the stranger (Deut. 10: 18–19). In this framework, a scriptural ideal is presented of a just society in a specific land governed by a set of laws that serve to ensure the material well-being of the various inhabitants of the land.

These biblical values and obligations are later carried over into the core texts of classical rabbinic Judaism. However, one significant difference from the biblical portrayal lies in the fact that, whereas the setting of the biblical laws is one of an independent society under the rulership of God, rabbinic Judaism arises in a context of military occupation under the Roman Empire. Accordingly, the communal orientation of rabbinic literature is one of 'not being in charge' and in which the notion of exile (*galut*) plays a key theological role. Following the destruction of the Temple, God's direct presence on earth is held to be suspended, and both Israel and the world as a whole are left in a state of exile. In the rabbinic framework, Israel's task is to accept exile as part of God's plan, and to wait faithfully for God to send the Messiah as part of the future redemption of Israel and of the world (see Neusner 1987). In the present period, however, in which the Messiah has not yet come, Israel's distinctive calling is not to engage in political affairs of state-sovereignty like the rest of 'the nations', but instead to cultivate justice and righteousness on the smaller political scale of the local community.

Thus, in classical rabbinic Judaism, the concept of *tzedakah* comes to play a central role in relation to questions of need, poverty and justice. While *tzedakah*, in the rabbinic context, denotes monetary and material support given to the poor and needy, and so is often translated in English as 'charity', it is notable that the term itself comes from the Hebrew root for 'justice' or 'righteousness'. In connection to the latter concepts, the giving of *tzedakah* is understood not simply as a matter of voluntary love on the part of the giver; rather, that which is given is rightly or justly due to the poor person herself. That is to say, the obligation to give is predicated not on the subjective feeling of the giver (although this is also important) but on the objective situation of the poor person: the condition of poverty mandates the giving of support as a matter of duty and justice in the eyes of God.

These central theological concepts of exile and of *tzedakah* give rise in the continuing rabbinic tradition to local communal structures of support for the poor. Thus, for instance, the Talmud describes the *kuppah*, a communal alms fund for the poor, redistributed each Sabbath eve, and the *tamchui*, for distributing food to those in need (BT Bava Batra 8a–b; Jacobs 2009: 67–8). While there was also an obligation to 'support the poor of the non-Jews along with the poor of the Jews' (BT Gittin 61a), the widespread legal oppression and social isolation of Jews during the Middle Ages meant that Jewish charitable giving ended up focusing primarily on the impoverished members of the Jewish community within a given locale (cf. BT Bava Metzia 71a; Jacobs 2009: 87–91). Moreover, since exclusion from broader culture and politics meant that Jews lacked access to mechanisms for addressing poverty through national- or state-level social or political programmes, the overall Jewish orientation to poverty remained largely at the communal level, in accord with both practical constraints and the theological framework of exile (see Penslar 2001).

The coming of modernity, which saw increased integration of Jews into wider society and culture, has led to the rise of a new theological concept in connection to poverty and justice. Alongside *tzedakah*, which traditionally focused on smaller-scale attempts to address the immediate needs of the poor, the notion of *tikkun olam* has come to play a prominent role in contemporary Jewish programmes and discourse surrounding the question of poverty. Often translated as 'repairing the world', the phrase *tikkun olam* can be found in earlier rabbinic and kabbalistic texts, but it has taken on a notably different meaning in twentieth- and twenty-first-century contexts. Whereas in kabbalistic texts it refers to the ways in which prayer and enactment of religious practices can help to repair the 'broken' metaphysical structure of the divine realm, the modern usage transfers it to the sphere of systemic social justice, often on a national or even global level. Thus, for instance, campaigning for living wage legislation, advocating for environmental regulations or promoting fair trade food products are representative activities that would fall under the modern usage of *tikkun olam*. Through this new concept, activities that might otherwise simply be part of one's political efforts as a citizen of the modern liberal state are given a specifically theological framing and are thus represented as Jewish religious duties and not merely as secular social endeavours.

The shift towards broader societal or systemic efforts to address poverty, as exemplified by the notion of *tikkun olam*, has more recently produced various Jewish organizations focused on matters of global development. Thus, in addition to Jewish organizations established to aid Jewish refugees in other countries, particularly after the Nazi Holocaust, recent decades have seen the establishment of organizations such the American Jewish World Service in the US in 1985 (American Jewish World Service n.d.) and Tzedek in the UK in 1990 (Tzedek n.d.), geared specifically towards general relief and development efforts in countries around the globe. This global scope – as highlighted by the term *olam* ('world') in *tikkun olam* – marks a prominent way in which Jewish philanthropic impulses have come to align themselves with broader humanitarian trends in contemporary Western society and culture with regard to concepts of poverty, need, justice and development.

Existing theological approaches to development

In this section of the chapter our aim is to examine existing theological approaches to development before then making some suggestions about the potential directions future commentary and action could take within both traditions. In the contemporary Jewish context, however, to date there have been few sustained theological engagements with the specific question of development, compared to Christianity, although a notable instance of Jewish interaction with the tradition of liberation theology is Marc Ellis's *Towards a Jewish Theology of Liberation* (2004 [1987]), with additional subsequent contributions in the collection edited by Otto Maduro (1991) and, more recently, the work of Santiago Slabodsky (2014). This comparative paucity may be due in part to the smaller size of Judaism as a religious tradition in the present context, with correspondingly smaller numbers of Jewish theologians, as well as differing areas of focus among contemporary Jewish religious thinkers and writers. As indicated below, however, the tradition of rabbinic Judaism contains rich potential for engaging theologically with questions of development and provides important complements and counterpoints to the types of questions raised by Christian theological reflection.

It is plain to any intelligent observer that Christianity is extraordinarily diverse with respect to its beliefs, ethics, cultural and institutional forms, and patterns of worship. This diversity has, unsurprisingly, given rise to several theological approaches to development. To illustrate, rather than to sum up, this diversity we may note three particularly distinctive examples.

Natural law (Catholic Social Teaching)

In March 1967 Pope Paul VI published his encyclical letter *Populorum Progressio*, 'On the Development of Peoples'. The letter was rooted in the conviction that there is a universal natural moral law undergirding all moral rights and duties irrespective of one's religious beliefs. The natural law originates with God, whether or not he is acknowledged as its author, and infuses the whole created order. Because of this natural law, different cultures – and different religious traditions – tend to arrive at very similar conclusions about, for example, murder, or respect for one's parents: not only, then, is natural law universal, it is immutable.

Populorum Progressio was a strikingly forthright, even advanced, statement of how natural justice should shape the development of peoples. Natural law or natural justice suggests that there should be a fair distribution of the world's resources, but left to its own devices capitalism 'works rather to widen the differences in the world's levels of life, not to enjoy them: rich peoples enjoy rapid growth whereas the poor develop slowly' (*Populorum Progressio*, para. 8). Though the Church is concerned with charity as a proper response, it is also concerned with the *rights* of the poor, and with the economic and social conditions that conspire to frustrate the exercise of those rights. Catholic Social Teaching is committed to several principles that form the basis for a fairer world. These include:

1   the universal destination of goods, i.e. that each person has the right to find in the world what is necessary for her or his well-being;
2   the option, or preferential love, of the Church for the poor;
3   the principle of subsidiarity, on the basis of which societies of a 'superior order' must adopt attitudes of help for 'lower-order' societies, e.g. the state should support, promote and develop the family.

Catholic Social Teaching (see, for a summary, Pontifical Council for Justice and Peace 2005) has continued to be the primary discourse of Catholics engaging with development, in the more recent papal encyclicals, e.g. Benedict XVI's *Deus Caritas Est* of 2005.

Liberation theology

Theologies of liberation have arisen in several contexts, for example Black theology (North America and South Africa), Minjung theology (South Korea), Dalit theology (India) and Coconut theology (Pacific). The particularizing of Christian theology to context is an important shared feature of such theologies. For reasons of space, however, we will focus on Latin America, where liberation theology has played a particularly important role.

In Latin American theologies of liberation several streams came together in response to inequality, poverty and brutal political oppression. One stream was Catholic Social Teaching; another was the 'political theology' that found expression in several German theologians of the 1960s, in which both political radicalism and liberal theology played a part. Latin American anti-colonial political thought was also added to the mix. Finally, liberation theology, certainly in its earliest period, made use of Marxist economic and social analytical tools in ways that remain a subject of theological controversy. In consequence of the use of Marxist tools and in spite of sharing with liberation theologians the principle of a 'bias to the poor', the Roman Catholic Church's Congregation for the Doctrine of the Faith, under the leadership of Cardinal Ratzinger, in 1984 published an 'Instruction on Certain Aspects of the "Theology of Liberation"' that challenged the use of Marxist analysis by asserting that 'atheism and the denial of the human person, his liberty and rights, are at the core of the Marxist theory', directly threatening 'the truths of the faith'.

Whatever the merits of the case against certain forms of liberation theology – and the claim that one cannot use Marxist analysis without promoting atheism seems, at the very least, debatable – Cardinal Ratzinger was undoubtedly correct to point out the central importance of Marxist analytical tools in liberation theology. With respect to development, the use of Marxist analysis by many liberation theologians results in an approach that shares features with Marxist critiques. A good early example of this approach is found in Gustavo Gutiérrez's foundational book *A Theology of Liberation* (Spanish 1971, English translation 1973). Gutiérrez recognizes the aspiration to end poverty and injustice lying behind many uses of the term 'development', though sceptical about the intent behind 'Western' assumptions about 'underdevelopment'. However, acknowledging that initial conceptualizations of development in purely economic terms have given way to understandings of development as a total social process, Gutiérrez believes that this does not go far enough towards the fundamental social revolution required permanently to liberate the poor. Development is synonymous, for him, with reform, and reform is not enough. This view and the importance of Marxist analysis are both neatly captured in his conclusion that:

> *Liberation* expresses the aspirations of oppressed peoples and social classes, emphasizing the conflictual aspect of the economic, social, and political process which puts them at odds with wealthy nations and oppressive classes. In contrast, the word *development*, and above all the policies characterized as developmentalist (*desarrollista*), appear some-what aseptic, giving a false picture of a tragic and conflictual reality.
>
> (Gutiérrez 1988: 24)

However, theologies of liberation cannot simply be reduced to a method of social analysis. Connected with Marxist tools of social analysis, theologies of liberation involve two further methodological features that shape the theologies' engagement with poverty and injustice. The first is a way of reading the Bible, in which a distinctive 'hermeneutic of suspicion' engages with biblical texts by reading them critically on behalf of the poor. Secondly, theologies of liberation · are committed to a theological method that leads from reading and reflection to action on behalf of the poor – a method often described using the Marxist terms 'theory' and 'praxis'.

Transformational development

A third, more recent theological approach has arisen in agencies such as World Vision and Tearfund with roots in Protestant evangelical churches. A commitment to social justice has frequently played an important part in the history of Protestant evangelicalism – one thinks, for example, of the roles of John Wesley and William Wilberforce in the campaign against the slave trade in eighteenth- and nineteenth-century England. In the late twentieth century, however, an emphasis on evangelism tended to overshadow the historic commitment of evan-gelical Christians to social justice. Transformational development represents the attempt by evangelical Christians to engage practically with global poverty and injustice in an authenti-cally evangelical way. Another phrase used by the UK agency Tearfund to describe the same approach is *integral mission*.

Bryant L. Myers expresses a preference for the alternative 'transformational development' because the term 'development' is too suggestive of material or social change alone. The term 'development' is also suggestive of modernization or Westernization. He continues: 'I use the term *transformation development* to reflect my concern for seeking positive change in the whole of human life materially, socially, and spiritually' (Myers 2008: 3). Among the reasons for this holistic approach is that words and action belong together in the proclamation of the Christian Gospel. Human beings do not themselves effect transformational development: they are consid-ered to be participants in the transforming action of God.

One of the ways this understanding of development is expressed methodologically is a strong preference where possible for working with local churches in implementing relief and development programmes, though there is a very strong commitment to giving help on the basis of need, irrespective of factors such as religion or gender. This commitment to working through local partnership has frequently involved extensive use of participatory learning and action (PLA).

Theological questions

In this section of the chapter our aim is to outline some of the kinds of questions that are raised by global development for theologians and that theologians might contribute to development studies. From a Christian perspective we suggest four possible areas where theology and global development might engage in a mutually provocative conversation. Perhaps the most obvious question is the challenge raised for any doctrine of God by the persistence of injustice and suffering in the world. This problem, associated in Christian theology with the problem of evil, is known as theodicy, the attempt to answer the question of how a loving and all-powerful God allows suffering to exist. How can Christians speak of a loving God without mocking those who suffer? This is one of the most frequently asked theological questions and one to which there are some very unsatisfactory answers. But the challenge of extreme injustice and suffering extends far deeper into God than finding a plausible resolution to theodicy. Extreme injustice and suffering challenge *all* Christian theological proposals to be such that one would feel no shame in articulating them in the presence of those who suffer.

A second area where Christian theology and global development might engage with each other concerns the relationship between charity and justice, or love and rights. Both secular humanists and Christian theologians have argued that charity and justice are incompatible. A rights–based practitioner might hold that charity is a matter of giving by those who have to those who do not have; it may therefore be said to enact an *in*justice because it maintains a relation in which some have and some do not have what all should have intrinsically. On the other hand, some Christian thinkers have also maintained that an act of Christian love is distinct from an enactment of justice. Is it really the case that justice and charity, love and rights are incompatible? An alternative approach would be to see a true act of love as an act of recognition of the intrinsic worth of the other. Love enacts justice because it sees the other as one who is loved by God intrinsically: as 1 John 4: 19 puts this, 'We love, because he first loved us.' Is it possible that charity or Christian love, viewed, for example, as Thomas Aquinas views it, as an *enactment* of justice, can provide a new way of conceiving development work?

A third area where Christian theology might provoke conversation in development studies concerns ways of understanding or defining human flourishing. One of the best-known modes of Christian engagement with injustice in recent decades has been the discourse or practice known as liberation theology. Theologies of liberation, arising in the context of political and economic injustice in several Central and South American governments in the 1960s, 1970s and 1980s, in the South African Apartheid struggle, and also in the struggle by Dalit communities in India for equality of opportunity, articulated again the apostle Paul's concern for a Christianity that took seriously a concern with material as well as 'spiritual' salvation or healing.

Theologians of liberation have helped to bring to the fore the question of how human flourishing is defined, but this is a question that has been a central part of Christian theological reflection for some time. Augustine of Hippo, for example, writing after the fall of Rome to the Visigoths in AD 410, asked how Christians ought to regard such earthly goods as peace, order, security, availability of food and fairness in the exercise of justice. Augustine concluded that Christians, just like everyone else, make *use* of such temporal goods, but that they may only truly *enjoy* God. The question of how one defines human flourishing is now widely discussed in development studies, for example in the work of Amartya Sen. Christian theology has a distinct perspective to contribute to these debates.

A fourth area for conversation concerns the relationship between beliefs in human progress characteristic of many development theories and a Christian theology of hope, sometimes also called the doctrine of eschatology. A key difference between beliefs in progress and Christian theologies of hope concerns the capacity of human beings to effect their own salvation. The evangelist Matthew writes that an angel instructed Joseph that the son to whom Mary would give birth was to be called Jesus, 'for he will save his people from their sins' (Matthew 1: 21). It is a central claim in Christian theology that Jesus, who Matthew also tells us is Emmanuel, 'God with us', is the one who saves. In so far as Christians have hope for the world, a hope that will mean peace, justice, health and prosperity for all, it is a hope that can only be achieved by God. This is certainly not an excuse for Christian passivity; on the contrary, it obliges Christians energetically to participate by prayer and righteous action in bringing God's salvation about. What, then, is the relation between Christian hope and the belief in progress that is so central to theories and practices of global development?

In the context of Jewish theology, although a number of areas of continuity exist between past tradition and the ethical and political concerns prevalent today, the classical rabbinic conceptions of exile and of Israel's task in an unredeemed world stand also in theological tension, in significant ways, with contemporary notions of *tikkun olam* and of human efforts in global development. These tensions and questions manifest themselves in relation to distinctions between divine agency and human agency, between the global and the local, and between present exile and future redemption.

From the Jewish perspective, a range of theological concerns and questions arise from the fact that many key conceptual roots of modern global development lie in specifically Christian theological notions of global mission, which were dominant in the Western cultural context in which notions of development took shape. Long-standing Christian theological notions held that, with the coming of Christ, the age of redemption had begun, and accordingly Christians are charged with the missionary task of spreading salvation to the rest of the world. In this framework, the notion would be: salvation has been brought to us and has raised us from out our previous state of non-redemption; now, we are called to bring it to others so that they too can be brought to the same state of redemption that we already enjoy. Scholars have noted ways in which certain dynamics in modern notions of development can be viewed as reconfigurations of earlier Christian views, wherein those in what was termed the 'developed world' (who have, supposedly, already been raised up to the higher state of development) have the obligation to bring the means of development to others around the world (the nations designated as currently still in a state of 'underdevelopment') so that they too can enjoy the material and economic benefits of 'progress' and development, and can thus be redeemed from their current state of poverty and need (Gronemeyer 2010: 55–73; Rist 2014: 21ff., 77). While shifts from 'spiritual salvation' towards 'material and economic salvation' are significant, the elements of global mission, of qualitative transformation and of bringing others to the state that we already enjoy can be seen as important points of continuity between earlier Christian theology and modern ideas of development.

From a traditional rabbinic theological perspective, the notion of 'bringing others to the state of redemption that we already enjoy' is problematic precisely because a core element of rabbinic theology is that Israel does *not* currently partake in redemption, as the age of redemption has not yet begun. Rather, as Amnon Raz-Krakotzkin emphasizes, the present is an era of non-redemption and of spiritual and metaphysical exile for both Israel and the world; instead, redemption is held to be a specifically future event (Raz-Krakotzkin 2007: 532, 535–6). In this framework, 'we' have not yet ourselves entered into a state of redemption and of salvation, and so the notion of bringing 'others' to such a state simply does not make sense. While there is certainly a place for seeking to improve the material condition of the poor, the notion of a task to bring about a qualitative transformation, of a transition to a qualitatively different state of affairs, is problematic, precisely because, from the rabbinic point of view, it fails to acknowledge the currently unredeemed state of the world. While for rabbinic theology a qualitative transformation *will* come about in the future, the assumption prevalent in global development efforts, that such a transformation has already been brought about in 'developed countries' and can now be spread to the rest of the world, raises concerns of premature messianic claims.

Likewise, while rabbinic theology holds the notion of a messianic future in which 'the Lord will be one and his name one' (Zech. 14: 9) there is not a present obligation on the part of human beings to establish a worldwide state of unity and sameness. In this regard, the premise of development wherein the developed world seeks to help transform the Third World so that it can be 'like us' stands in tension with the notion that the present era is one of metaphysical brokenness and that it is only with God's future redemption that a state of global human oneness will be brought about. Moreover, the historical experience of Jews, particularly in Europe, vis-à-vis Christian missionary attempts has meant that efforts to 'transform others to be like us' are associated theologically not with love and salvation, but with power and coercion. From the rabbinic perspective, while seeking justice and alleviating poverty are important obligations, the additional presence of a drive to establish unity before its proper time increases the risk that well-intended efforts of help and justice can easily slide into becoming acts of oppression and destructive homogenization.

Finally, notions of global development, in common with both the Christian missionary tradition and the contemporary concept of *tikkun olam*, take 'the world' as a whole as the proper scope and domain of human efforts of transformation. By contrast, while earlier rabbinic theology did indeed hold that the world will ultimately be repaired in a manner that encompasses prosperity, abundance, and material and economic justice, it was specifically God, and not Israel, who was tasked with this 'global transformation'. Thus, in the text of the *Aleinu* prayer, which was part of the early rabbinic liturgy and which is still found in contemporary Jewish liturgy, the worshipping community calls upon God 'to repair the world under the kingship of the Almighty [*le-takken olam be-malchut shaddai*]' but does not indicate that Israel itself is called to effect global changes in the economic or political realms. Instead, the rabbinic assumption appears to be that Israel's religious task in the present era of exile, while including active obligations of addressing poverty and material need under the framework of *tzedakah*, nevertheless remains on the level of local communities and does not extend to an encompassing 'global' sphere. Accordingly, one theological question raised by the notions of global development and by the modern sense of *tikkun olam* is whether such notions implicitly arrogate to human beings what should properly be a task designated specifically for God. Again, the salient point for this chapter's analysis is not so much this or that concrete element of contemporary development projects, but rather the *conceptuality* that underlies such projects, and the extent to which it may be linked to elisions of the distinctions between God's agency and human agency, and between the unredeemed present and the future redemption.

To be sure, although changes in the modern world have brought about significant theological changes and shifts with the contemporary Jewish community, this need not mean that these new orientations are inherently illegitimate. While modern notions of global development raise important theological questions vis-à-vis traditional Jewish theological conceptions, the answers to such questions are by no means obvious or predetermined. One can certainly construct contemporary theological accounts that emphasize continuities with modern efforts at development, just as one can construct theological accounts that emphasize discontinuities. Thus, while a wide range of answers might be given, the important point is to highlight the specific places where the questions and tensions might arise and require reflection.

Conclusion

In this chapter we have attempted to point out ways in which Jewish and Christian theological reflection can illuminate the interactions of contemporary religious communities with global development projects and efforts. By looking at earlier streams of thought within each of the two traditions, one can gain a better sense of how modern changes both pose challenges and present new opportunities to existing religious groups. Importantly, while Jewish and Christian traditions may share important conceptual understandings of certain aspects of human tasks and obligations before God, there are also equally important ways in which the two traditions may come to contemporary problems with quite different theological questions or concerns. Thus, by exploring the two different theological traditions in this chapter, our aim has been to convey the specificities of each, and therefore show the ways in which a 'one size fits all' approach to religion and development is insufficient. At the same time, recent traditions in global development present *both* traditions with new questions, for which there are no obvious or indisputable answers. Precisely this uncertainty and newness, however, underscore the fact that careful theological considerations and reflection are crucial for a full conceptual understanding of the relation between religion and development in the historical and contemporary contexts, and that such approaches can uncover additional angles and insights not available through social scientific approaches alone.

Note

1 Although if we take theology to be about *theos* – God – then this may not be an appropriate term to use with respect to Buddhism, which is often viewed as not accepting with belief in God or gods particularly in the sense of a supreme creator deity.

References

Biblical citations are from the New Revised Standard Version, Anglicized Edition (Oxford: Oxford University Press, 1998).

Alföldy, Géza (1985) *The Social History of Rome*, London: Croom Helm.
Alvey, Norman (1995) *From Chantry to Oxfam*, Salisbury: British Association for Local History.
American Jewish World Service (n.d.) Home page, www.ajws.org (accessed 1 July 2014).
Anselm of Canterbury (2008) *The Major Works*, ed. Brian Davies and G. R. Evans, Oxford: Oxford University Press.
Ben-Amos, Ilana Krausman (2008) *The Culture of Giving: Informal Support and Gift-Exchange in Early Modern England*, Cambridge: Cambridge University Press.
Cohen, Hermann (1995 [1919]) *Religion of Reason out of the Sources of Judaism*, trans. Simon Kaplan, Atlanta, GA: Scholars Press.
Cowen, M. P. and Shenton, R. W. (1996) *Doctrines of Development*, London: Routledge.
Ellis, Marc (2004 [1987]) *Toward a Jewish Theology of Liberation*, 3rd expanded edn, Waco, TX: Baylor University Press.
Ferngren, Gary B. (2009) *Medicine and Health Care in Early Christianity*, Baltimore, MD: Johns Hopkins University Press.
Gronemeyer, Marianne (2010) 'Helping', in Wolfgang Sachs (ed.), *The Development Dictionary*, 2nd edn, London: Zed Books, pp. 55–73.
Gutiérrez, Gustavo (1988) *A Theology of Liberation*, London: SCM.
Jacobs, Jill (2009) *There Shall Be No Needy: Pursuing Social Justice through Jewish Law and Tradition*, Woodstock, VT: Jewish Lights Publishing.
Maduro, Otto (ed.) (1991) *Judaism, Christianity, and Liberation: An Agenda for Dialogue*, Maryknoll, NY: Orbis.
Meggitt, Justin J. (1998) *Paul, Poverty and Survival*, Edinburgh: T&T Clark.
Myers, Bryant L. (2008) *Walking with the Poor*, New York: Orbis Books.

Neusner, Jacob (1987) *Vanquished Nation, Broken Spirit: The Virtues of the Heart in Formative Judaism*, Cambridge: Cambridge University Press.

Ochs, Peter and Levene, Nancy (eds) (2002) *Textual Reasonings: Jewish Philosophy and Text Study at the End of the Twentieth Century*, Grand Rapids, MI: Eerdmans.

Penslar, Derek S. (2001) *Shylock's Children: Economics and Jewish Identity in Modern Europe*, Berkeley: University of California Press, 2001 (esp. chap. 3, 'The Origins of Modern Jewish Philanthropy, 1789–1860').

Pontifical Council for Justice and Peace (2005) *Compendium of the Social Doctrine of the Church*, London: Burns & Oates.

Raz-Krakotzkin, Amnon (2007) 'Jewish Memory between Exile and History', *Jewish Quarterly Review*, 97 (4), 530–43.

Rist, Gilbert (2014) *The History of Development: From Western Origins to Global Faith*, 4th edn, London: Zed Books.

Slabodsky, Santiago (2014) *Decolonial Judaism: Triumphal Failures of Barbaric Thinking*, New York: Palgrave Macmillan.

Tomalin, Emma (2013) *Religions and Development*, London: Routledge.

Tzedek: Jewish Action for a Just World (n.d.) Home page, www.tzedek.org.uk (accessed 1 July 2014).

5

A HISTORY OF FAITH-BASED AID AND DEVELOPMENT

Gregory Deacon and Emma Tomalin

Introduction

Historically, religious organizations very much prefigured states in the provision of social services, welfare and health: be they hospitals in the Middle Ages in Europe or the role of *zakat* at the dawn of Islam (Ferris 2005). However, concepts of development that were dominant from the end of the Second World War, as European colonialism retreated and late capitalism reigned across much of the globe (cf. Larrain 1989), explicitly or implicitly contained expectations that as societies modernized so religion would retreat, at the very least to the private lives of individuals. With that shift, religion would become publicly irrelevant and, at its extreme conception, this would lead to its eventual demise beyond anything other than perhaps mental aberration or a quaint hobby (Deneulin and Rakodi 2011; cf. Wilson 1966). Such expectations of secularization meant that religion was little discussed in Western social science, and large mainstream development organizations and institutions had very limited engagement with religious organizations. However, in contrast to the expectations of modernization theory, religion had not only been immensely important in and for development to that point, but it remained so. Indeed religious actors became increasingly significant providers of social services and welfare provision with the retreat of the state in many developing contexts in the 1980s, and since the 1990s secular agencies and analysts (re)discovered religion (the 'turn to religion') and have increasingly sought to work with and fund religious actors and organizations of different types.

The history of faith-based aid and development is by no means simple or uncontested. Christianity's role, or the actions of those in its name, has included the ravages of Iberian *conquistadors*, for example, or the construction of mission stations, schools and hospitals by European Christian missionaries in the colonies and protectorates of their home nations, and their portrayal as 'arrogant and rapacious imperialists' (Andrews 2009: 2). Nonetheless, in important ways religious organizations have played 'development' roles since they emerged many centuries ago. In fact, Manji and O'Coill (2002) have argued that the evolution of the role of development non-governmental organizations (NGOs) in Africa 'represents a continuity of the work of their precursors, the missionaries and voluntary organizations that cooperated in Europe's colonization and control of Africa' (2002: 568). This echoes Woodberry's challenge to traditional theories of modernization that 'liberal democracy and other social transformations traditionally associated with "modernity" developed primarily as the result of secular rationality, economic development, urbanization, industrialization, the expansion of the state, and the development of new class structures' (2012: 244). Instead, he argues that, although these factors matter, 'Western modernity, in its current form, is profoundly shaped by religious factors, and although many aspects of this "modernity" have been replicated in countries around the world, religion shaped what spread, where it spread, how it spread, and how it adapted to new contexts' (2012: 244). Nevertheless, this religious underpinning of modernity and its associated development project has been to a large extent ignored or underestimated (see also Fountain, Chapter 6).

In this discussion of the history of faith-based aid and development, our aim is first to make some initial comments about traditional forms of 'faith-based aid', including the extent to which these reflect a model of charity or development. We will then discuss modern Western faith-based development and aid within a broader history of colonialism and Christian missionary activity. While Christianity played an important role in colonialism, which was arguably the precursor to the modern development project that emerged after the Second World War, this legacy of religion has been obscured. Since the 1990s, though, there has been a 'new' (or newly acknowledged) reliance on faith-based organizations (FBOs) as partners on the part of Western development actors (the bilaterals, in particular), and this has led to increased support for FBOs. This shift has been resisted in some quarters, and at least subject to great suspicion in others. Nevertheless, the change has been, when considered in terms of funding levels if nothing else, immense and it is notable that what has really been a paradigmatic shift remains underreported. Once again, the deep-rooted role of faith-based aid and development sits uneasily with Western views, which are arguably shaped by religion, but whose authors are unwilling to acknowledge that influence amidst continuing, also unacknowledged, domination by the rubric of modernity.

Traditional forms of faith-based aid and development

Within all religions we can find long traditions of charitable work, including giving food and other items to the poorest, as well as caring for orphans and the sick and dying. Humanitarian impulses are also deep seated, where the impulse to rush to the assistance of those affected by natural disasters or war is common. It is not surprising, therefore, that a central feature of most religious traditions is the existence of mechanisms for helping the poor and destitute. For instance, by the time Muhammad had established the first Islamic state in 622 CE, the giving of *zakat* had become mandatory (one of the 'five pillars' of Islam). The primary form of charitable giving in Islam is in fact *zakat* (which may only be used to benefit Muslims), given at the end of every year, calculated at 2.5 per cent of any disposable wealth above a minimum amount. In addition to *zakat*, which today is often given via an intermediary, including the state (for example in Sudan, Malaysia and Pakistan[1]), there are other mechanisms for direct giving. For instance, *sadaqah* (voluntary charity) consists of an individual devotion where charity is given directly to a beneficiary, and during Ramadan, the yearly month of fasting:

> Muslims are expected to feed the destitute while fasting themselves. A special contribution called *zakat al-fitr* has to be made at the end of the fasting month, being sufficient food to feed one person in need or its monetary equivalent. Similarly, during *Hajj* period, Muslims, whether performing pilgrimage or not, are expected to sacrifice a cow, goat or camel to feed the needy.
>
> (Kroessin 2008: 48)

Similarly, the concepts of *dana* (selfless giving) and *seva* (service) are important with the Indic religions, Hinduism, Sikhism and Buddhism. These practices are part of the duty of each individual and are to be performed without attachment to personal gain or reward. Often people will donate food or clothing, for instance, directly to those in need as part of this spiritual practice or today will contribute towards the activities undertaken by different religious charities and FBOs. In Sikhism, *Dasvandh* or *Dasaundh* refers to the practice among Sikhs of giving a tenth of one's income towards common community resources, including to support the poor (Singh 2001: 131). In Christianity, we find an emphasis upon Jesus's social teachings across all Christian denominations upon which Christians should model their behaviour. Individual Christians have a moral responsibility to follow Jesus's example, in helping the poor and reducing their suffering, and this is also taken seriously by Christian churches as institutions.

However, much of the activity these religious institutions have traditionally undertaken might seem to resemble 'charity' rather than social or human development. While the distinction between 'charity' and 'development' is not always clear cut and has been much debated, a distinction is often drawn between activities that simply provide much-needed immediate support or relief in times of disaster (today this would come under the heading of disaster or humanitarian relief) and activities that engage with people in ways that could enable them to take their own development forward and contribute towards long-term and sustainable change. From the 1980s, bottom-up and participatory approaches to development sought to shift away from a charitable model and to embrace participation and cooperation to enable people to help themselves rather than relying on others to provide assistance to them. Today, however, many FBOs do explicitly adopt the language of 'development' and are keen to demonstrate that their work with the poor goes beyond just providing short-term charity. However, if we take development to mean a process of 'social transformation', then this has close resemblances with the underlying project of many religions, which have at their core a desire not only to transform the individual but in doing so to create a community that is capable of delivering better social and political standards for people in accordance with religious teachings. It is in practice difficult to separate charitable acts from their embeddedness in broader visions of social change and development.

However, the extent to which religious approaches to development and social change in the past coincide with what we call 'development' today is far from clear. Indeed many religions have been quite critical of the donor-driven development project that has emerged since the Second World War for its emphasis upon economic growth at the expense of other understandings that focus on human 'development', understood 'as a process of enlarging people's choices and enabling them to live happy and fulfilling lives: it considers human beings to be the ends as well as the means of development' (Hulme 2007: 2). While donor-driven development today reflects a broader range of values and activities than it did during the 1950s and 1960s, there continues to be much disagreement in the development studies literature about what is meant by development and of what it should consist.

There is also disagreement about when development is thought to have emerged. Kothari (2005) and other 'post-development' thinkers are critical of those who locate the origins of development in the 1940s, following the Second World War, and instead consider that it is a continuation of colonialism. As Kothari writes, 'there has been a political imperative to distance the international aid industry from the colonial encounter, so as to avoid tarnishing what is presented as an humanitarian project far removed from the exploitation of the colonial era' (2005: 51). This account is compelling, and in the next section we extend it to also include the role that religion played in shaping the colonial project and hence modern donor-led development. In particular we will focus on the literature that explores the role of Christian missions in Africa as bolstering the imperial project and heralding the beginnings of 'development'. The history of colonialism and Christian missionaries extends beyond Africa, and the links between missionaries, imperialism and 'development' could be explored in other settings.

However, Africa provides an interesting case study, since in the post-colonial era African Christianity has undergone sweeping changes, with an attendant and growing literature considering the positive and negative aspects of this for development. Moreover, Africa is said to have seen a 'transition from state-led development to development-by-NGO' and there are significant 'critiques [of] the mode of operation of NGOs and their effectiveness as agents of change' (Freeman 2013: 3) as well as accusations that this stems from the initial models of development introduced to Africa by Christian missionaries. A further literature provides an interesting nuance to these debates, though, by considering the ways in which religion has functioned in terms of contestation of and resistance to processes of colonialism, and continues to provide alternative models and questions regarding dominant modes of development and modernity (e.g. Ranger 1968; Kalu 2008; Carson 1992; Freeman 2013).

Christianity in Africa, the imperial project and the beginnings of 'development'

The beginnings of colonialism can be located in the European global expansion beginning in the early fifteenth century, led by the Spanish and Portuguese, which enabled Christianity to be spread to other parts of the globe by missionaries. This process of exploration eventually gave way to the setting up of colonies by the Spanish and Portuguese, as well as other countries including France, Belgium, the Netherlands and Britain. While Christian missionaries accompanied explorers and colonialists, often shaping and assisting their work, they were not the only relevant religious actors, and in all colonial settings missionaries interacted in different ways with local religions, often replacing them and always radically transforming them (see Tomalin, Chapter 13) but also being transformed by them (Peel 1990; Peterson 1997).

Certainly the historical, mission or what Paul Gifford calls 'mainline' (2004: 20) churches in African settings – 'Anglicans, Catholics, Presbyterians, Methodists (even the Quakers) – have a long history of development work', with significant contributions to health, education and infrastructure provision (Gifford 2009: 46). From the early construction of isolated mission stations came forth the building of roads, schools and hospitals, as well as, of course, churches. The period when the connections between religious organizations and colonialism in Africa may be viewed as particularly 'strong' (Clarke and Jennings 2008: 2) or as 'vital and consistent' (Comaroff and Comaroff 1986: 2) is the New Imperialism in Africa from roughly the middle of the nineteenth century to the 1960s – taking in late exploration, the 'scramble for Africa' and the 1884 Conference of Berlin, consolidation of colonial roles, both world wars and the independence of East, West and Central African Anglophone and Francophone countries in the 'Wind of Change' period (cf. Ovendale 1995; Chamberlain 2014). Initial reporting or discussions of the role of missionaries, churches and colonialism from this era tended to consist simply of 'chronicles of events and actions' (Comaroff and Comaroff 1986: 2), but critical post-colonial writing on mission Christianity moved into the realms of 'polemics, historical analyses, and contemporary accounts of missionary activity by authors suggesting that there was an intimate, inevitable connection between missions and "cultural imperialism"' (Porter 1997: 367).

In broad terms, post-colonial critiques have argued that, in the theology they taught and through the structures they built, Christian missionaries laid the groundwork for the arrival of colonialists (Beidelman 1981), with missionaries acting as 'ideological shock troops' (Silverman 2005: 144); that missionaries justified the colonial project to Africans through indoctrination in new and alien ideals that were damaging for their development (Mackenzie 1993); and that social welfare projects and infrastructure were provided by missions (often funded by subscription and collections in Europe) and this supported colonial states that would have been unable to fund such activities otherwise (Manji and O'Coill 2002: 569). Biblical translation and education in churches, for example, can be seen as involved in the development of literacy, but also in the control and utilization of language to particular ends (Welmers 1974; Schiffman 1996; Harries 2001; Pennycook 2005). Furthermore, schooling by missionaries has been discussed as being important for producing elites, who came to take control of national development beholden to particular conceptions of state, race and development (Ajayi 1965). In this manner, John and Jean Comaroff speak of the 'incorporation of human subjects into the "natural", taken-for-granted forms of economy and society' or 'the internalization of a set of values, an ineffable manner of seeing and being' (1986: 2). To further distil these arguments, they might be put into two broad categories suggesting that, on the one hand, mission Christianity justified the colonial project with faith, and that, on the other, it supported it with faith-based development projects. Anger at the perceived role of Christianity in colonialism is perhaps best summarized in a widely reported statement (of disputed origin) that 'the missionaries came with the Bible, and we had the land: when they left, they had the land, and we still have the Bible'.[2]

In these terms, mission Christianity during the colonial period is in essence subject to the claims and counter-claims that are made regarding colonialism in Africa in general (Rodney 1972; Clarence-Smith 1979; Comaroff and Comaroff 1986; Jarrett 1996). Questions have, however, been raised over the range, extent and pervasiveness of mission involvement in colonialism. Many early Christian communities were small and reliant on limited communities of former slaves (Strayer 1978) or marginalized, landless members of communities, for example (Sandgren 1982). Consideration also needs to be given to other religions and attendant limitations on Christian influence – especially given the dominance of Islam in many regions (Heap 1998; Newbury 2004) and the extent to which Africans adopted or adapted Christian ideas according to traditional religious worldviews (Sundkler 1961). Furthermore, arguments have been made that Christianity in colonial Africa might represent resistance, rather than something more akin to brainwashing. In fact, Christianity in Africa has been cast by some in quite the opposite role, as instead introducing and facilitating protest and contestation of and resistance to colonialism (Ranger 1968). Terence Ranger, originally a proponent of this position later 'abandoned the attempt to demonstrate that African independent church movements in Central Africa constituted a stage in the evolution of anti-colonial protest, lying between early armed resistance and the rise of modern mass nationalist parties' (Ranger 1986: 2). However, many mission-educated subjects do seem to have questioned their altered universe: mission education often meant that Biblical texts were interrogated and those who had attended mission schools were the first to express 'open resistance to the colonial order by pointing to its inconsistency with biblical injunction, and by freeing from the holy text itself a charter for liberation: the message of the chosen suffering in exile, whose historical destiny was to regain their promised land' (Comaroff and Comaroff 1986: 2).

Nevertheless, Manji and O'Coill contend that contemporary NGOs are involved in carrying on 'the work of their precursors, the missionaries and voluntary organizations that cooperated in Europe's colonization and control of Africa' (2002: 568). In establishing this historical narrative they aim not only to explain how things have developed but also to make a moral judgement about the ideological similarities between the colonialists, Christian missionaries and modern NGOs, arguing that today NGOs contribute greatly to 'undermining the struggle of African people to emancipate themselves from economic, social, and political oppression' and only 'marginally to the relief of poverty' (ibid.). Their narrative suggests that following independence and the involvement of a range of external international relief and development agencies (including those that were faith based) most of these agencies and organizations (as well as many of the governments of new African nations) in fact took little notice of the work carried out by religions or of the role that religions were playing in local conceptions and practices of development, whilst remaining beholden to pre-existing, Christian ideas of commerce and civilization.

Another reason for the low profile of mission churches at this point (despite their continuing significance in development), was their acquiescence with post-colonial states (Joseph 1993: 232) in the face of accusations of neo-colonialism and fear that 'any kind of critical stance' might have resulted in the detention of clergymen (Newell 1995: 246). However, many mission churches continued to focus on infrastructure-led development – in short, roads, hospitals and schools (cf. Gifford 1998); as Paul Gifford puts it, 'Blessed with enormous resources, educated personnel and extensive grassroots networks, the Catholic Church [for instance] is a development agency without parallel' (Gifford 2009: 81). Moreover, as civil conflicts increasingly took their toll in nations that lacked such services even before the ravages of war, faith-based relief and medical groups responded to particular events and conflicts, such as the Biafran war. Such groups include Christian Aid, Habitat for Humanity, Care International, Church World Service, Oxfam, World Vision and Caritas (consisting of groups such as Catholic Relief Services, formed in 1943) amongst others. Even The World Council of Churches (WCC), formed in 1948, began as a fellowship of churches, but spent much of its programmatic work in its early years dealing with humanitarian issues. This was also very much the case with regard to the Lutheran World Federation (LWF), founded in 1947.

It was not until the 1980s and the subsequent ending of the Cold War that the Christian churches showed significant moves towards critical engagement with oppressive regimes, support for democratization and suggestions regarding other modes of development than existing state-enforced, top-down imposition. In March 1992 the Malawian Catholic bishops, acting as the Episcopal Conference of Malawi (ECM), released a Lenten pastoral letter (Mitchell 2002: 5), which is credited with breaking the 'spell of the Banda dictatorship and awaken[ing] Malawians to the need and possibility of radical political reform' (Road 2003: 132). The picture is complex, though, and in many, especially French-speaking, countries leading Catholics took part in national conferences, and these were often utilized by rulers to restrict dissent. In Zaire, 'It is claimed that senior Catholic figures were bought off by material inducements, quite apart from the fact that the institutional role of the Church was believed to be supportive of almost any temporal regime, including Mobutu's authoritarian rule' (Haynes 2004: 69). Perhaps most odiously the Christian churches 'were deeply implicated in the 1994 genocide of ethnic Tutsi in Rwanda' (Longman 2001: 163).

Away from the mainline churches, though, African Christianity was undergoing paradigmatic changes, particularly through the increasing influence of Pentecostalism and Evangelicalism. As discussed further in Chapter 8, Birgit Meyer, amongst many others (Gifford 2004; Maxwell 2006; Marshall 2009; Deacon and Lynch 2013), states that 'the appropriation of Christianity in Africa has entered a new phase' moving from mainline domination and schismatic African independent churches (AICs) (see also Chapter 7) to 'current Pentecostal–Charismatic Churches (PCCs)' that have a powerful, visible 'mass appeal' (Meyer 2004: 448). In the realm of conceptualizing economic development, New Pentecostal and Evangelical theologies are notable for beliefs in and attempts to 'leap over the local national environment to embrace a global modernity' (Martin 2005: 149) as promised by a very personal spirituality and Jesus figure. The way in which Pentecostalism engages with development questions precisely what is meant by 'development', demanding alternatives to a 'secular' definition, and replacing it instead with one that sees development as part of God's plan (Freeman 2013: 2). Such new churches or movements, linked by what is called the Faith Gospel, hold ideas regarding 'the reversal of [personal] economic desolation' (Kalu 2008: 213) and a search 'for [individual] excellence' (Carson 1992: 153) that are expected to lead to one's 'financial prosperity' (Gifford 2004: 49).

Thus, Christianity was of great importance for colonial development in Africa (and continues to be so to this day) in a variety of ways and correspondingly appears to have played a role in creating the foundations for the modern development project – described by Manji and O'Coill as 'a vast institutional and disciplinary nexus of official agencies, practitioners, consultants, scholars and other miscellaneous "experts" producing and consuming knowledge about the "developing world"' (2002: 568). As critics argue, once the formal colonialists withdrew they were shortly afterwards replaced with a 'neo-colonialism' in the form of the modern development project, which through provision of aid could effect the global spread of Western values, including capitalism. In this way we may argue that religion (i.e. Christianity) was a driver of formal colonialism. In the next section of this chapter we will consider the role that it has played in the post-colonial (or even 'neo-colonial') development project.

Institutional (re-)engagement with faith-based development

Despite the existence of a vibrant range of religious actors in African settings, as Bompani notes in Chapter 7, in post-colonial Africa as elsewhere there were dominant discourses that predicted that development and modernization would be accompanied by secularization. Similarly, large international development institutions, since their inception following the Second World War, maintained a position of secularism and thereby distance from religious organizations. The donor-driven development project has typically viewed these aspects of life as outdated and likely to disappear as societies develop and modernize. Additionally, 'culture' more broadly, of which religion is often viewed as a manifestation, has been understood as something that potentially gets in the way of development. As Eade writes, '"local" or "traditional" cultures have been seen as a brake on development, while the international development agencies and their national counterparts regard themselves as culturally neutral – if not superior' (2002: ix). Moreover, according to Eade, development policies and practices 'for the most part . . . proceed as though all cultures are, or seek to be, more or less the same: development, from this perspective is a normative project' (2002: ix).

However, in the 1990s a range of factors (for further detail see Occhipinti, Chapter 22) resulted in a significant re-engagement with religion by Western governments and international development NGOs. A shift to government funding for religious organizations occurred in the US, for example, with the 1996 Welfare Reform Act and its facilitation of the 2001 Faith-Based and Community Initiatives Act. Following this legislation, which allowed government funding of FBOs, directly or through agencies such as USAID, a survey identified 159 faith-based organizations that received more than $1.7 billion in USAID prime contracts, grants and agreements from 2001 to 2005 (*Globe*, Boston, 8 October 2006). Overall, in the US, government funding to FBOs almost doubled from 10.5 per cent of aid in 2001 to 19.9 per cent by 2005 (ibid.).

As regards international or multilateral development, the Zeitgeist in the late 1990s into 2000s was more widely one of holistic, alternative and even spiritual approaches to development. The damaging impact of International Monetary Fund (IMF) imposed Structural Adjustment Programmes (SAPs) on education, health and other basic rights throughout the developing world had proven increasingly hard to ignore. There was a wide reassessment amongst development practitioners of the meaning of development and the dominant conception of growth in gross domestic product (GDP) as sufficient or necessary. As early as 1990 the United Nations (UN) introduced its Human Development Indicators, and arguably a growing sense of a need for more compassionate, broad-based or even caring development began to emerge. In fact, it might be claimed that the UN had always been something of an FBO, dominated by Judaeo-Christian ideals (Linden 2008). Christian churches in particular were instrumental in pushing for the creation of the institution and arguing for human rights references to be included in the 1945 UN Charter. The Federal Council of Churches, for example, was extremely active in drafting text for the charter and then moved to push its thoughts through American committee representatives. More than 1,200 non-governmental organizations (NGOs) attended the conference to finalize the UN charter in San Francisco. Beyond the Christian organizations involved, Jewish groups and especially the American Jewish Committee exerted a powerful presence. However, it was in the 1990s that a new religious acceptance came to be signalled publicly, and spirituality was mentioned in calls for action and communiqués by, for example, the United Nations Conference on Environment and Development in 1992, the United Nations World Summit for Social Development in 1995, the United Nations Fourth World Conference on Women in 1995[3] and the United Nations Conference on Human Settlements in 1996 (Berger 2003).

At the World Bank the decision was taken as early as 1982 to 'explore cooperation between NGOs and the Bank' (Pallas 2005: 677), though at that early stage Christopher Pallas at least suggests that 'Little of note was accomplished' (ibid.). However, he argues that this was followed by lobbying on the part of NGOs that deemed Bank projects to be unproductive or directly damaging, that this culminated in obstruction of the Bank's activities[4] and that in response to these protests the Bank reluctantly acknowledged the work of NGOs and as a result 'poverty/ church groups' came to be listed in its strategic planning. The development of the World Bank's engagement with religions represents an intricate and disputed history that can be followed at length and from different angles elsewhere (Thomas 2004; Pallas 2005; Katherine Marshall and Van Saanen 2007; Jones and Juul Petersen 2011; Katherine Marshall 2013). What has been widely reported, though, is that, as the Bank looked, in part at least, to change the nature of this engagement, in 1998 it launched the World Faiths Development Dialogue to be a vehicle that would 'promote a dialogue on poverty and development, both among the different faith traditions and between them and development agencies' (WFDD 2003). The next year also saw the Churches of Africa and World Bank Conference on Alleviating Poverty in Africa, in Nairobi – as an initiative of the churches. The Bank then set up a (now defunct) internal office for faith relations (the Development Dialogue on Values and Ethics).

The UN and World Bank are but two examples of this shift towards consideration of faith-based development on the part of international, multilateral agencies. And by 2009, in Kenya alone, the following range of religious organizations, engaging in development work, and gaining 'most, even all, of their funds from governments or world bodies – for example from USAID, the EU or the UN', were to be found:

> World Vision International, Catholic Relief Services, the Lutheran World Foundation . . . and other significant players like Christian Aid, Cafod and Tear Fund (from UK), DanChurchAid, Norwegian Church Aid, Diakonia (Sweden), Cordaid (Holland), Trocaire (Ireland), Church World Service, Christian Reformed World Relief Committee, Samaritan's Purse and Medical Assistance Plan (MAP) International (USA), Misereor and Bread for the World (Germany), Caritas Switzerland, Jesuit Refugee Services, and the Adventist Development and Relief Agency.
>
> (Gifford 2009: 48)

Despite this new, apparently open and accepting acknowledgement of religion on the part of the major donors and agencies, as is argued elsewhere in this *Handbook*, commentators have been critical that in general this re-engagement has been not with small, diverse, new religious movements but with more historically rooted, hierarchical, 'carefully codified "book" religion[s]' (Clarke and Jennings 2008: 5). The framework for this engagement has assumed an interaction between distinct secular and religious actors, with particular religious actors favoured for resembling the methods and processes of secular development (as well as passively expressing their faith position). Certainly the religious make-up of those involved is not homogeneous or exclusively Christian, but, even where the religious organizations have not been Christian, engagement has tended to be with those organizations most similar to or at least agreeably polite to such churches regarding conceptions and structure.

Moreover, this engagement between development actors and 'faith-based organizations' has been critiqued for only recognizing a narrow range of religious actors as well as for constituting an instrumentalization of religion to serve the ends of Western development rather than considering whether certain faith communities might aspire to different goals altogether (Deneulin and Bano 2009). Jones and Juul Petersen argue that international institutions are using religion 'to do development "better"' (Jones and Juul Petersen 2011: 1291). In response to this 'turn to development', new organizations have arisen and old ones have reshaped themselves in response to the political climate, which has sought to elevate the role that faith traditions can play in many aspects of public life, including international development. At the same time, groups outside the mainstream continue to question dominant approaches to development, and it may also be a time for a reassessment of the extent to which large development institutions are slowly being altered, if not transformed, by religion, rather than acting only as cynical appropriators of faith as vehicles for ongoing cultural hegemony.

Conclusion

In this chapter we have highlighted that, until recently, the religious contribution to aid and development has tended to be ignored by Western development policy and practice. While religious traditions were involved in the provision of social welfare and service provision, including health and education, long before the dawn of modern development policy and practice, this legacy was obscured and sidelined by the secular modern development project, which emerged in the post-Second World War period. Moreover, as a number of scholars have convincingly argued, the contemporary development project can itself be traced back to the work undertaken by Christian missionary organizations, for example, in Africa, which enabled the colonial state to expand and consolidate its rule. Thus, parallels have been drawn between missionaries as facilitators of colonialism, and modern development NGOs as spreading and solidifying Western development goals and interests (Manji and O'Coill 2002). However, just as the colonial project badly needed and benefitted from the support of religion, the modern – some would argue neo-colonial – development project is also finding ways of drawing religion into its programmes. While these new manifestations of faith-based aid and development could be viewed as a counterpoint to critiques that mainstream development is homogenous and restricts the space for alternative conceptions of development, critical voices have challenged the renewed interest of major development institutions in religions, not least for engaging with them instrumentally. This is undoubtedly a concern but at the same time there is a broader set of faith-based development actors that have yet to be adequately taken into consideration, undoubtedly because they do not comfortably fit with the style of religious expression and structure that mainstream development actors feel comfortable with. Faith-based aid and development is a complex and contested terrain that is rapidly shifting and innovating, at times coinciding with the modern Western development goals and at other times seeking to challenge and transform them. Nevertheless, whilst some faith-based approaches may be anti-development, in the extreme sense of supporting terrorism and gender inequality, others continue to question development in productive and challenging ways.

Notes

1 Shi'a Muslims do not believe that *zakat* should be collected and administered by the state. Today many Islamic FBOs use these traditions of giving to raise money for their causes and to enable people not living in Islamic states to fulfil their obligations.
2 For example Carmichael (1966); and http://www.youtube.com/watch?v=dFFWTsUqEaY.
3 Although the challenges of faith-based development were demonstrated clearly at this event, where there were strong conflicts between the Vatican and Muslim states.
4 In particular funding of the International Development Association.

References

Ajayi, J. F. A. (1965) *Christian Missions in Nigeria 1841–1891: The Making of a New Elite*, London: Longman.
Andrews, Edward (2009) 'Christian Missions and Colonial Empires Reconsidered: A Black Evangelist in West Africa, 1766–1816', *Journal of Church and State*, 51 (4), 663–91.
Beidelman, Thomas (1981) *Colonial Evangelism*, Bloomington: Indiana University Press.
Berger, Julia (2003) 'Religious Nongovernmental Organizations: An Exploratory Analysis', *Voluntas: International Journal of Voluntary and Nonprofit Organizations*, 14 (1), 15–39.
Carmichael, Stokely (1966) 'Black Power', speech at Berkeley University, 29 October.
Carson, Ben (1992) *Think Big: Unleashing Your Potential for Excellence*, Grand Rapids, MI: Zondervan.
Chamberlain, Muriel (2014) *The Scramble for Africa*, Abingdon: Routledge.
Clarence-Smith, William Gervase (1979) 'The Myth of Uneconomic Imperialism: The Portuguese in Angola, 1836–1926', *Journal of Southern African Studies*, 5 (2), 165–80.
Clarke, Gerard and Jennings, Michael (2008) 'Introduction', in Gerard Clarke and Michael Jennings (eds), *Development, Civil Society and Faith-Based Organizations: Bridging the Secular and the Sacred*, Houndmills: Palgrave Macmillan.
Comaroff, John and Comaroff, Jean (1986) 'Christianity and Colonialism in South Africa', *American Ethnologist*, 13 (1), 1–22.
Deacon, Gregory and Lynch, Gabrielle (2013) 'Allowing Satan In? Toward a Political Economy of Pentecostalism in Kenya', *Journal of Religion in Africa*, 43 (2), 108–30.
Deneulin, Séverine and Bano, Masooda (2009) *Religion in Development: Rewriting the Secular Script*, London: Zed Books.
Deneulin, Séverine and Rakodi, Carole (2011) 'Revisiting Religion: Development Studies Thirty Years On', *World Development*, 39 (1), 45–54.
Eade, Deborah (2002) 'Introduction', in *Development and Culture: Development, NGOs and Civil Society: Selected Essays from Development Practice*, Oxford: Oxfam.
Ferris, Elizabeth (2005) 'Faith-Based and Secular Humanitarian Organizations', *International Review of the Red Cross*, 87 (858), 311–25.
Freeman, Dena (ed.) (2013) *Pentecostalism and Development: Churches, NGOs and Social Change in Africa*, Basingstoke: Palgrave Macmillan.
Gifford, Paul (1998) *African Christianity: Its Public Role*, London: Hurst.
Gifford, Paul (2004) *Ghana's New Christianity: Pentecostalism in a Globalising African Economy*, London: Hurst.
Gifford, Paul (2009) *Christianity, Politics and Public Life in Kenya*, London: Hurst.
Harries, Patrick (2001) 'Missionaries, Marxists and Magic: Power and the Politics of Literacy in South-East Africa', *Journal of Southern African Studies*, 27 (3), 405–27.

Haynes, Jeff (2004) 'Religion and Democratization in Africa', *Democratization*, 11 (4), 66–89.

Heap, Simon (1998) '"We Think Prohibition Is a Farce": Drinking in the Alcohol-Prohibited Zone of Colonial Northern Nigeria', *International Journal of African Historical Studies*, 31 (1), 23–51.

Hulme, David (2007) *The Making of the Millennium Development Goals: Human Development Meets Results-Based Management in an Imperfect World*, Brooks World Poverty Institute, Working Paper 16, http://www.bwpi.manchester.ac.uk/resources/Working-Papers/bwpi-wp-1607.pdf (accessed 12 September 2012).

Jarrett, Alfred Abioseh (1996) *The Under-Development of Africa: Colonialism, Neo-Colonialism and Socialism*, Lanham, MD: University Press of America.

Jones, Ben and Juul Petersen, Marie (2011) 'Instrumental, Narrow, Normative? Reviewing Recent Work on Religion and Development', *Third World Quarterly*, 32 (7), 1291–1306.

Joseph, Richard (1993) 'The Christian Churches and Democracy in Contemporary Africa', in John Witte (ed.), *Christianity and Democracy in Global Context*, Boulder, CO: Westview.

Kalu, Ogbu (2008) *African Pentecostalism: An Introduction*, New York: Oxford University Press.

Kothari, Uma (ed.) (2005) *A Radical History of Development Studies: Individuals, Institutions and Ideologies*, Cape Town: David Philip, and London: Zed Books.

Kroessin, Mohammed Ralf (2008) *Concepts of Development in 'Islam': A Review of Contemporary Literature and Practice*, Birmingham: Religions and Development WP 20.

Larrain, Jorge (1989) *Theories of Development: Capitalism, Colonialism and Dependency*, Cambridge: Polity Press.

Linden, Ian (2008) 'The Language of Development: What are International Development Agencies Talking About?', in Gerard Clarke and Michael Jennings (eds), *Development, Civil Society and Faith-Based Organizations: Bridging the Secular and the Sacred*, Houndmills: Palgrave Macmillan, pp. 72–93.

Longman, Timothy (2001) 'Church Politics and the Genocide in Rwanda', *Journal of Religion in Africa*, 31 (2), 163–86.

Mackenzie, Clayton (1993) 'Demythologising the Missionaries: A Reassessment of the Functions and Relationships of Christian Missionary Education under Colonialism', *Comparative Education*, 29 (1), 45–66.

Manji, Firoze and O'Coill, Carl (2002) 'The Missionary Position: NGOs and Development in Africa', *International Affairs*, 78 (3), 567–83.

Marshall, Katherine (2013) *Global Institutions of Religion: Ancient Movers, Modern Shakers*, Abingdon: Routledge.

Marshall, Katherine and Van Saanen, Marisa (2007) *Development and Faith: Where Mind, Body and Soul Work Together*, Washington, DC: World Bank.

Marshall, Ruth (2009) *Political Spiritualities: The Pentecostal Revolution in Nigeria*, Chicago: University of Chicago Press.

Martin, David (2005) *On Secularization: Towards a Revised General Theory*, Aldershot: Ashgate.

Maxwell, David (2006) *African Gifts of the Spirit: Pentecostalism and the Rise of a Zimbabwean Transnational Religious Movement*, Oxford: James Currey.

Meyer, Birgit (2004) 'Christianity in Africa: From African Independent to Pentecostal–Charismatic Churches', *Annual Review of Anthropology*, 33, 447–74.

Mitchell, Maura (2002) 'Living Our Faith: The Lenten Pastoral Letter of the Bishops of Malawi and the Shift to Multiparty Democracy, 1992–1993', *Journal for the Scientific Study of Religion*, 41, 5–18.

Newbury, Colin (2004) 'Accounting for Power in Northern Nigeria', *Journal of African History*, 45 (2), 257–77.

Newell, Jonathan (1995), 'A Moment of Truth? The Church and Political Change in Malawi, 1992', *Journal of Modern African Studies*, 33 (2), 243–62.

Ovendale, Ritchie (1995) 'Macmillan and the Wind of Change in Africa, 1957–1960', *Historical Journal*, 38, 455–77.

Pallas, Christopher (2005) 'Canterbury to Cameroon: A New Partnership between Faiths and the World Bank', *Development in Practice*, 15 (5), 677–84.

Peel, J. D. Y. (1990) 'The Pastor and the Babalawo: The Interaction of Religions in Nineteenth-Century Yorubaland', *Africa*, 60 (3), 338–69.

Pennycook, Alistair (2005) 'The Modern Mission: The Language Effects of Christianity', *Journal of Language, Identity, and Education*, 4 (2), 137–55.

Peterson, D. (1997) 'Colonizing Language? Missionaries and Gikuyu Dictionaries, 1904 and 1914', *History in Africa*, 24, 257–72.

Porter, Andrew (1997) '"Cultural Imperialism" and Protestant Missionary Enterprise, 1780–1914', *Journal of Imperial and Commonwealth History*, 25 (3), 367–91.

Ranger, Terence (1968) 'Connections between "Primary Resistance" Movements and Modern Mass Nationalism In East and Central Africa, Part I', *Journal of African History*, 9, 437–53.

Ranger, Terence (1986) 'Religious Movements and Politics in Sub-Saharan Africa', *African Studies Review*, 29 (2), 1–69.

Road, Kenneth (2003) 'Church Life, Civil Society and Democratisation in Malawi 1992–96', in James L. Cox and Gerrie ter Haar (eds), *Uniquely African? African Christian Identity from Cultural and Historical Perspectives*, Trenton, NJ: Africa World Press.

Rodney, Walter (1972) 'How Europe Underdeveloped Africa', in P. Rothenberg (ed.), *Beyond Borders: Thinking Critically about Global Issues*, New York: Worth, pp. 107–25.

Sandgren, David (1982) 'Twentieth Century Religious and Political Divisions among the Kikuyu of Kenya', *African Studies Review*, 25 (2/3), 195–207.

Schiffman, Harold (1996) *Linguistic Culture and Language Policy*, Hove: Psychology Press.

Silverman, David (2005) 'Indians, Missionaries, and Religious Translation: Creating Wampanoag Christianity in Seventeenth-Century Martha's Vineyard', *William and Mary Quarterly*, 62 (2), 141–74.

Singh, Wazir (2001) 'The Sikh View of Charity', in W. Singh and N. K. Singh (eds), *Spiritual Value of Social Charity*, Delhi: Global Vision.

Stockman, Farah, Kranish, Michael, Canellos, Peter S. and Baron, Kevin (2006) 'Bush Brings Faith to Foreign Aid: As Funding Rises, Christian Groups Deliver Help – with a Message', *Boston Globe*, October 8.

Strayer, Robert (1978) *The Making of Mission Communities in East Africa: Anglicans and Africans in Colonial Kenya, 1875–1935*, New York: SUNY Press.

Sundkler, Bengt (1961) *Bantu Prophets in South Africa*, Cambridge: James Clarke & Co.

Thomas, S. M. (2004) 'Faith and Foreign Aid, or How the World Bank Got Religion and Why It Matters', *Review of Faith and International Affairs*, 2 (2), 21–30.

Tomalin, Emma (2013) *Religions and Development*, London: Routledge.

UNFPA (2004) *Culture Matters: Working with Communities and Faith Based Organizations*, New York: UNFPA.

Welmers, William (1974) 'Christian Missions and Language Policies in Africa', in J. Fishman (ed.), *Advances in Language Planning*, The Hague: Mouton, pp. 191–203.

WFDD (World Faiths Development Dialogue) (2003) *Cultures, Spirituality and Development*, Washington, DC: WFDD.

Wilson, Bryan (1966) *Religion in Secular Society: A Sociological Comment*, London: C. A. Watts.

Woodberry, Robert (2012) 'The Missionary Roots of Liberal Democracy', *American Political Science Review*, 106 (2), 244–74.

6

PROSELYTIZING DEVELOPMENT

Philip Fountain

Introduction: the prickliest of subjects

One of the most frequent questions asked of me by new acquaintances when they learn about my ethnographic research into the Mennonite Central Committee, a North American Christian development organization, and its work in the context of Indonesia is: *Do they proselytize?* The sheer predictability of the question in both academic and development industry contexts would be a bore if it was not also so thoroughly revealing. The fact that 'religious NGOs' are imagined as having a predilection for illegitimate extensions of religious concerns says something important about the imaginations at work. The question almost always presumes that there is something inherently illegitimate, immoral, or just downright distasteful when development is intermixed with religious propagation. In fact, this is a veritable article of faith in development circles, and suggesting otherwise is tantamount to heresy. Proselytism is arguably the prickliest subject in the emerging field of religion and development.[1]

This chapter argues that it is pivotal to *think with* concepts and practices of 'proselytization' – and various close synonyms including 'conversion', 'evangelism', and 'missionization' – for research into the cultural politics of development. The chapter does so by rethinking the questions that are asked about the subject. Rather than presuming an essential link between religious actors and proselytism, and rather than presupposing that all forms of conversionary impulses are necessarily illicit, this chapter instead probes the logics undergirding the questioning itself. In so doing I invite further critical attention into what I have termed 'proselytizing development', a phrase that intentionally maintains ambiguity over the object of referral: does it evoke a particular sub-set of development actors who do proselytizing or does it rather infer that all development, whether labelled religious or otherwise, is incurably proselytizing?

Proselytization as problem

Development has a problem with proselytization. Because problems are privileged windows into the study of cultural and political processes, development's problem with proselytization offers an invaluable starting point for a critical examination of development. The work of de-linking proselytization and development is premised on the belief that their intermixing is illegitimate, coercive, and dangerous. These themes are frequently regurgitated in Western media

80

reports, with a marked insistence on the moral imperative for clear demarcation.[2] While such discursive policing is certainly influential and deserves closer attention than it has received to date, I focus my analysis on two particular instances of institutional-legal separation. The 'problem' of proselytization is particularly apparent within the policy frameworks used by development institutions.

The first example concerns legal measures separating proselytization and development that have been instituted by most major donor governments around the world (though notably less so among 'emerging' donors from the Middle East and elsewhere). The Australian government, for example, deploys a series of overlapping regulatory mechanisms to achieve this separation.[3] The repetition of these divisions points toward their central location, and their orthodox status, within the Australian aid programme. The mechanisms include the Code of Conduct of the Australian Council for International Development (ACFID), the umbrella body for Australian NGOs involved in international development work, which states that there must be a 'clear separation' between all funds designated for aid or development and those to be used 'to promote a particular religious adherence'.[4] In order to channel funding from the Australian government's aid programme, an enticing arrangement for many such organizations, an NGO must gain accreditation under the Australian NGO Cooperation Program (ANCP), for which, according to the 2012 *NGO Accreditation Guidance Manual*, they will be required to demonstrate that they are able philosophically and programmatically to 'differentiate' between development and evangelism.[5]

Another legal mechanism for separation is tax deductibility, a status granted by the Australian government to particular activities and not for others. The explanation of requirements for the Overseas Aid Gift Deduction Scheme (OAGDS), which provides guidelines for eligibility relating to tax-deductible donations, states that 'evangelical' activities '*cannot* be considered under the OAGDS' (emphasis in original).[6] It is necessary for those agencies that engage in evangelism to indicate how these activities are adequately 'distinguished' from development, and how the two are 'managed separately'. Whereas the other legal mechanisms for separating proselytization and development are notably generic and vague on their use of terminology, the OAGDS includes the most substantial discussion, defining evangelism as 'the practice of attempting to convert people to another religion or faith'. Acknowledging the Christian origins of the term, the guidelines nevertheless insist on the ability of the term to refer to 'other religions' attempts to convert people to their religion or faith'. Evangelistic activities include discriminating against those belonging to particular religious groups or aiming to 'persuade or develop religious beliefs and faith practices among project beneficiaries', which may include 'theological training and training in and study of works of religious wisdom such as the Koran, Torah or Bible'. The 'building and maintenance of places of worship' is also exempt from tax deductibility.

These policy documents all assume that proselytization is an exclusively religious affair. But if proselytization is something *only* religions do then it is necessary also to ask 'What is religion?' Unfortunately, none of the documents in question attempt to provide an answer, and the working definition is therefore left implicit.[7] The absence of a working definition of religion is not merely a semantic concern. At stake are crucial issues of power, control, and money. But the absence of an attempt to provide a working definition is also hardly surprising. An adequate definition must be broad enough to encompass a culturally diverse set of practices; that is, it must be a definition that can travel and therefore one that has universal applicability, and yet narrow enough not to include everything, which would clearly be counter to the de-linking thrust already described. Such definitions are notoriously difficult to obtain. Nevertheless, religion is clearly imagined here as a defined object that is always and everywhere distinguishable from other practices. That is, religion is *sui generis* ('of its own kind'), boundable, ahistorical, and transcultural.

Work by Talal Asad (1993, 2003), Russell McCutcheon (1997), Peter van der Veer (2001), Timothy Fitzgerald (2003, 2011), Tomoko Masuzawa (2005), and William Cavanaugh (2009) – and a slew of other critics of 'religion' from anthropology, religious studies, and theology – has engaged critically with precisely this understanding of religion such that it is flatly rejected – and for good reason. Rather than assuming that religion is always easily identifiable, they point instead to its *historicity*. The idea of 'religion', for Benson Saler (2000), is a Western 'folk category' that developed out of a particular context and which has mistakenly been assumed to be globally applicable. But not all societies have straightforward analogues for 'religion' in their own languages, and in any case the meanings of religion are changed and are reworked over time and space. Given that the issue of the definition of religion is central to financial flows and power dynamics associated with Australian government aid, the lack of definition is really quite a problem.[8]

A second example is the Code of Conduct for the International Red Cross and Red Crescent Movement and Non-Governmental Organisations (NGOs) in Disaster Relief of 1994. At the time of writing over 515 humanitarian organizations were signatories of the Code, including many of the largest and most influential humanitarian actors.[9] It is widely regarded as definitive for laying out the basic standards of humanitarian action. On questions of proselytization it too engages in explicit boundary policing. Point 3 of the Code stipulates that 'Aid will not be used to further a particular political or religious standpoint.' The proceeding explication acknowledges 'the right of NGHAs [non-governmental humanitarian agencies] to espouse particular political or religious opinions' and yet affirms that 'assistance will not be dependent on the adherence of the recipients to those opinions'. Point 3 also offers a guarantee that signatories 'will not tie the promise, delivery or distribution of assistance to the embracing or acceptance of a particular political or religious creed'.

Point 3 addresses religion and politics together, and the comparison is illuminating. Recent critiques of both development and humanitarianism have highlighted the impossibility of engaging in non-political activity (Ferguson 1994; Escobar 1995; Rist 2002; Li 2007; Barnett 2011; Donini 2012). Even when aid actors avoid engaging directly with party politics, elections, or advocacy and lobbying they nevertheless make decidedly political interventions. To engage in issues of poverty is to be immersed in questions of power and inequality. Of course, there are good *political* reasons to frame one's actions as apolitical and purely technical interventions (Li 2007), but this is not the exclusion of politics but rather a kind of discursive cosmetics that enables political work to be carried out, as it were, under the radar. Given this vociferous critique it is revealing, therefore, that a parallel critique about the bracketing of religion has hardly begun. Yet, even if we accept that there may be good reasons for humanitarian organizations to appear a-religious, the line drawing on this matter is more easily said than done, even within the Code.

The general thrust of the Code's point 3 is clear – the goal is to de-link the intent to spread 'religious opinions' from humanitarian action. Beyond the issue of whether religion is best understood as a matter of 'opinions' – it could also be about practices, dispositions, or, as some would have it, the truth – the very act of marking the boundary draws attention to frayed edges. These gaps are apparent in the shift from the initial statement to the explication of this in the text that follows. The initial framing disallows the use of aid to 'further' a religious standpoint. However, in keeping with the Universal Declaration of Human Rights, which in Article 18 declares that 'Everyone has the right to freedom of thought, conscience and *religion*' (my emphasis),[10] humanitarian agencies are granted the ability to 'espouse' religious positions. The exact difference between 'espousing' and 'furthering', however, is entirely unclear. It is difficult to imagine any clear distinction between articulating a position, or even merely identifying oneself as adhering to a position, and the promotion of it. The lack of clarity opened by the non-difference between espousing and furthering is made all the more blurry by the Code's commendation, in point 6, to 'strengthen' local capacities. Again, questions centre on whether, or how, a distinction between 'furthering' religion can be separated from 'strengthening' local capacity, when mosques, churches, temples, ritual activities, and various congregational formations are often key elements of, and indeed also indistinguishable from, local 'civil society' (Weller 2001). Given that strengthening local capacities may well require the enhancement of 'religious' institutions – resourcing their capacity to engage and service communities and thereby also cementing their moral authority – then these two imperatives may frequently be in direct conflict.

Another shift between the initial point 3 statement and the explanatory text that follows is that, while the former implies a blanket ban of religious 'furthering', the latter focuses exclusively on restrictions directed against what can be regarded as 'coercive conversion', that is, the deployment of aid as a tool to manipulate changes in the recipients' religious adherence by tying aid to changing religious affiliation and/or the embrace of particular beliefs. But are these two necessarily synonymous? For example, in situations of common Islamic adherence would the furthering of religion, say in the provision of theological resources and the active leadership of aid staff in rituals of worship, be a flagrant and distasteful breaching of trust or the compassionate practice of fraternal relationships and (in accordance with the above) the enhancement of local capacity? Indeed, would the refusal to engage in a community's communal practices be itself a betrayal of trust and an impediment to effective relief? The fact that such an outcome is conceivable suggests that even if a line between furthering and espousing religion could be effectively drawn it is far from clear that furthering is itself inherently something that should be avoided.

Benthall and Bellion-Jourdan (2009: 156) have correctly argued that 'Christian missionary activity and humanitarian aid have been progressively de-linked from each other since the founding of the Red Cross movement'. The legal-institutional examples just discussed point also to this impulse for demarcation and separation. However, the ambiguity in both examples opens up uncertainty as to how this de-linking is operationalized. It is clear that the de-linking of proselytization from humanitarian and development activities may be considerably more complex than is often imagined, not least because of severe problems associated with defining and locating 'religion'.

Purification and amnesia

The preceding examples highlighted a pervasive moral project which has systematically sought to draw sharp distinctions between proselytization and development. Given the general acceptance within the mainstream Western development industry of the need for such a rigid separation, and given the difficulty of instituting clear-cut demarcations, it is necessary to ask why such a project came to be regarded as unquestionable orthodoxy.

There are, of course, pragmatic reasons for de-emphasizing 'religious motivations' for all sorts of activities. Explicit Christian proselytizing in particular, but by no means exclusively, can provoke vigorous responses.[11] But while this could justify a *strategic* de-linking – that is, targeted and occasional separations as deemed politically prudent – this hardly explains the felt necessity for broad-sweeping universal declarations of demarcation, as is actually the case. Other explanations need to be sought. These are, I suggest, best found by paying attention to the logics and politics of *modernity*. There are two closely connected processes that deserve particular attention: (1) a passion for *purification*, which insists on the moral imperative for clear demarcation; and (2) the compulsive forward movement associated with dreams of progress, which is accompanied by a concomitant *amnesia*.

Modernity can be understood as an age in which a particular social imaginary has become dominant, a key feature of which is secularity (Taylor 2007). The secular can be defined in a variety of ways. A particularly helpful approach is to see the secular as a matter of 'institutional differentiation' through which human activity is parcelled out (with varying degrees of success) into distinct spheres.[12] The processes of categorizing, separating, mapping, and taxonomic ordering are features of a peculiar optic which is integral to the modern apparatus of governmentality (Scott 1998). Whether secular modern demarcation necessarily involves the *removal* of religion from the 'public sphere' and its isolation as 'private' reason, as is often thought, or whether it can involve various other configurations of boundary activation and differentiation remains contested.[13] Yet the key point is not the specific location of religion in contemporary society; it is rather the assumption that 'religion' and 'society' are separable and that, therefore, it is possible to locate religion somewhere and not elsewhere. In modernity religion becomes imaginable as being confined to something called the 'the religious sphere' (Milbank 2006: 144). Talal Asad (2003) has argued that secularism is best understood not as a discrete set of practices but rather as instituting a *redefinition of religion* such that religion becomes imagined as being locatable and boundable. Situating religion as an ahistorical and transcultural object renders it available for techniques of management through the policing of boundaries.

In an important paper Jonathan Benthall (forthcoming) argues that all attempts at maintaining boundaries should be regarded as acts of *purification*. The institution of boundaries is a kind of purity-seeking. Drawing on Mary Douglas's seminal *Purity and Danger* (1966), Benthall weaves within secular–religious dichotomization to argue that both humanitarianism and various religious traditions, and he is particularly concerned with Islam, exhibit parallel 'puripetal' dynamics through which polluting influences are expunged in order to avoid contamination. This analysis is illuminating for the problem of proselytization. Proselytization is a polluting threat to the purity of the secular development enterprise. The mixing of the two endangers development's moral authority, and calls into question its ability to stand above cultural traditions (and thereby exceed history) or to expand across spatial gaps (and thereby exceed geography). Proselytizing development is polluting because it breaks the taboo of proper demarcation. It is for this reason that proselytization is consistently and forthrightly rejected among development actors; the problem of proselytism is the danger of pollution.

However, acts of purification are always chronically incomplete. Boundaries are never watertight. Ring-fencing always leaves gaps. Because the bounding of religion is never total, the borderlands of separation must be continually policed and the dividing lines frequently redrawn. Following Bruno Latour (1993) we should even reconsider whether acts of purification and their dissolving or admixture are mutually exclusive processes. Latour argues that, to the contrary, the greater the emphasis on purification the more profuse the proliferation of hybrids, translations, and in-betweens. It is within the context of the modern fetish for purification that the *de-religionization* of development in the post-Second World War era is best understood. Indeed, it is an archetypal instance of modern purification, all the more so because it remains incomplete and therefore necessitates continual reiteration through codes, laws, and discursive policing.

A de-religionization of development was necessary because development and humanitarianism are so profoundly indebted to particular religious histories, including a missionary heritage. De-religionization is an act of purification, but it is also a kind of *amnesia*. Because development is 'a ruthlessly future-oriented concept' (Ekbladh 2010: 272) it is particularly prone to forgetfulness. For David Lewis, development agencies operate in a 'perpetual present', with a resulting neglect in historical reflection (Lewis 2009). The compulsive forward movement accompanying ideologies of progress is crucial for discussions of proselytization. This cultivated amnesia enables a particular imagination to be considered plausible in which mainstream development shares no affiliation with missionary endeavours. Ongoing continuities, lessons unlearned, and the unnerving proximity of the past can all be sidestepped for a belief in our own uniquely potent veracity, different in type and kind from all that came before. This is, of course, patently not the case.

A child of missionaries

As also discussed in Chapter 4 (Plant and Weiss), contemporary Western development is a direct descendent of Christian proselytizing impulses, dispositions, practices, and organizational forms. This lineage is part of what is now being described as the ongoing imbrications of post-Enlightenment secularity in Christian genealogies (Asad 1993, 2003; Milbank 2006; Keane 2007; Taylor 2007; Agamben 2011). While long occluded both in development scholarship and among development organizations themselves, such associations are now receiving close scholarly attention.

In his narration of humanitarianism in the *longue durée*, Michael Barnett (2011) examines how Western humanitarianism interacted with, drew upon, and emerged out of a specifically Christian ethos. He points specifically to the prominent role played by evangelicalism in the birth of humanitarianism. The humanitarian 'big bang', for Barnett, was a sea change in ideas of compassion which emerged during the religious experimentation of the seventeenth and eight-eenth centuries in Europe. Evangelicalism[14] was central to these changing moral sentiments. The emphasis on believers' salvation and the felt need to go about furnishing this salvation to others – and therefore also the belief that others, given the opportunity, could be saved – spurred pervasive 'moral ambitions' (cf. Elisha 2011) among evangelicals to remake society. This was because, providing sufficient will was present, society was considered *remakeable*. A power-ful 'missionary impulse' (Barnett 2011: 54) gave rise to a burst of charitable activities and social reform. Obstructions to the path of salvation – and this included not merely inadequate infor-mation about one's salvific opportunities but also social vices including poverty, alcoholism, and inadequate education – should be removed. To do so, the science of government was deployed to ensure appropriate programmes were implemented. It was evangelicals who believed that, with appropriate techniques and technologies of intervention, the world could be reformed, if not in a heavenly image as such, then at least in a heaven-bound direction. This was, of course, a deeply paternalistic pursuit. But Barnett argues that it was from these origins that humanitarian-ism sprang. Motivated by a belief in the unity of humanity and a confidence in the superiority of Christian or European civilization, and accompanying colonial and capitalist routes, humanitari-anism spread from its domestic origins and circulated around the world. Contemporary Western humanitarianism is the product of the evangelical passion for saving distant others.

In *The Great American Mission*, David Ekbladh's (2010) seminal history of American develop-ment, the place given to Christian missionaries is less dramatic than in Barnett's (2011) account, but no less pervasive. In the early years of American modernization programmes (1930s–1960s) missionaries were perennial actors in planning meetings and international cooperation activi-ties, and powerful advocates for American involvement in international development. Indeed, expanding American missionary activity in the nineteenth century, influenced by a rise of the Protestant 'social gospel' which sought to attack social ills in both the US and overseas through the transfer of education and technology, preceded and directly fed into the emphasis on devel-opment that emerged in the twentieth century. It was during this early period that formative ideas were established within American self-understandings of their place in the world, includ-ing particularly faith in the superiority of American civilization and the moral imperative to be a beacon of light for other, less advanced peoples (Ekbladh 2010: 19–27). Missionary connections were also important in the post-war launch of the age of development, with missionaries playing influential roles as advocates for a proactive American state intervention as well as being important channels for government funding (2010: 106–09).

Further insight into the important role of the 'social gospel' in giving birth to contemporary aid and development is provided by Pamela Klassen (2011) in her study of Canadian liberal medical missions through the long twentieth century. Klassen's liberal Protestants were passionately formed through missionary engagements and propelled by moralities of compassion and concern for distant suffering others. As with Barnett's evangelicals, these liberals were committed to social, political, and economic transformation rooted in theological rationales. Liberal Protestants were also increasingly shaped by, and helped shape, thoroughly modern distinctions. They were at the forefront of critiquing imperialism and embraced aspirations for independence and development for the colonized. The Christian missionary enterprise, in so far as it sought conversions and church-planting, was increasingly seen as misplaced, with some liberal Protestants arguing that evangelism was a tool of control and should be discarded. But this rejection was not a complete dismantling of missionary endeavours. Alongside a growing disparagement of 'religious' interventions, liberal Protestants lionized other interventionary strategies, including promoting the dissemination of biomedicine and the truths of science to bring the benefits of modern progress to underdeveloped peoples. For these Protestants, 'medicine became a Christian vocation not measured by souls saved but by numbers of local doctors trained and surgeries performed' (Klassen 2011: 106). Liberal Protestants thereby became 'coworkers and forebears' of humanitarian organizations such as the Red Cross and Doctors without Borders (2011: xv),[15] and they had a direct impact on wider development methods and policies.[16] While liberals remained committed to both 'science and the social gospel' they also helped found central institutions in secular modernity and to institute an incipient, if increasingly distinct, religious–secular split (2011: 4–5). Their initiatives therefore helped lay the groundwork for the predominance of the same divisions in contemporary development.

Another, more genealogical approach to tracing the connections between Christianity and Western humanitarianism is proposed in the concluding chapter of Didier Fassin's *Humanitarian Reason* (2012: 248–57). Fassin's analysis of the emergence of a global humanitarian project offers a sweeping critique of the effects of the rise of a politics of compassion in reshaping transnational governance. His attention to Christian theology emerges in his analysis of a 'politics of life' and a 'politics of suffering', which lie at the heart of humanitarian logics and both of which are grounded in a Christian 'ethos'. Fassin argues that humanitarianism is a case of 'the religious after religion', whereby 'the ultimate victory of religion lies not in the renewal of religious expression throughout the world, but in its lasting presence at the heart of our democratic secular values' (2012: 249). Rather than it being devoid of religion, humanitarianism should be understood as a 'political theology' (2012: 251).[17] On the politics of life Fassin argues that the idea that human life is the highest good (though replete with contradictions and inconsistencies) is shaped by a Christian sacralization of humanness which persists in humanitarian logic. The iconic figure of the humanitarian 'saving lives' is indebted to Christian morality (2012: 250). Similarly, the emphasis on suffering derives from a Christian moral economy: 'the valorization of suffering as the basic human experience is closely linked to the passion of Christ redeeming the original sin. . . . The singular feature of Christianity in this respect is that it turns suffering into redemption' (ibid.). Modernity, however, presents a rupture in this genealogy such that now 'salvation emanates not through the passion one endures, but through the compassion one feels' (ibid.). Humanitarianism is heir to a Christian politics and therefore 'prolongs and renews the Christian legacy' (2012: 251).

Such arguments, individually and even more so cumulatively,[18] make for a compelling case for the missionary roots of contemporary development. It is these roots that have, for much of the past 60 years of development practice, been written out of development histories (Tvedt 2006). The reasons for a newfound ability to rewrite history at this present juncture may have much to do with the recent undermining of faith in development among diverse groups in the wake of environmental concerns, repeated economic crises, pronounced critiques, and ongoing poverty. Lacking the same moral suasion as it previously held, though by no means disarmed, it has become possible, perhaps even imperative, to relook at history to examine the complicated birth of development in Christian missionary activities.

Missionaries as contemporary development actors

But, of course, missionaries are not just past presences who have since been displaced by modern secular formations. Missionaries of various sorts remain as contemporary actors who continue to play important roles channelling development resources. Christian missionaries have received the greatest attention. This includes analysis of the developmental impacts (whether construed as positive or negative) of missionaries on poverty alleviation (Samuel and Sugden 1987; Meyers 1999; Oladipo 2001; Ilo 2011; Bradbury 2013), health care (Loewenberg 2009; Klassen 2011; Pallant 2012; Watson 2012), literacy and language (Pennycook 2005; Hartch 2006; Sanneh 2009), education (Close 2012), microfinance (Bussau and Mask 2003), agriculture (Sinclair 1980; Bornstein 2002; Abbink 2005; Fountain 2012), sustainability (Moyer *et al.* 2012), nation building (Clarke 2012), disaster relief (Ensor 2003; Fountain *et al.* 2004), and peace building (Sampson and Lederach 2000). That is to say, Christian missionary development impacts have worked, and continue to work, right across the spectrum of development activity today. Anthropological accounts, such as the following examples, have proved particularly insightful for exploring contemporary missionary entanglements with development.

Erica Bornstein's (2003) ethnographic study of Christian NGOs in Zimbabwe, focusing on World Vision as a local (if also globally connected) actor inspired by Zimbabwean Pentecostal theologies, provides one of the richest ethnographic studies of Christian proselytizing woven into development practice. Bornstein describes an 'enchanted' development in which paradigms and practices of the mainstream development industry are deployed according to spiritual goals. Bornstein challenges the understanding that economic development and technical, scientific interventions necessarily involve a move away from religion. She concludes that far from abnormal intrusions into an otherwise secular development ecology World Vision's proselytization worked according to a distinctly Zimbabwean spiritual discourse in which theological questions and spiritual practices were both public and pervasive. The apparent intrusion of missionary ambitions was therefore considerably less peculiar than was its absence, such as was practised by various secular NGOs.

Another important study provides complications in a different trajectory. Lorraine Aragon's (2000) account of Christian evangelism in Indonesia – focusing particularly on the Salvation Army's work among the Tobaku peoples of Central Sulawesi – locates the conversionary impulse within a wider political context. Aragon argues that foreign missionaries were strategically deployed by Suharto's New Order state to help achieve the state's programmes of 'human engineering' (2000: 275). Western missionaries 'facilitated government aims', including 'creating nuclear family households, defining individual economic responsibilities, increasing ties to the national and global economies, introducing biomedicine, and expanding school attendance', as well as promoting 'national regulations, the use of money, government rhetoric concerning the benefits of progress, and regional record keeping' (2000: 24). By controlling access and granting or withholding visas the Indonesian state ensured that missionaries remained pliant and dependent on state support (2000: 276). As a consequence highland churches in Sulawesi increasingly 'became proxies for the New Order state' (2000: 277) and missionaries were enrolled into the state's governance apparatus. The state was therefore itself an evangelistic agent. No clear separation can be drawn here between politics, development, and religion. Instead, this is an example of how '[r]eligious devotion and economic development' became 'quietly indexed to one another' (2000: 305).[19] Yet, while the state used missionaries to further its own reach, the Tobaku highlanders also made use of Christianity for their own purposes, which did not necessarily align with either missionary or state goals. Aragon argues that Protestantism provided the Tobaku with connections to 'super-regional symbolic and political networks' (2000: 44) that allowed them to counter the Indonesian state's narrative of their backward and marginalized status. Connected via missionaries to foreign development agencies, education opportunities, and finances, the Tobaku sought to buttress their (limited) autonomy and preclude other Indonesian government programmes which threatened other forms of intrusive intervention. In this way, for Aragon, Christian missionary activity is an ambivalent subject, and its propagation and flourishing in Central Sulawesi rested upon diverse and competing interests.[20]

Even when missionaries are strictly concerned with 'saving souls', the impact of their proselytizing activity is often much broader and far-ranging. As Robert Woodberry (2012) has argued for the missionary influences on liberal democracy, missionary work can have unforeseen yet influential effects. Missionary work can be *cascading* in that the implications of missionizing can ripple out of individual conversions into wider societal impacts. For example, the missionary desire to spread understanding of the Christian scriptures in order to secure salvation led to the establishment of primary schools for the general public, which led to increased literacy, which in turn directly influenced economic, political, social, and technological processes of transformation. Mission work is often also *catalysing* in that, even when missionary impacts were limited, the responses to the incursions of missionary activity frequently helped influence factors well beyond mission stations or those in direct contact with missionaries. Again with the example of education, when missionaries set up schools other groups who opposed Christian missionary activity could also be spurred to establish schools in order to counter the perceived competition. Through these processes, missionary impact on development can be extensive.

Christian missionary activity clearly remains important for development interventions around the world. Indeed, Hearn (2002) argues that Christian missionary activity is more politically and socially influential now than during any previous era. They are not and never have been, however, the only missionary actors involved in development and humanitarian interventions. I provide two examples drawn from emerging literature.

Julia Huang's (2009) ethnographic analysis of Tzu Chi is an insightful and textured analysis of a major Taiwanese Buddhist NGO founded by the venerable Cheng Yen. Huang pays nuanced attention to the explicit proselytizing agenda of the organization. The Tzu Chi movement is a significant innovation of Taiwanese Buddhism in its focus on mobilizing communal resources to provide a public, outwardly focused service. The key figures in Tzu Chi's proselytization are the (female) Commissioners (*Weiyuan*), who are responsible for overseeing social services (to, for example, low-income families and disaster victims), organizing Tzu Chi branch activities and small group meetings, and also 'exemplifying the spirit of compassionate contribution . . . [and] joyfulness' so as to 'educate' the well-to-do donors and volunteers in the organization (2009: 66–72). The location of each of these tasks within the same position or persons suggests a lack of clear separation between them. Indeed, the Commissioners certainly are tasked with adding additional members to the Tzu Chi movement, and one of the basic conditions for becoming a Commissioner is an active proselytizing of a fixed number of households. However, almost all who join the organization derive from Chinese Buddhist backgrounds. The proselytization of Tzu Chi could therefore be said to be focused primarily within Buddhism itself in an attempt to reform individuals, communities, and the Taiwanese nation. The primary objects of this transformative proselytizing agenda are the volunteers themselves, who in the process of volunteering and embodying a compassionate response to the poor and suffering are remoulded into 'exemplary citizens' such that they come to embody a *bodhisattva* (enlightened being) and serve as models of 'civility' (2009: 191–6).

Jonathan Benthall and Jérôme Bellion-Jourdan's (2009) important study of Islamic aid includes discussion of Islamic discourses of 'seamlessness'. This prominent discourse refuses to acknowledge 'a distinction between aspects of life in which religion, politics, economics and morality are interfused' (2009: 105). While the authors express scepticism about whether this always corresponds to actual practices, and while a number of modern Islamic charities are increasingly attempting to de-link these elements, nevertheless it is apparent that many Islamic charities are concerned with 'furthering the Muslim cause as well as benefiting already committed Muslims' (ibid.).[21] Discussing the work of transnational Islamic networks in Bosnia-Herzegovina in the 1990s, they point to the ways in which some Islamic NGOs deployed '*ighatha* (material relief) to undertake *da'wa* (spiritual relief)' to further a comprehensive 'reislamization' of the Balkans (2009: 142–4). Implicit here was an understanding among some Islamic aid workers that Muslims in the Balkans were no longer practising orthodox Islam and that a return to the correct path was a necessary element of recovery. The conspicuous permeability of relief goals was found in the recruitment of staff who were committed to Islam, practices of aid distribution including selective distribution based on visible markers of religiosity and the distribution of Islamic literature, and the focus on reconstructing mosques and Quranic schools, though the exact nature of such practices varied among, and also within, the various Islamic organizations. Reislamization in the Balkans involved diverse transformative projects aimed at reshaping physical landscapes, corporeal practices, ideological commitments, and communal dynamics.[22]

Proselytizing development

At the outset of their chapter examining Saudi Arabian NGOs in Somalia, Kroessin and Mohamed (2008: 187–8) raise the provocative question about what exactly constitutes the definition of 'missionary'. They argue that, '[a]t an abstract level of analysis, all humanitarian and development actors ought . . . to be regarded as "missionaries", although not necessarily in a religious sense. They are underpinned by a particular value set that drives them to promote social change and to shape the world in their image.' I suggest that their proposition for expanding the term 'missionary' is essentially correct, even if Kroessin and Mohamed are a little too timid in making their case. In fact, as I have argued above, there is no generic ahistorical or transcultural 'religious sense' which is identifiable as a distinctive feature of *only* certain missionary organizations. Given the impossibility of identifying a universally applicable 'religious sense', a clear implication is that there is also nothing inherently 'religious' about proselytization.

Rather than identifying proselytizing with some kind of essentially religious practice it is much more helpful – for the sake of analytical clarity and to enable comparative research, as well as to facilitate attention to the political work of demarcations – to identify proselytization with *intentional moral practices of transformative interventions aimed at reworking the social practices of others.* 'Proselytizing development' therefore should be expanded beyond the imagined boundaries of religious institutions to include an examination of all practices that seek social transformation, which is to say that *all* development is proselytizing. What differentiates development and humanitarian projects is not a religious–secular divide, but rather diverse transformative goals, methods of intervention, the targeted 'others', and the ethics of change-seeking practices. Needless to say, over these issues there is indeed substantial, pervasive disagreement. What this approach enables is a thoroughgoing comparative analysis of divergences and continuities without assuming *a priori* that a particular category of analysis is necessarily the most appropriate.

This broader conceptualization of proselytization facilitates attention to the proselytizing work of mainstream development actors, including the desire to expand secular formations, logics, and practices. The attempt to carve out or *invent* a realm separate and autonomous from any religious incursion should be understood as a remarkably transformative project of intervention. This is precisely the project which Flanigan (2010) commends in her recommendation that donors seek to avoid religious institutions in the delivery of relief and instead seek to support, enhance, and initiate the work of a local secular sector as a realm supposedly more neutral than other alternatives. It is also apparent in the work of major development donors, such as with the examples of the Australian government and the Red Cross Code of Conduct discussed above, which seek to carve out a space separated from religious influence. As I have argued elsewhere, the invention of a secular sphere devoid of religion is 'a radical disciplining and re-construction of religion and should be seen as a potentially transformative attempt to re-work religious subjectivities in ways that run parallel to explicit proselytizing' (Fountain 2012: 146).

The case of the American pursuit of modernization projects during the post-war growth of development cooperation is a prime example of missionary zeal. Gilbert Rist (2002: 77) has described how President Truman's famous Four Point speech, delivered in early 1949, was thoroughly evangelistic. Describing the speech as containing four components – the current 'desperate straits', the 'good news' of possible happiness, the need to mobilize collective energies, and the eschatological promise of a future 'era of happiness, peace and prosperity' – Rist concludes that an 'American evangelist would have said much the same thing'. This '*structural homology*' (emphasis in original) between salvationist religion and development speech has been repeatedly deployed in development discourse ever since. Indeed, for Rist, development is a form of 'secularized messianism' which 'took flight' soon after President Truman's speech with the promise 'to bring heaven down to earth' (2002: 218).

In his analysis of American 'secular missionaries', Larry Grubbs (2009) also points to the desire of development workers to bring about the 'salvation' of distant others. Grubbs focuses on the US's ambitions for Africa in the 1960s and their promotion of a 'gospel of modernization' (2009: 54–73). Their 'doctrine' operated as both an analytical framework and a normative project for how to pursue vast continental transformation. Armed with extraordinary self-confidence, an absolute faith in their mission, and an enduring belief in American exceptionalism and expertise, development workers sought not just to influence economic processes but to institute 'changes in incentives, attitudes, and aspirations, [such that] nothing about African societies or cultures was irrelevant'.[23]

The proselytizing nature of development – the moral project of enacting transformative interventions in the lives of others – could similarly be traced throughout the development and humanitarian infrastructure of today. The need for participation in development can be seen as a kind of 'spiritual duty' (Henkel and Stirrat 2001). WID, WAD, and GAD (Women in Development, Women and Development, and Gender and Development), differences notwithstanding, are all aimed at instituting changes in gender relationships through development interventions, an attempt premised on the moral necessity of instigating transformative gender change and implementing new normative moralities. Environmental sustainability projects aim directly at reforming the ethics of human–environment relationships. The dissemination of 'freedom', democracy, and human rights is, similarly, a particular cultural project of intervention intended to reshape entire societies. But perhaps no intervention is as far-ranging, pervasive, and penetrating as the dissemination of consumer capitalism. A thoroughgoing comparative analysis of proselytizing development would interrogate each of these projects of change-making in order to examine the forms, moralities, logics, and practices deployed in each, and the effects – intended or otherwise – engendered by them.

Conclusion: toward a new research agenda

This chapter has sought to locate the problem of proselytizing as central to the discipline of development studies. Development as a field has been constituted in relation to this problem, both through its exclusions (via processes of purification and amnesia) and by way of genealogical continuities. This is not an argument intended solely for specialists in the emerging field of 'religion and development'. Instead, I suggest that no adequate study into the cultural politics of development can afford to ignore or undervalue the topic of proselytization. We neglect, if not at our peril, than at least to our profound analytical impoverishment. Drawing on the argument I have advanced in this chapter, I propose three areas which will be key (though not exhaustive) for the research agenda on proselytizing development.

First, research must move beyond predetermined pejorative conceptualizations to a more expansive discussion of ethics. Academic understandings of proselytization, which are also widespread in mainstream development organizations, tend to perceive proselytizing activities as illegitimate, coercive, and dangerous. To label someone a 'missionary' is an unambiguous insult. The argument I have advanced here, however, invites a reconsideration of this approach.[24] Eschewing a tired and inadequate secular–religious dichotomy and an accompanying essentialist framing of religion I have proposed instead that proselytization be redefined so as to encompass all moral practices of transformative interventions. Notably absent from this framing is any sense that such practices be construed as inherently ethically erroneous. This is not to cast aside moral critique altogether, but rather it is intended to have the opposite effect: the goal is to force a new conversation about the ethics of proselytization and development. This conversation will include wide-ranging debate about the diverse modes of doing proselytization and development, the various kinds of creeds proffered, the moralities informing it, the hostilities surrounding it, and the practices enacting it. Discussion of the ethical is not, therefore, reduced to mere judgements 'for' or 'against'. Rather, ethical debates are configured according to an expansive horizon which will include, no doubt, considerable disagreement about the grounds of ethics itself.

An effect of this approach, and this is the second key area of the new research agenda, is to make apparently secular initiatives available for critical ethical investigation. No longer concealed behind the pretence of secular neutrality, all development projects can and should be analysed as value-laden initiatives generated from within particular traditions, including the ways diverse theological traditions engage in proactive work outside the formal development sector as well as the ways mainstream development continues to imbue theological traditions of thought and practice. Of particular interest is the question of the relationship of Christianity – and perhaps especially its modern and Protestant varieties – with contemporary development. To illuminate the contours of the Christian legacy it will be necessary to engage in comparative analysis between diverse 'religious' and 'secular' traditions. The focus on the secular will also include attention to the ways in which secular–religious distinctions are negotiated in both imagination and practice.

A third key area of the new research agenda is to furnish a detailed 'thick' description of proselytizing and development field encounters. The challenge is to move past merely engaging with proselytization discourses in order to explore the ways in which diverse agendas are translated into particular contexts. This will include examining the ways in which diverse, even contradictory, projects become entangled in the process of implementation. Such studies will involve paying attention to the unintended consequences of particular projects on 'religious' and 'secular' fields. This task will rely heavily on ethnographic, biographical, and historical research methodologies.

A vibrant debate about these three concerns, and other questions related to proselytizing development, promises illuminating insights and compelling investigations. This is the stuff of a dynamic field of study. The implications of such debates are also far-ranging, and therefore potentially influential for the ways in which programmes in poverty alleviation and other tasks are conceptualized and practised. For these reasons proselytizing development should become a central theme in development debates.

Notes

Acknowledgements: Grateful thanks for critical readings on earlier drafts of this chapter by Robin Bush, Kyuhoon Cho, Scott Flower, Josh Gedacht, Jesse Grayman, Emma Tomalin, and an anonymous reviewer. I also benefited from feedback following seminar presentations on the topic at the anthropology departments of Massey University and Victoria University of Wellington. Thanks to Trisia Farrelly, Regina Scheyvens, and Lorena Gibson for arranging and hosting these seminars. Conversations with Michael Feener have been especially formative for my argument, though as with the others I thank he should not be blamed for the outcome.

1 Neither 'religion' nor 'development' is a fixed, stable category. Recognizing the *historicity* of both 'religion' (Asad 1993; Masuzawa 2005) and 'development' (Rist 2002; Ekbladh 2010) facilitates analysis which is attentive to how each is reworked across time and space. 'Development' here denotes a field of encounters involving diverse projects of socio-economic engagement. Much of this chapter is concerned with the 'mainstream development industry', including international NGOs, humanitarian actors, and donor agencies. However, 'development' can be expanded to include a wide range of actors and practices involved in disaster relief, charity, philanthropy, voluntarism, welfare, and social activism. Recognizing that 'religion' is a constructed category, albeit one that has real-world political effects, helps move us beyond generic analyses to explore the complex contemporary manifestations of diverse traditions, including secularism.

2 See for example the *Time* magazine report 'Missionaries under Cover' (van Biema 2003), a *Mother Jones* report by Yeoman on 'The Stealth Crusade' (2002), and Ahmed's (2005) much-cited 'A Dangerous Mix', which was originally published on the Women's Human Rights website.

3 See also Bradbury (2012, 2013) for further discussion of the Australian regulatory framework. Bradbury's analysis includes discussion of the now defunct AusAID, though his examples closely parallel those I provide here. Alongside Australian policy frameworks, Bradbury also addresses the policy contexts of the US and the UK. Hovland's (2008) insightful study of the Norwegian context likewise draws out important parallels.

4 The current version of the ACFID Code was substantially revised in 2010. It was accessed at www.acfid.asn.au/code-of-conduct/files/code-of-conduct-small-format (accessed 30 October 2013). While the Code is voluntary, all NGOs wishing to be accredited with the Australian government are required to become signatories.

5 The *Manual* was accessed at www.ausaid.gov.au/ngos/Documents/ngo-accreditation-manual.doc (accessed 30 October 2013). The *Manual* refers readers to the Recognised Development Expenditure (RDE) Explanatory Notes (June 2010) for definitions. The RDE is used to calculate the annual level of funding available to each accredited NGO from AusAID. The entry under 'evangelistic' is: 'Promoting a particular religious adherence, such as activities undertaken with the intention of converting individuals or groups from one faith and/or denominational affiliation to another.' The Explanatory Notes further indicate that it is necessary to document the separation of development and evangelism not only in the organization's programmes but also with local partners. The RDE Explanatory Notes were accessed at www.ausaid.gov.au/ngos/ancp/Documents/rde_notes.doc (accessed 30 October 2013).

6 The document was produced in May 2009 and updated in April 2013. It is available at www.ausaid.gov.au/ngos/Documents/oagds-guidelines-april2013.docx (accessed 30 October 2013).

7 The Australian Tax Office (ATO) does provide a working definition of religion in relation to goods and service tax regulations, which states that the 'two most important factors for determining whether a particular set of beliefs and practices *constitute a religion* are: belief in a supernatural being, thing or principle; and acceptance of canons of conduct which give effect to that belief, but which do not offend against the ordinary laws' (emphasis in original). The ATO is clearly indebted to nineteenth-century English anthropologist Edward Burnett Tylor, whose influential substantivist and cognitivist definition proposed that religion be understood as 'belief in spiritual beings'. His approach is now heavily discredited within his own discipline and regarded as entirely inadequate. Nevertheless, it is unclear whether all Australian policy documents about proselytization and development assume this definition, including those produced by the ATO. The ATO's definition is available at www.ato.gov.au/Business/GST/In-detail/GST-industry-partnerships/Charities-consultative-committee-resolved-issues-document/?page=32 (accessed 31 October 2013).

8 For further discussion of the ways critical scholarship on 'religion' might help reshape the research agenda on 'religion and development', and development studies as a whole, see Fountain (2013).

9 The Code was accessed at http://www.icrc.org/eng/resources/documents/publication/p1067.htm. For the list of signatories see http://www.ifrc.org/Global/Publications/disasters/code-of-conduct/codeconduct_signatories.pdf (accessed 22 October 2013).

10 Article 18 also explains that 'this right includes freedom to change his religion or belief, and freedom, either alone or in community with others and in public or private, to manifest his religion or belief in teaching, practice, worship and observance'. This wording suggests that if the dissemination of faith is considered vital and obligatory for any particular tradition then inhibiting its dissemination could constitute a curtailing of the 'freedom of religion' and therefore a violation of the Declaration of Human Rights. See also Bradbury (2013: 424–5).

11 For example, recent research on post-tsunami Sri Lanka has examined tensions that emerged around the purported mixing of Christian proselytization and disaster relief (Woods 2012a, 2012b, 2013; Mahadev 2014; Hertzberg forthcoming). These tensions resulted in attempts to legislate against 'unethical conversions'. Although eventually aborted, this process was thoroughly paternalistic in its attempt to undermine conversionary agency through hierarchical imposition.

12 The quote is from Riesebrodt (2010: 175–7). I thank Michael Feener for drawing this to my attention.

13 The primary question in relation to this debate is whether a 'public–private' dyad is useful analytically. Difficulties in proffering adequate definitions for 'public' and 'private', grey areas operating between them, contrasting ways of imagining and enacting the distinction, and possibilities beyond a rigid binary opposition all point to limitations in assuming that religion will always fit neatly into such a categorization.

14 Barnett defines evangelicalism as a broad movement characterized by 'an emphasis on the conversion experience and being saved; the Bible as the only source of religious authority; a duty to share one's beliefs with others in various kinds of settings; and a focus on Jesus' death on the cross and his good works as the pathway to salvation' (2011: 53).

15 Though see also Redfield's (2013: 45–50) differentiation of Doctors without Borders (MSF) from prior missionary operations undertaken by such figures as David Livingstone and Albert Schweitzer. Redfield also locates the secularity of MSF against the Christian origins of the Red Cross, apparent in the theologies and politics of Henry Dunant and the other founding figures.

16 This included, for example, shaping the World Health Organization's adoption of strategies of 'Primary Health Care' in the 1970s, which refocused medical activity away from privileging large government hospitals located in primary cities to providing support for dispersed networks of local health workers (Klassen 2011: 54).

17 For his approach here Fassin draws on famous Weimar-era political philosopher Carl Schmitt (2005: 36), who argued that political ideas should be understood as 'secularized theological concepts'.

18 Other authors advance similar arguments to those discussed. For example, see also: Tusan's (2012) depiction of the roots of development interventions as evolving out of nineteenth-century British missionary engagements in the 'Eastern Question'; Sirota's (2014) analysis of the pivotal role played by the Church of England in the rapid increase of voluntarism and charitable activity during the Age of Benevolence (1680–1730), which gave birth to what is now called civil society; Harries and Maxwell's (2012) edited collection of missionary entanglements in the scientific enterprise and knowledge construction of Africa; Abruzzo's (2011) account of innovations against suffering undertaken by American Quaker activists in their opposition to the slave trade; Stamatov's (2010) discussion of activist Christian networks lying at the origins of contemporary transnational activism; and Tvedt's (1998: 43–5) proposal that missionaries be recalled as being the first in a series of development phases of Norwegian development activity.

19 For further discussion of Aragon's argument and for discussion of a parallel example also drawn from Indonesia, see Fountain (2012).
20 See also Hartch's (2006) important study of the Summer Institute of Linguistics (SIL) and its relationships with the state and indigenous peoples in Mexico.
21 The authors also argue that, rather than merely noting the permeability of charity, politics, and *da'wa* in Islamic aid practices it is also necessary to ask 'how intellectually and practically sustainable is the sharp distinction between the two that the Euro-American law of charities strives so hard to enforce' (Benthall and Bellion-Jourdan 2009: 105). This is also the line of questioning that this chapter pursues.
22 For other helpful studies on Islamic charitable practices, including examinations of Islamic 'seamlessness', see Kroessin and Mohamed (2008), Singer (2008), Latief (2012), and Feener (2013).
23 See also Ekbladh (2010), who describes the way American development workers engaged in a 'mission of development' (p. 5) which aimed at introducing 'psychological' and 'worldview' transformations across Asia (p. 103).
24 The analytical possibilities opened up through a non-pejorative approach to Christian proselytizing are provided, for example, by Dunch (2002), Hartch (2006) and Roberts (2012).

References

Abbink, J. (2005) 'Converting Pastoralists: Reflections on Missionary Work and Development in Southern Ethiopia', in O. Salemink, A. van Harskamp and A. K. Giri (eds), *The Development of Religion/The Religion of Development*, Delft: Eburon, pp. 121–30.
Abruzzo, M. (2011) *Polemical Pain: Slavery, Cruelty, and the Rise of Humanitarianism*, Baltimore, MD: Johns Hopkins University Press.
Agamben, G. (2011) *The Kingdom and the Glory: For a Theological Genealogy of Economy and Government*, Stanford, CA: Stanford University Press.
Ahmed, E. (2005) 'A Dangerous Mix: Religion and Development Aid', *WHRNet*, http://www.whrnet.org/fundamentalisms/docs/issue-aid_religion0507.html (accessed 3 March 2006).
Aragon, L. V. (2000) *Fields of the Lord: Animism, Christian Minorities, and State Development in Indonesia*, Honolulu: University of Hawai'i Press.
Asad, T. (1993) *Genealogies of Religion: Discipline and Reasons of Power in Christianity and Islam*, Baltimore, MD: Johns Hopkins University Press.
Asad, T. (2003) *Formations of the Secular: Christianity, Islam, Modernity*, Stanford, CA: Stanford University Press.
Barnett, M. (2011) *Empire of Humanity: A History of Humanitarianism*, Ithaca, NY: Cornell University Press.
Benthall, J. (forthcoming) 'Puripetal Force in the Charitable Field'.
Benthall, J. and Bellion-Jourdan, J. (2009) *The Charitable Crescent: Politics of Aid in the Muslim World*, London: I. B. Tauris.
Bornstein, E. (2002) 'Developing Faith: Theologies of Economic Development in Zimbabwe', *Journal of Religion in Africa*, 32 (1), 4–31.
Bornstein, E. (2003) *The Spirit of Development: Protestant NGOs, Morality, and Economics in Zimbabwe*, New York: Routledge.
Bradbury, S. (2012) 'The Micah Mandate: An Evangelical View', in M. Clarke (ed.), *Mission and Development: God's Work or Good Works?*, London: Continuum, pp. 103–22.
Bradbury, S. (2013) 'Mission, Missionaries and Development', in M. Clarke (ed.), *Handbook of Research on Development and Religion*, Cheltenham: Edward Elgar, pp. 413–29.
Bussau, D. and Mask, R. (2003) *Christian Microenterprise Development: An Introduction*, Oxford: Regnum Books International.
Cavanaugh, W. (2009) *The Myth of Religious Violence: Secular Ideology and the Roots of Modern Conflict*, Oxford: Oxford University Press.
Clarke, M. (2012) 'God i givim ples ya long yumi (God Has Given Us This Land): The Role of the Church in Building Pacific Nations', in M. Clarke (ed.), *Mission and Development: God's Work or Good Works?*, London: Continuum, pp. 67–82.
Close, K. (2012) 'Fiji's Methodist Mission and Its Role in Development through Education, Agriculture and Self-Governance in the Early Twentieth Century', in M. Clarke (ed.), *Mission and Development: God's Work or Good Works?*, London: Continuum, pp. 51–66.
Donini, A. (2012) *The Golden Fleece: Manipulation and Independence in Humanitarian Action*, Sterling, VA: Kumarian Press.

Douglas, M. (1966) *Purity and Danger: An Analysis of Concepts of Pollution and Taboo*, London: Routledge.

Dunch, R. (2002) 'Beyond Cultural Imperialism: Cultural Theory, Christian Missions, and Global Modernity', *History and Theory*, 41, 301–25.

Ekbladh, D. (2010) *The Great American Mission: Modernization and the Construction of an American World Order*, Princeton, NJ: Princeton University Press.

Elisha, O. (2011) *Moral Ambition: Mobilization and Social Outreach in Evangelical Megachurches*, Berkeley: University of California Press.

Ensor, M. O. (2003) 'Disaster Evangelism: Religion as a Catalyst for Change in Post-Mitch Honduras', *International Journal of Mass Emergencies and Disasters*, 21 (2), 31–49.

Escobar, A. (1995) *Encountering Development: The Making and Unmaking of the Third World*, Princeton, NJ: Princeton University Press.

Fassin, D. (2012) *Humanitarian Reason: A Moral History of the Present*, Berkeley: University of California Press.

Feener, R. M. (2013) *Sharī'a and Social Engineering: The Implementation of Islamic Law in Contemporary Aceh Indonesia*, Oxford: Oxford University Press.

Ferguson, J. (1994) *The Anti-Politics Machine: 'Development', Depoliticization, and Bureaucratic Power in Lesotho*, Minneapolis: University of Minnesota Press.

Fitzgerald, T. (2003) *The Ideology of Religious Studies*, New York: Oxford University Press.

Fitzgerald, T. (2011) *Religion and Politics in International Relations: The Modern Myth*, London: Continuum.

Flanigan, S. T. (2010) *For the Love of God: NGOs and Religious Identity in a Violent World*, Sterling, VA: Kumarian Press.

Fountain, P. (2012) 'Blurring Mission and Development in the Mennonite Central Committee', in M. Clarke (ed.), *Mission and Development: God's Work or Good Works?*, London: Continuum, pp. 143–66.

Fountain, P. (2013) 'The Myth of Religious NGOs: Development Studies and the Return of Religion', *International Development Policy: Religion and Development*, 4, 9–30.

Fountain, P., Kindon, S. and Murray, W. (2004) 'Christianity, Calamity, and Culture: The Involvement of Christian Churches in the 1998 Aitape Tsunami Disaster Relief', *Contemporary Pacific*, 16 (2), 321–55.

Grubbs, L. (2009) *Secular Missionaries: Americans and African Development in the 1960s*, Amherst: University of Massachusetts Press.

Harries, P. and Maxwell, D. (eds) (2012) *The Spiritual in the Secular: Missionaries and Knowledge about Africa*, Grand Rapids, MI: Eerdmans.

Hartch, T. (2006) *Missionaries of the State: The Summer Institute of Linguistics, State Formation, and Indigenous Mexico, 1935–1985*, Tuscaloosa: University of Alabama Press.

Hearn, J. (2002) 'The "Invisible" NGO: US Evangelical Missions in Kenya', *Journal of Religion in Africa*, 32 (1), 32–60.

Henkel, H. and Stirrat, R. (2001) 'Participation as Spiritual Duty; Empowerment as Secular Subjection', in B. Cooke and U. Kothari (eds), *Participation: The New Tyranny*, London: Zed Books, pp. 168–84.

Hertzberg, M. (forthcoming) 'Waves of Conversion? The Tsunami, "Unethical Conversions" and Political Buddhism in Sri Lanka', *International Journal of Mass Emergencies and Disasters*.

Hovland, I. (2008) 'Who's Afraid of Religion? Tensions between "Mission" and "Development" in the Norwegian Mission Society', in G. Clarke and M. Jennings (eds), *Development, Civil Society and Faith-Based Organizations: Bridging the Sacred and the Secular*, Basingstoke: Palgrave Macmillan, pp. 171–86.

Huang, C. J. (2009) *Charisma and Compassion: Cheng Yen and the Buddhist Tzu Chi Movement*, Cambridge, MA: Harvard University Press.

Ilo, S. C. (2011) *The Church and Development in Africa: Aid and Development from the Perspective of Catholic Social Ethics*, Eugene, OR: Wipf & Stock.

Keane, W. (2007) *Christian Moderns: Freedom and Fetish in the Mission Encounter*, Berkeley: University of California Press.

Klassen, P. E. (2011) *Spirits of Protestantism: Medicine, Healing, and Liberal Christianity*, Berkeley: University of California Press.

Kroessin, M. R. and Mohamed, A. S. (2008) 'Saudi Arabian NGOs in Somalia: "Wahabi" Da'wah or Humanitarian Aid?', in G. Clarke and M. Jennings (eds), *Development, Civil Society and Faith-Based Organizations: Bridging the Sacred and the Secular*, Basingstoke: Palgrave Macmillan, pp. 187–213.

Latief, H. (2012) 'Islamic Charities and Social Activism: Welfare, Dakwah and Politics in Indonesia', unpublished doctoral dissertation, Utrecht University, Utrecht.

Latour, B. (1993) *We Have Never Been Modern*, Cambridge, MA: Harvard University Press.

Lewis, D. (2009) 'International Development and the "Perpetual Present": Anthropological Approaches to the Re-Historicization of Policy', *European Journal of Development Research*, 21 (1), 32–46.

Li, T. M. (2007) *The Will to Improve: Governmentality, Development, and the Practice of Politics*, Durham, NC: Duke University Press.

Loewenberg, S. (2009) 'Medical Missionaries Deliver Faith and Health Care in Africa', *Lancet*, 373 (9666), 795–6.

Mahadev, N. (2014) 'Conversion and Anti-Conversion in Contemporary Sri Lanka: Pentecostal Christian Evangelism and Theravada Buddhist Views on the Ethics of Religious Attraction', in J. Finucane and R. M. Feener (eds), *Proselytizing and the Limits of Religious Pluralism in Contemporary Asia*, Singapore: Springer, pp. 211–35.

Masuzawa, T. (2005) *The Invention of World Religions: Or, How European Universalism Was Preserved in the Language of Pluralism*, Chicago: University of Chicago Press.

McCutcheon, R. T. (1997) *Manufacturing Religion: The Discourse on Sui Generis Religion and the Politics of Nostalgia*, New York: Oxford University Press.

Meyers, B. L. (1999) *Walking with the Poor: Principles and Practices of Transformational Development*, Maryknoll, NY: Orbis Books.

Milbank, J. (2006) *Theology and Social Theory: Beyond Secular Reason*, 2nd edn, Malden, MA: Wiley-Blackwell.

Moyer, J. M., Sinclair, A. J. and Spaling, H. (2012) 'Working for God and Sustainability: The Activities of Faith-Based Organizations in Kenya', *Voluntas: International Journal of Voluntary and Nonprofit Organizations*, 23 (4), 959–92.

Oladipo, J. (2001) 'The Role of the Church in Poverty Alleviation in Africa', in D. Belshaw, R. Calderisi and C. Sugden (eds), *Faith in Development: Partnership between the World Bank and the Churches of Africa*, Oxford: Regnum Books, pp. 219–36.

Pallant, D. (2012) *Keeping Faith in Faith-Based Organizations: A Practical Theology of Salvation Army Health Ministry*, Eugene, OR: Wipf & Stock.

Pennycook, A. (2005) 'The Modern Mission: The Language Effects of Christianity', *Journal of Language, Identity and Education*, 4 (2), 137–55.

Redfield, P. (2013) *Life in Crisis: The Ethical Journey of Doctors without Borders*, Berkeley: University of California Press.

Riesebrodt, M. (2010) *The Promise of Salvation: A Theory of Religion*, Chicago: University of Chicago Press.

Rist, G. (2002) *The History of Development: From Western Origins to Global Faith*, 2nd edn, London: Zed Books.

Roberts, N. (2012) 'Is Conversion a "Colonization of Consciousness"?', *Anthropological Theory*, 12 (3), 271–94.

Saler, B. (2000) *Conceptualizing Religion: Immanent Anthropologists, Transcendent Natives, and Unbounded Categories*, Leiden: Brill.

Sampson, C. and Lederach, J. P. (eds) (2000) *From the Ground Up: Mennonite Contributions to International Peacebuilding*, Oxford: Oxford University Press.

Samuel, V. and Sugden, C. (eds) (1987) *The Church in Response to Human Need*, Grand Rapids, MI: Eerdmans.

Sanneh, L. O. (2009) *Translating the Message: The Missionary Impact on Culture*, 2nd edn, Maryknoll, NY: Orbis Books.

Schmitt, C. (2005 [1922]) *Political Theology: Four Chapters on the Concept of Sovereignty*, trans. George Schwab, Chicago: University of Chicago Press.

Scott, J. C. (1998) *Seeing like a State: How Certain Schemes to Improve the Human Condition Have Failed*, New Haven, CT: Yale University Press.

Sinclair, M. (1980) *Green Finger of God*, Exeter: Paternoster Press.

Singer, A. (2008) *Charity in Islamic Societies*, Cambridge: Cambridge University Press.

Sirota, B. (2014) *The Christian Monitors: The Church of England and the Age of Benevolence, 1780–1830*, New Haven, CT: Yale University Press.

Stamatov, P. (2010) 'Activist Religion, Empire, and the Emergence of Modern Long-Distance Advocacy Networks', *American Sociological Review*, 75 (4), 607–28.

Taylor, C. (2007) *A Secular Age*, Cambridge, MA: Harvard University Press.

Tusan, M. (2012) *Smyrna's Ashes: Humanitarianism, Genocide, and the Birth of the Middle East*, Berkeley: University of California Press.

Tvedt, T. (1998) *Angels of Mercy or Development Diplomats? NGOs and Foreign Aid*, Oxford: Africa World Press.

Tvedt, T. (2006) 'Understanding the History of the International Aid System and the Development Research Tradition: The Case of the Disappearing Religious NGOs', *Forum for Development Studies*, 33 (2), 341–66.

van Biema, D. (2003) 'Missionaries under Cover', *Time*, 161 (26), 36–44.

van der Veer, P. (2001) *Imperial Encounters: Religion and Modernity in India and Britain*, Princeton, NJ: Princeton University Press.

Watson, B. (2012) 'The God Factor: Adventism, Medical Missionaries and "Development" in Papua New Guinea', in M. Clarke (ed.), *Mission and Development: God's Work or Good Works?*, London: Continuum, pp. 83–99.

Weller, R. P. (2001) *Alternate Civilities: Democracy and Culture in China and Taiwan*, Boulder, CO: Westview.

Woodberry, R. D. (2012) 'The Missionary Roots of Liberal Democracy', *American Political Science Review*, 106 (2), 244–74.

Woods, O. (2012a) 'Sri Lanka's Informal Religious Economy: Evangelical Competitiveness and Buddhist Hegemony in Perspective', *Journal for the Scientific Study of Religion*, 51 (2), 203–19.

Woods, O. (2012b) 'The Geographies of Religious Conversion', *Progress in Human Geography*, 36 (4), 440–56.

Woods, O. (2013) 'The Spatial Modalities of Evangelical Christian Growth in Sri Lanka: Evangelism, Social Ministry and the Structural Mosaic', *Transactions of the Institute of British Geographers*, 38 (4), 652–64.

Yeoman, B. (2002) 'The Stealth Crusade', *Mother Jones*, http://www.motherjones.com/politics/2002/05/stealth-crusade (accessed 23 October 2013).

PART 2

Sub-Saharan Africa

7

RELIGION AND DEVELOPMENT IN SUB-SAHARAN AFRICA

An overview

Barbara Bompani

Introduction

The relationship between religion and development in Africa in many ways runs contrary to the normative narrative of development as a linear project of modernization and progress, framed 60 years ago, driven by a predominantly Western-led development apparatus that *a priori* excluded non-Western alternatives.

Mainstream development has, indeed, been driven by a predominantly modernist, Western, secular view of the world. This encapsulates two central assumptions regarding the role that religion plays in people's lives in the Global South (Casanova 1994). The first assumption is that religion will wither and die as Africa develops, despite the evidence of constant growth and renewal within African religiosity. The second assumption implies that religion is antithetical to development and progress, despite the fact that development is 'inherent in what members of religious communities have been doing for a long time' in colonial and post-colonial African contexts (Deneulin and Bano 2009: 73). Neither assumption has been demonstrated to be strictly true, which has had important implications for religion, development and how one encounters the other, in Africa.

In trying to understand the relationship between religion and development in the African continent, we need to consider the limits of narrow theories of modernization in non-Western contexts, and in doing so consider the realities of the interstices between religion in development and religious ideas and institutions more broadly. Development has not replaced religion any more than religion naturally rejects or contradicts development. For instance, Christian missions in Africa have always been identified as the historical cornerstone for the promotion of Western-style wealth, health, welfare and education. In the kingdom of Buganda, in what is now Uganda, the elite embraced Christianity as a vehicle to modernity, as one way of participating in the colonial culture and an opportunity to take advantage of its benefits (Mukasa and Gikandi 1998). In pre-colonial and colonial times Islam played a role as a vehicle for helping urban Africans move into elite and educated circles of power (Mazrui 1986). In more recent times transnational Islamic non-governmental organizations (NGOs) have been active in many parts of the continent, mostly in West and East Africa. In addition to offering medical help, food and educational facilities, they also offer conducts of behaviour and a broader sense of belonging to the global community, the *Umma* (Kaag 2008). African traditional religions (ATRs) have often been depicted by their critics as the 'backward' product of human fears towards irrational conceptions of 'nature', and their collective interpretations have been defined as constituting a tyranny towards individualism, while their conservative character was a limitation to progress. This excluded an understanding and appreciation of the contribution of ATRs to community life, to shaping forms of solidarity and respect towards the natural world, and of building strong social networks. Historically, owing also to the lack of written sources (Ranger 1998: 106), ATRs have been particularly mistreated with regard to their contribution to social, political and economic transformations across the continent. Nonetheless, African traditional cosmologies still play an important role in contemporary Africa, as highlighted by analyses on guerrilla war and resistance techniques in Zimbabwe (Ranger 1998; Fontein 2006) and ideas of sustainable development (Mebratu 1998). Indigenized forms of African Christianity that brought together elements of African traditions and more Western forms of Christianity (Sundkler and Steed 2000) have not received a great deal of attention by social science literature, and their contributions to development and progress have frequently been underestimated (Bompani 2010).

The chapter presents examples of the complexities of religion and its public role in promoting and hindering development projects in Sub-Saharan Africa, which in many respects reflect broader debates about the evolving and contested role of religion in African societies. Contemporary case studies are presented that reflect different religious traditions in different parts of Africa. The chapter is organized into three main sections: first, it provides an overview of changes that occurred within and towards public religion in the continent from colonial to post-colonial and to more contemporary times; second, it presents cases of churches as central actors in mediating the relationship between state and society; third, it presents cases where religion might be said to have hindered development. This structure is somewhat artificial in that it presents cases that might be considered to be more 'positive' or 'negative' in weighing up the relationship of the religious organization or religion and development as a broad process of social and economic change. This approach has been adopted as a simple means to reflect the diversity of this engagement, not artificially to dichotomize it. The reality of the relationship between religion and development is complex, historical, contextual and often contested.

Old and new developments within religion and development in Africa

The great majority of people in Sub-Saharan Africa are deeply and actively religious,[1] and spirituality is integral in their understanding of the world (Ellis and ter Haar 2004: 2). The transformative power of religion with its related passion, norms, visions, reforming zeal, organizational forces and discipline that act as embodied cultural norms and play an important role in determining economic performance and social change (Leys 1996) deserves a better understanding in academic studies, policy analyses and development interventions.

Dominant post-colonial discourses that Africa would inevitably become less religious and more secular predicated neither the role of religion in navigating and making sense of rapid external change nor its enduring role in individual, institutional or public life in the continent. There was a limited understanding that religious organizations such as missionary or Islamic schools had often been a driver of change and transformation, and thus religious belief would almost inevitably gain traction in Africa, in the face of change, not disappear.

The above reality, easy to understand in retrospect, was not foreseen. Literature from the 1960s and 1970s that dealt with religion in the continent gave a sense that there was little left to study, and little need to do so, as Africa was inevitably going to follow a Western path of modernization. For example, in contrast to the everyday reality of African societies invariably strongly influenced by religion, curricula in schools and academic institutions in the newly decolonized African states in the middle of the twentieth century included European and African readings and texts that predicted the disappearance of religion from the public and fore-saw only the process of secularization advancing across Africa. Africa was supposed to shape its newly independent states and societies around a very Western model. So powerful was this dis-course that more recent analyses highlighting the enduring reality of religion have simply been portrayed as a negation of or a deviation from a so-called Western normality (Mbembe 2001). As Mbembe phrased it, Africa became known to the West through 'absence' and strangeness (Mbembe 2001: 3–4). If religion was relevant in the public arena in Africa, then this must have been a blip or slight diversion from the (inevitable) correct secular path. But, if it is the case that secularization in the contemporary era is inevitable, it is hard to explain away the United States of America (Pew Forum 2002; Gallup 2012), the most Westernized of all states, which has not lost all sense of the spiritual,[2] or the increasingly influential and changing role that religion plays in public life in many European states, driven by migration and globalization (P. Berger *et al.* 2008).

Instead of inevitably diminishing, religions are taking an increasingly central role in African political and developmental life (ter Haar and Ellis 2006). Religions have offered people modes of engagement that allow them to anchor meaning within their daily life experiences in rapidly changing social and political contexts. Religious organizations and religious institutions under-take their own 'development' work because it fits their ethos; notions of social justice, charity and service are critical to the work of many religious groups, and the failures of the African state to deliver services and of mainstream development organizations to properly engage create spaces and opportunities for religious groups.

After the relatively small success achieved in the first years after decolonization in the 1960s, African countries were hit by years of economic crisis, rising inflation and a drastic reduction in commodity prices. All this inevitably led to massive increases in national debt and ultimately huge reductions in social spending, often promoted by multilateral development organizations. Structural Adjustment Programmes (SAPs), introduced by the World Bank and the International Monetary Fund (IMF) during this period, with their focus on privatization and liberalization, did not help to ameliorate the situation but instead aggravated and caused the deterioration of the material standard of living in African countries (Riddell 1992). During this period in Africa, churches, mosques, interfaith programmes and faith-inspired non-governmental organizations often picked up the slack precipitated by these failures of development and shortcomings of the state owing to their inherent ability to connect to local contexts, communities and their beliefs. There was tremendous growth in the number and levels of activity of religious-related actors 'doing development'. According to a World Bank report, 50 per cent of health and education services in Sub-Saharan Africa in 2000 were provided by faith-inspired organizations (World Bank 2008), and these figures are even higher (up to 70 per cent) in certain countries. The total number of Islamic faith-based organizations (FBOs) providing education rose from 138 (out of a total of 1,854 NGOs) in 1980 to 891 (out of a total of 5,896) in the early 2000s (Salih, cited in Haynes 2007: 189). In some areas, faith-based hospitals or clinics are the only healthcare facilities that exist. FBOs are also a major source of funding for HIV/AIDS treatment and programmes, owing to their capacity to fundraise from both religious and secular networks in developed countries (which, of course, can in itself create problems about what sort of interventions might be prioritized, for example abstinence over protection). For example, an African Religious Health Assets Programme and World Health Organization (WHO) report found that FBOs were providing up to 40 per cent of all HIV healthcare and treatment services in Zambia and Lesotho, much of it funded from faith-based communities outside Africa (ARHAP 2007). It is also relevant to note that, at the beginning of the twenty-first century, Africa had the highest number of expatriate missionaries in its entire history, to the point that the beginning of the millennium has been defined as the 'greatest missionary era' (Hearn 2002: 32).

The importance of religion in understanding and promoting development has undergone a process of critical reconsideration in the last 15 years, especially since post-development critiques have produced alternative visions and conceptualizations of well-being and needs (Sen 1999).[3] Analyses of the relation between religion and development are beginning to produce studies and are acquiring some recognition in both academia and applied development (J. Berger 2003; Tyndale 2006; Marshall and Van Saanen 2007; Clarke and Jennings 2008; Deneulin and Bano 2009); nonetheless there are still several key areas that warrant deeper investigation, especially in relation to African contexts. One of these areas is in understanding the capacity of many local and national faith-based organizations to connect with the local and to translate 'modernist' complex discourses into understandable practices. Another important aspect that needs to be carefully investigated is the role that religious leaders play in shaping development interventions. The leadership in religious organizations is important and affects the vision, regular functioning and decision making of the organization, especially in forms of religious expression that are not strongly hierarchical, such as Pentecostal–Charismatic Christianity. Understanding the internal workings of religious organizations is extremely important if development organizations are to understand them and engage effectively with them. Furthermore, it is advantageous to remember that FBOs encompass a diversity of organizations that differ in numerous dimensions and change dynamically through time. Their relationships with the African state and historical, social and cultural contexts can be crucial in untangling how ideas, ideologies and actors change and are shaped and to understand where power and potential lie. At this point in Africa, analysis still appears to have a strong focus on forms of established Christianity and certain forms of Islam, rather than on forms such as Sufism, African Christianity, Hinduism and new religious movements (Clarke and Jennings 2008).

Religions and the African state

Religious organizations are affected by their own history, which determines their attitudes and behaviour towards the public and to local systems of power. In order to understand the work and operative power of religious organizations we need to understand their relation with the state, society and the historical moment (the dominant ideas, ideologies and interactions) in which they exist. For example, in Kenya, churches and other faith groups in the 1980s and the greater part of the 1990s, along with other civil society organizations, did not enjoy much freedom of expression and public action and suffered from the repressive strategies of the Moi government that ended in December 2002, following 24 years in power.[4] In contrast, in the past 15 years religious leaders and religious organizations became more and more involved in the national reconstruction programme, and they are now very visible actors in the public sphere. As James Howard Smith (2008) argued, the shift in the national concept of development, which moved away from the state-controlled and centralized approach of Moi's era, in the new multiparty democratic Kenyan setting promoted the flourishing of 'horizontal' and dynamic organizations like NGOs and FBOs, which during the previous regime had limited freedom and were kept almost silent (Hearn 2002).

Michael Jennings (2013) in his analysis of the voluntary sector in Tanzania highlights the importance of understanding historical relations between religious organizations and the state in African contexts. Developmental, historical and political narratives tend to forget, or not sufficiently elaborate upon, the fact that the organizational and political behaviour and attitudes of FBOs (and missions during colonial times) have historical roots and are still influenced in the present by old links and operational attitudes that were created in the past. Nonetheless, despite the significance of the faith-inspired development sector, Jennings points out how the broader voluntary sector in Africa has usually been defined through, and often treated as synonymous with, secular, professional NGOs. In this way, the boundaries of understandings of the 'third sector'[5] space occupied by the vast number of NGOs – its origins, the nature of the relationship of voluntary sector actors to the state, and the types of organizations that characterize the sector – have tended to reflect a narrow concern with the secular NGO type and its experiences. His analysis suggests that in contrast to this limited view the voluntary sector was not the singular creation of a post-colonial development crisis. Instead this came about as the result of evolving relationships between colonial non-state (voluntary) actors and governments that were determined to demonstrate their commitments to the well-being of Africans in colonial times (ibid.). Mission schools and mission welfare services, expanding across much of rural Sub-Saharan Africa by the beginning of the twentieth century, created the foundations for the emergence of much of Sub-Saharan Africa's formal (and informal) voluntary sector as it exists today. This recognition is valuable to a better understanding of contemporary relationships between religious development agencies and the state, their operational memory (Lewis 2001) and again dismantling another piece of the secular narrative that sees explanations for the implementation of development only in terms of non-religious actors and non-religious dynamics.

The case study described below will offer an examination of the ways in which the relationship between religion, the African state and society impacts upon the role that religion plays in development projects and outcomes. This section highlights how religious organizations' public role is partially mediated through their relationship with the state, in this case the South African state, and how the socio-political context in which they must operate shapes the work that religious organizations can do for development.

African independent churches in South Africa

Religion has always played a relevant role in the public sphere in South Africa, although different religious actors contributed in different ways in different historical periods. The Dutch Reformed Church (DRC), for example, had provided strong political support and theoretical justification to the past apartheid state (Chidester 1992). In contrast, mainline missionary churches, especially from the 1960s, developed strong links with the then African National Congress (ANC) liberation movement (now the ruling party, in power since 1994) (Gifford 1995). This link has remained strong in the post-apartheid period (Bompani 2006).

In contrast to the distinct, clear relationships of the DRC and mainline missionary churches, African independent churches (AICs) in South Africa have always had a problematic relationship to politics and to the state. During apartheid, owing to their neutral position and for not publicly having provided support to the ANC movement in the liberation struggle, they were often regarded as far from critical and subversive politics.[6] In the years immediately following the first democratic election in April 1994 there was a period of consensus between the state, civil society and English-speaking mainline churches. The relationship between state and AICs in this period was more complex. In the post-1994 context AICs continued to disengage with the state, not publicly engaging with the newly democratic government and not playing a public and vocal role in the nation-building process. However, more recent analyses highlight how AICs played a strong and supportive role among black Africans in particularly deprived economic situations where there was often little support from mainstream development organizations (Garner 2000, 2004; Bompani 2010). AICs tended to operate locally and almost invisibly, owing both to their lack of political profile and voice and to their disengagement with, and by, the typical Western development actors. Subsequently, their tangible contributions were recognized neither during apartheid nor in the post-apartheid era. Likewise, intellectually they have not received due recognition until relatively recently.

Emerging shortly before the end of the nineteenth century, generally AICs have since the late 1920s been virtually ignored by the rest of the Christian community, or regarded as apolitical and socially impotent, if not reactionary. Since the 1980s and especially in the post-apartheid, democratic era, independent churches have grown rapidly in the country,[7] and they represent a significant percentage of South Africa's black population,[8] most of whom are very poor with very few resources. They constitute a universe made up of many small churches that embrace a form of Christianity interpreted through local traditions and customs. For a long time politics and established Christianity misunderstood AICs' roots in African tradition and their consequent distance from the West as anachronistic, as a symptom of backwardness and of 'incomplete' development (Bompani 2010). 'Underdeveloped' black Africans were not thought to have the ability to deal with contemporary political issues owing to their personal, cultural, religious and economic underdevelopment. In order to move towards more modern types of economic existence it was thought that people had to leave behind their old mythologies and systems of belief which 'held them back' from political and economic advancement. Studies on AICs in South Africa gave significant emphasis to certain beliefs and focused on the link between tradition and independent churches without paying attention to (or refusing to see) another possibility, that AICs as an important component of associational life among poor communities could shape a relationship with modernity and therefore could play a role within the 'modernization' process. Their 'developmental' ethos is particularly evident with the promotion of communities' initiatives and the sustainment of their own improvement through local techniques like protection from evil spirits (Ashforth 2005), the promotion of strong networks for community support and the running of traditional financial schemes of assistance in poor economic situations (Bompani 2010).

AICs offer, alongside their religious inputs, concrete resources that attract and sustain new believers. AICs are involved in important economic activities such as savings clubs, lending societies, *stokvels* (informal savings funds) and burial societies that encompass substantial amounts of money. On their own or in partnership, AICs generate social capital and they add value to development projects, for example through the great attention given to trust and community relations, through leadership that is perceived as clean and committed, through local roots and sources of accountability and through a commitment to values compatible with democratization, good governance and other forms of sustainability, as well as participation (Bompani 2008). However, as mentioned above, AICs have constantly been marginalized and excluded from development analyses and interventions and have had an ambiguous relationship with the South African state, both in the apartheid and in the post-apartheid period,[9] though attitudes and public involvement of these organizations seemed to have changed with the leadership of President Jacob Zuma since 2009. In fact, as part of the narrative of 'Africanness' and what has been defined as 'rational populism' (Marais 2010) promoted by the current South African president, these churches have started to be publicly recognized by the political establishment, and this seems to have led to a greater involvement in official national development projects. For example, along with many well-publicized visits to AICs, President Zuma delivered several public speeches in which he invoked history and the role played by AICs in bringing together 'tradition' and new visions for the future of the country. In his speech 'ANC's History and Moral Vision' at the Religious Summit in Johannesburg in November 2008, President Zuma highlighted the relationship between the nascent ANC movement in 1912 and AICs' independent spirit:

the Ethiopian Church Movement [one of the three types of AICs along with Zionist and Apostolic churches] was formed as a response to the rapid land dispossession from the 1800s. The African clergy sought to free themselves from the fetters of the missionaries by establishing African Independent Churches that came to be known as Ethiopian Churches. . . . The founders of the Congress Movement [which evolved in the ANC] also received spiritual support and guidance from Zionist and Apostolic churches founded during the beginning of the twentieth century.

(Zuma 2008)

More recently, speaking at a ceremony in Limpopo, a province in the North at the border with Zimbabwe, President Zuma invited all traditional leaders and independent churches to be an active part in the new National Development Plan (NDP):[10] 'our government cannot succeed alone without the active partnership with the institution of traditional leadership. They will continue to play a pivotal role to make our country prosperous' (SABC 2013).

This may represent the beginning of a change in the relationship between AICs and the state, recognizing the important role they have had and continue to have in supporting poor communities and providing micro-level development. However, this shift of political relationship is recent, nascent and possibly simply populism. It needs to be understood in its entirety, but for this analysis it is sufficient to recognize and highlight the relational dynamic between state and this kind of religious organization.

When religions can 'hinder' development

Beliefs are, of course, of particular relevance when dealing with religious organizations. Religious institutions may not always have been positive influences, and the added 'complication' of different or opposing worldviews that theology may introduce might not always lead people to a path of transformation and emancipation and may in fact lead to greater dependence and poverty (Alkire 2006). Although it is true of almost any intervention designed to transform society, religious values can become extremely powerful in promoting ideas or countering ideas of change. This section will present two case studies, one examining healthcare and vaccination in predominantly Muslim northern Nigeria and another one examining Christianity and sexuality in Uganda, in order to explore the often ambiguous relation of religion and development and ways in which religion might have blocked or hindered 'development'.

Polarization of health interventions along religious lines

De Cordier (2009) has highlighted in his analysis of aid workers in development and humanitarian projects in predominantly Islamic contexts that the development and relief sector has been confronted with a global climate of polarization between what is perceived as 'the West' on the one hand and 'the non-West' on the other. This may be seen in terms of 'Christianity' versus 'Islam' or as 'the secular West' versus 'African ways'. At the same time, Western or Western-associated secular development models have either failed or encountered constraints or roadblocks in several contexts in the Global South.

The Global Polio Eradication Initiative (GPEI) established the target of eradicating polio in 125 countries by mid-2005. By 2003, polio remained endemic in only seven countries, one of which was Nigeria. The eradication project found considerable resistance, especially in northern Nigeria, and it was marred by the boycott of the polio vaccination campaign (Yahya 2007). Trouble began in July 2003 as religious and political leaders in northern Nigeria stoked fears that the vaccines were deliberately contaminated with anti-fertility agents and the HIV virus by Western actors. Under the powerful and symbolic threat of a perceived anti-fertility plot, the umbrella of the Supreme Council for Sharia in Nigeria (SCSN) publicly asserted that the Polio Eradication Initiative (PEI) in the country was part of a plot by Western governments to reduce Muslim populations worldwide (Kaufmann and Feldbaum 2009). The 16-month controversy delayed the immunization of children, resulting in the spread of new polio infections within Nigeria and allegedly to other parts of Western and Central Africa, jeopardizing previous accomplishments of the global campaign (Renne 2006). The immunization project was eventually restarted. The World Health Organization (WHO) engaged with and gained the support of the Organization of the Islamic Conference (OIC), the African Union and the Arab League to urge a resumption of the Nigerian immunization drive. In November 2003, the OIC adopted a resolution to pressure Islamic countries to make greater efforts to eradicate polio through the procuring of vaccines from companies in Muslim parts of Asia, which seemed a viable solution. Ideas of purity (associated with correct and theologically sound procedures according to the Koran) and the idea of 'safe vaccines' produced in a Muslim state would further challenge the fears and anti-vaccine sentiments (Yahya 2007). The religiously and politically motivated opposition to the vaccine project was resolved through religious solutions. However, as a few episodes highlighted, the resistance and opposition towards the alleged Western conspiracy have not been completely sedated. Sadly, a series of assaults took place and killed polio vaccinators in northern Nigeria in February 2013 as well as in Pakistan in December 2012 (D. Smith 2013). In mid-2013, Islamic Pakistan, Nigeria and Afghanistan remained the only countries where polio had not been formally eradicated.

For many people in northern Nigeria, however, anxieties about polio vaccines were shaped not just by perceptions of global religious politics and rumours (as has often been portrayed by policy makers and media commentators). They also made sense in relation to past incidents concerning alleged malpractices in the meningitis vaccine delivery in 1996, when families in Kano accused the US pharmaceutical company Pfizer Inc. of using an experimental meningitis drug on patients without fully informing them of the risks. There are political and cultural dynamics to this controversy, revealing the deeper dimensions and complex factors that have contributed to the rejection of the oral polio vaccine in northern Nigeria. This region is inhabited by a predominantly Muslim population, the great majority Sunni from the Maliki school, and this coincidence helped create a perception that Muslims were being deliberately targeted. Furthermore, there is a strong relationship between religious and political power, and using one to evoke the other has long been key to power politics in the region. The polio vaccination boycott in northern Nigeria provides an illustrative case study of the realities of global health and development interventions in areas in which public religion counts, where religious beliefs are influential and religious organizations have practical potential, both in hindering development projects and towards promoting solutions. There are contextual and historical dynamics regarding the relationship between political power and religious authorities, and certainly there are strong elements of this in the case of northern Nigeria. It remains too simplistic to think of religion as universally antithetical to development or progress; rather religion in Africa remains a powerful tool through which power may be exercised for politics and development.

Pentecostal–Charismatic churches and the sexuality discourse in Uganda

There is an increasingly tense debate around issues of homosexuality in Africa and its centrality to contemporary politics. Historically homosexuality throughout the African continent has largely remained a marginal and often conflicted issue (Tamale 2011). Consequently, research remains relatively limited and has tended to focus on the history of homosexuality in Africa, lacking engagement with contemporary development, politics and human rights, and generally embedded in Western theoretical framings of homosexuality, which have not been useful in understanding the African context (see for example van Klinken and Chitando, Chapter 9). Upon closer reading it is possible to discern that those political discourses are often supported by religious voices, drawing from religious symbols, languages and moral values. For example, according to human rights activists in Cameroon, life for homosexuals became more difficult after 2005 when a Catholic archbishop made homosexuality part of his Christmas homily, blaming it for youth unemployment. According to the archbishop, high-profile Cameroonians gave jobs to those who favoured same-sex activities (Bowcott 2011). In a public speech Zimbabwean president Robert Mugabe said homosexuals would be punished severely for their behaviour, which is inconsistent with African and Christian values, and 'it becomes Satanic when you get a Prime Minister like [David] Cameron saying countries that want British aid should accept homosexuality' (Mashavave 2011).

Sub-Saharan Africa throughout the past two decades has experienced a religious transformation with the massive growth of Pentecostal–Charismatic churches (PCCs) (Corten and Marshall-Fratani 2001; Anderson 2004; Meyer 2004). According to Epstein (2007: 192), in the past 15 years nearly one-third of Ugandans have converted to Pentecostal–Charismatic Christianity, and Ugandan Pentecostalism aims to produce a new generation of Charismatic politicians and leaders (Gusman 2009). In this altered religious landscape new voices and leaders are emerging. Driven by their theological understanding of morality, rightness and the common good, these actors are profoundly influencing both public space and political decisions. This ties in with a more detailed look at Pentecostalism and homosexuality in the following chapters.

Discourses on morality, family values and sexuality are promoted and shaped both by external voices like US evangelical churches that are finding extremely fertile terrain in East Africa (Hearn 2002) and by local churches and leaders who are proposing their own interpretation of morality infused with existing and sometimes not so genuine local or African traditions. Conservative interpretations of Christianity are having a real negative impact and affecting the life of LGBT people on a daily basis. Beyond the political and human rights implications and challenges that LGBT people face on an everyday basis in Uganda (and in other African contexts), there are several healthcare problems that this religiously inspired narrative produces. With the increase of HIV/AIDS infection rates throughout Sub-Saharan Africa, religion and public health are further intertwined with gay rights movements, as legislation threatens the freedoms and often the very lives of homosexual Africans. The HIV/AIDS crisis has become inextricably linked to religious movements, as church membership has exponentially grown throughout the continent, particularly evidenced within the Charismatic–Pentecostal movement. Consequently, the implementation of the President's Emergency Plan for AIDS Relief (PEPFAR) in 2004 under US president G. W. Bush introduced a further morally framed discourse around HIV/AIDS and prevention, prioritizing 'faith-based' initiatives of abstinence and monogamy over the use of condoms and sexual education, as briefly mentioned above (Epstein 2007; Sadgrove 2007: 121). The distribution of PEPFAR funds to heavily donor-dependent nations like Uganda has granted American evangelicals further influence throughout the region. To further complicate matters, the majority of conservative American evangelicals denounce homosexuality, reinforcing numerous indigenous formations. Consequently, 'AIDS has created an evangelism opportunity . . . unlike any other in history' (Isaacs 2003: 194). During Congressional debates Ugandan first lady Janet Museveni presented a statement before Congress, crediting abstinence in the Ugandan epidemic (Tumushabe 2006: 11). The increasing influence of PEPFAR, coupled with the increasing influence of religious organizations throughout Uganda, has led to HIV/AIDS programmes framing transmission within moral parameters, reducing remaining HIV-negative to a simple choice of the individual. Subsequently, sexual behaviour – and especially 'non-normative' sexual behaviour – is increasingly predicated upon individual behavioural choice in line with Christian conservative interpretations of morality.

This is compounded by the influence of religious beliefs on medical professionals' values and work in clinics and hospitals. During fieldwork in Kampala in January and February 2013, I found many cases of medical doctors who refused to treat LGBT people in the name of religion and traditional culture (fieldwork notes, February 2013). As long as African homosexuality remains marginalized, issues greater than homophobia will persist, as homosexuality intertwines with practical issues of underdevelopment, race, class, public health, well-being and feelings.

Conclusion

Modernity-inspired (or -obsessed) international development has repeatedly disappointed when not taking sufficient account of local context, local actors, cultures and beliefs. From a not dissimilar perspective, Richard Dawkins (2006) has proclaimed faith as a delusion and religion as a dangerous 'mind virus' that can spread across societies, slowing their progress. One might argue that there is a corresponding danger or delusion in a refusal to acknowledge the enduring societal role of religion, or to place faith in faith. This is not necessarily to argue that faith may be right (or wrong), but simply that faith cannot be dismissed as unnecessary. Rather we need to acknowledge religion as a fundamental social, political and development force in many African contexts. Studying or engaging with religion and its role in the public is not a simple matter, but failing to consider religion and religious ideas risks the failure of enduring and meaningful social change. Engagement with and acknowledgement of faith and belief seem a more productive and appropriate way of understanding and framing societies and people's lives, rather than a simple negation of an important dimension through which people understand the world and through which the fabric of society is bound. This is more true in Africa, with its growing spirituality and enduring poverty, than anywhere else.

Notes

1 The great majority of people in Africa belong to one of the world's two largest religions, Christianity and Islam, while many still practise, often in coexistence, forms of African religious beliefs (Pew Forum 2010).
2 According to a Gallup survey, the large majority of Americans, 77 per cent of the adult population, identify with a Christian denomination (Gallup 2012). Six in ten (59 per cent) people in the US say religion plays an extremely important role in their lives. Americans' views are closer to those of people in low-income countries than to the publics in the Global North (Pew Forum 2002).
3 Particularly influential has been the human development approach, based on the analysis of Amartya Sen (1999) and his 'capability approach', which has enabled different organizations and actors to generate their own perspectives of development and in turn to provide alternative ways of intervening, delivering services and organizing politics and social relationships in given communities.
4 In Kenya in the 1970s the central government started eroding local authorities' powers. Moi's government adopted a very top-down and vertical approach to development, and the responsibility for delivering the basic social services of health and education was moved from local authorities to centralized national organizations.
5 The 'third sector' is intended as the sphere of social activities undertaken by non-profit and non-governmental organizations. These are defined as 'third sector' in relation to public sector and private sector. This is also known as the voluntary sector.

6 Two of the oldest and largest AICs, the Zion Christian Church (ZCC) and the Shembe Church (Ibandla lamaNazaretha), during the Truth and Reconciliation Commission faith community hearings took the view that they had nothing to apologize for, and both rejected the long-standing view that they had been apolitical or apathetic. The ZCC's stance is that silence under particular conditions is a rite of resistance in itself.

7 For an explanation on the AICs' growth since the 1980s, see Bompani (2008, 2010).

8 In 2001 they represented around 32 per cent of the entire South African population (in terms of black population the percentage would be higher) according to Statistic SA, Pretoria, 2004 (http://www. statssa.gov.za/census01/Census/).

9 AICs have been generally perceived by South African social scientists and religious studies researchers as phenomena unable to promote development, understood as Western-led modern progress, because they were too anchored in African tradition. For this reason AICs have not been included in development projects promoted by secular NGOs, the South African state and FBOs.

10 The National Development Plan is a governmental blueprint for economic and socio-economic development strategies for the country that was launched in 2013. This national framework comes after four previous national development strategies: Reconstruction and Development Programme (RDP) in 1994; Growth, Employment and Redistribution (GEAR) in 1996; Accelerated and Shared Growth Initiative for South Africa (ASGISA) in 2006; and New Growth Path (NGP) in 2010.

References

Alkire, S. (2006) 'Religion and Development', in D. A. Clark (eds), *The Elgar Companion to Development Studies*, Cheltenham: Edward Elgar, pp. 502–10.

Anderson, A. (2004) *An Introduction to Pentecostalism: Global Charismatic Christianity*, Cambridge: Cambridge University Press.

ARHAP (African Religious Health Assets Programme) (2007) *Appreciating Assets: The Contribution of Religion to Universal Access in Africa*, Cape Town: ARHAP, http://www.arhap.uct.ac.za/publications.php.

Ashforth, A. (2005) *Witchcraft, Violence and Democracy in South Africa*, Chicago: University of Chicago Press.

Berger, J. (2003), 'Religious Non-Governmental Organisations: An Exploratory Analysis', *Voluntas: International Journal of Voluntary and Nonprofit Organizations*, 14 (1), 15–39.

Berger, P., Davie, G. and Fokas, E. (2008), *Religious America, Secular Europe? A Theme and Variations*, London: Ashgate.

Bompani, B. (2006) 'Mandela Mania: Mainline Churches in Post-Apartheid South Africa', *Third World Quarterly*, 27 (6), 1137–49.

Bompani, B. (2008) 'African Independent Churches in Post-Apartheid South Africa: New Political Interpretations', *Journal of Southern African Studies*, 34 (3), 665–77.

Bompani, B. (2010) 'Religion and Development from Below: Independent Christianity in South Africa', *Journal of Religion in Africa*, 40 (3), 307–30.

Bowcott, O. (2011) 'Cameroon Gay Rights Lawyer Warns of Rise in Homophobia', *Guardian* online, 16 November.

Casanova, J. (1994) *Public Religion in the Modern World*, Chicago: University of Chicago Press.

Chidester, D. (1992) *Religions of South Africa*, London: Routledge.

Clarke, G. and Jennings, M. (eds) (2008) 'Introduction', in G. Clarke and M. Jennings (eds), *Development, Civil Society and Faith-Based Organizations: Bridging the Sacred and the Secular*, London: Palgrave Macmillan, pp. 1–16.

Corten, A. and Marshall-Fratani, R. (eds) (2001) *Between Babel and Pentecost: Transnational Pentecostalism in Africa and Latin America*, Indianapolis: Indiana University Press.

Dawkins, R. (2006) *The God Delusion*, London: Bantam Press.

De Cordier, B. (2009) 'The "Humanitarian Frontline", Development and Relief, and Religion: What Context, Which Threats and Which Opportunities?', *Third World Quarterly*, 30 (4), 663–84.

Deneulin, S. and Bano, M. (2009) *Religion in Development: Rewriting the Secular Spirit*, London: Zed Books.

Ellis, S. and ter Haar, G. (2004) *Worlds of Power: Religious Thought and Political Practice in Africa*, Oxford: Oxford University Press.

Epstein, H. (2007) *The Invisible Cure: Africa, the West and the Fight against AIDS*, London: Penguin Books.

Fontein, J. (2006) 'Shared Legacies of the War: Spirit Mediums and War Veterans in Southern Zimbabwe', *Journal of Religion in Africa*, 36 (2), 167–99.

Gallup Politics (2012) 'In U.S., 77% Identify as Christian', http://www.gallup.com/poll/159548/identify-christian.aspx.

Garner, R. C. (2000) 'Safe Sects? Dynamics Religion and AIDS in South Africa', *Journal of Modern African Studies*, 38 (1), 41–69.

Garner, R. (2004) 'African Independent Churches and Economic Development in Edendale', in D. Venter (eds), *Engaging Modernity: Methods and Cases for Studying African Independent Churches in South Africa*, London: Praeger.

Gifford, P. (ed.) (1995) *The Christian Churches and the Democratisation of Africa*, Leiden: Brill Press.

Gusman, A. (2009) 'HIV/AIDS, Pentecostal Churches, and the "Joseph Generation" in Uganda', *Africa Today*, 56 (1), 67–86.

Haynes, J. (2007) *Religion and Development: Conflict or Cooperation?*, Basingstoke: Palgrave Macmillan.

Hearn, J. (2002) 'The Invisible NGO: US Evangelical Missions in Kenya', *Journal of Religion in Africa*, 32 (1), 32–60.

Isaacs, K. (2003) 'Can Christian Aid Organisations Ignore the Crisis?', in T. Yamamori, D. Dageforde and T. Bruner (eds), *The Hope Factor*, Waynesboro, GA: World Vision Press, pp. 185–99.

Jennings, M. (2013) 'Common Counsel, Common Policy: Healthcare, Missions and the Rise of the "Voluntary Sector" in Colonial Tanzania', *Development and Change*, 4 (44), 939–63.

Kaag, M. (2008) 'Aid, Umma and Politics: Transnational Islamic NGOs in Chad', in B. Soares and N. Otayek (eds), *Islam and Muslim Politics in Africa*, London: Palgrave Macmillan, pp. 85–106.

Kaufmann, J. R. and Feldbaum, H. (2009) 'The Polio Immunization Boycott in Northern Nigeria', *Health Affairs*, 28 (4), 1091–1101.

Lewis, D. (2001) *The Management of NGOs*, 2nd edn, Abingdon: Routledge.

Leys, C. (1996) *The Rise and Fall of Development Theory*, Bloomington: Indiana University Press.

Marais, H. (2010) *South Africa Pushed to the Limit: The Political Economy of Change*, Cape Town: UCT Press.

Marshall, K. and Van Saanen, M. (2007) *Development and Faith: Where Mind, Heart and Soul Work Together*, Washington, DC: World Bank.

Mashavave, R. (2011) 'Mugabe Calls British PM "Satanic" for Backing Gay Rights', *Herald* (Zimbabwe) online, 24 November.

Mazrui, A. (1986) *The Africans: A Triple Heritage*, London: Little, Brown.

Mbembe, A. (2001) *On the Postcolony*, Berkeley: University of California Press.

Mebratu, D. (1998) 'Sustainability and Sustainable Development: Historical and Conceptual Review', *Environmental Impact Assessment Review*, 18, 493–520.

Meyer, B. (2004) 'Christianity in Africa: From African Independent to Pentecostal–Charismatic Churches', *Annual Review of Anthropology*, 33, 447–74.

Mukasa, M. and Gikandi, S. (1998) *Uganda's Katikiro in England*, Manchester: Manchester University Press.

Pew Forum (2002) *Among Wealthy Nations: U.S. Stands Alone in Its Embrace of Religion*, http://www.pew-global.org/2002/12/19/among-wealthy-nations/.

Pew Forum (2010) *Tolerance and Tension: Islam and Christianity in Sub-Saharan Africa*, http://pewforum.org/executive-summary-islam-and-christianity-in-sub-saharan-africa.aspx#quickdefinition.

Ranger, T. O. (1998) 'African Traditional Religion', in S. Sutherland and P. Clarke (eds), *The World's Religions: The Study of Religion, Traditional and New Religion*, London: Routledge, pp. 106–14.

Renne, E. (2006), 'Perspectives on Polio and Immunization in Northern Nigeria', *Social Science and Medicine*, 63 (7), 1857–69.

Riddell, B. (1992) 'Things Fall Apart Again: Structural Adjustment Programmes in Sub-Saharan Africa', *Journal of Modern African Studies*, 31 (1), 53–68.

SABC (2013) 'Zuma Urges Traditional Leaders to Work with the Government', 8 August, http://www.sabc.co.za/news/a/2ade698040a6bc2bb751f7ff48b0571c/Zuma-urges-traditional-leaders-to-work-with-govt-20130808.

Sadgrove, J. (2007) '"Keeping Up Appearances": Sex and Religion amongst University Students in Uganda', *Journal of Religion in Africa*, 37, 116–44.

Sen, A. (1999) *Development as Freedom*, Oxford: Oxford University Press.

Smith, D. (2013) 'Polio Workers in Nigeria Shot Dead', *Guardian* online, 8 February 2013.

Smith, J. H. (2008) *Bewitching Development: Witchcraft and the Reinvention of Development in Neoliberal Kenya*, Chicago: University of Chicago Press.

Sundkler, B. and Steed, C. (2000) *A History of the Church in Africa*, Cambridge: Cambridge University Press.

Tamale, S. (eds) (2011) *African Sexualities: A Reader*, Cape Town: Pambazuka Press.

ter Haar, G. and Ellis, S. (2006) 'The Role of Religion in Development: Towards a New Relationship between the European Union and Africa', *European Journal of Development Research*, 18 (3), 351–67.

Tumushabe, J. (2006) *Politics of HIV/AIDS in Uganda*, United Nations Research Institute for Social Development, Social Policy and Development Paper 28, Geneva: United Nations.

Tyndale, W. R. (ed.) (2006) *Visions of Development: Faith-Based Initiatives*, Aldershot: Ashgate.

World Bank (2008) *The World Bank's Commitment to HIV/AIDS in Africa: Our Agenda for Action, 2007–2011*, Washington, DC: World Bank.

Yahya, M. (2007) '"Polio Vaccines – No Thank You!" Barriers to Polio Eradication in Northern Nigeria', *African Affairs*, 106 (423), 185–204.

Zuma, J. (2008) 'ANC's "History and Moral Vision" Rooted in Religion', 27 November, http://www.politicsweb.co.za/politicsweb/view/politicsweb/en/page71654?oid=111176&sn=Detail.

8

PENTECOSTALISM AND ECONOMIC DEVELOPMENT IN SUB-SAHARAN AFRICA

Dena Freeman

Introduction

[handwritten margin note: Philosophy of Rostow and others of development without considering culture.]

Up until the 1980s scholarly thinking about development was largely focused on macro-scale economic matters: it was just a case of getting the right economic structures in place and, bingo, 'economic take-off' would occur. Walt Rostow's 'five stages of economic growth' was one of the most influential of these types of theory and postulated that for a traditional society to develop it had first to manifest the 'preconditions for take-off' (largely a new external demand for raw materials, which would *somehow* stimulate increasing production and investment and drive social change) before it would indeed 'take off' (by developing manufacturing, transport systems and schools and universities), and so on until it reached the fifth and final stage of 'mass consumption' (Rostow 1960). While there was a certain neatness to this approach, it turned out that it did not actually work in practice. External demand for raw materials grew, but it did not appear to stimulate all the other changes that Rostow postulated. The 'somehow' that Rostow had glossed over seemed to be more complicated than originally envisaged.

[handwritten margin note: since then more important based on culture]

Since then development studies has broadened out considerably, and more attention has been paid to the human aspects of development, through for example the livelihoods approach (e.g. Chambers and Conway 1991; Scoones 1998), Amartya Sen's human development approach (Sen 1999; Alkire 2005), and the more recent interest in development and well-being (Gough and McGregor 2007). In one way or another all of these approaches try to shed light on the 'somehow' of how individuals choose new behaviours and societies actually change. Increasingly scholars have come to the realisation that human beings are not rational economic agents and do not make their life decisions solely based on economic criteria and the soulless and lonely goal of economic maximisation. Instead there has been an increasing appreciation for the importance of non-material matters – such as beliefs, values and morality – in the development process (e.g. Goulet 1997). It is slowly becoming clear that these ephemeral and non-rational factors actually form a large part of the 'somehow' of how individuals decide to make changes, to take on new behaviours and to transform their social relations – activities that make up some of the key aspects of the developmental process.

Beliefs, values and morality traditionally reside in the realm of religion and culture, and thus a number of scholars from various different disciplines have recently started to look at the role of religion in development (e.g. Ver Beek 2002; Goody 2003; Berger 2004, 2009; Selinger

2004; ter Haar and Ellis 2006; K. Marshall and Van Saanen 2007; Rakodi 2007; Tomalin 2008; Deneulin 2009; Deneulin and Rakodi 2011; Freeman 2012a). Anthropologists, as specialists in culture, have also engaged with these questions, and the anthropological literature is now full of case studies which show how various development projects did not work because the proposed innovations clashed with local people's ideas, values and social forms. In one place, for example, people did not behave as economic rationalists as expected but instead invested new-found wealth in religious rituals or gift-giving ceremonies, while in another it was impossible to create a bounded target group of farmers because the whole community was linked through kinship ties. These cultural factors, often poorly understood by development practitioners, have led to the downfall of many a well-meaning development project.

Key questions for development actors, then, are how to design interventions which fit with local people's beliefs and values or, more radically, *how to change people's beliefs and values to fit with the behaviours necessary for economic development*. In the rest of this chapter I will focus on the second question and consider the role that Pentecostal Christianity can play in this regard. First, I will give a brief outline of the rise of Pentecostalism in Africa and the form that it currently takes. Second, I will briefly discuss how Pentecostal churches rarely run explicit development projects themselves and do not in fact separate 'religion' from 'development'. Then finally, drawing on examples from across the continent, I will show how Pentecostalism's impact on development is not through consciously defined 'development' activities, but rather through the very nature of Pentecostal belief and practice itself. I will focus on the Pentecostal transformation of the person and show that Pentecostalism does indeed shift people's beliefs, values and morality in such a way that, when other factors are favourable, very often leads these people to make quite radical social and economic changes, which then lead them in the direction of development.

The Pentecostal explosion

In the last 30 years there has been a massive 'Pentecostal explosion' that has radically altered the religious landscape in much of the developing world. Millions of people in Africa and elsewhere have joined Pentecostal churches. From humble beginnings as an early twentieth-century revivalist movement among America's poorer socio-economic groups, Pentecostalism has spread across the globe to become what is widely believed to be the fastest-growing Christian movement today (Hollenweger 1997; Burgess and van der Maas 2002; Anderson 2004: 1). In just over 100 years Pentecostal and charismatic Christianity has won over half a billion souls worldwide (Barrett 2001), representing almost 28 per cent of organised global Christianity (Barrett and Johnson 2002). David Martin has called the phenomenal uptake of Pentecostalism 'the largest global shift in the religious market place' in recent years (Martin 2002).

By far the majority of the new Pentecostal and charismatic converts are to be found in the non-Western world, particularly in Latin America, Asia and Africa. In Africa alone there are estimated to be some 126 million Pentecostals and charismatics, constituting about 11 per cent of the continent's total population. The vast majority of them, some 109 million, have joined since 1980 (Barrett and Johnson 2002: 287). Christianity is, of course, not new to Africa, and there have been Protestants and Catholics in Africa since colonial times (Gifford 1995, 1998), but what is new about Pentecostalism is that it is a form of Christianity that, even though it first emerged in the United States, fits extremely well with African ontologies and sensibilities. Whereas earlier forms of Christianity were essentially transposed from Europe and ignored African traditional beliefs in spirits and demons, Pentecostalism shares the basic African ontology of good and bad spirits, and embraces supernatural beings (God, Jesus, demons) that can have

Spread of Pentecostal Christianity

a direct influence in the world (Meyer 2004). In this way Pentecostalism becomes a lot more meaningful and powerful to Africans than earlier forms of Christianity. And in this power we find an astonishing ability to bring about change and transformation – often in the direction of what we usually call 'development'.

There is a huge variety of different Pentecostal and charismatic churches in Africa, and it is impossible to generalise across them all. Nonetheless, it is broadly accepted that there are three broad categories of Pentecostal and charismatic Christianity: classical Pentecostal, charismatic and neo-charismatic (Hollenweger 1997; Anderson 2004). Classical Pentecostal refers to churches with links to the early American and European Pentecostal churches and which stress the importance of speaking in tongues, or glossolalia, as evidence of baptism by the Holy Spirit. Examples include the Assemblies of God, the Church of God in Christ and the Pentecostal Church of God. Charismatic Christians are those members of mainline Christian denominations – Lutheran, Presbyterian, Catholic and so on – who began to experience the gifts of the Holy Spirit in the form of speaking in tongues, spiritual healing, miracles and the like. This 'Pentecostalisation' of mainstream Christianity started in the 1960s, and there are now charismatic churches across virtually all Christian denominations (e.g. Csordas 1992, 2007; Coleman 2000, 2002). The third wave, or neo-charismatics, is the broadest category, serving much as a catch-all for the vast number of non-denominational or post-denominational churches and fellowships that have exploded on to the scene since the 1980s. Neo-charismatics have been particularly creative and innovative in their adaptation of Pentecostal doctrine and styles to new settings and contexts. Examples could include Mensa Otabil's International Central Gospel Church, David Oyepedo's Winner's Chapel, the Rhema Church and the Vineyard Fellowship (Luhrmann 2004; Bialecki 2008). Churches from all three waves are flourishing in Africa today, and they are having an extraordinary effect on the continent. This chapter mainly focuses on the neo-charismatics, although much of what is said here also applies to the charismatics and, to a rather lesser extent, to the classical Pentecostals.

Pentecostal development projects

Mainstream Christian churches have been active in development work in Africa for many decades. In recent years, particularly since the 1980s, many of them have set up separate 'development wings' to expand their development work and tap into the increased flow of donor money to civil society organisations. However, perhaps surprisingly, Pentecostal churches have been far slower in setting up 'development wings' and joining in with explicitly development-focused activities. Although there are some exceptions, particularly in the area of HIV/AIDS (e.g. Dilger 2009; Burchardt 2013), it is actually quite noticeable that Pentecostal churches have *not* got actively involved with development-focused projects. As just one example, in Ethiopia most of the large mainline churches have development wings that source donor money and carry out development projects in both Christian and non-Christian communities, while none of the Pentecostal churches have set up similar development wings or carry out explicitly development-focused activities.

This is not to say that Pentecostals are not involved in development projects. It is just that for the most part, and in contrast to mainstream Christianity, the churches themselves do not run development projects. There are however a number of Pentecostal NGOs, or faith-based organisations (FBOs), that carry out development work from a Pentecostal perspective. These FBOs are often not linked to any particular church, and their activities are outside the remit of this chapter (but see Kamsteeg 1998; Hofer 2003; DeTemple 2006).

By far the greatest impact that Pentecostals have on development in Africa comes not from these FBOs, but from the changes instilled in 'believers' by the religious activities of the

Answer to 6

churches themselves. In these churches 'religion' is not separated from 'development'. Church leaders take a holistic focus on the 'whole person' and try to bring about change socially and economically, as well as spiritually. The rest of this chapter will focus on the type of change that Pentecostal churches bring about in their followers and will seek to show how in very many cases this change impacts on people's economic activities and leads them in the direction that we tend to call 'development'.

Pentecostal transformation

Transformations of subjectivity

It is well known that Pentecostals and charismatics are extremely effective in bringing about dramatic changes in subjectivity. Numerous scholars have noticed this tendency, dubbing it a 'revision of consciousness' (Martin 1990: 287), a 'remaking of the individual' (Maxwell 1998: 352) or a 'reorientation of persons' (Barbalet 2008: 75). What has been less noted is how the re-formed Pentecostal subjectivity is very similar to the neoliberal subjectivity required to succeed in the contemporary capitalist economy (although see Comaroff and Comaroff 2000; Maxwell 2005). Whereas 'traditional' Africans are embedded in tight-knit webs of kinship and community, with the associated economic demands of helping less wealthy relatives and contributing to costly individual and communal rituals and ceremonies, the ideal Pentecostal African is an individual (or a member of a small nuclear family), with no economic demands beyond his or her immediate household. While the 'traditional' African is reticent to become wealthier than his peers lest he be accused of witchcraft or sorcery, the Pentecostal African *Lukas* strives to become rich because he believes that this is what God wants for him. While the 'traditional' African is generally rather fatalist and accepts her lot, the Pentecostal African has a strong sense of agency and believes that she can improve her situation with hard work and deeply felt prayer. While the 'traditional' African favours stability and is slow to take risks, the Pentecostal African strives for improvement and is more likely to try something new. These changes to individuals, and to the web of social relations in which they find themselves, have a huge impact on economic behaviour.

Thus, Pentecostal churches are exceptionally effective at bringing about the type of change that is often called 'development' – sustained social and economic transformation from 'traditional' modalities to forms of behaviour and relationship that fit well with the prevailing neoliberal capitalist system. How is this radical transformation brought about? As I will show in more detail below, there are three key interlinked processes of change that are brought about by Pentecostalism: firstly, a major embodied personal transformation and empowerment of the individual; secondly, a shift in values that provides moral legitimacy for a set of behaviour changes that would otherwise clash with local sensibilities; and thirdly, if other factors are favourable, a radical reconstructing of the social and economic relationships in families and communities. *Answer to 6*

Most of the followers of Pentecostalism in Africa come from either the poor or the new middle class (or relatively more wealthy farmers in rural settings). Pentecostalism caters to these two groups in quite different ways, often having different churches for different socio-economic groups (e.g. Comaroff 2012; Hasu 2012). Many poor people, particularly the urban poor, first come to Pentecostal churches feeling wretched, despised and hopeless. Often newly disembedded from tightly knit communities in the countryside, they feel lost and bewildered in the urban environment and struggle to find somewhere to live and enough to eat. Their self-esteem is low and they feel powerless to change their situation. In many countries, including *Answer to 2* for example Tanzania and South Africa, people in this situation often complain of being turned into 'zombies' (*misukule* in Swahili), people who are thought to be taken to carry out nocturnal unpaid labour for witches while their bodies lie in bed at night (e.g. Hasu 2009, 2012). Victimised and slaving away for their imaginary owners in an underground occult economy, these people wake up listless and exhausted and suffer from many of the symptoms that we might call depression. Engagement with a Pentecostal church, and their ensuing conversion, can radically change these people's sense of themselves and their place in the world. Through their engagement with pastors and other church members, in study, prayer and healing, these people begin to see themselves as valued individuals, part of God's people, a 'somebody' rather than a 'nobody'. Most importantly of all, they begin to move beyond a passive fatalism and come to realise that they have agency in their lives (Maxwell 2005). Eventually they shift from seeing themselves as victims to seeing themselves as victors.

This transformation is often brought about by spiritual healing and deliverance. Many churches offer healing services where pastors and lay people pray for those with problems, lay on hands and attempt to heal 'in the name of Jesus'. For people going through such a healing ceremony it can be a very powerful experience – suddenly finding themselves at the centre of a crowd of praying or chanting people, all focusing on them, supposedly channelling the divine healing force into their body and their soul. Often simply accepting the possibility that Jesus might be able to help them opens a mental door out of the preceding blackness.

Pentecostal ontology is binary, with right and wrong, Jesus and devil, as polar opposites. So another type of healing ceremony is the 'spiritual warfare' against, and deliverance from, the devil or associated evil spirits who are believed to be the cause of the person's suffering and distress. Many Pentecostal churches carry out exorcisms where evil spirits are cast out of the sufferer with much crying, weeping and wailing. Again, these emotive services have the power to touch individuals deeply and enable them to reframe their situation so that they can more easily deal with it.

Päivi Hasu, for example, describes the case of Neema, a 17-year-old girl she met in Dar es Salaam, Tanzania, who had dropped out of school, argued with her family in Moshi, and eventually come to the capital city, feeling lonely, tired and listless, with headaches and chest pains, and complaining of having been taken as a 'zombie' and having to work in the 'land of the witches'. She writes how Neema described her personal transformation at the hands of the Glory of Christ Tanzania Church:

> Neema described how, one day in the land of the witches, she heard somebody calling her name from afar. She heard the voice calling her: 'Neema come, Neema come!' Then she saw a white person resembling pastor Gwajima who came and took her hand and said that Neema had been tormented enough and that it had to stop. She then unexpectedly found herself at Glory church. At the beginning she was possessed by spirits (*mapepo*), but she was prayed for and since that day she has not had any more headaches or chest pains. . . . She received Jesus as her personal saviour and wanted to serve God. She saw a clear difference in her life compared with what it had been before. Previously she was ill all the time and had no direction in her life. Now she had received Jesus and was not ill any more. She had joy in her life as well as direction. She wanted to go back to school and complete her education. Despite her bleak circumstances, Neema had begun to feel more hopeful about the future.
>
> (Hasu 2012: 82–3)

In a similar although less dramatic fashion, Charles Piot quotes from an interview with a Pentecostal convert in Lomé, Togo:

Prosperity wealth: Belief that God rewards faith with health and wealth.

> When I walk down the street as a Christian, I hold my head high. I know I have something that others don't. I am not wealthy and I am not classed ['classé'], but I have something even better. I have Jesus on my side, and with Jesus anything is possible. Others look at me and wonder where this confidence comes from, because they don't see money or class. But this is what Jesus does for you. Every day I get out of bed and feel that today will be even better than the day before.
>
> (Piot 2012: 122–3)

These subjective transformations can radically change a person's life. From being wretched and helpless, new believers find inner strength, hope and purpose. They become motivated to work or to study; they seek to improve their lives. Most importantly they develop a sense of agency, of personal power. They move from a fatalistic acceptance of their situation to an awareness of the importance of their actions and the potential of their own efforts to bring about the social and economic changes that they desire. The ecstatic ritual and worship that are so characteristic of Pentecostalism play a fundamental role in this transformation of embodied subjectivities and in creating the felt experience of newness which makes the rhetoric of rebirth feel actual (cf. Csordas 2002; Maxwell 2005). Such charismatic experiences make possible a fundamental rupture in the social order and then lead to the possibility of the establishment of a new order (Keyes 2002: 249). What other forms of Protestantism may seek to do with sober stories and prayer, and what secular development organisations may seek to do with dull workshops, micro-credit schemes and the like, Pentecostalism achieves far more effectively with its exuberant rituals, exorcisms and gifts of the Spirit. Many people shift from begging or dependency on relatives to getting a job or operating in the informal economy, becoming productive members of society. This shift has major implications for development.

Nonetheless, it is important to stress that such changes in subjectivity on their own do not always lead to shifts in people's social and economic actions. The shift in subjectivity reorients people so that they become able to grasp new opportunities when they are available. However, new opportunities are not always available, and in these situations the change in subjectivity can both empower and frustrate people, as they seek to change their lives but find themselves unable to do so. Gregory Deacon describes such a situation in the slums of Nairobi (Deacon 2012; Deacon and Lynch 2013). In this case Pentecostalism offers people defence mechanisms and survival strategies, but does not lead to any significant change in their economic behaviour, as there simply are no new options available to them. In a similar fashion my own work in rural Ethiopia shows how, after their initial conversion to Pentecostalism, many young men started to desire new ways of living and more independence, but were then left frustrated when they could not find a way to break from the traditional production system in which they remained structurally dependent on their fathers. It was only several years later when a development NGO came to the area and started a market-based development project that these young men found the opportunity for something new, and they were indeed the first people in the community to take the chance and participate in the new project, and in so doing eventually became very economically successful (Freeman 2012c).

For relatively wealthy rural people or those in the urban middle class, Pentecostalism offers a somewhat different reformulation of subjectivity. For these people their major problem is generally not loneliness and poverty, but rather how to make more money and how to deal with the social and moral dilemmas of becoming newly rich while their neighbours and kin continue to struggle.

While earlier forms of classical Pentecostalism promoted a rather ascetic approach to the material world, shifts since the 1980s have led to a fundamental realignment with regard to views about the material life and this-worldly concerns. The new view, often termed the 'prosperity gospel', was taken up with phenomenal enthusiasm in churches with more middle-class members in post-1980s Africa, and promises an 'economically advantageous redemption' (Bialecki *et al.* 2008: 1149). Salvation, in this view, can take place in this life, because Jesus wants his people to enjoy abundance and prosperity (Ruth Marshall 1991; Maxwell 1998; Ukah 2005; van Dijk 2005). Churches that preach the prosperity gospel encourage their members to pray to Jesus for wealth and abundance, and also to do their part in the bargain, by engaging in business and working hard. Sermons are often blatantly materialistic. Birgit Meyer describes a visit to a 'prosperity gospel' Pentecostal church in Ghana, during which:

> I heard the pastor ask all members to rise, close their eyes and fill in a cheque in their minds which was then sent up to heaven; the people were assured that God would sign this cheque and that they would, in the future, receive the money requested – if only they believed.
>
> (Meyer 1998b: 762–3)

Furthermore, many of the new Pentecostal churches encourage people to start businesses, and they play a major role in stimulating and shaping business behaviour. They empower people to be courageous and aim high, to take risks and follow their dreams, and to start enterprises, large and small. Paul Freston, for example, quotes a Pentecostal pastor telling his congregation: 'It's not enough just to give the "sacrifice" (a special offering) and cross your arms. You have to leave your job and open a business, even if it's only selling popcorn on the street. As an employee you'll never get rich' (Freston 1995: 132). In many of these churches, pastors are actively training their members in business and management skills. Van Dijk has commented that various Pentecostal churches in Ghana and Botswana 'devote extensive time and energy to the particular matter of how a modern believer is to be transformed and developed into a proactive and goal-oriented agent' (van Dijk 2012: 96). In several publications (e.g. van Dijk 2009, 2012) he describes how these churches run courses in planning, goal setting, time management and budgeting. These churches are not an anomalous few, but a growing trend throughout Africa. They draw on the works of several well-known African Pentecostal preachers who write books about how to understand the workings of the market and how the gospel can help one to reach economic success. Some of the most well-known publications include Mensa Otabil's *Four Laws of Productivity*, Dag Heward-Mills's series of booklets entitled *Success and the Ministry*, Michael Ntumy's *Financial Breakthrough: Discovering God's Secrets to Prosperity*, and David Oyepedo's *Maximise Your Destiny*. Through church training courses and books such as these, Pentecostal preachers take the role of instructing Africa's newly emerging middle class in how to engage with the market, build a business and manage their time. (For other examples across the continent see Maxwell 1998; Comaroff and Comaroff 2000; Ukah 2005; Meyer 2007; and Schlemmer 2008.) These are skills that development organisations have long sought to instil in their African 'beneficiaries', with little success. On their own they seem alien and unnecessary, but, when packaged up with the Pentecostal message of economic salvation and God's desire for abundance, they become useful tools to create a good and meaningful life.

Transformations in values and social relationships

The Pentecostal enthusiasm for material wealth is not without its dilemmas, often associated in Africa with witchcraft, and in some cases churches acknowledge traditional fears of wealth accumulation and create practices that purify potentially dangerous commodities and legitimise accumulation by good Christians (Meyer 1998b). In other cases Pentecostal teachings encourage followers to withdraw from social obligations that would block them from reaching their financial goals. For many Africans one of the main barriers to accumulating wealth is the pressure to spend any money they have on costly traditional rituals, such as rites of passage or rituals of commensality. Redistribution, in one form or another, is inherent in most traditional African religions and moral systems, and it makes personal accumulation virtually impossible. Pentecostal theology links traditional African religion with the devil and labels all traditional practices as forms of devil worship. In this way, Pentecostalism makes avoidance of traditional religious obligations, and separation from more distant kin, intensely and aggressively moral, and thus enables the emergence of previously impossible behaviours, such as not participating in expensive ceremonies or refusing to contribute to communal rituals.

In my own research in rural Ethiopia, this new-found ability to absent oneself from expensive redistributive rituals, and the concomitant ability to reinvest one's wealth into education and new business opportunities, was something that made Pentecostalism very appealing in an otherwise traditional farming community. Farmers in the village of Doko in the Gamo Highlands of southwest Ethiopia had recently started earning money through the production of a cash crop – in this case, apples. Those who were among the earliest to take up apple production soon found themselves in an uncomfortable situation: they were successfully generating a fair amount of wealth, but suddenly the community elders were asking them to sponsor the large redistributive rituals and to become initiated. If they accepted this offer they would have no choice but to spend the most part of their newly earned wealth on huge feasts for the community. Many of them had other ideas for their money, such as investing in more apples, opening local bars or hotels or sending their children to school. Until recently there had been no morally legitimate way to refuse this request from the elders (Halperin and Olmstead 1976). At most people could put off sponsoring the feasts for a year or two, but any longer than that would bring about severe social discord, and communities had ways to force potential initiates to comply (Freeman 2002a, 2002b). However, with the introduction of the small Pentecostal church in the village, people finally had a way out. By joining the church people could effectively exit most aspects of the traditional culture – by claiming that it was devil worship and that they now followed Jesus. This was not just a rhetorical discourse; these people had lived in fear of the spirits for most of their lives and had therefore carried out the required traditional practices. Now that they felt that Jesus was more powerful than the spirits, and would be able to keep them safe if they did not carry out the traditional rituals, they finally had a safe way out. As one of these farmers told me: 'Before there was no way out. You had to follow *dere woga* [traditional practice]. There was no other option. You can't stop *dere woga* unless you believe. The community will force you back. The only way out is to believe. Then Jesus helps you and then you have peace.' By joining the Pentecostal church, apple farmers found a way to hold on to their new-found wealth, and this enabled many of them to become relatively rich in a fairly short period of time. Eventually, as apple production spread amongst the community, nearly everyone converted to Pentecostalism, the initiation rituals largely stopped and social and economic relations were radically reformulated (Freeman 2012c, 2013).

This type of behaviour is often framed as 'making a break with the past' (Meyer 1998a), where believers make every effort to separate themselves from former social networks and to actively shun traditional cultural practices. Despite the challenges of doing this in practice, this push to break with the past is paradoxically one of the main attractions of Pentecostalism, as people increasingly seek a 'way out'. It is worth noting that Pentecostal theology does not deny the existence of evil spirits, as do many other branches of Christianity and most secular development organisations; it rather accepts their existence but overcomes them with the superior power of Jesus. By acknowledging the existence and power of spirits and demons and simultaneously providing a route for believers to distance themselves from them – to make a break – Pentecostalism offers its followers a way out of traditional practices that is at once both safe and legitimate (Robbins 2004).

In many urban centres across Africa the dilemmas of separating oneself from traditional religions and from distant kin 'in the village' are ubiquitously visible in the increasingly popular genres of Pentecostal film and teleserial. In these media, seeking both to entertain and to evangelise, protagonists are seen trying to live a good Christian life while their domestic sphere gets invaded by demons, witches or other supernatural beings from the village. Mirroring the polar ontology of African Pentecostalism, these films and teleserials portray the struggle of good against evil, as played out in the lives of the urban middle classes, and show the ways in which a good Pentecostal must act in order to disengage herself successfully from occult traditional practices and distant village kin. In her study of Pentecostal teleserials in Kinshasa, Congo, Katrien Pype thus describes the key scenario that is repeatedly explored in numerous Pentecostal television dramas as:

> Life in Kinshasa is hazardous because of the working of the Devil and his demons. They invade the domestic sphere with the help of witches, who threaten collective and individual health (in a physical and social sense). Christians can however arm themselves against evil through prayer and by listening closely to the advice of pastors.
>
> (Pype 2012:10)

Similarly, Birgit Meyer claims that Pentecostal films in Accra, Ghana:

> represent modern life in the city – in a beautiful, well-furnished house, which is only inhabited by a caring husband, his loving wife, and their children, who all lead a Christian life – as ultimately desirable. And yet, this ideal is so difficult to attain because it is threatened from so many angles. Films thrive on a moral geography that opposes the village, which is the realm of the extended family, and the forces of nature, on the one hand, and the secluded house in the city, on the other.
>
> (Meyer 2003: 212)

Pentecostal films and teleserials saturate the media in many African cities. They are enormously popular with the growing middle class, who are often trying in their real lives to fathom the very same dilemmas that the films and teleserials portray. They are frequently discussed on television chat shows, used as examples in church sermons and talked about avidly amongst friends. The Pentecostal promise of individualisation and modernisation is strongly desired, but difficult to fully attain. Nonetheless, many Africans are moving in this direction using the faith, teachings and reconfigured morality of the Pentecostal churches.

Pentecostal preachers also encourage believers to be thick-skinned and to ignore the constant requests for help that they receive from poorer relatives, particularly distant relatives in the village. In many cases this leads to cutting or weakening kin ties, and Pentecostal belief has been shown to bring about a dramatic restructuring of families, as believers loosen ties with the extended family and focus on the nuclear family – as represented in so many Pentecostal films – as the central unit of production and consumption. In a similar way Pentecostalism challenges traditional power structures and modes of social organisation – particularly in rural contexts – and instead emphasises individualism and personal achievement.

Another way that Pentecostalism changes economic behaviour, for both the rich and the poor, is by changing consumption patterns. Across the continent Pentecostals call on their followers to abstain from alcohol, tobacco and extramarital relationships (including visits to prostitutes). As believers make strong efforts to change their behaviour in the name of Jesus, they bring about a highly significant change in their spending patterns. Money that is earned is no longer distributed among kin and community, and no longer frittered away on unproductive endeavours. Instead there is a marked limitation of 'wasteful consumption' and a reorientation towards investment and accumulation.

Whilst Pentecostalism goes far beyond these social and economic impacts for its followers, providing a new type of community, new form of moral framework and an intensely powerful embodied experience of a new belief and way to be in the world, for our purposes here it is these social and economic changes that show us how Pentecostalism affects development in Africa.

Conclusion

In *The Protestant Ethic and the Spirit of Capitalism*, Weber (2008 [1904–05]) argued that there was an elective affinity between the spread of Protestant Christianity and the growth of capitalism in sixteenth- and seventeenth-century Europe. He sought to show that Protestant belief led to an ethic of hard work and limited consumption that had the *unintended consequence* of leading to successful enterprise and capital accumulation, and thus the further growth and spread of capitalist economic practice. While there are many differences between sixteenth-century Calvinism and twenty-first-century Pentecostalism (see Freeman 2012b), there are nonetheless also many parallels, and I have sought to show here how Pentecostalism plays a similar role in Africa today. It is a form of Protestantism that stimulates a transformation of behaviour that can lead to success, or at least upward mobility, in the contemporary neoliberal economy. It motivates new behaviours and renders them moral. It promotes hard work, saving and a limitation on certain types of unproductive consumption. Thus it leads people to participate, and succeed, in the capitalist economy. This, at least in present thinking, is what we generally mean by 'development'.

References

Alkire, Sabina (2005) *Valuing Freedoms: Sen's Capability Approach and Poverty Reduction*, Oxford: Oxford University Press.

Anderson, Allan (2004) *An Introduction to Pentecostalism: Global Charismatic Christianity*, Cambridge: Cambridge University Press.

Barbalet, Jack (2008) *Weber, Passion and Profits: 'The Protestant Ethic and the Spirit of Capitalism' in Context*, Cambridge: Cambridge University Press.

Barrett, David (2001) *World Christian Trends, AD 30–AD 2200*, Pasadena, CA: William Carey.

Barrett, David and Johnson, Todd (2002) 'Global Statistics', in Stanley Burgess and Eduard van der Maas (eds), *The New International Dictionary of Pentecostal and Charismatic Movements, Grand Rapids*, MI: Zondervan.

Berger, Peter (2004) 'Max Weber Is Alive and Well and Living in Guatemala: The Protestant Ethic Today', paper prepared for the conference on Norms, Beliefs and Institutions of Twenty First Century Capitalism: Celebrating Max Weber's *The Protestant Ethic and the Spirit of Capitalism*, Ithaca, NY, 8 October.

Berger, Peter (2009) 'Faith and Development', *Society*, 46, 69–75.

Bialecki, Jon (2008) 'Between Stewardship and Sacrifice: Agency and Economy in a Southern Californian Charismatic Church', *Journal of the Royal Anthropological Institute* (NS), 14, 372–90.

Bialecki, Jon, Haynes, Naomi and Robbins, Joel (2008) 'The Anthropology of Christianity', *Religion Compass*, 2 (6), 1139–58.

Burchardt, Marian (2013) '"We Are Saving the Township": Pentecostalism, Faith-Based Organisations, and Development in South Africa', *Journal of Modern African Studies*, 51 (4), 627–51.

Burgess, Stanley and van der Maas, Eduard (eds) (2002) *The New International Dictionary of Pentecostal and Charismatic Movements*, Grand Rapids, MI: Zondervan.

Chambers, Robert and Conway, Gordon (1991) *Sustainable Rural Livelihoods: Practical Concepts for the 21st Century*, IDS Discussion Paper 296, Brighton: Institute of Development Studies.

Coleman, Simon (2000) *The Globalisation of Charismatic Christianity: Spreading the Gospel of Prosperity*, Cambridge: Cambridge University Press.

Coleman, Simon (2002) 'The Faith Movement: A Global Religious Culture?', *Culture and Religion*, 3, 3–19.

Comaroff, Jean (2012) 'Pentecostalism, Populism and the New Politics of Affect', in Dena Freeman (ed.), *Pentecostalism and Development: Churches, NGOs and Social Change in Africa*, London: Palgrave Macmillan.

Comaroff, Jean and Comaroff, John (2000) 'Privatizing the Millenium: New Protestant Ethics and the Spirits of Capitalism in Africa, and Elsewhere', *Afrika Spectrum*, 35 (3), 293–312.

Csordas, Thomas (1992) 'Religion and the World System: The Pentecostal Ethic and the Spirit of Monopoly Capital', *Dialectical Anthropology*, 17, 3–24.

Csordas, Thomas (2002) *Body/Meaning/Healing*, New York: Palgrave Macmillan.

Csordas, Thomas (2007) 'Global Religion and the Re-Enchantment of the World: The Case of the Catholic Charismatic Renewal', *Anthropological Theory*, 7 (9), 295–314.

Deacon, Gregory (2012) 'Pentecostalism and Development in Kibera Informal Settlement, Nairobi', *Development in Practice*, 22 (5–6), 663–74.

Deacon, Gregory and Lynch, Gabrielle (2013) 'Allowing Satan In? Moving toward a Political Economy of Neo-Pentecostalism in Kenya', *Journal of Religion in Africa*, 43, 108–30.

Deneulin, Séverine (2009) *Religion in Development: Rewriting the Secular Script*, London: Zed Books.

Deneulin, Séverine and Rakodi, Carole (2011) 'Revisiting Religion: Development Studies Thirty Years On', *World Development*, 39 (1), 45–54.

DeTemple, Jill (2006) '"Haiti Appeared at My Church": Faith-Based Organizations, Transnational Activism and Tourism in Sustainable Development', *Urban Anthropology*, 35, 155–81.

Dilger, Hansjorg (2009) 'Doing Better? Religion, the Virtue-Ethics of Development, and the Fragmentation of Health Politics in Tanzania', *Africa Today*, 56 (1), 89–110.

Freeman, Dena (2002a) *Initiating Change in Highland Ethiopia: Causes and Consequences of Cultural Transformation*, Cambridge: Cambridge University Press.

Freeman, Dena (2002b) 'From Warrior to Wife: Cultural Transformation in the Gamo Highlands of Ethiopia', *Journal of the Royal Anthropological Institute (NS)*, 8, 34–44.

Freeman, Dena (ed.) (2012a) *Pentecostalism and Development: Churches, NGOs and Social Change in Africa*, London: Palgrave Macmillan.

Freeman, Dena (2012b) 'The Pentecostal Ethic and the Spirit of Development', in Dena Freeman (ed.), *Pentecostalism and Development: Churches, NGOs and Social Change in Africa*, London: Palgrave Macmillan.

Freeman, Dena (2012c) 'Development and the Rural Entrepreneur: Pentecostals, NGOs and the Market in the Gamo Highlands, Ethiopia', in Dena Freeman (ed.), *Pentecostalism and Development: Churches, NGOs and Social Change in Africa*, London: Palgrave Macmillan.

Freeman, Dena (2013) 'Pentecostalism in a Rural Context: Dynamics of Religion and Development in Southwest Ethiopia', *PentecoStudies*, 12 (2), 231–49.

Freston, Paul (1995) 'Pentecostalism in Brazil: A Brief History', *Religion*, 25, 119–33.

Gifford, Paul (ed.) (1995) *The Christian Churches and the Democratization of Africa*, Leiden: Brill.

Gifford, Paul (1998) *African Christianity: Its Public Role*, London: Hurst.

Goody, Jack (2003) 'Religion and Development: Some Comparative Considerations', *Development*, 46 (4), 64–7.

Gough, Ian and McGregor, J. Allister (eds) (2007) *Wellbeing in Developing Countries: From Theory to Research*, Cambridge: Cambridge University Press.

Goulet, Denis (1997) 'Development Ethics: A New Discipline', *International Journal of Social Economics*, 24 (11), 1160–71.

Halperin, Rhoda and Olmstead, Judith (1976) 'To Catch a Feastgiver: Redistribution among the Dorze of Ethiopia', *Africa*, 46, 146–66.

Hasu, Päivi (2009) 'The Witch, the Zombie and the Power of Jesus: A Trinity of Spiritual Warfare in Tanzanian Pentecostalism', *Suomen Antropologi: Journal of the Finnish Anthropological Society*, 34 (1), 70–83.

Hasu, Päivi (2012) 'Prosperity Gospels and Enchanted Worldviews: Two Responses to Socio-Economic Transformation in Tanzanian Pentecostal Christianity', in Dena Freeman (ed.), *Pentecostalism and Development: Churches, NGOs and Social Change in Africa*, London: Palgrave Macmillan.

Hofer, Katharina (2003) 'The Role of Evangelical NGOs in International Development: A Comparative Case Study of Kenya and Uganda', *Afrika Spectrum*, 38 (3), 375–98.

Hollenweger, Walter (1997) *Pentecostalism: Origins and Developments Worldwide*, Peabody, MA: Hendrickson.

Kamsteeg, Franz (1998) *Prophetic Pentecostalism in Chile: A Case Study on Religion and Development Policy*, Lanham, MD: Scarecrow.

Keyes, Charles (2002) 'Weber and Anthropology', *Annual Review of Anthropology*, 31, 233–55.

Luhrmann, Tanya (2004) 'Metakinesis: How God Becomes Intimate in Contemporary US Christianity', *American Anthropologist*, 106, 518–28.

Marshall, Katherine and Van Saanen, Marisa (2007) *Development and Faith: Where Mind, Heart and Soul Work Together*, Washington, DC: World Bank.

Marshall, Ruth (1991) 'Power in the Name of Jesus', *Review of African Political Economy*, 52, 21–37.

Martin, David (1990) *Tongues of Fire: The Explosion of Protestantism in Latin America*, Oxford: Blackwell.

Martin, David (2002) *Pentecostalism: The World Their Parish*, Oxford: Blackwell.

Maxwell, David (1998) '"Delivered from the Spirit of Poverty": Pentecostalism, Prosperity and Modernity in Zimbabwe', *Journal of Religion in Africa*, 28 (3), 350–73.

Maxwell, David (2005) 'The Durawall of Faith: Pentecostal Spirituality in Neo-Liberal Zimbabwe', *Journal of Religion in Africa*, 35 (1), 4–32.

Meyer, Birgit (1998a) '"Make a Complete Break with the Past": Memory and Post-Colonial Modernity in Ghanaian Pentecostalist Discourse', *Journal of Religion in Africa*, 28 (3), 316–49.

Meyer, Birgit (1998b) 'Commodities and the Power of Prayer: Pentecostalist Attitudes towards Consumption in Contemporary Ghana', *Development and Change*, 29, 751–76.

Meyer, Birgit (2003) 'Ghanaian Popular Cinema and the Magic in and of Film', in Birgit Meyer and Peter Pels (eds), *Magic and Modernity: Interfaces of Revelation and Concealment*, Stanford, CA: Stanford University Press.

Meyer, Birgit (2004) 'Christianity in Africa: From African Independent to Pentecostal–Charismatic Churches', *Annual Review of Anthropology*, 33, 447–74.

Meyer, Birgit (2007) 'Pentecostalism and Neo-Liberal Capitalism: Faith, Prosperity and Vision in African Pentecostal–Charismatic Churches', *Journal for the Study of Religion*, 20 (2), 5–28.

Piot, Charles (2012) 'Pentecostal and Development Imaginaries in West Africa', in Dena Freeman (ed.), *Pentecostalism and Development: Churches, NGOs and Social Change in Africa*, London: Palgrave Macmillan.

Pype, Katrien (2012) *The Making of Pentecostal Melodrama: Religion, Media and Gender in Kinshasa*, Oxford: Berghahn Books.

Rakodi, Carole (2007) 'Understanding the Roles of Religion in Development: The Approach of the RaD Programme', Working Paper 9, Religions and Development Research Programme, Birmingham: Religions and Development.

Robbins, Joel (2004) 'The Globalisation of Pentecostal and Charismatic Christianity', *Annual Review of Anthropology*, 33, 117–43.

Rostow, Walt (1960) *The Stages of Economic Growth: A Non-Communist Manifesto*, Cambridge: Cambridge University Press.

Schlemmer, Lawrence (2008) *Dormant Capital: Pentecostalism in South Africa and Its Potential Social and Economic Role*, Johannesburg: Centre for Development and Enterprise.

Scoones, Ian (1998) *Sustainable Rural Livelihoods: A Framework for Analysis*, IDS, Working Paper 72, Brighton: Institute of Development Studies.

Selinger, Leah (2004) 'The Forgotten Factor: The Uneasy Relationship between Religion and Development', *Social Compass*, 51 (4), 523–43.

Sen, Amartya (1999) *Development as Freedom*, Oxford: Oxford University Press.

ter Haar, Gerrie and Ellis, Stephen (2006) 'The Role of Religion in Development: Towards a New Relationship between the European Union and Africa', *European Journal of Development Research*, 18 (3), 351–67.

Tomalin, E. (2008) 'Faith and Development' in V. Desai and R. Potter (eds), *Companion to Development Studies*, London: Hodder Education.

Ukah, A. F.-K. (2005) 'Those Who Trade with God Never Lose: The Economies of Pentecostal Activism in Nigeria', in T. Falola (ed.), *Christianity and Social Change in Africa: Essays in Honor of J. D. Y. Peel*, Durham, NC: Carolina Academic Press.

van Dijk, Rijk (2005) 'The Moral Life of the Gift in Ghanaian Pentecostal Churches in the Diaspora: Questions of (In-)dividuality and (In-)alienability in Transcultural Reciprocal Relations', in W. van Binsbergen and P. Geschiere (eds), *Commodification: Things, Agency and Identities*, Hamburg: LIT Verlag.

van Dijk, Rijk (2009) 'Social Catapulting and the Spirit of Entrepreneurialism: Migrants, Private Initiative and the Pentecostal Ethic in Botswana', in Gertrud Hüwelmeier and Kristine Krause (eds), *Traveling Spirits: Migrants, Markets and Mobilities*, New York: Routledge.

van Dijk, Rijk (2012) 'Pentecostalism and Post-Development: Exploring Religion as a Developmental Ideology in Ghanaian Migrant Communities', in Dena Freeman (ed.), *Pentecostalism and Development: Churches, NGOs and Social Change in Africa*, London: Palgrave Macmillan.

Ver Beek, K. (2002) 'Spirituality: A Development Taboo', in D. Eade (ed.), *Development and Culture: Selected Essays from Development in Practice*, Oxford: Oxfam GB.

Weber, Max (2008 [1904–05]) *The Protestant Ethic and the Spirit of Capitalism*, trans. Talcott Parsons, Miami, FL: BN Publishing.

9

MASCULINITIES, HIV AND RELIGION IN AFRICA

Adriaan van Klinken and Ezra Chitando

Introduction

Exploring and examining the intersections of masculinities, religion and the HIV epidemic in Africa, this chapter engages in various fields of study: masculinities and development, masculinities and HIV and AIDS, masculinities and religion, and religion and HIV and AIDS (cf. Haddad 2011). Within development studies gender is a central theme, but until recently discussions often narrowly focused upon women. Only with the turn of the new millennium, as a late reception of masculinity studies, did development scholarship and practice begin to widen its scope to include 'the other half of gender'. However, this trend is not yet reflected in studies of religion and development, where gender continues to be conceptualised predominantly as referring to issues that concern women. Cleaver (2002) identifies several arguments for the need to pay attention to men and masculinities in global development, and three of them are particularly relevant to the focus on HIV and AIDS in Africa in this chapter: arguments concerned with gendered vulnerabilities, the crisis of masculinity and strategic gender partnerships. The idea of gendered vulnerabilities means that not only women but also men can be disadvantaged by certain concepts of masculinity. This has proved to be especially true in the context of the HIV epidemic, where the virus infects and affects both men and women. The notion of 'crises of masculinity' refers to multiple processes of social, economic and cultural change that undermine and challenge traditional men's roles and forms of masculinity, and it is clear that in contemporary Africa the epidemic has posed serious threats to men and masculinity. Finally, if the HIV epidemic in Africa is a gendered phenomenon, as is now generally acknowledged, then the response to the epidemic should also be gender-based and thus involve men and address questions of masculinity. To build such a strategic partnership, men indeed have become special 'targets for a change' in Africa (Bujra 2002). In this chapter we explore these and other themes related to men, masculinities and HIV in Africa, critically examining their intersections with religion. In the process, our focus is on Sub-Saharan Africa, and the discussion is limited to the three major religions on the continent: African traditional religion, Christianity and Islam, with one section looking in particular at Pentecostal strands of Christianity.

As a preliminary remark, we acknowledge the risk that 'scholarship and policy-related research on masculinities can covertly reinforce colonial myth-making about the "essential" nature of African masculinity' (Lewis 2011: 205). In much of the literature, including our own work, there is a tendency to problematise African male sexuality as the cause of high-risk behaviour and sexual aggression, while the discourse of transforming masculinities may implicitly reflect a project of 'civilising' African men. Most scholars have engaged with the social constructivist theory of masculinities as a plural (Connell 2005) to avoid essentialist and monolithic representations of masculinity, but this has not completely prevented generalising accounts that indeed echo colonial perceptions of African sexuality and black masculinity. The challenge, therefore, has been about how to continue to agitate for more responsible masculinities, without slipping into colonising discourses.

Gender and HIV: the turn to masculinities

Since the early 1990s, it is increasingly acknowledged that the HIV epidemic in Africa has a gendered face: women get disproportionately infected with the virus, partly because of physiological aspects but also because of structural gender inequalities and their impact on sexual economies that make women more vulnerable to the virus than men. Women also suffer more from HIV-related stigma and carry a disproportionate burden of AIDS-related care (Baylies and Bujra 2000). As a result of this awareness, both scholarship and intervention programmes came to focus on women, and a discourse on women's empowerment in relation to HIV and AIDS emerged. Slowly but surely, it was realised that women's vulnerabilities are related to behaviours of men that are undergirded by ideologies of masculinity which actually also put men themselves at risk. This realisation has led to a shift in the understanding and response to gender and HIV and AIDS in Africa, with an increased focus on men and masculinities as part both of the problem and of the possible solution for the enormous challenges posed by the epidemic (Foreman 1999; Bujra 2002). As UNAIDS (2000: 7) points out, this new focus 'does not mean an end to prevention programmes for women and girls' but rather aims 'to complement these by work which more directly involves men'.

There is now a rapidly growing body of literature on men, masculinities and HIV in Africa. This literature mainly explores how prevalent types of masculinity, often referred to with Connell's (2005) concept of hegemonic masculinity, critically intersect with issues of HIV, while at the same time it contextualises these forms of masculinity by highlighting the historical and socio-cultural conditions that have shaped them. Exemplary here are the studies of Silberschmidt (2005) and Hunter (2005, 2010) on male sexuality in Kenya and South Africa respectively. Going beyond (and in fact questioning) popular ideas about a 'natural' African male promiscuity underlying the HIV epidemic, they argue that contemporary patterns of multiple sexual partnerships and high-risk sexual behaviour among men are shaped by material realities: in a context where poverty and unemployment disempower men economically, previous notions of masculinity such as being the breadwinner of the home are threatened and sexual conquest becomes an alternative way of strengthening male identity. Reviewing how the socialisation and behaviour of young men contributes to the spread of HIV in Sub-Saharan Africa, Barker and Ricardo (2006) show how critical issues such as multiple sexual partnership, cross-generational sex, sexual violence against women, the lack of condom use, and the low level of HIV testing are all related to a complex and dynamic matrix of cultural values, economic conditions and processes of social change. The edited volume by Meyer and Struthers (2012), though not strictly academic, stands out in that it debunks the stereotype of men as typically irresponsible, refusing to care for their partners when they develop AIDS, or that they are abusive fathers. The volume shows that, in the light of pressing socio-economic conditions, men often make sensitive and effective decisions.

Where hegemonic forms of masculinity are implicated in the HIV epidemic in various and complex ways, the social-constructivist notion of the plurality and diversity of masculinities entails some important insights to discussions about men, masculinities and the HIV epidemic. First, not all men are the same, and generalising and monolithic accounts on masculinity should therefore be avoided. There has been a tendency to blame men for the spread of HIV, such as in the statement that 'without men there would be no AIDS epidemic' (Foreman 1999: vi). This tone of blame not only is strategically unhelpful but also reveals a failure to differentiate between the individual and the social, because it oversimplifies social structures (Mane and Aggleton 2001). Second, what is constructed can also be actively deconstructed and transformed. Thus, it is possible to engage in masculinity politics and embark on a transformation of masculinities. Third, the idea that masculinity is subject to various and competing discourses implies that to a certain extent men do have agency to configure and reconfigure their identity and performance as men. It is important to acknowledge this notion of male agency, on the one hand to avoid the idea that men are just victims of hegemonic norms of masculinity, and on the other hand because it opens up the possibility of change among men.

If masculinity is a social and discursive construction, religion is one of the factors playing a role in the processes in which masculinities are constantly (re)configured. This is particularly the case in Africa, given the centrality and significance of religion in African societies and in people's lives. As Ellis and ter Haar (2004: 2) contend, 'it is largely through religious ideas that Africans think about the world today, and . . . religious ideas provide them with a means of becoming social and political actors'. Yet social scientists and gender scholars pay remarkably little attention to religion in their work on men, masculinities and AIDS. Some African theologians, in contrast, have made this a primary field of research and critical reflection. From the early 2000s, the Circle of Concerned African Women Theologians has addressed women's vulnerability in the context of the epidemic, and the organisation invited a number of male theologians to its 2007 pan-African conference on gender and the epidemic to participate in a session on 'liberating masculinities'. The resulting body of literature is centred on the idea that religion 'is a double-edged sword in relation to masculinities in the face of gender-based violence and HIV and AIDS. On the one hand, religion reinforces dangerous masculinities, while on the other it has an enormous potential to transform masculinities' (Chitando and Chirongoma 2012: 17). To begin with the former, how does religion interplay with forms of masculinity that are critical in the context of HIV?

Religion and HIV – critical masculinities

With HIV being a sexually transmittable disease, any discussion of gender and HIV immediately is also about sexuality and power. Social and economic inequalities in gender relations are reflected in sexual relationships between women and men. These inequalities contribute to women's relative powerlessness when it comes to sexual decision making and thus to their vulnerability to HIV. This realisation draws attention to the religious support of patriarchal notions of masculinity. African feminist theologians like Musa Dube, Isabel Phiri and Fulata Moyo have argued that both African traditional religion and Christianity uphold notions of male supremacy, such as the idea of male headship, which directly or indirectly assign all authority and power to control to men, including the control of women's bodies and female sexuality. Moyo (2004: 73), for example, states: 'Sexuality is about power for those who determine the what, when, where and how of sex, be it socio-economic and/or religio-cultural. In heterosexual relationships, those who have this power are men.' She then points out how this gendered structure of sexual decision making is reinforced by the teachings in both the traditional and the Christianised female initiation rites, where women are taught to serve men's sexual needs and to subordinate their sexual lives to those of men. Similar arguments about sexuality and power have been made with regard to Islamic masculinity in the context of HIV, since Islam, according to Godsey (2009: 130), also gives a man power and authority over his wife. Religious teachings like these are popularly embraced by men even when personally they are not very religious, as Simpson (2009: 149) found among a group of Zambian men who regularly cite the Genesis creation story as evidence of male superiority in gender relations. Of course, patriarchal ideals of masculinity found in and/or promoted by religious traditions do not directly contribute to the spread of HIV. One could argue that religious resources are used, or abused, by men to continue engaging in risky sexual behaviour and oppressive attitudes towards women, which is dangerous in times of HIV. This calls for a further study of the specific meanings of patriarchal notions of masculinity in religion, and of the different ways they are interpreted and applied by men.

With regard to male sexuality more specifically, prevalent patterns of multiple sexual partnerships are, of course, highly problematic in the context of HIV. Although such patterns do not reflect a natural essence of African or black masculinity but need to be understood within specific historical trajectories and socio-economic contexts, they may also be informed, directly or indirectly, by some deeply rooted cultural values and religious beliefs. Contemporary popular norms among young men which equate masculinity with sexual conquest, for example, reflect a preoccupation with virility and potency that could be related to the obligation to transmit 'the vital force of life' and ensure immortality which is at the heart of indigenous religious systems. Where in traditional African societies men observed this obligation within clearly demarcated structures of marriage and kinship, these structures have largely collapsed in the modern period as a result of colonialism and urbanisation, leaving male sexuality relatively unrestrained. Moreover, as Achille Mbembe reminds us, colonialism (and its companion, missionary Christianity) itself imposed a form of phallic domination on Africa which, in the colonial era and its aftermath, made the phallus the focus of ways of constructing masculinity and power in African societies. This concretely led to an emphasis in African (post)colonial masculinities on 'the individual male's ability to demonstrate his virility at the expense of a woman and to obtain its validation from the subjugated woman herself' (Mbembe 2001: 13).

Discussions about gender, masculinity and HIV in Africa tend to focus on heterosexuality. This reflects the widespread myth of a presumed exclusively heterosexual African HIV epidemic (Epprecht 2008). Only recently has attention started to be paid to the transmission of HIV through same-sex relationships. However, HIV prevention and treatment among the high-risk and highly vulnerable category of men having sex with men are being hindered by the enormous social, cultural and religious taboo on homosexuality in African societies and by the fact that in many countries same-sex relations are criminalised. In the current climate of public debates about homosexuality and 'gay rights' in Africa, religious leaders frequently are in the forefront of propagating homophobia. Specifically in relation to masculinities, religions not only reinforce heteronormative ideals of masculinity but also, directly or indirectly, legitimate discrimination and violence against people involved in alternative sexualities, which raises serious human rights and public health concerns.

Religion and HIV – constructive masculinities

As much as religion is intricately related to masculinities that are critical in the context of the HIV epidemic, can it also play a role in the transformation of masculinities so that they become more constructive? This section discusses various ways in which religions – religious practices, religious beliefs, religious texts, religious institutions and religious leaders – indeed play, or are envisioned to play, such a role.

In many traditional African societies circumcision was part of the rites of passage through which young men reached adulthood. Though it became less common in regions that in the twentieth century became Christian, it remains an important practice in other regions, and even when it is no longer practised it is culturally acceptable (Shapiro and Kapiga 2002). Several studies associate the cultural-religious practice of male circumcision with lower levels of HIV infection among men. This may be one factor explaining why African countries with major Muslim populations are less severely affected by the HIV epidemic, since Islam requires circumcision of male infants (Gray 2004). In recent years, organisations such as UNAIDS and the World Health Organization have come to advocate male circumcision as a protective measure against HIV. In these large-scale campaigns circumcision becomes a medical measure, but efforts are made to involve religious and traditional leaders to ensure that its cultural and religious significance is retained or (re)invented. An example of an invention of a religious meaning in this context is the slogan of some Christian pastors who promote male circumcision by saying 'Jesus was circumcised.' When accompanied by religious or cultural ritual and teaching on sexuality, relationships and HIV, circumcision is not just a medical measure, but can be a rite to institute constructive forms of masculinity and to encourage male agency in HIV prevention (cf. Phiri and Nadar 2012).

Some African theologians, working in collaboration with the above-mentioned Circle of African Women Theologians, have recently provided constructive religious accounts on masculinity, specifically addressing issues of HIV and gender-based violence. Employing resources in Christian and indigenous religious traditions, they present a vision of 'liberating' and 'redemptive' masculinities (van Klinken 2013b: 52–5). The notion of 'liberating masculinities' means that men have actively to support the liberation of women, willingly 'forgo the patriarchal dividend' and 'identify with women and children, and work towards gender justice' (Chitando and Chirongoma 2008: 66). Accompanying this process men themselves will also be liberated from the burden and risks of patriarchal norms of masculinity. The notion of 'redemptive masculinities' refers to 'masculinities that are life-giving in a world reeling from the effects of violence and the AIDS pandemic' (Chitando and Chirongoma 2012: 1). The resources to develop these notions come, for example, from the philosophy and spirituality of *ubuntu* (Manda 2012) or from the New Testament letters of St Paul (Togarasei 2012). Several Christian theologians refer to Jesus Christ as an example of liberating and redemptive masculinity, while Godsey (2009), writing from an Islamic perspective, presents Muhammad as the model of a transformative Muslim masculinity that supports responsibility and gender equality in the context of HIV. These accounts illustrate the creative and constructive engagement with religious traditions in the quest for transformative masculinities among progressive theologians. Since these theologians often work in institutions where they teach the pastors and religious leaders of tomorrow, their work potentially has a wider impact than the academy. Moreover, they are often involved in church programmes and community work. Exemplary here is the work of the Ujaama Centre for theological community development and research of the University of KwaZulu-Natal, who have rolled out a campaign in South Africa and other African countries in which they use a biblical story about rape to address issues of sexuality and violence in local men's groups in churches and other communities. According to West (2012), these bible studies open up a social space where hegemonic forms of masculinity are disrupted and where alternative masculinities can be articulated, leading to social transformation.

The discourse of redemptive and liberating masculinities is also adopted by the Ecumenical HIV/AIDS Initiative in Africa (EHAIA), an initiative of the World Council of Churches which works in close collaboration with the above-mentioned African theologians. Among other programmes, EHAIA seeks to involve local churches in the transformation of masculinities, and to this aim it facilitates training workshops for pastors and church leaders. The idea is that churches in Africa are rooted in local communities and therefore are influential institutions that can be a force for social transformation in view of the HIV epidemic. As Chitando (2007a), who serves as a theology consultant of EHAIA, points out, it is therefore crucial that churches rethink their mission towards men and start to play a major role in the transformation of masculinities, through preaching, youth activities and men's groups in the church, by reaching out to men in prisons and the army, and by collaborating with NGOs and non-religious men's organisations. For Chitando this also includes a particular attention to the sexual health needs of men who have sex with men, and he underlines the need for churches to discuss human sexuality in an open and liberating way.

With regard to NGOs, it is interesting to observe that in recent years in various African countries programmes have been launched specifically targeting men and aiming at a trans-formation of masculinities. An example is the Padare/Enkundleni Men's Forum on Gender (Zimbabwe), which was established in 1995, utilising the HIV epidemic as an opportunity to address prevailing notions of sexuality and masculinity and to work with men around the con-cept of responsibility. Another example is MenEngage Africa, an alliance of NGOs working in various African countries, which recently has launched a training initiative on masculinities, leadership and gender justice that seeks to promote men's and boys' involvement in HIV pre-vention, response to gender-based violence, and defence of all human rights (including LGBT rights). Both organisations work from a secular perspective and do not explicitly take a religious approach, but working in African contexts it seems unavoidable that religious issues emerge in their activities. This raises the question about the relation between secular and religious forms of masculinity politics in Africa, opening a new field of scholarly inquiry. This question also applies to another NGO, the Young Men's Christian Association (YMCA), whose original Christian-ecumenical background is accentuated or mitigated depending on the local organisation. The YMCA has recently launched a transformative masculinity programme in various Southern African countries, as a response to HIV, sexual violence and other problems among male youths, but it is not clear to what extent and in which ways religion is included here.

At a more grassroots level, faith communities and religious movements do implicitly or explicitly promote certain norms and ideals of masculinity among men, and they may actively address issues concerning men and masculinity in their communities. Most research in this area so far has focused on masculinities in Pentecostal Christianity (see the next section). However, as far as Christianity is concerned, many denominations in Africa do have youth groups, men's fellowship groups and marriage courses, but little is known about the ideals of masculinity pro-moted here or about the way in which gender and sexuality more generally are discussed here. In a study of a Catholic men's organisation in Zambia that presents its patron saint, St Joachim, as a universal model of Catholic manhood, van Klinken (2013a) shows how this model in fact is contextually shaped to address issues of HIV and gender-based violence and to promote an alternative, religious ideal of masculinity among Catholic men. More comparative research is needed to investigate whether similar processes take place in other Christian men's groups, in Islamic faith communities or in groups inspired by indigenous religious traditions.

Pentecostal trajectories to transform masculinities

Pentecostal types of Christianity have attracted substantial attention from researchers on religion and masculinities in Africa. This may have to do with the association of Pentecostalism with a particular capacity to bring about social change – in general as well as more specifically in gender relations. With regard to men and masculinities, the Pentecostal rhetoric about 'a new man' suggests that it is a religious ideology that can wean men from destructive expressions of masculinity. In particular, Pentecostalism's emphasis on sexual faithfulness in relationships has attracted attention. Chitando has examined the extent to which the Zimbabwe Assemblies of God Africa (ZAOGA) has sought to encourage men to be loving, non-violent and accommo-dating in relationships (Chitando 2007b; Chitando and Biri 2013). Van Klinken (2013b) has explored the broader notion of 'responsible manhood' in a Zambian Pentecostal church. These studies suggest that the religious ideals of masculinity promoted in Pentecostal churches are helpful to the struggle against HIV, as men are encouraged to be faithful and responsible and not to perpetrate violence against their partners. Furthermore, these ideals are promising in terms of building and strengthening family systems and partnership with women. Many Pentecostal churches and ministries invest heavily in sensitising boys and young men, among other ways through the establishment of boys' and youth groups that provide crucial social spaces for learn-ing and support. They also have fellowship groups for adult men, where concrete issues and challenges in areas varying from marriage and relationships to business and investments are discussed.

'Born-again masculinity' is not just an abstract ideal preached by Pentecostal pastors, but also a model male converts strive to embody in their daily lives. This is reflected in their conversion stories. Such stories usually have an element of biographical reconstruction and, in a study with Zambian Pentecostal men, van Klinken (2012) shows how these men narrate their conversion in terms of a radical change of their male identity. The narratives thrive on a 'before' and 'after' scheme in which converts describe the 'dangerous' masculinity they embodied prior to becom-ing born again. 'Dangerous masculinity' is expressed in terms of having multiple concurrent sex partners, perpetrating violence against partners, and reckless drinking. Upon conversion, the 'born-again' male adopts a new pattern of behaviour that entails faithfulness in relationships, bonding with his partner and stopping alcohol consumption. While giving up their previous 'manly' behaviour can be a threat to men's male identity, van Klinken shows how the men in his study actually redefine the meaning of manhood so that retrospectively they conclude that only after conversion have they become 'real' men. It appears that, in contemporary contexts of HIV and other social and spiritual challenges, Pentecostal Christianity is a discursive regime that empowers men spiritually to make a break with the past, including dangerous forms of masculinity, and to embark on the existential project of *being* born again and transforming the male self.

Although in practice it is difficult to ascertain the extent to which men actually live up to the ideals held by Pentecostal churches, it is important to acknowledge the quest for, and effects of, 'born-again masculinity'. The Pentecostal gospel of fidelity, self-control and responsibil-ity addresses men's vulnerability, and the related crisis of masculinity, in the shadow of AIDS (Simpson 2009). In contexts where men socio-economically are disempowered (Silberschmidt 2005), the notion of loving, caring and responsible men is an attractive one and can be advanta-geous to men *and* women. David Maxwell (2006), in his study on the Zimbabwe Assemblies of God, points out that male converts and their families often become more successful economi-cally, since money once spent on drinking and womanising is now invested in the home, par-ticularly in education. This argument echoes the Weberian thesis of the Protestant ethic with which Pentecostalism often is associated. Thus, Pentecostalism plays a major role in transform-ing masculinity in contemporary Africa, explicitly responding to issues such as poverty, sexual and gender-based violence, and HIV. It is critical to note, however, that the Pentecostal trajec-tory to transform masculinities is often based on the deployment of patriarchal themes, such as rhetoric of male headship. Even though this notion is discursively dissociated from its assumed 'traditional' or 'African' connotation of male supremacy and domination and is redefined in terms of responsibility and servant leadership, it may easily reinforce or be used to legitimate the very forms of masculinity that Pentecostalism seeks to overcome (Chitando 2007b). At the same time, the Pentecostal understanding of male headship mobilises a sense of agency in men that enables a transformation of masculinity: precisely because men are believed to have been given the role of headship by God, Pentecostalism can invoke a sense of responsibility in men (van Klinken 2011). Feminist-minded scholars and gender activists are faced with a dilemma here: Pentecostalism is not so much concerned with gender equality as such but with male responsibility, and it is precisely through the deployment of patriarchal themes, presented in a religious and spiritual discourse, that Pentecostal masculinity politics are productive and can have transformative effects.

Pressing academic and political issues

Overviewing the recent engagement in academic and gender activist circles with issues of masculinity, HIV and religion, some urgent academic and political issues emerge. To begin with, our above discussion on Pentecostalism reminds us that religious trajectories to transform masculinities often do not follow the 'liberal' or 'progressive' agenda of gender equality that dominates most of the gender and development policies and programmes (Greig *et al.* 2000). Intellectually and politically, this raises challenging questions about the understanding and evaluation of religious forms of masculinity politics that may deploy patriarchal themes but do have constructive effects. The postcolonial contexts in which African Pentecostal and other religious trajectories to transform masculinity manifest themselves, as well as the post-secular turn in Western academia, make scholars more sensitive to these questions and call for a nuanced analysis of religious masculinity politics in a self-reflexive mode (van Klinken 2013b).

Related to this, a critical question is whether programmes aiming at 'transformative masculinities', initiated in Africa by international faith-based bodies such as the World Council of Churches as well as by secular NGOs, are informed by local issues and concerns or represent yet another Western project. To what extent do such programmes, perhaps even subconsciously, perpetuate a colonial and colonising agenda that stereotypes African men as dangerous, backward and unproductive? Are there indigenous resources for the transformation of masculinities? Contestations around these issues will persist into the foreseeable future, as they are related to broader fundamental questions about gender politics and policies of social change in contemporary African societies.

A critical gap in current research and available literature on religion, masculinities and HIV is the lack of knowledge about men living with HIV and the role of religion – as a source of stigmatisation and of coping strategies – in their lives. All over Sub-Saharan Africa, men living with HIV have been actively involved in forming support groups, sometimes in religious settings, and one can imagine that such groups are crucial sites where the fragility and instability of masculinity become visible and are negotiated. Men living with HIV have also emerged in the forefront of discussions about masculinity in Africa. A noteworthy example here is Canon Gideon Byamugisha of Uganda, who in 1992 became the first African religious leader to announce publicly that he was HIV positive. Since then, he has not only been fighting the stigma surrounding HIV in religious communities, but also been advocating that men concede they are vulnerable to HIV and take up more caring and responsible roles. As a founding member of the International Network of Religious Leaders Living with or Personally Affected by HIV and AIDS (INERELA+), Byamugisha has emerged as one of the prime movers of the agenda to transform masculinities in the era of HIV (Chitando 2010). Men who are members of INERELA+ consider religion a valuable resource that empowers them to face HIV. Future research needs to examine the role of religion for men who are living positively but who do not belong to organised religions or institutions. In addition, studies on how HIV has had an impact on masculinities, as well as on the new dynamics caused by the increasing availability of anti-retroviral therapy, are required.

Another relevant issue for future research is the role of women in the shaping of masculinities. If men are largely absent or ineffective fathers, as much literature suggests, then boys to a greater or lesser degree are being raised and shaped into adult men by women. Furthermore, women influence men's behaviour as partners, sisters and friends. It is indeed critical to investigate the values and understandings of masculinity that (grand)mothers inculcate in boys from very early on, and to examine women's perception of masculinity and their role in (re)shaping male behaviour more broadly. However, we should be cautious of the risk of 'blaming the victim', where women are being blamed for the kind of people that their sons and partners turn out to be. It is important to realise that, apart from upbringing, there are many other factors that shape masculinity. Women do not have control over institutions such as the media that play a major role in defining masculinity.

Some of the most pressing political and academic issues regarding masculinities, HIV and religion concern homosexuality. Same-sex relationships have often been excluded or ignored as a relevant factor in the transmission of HIV in Africa, meaning that men having sex with men (MSM) have rarely been targeted in programmes for HIV prevention, testing and treatment. It is now increasingly realised that male same-sex sexuality should be taken into account, not least because most MSM are likely also to have relationships with women, making the taboo on homosexuality also a critical factor in the heterosexual transmission of the virus. However, attempts to incorporate MSM in HIV programmes have been hampered, not only by the social, cultural and religious taboo surrounding homosexuality in many African societies, but also by the legal criminalisation of same-sex practices in many countries, which seriously limits the access of MSM to health services and renders them more vulnerable to HIV. Academically, more research needs to be conducted, first, on the complex interplay of politics, religion, and norms of masculinity that inform the continuing taboo on homosexuality and that give rise to exclusion, discrimination and violence and, second, on the experiences of MSM and the strategies they have developed to cope with, and survive in, the current hostile climate surrounding homosexuality and the life-threatening reality of HIV and AIDS. Politically, more advocacy work needs to be done to create awareness about the public health consequences of homophobia and to target MSM in HIV prevention and treatment programmes. This is particularly critical for religious communities and faith-based organisations that have generally struggled to address the issue of sexuality, and for which homosexuality is particularly controversial and divisive. It is promising, but only a beginning, that some African theologians and activists, mainly within Christianity, have recently broken the taboo and have called for a greater realism, pointing out that HIV thrives in contexts of human rights violations and the marginalisation of MSM (Chitando 2012; Njoroge 2012; van Klinken and Gunda 2012).

Conclusion

It is clear that the HIV epidemic has given rise to critical reflections on masculinities in Africa. This has seen faith-based organisations and NGOs calling for transformative masculinities, as well as grassroots religious communities trying to inculcate new values and perceptions of masculinity among men. In this chapter we have identified and discussed some of the most crucial issues at the intersection of masculinities, HIV and religion, highlighting emerging political and academic challenges. Given that masculinities, religion and the HIV epidemic are multifaceted and highly dynamic, the relations between them are varied and complex as well as constantly changing. This underlines the need to continue examining the developments concerning men and masculinities in Africa, in relation to broader issues of HIV and religion, as these are key to academic and activist practice in the field of gender, religion and development.

References

Barker, G. and Ricardo, C. (2006) 'Young Men and the Construction of Masculinity in Sub-Saharan Africa: Implications for HIV/AIDS, Conflict, and Violence', in I. Bannon and M. C. Correia (eds), *The Other Half of Gender: Men's Issues in Development*, Washington, DC: World Bank, pp. 159–93.

Baylies, C. and Bujra, J. (eds) (2000) *AIDS, Sexuality and Gender in Africa: Collective Strategies and Struggles in Tanzania and Zambia*, London: Routledge.

Bujra, J. (2002) 'Targeting Men for a Change: AIDS Discourse and Activism in Africa', in F. Cleaver (ed.), *Masculinities Matter! Men, Gender and Development*, London: Zed Books, pp. 209–34.

Chitando, E. (2007a) *Acting in Hope: African Churches and HIV/AIDS 2*, Geneva: WCC Publications.

Chitando, E. (2007b) 'A New Man for a New Era? Zimbabwean Pentecostalism, Masculinities and the HIV Epidemic', *Missionalia*, 35 (3), 112–27.

Chitando, E. (2010) 'One Man Can: Gideon Byamugisha and Redemptive Masculinity', *Boleswa*, 3 (2), 46–62.

Chitando, E. (2012) '"Even When There Is No Rooster, the Morning Will Start": Men, HIV and African Theologies', *Journal of Feminist Studies in Religion*, 28 (2), 141–7.

Chitando, E. and Biri, K. (2013) 'Faithful Men of a Faithful God: Masculinities in the Zimbabwe Assemblies of God Africa', *Exchange*, 42 (1), 34–50.

Chitando, E. and Chirongoma, S. (2008) 'Challenging Masculinities: Religious Studies, Men and HIV in Africa', *Journal of Constructive Theology*, 14 (1), 55–69.

Chitando, E. and Chirongoma, S. (2012) 'Introduction', in E. Chitando and S. Chirongoma (eds), *Redemptive Masculinities: Men, HIV and Religion*, Geneva: WCC Publications, pp. 1–28.

Cleaver, F. (2002) 'Men and Masculinities: New Directions in Gender and Development', in F. Cleaver (ed.), *Masculinities Matter! Men, Gender and Development*, London: Zed Books, pp. 1–27.

Connell, R. W. (2005), *Masculinities*, 2nd edn, Berkeley: University of California Press.

Ellis, S. and ter Haar, G. (2004) *Worlds of Power: Religious Thought and Political Practice in Africa*, London: C. Hurst & Co.

Epprecht, M. (2008) *Heterosexual Africa? The History of an Idea from the Age of Exploration to the Age of AIDS*, Athens: Ohio University Press.

Foreman, M. (ed.) (1999) *AIDS and Men: Taking Risks or Taking Responsibility?*, London: Panos Institute.

Godsey, T. (2009) 'The Muslim Man and AIDS: Negotiating Spaces for New Conceptualizations of Masculinity', in F. Esack and S. Chiddy (eds), *Islam and AIDS: Between Scorn, Pity and Justice*, Oxford: Oneworld Publications, pp. 119–36.

Gray, P. B. (2004) 'HIV and Islam: Is HIV Prevalence Lower among Muslims?', *Social Science and Medicine*, 58 (9), 1751–6.

Greig, A., Kimmel, M. and Lang, J. (2000) *Men, Masculinities and Development: Broadening Our Work towards Gender Equality*, Gender in Development Monograph Series 10, New York: United Nations Development Programme.

Haddad, B. (ed.) (2011) *Religion and HIV and AIDS: Charting the Terrain*, Scottsville: University of KwaZulu-Natal Press.

Hunter, M. (2005) 'Cultural Politics and Masculinities: Multiple-Partners in Historical Perspective in KwaZulu-Natal', *Culture, Health and Sexuality*, 7 (4), 389–403.

Hunter, M. (2010) *Love in the Time of Aids: Inequality, Gender, and Rights in South Africa*, Scottsville: University of KwaZulu-Natal Press.

Lewis, D. (2011) 'Representing African Sexualities', in S. Tamale (ed.), *African Sexualities: A Reader*, Cape Town: Pambazuka Press, pp. 199–216.

Manda, D. L. (2012) 'Religions and the Responsibility of Men in Relation to Gender-Based Violence and HIV: An Ethical Plea', in E. Chitando and S. Chirongoma (eds), *Redemptive Masculinities: Men, HIV and Religion*, Geneva: WCC Publications, pp. 471–90.

Mane, P. and Aggleton, P. (2001) 'Gender and HIV/AIDS: What Do Men Have to Do with It?', *Current Sociology*, 49 (6), 23–37.

Maxwell, D. (2006) *African Gifts of the Spirit: Pentecostalism and the Rise of a Zimbabwean Transnational Religious Movement*, Harare: Weaver Press.

Mbembe, A. (2001), *On the Postcolony*, Berkeley: University of California Press.

Meyer, M. and Struthers, H. (eds) (2012) *(Un)covering Men: Rewriting Masculinity and Health in South Africa*, Auckland Park, South Africa: Fanele.

Moyo, F. L. (2004) 'Religion, Spirituality and Being a Woman in Africa: Gender Constructions within the African Religio-Cultural Experiences', *Agenda*, 61, 72–8.

Njoroge, N. N. (2012) 'A Body of Knowledge for HIV Resources', *Journal of Feminist Studies*, 28 (2), 129–33.

Phiri, I. A. and Nadar, S. (2012). 'Cutting Cultural Corners: Ritual Male Circumcision as a Health Asset for HIV Prevention? An African Feminist Perspective', in J. R. Cochrane, E. Bongmba, I. A. Phiri and D. van der Water (eds), *Living on the Edge: Essays in Honour of Steve de Gruchy, Activist and Theologian*, Pietermaritzburg: Cluster Publications, pp. 139–54.

Shapiro, R. L. and Kapiga, S. H. (2002) 'Male Condoms and Circumcision', in M. Essex, S. Mboup, P. J. Kanki, R. G. Marlink and S. D. Tlou (eds), *AIDS in Africa*, 2nd edn, New York: Kluwer, pp. 498–505.

Silberschmidt, M. (2005) 'Poverty, Male Disempowerment, and Male Sexuality: Rethinking Men and Masculinities in Rural and Urban East Africa', in L. Ouzgane and R. Morrell (eds), *African Masculinities: Men in Africa from the Late Nineteenth Century to the Present*, New York: Palgrave Macmillan, pp. 189–204.

Simpson, A. (2009) *Boys to Men in the Shadow of AIDS: Masculinities and HIV Risk in Zambia*, New York: Palgrave Macmillan.

Togarasei, L. (2012) 'Pauline Challenge to African Masculinities: Reading Pauline Texts in the Context of HIV/AIDS', *Acta Theologica*, Supplement 16, 148–60.

UNAIDS (2000) *Men and AIDS: A Gendered Approach*, Geneva: UNAIDS.

van Klinken, A. S. (2011) 'Male Headship as Male Agency: An Alternative Understanding of a "Patriarchal" African Pentecostal Discourse on Masculinity', *Religion and Gender*, 1 (1), 103–24.

van Klinken, A. S. (2012) 'Men in the Remaking: Conversion Narratives and Born-Again Masculinity in Zambia', *Journal of Religion in Africa*, 42 (3), 215–39.

van Klinken, A. S. (2013a) 'Imitation as Transformation of the Male Self: How an Apocryphal Saint Reshapes Zambian Catholic Men', *Cahiers d'Études africaines*, 209–210, 119–42.

van Klinken, A. S. (2013b) *Transforming Masculinities in African Christianity: Gender Controversies in Times of AIDS*, Farnham: Ashgate.

van Klinken, A. S. and Gunda, M. R. (2012) 'Taking Up the Cudgels against Gay Rights? Trends and Trajectories in African Christian Theologies on Homosexuality', *Journal of Homosexuality Studies*, 59 (1), 114–38.

West, G. (2012) 'The Contribution of Tamar's Story to the Construction of Alternative African Masculinities', in E. Chitando and S. Chirongoma (eds), *Redemptive Masculinities: Men, HIV and Religion*, Geneva: WCC Publications, pp. 173–92.

PART 3

Latin America

10

DEVELOPMENT AND RELIGIOUS CHANGE IN LATIN AMERICA

Paul Freston

Introduction

This chapter will concentrate on Pentecostalism as the engine of religious change in Latin America, and on Brazil as both world capital of Pentecostalism and a 'BRIC' country. I begin with relevant portions of the debate on religion and development, before discussing religious changes in Latin America and Pentecostalism as their key component. I then examine the state of play in works on Pentecostalism and development in the region. The conclusion cautiously attempts to discern what can be said with any confidence regarding the relationship between Pentecostalism and development.

Pentecostalism and the 'religion and development' debate

Marginalized by modernization theory (and by Marxism), religion was for long peripheral in the development arena. Even Max Weber's thesis on the historical role of the 'Protestant ethic' and his explorations of the 'economic ethic' of the other world religions do not claim any lasting role for religion in general or Protestant Christianity in particular. Little wonder that the 'secular missionaries' of the development NGOs, if they regard religion as more than part of the problem, have usually reduced it to 'thin' practices appealed to in terms of Enlightenment rationality, supporting a narrow range of local NGOs that fit secular utilitarian concepts, or at most accept the collaboration of faith-based organizations as long as they do not proselytize or try to influence the *content* of development (Thomas 2005).

But talk of 'modernization' has been in large part replaced by 'globalization', which (as Beyer 2006: 18 explains; see Tomalin, Chapter 1) cannot blithely be used as a successor term with impunity, since the old concept of a unitary modernity has been (implicitly, at least) dethroned either by Eisenstadt's concept of 'multiple modernities' or by Huntington's 'clash of civilizations'. Religion and modernity may be related in unsuspected ways.

These ways should not be imagined purely as a possible role for religion in developing countries as an 'authentic' alternative to the modernization paradigm (Selinger 2004), as a 'revolt against the West' in which 'authenticity' rivals 'development' for primacy in political aspirations (Thomas 2005). Such a search for authenticity is of course relevant to Africa and Asia, where decolonization and high hopes for development were followed a generation later by religious resurgence in public life. But Latin America is outside this framework, since it was decolonized nearly a century and a half earlier, with Westernized elites remaining largely in control. There was not, therefore, the same crisis of the secular modernizing state as such. Yet there is still the need to take religious pluralism seriously, not as a postmodern celebration of diversity which argues that any normative truth claims are to be censured as divisive, but by accepting that real pluralism includes clashing normative claims.

Taking 'actually existing pluralism' seriously is important for the ability to analyse empathetically a non-traditional, proselytizing, spirit-infused and strongly congregational religion such as Pentecostalism in Latin America. It illustrates Deneulin and Bano's (2009) argument that there is no separation between religion and development, since the 'spiritual' and the 'temporal' are intertwined, and that conflicts should be faced by engaging a religion in its entirety. And we shall see the force of ter Haar's (2011) view of 'integral development' as the merging of a religious perspective of internal transformation (Pentecostalism's strong suit) and a development perspective of external transformation (Pentecostalism's weak suit).

Religious change in Latin America

In tune with Marshall's (2011) exhortation to development scholars and practitioners to pay attention to *changing* religious demography, and ter Haar's (2011) reminder that Christian organizations outside the mainstream have been especially under-researched, a concentration on Pentecostalism is justified both because it is large and growing, and because it may lead to a 'worst of both worlds' situation for the role of religion in Latin America.

Latin America is the major region in which Western Christianity (still vibrant among the native-born) meets poverty and geopolitical humiliation. Specifically, what light is thrown by the globalization of Pentecostalism on the historical correlation between Protestantism and economic development?

At the same time as Catholicism has become globally centred in Latin America, its hegemony there has been eroded. The main beneficiaries have been Pentecostalism and the category of 'no religion'. The 2010 census in Brazil, for example, points to an increasingly pluralistic field consisting of Catholics (64.6 per cent, largely non-practising), Protestants (22.2 per cent and heavily practising, of whom nearly two-thirds are Pentecostals) and 'non-religious' (8 per cent, very few of whom are atheists).

Ter Haar (2011) reminds us that, while in the modern West religion might be conceived primarily as a provider of meaning, elsewhere it is primarily belief in an invisible spirit world, distinct but not separated from the visible, whose resources can be employed to sustain material life. Pentecostalism, with its strong concept of the Holy Spirit and of the evil spirits, illustrates this.

Pentecostalism is generally associated disproportionately with the Latin American poor. In Brazil, its expansion has been fastest in the most economically and demographically dynamic spaces, i.e. in the metropolitan areas of the South-East and the agricultural frontiers of the North and Centre-West. In metropolitan regions, Pentecostals are located heavily in the poor peripheries, owing not just to poverty but to the virtual absence there of the state or the Catholic Church.

Apart from its greater prevalence among lower-income sectors (a Brazilian survey of 2009 showed 15.3 per cent in class D, the lowest-but-one, versus only 6.3 per cent in A–B, the upper and middle classes), Pentecostalism is even more skewed towards the less educated.

The worst of both worlds?

The Berkley Center reports on Latin America in its Religion and Global Development project point to a concern that the region might be harmed by both Pentecostal growth and its correlate, Catholic decline. Because the Catholic Church has such a 'long standing and wide presence' (over 1,200 hospitals, 5,000 dispensaries, 2,400 elderly care facilities and nearly 2,000 orphanages in Latin America; Berkley Center 2009b: 26), a shift towards a more pluralistic situation could have a profound effect, as could the circumstances of the shift: a 'religious marketplace' in which 'what prevails is the desire to win customers' (Berkley Center 2009a: 15) rather than to serve the poor. A Catholic participant in the Berkley Center consultation on Latin America says Pentecostals 'very effectively separate people from vice . . . [but] spread a message of, 'We should only worry about ourselves.' . . . Faith might not be an impulse of solidarity any more' (2009a: 24).

But the reports also contain a different perspective on this transition. Zilda Arns, founder of the Brazilian Catholic Pastoral da Criança, says: 'We have been working with Pentecostal groups' for 30 years (Berkley Center 2009a: 21). The vice-president for Latin America of the evangelical organization World Vision adds: 'We work with many [Pentecostals], though our work to date has been more significant among the historical Protestant denominations. . . . What we are seeing among the Pentecostals are . . . new ways of addressing social issues' (2009a: 23). Sociologist Cecilia Mariz is quoted to the effect that the difference between Catholics and Pentecostals is often mainly in discourse and 'coping strategies' (Berkley Center 2009b: 18). And the Berkley Center admits that its overview is 'rather biased against faith organizations at the grassroots that have not published information on the web or joined in partnerships with international donors' (2009b: 10).

Pentecostal social projects

One way to look at the relationship between Pentecostalism and development is with regard to specific efforts to promote development. Global evangelicalism awakened to such involvement after the Lausanne conference of 1974, a 'Vatican II'-style *aggiornamento* at which Latin American evangelicals (non-Pentecostal) played an important role. Lausanne liberated evangelicals to be involved in development. Evangelical relief agencies now developed theologies and strategies of development. At the same time, the major evangelical development agencies generally accepted the 'Oxfam model' (relying on local communities to determine their own development needs, abstaining from proselytism) rather than the 'missionary model' (Thomas 2005). This has led to a considerable number of evangelical NGOs, whether local or transnational, such as World Vision.

World Vision was neither founded in Latin America nor by Pentecostals but is increasingly Latin American in staff and ethos and exemplifies the sort of evangelical organization that works with Latin American Pentecostal churches and incorporates Pentecostal activists. Besides relief and development, it has acted in human rights issues and raised awareness in churches (especially regarding children's rights and global economic justice).

At a more homespun level, however, there has always been some Pentecostal social involvement; there were orphanages and other projects from the beginning in the early twentieth century, although on a relatively small scale. The theological emphasis was heavily evangelistic, and sometimes the strong feeling of living in the 'last times' inhibited social concern. In Latin America, until recently people would say that 'traditional' Protestants had social projects but Pentecostals did not. That has changed considerably in the last 20 years, possibly because of weaker states and the effects of globalization, but also because of the growing numbers of Pentecostals and growing expectation (from Pentecostals themselves and society in general) that numbers should result in greater social impact. Some newer denominations, at both lower- and middle-class levels, have become heavily involved in diverse social programmes.

This involvement is often of an *assistencialista* type (charitable help) rather than more sophisticated projects of 'conscientization', community mobilizing and empowering. But over time there has been growing reflection on what works. In some cases that leads to a growing awareness of structural dimensions of social reality. Gradually, some Pentecostals have concluded that not everything is solved by transforming individuals, but there are other dimensions that must be tackled through lobbying, social pressure, community mobilization and perhaps involvement in the political system.

On the whole, though, the Pentecostal approach to social action has been a straightforward one based on the 'holistic' ministry of Jesus (teaching, helping, healing). There are many grassroots initiatives which are distant from global Christian reflection on social involvement, although sometimes such initiatives do later connect with national or international evangelical NGOs. Miller and Yamamori (2007) talk of 'progressive Pentecostalism', a new wave of social ministries carried out by Pentecostal and charismatic churches in the name of a gospel 'holism'.

Another factor in this change is what Mourier (2013) calls 'supplemental secularism'. The state has become more a financial backer than a provider of public social services and, in a highly religious context, the results are 'public–religious partnerships' in which religious social action (Catholic, evangelical, spiritist) dominates the 'third sector'. In line with the Constitution of 1988, which allowed governmental alliances with religions for 'cooperation for the public interest', key laws of the early 1990s encouraged the participation of civil society. At the same time, and especially since the turn of the century, Brazil has ceased being an international development priority, leading Brazilian religious NGOs to depend more heavily on state funding.

Two major actors: Renas and the UCKG

Renas (the Evangelical National Network of Social Action) was founded in Brazil in 2003, uniting traditional Protestant and Pentecostal sectors. It emphasizes networking, training and community development, as well as 'disseminating the codes which are relevant for talking to the state and to organized civil society' (Scheliga 2010: 40). It is also aware that, increasingly, Christian NGOs share a practical and discursive repertoire with secular development actors, which introduces the risk of a creeping secularization, which Renas combats by an emphasis on the evangelical concept of 'holistic mission'. It has carried out a mapping of evangelical social action in Brazil (in late 2010 it had counted 548 organizations, of which only 34 were connected to Renas); it promotes discussion on public policies in the areas of youth, social assistance and food security, and is indirectly represented on several governmental councils.

Renas, however, does not include the huge neo-Pentecostal Universal Church of the Kingdom of God (UCKG). The UCKG's strong prosperity theology might be thought to preclude any social projects, or to make them merely tools in the church's electoral ambitions. But the UCKG opted to cultivate a new public image by means of social projects, while also following the Catholic tradition of using its social role as a channel for building a positive relationship with the state.

The UCKG's plethora of social projects have included a partnership with the Fundação Pestalozzi (a traditional charity oriented to children), a large agricultural project in the impoverished North-East called Fazenda Nova Canaã, and the Associação Beneficente Cristã, which has accompanied the church in many of the countries to which it has spread. The UCKG also has projects started by its parliamentary representatives, and a television programme on its own television network which discusses 'third sector' questions.

As Rosas (2011) concludes, the social work of the UCKG is diverse, from traditional charitable practices, to efforts to promote 'citizenship', to the political action of its many parliamentarians.

Its motives are constantly impugned (being attributed to desire for success in the religious marketplace, social legitimacy or political advantage). But Rosas's study of one locality reveals a more complex reality, indifferent to such factors, but also strangely indifferent to any notion of efficacy in development. At the same time, it selectively reinforces the prosperity gospel preached by the church, encouraging perseverance in those who have yet to prosper.

The expectation of material reward through religious means is far from unique to Pentecostalism: 64 per cent of all religious Brazilians believe God grants believers prosperity; Pentecostals merely up the percentage to 83 per cent (Pew Forum 2006). Zaluar's study of Cidade de Deus, a peripheral area of Rio de Janeiro, discovered that 'the urban poor now experience poverty as a privation. . . . The religious meaning of redemption through suffering has been lost' (1985: 115f.). This is an opening for prosperity theology, which proclaims that God intends all his people to be prosperous, if we only have faith to 'claim' what should be ours and demonstrate that faith by giving generously to God so that he will reward us many times over. But prosperity theology coexists tensely with a religious 'populism' which glories in God's choice of the poor and is suspicious of the spiritually deleterious effects of wealth. The more traditional Pentecostal ethic was that of primitive capitalism, a long and arduous struggle to reach modest respectability. Today, that ethic has lost ground (especially within the newer churches) to prosperity teachings. But, even in these churches, the recipe for prosperity is not just giving to the church; they also make a fairly realistic analysis of economic opportunities. As a sermon I heard in the UCKG said, 'It's no good just giving an offering. You must quit your job and open a business, even if it's only selling popcorn in the street. As an employee you'll never get rich.' Previous Pentecostal churches had valued self-employment only because it offered flexibility (the chance to give time to the church) and avoidance of spiritually damaging environments. Now, it is valued as a means to enrichment, as a stage on the way to becoming an employer. UCKG publications contain practical suggestions on branches of business and initial capital needed. Their message may reinforce petty entrepreneurial initiative in an adverse context.

Interestingly, this same church's publications contain critical evaluations of global capitalism. One of its bishops writes that 'globalisation is the fruit of an economic policy dictated by the developed countries to expand their markets . . . giving their citizens all the things they "steal" from ours' (*Folha Universal*, 17 October 1999). Another bishop reconciles anti-neoliberalism with prosperity theology:

> There is a Satanic trinity in capitalism: the great 'god' is the market, the great world religion is capitalism and the Holy Spirit is the IMF. . . . When we do a Prosperity Chain [meetings dedicated to obtaining prosperity] we are going against the elementary principles of the market, which include 'you are poor, you were born to be poor, you will die poor'.
>
> (*Folha Universal*, 25 April 1999)

At a higher social level, we find Pentecostal associations for businesspeople which teach, for example, 'seven ways of taking over your rival's market'. These ways include practical advice (choose the right partners), moral exhortations (don't occupy a new market with manipulation and fraud, as otherwise you will lose the support of the angels), psychological galvanizing based on religious identity (there is nowhere that a servant of the Lord may not enter; there are no impenetrable markets if you have the Lord's anointing), and financial loyalty to the church (do not hold back anything that belongs to God).

Pentecostal treatment of financial donations is highly controversial in Brazil. The neo-Pentecostal groups are especially criticized for their strong emphasis on giving to the church.

On the other hand, Mariz (1995) says that, in the popular mentality, giving is power, whereas submission is symbolically reinforced by receiving. In Pentecostalism, the poor discover they are capable of giving and not just of receiving. In addition, it should be remembered that donations often replace previous spending on medicines, gambling, drink or drugs. For many members, giving to the church and a rationalization of overall economic behaviour are inseparable. They came together as a package of transformations, a package constantly threatened by old habits. Repeated giving incarnates this precarious commitment to the new pattern.

Talk of rationalization with regard to Pentecostalism may seem contradictory. Yet Mariz (1994), discussing Pentecostalism's approach to alcoholism, stresses how exorcism becomes an ethicization of the supernatural and therefore a way of rationalizing religion. In Pentecostalism, she says, magical and ethical religion are not opposed but reinforce each other through the concept of 'deliverance'. Although in itself 'magical', deliverance is the first step in a process of rationalization, leading believers to see themselves as 'individuals' with a certain power of choice, and not as 'persons' subject to traditional roles. The main cause of alcoholism is seen as an amoral magical force, which can be conquered only by an absolute and ethical force. The magical world is subdued by a stronger magic, one that is moral. Thus, Mariz concludes, the Pentecostal churches do not contradict Weber's thesis of a greater rationalization of religion accompanying social development.

Ongoing research in El Salvador by Ronald Bueno (forthcoming) asks whether Pentecostals can contribute to broader change through engagement in community initiatives alongside non-church partners such as community associations. A small but growing number are, he finds, and they have changed their structures and liturgies to adapt to the new practice. But many are opposed, because of the redefinition of mission as including social engagement and the lack of control over outcomes which it implies. Not only is the closed 'sectarian' self-image threatened, but mission comes to be defined as including tasks in which non-believers may have more expertise. This has led to congregational-level and denominational-level opposition to such initiatives, but without managing to impede their expansion.

Pentecostalism and development in Latin America: contours of a debate

The debate about Pentecostalism and development, of course, goes way beyond the efforts of religiously inspired 'development agencies'. It is related to the whole 'embeddedness' of the economy in value systems and non-economic institutions, and is bedevilled by methodological difficulties. The first methodological question is the direction of causality alleged by each analyst of Latin American Pentecostalism, and the problem of separating causation and correlation. Inevitably the ghost of Weber looms large whenever any form of Protestantism expands in a new part of the globe. Thus, Gill examines whether the rise of evangelicalism in Latin America might be influencing the Catholic historical legacy in ways that transform the region's development. Given that evangelicals preach thrift, trustworthiness and personal responsibility, he says, one might expect this to bolster capitalism's prospects. He comments that some scholars reverse Weber's causality: rather than Protestantism promoting capitalism, they see individuals converting to Protestantism because it is more congruent with the previous advance of capitalism in their part of the world. Gill thus seeks to test the linkage between church affiliation and economic predispositions using the World Values Survey data from 1990. He concludes that Protestants and Catholics do not differ substantially in economic preferences, and that other factors such as age, gender and socio-economic status matter more. Weber is therefore 'not at work in Latin America', at least in terms of the culturally defining role of Protestantism (Gill 2004). This is the polar opposite of Berger's assertion that 'Max Weber is alive and well and living in

Guatemala' and that the growth of Protestantism in Latin America will lead to 'the emergence of a solid bourgeoisie, with virtues conducive to the development of a democratic capitalism' (in David Martin 1990: ix). For Berger, Weber is not only alive but standing on his feet, rather than the 'inverse causality' version mentioned by Gill, which we can describe as Weber standing on his head. A third possibility, of course, would be Weber lying down, that is, a mutually reinforcing relationship between Pentecostalism and development in Latin America.

The second methodological question concerns the social level at which any relationship is thought to operate. Weber wrote about a specific historical juncture (early modern northern Europe), a specific group of Protestants (those influenced by what should really be called the 'Puritan ethic' rather than the 'Protestant ethic') and a specific social location (the rising bourgeoisie). He himself did not imagine that a constant repeat of that process would be necessary to maintain capitalism where it was already established or to establish it where it was not. That does not mean one should not examine whether Latin American Pentecostalism is not assisting 'the emergence of a solid bourgeoisie'; Weber, after all, may have been wrong. But it does mean the discussion should not be restricted to that. Pentecostalism may affect capitalist development at other levels, more suited to the social location of its constituency, or to the structural position of the Latin American economy today, or to the specific ethic that these Pentecostals incorporate. With regard to these questions, it should be stressed that Latin American Pentecostals operate on the periphery of established global capitalism and cannot have the same macro-economic effect that Weber's Puritans had. In any case, they do not usually have the classic Protestant work ethic and frugal consumption patterns, lacking the theological ideas of predestination and worldly vocation, with the attendant psychological mechanism (anguish about eternal destiny) which supposedly impelled Puritans in their rational search for prosperity. Nevertheless, Pentecostals may be energized economically by various aspects of their faith (greater optimism and self-belief, new patterns of honesty, sobriety and diligence) and by skills learnt in the churches.

The third methodological question has to do with what constitutes evidence. In the examples cited, Berger is basing himself (and perhaps going beyond) David Martin's work on Latin American Protestantism, a review of the literature supplemented by personal observation and the collecting of Pentecostal life histories. Gill, on the other hand, is using the World Values Survey. It might be thought that the latter is a more solid basis. Yet, besides the traditional limitations of a survey, what can really be determined from such data? Hard evidence of conversion causing upward mobility (or even attitudinal change) rather than the reverse (mobility causing conversion) requires longitudinal studies, which are difficult to do, especially for a conversionist religion which is constantly gaining new members (and even losing some old ones). Such a study is far harder than for an ethnic minority whose mobility over time can readily be traced. A recent study showed 62 per cent of Brazilian Pentecostals were not born into the religion but have converted to it (Pew Forum 2006). This makes causal relationships very difficult to trace. It proves very little merely to cite a survey showing that Pentecostals are accentuatedly lower-class, or even two surveys 20 years apart to the same effect. None of this proves Pentecostalism does not cause upward mobility, still less that it causes downward mobility (which, significantly, no one seems to suggest). Without the right sort of data over long periods of time, we are reduced to using 'softer' indicators. Pentecostal 'testimonies' (the recountings of elements of their life histories) do allege a causality, but implicitly of the counter-factual type (such an outcome would not have happened if I had not converted or not trusted God). Since we cannot rerun our lives, such allegations are impossible to prove or disprove.

So should we just ignore Weber (at least Weber of the 'Protestant ethic' rather than of the American sects) and invoke Ho Chi Minh regarding the French Revolution ('too early to say')? Perhaps. Hard evidence for upward mobility is scarce, and signs of a macro effect on

Paul Freston

Latin American economies even scarcer (the countries with larger percentages of Protestants are distributed across the region's range of macro-economic performance, from relatively successful Chile to far less successful Guatemala and El Salvador).

Amy Sherman (1997), however, claims it is not too early to say: Protestantism in Guatemala is already having a positive effect, including receptivity to entrepreneurialism, educational attainment and literacy for both sexes. However, the problem of separating causation and correlation remains. Sherman employs causal language, even though her only before-and-after data are converts' own testimonies.

Annis's (1987) work on an indigenous Guatemalan town also finds Protestantism to be the strongest predictor of which families will be upwardly mobile and end up in micro-business ownership. But Protestantism as compared to what? If the term of comparison is 'Catholicism', the effect of Protestantism can seem immense; if, however, it is 'practising Catholics', the effect is much diminished. But, since most Protestant converts come from the 'non-practising Catholic' category, at least they seem to be increasing the overall number of people acquiring such characteristics.

Nevertheless, Bernice Martin (1995) reminds us that there might still be a way to invoke a nearly 'full' Weber. The entrepreneurial class is constantly replenished by new recruits who, as individuals, encounter for the first time the need to make money but not dissipate it. With the expansion of postmodern capitalism, there may be a continuing role for inner-worldly asceticism in the small business sector. This is perhaps a rising petty bourgeoisie rather than a bourgeoisie, but the author points out that most Pentecostals in Latin America have to create work for themselves and set their own schedules. This is 'survival entrepreneurship', putting a premium on internalized discipline rather than on the traditional pietistic ethic of the good functionary.

David Martin looked at Pentecostalism in this 'new phase of global capitalism in which culture is increasingly recognised as a key variable' (2002: 71), where the ability to be punctual, regimented and obedient (important in the Fordist factory system) is less relevant than the capacity to be self-motivated and self-monitoring, and to manage interpersonal encounters skilfully. Pentecostalism, he admits, does not have the Weberian notion of vocation, but it operates a psychic mutation towards independence and initiative. Its 'reformation of manners' has implications for development, giving a new sense of agency, equipping for seizing opportunities and not merely consoling the victims of social change. Yet the tension with evangelical disciplines remains. Pentecostalism's consonance with global capitalism is partial, and its consumerism is selective.

As for upward mobility, it depends on facilitating conditions. People advance by the margins available. At the least, economic advancement and evangelical religion often go together and appear to reinforce each other. But capacities may take generations to come to fruition, says Martin, recognizing that hard evidence is scarce.

A fascinating 1999 documentary film (Santa Cruz), on the first year in the life of a small Pentecostal church on the periphery of Rio de Janeiro, tells how in one neighbourhood virtually everyone has converted and property values have risen. The location is considered safe, people concern themselves with their neighbours, families are more structured, men no longer drink and beat their wives, and it is generally considered a more desirable place to live, despite the visible poverty still reigning there.

None of this, evidently, proves mobility through conversion; a Pentecostal group ideology may precondition people to believe they have experienced 'uplift'. Perhaps Pentecostalism raises people from misery to poverty (for example, through combating alcoholism), but no further than that. It changes attitudes to consumption rather than to work, offering a new plausibility for saving in an adverse context. Its ethic reinforces capitalist values among people who have already embraced such values but have not been materially rewarded for them.

An interesting recent study (Sullivan 2014) looks at a possible relationship between the Bolsa-Família, the large conditional cash transfer programme introduced by the Brazilian government since 2003, and Pentecostalism. Studies have shown the Bolsa-Família to be largely successful at reducing inequality and targeting systemic poverty through incentives for building human capital such as education and health; but a possible role in this for the 'Pentecostal ethic' has not been examined. Conditional cash transfer programmes rely on recipients making rational decisions to invest the transfers wisely in accumulating human capital and breaking the transmission of poverty. The Brazilian programme requires educational and health conditionalities, and to that end women are overwhelmingly preferred as the legal beneficiaries. This, says Sullivan, matches well with the 'Pentecostal ethic' of female empowerment and valuing of family life and education, and may account for a certain degree of the programme's success.

Pentecostalism, education and female empowerment

Talk of a Pentecostal ethic of female empowerment and valuing of education may surprise those who associate Pentecostalism with benightedness and patriarchy. In Brazil, there has been a general rise in educational levels among Pentecostals, thanks both to larger social processes and to the way Pentecostalism specifically promotes investment in education.

Among the lowest educational level (three years or fewer of schooling), Pentecostals are 13.6 per cent, a rate which changes little at the next two levels. However, among those with 12 years or more of schooling, Pentecostals are still only 6.7 per cent. However, they are over-represented (14.8 per cent) among the *pré-vestibular* category, i.e. those taking preparatory courses for competitive university entrance exams (Freston 2013: 80–81). This suggests a repressed demand for higher education, and means that a large-scale Pentecostal arrival in the universities might be about to occur. An interview of mine (Freston 2013: 81–82) with a female Pentecostal pastor is illustrative. She grew up in a backwater of the impoverished North-East, and 'the church taught us to read because we had to read the Bible and the Sunday School magazine. We were taught to take care of our parents, and for that we had to have jobs, which meant we were encouraged to study.' But in the past, I interject, it was said that Pentecostals were indifferent or resistant to education, even demonizing it as bad for faith.

> That's definitely not what I experienced! Pentecostal young people spend a lot of time together, and one pulls the other along. If one gets into university, the others want to go too. In church we learned we had to go to school and respect the teacher and get the best grades, without cheating! So the Pentecostal church did not reach the school through a miracle. It sought out the school.

In a context of increasing female employment and male irresponsibility and violence, Pentecostalism restores the family largely through reformation of the male and the elimination of the double standard. An increasing number of scholars, especially female sociologists and anthropologists, have addressed the gender dimension of Latin American Pentecostalism, which appeals disproportionately to women. Sometimes this is a puzzle to scholars, because they perceive in Pentecostalism what seems to be a traditional patriarchal discourse. But the effects for poor women are usually positive, especially in domesticating their menfolk, weaning them off machista culture and helping them value the same things as the women themselves, especially in how money and time are spent.

149

Looking beyond the patriarchal rhetoric, the advantages to poor women are seen to be financial, emotional and physical. Elizabeth Brusco (1993) shows how Pentecostalism in Colombia helps women resocialize men away from the destructive patterns of machismo, even though (or precisely because) it maintains the rhetoric of male control. Pentecostalism's reconciliation of gender values is something middle-class feminism has not achieved. Thus, it serves the practical interests of poor women, even when it legitimizes male authority (although in fact a 2006 survey found Pentecostals to be as favourable as the general population to having women as religious leaders; Pew Forum 2006: 46).

In fact, an interpretation of religious change in Brazil calls attention to the parallel curves of religious conversion and increasing female participation in the labour market. Neri (2005) talks of 'elective affinities' between religious choices and economic changes affecting women. In 1940, women were more Catholic than men; today, the opposite is true. While men have remained Catholic or joined the 'non-religious' category, women have migrated disproportionately to other religions, especially Pentecostalism. Neri attributes this to the Catholic Church's difficulty in questions of female emancipation such as contraception, divorce and professional success. In the mid-1990s, a survey in greater Rio de Janeiro found that Protestant affiliation made a greater difference in reproductive behaviour (fewer children) the lower the social class involved.

But, as Brusco (2010) clarifies, Pentecostalism effectively addresses the problems of machismo, but not those of patriarchy. We can add that, in consequence, Pentecostalism's advantages for women at lower social levels seem clear: despite its patriarchal discourse, it is efficacious in restoring the dignity of women and often also in domesticating their menfolk. In any case, other discourses of female empowerment are inaudible in that social context, or virtually impossible to appropriate. But, at the middle-class level in Brazil, the situation is different. The middle class is very Western and capable not only of hearing but of appropriating such alternative discourses. If Pentecostal growth is slowing now in Brazil (as recent figures seem to show), it may be partly because it is less attractive to women who are moving into the lower middle class and accessing higher levels of education. But, for some time yet, the relationship will continue to be largely positive: since social assistance has been historically preponderantly female, and the Pentecostal field also, this makes women both 'preferential agents of giving' and central figures in the Pentecostal relationship to poverty (Machado and Mariz 2008).

Pentecostalism and human rights

The difficulty of incorporating Pentecostalism into formal human rights activities is related partly to the apolitical and individualistic tendencies in its theology, but also to its proselytizing impulse and its heavily lower-class character (distancing it from the social environments in which rights discourse is widely disseminated). Nevertheless, in informal settings Pentecostalism is widely recognized as making a significant contribution to dignifying and protecting the most vulnerable.

The perceived aggressiveness of much Pentecostal proselytizing creates some social tension in Brazil. Yet the clash between Pentecostals and Afro-Brazilian religions has very rarely been violent. Rather, it is a verbal dispute between social equals at the grassroots level. Undoubtedly, however, many churches have often shown a lack of respect for other religions and have a demonizing discourse.

The questions of proselytization and class location represent a Brazilian refraction of an international tension between religion and human rights movements. The latter often present the face of a 'worldwide secular religion' governed by an internationalized elite (Hackett 2004: 190). We see an example of this in a brochure produced by the Brazilian National Programme on Human Rights (a governmental body), called 'Religious Diversity and Human Rights' (http://www. portaldoservidor.ba.gov.br/sites/default/files/cartilha_sedh_diversidade_religiosa%5B1%5D. pdf). Its aim is 'to encourage dialogue between religious movements'. But, instead of seeking a basis for human rights in the teaching of each confession, the document tries to construct a common creed which, in effect, approves of certain religions and disapproves of others. All the behaviours referred to with disapproval are real or supposed activities of Pentecostals: 'invasion of Umbanda and Candomblé temples'; 'disrespect for the spirituality of indigenous peoples'; 'Wicca rituals called "Satanic"'. But this is not an analysis of actual incidents of Pentecostal intolerance; instead, it exemplifies a hijacking of the prestigious language of human rights by a particular approach to religion, endorsing a religiously specific view of the relationship of 'the Creator' to human beings. Although based on real incidents of reprehensible behaviour, the underlying problem seems to be Pentecostalism's proselytistic success. But, as Appleby (2000: 280) stresses, to be effective human rights discourse cannot ignore what individuals and communities hold sacred, but instead needs 'translators' who comprehend believers' sensibilities while weighing their conduct against universal norms. It is the absence of an attempt to 'translate' rights discourse in terms of Pentecostal sensibilities which makes the document ineffective.

Spickard (1999) refers to Muslim and Confucianist attempts at alternative rights philosophies. Is Latin American Pentecostalism part of this? Does it, as Spickard says of these counter-movements, place the group above humanity? Does it refuse to treat as equals those whom it opposes, and would it deny them political, civil, economic and social rights? Would it construct an alternative rights philosophy?

In its origins in popular Western Christianity, Pentecostalism is part of the culture which developed the dominant international concepts of rights. It questions liberal understandings without going as far as 'communitarian' questioning of the whole idea of universal rights. It stands within the dissenting Protestant tradition which talks neither of the modern liberal 'individual' nor of stable 'ascriptive communities', but of 'achieved communities' peopled by accountable individuals.

In the survey already mentioned (Pew Forum 2006), Brazilian Pentecostalism does not appear as a barrier to the advance of human rights. To the question whether it is important that there be freedom for religions other than one's own, Pentecostals were as affirmative as the general population. Similarly, the view that Pentecostals' liking for charismatic leaders renders them more favourable to authoritarian political systems is challenged. When asked whether, to solve the country's problems, it would be better to have a more participatory government or a strong leader, Brazilian Pentecostals are even more favourable to the participatory solution than the general population.

Pentecostalism and violence

Since it is concentrated in the poor urban peripheries, Pentecostalism's relationship to violence is key for its possible relationship to development. In marginal areas virtually untouched by other sectors of civil society or the state, the Pentecostal presence is generally perceived as vital. This is Pentecostalism's 'civilizing' mission, providing ways of escape from criminality, prostitution and drug addiction. Zaluar says: 'the few stories of regeneration which I heard involved sessions of healing in Pentecostal churches or a radical conversion' (in Novaes 2001: 70). Lins and Silva confirm this: 'the myth that there is no way back from the world of crime finds a clear exception in criminals' conversion to evangelical churches. . . . The convert has the right to be pardoned by other criminals' (1990: 172).

Urban violence is related to perceptions of the demonic in Brazilian society. Birman and Leite (2000) analyse the relationship of urban violence and religion, in which certain religious interpretations have lost credibility and others have gained plausibility. The Catholic Church is perceived as helpless to deal with the causes of urban violence, but Pentecostal pastors are widely regarded as possessing more power than Catholic priests. They interrupt the flow of violence with the word of God and exorcisms.

Conclusions

I have written elsewhere (Freston 2010) of forthcoming transitions in Brazilian religion: a 'Catholic transition', in which numerical decline, relative institutional weakness, and the effects of democracy and a fragmented civil society will make Catholicism's old socio-political roles unsustainable; and a 'Protestant transition', in which a ceiling will be reached on Protestant growth and social aspirations, caused partly by Pentecostalism's limited ability to produce social transformation (unlike individual transformation, at which it is undeniably successful).

Many things will change after these transitions, and perhaps a slimmer but more committed Catholicism and a maturing Protestantism may represent a net gain for development. The current moment, however, may be the worst of both worlds.

Not that Brazilian Pentecostalism is intrinsically inimical to development. While Marshall (2011: 45) warns that 'development practitioners surely need to avoid associating with advocates of violence and with bitter critics of other faiths', Brazilian Pentecostals are almost never violent and their criticism of other faiths usually does not imply inability to cooperate in civic life. Similarly, when Deneulin and Bano (2009: 105) mention four sticking-points (religious decrees which prohibit women working; religious groups which consider each other as enemies to be converted or killed; denial of contraception to women with HIV-positive partners; and religious education which teaches children to hate those of other religions), none of these really characterizes Brazilian Pentecostalism. Some existing tensions have other sources. As ter Haar (2011: 297) warns, people whose views of rights are oriented towards religion can easily become the ideological enemies of those whose commitment to rights is based on secular sources. And since, as Fountain (2013: 26) stresses, development work emerged from missionary work, and proselytization is not unique to churches but is also practised by 'development projects that . . . seek to transform the behaviour and attitudes of others', one wonders why Pentecostalism's propensity to proselytize is so hard to swallow. Is it because it appears as a rival mission to those secular development workers who implicitly claim the morality and universality they now deny to their precursors, the missionaries?

Pentecostalism rarely has an explicit discourse of development, because of its social location. Of course, some Pentecostal sectors are increasingly well educated and incorporate mainstream evangelical discourse on development. But most of the Pentecostal world is still distant from all that. When discussing Pentecostalism, verbs should be in the reflexive. They rarely 'do development work' for others; rather, they 'develop themselves'. Pentecostalism is a self-development in community.

As for a 'Pentecostal ethic', we should remember that this is economically well nigh necessary at lower social levels in modern Brazil, whereas the Weberian Protestant ethic was precisely *not* economically necessary for the rising seventeenth-century bourgeoisie, and therefore needed a strong doctrinal justification. For Weber's Calvinists, religion led to an economic ethic; in Brazil today, the need for an economic ethic encourages a religious option, because it needs not doctrinal justification but personal and communitarian motivation.

Work on Brazilian Pentecostalism and development lags behind that on African Pentecostalism and development, so it is interesting to place Brazil within Freeman's (2012) Africa-inspired reflections (see Freeman, Chapter 8). Pentecostalism, she says, for the most part does not set up FBOs, but it does bring a radically new conception of development, based on a 'war against the demons'. However, she also notes that European Protestantism originated in a Catholic environment which promoted an ascetic ideal, whereas African Protestantism has grown in a context of traditional religions which emphasize health and wealth. Brazil is a mixture of these heritages, and its Protestantism is similarly ambivalent.

For Freeman, Pentecostal churches are often more effective change agents than development NGOs, because they are home grown, focus on transforming subjectivities, create moral legitimacy for behaviours that clash with local values, and are often very democratic and thus seen as 'moral and meaningful institutions' (2012: 24–6). In Brazil, however, NGOs are more often equally home grown; the cultural obstacles to developmentally appropriate behaviours are smaller; the state is stronger; and the representative legitimacy of ecclesiastical institutions vis-à-vis the state is less obvious. I am thus less sanguine regarding Pentecostalism's potentialities in the Brazilian context. As for its 'new conception of development', even though Robbins's work on global Pentecostalism talks of 'spiritual warfare' as 'locally meaningful idioms for talking about social problems' (2004: 124), this has severe limits in Brazil, which is more Western than Africa and Asia and where there is increasing need for dialogue with secular ideologies.

Freeman's verdict that Pentecostalism offers a third approach to development (distinct from mainstream and post-developmentalist views) because it embraces consumption while maintaining a magico-religious worldview, and acknowledges traditional values while seeking to break from them, is correct in its details but exaggerates in elevating it to a 'third approach to development'. Nevertheless, as van Dijk (2012: 103) recognizes, Pentecostalism sits uneasily both with modernist disenchantment of the world and with the post-developmentalist bias towards 'authenticity', cultural relativism and romanticizing of local traditions.

Van Wensveen (2011) talks of two historical patterns of religious engagement in development. The 'additive' pattern adopts a mechanistic paradigm and an instrumental approach to religion, whereas the 'integral' pattern uses an organic paradigm and integrates religion fully into the development process. The author gives a rather unsympathetic portrayal of the 'additive pattern', such that one wonders whether its rejection is not a case of misplaced utopianism. The 'integral' alternative seems close to the non-Abrahamic religions. Certainly, few trends are more antipathetic to Pentecostalism than Western ideas about what local peoples worldwide should really want when being 'authentic'. Van Wensveen does end up recognizing that the additive pattern's 'linear and anthropocentric view' tends to accompany a transcendent concept of the divine, and thus may be more acceptable in the case of Christianity because development theory arose out of a society imbued with Christianity and represented a sort of secularized version of it (2011: 83, 102). She also admits that the additive and integral may not be logically exclusive, and that studies which identify parallelisms are beneficial to the additive pattern. I have tried here to do just that in relation to Brazilian Pentecostalism; but is her apparent relegation of the additive pattern to inferior status not too condescending about both it and the religious forms with which it fits most easily?

Nevertheless, there will be limits to Brazilian Pentecostalism's contribution to development. As I have written elsewhere (Freston 2013), there are reasons for doubting its ability to continue its headlong growth, and to achieve the social influence that its size might lead us to expect. In fact, we see the beginnings of a process of adoption of broader Protestant thinking and practices in particular areas. This is deemed necessary because Pentecostalism is perceived as insurmountably deficient in social and political dimensions. It seems that being good at personal transformation and poor at societal transformation might be two sides of the same coin, and that Pentecostalism's intense self-belief and pragmatism discourage a humble and teachable perseverance through long learning processes. Pentecostals rarely use the language of 'empowerment' but talk much of 'power'. Empowerment is from without, whereas power is from within; or, if one prefers, empowerment is through other humans, whereas power comes unmediated from 'above'. The latter is very effective for personal transformation but runs into evident limits for social transformation; with the former, the opposite occurs. Yet some combination of power and empowerment seems a stretch too far for Pentecostalism, as its history shows. Its initial universalist thrust, overcoming ethnic, gender and other barriers through the experience of the Holy Spirit, always gets clawed back over time. Against this clawing back, it is not enough simply to reaffirm the Spirit. The hardness and durability of cultural forms and social structures need to be recognized. Pentecostalism, as a strongly 'third-person' Christianity (emphasizing the Holy Spirit), does not call a spade a spade in sociological terms, but tends to generalize and spiritualize and shy away from facing up to social realities. As a result, Pentecostalism, while certainly not inimical to development, may not be as useful an ally as is sometimes thought.

References

Annis, Sheldon (1987) *God and Production in a Guatemalan Town*, Austin: University of Texas Press.

Appleby, R. Scott (2000) *The Ambivalence of the Sacred*, Lanham, MD: Rowman & Littlefield.

Berkley Center for Religion, Peace and World Affairs (2009a) *Global Development and Faith-Inspired Organizations in Latin America: Meeting Report*, Washington, DC: Georgetown University.

Berkley Center for Religion, Peace and World Affairs (2009b) *Faith-Inspired Organizations and Global Development Policy*, Washington, DC: Georgetown University.

Beyer, Peter (2006) *Religions in Global Society*, London: Routledge.

Birman, Patrícia and Leite, Marcia Pereira (2000) 'Whatever Happened to What Used to Be the Largest Catholic Country in the World?', *Daedalus*, 129 (2) (Spring), 239–70.

Brusco, Elizabeth (1993) 'The Reformation of Machismo: Asceticism and Masculinity among Colombian Evangelicals', in Virginia Garrard-Burnett and David Stoll (eds), *Rethinking Protestantism in Latin America*, Philadelphia: Temple University Press, pp. 143–58.

Brusco, Elizabeth (2010) 'Gender and Power', in A. Anderson, M. Bergunder, A. Droogers and C. van der Laan (eds), *Studying Global Pentecostalism*, Berkeley: University of California Press, pp. 74–92.

Bueno, Ronald (forthcoming) 'Translating Pentecost into Transformed Communities in El Salvador: Social Engagement as a New and Contested Ritual'.

Deneulin, S. and Bano, M. (2009) *Religion in Development*, London: Zed Books.

Fountain, Philip (2013) 'The Myth of Religious NGOs: Development Studies and the Return of Religion', in G. Carbonnier (ed.), *Religion and Development*, Basingstoke: Palgrave Macmillan, pp. 9–30.

Freeman, Dena (2012) 'The Pentecostal Ethic and the Spirit of Development', in D. Freeman (ed.), *Pentecostalism and Development*, New York: Palgrave Macmillan, pp. 1–38.

Freston, Paul (2010) 'As Duas Transições Futuras: Católicos, Protestantes e Sociedade na América Latina', *Ciencias Sociales y Religión/Ciências Sociais e Religião*, 12 (12) (October), 13–30.

Freston, Paul (2013) 'The Future of Pentecostalism in Brazil: The Limits to Growth', in Robert Hefner (ed.), *Global Pentecostalism in the 21st Century*, Bloomington: Indiana University Press, pp. 63–90.

Gill, Anthony (2004) 'Weber in Latin America: Is Protestant Growth Enabling the Consolidation of Democratic Capitalism?', *Democratization*, 11 (4) (August), 42–65.

Hackett, Rosalind (2004) 'Human Rights: An Important and Challenging New Field for the Study of Religion', in P. Antes, A. Geertz and R. Warne (eds), *New Approaches to the Study of Religion*, Berlin: Walter de Gruyter, pp. 165–93.

Lins, Paulo and Silva, Maria de Lourdes (1990) 'Bandidos e Evangélicos: Extremos que se Tocam', *Religião e Sociedade*, 15 (1), 166–73.

Machado, M. D. C. and Mariz, C. (2008) 'Religião, trabalho voluntário e gênero', *Interseções*, 9, 309–26.

Mariz, Cecilia (1994) 'Libertação e Ética: Uma Análise do Discurso dos Pentecostais que se Recuperam do Alcoolismo', in A. Antoniazzi *et al.* (eds), *Nem Anjos Nem Demônios*, Petrópolis: Vozes.

Mariz, Cecilia (1995) 'El Debate en Torno del Pentecostalismo Autónomo en Brasil', *Sociedad y Religión*, 13, 21–32.

Marshall, Katherine (2011) 'Development and Faith Institutions: Gulfs and Bridges', in G. ter Haar (ed.), *Religion and Development*, London: Hurst & Co., pp. 27–53.

Martin, Bernice (1995) 'New Mutations of the Protestant Ethic among Latin American Pentecostals', *Religion*, 25, 101–17.

Martin, David (1990) *Tongues of Fire*, Oxford: Blackwell.

Martin, David (2002) *Pentecostalism: The World Their Parish*, Oxford: Blackwell.

Miller, D. E. and Yamamori, T. (2007) *Global Pentecostalism*, Berkeley: University of California Press.

Mourier, Eliott (2013) 'Religion as a Social Substitute for the State: Faith-Based Social Action in Twenty-First Century Brazil', in G. Carbonnier (ed.), *Religion and Development*, Basingstoke: Palgrave Macmillan, pp. 79–94.

Neri, Marcelo (2005) 'A Ética Pentecostal e o Declínio Católico', Fundação Getúlio Vargas, Rio de Janeiro, www.fgv.br/cps/artigos/conjuntura/2005/a%20ética%20pentecostal%20e%20o%20declínio%20católico_mai2005.pdf.

Novaes, Regina (2001.) 'Pentecostalismo, política, mídia e favela', in Victor Vincent Valla (ed.), *Religião e Cultura Popular*, Rio de Janeiro: DP&A, pp. 41–74.

Pew Forum on Religion and Public Life (2006) *Spirit and Power*, Washington, DC: Pew Research Center, pewforum.org/publications/surveys/pentecostals-06.pdf.

Robbins, Joel (2004) 'The Globalization of Pentecostal and Charismatic Christianity', *Annual Review of Anthropology*, 33, 117–43.

Rosas, Nina (2011) 'As Obras Sociais da Igreja Universal: Uma Análise Sociológica', MA thesis, Universidade Federal de Minas Gerais.

Scheliga, Eva (2010) 'Educando sentidos, orientando uma práxis: Etnografia das práticas assistenciais de evangélicos brasileiros', Ph.D. thesis, Universidade de São Paulo.

Selinger, Leah (2004) 'The Forgotten Factor: The Uneasy Relationship between Religion and Development', *Social Compass*, 51 (4), 523–43.

Sherman, Amy (1997) *The Soul of Development*, New York: Oxford University Press.

Spickard, James (1999) 'Human Rights, Religious Conflict, and Globalization: Ultimate Values in a New World Order', *Management of Social Transformations (MOST)*, 1 (1), 2–19.

Sullivan, Kevin (2014) 'The Pentecostal Ethic and the "Spirit" of Capitalism', Walsh School of Foreign Service, Georgetown University, Washington, DC.

ter Haar, Gerrie (2011) 'Religion and Development: Introducing a New Debate', in G. ter Haar (ed.), *Religion and Development*, London: Hurst & Co., pp. 3–25.

Thomas, Scott (2005) *The Global Resurgence of Religion and the Transformation of International Relations*, New York: Palgrave Macmillan.

van Dijk, Rijk (2012) 'Pentecostalism and Post-Development: Exploring Religion as a Developmental Ideology in Ghanaian Migrant Communities', in D. Freeman (ed.), *Pentecostalism and Development*, New York: Palgrave Macmillan, pp. 87–108.

van Wensveen, Louke (2011) 'Religion and Sustainable Development: A Typological Analysis', in G. ter Haar (ed.), *Religion and Development*, London: Hurst & Co., pp. 81–108.

Zaluar, Alba (1985) *A Máquina e a Revolta*, São Paulo: Brasiliense.

11

INCA ROADS, PROTESTANT HOSPITALS, CATHOLIC CHEESE, AND THE FLUCTUATING STATE

Religion and development in Ecuador

Jill DeTemple

Introduction

Though geographically small with only 284,000 square kilometers within its borders, Ecuador is a diverse nation. The Pacific littoral plain at the western edge of the country is warm and home to almost half of Ecuador's inhabitants, many of whom make their living in shrimp and large-scale fruit cultivation, two of Ecuador's primary export industries (Instituto Nacional de Estadísticas y Censos del Ecuador 2013).[1] The Andean highlands to the east of the Pacific coast rise to heights of 6,000 meters, and feature fertile volcanic valleys and slopes suitable for agriculture, an activity that employs close to a quarter of all Ecuadorians in the early twenty-first century. Continuing east, the Andes fall away into the Amazon Basin, the least populated portion of the country, but one of supreme strategic and cultural importance as it is home to a diverse array of indigenous peoples and most of Ecuador's significant oil and mineral wealth.

This geographic compactness, combined with a rich cultural and historical mixture, makes Ecuador an ideal case study for the many ways that religion and development interact in Latin America. As in the more frequently studied cases of Guatemala, Mexico, and Brazil, Spanish conquest and colonization that began with Pizarro's arrival in 1530 melded radically new technologies with political and religious goals. This confluence remained intact until liberal reforms in the nineteenth century began to disentangle the formal union of church and state. Ecuador's pre-Columbian history of Inca conquest and trade routes between geographic zones, its relatively early embrace of Protestant missions, and its current political orientation that works to balance socialist leanings with decentralized economic and religious markets demonstrate a continual relationship between development and religion. These histories also reveal a fluctuating role of the state vis-à-vis religion and development which has at times bound them inextricably together and has at times worked to keep them apart when state powers felt threatened by their union.

This chapter analyzes these fluctuations in order to highlight the expansive settings in which religion and development interact. In academic contexts, both religion and development have been described as "narratives," or more broadly "discourses," which explain social constructs and create them (Escobar 1995; McCutcheon 1997). I adopt a similar view, taking "development" to mean programs of technological innovation linked to ideas of "progress," and "religion" to be the experiences, beliefs, rituals, practices, and institutions broadly concerned with cosmological understandings of reality and the relationship of that reality to human existence. To paraphrase sociologist Emile Durkheim, religion and development are "eminently collective thing[s]," produced and experienced in tension and concordance with social institutions as diverse as family, schools, and systems of government (Durkheim 1985: 44).[2] Under these conditions, development actors – be they religiously motivated or not – work within larger political, economic, and religious contexts which may support or constrain their goals. Considering the role of the state is thus essential as researchers continue to develop analytic models to better understand the ways in which religion and development interact in local, national, and global settings.

This chapter contributes to this work by examining religion and development in Ecuadorian history as social vectors: dynamic bundles of ideas, institutions, and actions that carry values, relational hierarchies, and cosmological explanations for historical events and social positioning. Though the relationship of these social vectors has changed, as has the expression of that relationship, what Ecuador's history demonstrates is that neither can be adequately explored without concomitant attention to the political and economic realities that condition their existence. For many Ecuadorians, to speak of religion has always been to speak of the possibility of attendant technological change. To speak of development has always been to hint at cosmological conditions and consequences. What has changed, and continues to change, is the relationship of both vectors to various state institutions and ideologies. Attention to all of these factors is thus vital to a nuanced understanding of their historical importance and future possibilities.

Native lords and Inca roads: pre-Columbian Ecuador

Though the land that is now encapsulated in the nation of Ecuador has been inhabited for more than 10,000 years, the peoples living in the area were not brought into a major state entity until the Inca expansion into the territory in the fifteenth century. Prior to that time, "native lords," or regional leaders whom the Spanish would dub *caciques*, controlled chiefdoms in relatively small geographic areas (Salomon 1986). Though early communities in Ecuador were somewhat isolated, there is good evidence that they operated in a way similar to what archaeologist John Murra dubbed "Andean archipelagos," with communities in the highlands trading corn, potatoes, and fibers from their climatic zone for capsicum red peppers, hand axes, and other goods from lower elevations (Murra 1972). In this way, Ecuador has long been characterized by trade networks that allowed the exchange not only of goods, but of political structures, technology, and, presumably, religious ideas. Though not much is known about pre-Inca religion in Ecuador, religious objects appear to have been kept at the houses of the *caciques*, melding at least some religious power with indigenous political control (Salomon 1986: 126).

With the arrival of the Inca Empire in 1463, this union between religious and political power grew stronger as the Inca in Cuzco (and later in Cuzco and Quito as the empire faced a civil war) was not only the political leader, but also a deity with a divine right to rule. Inca civil administrators collected religious tribute from throughout the empire, and often collected local religious icons to take to Cuzco in order to cement control of outlying territories. Land, people, and goods were also pressed into religious service. Every community under Inca control was required to contribute harvests of grain and fibers to the empire, some of which went to the maintenance of the temple in Cuzco. Young girls from throughout the Inca territory were subject to becoming *aclla*, virgins taken to the Cuzco temple and tasked with spinning the fine *cumbi* cloth that nobles wore.

It is in the brief years of the Inca Empire (1463–1533), then, that strong connections between religion, technological innovation, and the state began to solidify in Ecuador. To be an Inca subject was, at least formally, to worship the Inca leader in Cuzco or Quito as a deity. It was also to enjoy some of the technological advances that the empire brought. The religious items, people, and goods traveling to Cuzco moved along an extensive system of roads that covered the Andean highlands, enabling communications via *chasqi* runners who could carry a message 2,000 kilometers from Cuzco to Quito in ten days. A complex structure of tax collection and warehouses also mitigated the worst effects of local climatic disasters, allowing for a relatively stable supply of food and other necessities. The experience of the Inca conquest of Ecuador was thus an experience that wedded rapid changes in technology and infrastructure to a theocratic government. While it is certain that no one of that era used the word "development," and "religion" as a broad concept also seems unlikely to have had any currency, the experience of Inca subjects was one where technology and cosmology were irrevocably entangled in governing structures.

When the bell sounded: Spanish conquest and colonization

This relationship became even more cemented as the Spanish established and expanded their empire in the New World in the early sixteenth century. The work of making indigenous peoples into Spanish subjects was done by Spanish soldiers who were then granted land and indigenous labor for their efforts. Conquistadors used guns, wheels, horses, metal weapons, roads the Inca had built, and their timely arrival during the Inca civil war to take land and peoples in their quest for New World wealth.

As in the case of the Inca Empire, the Audiencia de Quito, as Ecuador was known for much of the colonial period, was conquered and then administered through the introduction of new technology. And, as in the case of the Inca Empire, this new technology came married to new religious and political systems which were themselves intertwined. Unlike Inca administrators, however, who removed religious objects and young women to Cuzco in a unified political, religious, and technological effort, the Spanish divided their labors. The crown sent soldiers and others loyal to the empire to do the work of conquest and administration of New World resources, and employed Catholic religious orders to do the work of "civilizing" indigenous peoples. Spain conquered for gold, but, in the context of the 1492 *Reconquista* of Spain in which Muslims and Jews were expelled, conquering the world for Christianity was also a major motivation for Spanish action.

Early colonial history in Ecuador demonstrates this dual purpose, as well as the way such divided political administration shored up the link between Roman Catholic Christianity and technological innovation as a part of governmentality. Augustinians, Franciscans, Dominicans, Mercidarians, and Jesuits established missions throughout the Audiencia de Quito, many of which introduced European modes of farming and animal husbandry, as well as capitalist systems of agriculture, to indigenous peoples. The Jesuits, especially, knitted together technological advances with religious instruction in Roman Catholicism as they established universities and presses. They were also the primary order to run large settlements of indigenous people, often called "reductions" in other parts of Latin America, which introduced Catholicism alongside European agricultural techniques, European arts, and basic education.

One such settlement, established in the Ecuadorian Amazon in 1637, is an especially good example of the way technology and religious instruction were intertwined by religious orders in the colonial era. Located with the city of Borja at its head and extending as far as the Rio Negro, Mainas was founded at least partially in response to an uprising by indigenous peoples in the area against Spanish soldiers who had tried to implement an *encomienda* system similar to that in the highlands, wherein land was granted along with the labor of indigenous peoples living on it to those who had aided the crown in conquest. Contrasting the Jesuit fathers at Mainas to the conquistadors and *encomienda* owners, Jorge Villalba Freile, a modern-day Jesuit priest and historian, writes that:

> Seeing this disaster [maltreatment to the point of starvation at the hands of Spanish soldiers], the [Jesuit missionaries] understood that there had to be another system for Amazonian tribes: the missionary would enter their territory alone, accompanied only by Indian interpreters. Without soldiers, without any Spaniards. He would invite them to form villages, because within them there could be many of the advantages of European civilization: security, medicine, iron tools, education, and food security. The caciques would continue to rule, and they would maintain tribal customs, but under the paternal supervision of the mission.
>
> And so it happened that these children of the jungle, accustomed for centuries to living in scattered huts, delivered of unlimited liberty and vice, accepted the mission-ary's invitation and congregated in villages with houses ordered in a row all around the plaza and the church. They were subjected to a change in habits: instead of being hunters for firearms and the heads of their enemies, they became established farmers who loyally, when the bell sounded, went off to work in their communal gardens or in their private fields or to learn trades or a musical instrument.
>
> (Villalba in Carrión *et al*. 1987: 108–09)[3]

While Villalba's view of the mission is generous, it neatly encapsulates the goals of Jesuit mis-sions in Ecuador during the time of colonization. The missions combined religious instruction with "the advantages of European civilization," all at the behest of the regional governor, and all for the purposes of creating Christian Spanish subjects capable of adding to Spain's efforts at global expansion and continued success as a power within Europe. The fact that the mission in Mainas was established in response to a revolt against the *encomienda* system also points to tension between religious orders and the crown, and to indigenous resistance against colonization more broadly. That the Jesuits allowed a certain amount of indigenous leadership to remain intact at Mainas even as they introduced new religious and technological modes of life also indicates that the tight connection between religion, development, and government that the crown desired was never a complete nor easy colonial reality.[4]

"The most intensely Roman Catholic country in the world": state, church, and development in the age of independence

If the union between religion, development, and government was never seamless in the colo-nial period, neither was its dissolution as the formal tie between Ecuador and Spain was bro-ken. When Ecuador won its independence from Spain in 1822, it did not also seek to remove itself from the oversight of the Roman Catholic Church. Protestant Christianity was expressly prohibited in the country, and the church remained in charge of general education. Catholic programs also continued to give people access to technologies in areas such as agricultural pro-duction, printing, and trades. Indeed, in an 1881 report to the United States State Department, which was then passed along to the US Congress, George Earl Church describes Ecuador as "undoubtedly the most intensely Roman Catholic country in the world" (Church 1883: 34), an honor which he considered dubious at best. Much of Church's report documents Ecuadorian president Gabriel García Moreno's attempts to bring Ecuador closer to Rome, as well as a "purification" of extant religious orders, especially those involved in education, which were widely condemned as lazy and ineffectual after more than 200 years of unchallenged hegemony (Hurtado 2010: 67–8). In Church's colorful account:

> The work of purification began, aided by the iron will of García Moreno, until the convent and monastery were swept of their abuses, and holy, cenobitic life was for the first time in Ecuador reduced to the moral principles upon which its foundations rest. Friars and nuns then found welcome here in greater numbers, then came "Brothers of the Christian Schools," "Sisters of Charity" for the hospitals, "Sisters of Providence" to teach poor children, "Sisters of the Good Pastor" for the teaching of good habits, a "College of the Sacred Heart," numerous Jesuit colleges and schools, the establishment of missions among the tribes of the Amazon, until the zealous labors of priest and nun could in 1875 boast of eighteen towns flourishing under their care and 9,000 savages subjected to the teachings of civilization in five years' time. Ecuador was turned into a vast convent and church, where the good which is in the Roman Catholic religion had almost dominated its corruption, and its teachers, under the lead of Moreno, pushed on with their crusade with a zeal, a fanaticism, and a fierce bigotry comparable to that of a Hildebrand, a Torquemada, or a Cardinal Ximenes.
>
> (1883: 37)

Church goes on to mention the large *haciendas* (agricultural estates run with indigenous labor) owned and operated by Catholic orders, which historically have been amongst the largest land-owners in the nation. What stands out here is that, even for critics of the close connections between the Ecuadorian government and Rome in the post-independence era, there is no question that the mission of "civilizing," which includes education and agricultural techniques and technologies, is something best undertaken by religious authorities. For Ecuadorians in the nineteenth century, as for those before the Spanish Conquest and under Inca rule, religion and technological "progress" went hand in hand, and were closely tied to state mechanisms.

With the assassination of García Moreno in 1875, however, and the election of José Eloy Alfaro to the Ecuadorian presidency in 1895, the relationship between religion, development, and the state changed significantly. Alfaro, a liberal, believed that Ecuador had given too much to the church, and accordingly broke official ties with the Vatican, legalizing Protestantism even as he prohibited religious orders in the 1897 constitution which passed under his watch. It was during this liberal period that state-sponsored education, separate from the church, was established for the first time since the Conquest. It was also at this time that Protestant missionaries were first allowed into the country, though Protestant Bible salesmen had been present since the 1820s (Goffin 1994: 17).

The first non-Catholic missionaries in Ecuador were evangelical Christians of various denominational backgrounds working under the auspices of the Gospel Missionary Union and the Christian and Missionary Alliance. Most of these missions were small, and while many engaged in some educational programs, especially related to literacy, as Protestants placed an emphasis on reading the Bible, there were no large-scale technical programs along the lines of the Jesuit reductions or even the church-held *haciendas*. Neither did there seem to be a great deal of enthusiasm on the part of Ecuadorians for Protestantism. Most censuses at the time mark the Protestant population at less than 1 percent of the total population (Hamilton 1962: 34), a number that would not change significantly for a century.

What did change, especially with the expansion of Protestant missions in the interwar period and after World War II, was the ways in which religious and technological vectors intersected. While many Protestant missions continued Catholic traditions of combining religious and technological education, as well as religiously motivated medical aid, Protestants in Ecuador were notable for their novel use of new technologies with the aim of religious conversion. Sound trucks and boxcars, radio, movies, and airplanes became the hallmarks of Protestant faith, even as the infrastructure needed for their use necessitated a working relationship between missionaries and the Ecuadorian government.

The clearest example of this, and one of the most visible in various Ecuadorian landscapes, is an evangelical organization known by the call letters of its radio station, HCJB. Founded as the World Radio Missionary Fellowship in 1931 by North Americans Clarence Jones and Reuben Larson, HCJB aimed to utilize "the twin scientific marvels of radio communication and aviation" for the cause of Protestant mission work in Ecuador (Jones 1946: 7). Larson, a career missionary with the Christian and Missionary Alliance in the Amazonian town of Tena, successfully lobbied the Ecuadorian government in 1930 for permission to build a large antenna on the side of Mount Pichincha, the large volcano that borders Quito to the west. Permission was granted by the Ecuadorian congress, and after a transmitter was shipped from Chicago HCJB began broadcasting Spanish-language gospel messages, music, and news throughout Ecuador as one of the country's first and most far-reaching radio stations. When in 1949 a powerful earthquake leveled Ambato, an important commercial center in the highlands, HCJB engineers were the first to establish contact between the city and government officials in Quito (Hallock 1951: 60).

As indicated by Larson's invocation of aviation and radio as scientific marvels capable of changing the world, HCJB did not limit its use of technology to the airwaves. Early on, missionaries engaged in "boxcar evangelism," loading a car on Ecuador's single train line between Quito and Guayaquil with sound equipment and putting on evangelical revivals at every stop. More permanently, HCJB built a hospital in Shell-Mera, an Amazonian town initially built up by the Shell Oil Company in the late 1930s but abandoned by that corporation in 1948. In 1949, the Mission Aviation Fellowship, working with HCJB, established a mission in Shell-Mera, taking over an airstrip the oil company had left behind in order to extend Protestant religious instruction and technological aid to indigenous peoples. This mission post became an important center for medical care in the Amazon with the establishment of a hospital run by HCJB in 1958.[5] This hospital complemented Hospital VozAndes in Quito, which Larson saw completed in 1955, 30 years after having received permission from the Ecuadorian government to begin medical practice. VozAndes serves the greater Quito area, as well as patients referred to it by HCJB medical missions, and also regularly trains Ecuadorian medical students, most of whom are not otherwise affiliated with HCJB or evangelical Christianity.[6]

In these ways, HCJB, and certainly many other Protestant missions, mirror and augment government development initiatives that aim to bring medical care, transportation, and access to communications to Ecuadorian citizens. Protestant missions such as HCJB, however, introduced a new relationship between religion, technology, and state interests. Rather than more or less directly controlling religious orders to achieve political and economic ends, the Ecuadorian government in this case acted as facilitator and, in many instances, as a partner in development projects. In this manner, the direct link between religion, state, and development became much more blurred, variable, and negotiable by those whom these vectors target.

Catholics in the gap: Liberation Theology and the state

This is perhaps most clearly evidenced by the conflicts that arose in the golden era of Liberation Theology, beginning in the late 1960s, when Protestants were not the only religious group to challenge any easy relationship between the state, religion, and what was coming to be known as international economic development in the post-World War II period. After World War II, Ecuador became a receiving country for economic development assistance that was designed to raise the standard of living and industrial output of "poorer" countries, primarily those in the Southern Hemisphere. As this assistance was brokered at the national level, it was the Ecuadorian government that negotiated the terms of aid to be received from the newly formed World Bank and International Monetary Fund. This is the point when many scholars see a shift in historical mission and charity work to modern economic development, which becomes the work of nation states in often uneven international contexts (Escobar 1995; Rist 1997).

What the Ecuadorian experience with Liberation Theology demonstrates, however, is that religious vectors were never entirely disentangled from development, allowing Ecuadorians to negotiate the relationship between religion, development, and (inter)national government at local levels. This is neatly illustrated by the case of Leonidas Proaño, bishop of the highland city of Riobamba from 1954 until 1985.

Very few contemporary Ecuadorians, especially *mestizas/os* (Ecuadorians of mixed indigenous and European heritage) and whites living in the rural sectors of the country, claim much familiarity with Liberation Theology or its aims.[7] Most, however, are familiar with Proaño. Songs about him are regularly played on Catholic radio stations, and his name is frequently invoked as a "bishop of the people." During his tenure as bishop, Proaño founded many liberationist base communities (CEBs) in the Riobamba area, giving special attention to the many indigenous groups that surround the largely *mestizo* urban center. Proaño was a member of CELAM, the Latin American bishops' conference, which declared a "preferential option for the poor" within the Catholic Church, a stance for which he drew criticism from the conservative Catholic hierarchy as well as the Ecuadorian government, especially as he became actively involved in Ecuador's 1964 land reform.[8] In 1973, Proaño was tried in Rome on charges of guerrilla warfare, of which he was acquitted, only to be jailed by Ecuadorian dictator Guillermo Rodríguez Lara in 1976.[9]

Proaño is notable, however, not only for his political work, but for the religiously informed development enterprises he founded. Taking a cue from Protestant uses of technology, Proaño founded *escuelas radiofónicas populares* (public radio schools), an educational program broadcast via radio to remote regions that were either unserved or underserved by the government schools. He also founded Tepeyec, a warehouse and trade school designed to promote indigenous rights and to teach artisanal and agricultural skills.

To participate in the *escuelas radiofónicas* or in Tepeyec was thus to embrace a religiously motivated form of development which was not warmly received, and was at times directly suppressed, by the Ecuadorian government. It was to choose religiously motivated development instead of or in addition to government development programs which were legally separated from religious institutions and which often worked at the behest of the Alliance for Progress, a US program that tied development aid to compliance with US foreign policy goals and favorable contracts with US corporations. It was to negotiate a development, and often a religious identity, quite different from the one in formal power.

In this sense, Liberation Theology highlights a time in Ecuadorian history when religion and development came together as vectors, but did so in ways which drew criticism and opposition from state powers. Unlike in Inca or colonial times when opting for the state meant, de facto, opting for new religious systems, choosing a new expression of Catholicism in this era risked the ire of a dictatorial state and was, in significant ways, an act of resistance against state powers.

Catholic cheese: religious development in the liberationist and neoliberal eras

Despite the risk of state policies that many construed as hostile to liberal religious projects, many Ecuadorians, especially people living in indigenous communities that had been neglected and oppressed by the *mestizo* majority in the country for centuries, continued to opt for religiously sponsored development programs as the liberationist period continued.[10] While Bishop Proaño worked in Riobamba, a group of Salesian priests from Italy came to adjoining Bolívar Province to join the Bishop of Guaranda, Cándido Rada, and his development organization, Fondo Ecuatoriano Populorum Progressio (FEPP). FEPP, which continues to operate today, highlights a relationship to the state which is more conciliatory than that of Proaño, but which has continued to offer resistance to international models of development, specifically neoliberalism.

Bishop Rada founded FEPP in 1970, and named the organization after Pope Paul VI's 1967 encyclical *Populorum Progressio* (Development of the Peoples), in which the pontiff called for a "common fund" for the "assistance of the most disinherited." For development to be effective, wrote the Pope, it must not focus exclusively on economics at the state level, but should come from a spirit of "solidarity human development." "Development," he wrote, "cannot be restricted to economic growth alone. To be authentic, it must be well rounded; it must foster the development of each man and of the whole man" (Paul VI 1967).

While stemming from a Catholic notion of persons composed of mind, body, and spirit, Paul VI's language also reflected a burgeoning movement within development circles toward assessing development on its ability to meet the needs of populations rather than economic productivity at the national level. Basic needs approaches to development, as these were called, argued that economic growth at national levels could only come once people had regular access to healthcare, food, and education, the body and mind portions of Paul VI's "whole man."[11]

Certainly, both needs-based approaches to development and solidarity human development were reflected in Salinas, a small town where Salesian priests partnered with FEPP to form cooperatives and microlending enterprises, beginning in 1971. At the edge of the habitable zone in the high Andes, Salinas and its surrounding communities were populated almost exclusively by indigenous peoples forced from the lower, fertile valleys during the time of the Spanish Conquest. In the twentieth century, the local economy was dominated by a salt mine in which many indigenous laborers worked under brutal conditions. Father Antonio Polo, who arrived in Salinas in 1971 as a part of the larger Salesian Mato Grosso project in Ecuador, described the relationship of local peoples to the salt mine owners as "harshly exploitative" and "desperate" (Polo 2002: 18).

Polo, in conjunction with FEPP director José Tonello, started community savings and loan programs in Salinas shortly after his arrival so that people could better manage what money they had. He then moved to establish artisanal and textile programs in order to generate income apart from salt mining and sharecropping. Eventually, Polo worked with Tonello, fellow Salesian Matteo Panteghini, and Swiss technical consultant José Dubách to pioneer the production of hard cheeses. This industry has been widely successful not only in Salinas but throughout Bolívar Province and the greater region. The Salinas consortium in charge of artisanal crafts opened a store, Quesos de Bolívar, to market the cheeses in Quito in 1978, and in 1991 FUNCONQUERUCOM (Fundación de Consorcios de Queseras Rurales Comunitarias, or Foundation of Rural Community Cheese Plants) was founded to manage cheese production and markets.

The Salinas projects are often heralded as a successful example of community-based development, though Polo, who still lives in Salinas and oversees operations with Panteghini, sees his mission as religiously based. Speaking of the Salinas Mission (Misión Salinera), he points to the "orienting principle" wherein "The whole initiative of the mission is – and should be – ministry," that is, "evangelization, education ministry, health ministry, and social promotion ministry" (Polo 2002: 61). For Polo, and for many of those who work in a FUNCONQUERUCOM cheese plant, the Salesian project has been successful because it freely combines Roman Catholic understandings of community, solidarity, and development with local modes of production that are not controlled at the state level. Indeed, and as Liisa North has documented, as Ecuador entered the era of neoliberalism in the 1980s and 1990s the Salinas project combated many of the effects of economic policies that downplayed the role of the state. The project harnessed an overt sense of communitarianism to replace reduced state services at local levels even as it adopted the neoliberal preference for NGOs (North and Cameron 2003: 187–206). Here, the tension between religiously sponsored development and the state was less pronounced than during land reform or at the height of Liberation Theology's influence in the country, but it once again highlights the ways religious and development vectors are not always controlled by, or operate in concert with, political power at the national level.

Conclusion – a future in flux: changes in religion and development in twenty-first-century Ecuador

Finally, the Salinas project highlights two other realities which are shaping the nature of religion and development, and their intersection with the state, in the early twenty-first century. In a 2002 interview Polo responded to critics of the Salinas project who were worried that it had become too secular. In essence, several families in the region were reported to have responded that they had "no religion" in a survey. It was not that they have no religion, Polo explained, but that they confused the surveyor's question about Christianity more broadly with evangelical Christianity. They have a religion, in other words, but unlike many indigenous peoples in the region they are, and remain, Catholic (Polo 2002: 110).

That Polo was required to make this claim points to the rapidly changing religious landscape in Ecuador, the country Church had described as "the most intensely Roman Catholic country in the world" only 120 years before. Like much of Latin America, Ecuador has seen significant growth in Pentecostal and Charismatic Christianity beginning in the 1980s, though it has only begun to experience the demographic changes now familiar in places such as Guatemala and Brazil. In 1970, less than 2 percent of Ecuadorians identified as Protestant, with the remainder of its citizens identifying as Roman Catholic (Barrett *et al.* 2001: 246). In 2010, only 80 percent were estimated to be Roman Catholic (Instituto Nacional de Estadísticas y Censos 2013), and of these approximately 8 percent are Charismatic (Jacobson 2011: 58).[12] Mormons, Seventh Day Adventists, and Jehovah's Witnesses have also made gains in Ecuador, and while their populations remain relatively small they are a visible reminder that Ecuador's more or less unified religious identity is a thing of the past.

Also in flux is the relationship between development and the Ecuadorian government. As in many places, NGOs have proliferated wildly in the country since the 1990s, partially in response to critiques of top-down, monolithic international economic development and partially in response to international development structures such as the IMF and World Bank, which required recipient countries to privatize services as a part of neoliberal adjustment policies. In the 1980s, a typical Ecuadorian town had a state-run telephone service, a government-run health subcenter, and access to agricultural technologies via the Ministry of Agriculture. In the early twenty-first century, people carry cell phones from private companies and receive healthcare from a combination of government clinics, religious hospitals such as HCJB, and secular NGOs concerned with HIV/AIDS and other ailments. They also participate in agricultural projects run by organizations as diverse as subsidiaries of the European Union, World Vision (an evangelical Christian organization), and Plan International (a non-sectarian NGO founded in Britain). It is no longer a question of church or state, or some combination thereof, but of which church, which state, which private organization, or which combination of these entities may best assist communities in reaching their goals.

Ecuadorian history thus highlights not only the various and significant ways in which religion and development have intertwined since pre-Columbian times, but also the fluctuating role various government institutions, ideologies, and policies have had in creating, controlling, and resisting this combination. The state often wedded religious instruction and ritual practice to the proliferation of new technologies, as in the case of the Inca and Spanish conquests. Government institutions have also acted to keep these vectors apart, as in the case of early Liberation Theology and the incarceration of Bishop Proaño. These dynamics certainly merit careful attention from scholars interested in the intersection of religion and development. They also point to future projects which examine, in greater detail than this chapter is able, how decreasing state influence in the age of globalization may shift this center of entanglement or separation, once again altering the conditions under which the vectors of religion and development deploy.

Notes

1 The Galápagos Islands, as well as the west of the littoral plain, are also Ecuadorian possessions, are counted as a province within the country, and do have a small permanent population. Here I refer to the main geographic body of the nation.

2 Of course, given his strict separation of the sacred and the profane, Durkheim would most likely not agree with the assertion that development shares the transcendent qualities he attributes uniquely to religion. Many scholars, especially in the post-development vein, challenge this separation, arguing that development shares many of these transcendent characteristics. See especially Escobar (1995) and Rist (1997).

3 Translation from the Spanish by the author.

4 The relationship between clergy and the crown was certainly not without discord. As Las Casas's 1550 critique of Spanish treatment of indigenous peoples, and the later expulsion of the Jesuits from the Americas in 1716 demonstrate, while church and state shared a common interest in Christianizing and "civilizing" Native Americans, there was not widespread agreement about the best way to undertake the project (Las Casas 1974).

5 The mission is also notable for an act of indigenous resistance. Aviation missionaries Nate Saint, Ed McCully, Jim Elliott, and Peter Fleming were killed on January 8, 1956 when they landed on a beach by the side of an Amazonian tributary in an attempt to make contact with Waorani peoples. Men from the village killed the missionaries with spears, an event that has been the subject of the pro-mission movie *End of the Spear* (2006), as well as the documentary *Beyond the Gates of Splendor* (2002).

6 For more on HCJB practices and its relationship to medical students, see "Spiritual Cardiology: Wholeness, Becoming and (Dis)Integration" in DeTemple (2012: 169–95).

7 While the practices and theologies associated with the Liberation Theology movement in Latin America did reach many rural Ecuadorians in the forms of small church communities and an emphasis on "solidarity" and "justice," the term "Liberation Theology" does not appear to have widely employed. See DeTemple (2013).

8 The 1964 land reform in Ecuador attempted to break a cycle of indentured servitude in which indigenous peoples worked in debt peonage (*concertaje*) on large *haciendas* in the control of wealthy, usually white, landowners. Under the reform act, tracts over 2,500 hectares on the coast and 800 hectares in the highlands were seized by the state and distributed to the indigenous peoples, who assumed cooperative ownership. In addition, unused public lands were distributed to landless peasants. While land reform did ease some of the burdens of the *concertaje* system, it is generally considered to have been only partly effective, at best (see Blankenstein and Zuvekas 1973; and Lyons 2006).

9 Lara is also notable for his elision of "whitening," a notion that indigenous peoples should accept and practice dominant European culture, with development. In a 1972 speech in the Amazonian town of Puyo, Lara declared that: "There is no more Indian Problem. We all become white when we accept the goals of national culture" (as quoted in Stutzman 1981: 46). The linkage between whiteness and development was not unique to Ecuador, and also existed in South Africa (see Bompani, Chapter 7).

10 While I highlight the Salesian program in Bolívar Province here, this was certainly not the only religiously sponsored development program working in Ecuador at the time. Indeed, the 1970s were a period of rapid Protestant expansion in Ecuador, and many indigenous communities, especially, opted for faith-based development programs initiated by HCJB, World Vision International, and others.

11 Catholics are not the only religious organization to focus on development as more than physical. HCJB, for example, requires employees to read Daniel Fountain's (1989) book *Health, the Bible, and the Church*, which argues for the development of the "whole person," who is healthy in mind, body, and spirit.

12 Charismatic Catholics, who place an emphasis on charisms such as speaking in tongues, faith healing and prophecy, small group participation, emotional retreats, and a personal relationship with God, are quickly becoming a major influence in Latin American Roman Catholicism. For an especially detailed overview of the movement see Cleary (2011).

References

Barrett, David, Kurian, George and Johnson, Todd (eds) (2001) *World Christian Encyclopedia: A Comparative Survey of Churches and Religions in the Modern World*, 2nd edn, New York: Oxford University Press.
Beyond the Gates of Splendor (2002) Jim Hanon (director), Bearing Fruit Entertainment.
Blankenstein, Charles S. and Zuvekas, Charles (1973) 'Agrarian Reform in Ecuador: An Evaluation of Past Efforts and the Development of a New Approach', *Economic Development and Cultural Change*, 22 (1) (October), 73–94.
Carrión, Alejandro, Lara, Jorge Salvador, Dutari, Julio Terán and Villalva, Jorge (1987) *Los Jesuitas en el Ecuador*, Quito: Casa de Cultura Benjamín Carrión.
Church, George (1883) *Report of Mr. George Earl Church upon Ecuador*, Senate Document no. 69, Washington, DC: US Government Printing Office.
Cleary, Edward (2011) *The Rise of Charismatic Catholicism in Latin America*, Gainesville: University Press of Florida.
DeTemple, Jill (2012) *Cement, Earthworms, and Cheese Factories: Religion and Community Development in Rural Ecuador*, Notre Dame, IN: University of Notre Dame Press.
DeTemple, Jill (2013) 'Imagining Development: Religious Studies in the Context of International Economic Development', *Journal of the American Academy of Religion*, 80 (1) (March), 107–29.
Durkheim, Emile (1985) *The Elementary Forms of Religious Life*, trans. Karen Fields, New York: Free Press.
End of the Spear (2006) Jim Hanon (director), Every Tribe Entertainment.
Escobar, Arturo (1995) *Encountering Development: The Making and Unmaking of the Third World*, Princeton, NJ: Princeton University Press.
Fountain, Daniel (1989) *Health, the Bible, and the Church*, Wheaton, IL: Evangelism and Missions Information Service.
Goffin, Alvin M. (1994) *The Rise of Protestant Evangelism in Ecuador 1895–1900*, Gainesville: University Press of Florida.
Hallock, Constance M. (1951) *Looking South*, New York: Friendship Press.
Hamilton, Keith E. (1962) *Church Growth in the High Andes*, Lucknow, India: Lucknow Publishing House.
Hurtado, Osvaldo (2010) *Portrait of a Nation: Culture and Progress in Ecuador*, trans. Barbara Snipe, Lanham, MD: Madison Books.
Instituto Nacional de Estadísticas y Censos del Ecuador (2013).
Jacobson, Douglas (2011) *The World's Christians: Who They Are, Where They Are, and How They Got There*, Hoboken, NJ: Wiley-Blackwell.
Jones, Clarence W. (1946) *Radio: The New Missionary*, Chicago: Moody Press.
Las Casas, Bartolomé de (1974) *In Defense of the Indians*, DeKalb: Northern Illinois University.
Lyons, Barry (2006) *Remembering the Hacienda: Religion, Authority, and Social Change in Highland Ecuador*, Austin: University of Texas Press.
McCutcheon, Russell (1997) *Manufacturing Religion: The Discourse on Sui Generis Religion and the Politics of Nostalgia*, New York: Oxford University Press.
Murra, John (1972) 'El "Control Vertical" de un Máximo de Pisos Ecológicos en la Economía de Sociedades Andinas', in J. V. Murra (ed.), *Vista de la Provincia de Leon de Huanuco en 1562*, Huanuco, Peru: Universidad Nacional Hermilio Valdizán, pp. 427–76.
North, Liisa and Cameron, John D. (eds) (2003) *Rural Progress, Rural Decay: Neoliberal Adjustment Policies and Local Initiatives*, Bloomfield, CT: Kumarian Press.
Paul VI (1967) *Populorum Progressio*, Encyclical Letter on the Development of Peoples, 26 March, http://www.vatican.va/holy_father/paul_vi/encyclicals/documents/hf_p-vi_enc_26031967_populorum_en.html (accessed 10 January 2014).
Polo, Antonio F. (2002) *La Puerta Abierta: 30 años de aventura misionera y social en Salinas de Bolívar Ecuador*, Quito: Abya Yala.
Rist, Gilbert (1997) *The History of Development: From Western Origins to Global Faith*, London: Zed Books.
Salomon, Frank (1986) *Native Lords of Quito in the Age of the Incas*, Cambridge: Cambridge University Press.
Stutzman, Ronald (1981) 'El Mestizaje', in Norman Whitten (ed.), *Cultural Transformations and Ethnicity in Modern Ecuador*, Urbana: University of Illinois Press, pp. 41–94.

12

THE CATHOLIC CHURCH, CONTEMPORARY SEXUAL POLITICS AND DEVELOPMENT IN LATIN AMERICA

Juan Marco Vaggione

Introduction

The mid-1990s were a turning point in the way sexuality was debated and constructed worldwide. The arrival of reproductive rights, and later sexual rights, in the United Nations (UN) conferences challenged reductionist visions of health and population that had dominated development politics for decades (Pecheny and de la Dehesa 2011). The International Conference on Population and Development in Cairo in 1994 articulated an innovative perspective by emphasizing reproductive rights as human rights. The freedom of individuals and couples to make decisions regarding their reproductive and sexual health became a primary dimension of a vision of human development "concerned with justice, equality and dignity" (Sweetman 2008: 220). The trajectory of sexual rights was more complicated. However, there are important milestones like the Yogyakarta Principles in 2007, a UN declaration in 2008 and a Human Rights Council resolution in 2011. Each of these milestones, with different impacts and levels of formalization, recognizes sexual orientation and gender identity as central to human rights debates. Despite some contradictions, areas of disagreement and limitations (Miller 2010), the introduction of sexual and reproductive rights inaugurated, at least symbolically, a new stage in development politics. In tension with other approaches (such as population control, sexual violence, and health), the construction of sexuality came to revolve around a "complete state of physical, mental and social well-being" (UNFPA 1994).

The sexual and reproductive rights agenda defends a conception of sexuality that legitimizes desire and freedom. It seeks to dismantle, among other things, the construction of a sexual order that prioritizes reproduction while simultaneously marginalizing, criminalizing and delegitimizing distinct sexual identities and practices. It is thus not surprising that the success of feminist and sexual diversity movements in advancing their demands worldwide has generated resistance and counter-mobilization. The mid-1990s also saw the emergence of a transnational movement, with strong religious identifications, that mobilized for the precise purpose of opposing sexual and reproductive rights (Buss and Herman 2003; Butler 2006). The moment in which such rights begin to have legitimacy is thus interwoven with strong opposition from UN-affiliated actors that lobby against the demands of feminist and sexual diversity movements. Prominent among these actors is the Holy See, the only religion with UN permanent member state status, lending it a unique leadership position. Other actors include representatives of countries strongly identified with different religious traditions (Christianity, Catholicism and Islam) and the growing presence of formally recognized faith-based organizations.[1] This heterogeneous ensemble find common ground in their rejection of sexual and reproductive rights, permitting them to ally themselves with one another, despite their differences, to defend "family" or "life" values that they consider to be threatened. This alliance uses different strategies and discourses to avoid (and in some cases reverse) the inclusion of these rights in various agreements, resolutions and documents, thus preventing the consensus required by the UN. These groups have actively coordinated meetings and conferences and organized sessions with the goal of becoming a more effective lobby within the UN.

The Catholic Church, as a global institution, is not just the leader of this conservative block within the UN, but also one of the principal obstacles to the implementation of sexual and reproductive rights-based policies in Latin America. The Vatican not only constructs ethical-religious positions, but orchestrates strategies and disseminates discourses that seek to influence the political actions of those within its hierarchy and the faithful (Vaggione 2012). This political machine, the analysis of which constitutes the primary objective of this chapter, has adapted to different international and national scenarios in defense of a sexual order based on biological reproduction. While the feminist and sexual diversity movements have managed to fissure, at least partially, the hierarchy's power over sexual politics, including generating legal reforms that expand the legal boundaries of freedom and diversity, the Catholic Church has not given up its goal of supporting political regimes that reflect its ethical-religious positions.

Nevertheless, as this chapter demonstrates, this goal is channeled in dynamic ways that adapt to changing circumstances. First, this chapter considers the ways in which the Vatican, as the pillar of ecclesiastic power, structures the defense of the sexual order in reaction to advances by the feminist and sexual diversity movements. To understand the public actions taken by the Church in national or regional contexts, we must consider the Church as a transnational institution that acquires its principal strategies and discourses from the Vatican. Second, we consider Argentina's same-sex marriage debate in 2010 as a moment in which to observe the forms of political intervention employed by conservative Catholic sectors. Although this analysis focuses on Argentina, it permits us to consider the renewed strategies and discourses that characterize conservative Catholic activism in Latin America in general.

Through these analyses, the chapter seeks to address the debates surrounding the intersections between religion, development and sexual politics in contemporary societies. The failure of secularization theory has challenged the principal approaches to religion, in particular those that consider religion's influence in contemporary politics. Because the frameworks that reduced religion to taking place *outside* of politics in the context of western modernity were contested, analytical and normative approaches that accommodate complex political forms of religion became a priority. Sexuality is an ideal area in which to understand (present) religious political articulations, in particular those of the Catholic Church. Without giving up traditional forms of power, the institution of religion implements strategies, supports new actors and circulates discourses that demonstrate the limits of secularization theory as a theoretical and ideological framework for understanding contemporary sexual politics.

The Catholic Church confronts a (new) sexual politics

It is not uncommon for religious traditions to play a lead role in maintaining a restrictive sexual order. For centuries, they have constructed moral frameworks that continue to affect law and public policy. In the majority of contemporary societies, religious institutions transcend the boundaries of the religious sphere and condition the forms of ethical and legal regulation of the citizenry. Religious traditions are thus central to the organization of sexuality into a hierarchy, in which some practices are rendered legitimate while the majority are silenced, concealed or even criminalized. Latin America is no exception, since the historical influence of the Catholic Church on culture and politics has generated an overlap between religious doctrine and state regulations surrounding sexuality. Although the influence of the Catholic Church has fluctuated in accordance with distinct historical periods, the country in question and its governing body, the Church's power tends to determine the legal and moral boundaries that have historically sustained different restrictions. Catholicism legitimizes an order based on the linking of sexuality with reproduction (procreative) and within marriage (unitive), thus justifying ethical and legal constructions to this end. This construction gives pleasure a secondary, even negative, role; as the Catechism of the Catholic Church sustains, "Sexual pleasure is morally disordered when sought for itself, isolated from its procreative and unitive purposes" (Catechism of the Catholic Church, 2351).

The imbrication of sexuality and reproduction has been strongly criticized by the feminist and sexual diversity movements, initiating a new phase in sexual politics and legal thought (Vaggione 2011a). These movements' principal goals have been to make visible, criticize and confront the exclusions and inequalities generated by a traditional sexual order. Without downplaying the heterogeneity of these movements, the demand for recognizing sexual and reproductive rights is a primary strategy that can dismantle legal and cultural restrictions and generate policies that guarantee autonomy in reproductive and sexual decision making.

The new sexual politics generated by the feminist and sexual diversity movements challenges the Catholic Church in complex ways. One type of impact is occurring even within Catholic circles, where the process of secularization on morality is taking effect. These movements, at least partially, look to dismantle the standards used to govern forms of action, moral judgment and public manifestations that construct a series of sexual identities and practices as immoral, and simultaneously to circulate an alternative sexual ethic. This shift has increased the presence within the Catholic realm of members and debates that favor a more sexually inclusive and diverse Church. Groups like Dignity (1969) and Catholics for Choice (1973), which began to have a growing impact in the United States during the 1970s, were early examples of the forms in which feminism and pro-sexual diversity influenced religious identity. From these first protests, the number of individuals, organizations and theological debates that consider Catholicism a wide and plural tradition has only increased. They propose the use of contraception, termination of pregnancy, or rights for same-sex couples as ethical options that can be supported by the Catholic tradition. The election of the latest Pope in 2013 has generated expectations on a doctrine reform allowing for a more flexible sexual ethic.

Another impact of these movements is their dismantling of the Catholic Church's influence on law, public policy and the State. Although the Church recognized the independence and autonomy between religion and policy during the Second Vatican Council (Gaudium et Epes, 1965), in Latin America the institution has formal and informal privileges that call such autonomy into question. In exchange for material and symbolic perquisites such as economic sustenance, privileged legal status, constitutional norms that make Catholicism the official religion, and a clientelistic relationship between the Catholic hierarchy and legislators, the Church bestows valuable legitimacy on the government (because political legitimacy can be problematic in Latin America). These movements have reignited the struggle for secular states, which has been an ideological mechanism for limiting the influence of religion in politics throughout the region. Sexuality thus becomes a lens through which one can observe a lack of sufficient autonomy between Church and State. This "deficient" separation has resulted in, among other questions, the tendency for forms of state regulation regarding sexuality and reproduction to be soaked, if not saturated, with religious influence.

The feminist and sexual diversity movements have been successful in making historical practices more visible (like contraception, sexual relations between people of the same sex or voluntary termination of pregnancy) and converting them from legal marginality into laws and public policies. Although the situation in the region is diverse, there have been important changes through jurisprudence in cases like the decriminalization of abortion by the Colombian court or the existence of rulings that recognize the right of same-sex couples in different countries (Vaggione 2013). Sexual and reproductive rights have also been recognized through parliamentary debates and legal reforms, for example the legalization of abortion in the capital of Mexico (2007) and Uruguay (2012) or the marriage reforms for same-sex partners in Mexico City (2009) and Argentina (2010).

The demand for sexual and reproductive rights does not necessarily imply a change in practices and identities, but rather a critique of a hierarchical sexual order that hides, marginalizes and even criminalizes them. Sexual and reproductive rights, beyond recognizing and legitimizing subaltern identities, also imply the democratization of access to sexual and reproductive practices. Although the ways of regulating sexuality and reproduction have cut across population policies in various ways, sexual and reproductive rights create an alternative way of thinking about the intersections between sexuality, development and public policy. These rights look to guarantee decision-making autonomy about sexuality and reproduction, particularly in contexts like Latin America where there is high inequality and economic exclusion. Restricting access to contraception and abortion, or prioritizing certain familial arrangements over others, contributes to the economic inequality that characterizes the region. Although the feminist and sexual diversity movements have different positions with respect to economic inequality (ranging from reformist to radical), in general the goal of rights recognition is the attainment of greater sexual and reproductive justice and equality.

In response to these advances, the Catholic Church has (re)dogmatized its mandate and (re) designed its sexual politics in an effort to influence public and legal debates. In general, this redesign conforms to the Vatican's overarching direction and strategy, made visible and concrete in both national and international arenas. Although the Catholic Church has long defended a restrictive sexual order, the *Evangelium Vitae* encyclical of 1995 was a decisive milestone. The encyclical condenses decades of the religious institution's positions while clearly stating the principal characteristics of contemporary conservative Catholic activism. Through its establishment of an opposition between the culture of life and the culture of death, the encyclical conveys a strong and irreconcilable antagonism toward the demands of the feminist and sexual diversity movements. Although the decriminalization of abortion and euthanasia are the most visible aspects of this culture of death, the encyclical considers the primary problem to be a "contraceptive mentality." This mentality means that "the original import of human sexuality is distorted and falsified, and the two meanings, unitive and procreative, inherent in the very nature of the conjugal act, are artificially separated" (*Evangelium Vitae* 1995).

While the *Evangelium Vitae* encyclical reaffirms the religious hierarchy's role as a public actor in contemporary debates, it also outlines some principal characteristics of conservative Catholic activism that become visible when sexuality is debated in different countries. In particular it mentions two facets that constitute notable shifts in the forms of religious political intervention in contemporary democracies (Vaggione 2012). First, the encyclical emphasizes the role of the faithful, in particular, in resisting sexual and reproductive rights. Although the Catholic Church's call upon its faithful to publicly protest is not a new trend (even Vatican II is an example in this direction), what is notable is the central role of the call to citizens and politicians to defend the "culture of life," particularly since the 1990s. A "pro-life" or "pro-family" Catholic movement has emerged and become relevant in sexual politics. In connection with this, every three years John Paul II (Pope between 1978 and 2005) organized the World Meeting of Families, which served as a transnational space to consolidate an agenda after Cairo's impact. During the first of these encounters, in Rome in October 1994,[2] the Pope denounced the existence of a tendency during the International Conference on Population and Development (ICPD) in Cairo in 1994 to alter the meaning of the family by de-naturalizing it (John Paul II 1994).

Another change present in this encyclical is the shift toward secular arguments to justify the rejection of sexual and reproductive rights. The defense of a "culture of life" is not made exclusively from religious and ethical justifications; rather, secular arguments, in particular scientific research, become notable reasons to reject sexual and reproductive rights.[3] In 1995, the same year as the encyclical, John Paul II created the Pontifical Academy for Life, dedicated to "study, information and formation on the principal problems of biomedicine and of law, relative to the promotion and defense of life, above all in the direct relation that they have with Christian morality and the directives of the Church's Magisterium."[4]

The Vatican's discursive shifts and rearticulations have become visible in the distinct national and international spheres where the status of sexual and reproductive rights is debated. Other facets of religious politics, requiring new analysis and normative frameworks, are added to traditional forms of participation by the Catholic hierarchy. The debate regarding "homosexuality," and the legal recognition of same-sex couples in particular, permits the observation of some relevant dimensions of conservative Catholic activism, as explored in greater detail in the following section.

The Catholic Church as a heteronormative mechanism

The rights of same-sex couples are still among the most politicized demands within the broader scope of sexual rights. Without overlooking the continued existence of strong discrimination against homosexuality, including a significant number of countries where it is criminalized, the sexual diversity movement has managed to achieve formal recognition for same-sex couples in different places. Whether through judicial cases or legal reforms, the legal status of these couples has changed in notable ways. The judicial cases that bestow rights like social security, inheritance, adoption and conjugal visits are diverse. Also legal reforms have given rights to same-sex couples. An early example in this direction has been the creation of institutions like the civil union that formally recognize these couples while preserving marriage as an institution that is exclusively heterosexual. Finally, at the beginning of the twenty-first century, same-sex marriage began to be permitted, dismantling the requisite complementarity of the sexes.[5] Among the multiple questions raised by this legal change is the symbolic effect of separating (biological) reproduction as a mark of legitimacy within the hierarchy of sexuality. To recognize the marriage of couples characterized by a status *external* to biological reproduction implies a paradigmatic change in construction, hierarchy, and legalization of sexuality.

Along with the decriminalization of abortion,[6] this demand is a priority for the Catholic hierarchy, which along with reaffirming, even intensifying, its doctrine regarding homosexuality[7] also plays an active role in influencing legal debates. To give rights to same-sex couples implies legitimizing a sexuality that goes against natural law and is therefore illegal as well as immoral. In a clear response to the growing legitimacy and existence of Catholic groups that support sexual diversity,[8] the Catholic Church stiffened its mandate, instructing bishops not to permit agencies to present themselves as Catholic if they allow homosexuals to associate without "clearly establishing that homosexual activity is immoral" (Congregation for the Doctrine of the Faith 2003).

The Vatican orchestrates still more strategies and arguments that attempt to resist or overturn the recognition of rights. Two specific documents form the basis for constructing a policy toward homosexuality that was later taken up by the Catholic hierarchies in different countries. In reaction to anti-discrimination legislation in 1992, the Catholic Church maintains that there are areas where the explicit exclusion of people because of their sexual orientation does not constitute "unjust discrimination." The assertion concretely mentions adoption, the care of minors, admission to the military and employment as a physical education teacher (Congregation for the Doctrine of the Faith 1992). It directs bishops to oppose legislation that prohibits discrimination based on sexual orientation as well as that which would criminalize hate crimes against homosexuals.

The other document, from 2003, is entitled "Considerations Regarding Proposals to Give Legal Recognition to Unions between Homosexual Persons" (from here forward, "Considerations"). It deals specifically with the legal status of same-sex couples whose recognition is considered "not only the approval of deviant behaviour, with the consequence of making it a model in present-day society, but would also obscure basic values which belong to the common inheritance of humanity" (Congregation for the Doctrine of the Faith 2003). The document outlines the principal alignments regarding the forms in which the hierarchy and Catholic legislators should act, in their different roles, in response to proposals that would recognize the rights of same-sex couples. "Considerations" is central to understanding the discourses and strategies imposed by the Catholic hierarchy in countries where reforms along this trajectory were debated, as was the case in Argentina in 2010.

Conservative Catholic activism faces same-sex marriage in Argentina

The legal regulation of marriage in Latin America has been an issue where the overlap and articulation between the Catholic Church and the State have become apparent. In Argentina, for example, the 1869 Civil Code left the jurisdiction of marriage to the Catholic Church (it gave civil effects to religious marriage). From this moment the institution of marriage passed through various stages that slowly deinstitutionalized religious influences. Two decades afterward (1888) the Civil Marriage Law was introduced, and civil and religious marriage were distinguished – the State "regulated the civil contract . . . [while] the Church only concerned itself with the celebration of the religious sacrament" (Vaggione 2011a: 935) – despite the objections of the Catholic hierarchy. This distinction did not imply a complete secularization of the law, because marriage went on being defined according to the Catholic doctrine on topics such as divorce, which was prohibited. The Catholic Church's power over law was also made evident in the marches and counter-marches over the issue of divorce in the twentieth century. As a result of the process of democratization in the 1980s, legal regulation broke from Catholic doctrine, finally establishing in 1987 the right to dissolve the state of matrimony, despite strong opposition from the Catholic hierarchy and allied sectors.

The uneasy relationship between religious doctrine and secular law has more recently come to the fore in the decision by the Argentinian government to allow marriage between same-sex couples since July 2010. In the run-up to the passing of the law on same-sex marriage, Catholic objection gave rise to renewed debates about the "complementarity of the sexes" as a defining part of the institution of matrimony. Through official communications, media declarations and sermons, some members of the public began to manifest their opposition to legal reform. In particular, the Argentine Episcopal Conference (CEA), the ecclesial government's central organ, circulated two documents on the issue based on Vatican documents. At the end of 2009, the CEA made a declaration defining marriage as a "stable relationship between man and woman, who in their diversity complement one another for the transmission and care of life, a good that does as much for the development of persons as of society" (CEA 2009). In April 2010, the bill having already been introduced to Parliament, the CEA produced a document called "On the Unalterable Good of Marriage and the Family." This document defended marriage as an exclusively heterosexual union, offering arguments to reject the bill and appealing to "the conscience of our legislators so that, when deciding about such a grave question, they have these fundamental truths in mind, for the good of the homeland and her future generations" (Conferencia Episcopal Argentina 2010). Along with these declarations, the CEA also led a series of media protests from the principal representatives of the Catholic hierarchy in an attempt to impact public debate and prevent legal reform.

Although the Catholic Church continues to be a key actor in defense of a traditional sexual order, the forms in which this defense is presented allow us to see a complex web of actors, discourses and strategies that require new interpretive frameworks. When debating sexual and reproductive rights, we also see a renewed Catholic activism with diverse connections to traditional forms of influence, but with its own mutations and innovative strategies. One dimension of this activism is a growing shift toward secularism. Without ignoring the important presence of religious actors and arguments, it is also necessary to recognize the increasingly important role played by secular actors and arguments. This complicates our ability to understand the role of religion in sexual politics. In particular, it requires that we pay deeper attention to two previously mentioned characteristics of conservative Catholic activism: the increasing utilization of secular arguments by the Catholic hierarchy; and the growing importance of the self-defined "pro-life" or "pro-family" NGOs.

The religious hierarchy and secular arguments

One of the Catholic hierarchy's most notable interventions is a growing presence of secular justifications and arguments in its documents and public speeches. Although there continue to be references to the magisterium or the Bible that situate marriage as an element of divine creation or "not a purely human institution" (Catechism of the Catholic Church 1603), when the Catholic hierarchy intervenes in public debates it tends to privilege secular justifications. One major argument included in the CEA's 2010 document, following the Vatican's position, in reference to the need for complementarity between the sexes and the procreative potential that the sexual act should have, sustains the view that "the union of people of the same sex lacks the biological and anthropological elements of marriage and family" (Conferencia Episcopal Argentina 2010). This type of reasoning aligned well with the Catholic hierarchy's public manifestations that tended to associate homosexuality with promiscuity, unhappiness, health risks and violent conduct, among other characteristics presented as threats to social order (Morán Faundes and Vaggione 2012).

Along these lines, one of the Church's central positions concerns the defense of the child's interests as superior to all others. Documents from the Vatican and the CEA insist that the absence of sexual binarism creates obstacles to the normal development of children who are eventually integrated into these unions. In this sense, a law that permits same-sex marriage "does not only imply subjecting the children to grave risks, but also it could affect their normal emotional development . . . and the healthy development of their future sexuality."[9] The reference to supporting scientific documentation of the risks to children is one of the most repeated arguments, carrying the most symbolic weight (Morán Faundes and Vaggione 2012).

Another recurring line of argument emphasizes legal justifications to oppose recognizing the rights of same-sex couples. In connection with the Vatican's documents, the Argentine Catholic hierarchy affirms that differential legal treatment does not necessarily imply discrimination. The CEA's document, for example, states that the exclusion of same-sex couples from the right to marriage does not entail, as the sexual diversity movement argued, an act of unjust discrimination, because "to validate a real difference is not to discriminate. Nature does not discriminate when it makes us man or woman" (Conferencia Episcopal Argentina 2010). Along with this argument the Catholic hierarchy also holds that constitutional norms and international treaties prevent any legal reform. The CEA (2009), for example, maintains that various international documents, like the Universal Declaration of Human Rights, demand: "Men and women of full age, without any limitation due to race, nationality or religion, have the right to marry and to found a family."[10] In another document the CEA affirms that heterosexuality is not only required for the institution of marriage but also "protected by the National Constitution" (Conferencia Episcopal Argentina 2010).

These shifts have implied the growing presence of legal reasoning and scientific research and information on the part of religious actors. When the rights of same-sex couples are debated, scientific research and information are circulated to justify the inappropriateness of such rights.[11] In Argentina, a large part of this research was publicized in a report produced by the Universidad Austral, sponsored by Opus Dei, and published one month before the Senate vote on the same-sex marriage bill.[12] These arguments, while visible at the national level, are part of a strategy imposed by the Vatican that convenes research centers, universities and intellectuals to "place themselves at the service of a new culture of life by offering serious and well documented contributions, capable of commanding general respect and interest by reason of their merit" (*Evangelium Vitae* 1995). Beyond the veracity of the arguments and research, it is important to note that there is a strong shift toward the secular inherent in the Catholic hierarchy's interventions in sexual politics.

There was nevertheless a notable exception to the Church's strategic use of secular arguments. Several days before the final parliamentary debate, Jorge Bergoglio (current Pope and then Cardinal) circulated a letter in which he held that the bill was not just a political struggle, but rather a tool of the "destructive attempt on God's plan." The letter states: "Here also is the envy of the Devil, by which sin entered into the world, which cunningly seeks to destroy the image of God: man and woman receive the mandate to grow, multiply and subdue the earth."[13] Bergoglio's intervention represents a reactionary, fundamentalist discourse compared to other discursive constructions that emphasize scientific research and legal reasoning.

The type of expressions Bergoglio utilized, like the association of a legal proposal with a devil's plan, alienated certain sectors that had once identified with the official position of the Catholic Church. During the parliamentary debate, some self-identified Catholic senators distanced themselves from the words of their Church's highest representative (Vaggione 2011b). During the Senate debate, for example, Senator Alfredo Martínez said: "I've felt embarrassed by the words of he who should be my pastor, or rather, Monsignor Bergoglio. It seems to me that to suggest that the demon's envy is what wants to destroy God and what is within this bill, doesn't correspond to what an evangelist should be." It is difficult to evaluate how much the letter damaged the Church's position, but certainly the polemical change in strategy and discursive register left potential allies in an uncomfortable position. This exception, and the negative reaction it generated, shows not just that the secular shift is a strategy favored by Catholic activism, but also that it is potentially more effective when opposing sexual and reproductive rights.

NGOs in defense of religious doctrine

Another relevant factor that became visible during the equal marriage debate involved the complexity and heterogeneity of actors who accompanied the Catholic hierarchy in opposing the bill. The presence of evangelical sectors, for example, was notable, especially the perspectives of the extreme biblical conservatives (Wynarczyk 2009). These sectors participated in the public debate as well as calling citizens to mobilize in the streets (Jones and Vaggione 2012). A kind of "patriarchal ecumenism" (Vuola 2009) characterized the behavior of the Catholic and evangelical hierarchies; sectors that disagreed about diverse issues (above all in contexts in which Catholicism enjoys privileges denied to other religious traditions) united forces and agendas in common opposition to sexual and reproductive rights. Religious pluralism thus does not necessarily imply a diversity of positions with respect to sexual order; rather it can imply, as was the case here, the coordination of conjoined action to confront a "common enemy." Sexual and reproductive rights constituted a threat that generated once-improbable pacts and alliances.

In addition to the religious hierarchy, the presence of "pro-family" or "pro-life" nongovernmental organizations is particularly significant for our purposes. These NGOs have grown in importance as part of the strategy to resist sexual and reproductive rights.[14] In the case of Catholicism, it is important to consider the case of Human Life International, founded in the 1980s in the United States in reaction to the decriminalization of abortion. The organization opened chapters in different countries of the region; in the middle of the 1990s there were 18 such chapters in Latin America (González Ruiz 2005: 51).

In Argentina the existence of groups and associations defending the Catholic doctrine can be traced back to the beginning of the twentieth century (Morán Faundes 2013). However, the process of creation of "pro-life" and "pro-family" NGOs intensified during the 1990s, with the incorporation of sexual and reproductive rights into national agendas (Sgro Ruata *et al.* 2011; Morán Faundes 2013). These NGOs are heterogeneous, but in general tend to be strongly motivated by religious beliefs. Some expressly identify with the Catholic tradition (even in their names), whereas others position themselves as ecumenical and/or not religious, although their members share a strong religious affiliation. The initiatives that these NGOs have taken to combat the entrance of sexual and reproductive rights are notable. One prime example is their use of the judiciary as a strategy to resist or overturn the recognition of sexual and reproductive rights. In this sense, they have been successful in using the courts to generate jurisprudence that makes it difficult to establish rights that expand liberty and sexual diversity.[15]

These NGOs played an important role in opposing rights for same-sex couples. In 2010, numerous organizations came together with the concrete goal of intervening in the debate. This effervescence of organizations marks the importance of civil society as an arena for the organization and preparation of agendas defined by conservative Catholic activism. The level of institutionalization of these NGOs varied, from those known formally to those that only existed virtually. Along with the Catholic hierarchy and the evangelical churches found in the Association of Evangelical Churches in Argentina (ACIERA),[16] these organizations were central in mobilizing citizens to protest against "equal marriage" (Jones and Vaggione 2012). These NGOs were also highly visible during the intermediary and parliamentary debates. In the media as well as in Parliament, there was a constant presence of people who articulated their opposition to the proposed law while representing these NGOs (Sgro Ruata 2014). At the discursive level, their arguments coincide with those of the Catholic hierarchy. Their primary arguments include the necessity of the complementary and binary sexes for reproduction, the importance of conserving legal reforms, and the pathology of homosexual desire (Morán Faundes and Vaggione 2012).

Although the Catholic hierarchy has played a central role in resisting the sexual politics of the feminist and sexual diversity movements, it is also important to consider the increasing protagonism of the role played by "pro-life" and "pro-family" organizations in conservative Catholic activism. As with the use of secular arguments, this chapter does not argue that these are completely new strategies for the Catholic Church, but rather that they have been crucial in reactive politicization of the religious hierarchy with regard to sexual and reproductive rights (Vaggione 2005). In Latin America, the Catholic Church is an institution with power over the State that often undermines democratic rules, but it is also an institution that can adapt and mutate to achieve an impact. Conservative Catholic activism reinforces and simultaneously transcends the Catholic Church and the religious mandate by putting actors and discourses in motion, blurring the boundaries between the religious and the secular.

Conclusions

The feminist and sexual diversity movements have generated a new phase in sexual politics by criticizing a regime of reproductive governance in which an array of historical actors "use legislative controls, economic inducements, moral injunctions, direct coercion, and ethical incitements to produce, monitor, and control reproductive behaviors and practices" (Morgan and Roberts 2012: 243). One component of this phase is the growing legitimacy of sexual and reproductive rights as a strategy to dismantle restrictive legal regimens and generate public policies that democratize the sexual order. Within the distinct dimensions that characterize this set of rights is the need to dismantle models that legitimize sexuality through reproduction. The legal status of same-sex couples, the analytic focus of this chapter, is one relevant dimension that recently began to redefine the institution of matrimony by eradicating the complementarity of the sexes, and along with it biological reproduction, as a defining dimension.

As this chapter has analyzed, sexual and reproductive rights reveal the complex links between religion and politics in contemporary democracies. The debate about the regulation of sexuality and reproduction implies, in many contexts, dismantling the influence of religious institutions in politics and culture. In Latin America, the feminist and sexual diversity movements found the Catholic Church and its complex influence to be the principal obstacles to advancing public policy that would legitimize the autonomy between sexuality and reproduction. In this influence over sexual politics, the actions of the Catholic Church are commonly viewed in tension with the system of democracy. Examples of Church actions that could be considered "outside" of democratic logic include the existence of formal privileges from which the Church benefits, a clientelistic political culture between the government and Catholic hierarchy, and tactics such as threatening those who support sexual and reproductive rights with excommunication. Nonetheless, as this chapter has explained, the Church also participates within the spaces inhabited by the same democratic system. In recent years a conservative Catholic activism, in addition to reclaiming the right of the Catholic hierarchy to participate in public debates, has implemented a series of political intervention strategies in response to a new temporality opened by sexual and reproductive rights.

Although the Catholic hierarchy continues to be a central actor in defense of a reproductive sexual order, a political mechanism has developed alongside that includes a broad range of actors, arguments and intervention strategies. In this way, conservative Catholic activism overcomes any dichotomous thinking on the connection between religion and politics. To understand the hierarchy's actions in different countries, it is necessary to track the principal instructions, strategies and discourses generated by the Vatican. Although the debates generally occur within a national arena, it is the Vatican that designs the principal forms of public intervention by the Catholic Church. Furthermore, the analysis permits the observation of the ways in which the Catholic Church's participation in sexual politics displaces the religious–secular dichotomy. Although the Catholic hierarchy and its appeal to discourses based on the Bible and the religious order remain relevant, its reaction to the feminist and sexual diversity movements generates, among other questions, a strong shift toward using secular actors and justifications as a form of resistance. Finally, although not explicitly addressed in this chapter, the same-sex marriage debate made clear the heterogeneous politics that characterize Catholicism: in addition to the well-known distance between the hierarchy and its followers with respect to sexual morality, distinct Catholic sectors used their religious identification to support the legal reform (Vaggione 2012). For example, during the debate priests critical of the magistrate publicly protested in favor of same-sex marriage, thus showing that different sectors, including some parliamentarians, supported the bill from a religious perspective.

Latin American sexual politics are characterized not only by the impact of the feminist and sexual diversity movements, which have amplified the public debate regarding sexuality, but also by the complex and diverse reactions of the Catholic hierarchy and its allied sectors in defense of a hierarchical sexual order. Public policy in the region depends in large part on how this antagonism is resolved, which (for the moment) has had diverse impacts in different countries. While some countries have managed to reduce the Catholic Church's impact on law and public policy by extending the applicability of sexual and reproductive rights, governments in other countries have reinforced their defense of the Catholic hierarchy's position, particularly in Central America. The region is characterized by a strong heterogeneity; some countries recognize sex education, rights for same-sex couples or access to abortion, while in others the defense of life at conception or heterosexuality as the only family tie is the main point of agreement between governments and Catholic hierarchies.

The election of a Latin American Pope during this process raises distinct questions about the future of sexual politics in the region. On one hand, Pope Francis I has intensified the religious institution's symbolic power over governments. The presence of a global leader who grips governments and citizens, increasing the political impact of the Catholic Church, is added to the insufficient autonomy that characterizes the majority of Latin American states. For some analysts, on the other hand, this election implies a more democratic conduct that is less obsessed with sexuality. The Pope's diverse discourses and attitudes have been interpreted along these lines, although they have still not converted into significant change with respect to sexual morals. The principal challenge for this new Pope is the Vatican's disposal to unravel the religious and political machinery that conditions the design and implementation of public policies that guarantee sexual and reproductive freedom and autonomy in an economically unequal region.

Notes

1 In many cases these NGOs have formal status recognized by the Economic and Social Council (ECOSOC).

2 And then every three years in different cities (the last two were Mexico City in 2009 and Milan in 2012).

3 "A special task falls to Catholic intellectuals, who are called to be present and active in the leading centres where culture is formed, in schools and universities, in places of scientific and technological research, of artistic creativity and of the study of man. Allowing their talents and activity to be nourished by the living force of the Gospel, they ought to place themselves at the service of a new culture of life by offering serious and well documented contributions, capable of commanding general respect and interest by reason of their merit" (John Paul II, 98, *Evangelium Vitae*, 1995).

4 John Paul II, Motu Proprio *Vitae Mysterium* (11 February 1994), 4: *AAS* 86 (1994), 386–7.

5 There is disagreement within the sexual diversity movements on the importance of this legal reform; for example, from a queer theory perspective same-sex marriage represents a conservative demand.

6 See Kane (2008) for an analysis of the role of the Catholic Church in the politics of abortion in three Latin American countries.

7 A document entitled "Letter to the Bishops of the Catholic Church on the Pastoral Care of Homosexual People" (1986) affirms "Although the particular inclination of the homosexual person is not a sin, it is a more or less strong tendency toward an intrinsic moral evil; and thus the inclination itself must be seen as an objective disorder."

8 Dignity was founded in Los Angeles, United States, in 1969 with the purpose of integrating "gay Catholics" into the Church.
9 Monseñor Marcelo Martorell, Bishop of Puerto Iguazú, 17 June 2010, in Agencia Informativa Católica Argentina (AICA), http://www.aicaold.com.ar/docs_blanco.php?id=422 (accessed 8 June 2014).
10 The Universal Declaration of Human Rights, article 16.
11 A similar situation took place in Spain when same-sex marriage was debated in 2005 (Vaggione 2006).
12 Universidad Austral, June 2010, *Matrimonio homosexual y adopción por parejas del mismo sexo: Informe de estudios científicos y jurídicos de otros países*.
13 Jorge Bergoglio, 2010, "Carta a las Carmelitas," Boletín Eclesiástico del Arzobispado de Buenos Aires, Núm. 159, Año LII), translated by the author.
14 This phenomenon recognized as an antecedent the reaction, in the 1970s, to abortion decriminalization due to Roe vs Wade (1973).
15 In Argentina, Portal de Belén is a leading conservative case on the debate about the beginning of life and restricting access to emergency contraception.
16 La Asociación Cristiana de Iglesias Evangélicas de la República Argentina.

References

Buss, D. and Herman, D. (2003) *Globalizing Family Values: The Christian Right in International Politics*, Minneapolis: University of Minnesota Press.
Butler, Jennifer S. (2006) *Born Again: The Christian Right Globalized*, London: Pluto Press.
CEA (Comisión Ejecutiva de la Conferencia Episcopal Argentina) (2009) *Sobre los proyectos de ley de matrimonio homosexual*, Declaration, November, http://www.aicaold.com.ar//index2.php?pag=ceaComisionEjecutiva091105 (accessed 6 June 2014).
Conferencia Episcopal Argentina (2010) *Sobre el bien inalterable del matrimonio y la familia*, Declaración de la 99ª Asamblea Plenaria de la Conferencia Episcopal Argentina, April, http://www.aica.org/docs_blanco.php?id=226 (accessed 6 June 2014).
Congregation for the Doctrine of the Faith (1992) *Considerations Concerning the Response to Legislative Proposals on the Non-Discrimination of Homosexual Persons*, http://www.vatican.va/roman_curia/congregations/cfaith/documents/rc_con_cfaith_doc_19920724_homosexual-persons_en.html (accessed 8 June 2014).
Congregation for the Doctrine of the Faith (2003) *Considerations Regarding Proposals to Give Legal Recognition to Unions between Homosexual Persons*, June, http://www.vatican.va/roman_curia/congregations/cfaith/documents/rc_con_cfaith_doc_20030731_homosexual-unions_sp.html (accessed 8 June 2014).
González Ruiz, Edgar (2005), *Cruces y sombras: Perfiles del conservadurismo en América Latina*, www.letraese.org.mx/cruces_y_sombras.pdf (accessed 8 June 2014).
Jones, Daniel and Vaggione, Juan Marco (2012) 'Los vínculos entre religión y política a la luz del debate sobre matrimonio para parejas del mismo sexo en Argentina', *Civitas*, 12 (3), 522–37.
John Paul II (1994) *Discurso en el Encuentro Mundial con las Familias: A las Familias y Peregrinos en la Plaza de San Pedro*, October, http://www.vatican.va/holy_father//john_paul_ii/speeches/1994/october/documents/hf_jp-ii_spe_19941008_incontro-famiglie_sp.html (accessed 8 June 2014).
Kane, Gillian (2008) 'Abortion Law Reform in Latin America: Lessons for Advocacy', *Gender and Development*, Special Issue: Reproductive Rights: Current Challenges, 16 (2), 361–75.
Miller, Alice (2010) *Sexuality and Human Rights Discussion Paper*, Versoix, Switzerland: International Council on Human Rights Policy.
Morán Faundes, José Manuel (2013) 'Vidas que constriñen cuerpos: La política sexual y el discurso de la vida de los sectores "Pro-Vida" en Argentina', master's thesis, Centro de Estudios Avanzados (CEA), Universidad Nacional de Córdoba.
Morán Faundes, José Manuel and Vaggione, Juan Marco (2012) 'Ciencia y religión (hétero)sexuadas: El discurso científico del activismo católico conservador sobre la sexualidad en Argentina y Chile', *Contemporanea: Revista de Sociologia da UFSCar*, 2, 159–85.
Morgan, Lynn and Roberts, Elizabeth (2012) 'Reproductive Governance in Latin America', *Anthropology and Medicine*, 19 (2), 241–54.
Pecheny, Mario and de la Dehesa, Rafael (2011) 'Sexualidades y políticas en América Latina: Un esbozo para la discusión', in Sonia Corrêa and Richard Parker (eds), *Sexualidade e política na América Latina: Histórias, interseçoes e paradoxos*, Río de Janeiro: Sexuality Policy Watch, pp. 31–79.

Sgro Ruata, Candelaria (2014) 'Sexualidad: Significaciones y tensiones en el espacio público contemporáneo: Un estudio de la oposición al "matrimonio igualitario" en Argentina', doctoral thesis for Doctorado en Estudios Sociales de América Latina, Universidad Nacional de Córdoba.

Sgro Ruata, Candelaria, Rabbia, Hugo and Iosa, Tomas (2011) *El Debate sobre el Matrimonio Igualitario en Córdoba: Actores*, estrategias y discursos, Córdoba: Ferrerya Editor.

Sweetman, Caroline (2008) 'Editorial', *Gender and Development*, Special Issue: Reproductive Rights: Current Challenges, 16 (2), 219–26.

UNFPA (1994) *ICPD Programme of Action*, New York: UNFPA.

Vaggione, Juan Marco (2005) 'Reactive Politicization and Religious Dissidence: The Political Mutations of the Religious in Social Theory and Practice', *Social Theory and Practice*, 31 (2), 233–55.

Vaggione, Juan Marco (2006) 'Nuevas formas del activismo religioso: La Iglesia Católica frente al reconocimiento legal de las parejas del mismo sexo', *Orientaciones: Revista de Homosexualidades* (Fundación Triángulo, Madrid), 10, 123–38.

Vaggione, Juan Marco (2011a) 'Texto Panorámico: Sexualidad, religión y política en América Latina', in Sonia Corrêa and Richard Parker (eds), *Sexualidade e política na América Latina: Histórias, interseçoes e paradoxos*, Río de Janeiro: Sexuality Policy Watch, http://www.sxpolitics.org/pt/wp-content/uploads/2011/07/dialogo-la_total_final.pdf (accessed 8 June 2014).

Vaggione, Juan Marco (2011b) 'Sexual Rights and Religion: Same-Sex Marriage and Lawmakers' Catholic Identity in Argentina', *University of Miami Law Review*, 65, 935–54.

Vaggione, Juan Marco (2012) 'La "cultura de la vida": Desplazamientos estratégicos del activismo católico conservador frente a los derechos sexuales y reproductivos', *Religiao e Sociedade*, 32, 57–80.

Vaggione, Juan Marco (2013) 'Families beyond Heteronormativity', *Ius Gentium: Comparative Perspectives on Law and Justice*, 24, 233–77.

Vuola, Elina (2009) 'Patriarchal Ecumenism, Feminism and Women's Religious Experiences in Latin America', in Hanna Herzog and Ann Braude (eds), *Gendering Religion and Politics: Untangling Modernities*, New York: Palgrave Macmillan, pp. 217–38.

Wynarczyk, Hilario (2009) *Ciudadanos de dos mundos: El movimiento evangélico en la vida pública argentina 1980–2001*, Buenos Aires: Unsam Edita.

PART 4

South Asia

13

RELIGION AND DEVELOPMENT IN INDIA AND PAKISTAN

An overview

Emma Tomalin

Introduction

Across South Asia[1] religious actors (both individuals and organizations) have always played an important role in social and welfare activities, long before the emergence of the contemporary development project following the end of the Second World War. Indigenous mechanisms and institutions supported by religious bodies, providing basic services such as health, education and the distribution of water and donations of food, have been an important part of the social landscape of South Asia for centuries, and religious actors have continued to contribute towards these welfare and development-related activities since the advent of the post-colonial era (1947 for India, Pakistan and Bangladesh, and 1948 for Sri Lanka). However, as Bompani also notes in Chapter 7 with respect to Africa, western secularist and modernist ideas influenced narratives at independence. These predicted that, as the newly created nations developed and became economically stable, religion would dwindle and eventually disappear. Indeed for the newly elected and often western-educated elites that took up roles in the governments of countries such as India, Pakistan and Sri Lanka, religion as it was practised by the masses was typically viewed as superstitious, backward and likely to stand in the way of modernization and development. Like many new states emerging from colonial rule across the globe at this time, these countries initially adopted state-led models of economic development, with a strong leaning towards modernization and secularization. It is no surprise then that, upon separation from the British Empire in 1947, the founders of each of these states were committed to secularism. Despite the high levels of personal and communal religiosity in each, religion was to have no formal place in nation building and development. India[2] and Sri Lanka have both formally remained secular republics, while Pakistan has taken a different trajectory, becoming an Islamic republic by 1956, yet in each setting religious forces have been impossible to contain, with uneven and complex outcomes for development.

Religious actors do not operate in a vacuum, and the ways in which and the extent to which they can publicly express their faith, with concrete effects, are shaped in unexpected and unpredictable ways by the political settings within which they are situated. My aim in this chapter is to examine some of the ways in which religious actors in South Asia have engaged with social welfare and development-related activities in different periods, against the backdrop of differing political configurations between religions, the state and society. Given the size of the region and its immense political, religious, cultural and economic diversity, I will focus upon the two most demographically and economically important states: India and Pakistan. Not only does a shared colonial past link these countries, but the events at independence in 1947 have continued to reverberate in the relationships between religion, nationhood and development in each ever since. They are also the focus of the two chapters that follow, and one of my aims here is to provide context for those discussions.

The discussion will be divided into three main sections. First, I will provide some background on 'religion and development' activity in India and Pakistan in the pre-colonial and colonial periods, suggesting that religious traditions in both settings have long been associated with various types of welfare activities and philanthropic work that pre-date the emergence of development as a global concern, as well as the rise of the 'FBO' in the 2000s (see Occhipinti, Chapter 22). I will then explore the impact of colonialism upon religious configurations and activities in the region.

Second, I will examine the effects of independence on 'religion and development' by briefly describing the development strategies pursued as the new nations were formed and discussing the roles or responses of religious actors. In particular, I will present two case studies – one from Pakistan and one from India – that demonstrate some of the ways in which religious actors' engagement with development has been shaped by the political relationships between religions and the state in each country. These case studies will be preceded by an account of the relationships between religion, politics and development in each setting. What these case studies demonstrate is that, despite 'the triumph of the secular state at independence' (Jodhka 2008; Singh 2011: 17), the crisis of governance that affected both countries in the 1980s and 1990s 'witnessed the erosion or significant weakening of the political formations dating from the end of colonial rule', creating new spaces for religious formations (Singh 2011: 57). These included religious political parties and identity-based movements linked to religion. Religion never disappeared in South Asia, as proponents of the secularization thesis had predicted. Instead, during the 1980s and 1990s religious actors were given a new lease of life in ways that mirrored the so-called 'rise of religion' globally. This has continued into the 2000s, not least with the 'turn to religion' in some parts of the international development project which has included increasing recognition of and support for religious organizations as important civil society actors.

Third, I will shift the focus to look at the impact of the global development industry (the emergence of which more or less coincided with independence) upon economic development policies in India and Pakistan, especially the impact of the rolling back of the state with economic liberalization, which has facilitated renewed salience of religious actors with respect to welfare and development.

A history of religion and development in India and Pakistan[3]

Religion and social welfare in the pre-colonial and colonial eras

While academics and development agencies have only recently become interested in the role of religion in development, the historical context of 'faith-based' social service in South Asia is important to understanding its present-day form. All the religious traditions in the region have teachings about helping and giving to the poor, so that acts of welfare and philanthropy are encouraged or even expected. For instance, in India the teachings of the Vedas and later Hindu texts encourage charity and community service (Mujundar 1961; Tomalin 2009), while the Buddhist monastic orders, which were established from the sixth century BCE, have always engaged in service delivery to the poor (Tomalin 2009). In addition, by the eighth century BCE, Islam had arrived in South Asia, bringing new forms of philanthropy through mosques, *madrasas* and *khanqahs*,[4] as well as the establishment of *waqfs* (religious endowments, usually denoting land or buildings for religious or charitable use) to make the above sustainable (Iqbal and Siddiqui 2008: 16). Within Islam, *zakat*, a form of religiously mandated charity and the third of Islam's 'five pillars', involves the payment of alms for the purpose of distribution to the poor.[5]

Christians and Sikhs were also involved in forms of social service. While it is believed that the first Christian missionary to have come to India was St Thomas the Apostle in 52 BCE, missionary activity did not become established until much later, from the late fifteenth century onwards, with the arrival of Portuguese missionaries. Christian missions were later involved in setting up schools and other social services, such as health care, as part of their missionary activities. Sikhism, founded in the fifteenth century in the Punjab, has from its earliest days provided support to poorer community members, most notably through the *langar* (community kitchen), which provides free meals to people regardless of their caste (Tatla 2008: 16).

By 1600, the British East India Company had gained a foothold in the region, marking the beginnings of the British colonial period. From 1600 to 1858, the British presence in India was by way of the East India Company, but following the Indian Mutiny in 1857 the British Crown assumed direct control over India, until independence in 1947. During the period of British rule, voluntary organizations were institutionalized and laws regarding the registration and regulation of philanthropic and voluntary organizations passed in order to formalize, legalize and control their activities (Tomalin and Leurs 2012). Both religious and secular non-profit organizations proliferated during the British Raj. Many aimed to protect the interests of different religious and cultural groups in the face of changes brought about by colonialism. Their establishment was also made possible by the emergence of an educated middle class (Bano and Nair 2007). For instance, the Societies Registration Act was passed in 1860, primarily to regulate the voluntary associations that the British blamed for the Mutiny. Many currently active faith-based organizations (FBOs) emerged during the colonial period, and the spread of colonial modernity was accompanied by an increased presence of religion in the public sphere (van der Veer 2002: 179).

Initially, the British East India Company had been reluctant to allow Christian missionaries free rein to enter the country, but by 1813, under the Charter Act, Christian missions were allowed to work openly. Although the churches were not directly patronized by the colonial state, their activities, particularly in the field of education (without literacy, people were unable to read the Bible), expanded considerably with the establishment of colonial power in the subcontinent. To serve their mission, as well as from a desire to help the poor, missionaries also established hospitals, dispensaries, orphanages, hostels, infirmaries and seminaries, many of which have continued to operate since independence.

Apart from the growing strength of the churches during this period, the colonial presence had an impact on 'indigenous' religious traditions. In order to understand and control various forms of social life in India, the colonial state sought to categorize and draw boundaries around religions (and other types of group). As a result, for the first time people came to see themselves as members of discrete religious traditions, whereas previously the boundaries between the religions had been fluid (Oberoi 1994). Alongside this, various forms of religious revivalism emerged from within Islam, Hinduism and Sikhism.

For instance, revivalist forms of Islam became popular after the failure of the 1857 Mutiny, which led to the suppression of many Muslim leaders by the colonial state. Moreover, the displacement of Muslim rule by the British led to changes in the operation of *madrasas* and Sufi shrines (Bano and Nair 2007: 26). With the demise of the Mughal Empire, the support base for these dwindled, not least because of changes made by the British to *Madad-i-Ma'ash* (revenue-free land), which had sustained these institutions of Muslim education and learning (Bano and Nair 2007). The revivalist movements were both a response to British cultural and political hegemony and a reaction to Christian missionary criticism of Islam. They also aimed at protecting Muslim interests from western-educated Hindus, who were rapidly gaining indigenous elite status. One of the most significant was the Deobandi movement, which emerged following the setting up of the Darul Uloom Deoband Madrasa in 1866. This *madrasa* became an important centre for both learning and political organization during the struggle for independence (Metcalf 1978; Qasmi 2001: 17). Under its administrative and ideological guidance, a network of *madrasas* was forged across the subcontinent. These catered to the needs of those who could not afford education, especially in rural areas, contrasting with the earlier role of *madrasas* in Muslim India, when they were elite higher-learning establishments producing civil servants and judicial officials (Nair 2009).

Sikh and Hindu groups similarly became more clearly defined and politicized during this period, including revivalist groups, such as the Ad Dharm movement (representing Dalit Sikhs), which were largely confined to the Punjab (Oberoi 1994; Mahajan and Jodhka 2009; Jodhka and Kumar 2010), and reform movements within Hinduism such as the Brahmo Samaj (established 1828), Arya Samaj (1875), Ramakrishna Mission (1897), Satyashodhak Samaj (1873) and Indian National Social Conference (1887). These Hindu movements were influenced by modern western ideas of equality, liberty and rationality. Reformers campaigned against social evils such as child marriage and polygamy, and pressed for women's rights. In addition, the example of Christian missionaries' activities in education, health, relief and the welfare of poor and neglected sections of society were catalytic in spurring development-related activities by some of these Hindu groups. For instance, the Ramakrishna Mission was founded in 1897 by Swami Vivekananda, one of the important nineteenth-century 'Hindu reformers' and a disciple of the Bengali saint Sri Ramakrishna. On the basis of Ramakrishna's religious teachings, a successful welfare organization was established, offering services that included literacy projects, agricultural extension services and disaster relief, and which now has branches throughout the world. Vivekananda was one of the first Hindu teachers to travel to the west, not only to attract westerners to Hinduism but also to gain their financial support for his 'development' work in India. For the Ramakrishna Mission, social service is a *sadhana*, a religious path, based upon the (spiritual) realization that every person is divine, meaning that to serve others is considered to be a way of serving God (Miller 1999: 124).

Another important reformer at this time was the independence activist Mahatma Gandhi, and it is fitting – as we move to discuss the post-colonial era – also to mention him here. His combination of Hindu spirituality with a lifestyle model led him to identify what he regarded as crucial for the future of an independent India. In particular, he lacked trust in industrialization and capitalist expansion, promoting instead an economic system based upon the village system, with an emphasis on local production, traditional crafts and self-sufficiency. The image for an independent India that he favoured was that of a spinning wheel, which still appears on the Indian flag (Narayan 1970; Sharma 1997; Narendar 2002).[6] He was also a sharp critic of the idea of the partition of India and Pakistan.

Religion and development in the post-colonial era: setting the scene

Desai writes that 'the partition which occurred almost simultaneously with the independence of India and Pakistan meant that what was once an integrated economy, albeit with many local regional economies, was sundered into two countries and three regions' (2005: 271). Following independence from Britain in 1947, which was accompanied by the partition of

Pakistan from India (followed by the separation of West Pakistan and East Pakist
Pakistan and Bangladesh, in 1971 after the Bangladesh Liberation War), each st
and implemented policies for economic growth and social development. India
development programme in its first five-year plan in 1951, based on 'import substi
trialization',[7] founded on a belief that 'dynamic industrialisation would help to trigger off an
equally dynamic development in the field of agriculture' (Rothermund 2003: 127). In choosing
a 'mixed economy' as the basis for development, the 'state was not only to provide a regulatory
mechanism for the economy and markets to function in a manner that would bring growth and
prosperity, but was also to invest in building economic infrastructure and industrial production'
(Jodhka 2008: 8). The second five-year plan made it clear that increased incomes and improved
distribution of wealth were expected to be the key to raising standards of living. By providing
economic opportunities and social services, including education and health, it was anticipated
that society would prosper (2008: 8). As Jodhka tells us, Jawaharlal Nehru, the first prime minister of India, chose a brand of modernization which, according to Parekh, had seven interlinked
goals: 'national unity, parliamentary democracy, industrialisation, socialism, development of a
scientific temper, secularism and non-alignment' (2008: 8). Thus, religion had no place in this
developing economy, and the new political elite were 'suspicious of religious organisations and
their place in modern India' (2008: 9).

In 1947, unlike India, Pakistan had virtually no industry and was even more dismally underdeveloped. Not only was the country initially separated by thousands of miles, with West
Pakistan to the north and East Pakistan further south, but also, with partition, 'Pakistan lost its
bankers, merchants, shopkeepers, entrepreneurs and clerks – the wheels came off the machinery of the state' (Haq 2010: 145). As in India, a series of Soviet-inspired centralized economic
development plans began to be drafted, but owing to political unrest and shake-ups in the government the first five-year development plan was not completed until 1956. However, as Desai
tells us, 'although Planning in Pakistan started a bit later [than in India] and was not as articulated
as Indian planning until the 1960s, the overall policy in Pakistan was the same' (2005: 272). The
objectives of the first five-year plan were (Hussain 1956: 2):

1   to raise the national income and the standard of living of the people;
2   to improve the balance of payments of the country by increasing exports and by pro-
    duction of substitutes for imports;
3   to increase the opportunities for useful employment in the country;
4   to make steady progress in providing social services: housing, education, health and
    social welfare; and
5   to increase rapidly the rate of development, especially in East Pakistan and other rela-
    tively less developed areas.

Thus, the early years of the Pakistani state were politically tumultuous, with periods of democracy followed by periods of military rule, a pattern which has continued to the present day.
The founder of the country, Mohammad Ali Jinnah, had envisioned that Pakistan would be a
democratic secular state, as he famously made clear after partition in his first Presidential Address
to the Constituent Assembly (11 August 1947):

> Now I think we should keep that in front of us as our ideal, and you will find that
> in course of time Hindus would cease to be Hindus, and Muslims would cease to be
> Muslims, not in the religious sense, because that is the personal faith of each individual,
> but in the political sense as citizens of the State.[8]

However, by the time the constitution was written in 1956, Jinnah had died and Islamist forces insisted on an Islamic constitution and the creation of the Islamic Republic of Pakistan.

Colonial attitudes towards religion and the reverberations of partition have left a lasting impact upon the ways in which religious actors express themselves in contemporary South Asia. In both settings, styles of religious nationalism, or 'fundamentalism', which have their roots in the colonial period, have been able to survive and flourish. In both settings, conservative and illiberal religio-political parties and related organizations also play a role in humanitarian, welfare and development activities, even though they typically adhere to goals which do not easily map on to those of the secular development project (e.g. with respect to the pursuit of gender equality or the rights of minorities).[9] Below I will explore this with respect to the rise of the Muttahida Majlis-e-Amal (MMA, a coalition of religious political parties), which was successful in elections in the then North-West Frontier Province (NWFP) (now Khyber Pakhtunkhwa) in Pakistan and was in power there between 2002 and 2008.

However, the impact of religion in each post-colonial setting cannot simply be equated with the emergence of conservative religious political parties and their related organizations – the picture is more complex. With reference to India, I will explore the ways in which, in addition to the rise of religious political parties, religious identity movements have also flourished and have been able to take advantage of secular political structures to strengthen their cause. In particular, I will examine the emergence of the neo-Buddhist movement amongst Dalit groups in Maharashtra and the ways in which conversion from Hinduism to Buddhism has been seen as a way of escaping the caste system and improving converts' economic and social status.

Post-colonial Pakistan: religion, politics and development in an Islamic republic

Before we turn to the example of the coalition of religious political parties, the MMA, it is first necessary to provide an overview of relationships between religion, politics and development in Pakistan. Pakistan was originally established as a secular state for Muslims, as noted above, but this status was compromised in 1956, when a constitution was adopted that named the country the Islamic Republic of Pakistan, a democratic state based on Islamic principles. Furthermore, the constitution provided that the head of state was to be a Muslim, and no law was permitted to contradict the Quran and Sunnah (Waseem and Mufti, 2009: 25). While other religious traditions were permitted to exist and to establish their own organizational forms, many religious minorities have felt marginalized over the decades (and even victimized) by the dominance of Islam and by the rise of Islamist views in the country. Islamic political parties were permitted under the new constitution and have been allowed to continue under periods of military rule owing to their popular appeal. Following the death of Jinnah, the hopes for a secular Pakistan were undermined by the pressure of 'the traditionalist *ulama* [who] came to play a very major role in politics after independence in 1947 because of their mass appeal' (Ansari 2011: 48). They were represented by religious political parties that 'soon began demanding the introduction of an Islamic system in the country. To them, the notion of western parliamentary democracy was totally incompatible with the spirit of Islam' (2011: 48). Two of the most significant religious political parties were formed at this time, later became part of the MMA coalition and are still influential today: Jama'at-i-Islami (JI) was established in 1941 (led by Maulana Abul Ala Maududi) and Jamiat-i-Ulama-i-Islam (JUI) in January 1948 (led by Maulana Shabbir Ahmed Usmani).

In 1958–71 Pakistan experienced its first period of military rule under the auspices of Ayub Khan, 'who was avowedly modernist and who justified his military coup as an effort to save the country from an Islamic takeover' (Waseem and Mufti 2009: 26). Haqqani argues that 'Ayab

Khan was not a secularist; neither was he averse to the notion of Pakistan having a state [Islamic] ideology' (2005: 41). Rather, he did not think much of traditionalist clerics (*ulema*) and instead wanted the state to undertake 'the function of religious interpretation and wanted a modernist Islamic ideology that would help him in "defense and security and development" and the "welding" of Pakistan's different races into a unified whole' (2005: 41). Thus, while in the first years of his rule he attempted to keep the *ulema* and religious parties out of politics, even banning the Jama'at-i-Islami at one point 'under a new law regulating political parties' (2005: 43) because it had joined up with 'secular parties opposed to military rule' (2005: 43), over time he shifted his approach. In particular, with the transition to democracy in 1965, he needed the support of religious forces to secure his election – the result, according to Shafqat (cited in Ansari 2011: 50), was that he increased the 'regime-legitimizing role of the Traditionalists and also facilitated the Islamization of politics'. One example of the laws his government passed was the West Pakistan Waqf Properties Ordinance of 1959, which enabled the state to take control of Muslim endowments and institutions, such as mosques and religious shrines. While this had the effect of reducing the flow of money to religious organizations, it also led to the setting up of independent faith-based voluntary associations and charities by custodians and followers of the shrines.

In 1971, the Pakistan People's Party (PPP) replaced the military government, under the leadership of Zulfiqar Ali Bhutto (1971–73), who began a vigorous process of nationalization, which 'eroded the institutional base of the modern component of civil society' (Qadeer 1997). Whereas the state and the faith-based sector had largely worked in tandem during the 1950s and 1960s, in the 1970s the state assumed a dominant role in the provision of social services (Iqbal and Siddiqui 2008: 19). Educational institutions set up by religious organizations, especially the churches, were nationalized, although they were largely returned in the 1980s during the next phase of military rule (1977–88) under General Zia ul Haq. While initially Haq stated that his intention was to govern briefly, to resolve disputes over the fairness of the general elections, within days of coming to power he initiated the introduction of *shar'iah* law (Haqqani 2005: 133). In fact, he 'went farthest in defining Pakistan as an Islamic state and unlike other Pakistani rulers . . . was not averse to assigning the ulema and religious parties a significant role in the affairs of the state' (2005: 132). 'Indeed [a]gainst the backdrop of [this] Islamization drive, alongside the Afghan war (1979–89) and the liberal flow of foreign funds, pre-existing Islamic [organizations] flourished' (Iqbal and Siddiqui 2008: 19). There was also a rise in the number of Islamist organizations with a sectarian or militant outlook. The close relationship between the state and religious (Muslim) organizations continued with Musharraf's military regime (2001–08), although against the backdrop of the 'war on terror' his government did become more ambivalent towards them. Indeed:

> a reversal in Pakistan's pro-Taliban policy, followed by Musharraf's alliance with the Bush administration in its war against terror after 9/11, led 26 religious groups to form the Pak-Afghan Defence Council. . . . On 17 June 2001, leaders of the six main Islamic parties decided that they would contest the next elections . . . [as part of a] six party electoral alliance known as the MMA.
>
> (Waseem and Mufti 2009: 35)

The development performance of religious political parties in Pakistan

In Pakistan the religious political parties have variously been against or for the governing regime: being 'Prone to electoral marginalization during periods of democratization, historically these parties have thrived under military regimes because of their ideology and capacity for street mobilization' (Singh 2011: 35). In 2002, the MMA was successful in the provincial and national elections, winning in NWFP and 'establishing a strong presence in Baluchistan, Sindh and the National Assembly' (2011: 35). It fought its campaign on a range of issues, but in NWFP shortly after the elections it pursued a policy of Islamization that included a range of restrictions in line with *shari'ah* law, such as: the banning of alcohol and gambling; the appointment of female doctors to treat women; interest-free banking; and *shari'ah*-compliant punishments (e.g. *rajm*, stoning to death) (Singh 2011: 36). The passing of the Shari'ah Bill (2003) entrenched these moves and, in order to establish an executive authority to enforce the process of Islamization, the Hasba (accountability) Bill (2006) was passed. This effectively created a 'parallel administrative structure with an ombudsman likened to a "Taleban style vice and virtue department"' (Khan 2003). Although the Pakistan Supreme Court eventually rejected both bills, 'in passing these measures the MMA contributed significantly to creating an atmosphere of intolerance and radical change, in which its opponents were regularly castigated as anti-Islamic' (Singh 2011: 36).

Waseem and Mufti carried out an analysis of the MMA's development initiatives in health care and education in three districts of the NWFP. Their findings suggest that 'the coalition lacked a clear vision of development and operated very much according to traditional patron–client networks in seeking to consolidate and extend its support base' (Waseem and Mufti 2009: 49; Singh 2011: 37). As well as the MMA's own policies and lack of experience of governing, positive achievements were constrained by its dependence on funding from the national government (and international agencies). In addition, the targeted recipients of the government's policies 'did not clearly represent the economically and socially disadvantaged' (Singh 2011: 45), because Islamization and maintaining its own electoral support were higher priorities than poverty reduction (Waseem and Mufti 2009: 51). The emphasis on creating an Islamic society also had an impact upon the MMA's approach to gender and women, with restrictions on girls' access to education, efforts to 'erase' women from public life, by preventing them from voting or holding office, and toleration of so-called 'honour killings' of women (Waseem and Mufti 2009: 53–4). Particular hostility was shown towards women's non-governmental organizations (NGOs), with the pursuit of 'an unrelenting vision of "separate development", in which conventional assumptions about gender and development were turned upside down' (Singh 2011: 47). In response to these measures and the MMA's limited development achievements, its support declined and it was defeated in the 2008 election.

Post-colonial India: religion, politics and development in a secular democracy

In contrast to Pakistan, the post-colonial Indian state hung on to its secularist values, which assumed that economic development and secularization go together. Although the historical specificities of South Asia and the hold that religion had over the people of the region were recognized, the political leaders of independent India aspired to a modern nation with a scientific and secular outlook (Jodhka and Bora 2009: 3). Secularism was 'propagated by Nehru as the cement to hold together the newly independent India' (Desai 2005: 234). The Indian constitution provided a strict mandate not to favour one religion over another, in a bid to provide all citizens with equal status. It was expected that religion would slowly be privatized and lose its place in the public sphere. However, in practice, equal treatment was not achieved, with different religious groups at different times feeling that, in its policies, the state has shown priority to other traditions. One example of this tension is the existence of two forms of law in India – civil law (which is secular) and personal law (which is based on religion and governs issues around the family). As Bradley and Kirmani highlight in Chapter 15, the women's movement advocates creating a uniform civil code and doing away with separate sources of personal law, since, irrespective of tradition, religious systems of law do not treat women equally. These disparities, coupled with the colonial treatment of religion and the reverberations from partition, have contributed towards the rise of religio-political communal tensions between Hindus and Muslims, which have often resulted in bloodshed. Christians, Sikhs and Buddhists have also faced persecution at the hands of Hindu nationalists, who want India to be a Hindu state.

Hindu nationalism has its roots in the emergence of religious identities in colonial India, as well as the Hindu reform movements and nationalist politics of the pre-independence era. In all communities – Sikh, Hindu and Muslim – people began organizing along religious lines. For Hindus, this meant 'delineating a broad-based communal identity beyond caste that had not been strongly emphasised before' (Gold 1991: 537). In 1909, the Hindu Mahasabha was formed amongst members of the Arya Samaj (a prominent reform movement). It 'soon developed into a right-wing militant Hindu political party [which] has remained one of the national parties [despite being] based on a narrow definition of Hindu nationhood' (Klostermaier 1994: 463). V. D. Sarvakar, president of the Hindu Mahasabha from 1937 to 1942, wrote a famous book called *Hindutva: Who Is a Hindu?* while in prison (it was smuggled out in 1923), where he argued that only Indic religions were 'Hindu' and that other religions had no place in India. He promoted the idea of a Hindurashtra (Hindu nation), in which only members of the Indic religions would be considered to be truly Indian. In 1925 another prominent Hindu nationalist organization, the Rashtriya Swayamsevak Sangh (RSS), was formed by K. V. Hedgewar, a Hindu Mahasabha member. The RSS is not a political party, instead considering itself to be a cultural organization that emphasizes militaristic style training for men, women and children. M. S. Golwalkar, successor to Hedgewar, adopted a broader understanding of 'who is a Hindu', distinguishing between culture and religion and taking the latter to be a 'private' matter. In this view, although the public culture must be Hindu, people's private faith is a matter of personal choice.

Nevertheless, not only has the ideology of Hindutva ('Hinduness'), the key tenets of which include the idea that the Indian subcontinent is the homeland of Hindus and that Hindus are those who follow the original Indic religion of the Vedas (the most ancient Hindu texts), emerged from the Hindu nationalist movement, but so has a strengthening of the idea of Hinduism as a 'religion'. One of the most important groups propounding this view today is the Vishva Hindu Parishad (VHP), founded in 1964 as a religio-cultural organization that attempts to articulate a universal Hinduism (McKean 1996: 102). Hindutva is today promoted by a number of organizations, collectively known as the *sangh parivar* (family of organizations). In addition to the VHP and the RSS, perhaps most important is the Bharatiya Janata Party (BJP), founded in 1980. Between 1998 and 2004 this Hindu nationalist party was in overall power in the country, and it was re-elected in May 2014. Thus, even though constitutional secularism was intended 'to act as a counter to . . . communal riots and the communalism of the Hindu Mahasabha and the Rashtryia Swayam Sevak Sangh (RSS) movements' (Desai 2005: 234), the extent to which India today can really be called secular, in any meaningful sense, is debatable.[10]

The first government of India was formed by the Congress Party and was led by Nehru, who was a strong advocate of secularism. Nevertheless, between 1947 and 1951, he had to battle against right-wing Hindu influences amongst the leadership of the party, which 'took a religious view of nationhood' (Desai 2005: 252). In fact, as Desai tells us, there 'were discussions immediately after independence that advocated the merging of the Hindu Mahasabha and the RSS into the Congress party . . . and had it not been for Gandhi's assassination [by a former member of the RSS] this would have come to fruition' (2005: 252). Having bested the pro-Hindu faction, the Congress party ruled between 1947 and 1977 as 'the guardian of secularism'. While the RSS was briefly banned in 1948 and the Hindu Mahasabha vilified at this time, religious political parties were permitted to operate in India but had little chance of coming to power during the heyday of Congress. In 1951 the Jana Sangh formed with members of the RSS and replaced the Hindu Mahasabha as the main Hindu party. The Jana Sangh joined with other political actors to form the Janata Party in 1977 and Congress was finally toppled. However, in a bid to regain control, Congress began to demonstrate a 'more compromising attitude towards the communalists' and to court the Hindu vote (2005: 235). It was elected back into power between 1980 and 1989, followed by decade of coalition governments, under which the BJP (formed in 1980 by Jana Sangh affiliates leaving the Janata Party) became stronger and grew in popularity (2005: 257).

The rise of Hindu Right politics was also accompanied by communal tensions between Hindus and Muslims. Against a backdrop of inter-community conflicts, the question then arises as to whether religious communities have distinct development needs: 'Does the state need to address the concerns of distinct communities differently, through varied politics of recognition and distribution?' (Mahajan and Jodhka 2009: 20). In practice, apart from moves to elevate 'backward classes', Scheduled Castes and Scheduled Tribes (see below), there has been little attempt to introduce community-specific policies.

This issue is particularly germane for the Muslim population, the largest minority (13 per cent in 2001), which for the historical reasons outlined above has since independence existed in tension with the Hindu majority, and is significantly disadvantaged in terms of economic and educational opportunities when compared to the Hindu community, especially the middle and upper castes. Nevertheless, until the mid-2000s, the government resisted defining Muslims as a group eligible for positive discrimination policies. Eventually, in 2005, prime minister Manmohan Singh set up the Rajinder Sachar Committee to report on the social, economic and educational status of the Muslim community. The Sachar Committee's report in 2006 drew attention to the multiple ways in which Muslims are disadvantaged compared to most other communities in India, initiating a new debate about the need to target development policy towards Muslim groups (Mahajan and Jodhka 2009).[11]

Thus, despite the commitment to secularism in India, the role of religion in the public sphere has expanded since independence, with the most obvious examples being the increased presence of religion-based politics and the rise of religious identity movements among different groups, often building on the religious reform movements of the colonial period. In addition to the Hindu nationalist politics discussed above, important examples in modern India have been the different strategies adopted by Dalits, some of whom have campaigned for policies to address their disadvantage, while others have converted to Buddhism in order to escape the caste system and improve their material situation. Some of these alternative strategies are discussed further in the next subsection.

Marginalized religious communities and political mobilization in India

India has for long sustained a vision of society that is hierarchical and non-egalitarian by means of the caste system. Mosse in Chapter 14 argues that, although the caste system is typically associated with the Hindu tradition, caste is in fact found within all religious groups in India and the idea that it has a religious basis was actually a colonial and Christian missionary invention. The earliest texts associated with Hinduism, the Vedas, which date from the second millennium BCE, suggest that the society was already divided into four classes or *varnas*: the priestly Brahmin class; the warrior or *kshatriya* class; the merchant or *vaishya* class; and the servant or *shudra* class. However, this notion of *varna* is not identical to that of 'caste' (*jati*), and while there are only four *varnas* there are literally thousands of *jatis*. These are endogamous sections of society into which one is born, typically believed to be as a result of actions in a previous life (*karma*). Because caste was historically related to occupation and social hierarchy, its role in locking people into situations of poverty has long been acknowledged, giving rise to attempts to circumvent its negative impacts. For instance, the practice of 'untouchability' – under which the lowest castes were discriminated against in almost all areas of life – was outlawed in 1950, and the Indian State provides job and educational reservations for members of the low castes. Nonetheless, the former untouchable castes (now known as 'Dalits' – meaning downtrodden) still exist.

Moreover, defining which groups are eligible for this support and for what reasons has been the subject of debate and protest since the 1950s. The Indian constitution recognized so-called Scheduled Castes (SC) and Scheduled Tribes (ST) as in need of affirmative action policies to increase access to education and employment. Because caste is recognized as a Hindu institution, only Hindu Dalits are counted as SC. However, caste exists across all religious groups, and this meant that Dalit Christians, Muslims, Buddhists and Sikhs were not seen as SC and therefore were not treated in the same way as Dalit Hindus. Eventually Dalit Buddhists and Sikhs were included (in 1990 and 1956 respectively), on the basis that these religions emerged from within Hinduism, but Muslim and Christian Dalit groups are to this day not included as SCs. Thus, if Dalit Hindus convert to Islam or Christianity (this is sometimes done as a strategy to avoid caste stigma), they are no longer viewed as SCs and therefore eligible for the same affirmative action policies as they were when they were Dalit Hindus.

A category of Other Backward Classes (OBC) was also noted in the Indian constitution, but the identity of these groups was left unclear, and no affirmative action policies were initially applied to this group. Following the Mandal Commission report in 1980 OBCs were found to be 52 per cent of the population at that time, and the need for affirmative action to be extended was agreed. However, it was only in some states in the south that Dalit Muslims and Christians were included as OBC, and then only small levels of reservations were extended at the national level to Muslims and Christians via the OBC route after the Mandal Commission report. While this does mean that they benefit from some reservation policies, this places them in the same category as other dominant castes that have been the source of their oppression. For this reason they want to be classed as SC as well, to benefit from legal protection related to their being SC, for instance the 1989 SC/ST Prevention of Atrocities Act.

In addition to government policies those at the bottom of the caste system have increasingly responded to their situation by 'evolving alternative social visions or, indeed, new religiously-based social movements that aim to transcend religious and social inequality' (Singh 2011: 33). For some, this has involved conversion to another religion. For example, whereas Buddhism had died out in India by the thirteenth century, it returned in the 1950s under the leadership of a Dalit, Dr Ambedkar, in Maharashtra. Ambedkar, who was a lawyer, had been influential in national politics after independence, but came to the conclusion that Dalits would be unable to secure equal citizenship and socio-economic status under Hinduism, and so urged them to convert to Buddhism to escape the caste system. Many thousands did so, especially in Maharashtra. Both these Buddhist groups and the wider Dalit movement, including Sikhs, Muslims, Hindus and Christians, continue to fight for Dalit rights, seek to counter ongoing forms of discrimination and campaign for inclusion in state programmes of affirmative action as discussed above. However, as Singh writes, '[b]ecause of the size of the Dalit groups (which make up more than 50 percent of India's population), incentive structures have . . . been created for political parties to mobilize these communities' (2011: 33). Both secular and religious political parties have attempted to woo members of the Dalit communities, who make strategic use of their religious identities in their interactions with the government and political parties, while at the same time seeking to take advantage of affirmative policies based on caste.

A recent study of so-called 'neo-Buddhists' in Maharashtra shows how they have to some extent succeeded in improving their social status and social mobility (Singh 2011). While this can in part be attributed to their own efforts as a community, they were also able to use their religio-caste status to improve their socio-economic position, their ability to do so owing 'as much to the political incentives for such mobilization (for political parties) as internal community dynamics' (Singh 2011: 45). While neo-Buddhists have remained active in tackling discrimination against Dalits more generally, the improved socio-economic position of sections of the neo-Buddhist community has distanced them from the really disadvantaged (Mahajan and Jodhka 2009: 44–54; Singh 2011). In addition, as in other groups and movements, not only do women not have equal access to leadership roles, but they and male community leaders tend to 'place communal goals ahead of tackling patriarchy and marginalization' (Singh 2011: 47–8; see also Mahajan and Jodhka 2009: 81).

Thus, as Jodhka argues, while there has officially been little place for religion in Indian nation building and development, since the 1980s there have been 'some interesting new trends at the social and political levels, which have brought questions of culture and religion to the centre stage of Indian politics' (2008: 3). In both India and Pakistan, faith-based groups (including religious political parties and identity-based movements) have taken on a renewed significance. In the next section of this chapter, I will look more closely at the ways in which the 'withdrawal of the state' since economic liberalization in the early 1990s has not only encouraged private enterprise but also created a new political and developmental space for the voluntary sector, including a faith-based contribution. Because of the limited space available, I will confine the discussion to the scale and nature of faith-based welfare and development activity in modern Pakistan and India.

The liberalization of the economy and the global aid business: opening up spaces for faith-based welfare and development

In the second half of the 1950s, both India and Pakistan experienced food shortages and inflation. This coincided with the beginning of the Cold War, helping to 'generate a larger flow of foreign aid than anyone had hoped for in the early 1950s' (Desai 2005: 276). Although food production increased and industrialization continued, especially in India, the oil shocks of the 1970s caused increased inflation. While in some developing countries import-substitution policies were replaced with export-oriented industrialization, this type of reform did not happen in South Asia. While Pakistan had been forced to accept IMF assistance and conditionality in 1972, the second oil shock at the end of the 1970s contributed to a shift in the 'international context which made the strategy of undersaving and reliance on foreign recourses adopted by this region unfeasible' (Desai 2005: 279).

At the beginning of the 1990s, India and Pakistan started to liberalize their economies. In both, this meant a decrease in the involvement of the state in the economy and opening up to private investment. This rolling back of the state, which included the privatization of some previously state-provided services, resulted in an increased role for the not-for-profit sector, including both registered and unregistered providers. In Pakistan, in particular, the state has generally encouraged the development of an 'informal' social security sector, in which religious organizations play a significant role, largely because they are trusted by people, in part because they are often considered to provide services more successfully than the state. In contrast to the immediate post-independence period, when the state assumed control of social services and either nationalized or reduced its recognition of the services provided by religious organizations, since the 1980s there has been a rise in faith-based development activities not only in Pakistan but also in India. While this is in part attributable to the privatization of state services, it has also been a reaction towards the adverse socio-economic impacts of economic liberalization, as well as changing religio-political dynamics nationally and internationally, including the 'turn to religion' by some actors within the global aid business and increased support for FBOs (see Tomalin 2012).

The impact has been felt in both settings, not least through the influence and presence of international NGOs, including faith-based ones. Although the headquarters of these organizations are outside South Asia, they typically have regional offices and receive their funding from official donors, individual donations and other fund-raising efforts. The proliferation of and support for faith-based organizations such as Islamic Relief, Christian Aid, CAFOD or World Vision, have been well documented. What we know far less about is the local charities in developing contexts, many but not all of which are small, and which, although they are not formally linked to the global aid business, play important roles in welfare and development. Although it is impossible to quantify accurately the exact scale of their activities, some estimates are available.

For example, in 2008 Iqbal and Siddiqui estimated that numerically religious organizations in Pakistan make up a third of the non-profit sector (about 16,000 organizations out of a total of around 45,000), although not all of these were involved in development work (Iqbal and Siddiqui 2008; Ghaus-Pasha *et al.* 2002: 4).[12] While about 13,000 were *madrasas* (Ministry of Education 2006), most of the remaining organizations were linked to Islam, followed by Christianity, and relatively few with other religions (e.g. Hinduism and Zoroastrianism).

In contrast to Pakistan, where at times the state has actively encouraged religious involvement in social welfare, the government in India has remained committed to secular political and development models over the past 60 years. However, the non-profit sector in general, including religious involvement within it, has grown steadily, especially since the 1980s, following economic liberalization. Tandon and Srivastava (2005) estimate that in the early 2000s there were 1.2 million organizations in the non-profit sector as a whole (excluding *madrasas*), over a quarter of which were involved in a broad range of religious activities (ibid.). Overall, as expected, the majority of these roughly 300,000 organizations were Hindu. In both settings it is noticeable that the proportion of all faith-based organizations that are Christian – mostly schools and hospitals set up initially by missionaries – exceeds Christianity's share of adherents.

In both India and Pakistan, religious actors are mostly involved in the provision of relief, welfare and social services, especially education and health. In both, Christian missionaries have been important providers of health and education, and Hindu schools are gaining in popularity in India in parallel with the increasing prominence of the Hindu Right. Overall, *madrasas* constitute the largest part of the Muslim faith-based sector in both India and Pakistan, although Muslim involvement in health care is virtually non-existent. Many prominent *madrasas* also undertake philanthropic and humanitarian work through associated charities, trusts or relief organizations (Iqbal and Siddiqui 2008: 28).

Indigenous religious organizations play less of a role in development and advocacy than do international organizations. For example, in a study of the role of faith in the indigenous charity and development sector in Karachi and Sindh, Kirmani and Zaidi (2010) found that many of the charities they visited focused on meeting individual short-term needs rather than achieving longer-term 'development' objectives. In part, particularly for Muslim organizations, this can be attributed to the religious requirement for charitable giving to assist the poor and needy. Advocacy tends to be taken up by secular actors (not least, for instance, because religion is often part of the problem facing human rights advocacy campaigns), as well as international NGOs and FBOs. In Pakistan in particular, the predominance of conservative Islam, as well as the existence of powerful and restrictive *ulema*, means that it can be difficult for Muslim organizations to address 'sensitive' topics. For example, few Muslim organizations have publicly addressed HIV/AIDS, despite attempts by international organizations to involve religious leaders in this discourse. Indeed, women's rights, reproductive health and HIV/AIDS are often conceived of as part of a 'western agenda' (Iqbal and Siddiqui 2008: 45). However, there are exceptions. In practice, some Christian churches and organizations have been more willing to engage in advocacy; for example, in Pakistan, Kirmani and Zaidi (2010) found that the Christian churches in India have been involved in campaigning for caste equality and Dalit rights (see Mosse, Chapter 14), and some Christian organizations in Pakistan have engaged in advocacy and public debates surrounding controversial issues such as HIV/AIDS, contraceptive use and drug abuse.

However, difficulties in applying the categories of faith-based organization, welfare or service provider and development organization are clearly visible in the South Asian context. For example, although local charities were involved *both* in welfare activities, for example providing financial and material assistance to the needy, and religious activities, such as organizing religious ceremonial activities, many did not use the term 'faith-based organization' to describe themselves. Moreover, other organizations with a clear link to 'religion' actively denied that they were 'faith-based', including the Edhi Foundation (the largest welfare organization in Pakistan) and the Aga Khan Development Network (patronized by the Prince Aga Khan, the leader of the Ismaili faith) (Kirmani and Zaidi 2010). Finally, as noted above, 'development' rather than 'charitable' activities tended to be carried out by so-called professional development organizations, which are tied to the global aid business, attract funding from donors and are less likely to be rooted in a faith tradition (2010: 59).

The limitations of and sensitivities around the label 'faith-based' have been discussed elsewhere in this volume, but it is worth emphasizing here that, in both Pakistan and India, there are likely to be many more religious organizations involved in providing services and support to the poor that do not think of themselves as FBOs than those that do. Moreover, there are categories of religious organizations engaged in welfare and humanitarian relief (e.g. following the 2005 earthquake or with refugees displaced by the war with the Taliban in north-west Pakistan) that are not formally linked to the global aid business, are generally ineligible for official donor funding and may not even be recognized as faith-based organizations. In addition to some of the organizations already discussed, these include the welfare wings of religious political parties and so-called radical organizations. However, as Jodhka and Bora (2009: 19) note with respect to the impact of the global aid business on how such religious organizations depict themselves, some are beginning to 'present themselves explicitly as development agents, possibly reflecting broader shifts that have taken place with respect to the "NGO-ization" of civil society and also the reconfiguration of charity and welfare work (typically a mainstay of religious organizations) as "development"' (2009: 19).

Conclusion

The aim of this chapter was to explore the engagement between religious actors in India and Pakistan with social welfare and development-related work not only in different time periods but also against the backdrop of varied and shifting attitudes to the relationship between religion and the state. While India became a secular polity after independence in 1947, Pakistan had become an Islamic state by 1951, yet in both religion has played a significant role in political and development activities. However, the religion–development nexus in South Asia also has a global dimension, since the global development industry has had an impact upon economic development policies in both settings. Moreover, the rolling back of the state with economic liberalization from the late 1980s facilitated the growth of the non-profit sector at the level both of formal and informal organizations. This has included a renewed significance for religious actors with respect to welfare and development as they have increasingly stepped in to fill gaps left by a paucity in government provision.

Notes

1 There is a lack of agreement about exactly which countries constitute South Asia. Always included are a core of countries that were part of the British Empire – India, Pakistan, Bangladesh and Sri Lanka – but beyond this there are different formulations and rationales for drawing boundaries. The United Nations geographical region includes Afghanistan, Bangladesh, Bhutan, India, Iran, Maldives, Nepal, Pakistan and Sri Lanka (http://unstats.un.org/unsd/methods/m49/m49regin.htm#asia, accessed 8 June 2014). However, the South Asian Association for Regional Cooperation (SAARC), which originated in 1985, began life with seven countries – Bangladesh, Bhutan, India, Maldives, Nepal, Pakistan and Sri Lanka – and was extended to include Afghanistan in 2006. Different again is the United Nations Population Information Network (POPIN), which excludes Maldives, including it instead within the Pacific POPIN sub-region (http://www.un.org/popin/, accessed 8 June 2014).

2 In Indian politics, instead of secular denoting 'worldly' as opposed to 'religious' affairs (implying a rejection of religion), the term 'secular' refers to a constitution that bars the state from showing preference to one religion over another (Brass 2006). In a country where religion is seen as a 'way of life' (as true in important ways for religions other than Hinduism, i.e. Islam, Christianity, Sikhism, Buddhism and Jainism), however, there is arguably no possibility of a secular state in the western sense. The Indian model shows how the European model of secularism has mutated as it has spread to different locations.

3 Prior to 1947, when India gained independence from Britain but was also partitioned from East Pakistan (now Bangladesh) and West Pakistan, India and Pakistan were one country, so they will be dealt with together in this section.

4 *Khanqahs* are Sufi centres of spirituality, learning and social welfare. They rely on gifts, donations and charity, and often adjoin Sufi shrines, mosques and *madrasas*. In contemporary Pakistan, however, their role in poverty alleviation has declined, probably owing to the government taking over the shrines and associated *auqaf* (plural of *waqf*) in the late 1960s, leading to a decline in donations from the public (Iqbal and Siddiqui 2008: 43).

5 According to the Hanafi school of religious law, *zakat* is to be paid by Sunnis once a year on wealth held for more than a year. The rate is generally 2.5 per cent. Today, recipients of *zakat* can be individuals or organizations working for the welfare of people. Other forms of voluntary Islamic charity include *ushr*, *sadaqah* and *qurbani*.

6 The legacy of this thinking, which was rooted in the Swadeshi movement and Hindu spirituality, lives on in the present day. While India is overwhelmingly a capitalist economy, there are pockets of activity in which followers attempt to live by principles that reflect the ideas of these earlier thinkers. These include, for example, the continuation of the ashrams and communities inspired by Gandhi or Aurobindo.

7 'A trade and economic policy based on the premise that a country should attempt to reduce its foreign dependency through the local production of industrialized products' (http://www.princeton.edu/~achaney/tmve/wiki100k/docs/Import_substitution_industrialization.html, accessed 8 June 2014).

8 http://www.columbia.edu/itc/mealac/pritchett/00islamlinks/txt_jinnah_assembly_1947.html (accessed 8 June 2014).

9 Moreover, as a result of the massive population movements that occurred during partition, Hinduism is the largest religion in India (81 per cent in 2001), whereas in Pakistan Islam is the largest religion (96 per cent in 1998), with consequences for the minority traditions and religious freedom in both countries.

10 The principle of keeping 'the state equally distant from all religions and not letting it favor any one in public policy' (Varshney 1993: 259) has been criticized as 'shallow' or 'pseudo' secularism. In practice, the state, despite endeavouring to maintain a neutral position, has found it increasingly difficult to criticize practices carried out in the name of 'religion' or tradition, arguably laying the ground for an upsurge in communal problems grounded in various religious nationalisms (Varshney 1993: 250).

11 http://ncm.nic.in/pdf/compilation.pdf (accessed 8 June 2014).

12 This includes both formal registered organizations and informal unregistered organizations.

References

Ansari, Sarfraz Hussain (2011) 'Forced Modernization and Public Policy: A Case Study of Ayub Khan Era (1958–69)', *Journal of Political Studies*, 18 (1), 45–60, http://pu.edu.pk/images/journal/pols/pdf-files/Forced_Modernization%20-%204.pdf (accessed 8 June 2014).

Bano, Masooda and Nair, Padmaja (2007) *Faith-Based Organisations in South Asia: Historical Evolution, Current Status and Nature of Interaction with the State*, Religions and Development Research Programme, Working Paper 12, Birmingham: Religions and Development.

Brass, Paul (2006) 'Indian Secularism in Practice', *Indian Journal of Secularism*, 9 (1), 115–32.

Desai, Meghnad (2005) *Development and Nationhood: Essays in the Political Economy of South Asia*, New Delhi: Oxford University Press India.

Ghaus-Pasha, Aisha, Jamal, Haroon and Iqbal, Muhammad Asif (2002) 'Dimensions of the Nonprofit Sector in Pakistan', Johns Hopkins Comparative Nonprofit Sector Project Pakistan, SPDC Working Paper no. 1, Social Policy and Development Centre in collaboration with Aga Khan Foundation, Pakistan and Center for Civil Society, Johns Hopkins University, USA, http://www.spdc.org.pk/Publications/Working%20Papers/WP-01.pdf (accessed 8 June 2014).

Gold, Daniel (1991) 'Organized Hinduisms: From Vedic Truth to Hindu Nation', in Martin Marty and Scott R. Appleby (eds), *Fundamentalisms Observed*, Chicago: University of Chicago Press, pp. 531–93.

Haq, Farhat (2010) 'Pakistan: A State for the Muslims or an Islamic State?', in Ali Riaz (ed.), *Religion and Politics in South Asia*, London: Routledge.

Haqqani, Husain (2005) *Pakistan between Mosque and Military*, Washington, DC: Carnegie Endowment for International Peace.

Hussain, Zahid (1956) *The First Five Year Plan: Size, Objectives and Limitations*, http://pu.edu.pk/images/journal/pesr/PDF-FILES/1%20ZAHID%20The%20First%20Five%20Year%20Plan_v5_no1_1956.pdf (accessed 8 June 2014).

Iqbal, Muhammad Asif and Siddiqui, Saima (2008) *Mapping the Terrain: The Activities of Faith-Based Organisations in Development in Pakistan*, Religions and Development Research Programme, Working Paper 24, Birmingham: Religions and Development.

Jodhka, Surinder S. (2008) 'Religion and Development in India', in Religions and Development Research Programme (eds), *India: Some Reviews of Literature Related to Religions and Development*, Religions and Development Research Programme, Working Paper 10, Birmingham: Religions and Development, pp. 3–18.

Jodhka, Surinder S. and Bora, Pradyumna (2009) *Mapping Faith-Based Development Activities in Contemporary Maharashtra, India*, Religions and Development Research Programme, Working Paper 28, Birmingham: Religions and Development.

Jodhka, Surinder S. and Kumar, Avinash (2010) *Religious Mobilizations for Development and Social Change: A Comparative Study of Dalit Movements in Punjab and Maharashtra, India*, Religions and Development Research Programme, Working Paper 47, Birmingham: Religions and Development.

Khan, Ismail (2003) 'Peshwar: Mohtasibs to Get Sweeping Powers under Proposed Laws', *Dawn*, 3 May, http://www.dawn.com/news/100079/peshawar-mohtasibs-to-get-sweeping-powers-under-proposed-law (accessed 9 August 2014).

Kirmani, Nida and Zaidi, Sarah (2010) *The Role of Faith in the Charity and Development Sector in Karachi and Sindh, Pakistan*, Religions and Development Research Programme, Working Paper 50, Birmingham: Religions and Development.

Klostermaier, Klaus (1994) *A Survey of Hinduism*, Albany: University of New York Press.

Mahajan, Gurpreet and Jodhka, Surinder S. (2009) *Religion, Democracy and Governance: Spaces for the Marginalized in Contemporary India*, Religions and Development Research Programme, Working Paper 26, Birmingham: Religions and Development.

McKean, Lise (1996) *Divine Enterprise: Gurus and the Hindu Nationalist Movement*, Chicago: University of Chicago Press.

Metcalf, B. D. (1978) 'The Madrasa at Deoband: A Model for Religious Education in India', *Modern Asian Studies*, 12, 111–34.

Miller, David (1999) 'Modernity in Hindu Monasticism: Swami Vivekananda and the Ramakrishna Movement', *Journal of Asian Studies*, 34 (1), 111–26.

Ministry of Education (2006) *National Education Census, Pakistan*, Islamabad: Government of Pakistan, Academy of Education Planning and Management, Statistics Division, Federal Bureau of Statistics.

Mujundar, R. C. (1961) 'Social Work in Ancient and Medieval India', in A. R. Wadia (ed.), *History and Philosophy of Social Work in India*, Bombay: Allied Publishers.

Nair, Padmaja (2009) *The State and Madrasas in India*, Religions and Development Research Programme, Working Paper 15, Birmingham: Religions and Development.

Narayan, S. (1970) *Relevance of Gandhian Economics*, Ahmedabad: Navajivan Publishing House.

Narendar, U. (2002) *Inclusive Economics: Gandhian Method and Contemporary Policy*, New Delhi: Sage.

Oberoi, H. (1994) *The Construction of Religious Boundaries: Culture, Identity and Diversity in the Sikh Tradition*, Delhi: Oxford University Press.

Qadeer, Mohamed (1997) 'The Evolving Structure of Civil Society and the State in Pakistan', *Pakistan Development Review*, 36 (4), 743–62.

Qasmi, M. Burhanuddin (2001) *Darul Uloom Deoband: A Heroic Struggle against the British Tyranny*, Mumbai: Markazul Ma'arif India.

Rothermund, Dietmar (2003) *An Economic History of India: From Pre-Colonial Times to 1991*, London: Routledge.

Sharma, R. (1997) *Gandhian Economics*, New Delhi: Deep and Deep Publications.

Singh, Gurharpal (2011) *Religion, Politics and Governance in India, Pakistan, Nigeria and Tanzania: An Overview*, Religions and Development Research Programme, Working Paper 55, Birmingham: Religions and Development.

Tandon, Rajesh and Srivastava, S. S. (2005) 'How Large Is India's Non-Profit Sector?', *Economic and Political Weekly*, XL (19), 1948–52.

Tatla, Darshan S. (2008) *Sikhism and Development: A Review*, Religions and Development Research Programme, Working Paper 21, Birmingham: Religions and Development.

Tomalin, Emma (2009) *Hinduism and International Development: Religions and Development Background Paper*, Religions and Development Research Programme, Working Paper 19, Birmingham: Religions and Development.

Tomalin, Emma (2012) 'Thinking about Faith-Based Organisations in Development: Where Have We Got To and What Next?', *Development in Practice*, 22 (5–6), 689–703.

Tomalin, Emma and Leurs, Robert (2012) *Mapping the Development Activities of Local Faith-Based Organizations in Pakistan, India, Nigeria and Tanzania: A Comparative Analysis*, Religions and Development Research Programme, Working Paper 62, Birmingham: Religions and Development.

van der Veer, Peter (2002) 'Religion in South Asia', *Annual Review of Anthropology*, 31, 173–87.

Varshney, Ashutosh (1993) 'India's National Identity, Hindu Nationalism, and the Politics of Anxiety', *Daedalus*, 122 (3), 227–61.

Waseem, Mohammed and Mufti, Mariam (2009) *Religion, Politics and Governance in Pakistan*, Religions and Development Research Programme, Working Paper 27, Birmingham: Religions and Development.

14

CASTE AND THE CONUNDRUM OF RELIGION AND DEVELOPMENT IN INDIA[1]

David Mosse

Introduction

The emerging debate on 'religion' and 'development' has been challenged by some for unquestioningly deploying what are historically contingent, socially constructed and mutually constitutive categories. Arguably, separating out 'religion' renders development secular, as a value-free project of modernization, or the expansion of consumer capitalism and liberal democracy, while the paired idea of 'development' strips the political economy out of religion, making it available for instrumental packaging as the 'missing element' (faith, trust, values, commitment) now supplied by self-defined faith-based organizations (FBOs) (Fountain 2013). Such an idea certainly lies behind the complaint that the 'religion and development' agenda is normative and instrumental in its approach, agency-driven, and involves a narrow or overly institutional notion of religion, focused on 'faith agencies' (mostly Christian), as well as enclosing a Christian conception of religion as a matter of belief (Jones and Juul Petersen 2011).

A counterpart to religion *and* development is writing on religion *in* development, and of course religion *as* development or development as religion (Salemink *et al.* 2004). Among other things, this throws light on projects of moral or 'spiritual' improvement contained within various development interventions, and the material transformations through which religious reform movements are lived. The idea that modernizing development itself has gained a hold on the 'discursive imaginary', shaping expectations, dreams and aspirations, and in consequence imposing its goals and values so as to render people 'underdeveloped', to foster cultural self-denigration or cultural malaise, is at the heart of the long-running postmodern critique of development (Escobar 2012: xii–xiii). But introducing an opposition between development and indigenous cultural life is itself rather unhelpful. After all, however understood, 'development' takes place through existing categories and meanings (see Peel 1978; Robbins 2004); and articulating indigenous or local concerns in the language of development is also often a strategic means to engage with the state or other agencies in postcolonial societies (Gow 2008).

These debates arise precisely because social life is *not* arranged according to binary divides such as 'religion' and 'development'. The purpose of this chapter is not further to argue this point, but rather to explore how the division between 'religion' and 'development' (or economy or politics) nonetheless acquires significance, how institutions of various kinds – missionary, colonial and postcolonial state, NGO, activist – at different historical moments invest in these categorical distinctions in their approach to especially vulnerable people, and what the consequences are.

I focus on the case of Dalits, that is, members of inferiorized caste groups historically subordinated as 'untouchables', who constitute some 16–18 per cent of the population in India and remain among the most impoverished and excluded groups. The condition of Dalits has been part of the social policy of the state, missionaries and churches, activists, NGOs and other international organizations; and this social policy has produced and reproduced distinctions between religion and development (and analogously caste/class, ritual/economic, status/power and church/state) in ways that have an enduring impact on the life chances of Dalits themselves.

Dalit disadvantage and the categories of social policy

Until the latter part of the twentieth century the social and economic condition of Dalits in south India was truly grim: they were mostly landless, tied into various types of agrestic servitude to 'upper'-caste patrons and subject to a now well-known range of social-spatial-ritual exclusions and segregations articulated in various idioms including impurity and pollution. Where Dalits are concerned, poverty and the denial of dignity (the refusal of resources and recognition) were both public code and social identity. There was no meaningful distinction between Dalits economically exploited as labourers (a class) and religiously inferiorized and ritually humiliated as a caste (Viswanath 2014a). And, still today, control over labour and the distribution of rights to resources, access to public services (water, lighting, sanitation), educational opportunities and much more arises from historical inequalities of caste. This is not, however, to suggest a situation of social stability or passivity. Changes brought by British rule in the nineteenth century may in fact have conspired to make matters worse for the Dalits (Washbrook 1993), but at the same time colonialism offered new opportunities and broader identities, and engendered various forms of resistance or challenge that acquired momentum in the century that followed, including those opened up through new religious affiliation.

Since, as I will explain, significant numbers of Dalits are Christian converts, part of this discussion will concern Christianity and development. But my interest here is not in faith per se, but the societal conditions under which interventions and responses to them come to be defined as 'religious', or how religion and religious identities become part of the political system within which development policy is framed and resources allocated.

Inevitably central to this discussion is the effect, first, of separating religious and political-economic aspects of social life where this distinction has little prior meaning and, second, of abstracting the universal (identities and bases of claims) from the particularistic relations within which livelihoods are embedded. The effect is thus not the 'de-religionizing' of development (Fountain 2013) but rather the 'spiritualizing' (or 'culturalizing') of poverty, disembedded from the matrix of particular relations of power and economy. I will suggest that the imposition of categorical distinctions (religion versus economy) and the disembedding of universal from particularistic relations that were born of nineteenth-century missionary engagement with caste and untouchability in south India continue in other realms including both state-led development and international human rights activism in ways that constrain attention to the specific structural disadvantage of Dalits and interrupt their claims (cf. Viswanath 2014b).

Spiritualizing poverty: Protestant and Catholic approaches to caste

From the last quarter of the nineteenth century, for reasons still poorly understood, Christian missionaries of all denominations were astonished to find that the groups they called Pariahs, whom they had mostly overlooked in favour of sections of society thought to be more influential, began to convert en masse.[2] In consequence, the majority of Christians in India today are Dalit. We cannot be sure, but it is likely that conversion here was less a matter of signing up to a new belief than of new allegiance and commitment that might make a difference to a situation of oppression. Certainly, Protestant missionaries intervened as allies of people they regarded as subject to 'slavery' in ways that had economic effects – freedom from debt bondage, the acquisition of titles to house sites, or resettlement on agricultural wasteland (Viswanath 2010). However, to avoid the criticism that their converts were insincere, materially driven 'rice Christians', missionaries were constrained to represent this political-economic change as spiritual transformation, and Dalits as oppressed by a Hindu religious system and in need of salvation from 'spiritual slavery' (Viswanath 2008, 2010). Precisely because for their Dalit converts the misery of the body and the misery of the spirit were *not* separate, for the missionaries this separation became crucial, and caste and untouchability entered policy debate and colonial policy making as Hindu institution and practice (ibid.). Understood as spiritual servitude, caste was to be challenged by altering mental attitudes. It could be said that missionaries did not seek fundamental change in the structure of an agrarian system, but 'transformation [of] the attitudes and habits of Pariahs themselves' (Viswanath 2014a: 4), stripping out the 'Hindu excrescence' of caste to leave unchanged a 'rational core' of class (Viswanath 2010: 145).

Through missionary discourse on the 'Pariah problem' (Viswanath 2014b), Dalits gained access to the public realm (attention being drawn to the conditions of slavery from which India was thought exempt). However, this discourse also consolidated caste and untouchability as matters of religion separate from economic relations and exploitation (Viswanath 2008); and in these terms Hindu reform movements opposing missionaries shifted their perception of Christianity from being a threat to dominant caste interests (through the removal of biddable labour) to being a threat to Hindu religion (ibid.).

Viswanath traces a parallel 'conceptual apartheid' (2014a: 6) bifurcating the religious and the political-economic – caste and class – in the British colonial state's Labour Department and labour policy, especially under the influence of (upper-caste) native politicians. This brought about an artefactual distinction between policy on labour, on the one hand, and policy on the 'Depressed Classes' (the Dalits), on the other, a separation that, Viswanath explains, led to diminishment of the colonial and postcolonial capacity to address the reality of Dalit poverty. Like those of the missionaries, measures of state welfare for Dalits emphasized thrift, temperance and self-control, and involved a discourse of moral and economic change focused on domestic transformation and the family as the source of mobility – celebrating the thrift and self-sacrifice of Dalit women while making irresponsible alcoholic Dalit men the villains – entirely ignoring caste subordination as a structure of antagonistic agrarian relations (2014a: 14).

Of course, the categories and abstractions of missionaries or the colonial state were not determinant of the meaning of new opportunities and provisions for Dalits themselves. An extensive literature shows how religious conversion and Christianity became part of on-going contests within agrarian society. In a pattern that finds itself repeated in different development eras, the various measures for betterment – whether titles for house sites made available by the state, or chapels and Sunday services provided by the missions – were seized upon by Dalits as the means of struggle in an '*agonistic and relational* field' (Viswanath 2014a: 20, original emphasis), against caste landlords and for greater autonomy, even where (as was often the case) this led to short-term material loss or vulnerability. While external agents imposed a conceptual distinction between the caste-religious and the economic-political[3] that was irrelevant in practice, the local meaning of changes in wages, debt, access to land and other material benefits always exceeded the 'economic', being part of the struggles in the relational field of caste, just as at the same time innovations in religious ritual – having a place of worship of one's own and conversion itself – were essential elements in reworking agrarian relationships and entitlements.

Catholic missions in south India (for reasons explained at length elsewhere; Mosse 2012) imposed a very different kind of distinction between the religious and the secular, but with similar effects. Much earlier (in the early seventeenth century), before the Dalit conversion movements through which Protestants 'spiritualized' caste, Jesuits had concluded that caste was a secular or civil order irrelevant to eternal salvation and compatible with Christian conversion. This allowed the retention of caste among converts, based on a clear separation of the 'idolatrous' (to be rejected) and the 'civil' (to be tolerated).[4] Unlike the Protestants, they did not aim to bring spiritual release from the grip of caste, but rather to build the Catholic Church as a religious domain *beyond* caste society. The practical effect was paradoxical: Catholic communities and their ceremonial life and festival practices became profoundly embedded in the relational world of caste, its hierarchy and exclusions, and yet the Church claimed a realm in which people of all castes worshipped as equals in the eyes of God.

During the twentieth century the always fraught boundary between secular caste honour (the distinctions of caste that Jesuits tolerated among converts as 'civil') and sacred worship (the religious realm in which caste claims were illegitimate) shifted so as to bring more and more practices under ecclesiastical control. Until the late nineteenth century, the physical separation of castes within churches, and the separate administration of the Eucharist to Dalits at the back of or outside the churches were compatible with the spiritual equality of all. But by the 1930s these separations were regarded as an infringement of Dalits' religious rights as Christians. A range of practices, earlier part of the domain of 'secular' village headmen, caste landlords and Hindu rulers, were redefined as Christian so as to annul claims to caste rights. These included the caste-organized Catholic saint festival systems, which ascribed ranked duties and honours (and associated entitlement to village resources) to a hierarchy of castes. Dalit castes themselves found that Jesuit support for their struggles over entitlements to resources and caste honour depended upon the definition of the field of contest as religious rather than socio-political – that is, as a question of equal rights to worship as Christians.

In different ways, Protestant and Catholic missions provided Dalits with fields of action in which their struggles against exploitation and subordination could be rendered spiritual (or Christianized) and thereby secure missionary backing. This was especially important because the British government in India had adopted a policy of non-interference in affairs of native custom and religion, which precluded legal action against caste injustice, and meant that Dalits who were denied access to land or water, to temples or streets, or in other ways ill treated on the grounds of caste, had no recourse to colonial courts since (to Protestant-shaped policy) these deprivations arose from the practices of custom and religion.

Religion and entitlement to state development

Indian Independence changed things in interesting but difficult ways for Christian Dalits. The space of equality marked by the Christian religion was subsumed under a liberal paradigm of civil rights. Untouchability was secularized as a civic disability and socio-economic backwardness, and the Indian state introduced various protections, including laws which criminalized practices of caste discrimination, as well as reservations, welfare and development provision for the so-called Scheduled Castes. But although Dalits gained civic rights and development resources from the state, eligibility to these was defined in terms of *religion*. State provision was premised on the Protestant missionary idea of 'untouchability' as a debility arising from the practices of Hinduism. Thus, Dalits who were Christian or Muslim were (and are still) barred from legal protection as Scheduled Castes against the 'atrocities' (a legal category) of untouchability and from the development support of subsidized credit, scholarships, housing or a host of other schemes.

Dalits who are Christian face a dilemma. On the one hand, despite the importance of their Christian religious identity they continue to be subordinated as 'untouchables', and are unable to 'assert themselves as people other than as described by their birth' (Krishnan 2011). The churches never had the power to make Christian identity determinate in social life, because this was something always blocked by non-Dalit castes in the village community. On the other hand, the state allows them to be nothing but Christian, their religion determining identity and blocking access to the means of development. The situation leads many thousands of Christian Dalits to convert officially to Hinduism in order to progress (get jobs, houses, credit and so on): to convert for development. Eloquent autobiographical accounts capture the humiliation, guilt and betrayal that Christian Dalits experience when their faith is in question, as well as the absurd interrogation and surveillance of individual religious practice that accompany official verification of benefit entitlement (Gowthaman 2002; Krishnan 2011). Fifty years of Church-backed protest against this as unconstitutional religious discrimination have produced no result. The reason for this has much to do with electoral logic (the extension of development privileges to a section of the Christian minority being a vote loser). But it also reveals a rigidity of categories in the state system, equivalent in its impact to that of Christian missions.

As Krishnan (2011) points out (following Chatterjee 1999), it is a necessity of the modern state and its politics that social boundaries are simplified and reified, and that community identities are contained and enumerated in ways that disregard social reality: '[S]ince caste was considered [by the Indian state] to be a creation of Hindu scriptures it was deemed not possible for Christianity and Islam to have [their] followers identified by caste. If these religions admitted caste how [could] they be demarcated from Hinduism?' And Christians and Muslims themselves needed these demarcations from the majority religion, Hinduism, if they were:

> to have their social life governed by personal laws other than Hindu personal law and were to be awarded privileges for running their institutions without the supervision of the state, which found it incumbent to administer the Hindu endowments and temples. . . . Hence no matter if people could see as clearly as daylight that caste discrimination existed within Christianity in India, it could not be constitutionally recognised.
> (Krishnan 2011)

What is the effect of rigid categories on development? Any system of state provision that involves targeted categories constrains the articulation of demand and involves reflection by targeted groups on their own identity and entitlement – who they are and what they deserve (Still 2007: 280). Dalits who have become Christian (in pursuit of selfhood) are denied identity as the state's 'injured subjects' (Rao 2009: 177–8; Krishnan 2011: 14) or, if they seek progress by means of state support by adopting the religious identity of the welfare category Scheduled Caste, they have to retreat to the very untouchable and Hindu identities they left behind. Either way, Krishnan points out, Dalits experience an unbridgeable split between the pursuit of recompense or development in the public domain of schemes, scholarships, or legal protection against violence, on the one hand, and the pursuit of transformation in the inner private domain which refuses the pre-assigned identity and asserts difference (through religious conversion), that is, their development *through* (Christian) religion.[5] If missionaries disregarded the economic-political ('development') realities of Dalits by imposing on these the inner language of the spirit, the Indian state disregards the inner struggles for dignity, identity and spirit in the organization of outer categories of 'development' entitlement.

Christian Dalit development: Dalitizing Christianity and the culturalizing of caste

We should not of course presume that, because Dalit struggles against oppression were bound by the dichotomous categories of missionary and state agents, these provided the frameworks of meaning for Dalits themselves. The field of Christian religious action was inseparably political and economic. Thus the ritual honours over which Dalits mobilized claims at Catholic saint festivals were signifiers of opportunity and chits for access to wider resources and recognition. In fact, post-Independence Dalit political mobilization was born out of such contestation at saint festivals (Mosse 2012). The work on the self, enabled by Protestant Christianity, for example in changed clothing, diet, the confident speech that some could acquire from Bible reading, or giving up drink (Krishnan 2010), was also a political challenge to exclusion and stigma. As argued elsewhere (Mosse 2012: 181–6), Christianity has provided certain Dalits with a way of reflecting on difference and changeability, separating a shameful past from a better future, and is productive of a cultural capacity akin to what Appadurai (2004) calls the 'capacity to aspire'. Locally, this enabled renegotiation within villages of relationships of labour and services that could not be abandoned, and might even be accompanied by an 'upper'-caste Hindu perception of Christian Dalits as associated with tidiness or cleanliness, 'closer to education' and 'models of progress', as Krishnan's (2010) informants told him.

Those increasing numbers who join Pentecostal congregations also work to fashion lives anew in such ways, finding purpose and direction, in spite of persisting dangers and economic uncertainties. As Nathaniel Roberts notes of equally poor urban Dalit Pentecostals in Chennai, again Christianity is not a matter of *faith* apart from development (they are not fideists); it is not about change of culture. Christianity is about new knowledge and verifiable truth, about having reason to place trust in Jesus, and the confidence, transformation and displacement of fear that are said to follow. This new knowledge is not an accompaniment of modern development; it *is* development – a discovered universal, which makes the notion that Christianity is a cultural tradition, still less a western intrusion, absurd. As one Dalit tells Roberts: 'Do [people who reject Christianity as foreign] also reject tube lights because they are from the West?' 'Do they refuse to believe in airplanes?' (Roberts 2012: 278).

Christianity may itself have had powerful effects on Dalit lives, or perhaps its practices provided a coordination point for pre-existing elements of Dalit identification now brought together and articulated in new ways. Either way, Christian identity and action embodied development and dignity independent of the particularism of caste. However, from the late 1980s church leaders and activists influenced by a wider Dalit politics sought the recovery of socio-political caste – of Dalitness – that was concealed in this 'Christianization' of struggle.

In the more caste-embedded Catholic Church, this Dalit turn arose distinctively as a protest movement (the Dalit Christian Liberation Movement) within and against the Church and its tolerance of caste discrimination in worship, education institutions and the priesthood. This rebellious call to action by Dalit priests articulated the experience of Dalitness rather than Christianity. Indeed, Dalit activist leaders across the churches increasingly defined Christian Dalit difference in terms of *Dalitness* (rather than Christianity). As one prominent theologian (Nirmal 1990: 129) wrote, 'dalitness . . . is what is "Christian" about Dalit theology'; the 'broken Christ whom they [Dalits] can identify themselves with, follow behind and minister to, is for the most part non-Christian!' (Pieris 1993: 38). Protestant churches especially provided centres for theological and cultural production, articulating an honourable 'Christianized' Dalitness that fed into Dalit NGOs and movements connecting ideas of liberation and development to the assertion of cultural difference (a conversion discourse). Various types of symbolic reversal were drawn together to honour an 'outcaste' culture, Dalit art and religion. Publicly staged celebrations of Dalit arts in theological seminaries involved re-imagining formerly inferiorized drumming and dance forms, setting them apart from the relational context of servitude, and rendering Dalit arts as 'weapons for liberation'.[6]

Articulating Dalitness (and the political claim to Dalit development) from *within* Christianity may have been a way of challenging the state's categorical boundaries around caste and religion, forcing recognition of Christians as Scheduled Castes while drawing Christianity into the politics of caste. But the cultural and theological work of Dalit activists also rearticulated Dalit struggle as a *religio-cultural* struggle against Brahmanic Hinduism in a manner that echoed nineteenth-century missionary models of caste. The central role of seminaries, churches and theologians in the Dalitization of Christianity re-centralized religion in the matter of caste. These discourses of countercultural dissent were thus ironically aligned with the state interpretation of caste as based on a particular (Hindu, Brahmanic) religion.[7]

The effect of disembedding caste into the language of religion and culture has also been to fix the meaning of caste and ignore evidence on how caste is perpetuated in many different ways, serving various purposes of exclusion and domination, labour control, surplus extraction and opportunity hoarding (Mosse 2010). When caste is conceived as Brahmanical culture to be resisted through ideological challenges (including religious conversion), it is abstracted from the broader reality of caste as a system of graded economic rights or unequalized access to all sources of wealth (land, water, produce, education, employment, etc.) and from caste as a structure of agrarian and urban class relations, and a form of political domination that is compatible with *different* religions.[8]

Arguably the repeated process of 'rendering religious' for which caste provides a pretext has had a disabling influence on civil society actors working for Dalit development (see below); but it has also ensured the exclusion of the caste system from official (state and donor) frameworks for the analysis of poverty and the achievement of the Millennium Development Goals in India and South Asia. This is again because the Indian government's affirmative action is premised on the idea of compensation for historical disadvantage arising from the practices of Hinduism, rather than on caste discrimination as an *on-going* aspect of the economic system (Thorat and Newman 2010; Deshpande 2011). As a matter of religion (rather than socio-economics), caste falls outside the purview of the mainstream economic planning and development policy of the secular state. As a matter which is 'inner' or cultural, it is one to which the Indian state works hard to block international engagement, whether by development agencies or the UN human rights system. And international agencies become themselves complicit in the way religion as a category is the pretext for a narrowed conception of caste and development.[9]

The 'Dalitization' of development and human rights

There has been a two-decade-long effort to break the structure of categories of religion and development and to bring caste into Indian development discourse. I want briefly to explain aspects of this development effort as well as how it inadvertently reintroduced some of the categorical distinctions and distortions of Dalit experience which it sought to challenge.

I begin in the late 1980s when I was first closely involved with south Indian NGOs (by then the most visible agents intervening in the lives of Dalit communities) as Oxfam's Regional

Representative (in Bangalore). The prevailing policy categories at that time involved a still unchallenged 'economization' of poverty and a 'culturalization' of caste. Officially, caste was peripheralized as a religio-cultural accretion obscuring the class relations that were the proper focus of change – a view encouraged by the radical priests in Christian organizations whose Marxian and Liberation Theology training inspired the first generation of social action NGOs in the 1970s. Of course, in the villages, NGO schemes of various kinds were in actuality folded into caste struggles that focused simultaneously on fair wages and festival honours, land claims and teashop discrimination, electricity and temple entry, street lights, access to water and the refusal of ritual subordination at funerals. But the obdurate separation in policy of material from ritual relations, class from caste, and the inadequate representation of Dalit experience were especially apparent to NGO field coordinators who were themselves Dalit, working within familiar caste-structured village life, and who soon out of frustration with this formed their own NGOs. The rise of Dalit-led NGOs was one of several factors that moved caste and the fight against discrimination to the centre of NGO work in south India in the 1990s (see Mosse 2011).

The 'Dalitization' of NGO development policy was facilitated by the growing influence of Dalit activism and its multiplicity of movements, organizations and (later) political parties, including the American Black-influenced Dalit Panther movement (Gorringe 2005), as well as by the allied turn to Dalits within Church social policy (noted above), which for example recast the Jesuit 'preferential option for the poor' as an 'option for Dalits' in 1987 (see Mosse 2012: chap. 6). Such a reframing of development drew inspiration from the work of the preeminent Dalit leader Dr Bhimrao Ambedkar (d. 1956), whose birth centenary in 1991 brought national celebration and the availability of his writings newly in the vernacular. The centralization of Dalits in development was promoted too by the opportunities opened up by the 73rd Constitutional Amendment Act on local government, which reserved constituencies for Dalits and for women in elected bodies (Panchayats), and equally by the brutal denial to Dalits of these same constitutionally guaranteed political rights, and by a broader swathe of violence against Dalits across south India that manifested a reaction to Dalit acts of insubordination, self-respect and economic autonomy, targeting Dalit bodies (especially sexual attacks on Dalit women) and property, and marking out for destruction signs of Dalit development – radios, scooters, tiled houses – by dominant castes for whom development was emphatically a relational matter.

Thus, from within the NGO development field there appeared to come an approach that built on the everyday experience of the Dalit communities, and challenged the institutionalized separation of the religious–cultural and development. For the first time, caste was a development issue. The NGO capacity to articulate Dalit aspirations and to mobilize action in terms that were meaningful to the men and women with whom they worked was a hallmark of these initiatives. This 'Dalit development' approach could be (and came to be) articulated and sustained as a coherent discourse, capable of enrolling a wide range of actors and agencies – Dalit movements, state actors, lawyers, churches, donors and their European supporters, national campaigns and transnational advocacy groups.

However, the manner in which caste was brought into development had inadvertent effects that paralleled the earlier disembedding of caste from the 'totality of social relations' (Steur 2012: 64) by missionary and state discourses. Three aspects of this can briefly be highlighted: first, the relative autonomy of the framing of Dalit approaches to development from localized relations of caste power; second, the selectivity and reframing of Dalit experience involved; and, third, a change in the articulation of demand by Dalits themselves that is brought about.

On the first point, articulating a Dalit approach within the field of international development was never going to be simply a matter of transmitting local caste struggles for wider and wider support; it was not just a movement out from the local to 'the global' in order to solve village problems by linking them to 'higher levels' (Steur 2012). As in the earlier case of the missionaries, in order to build and sustain support, Dalit experience was abstracted and transformed as it came to be translated into other institutional agendas. Or, as Steur (2012) argues, 'Dalit activism and the articulation of Dalitness is not constituted at any particular "local" level but emerged in a transnational social field' (2012: 64). It was in the language of human rights (HR) (especially after the 50-year celebration of the Universal Declaration in 1998) that the Dalit turn in development policy was transnationally constituted, and through the set of pre-existing activist and institutional links that the HR discourse was afforded. Following the success (by 1994) of campaigns against apartheid, Steur points out, HR groups such as Human Rights Watch turned their attention to India and to the continuing caste discrimination and spectacular atrocities against Dalits (see HRW 1999), as did international Church networks (in particular the World Council of Churches and the World Lutheran Federation), concerned for the large (Dalit) Christian population subject to violation of their human rights (Steur 2012).[10]

The tabling of the issue of caste discrimination at the 2001 World Conference against Racism (WCAR) in Durban, and the large-scale presence of Dalit activists enabled by international support (Steur 2012) were focal for regional and local NGO networking on 'Dalit Human Rights' within India. What occurred in south India was a rapid expansion of Dalit NGO networks, and 'networks of networks' such as the Human Rights Forum for Dalit Liberation. Under the slogan 'Dalit rights are human rights' these networks served to articulate and consolidate a discourse on development as a question of Dalit rights (and underdevelopment – inequality of opportunity, persistent poverty, unemployment, ill-health or low education levels – as the effect of caste discrimination). International NGO donors (church and secular) found their own reasons to support a policy focus on Dalit rights and dignity, for example because this brought a desired holistic (material, social, spiritual) perspective to human development, or because, as a target for funding, NGO networks could be imagined as social action that was locally initiated but regionally interconnected into a kind of self-organizing social movement for 'structural' change.

The sheer speed of this process and the consequent weakness of underlying institutional structures meant that donor-supported Dalit NGO networks with their widening connections and high public profile were always going to be more significant as a discursive effect (Knox *et al.* 2006) than as an organizational structure fostering a sustained locally rooted social movement (see Mosse 2011 for an exploration of the implications of this). Here was a powerful representational machinery on Dalit human rights manifest in episodic events, and selectively foregrounding aspects of Dalit lives and struggles which could be subject to the available and effective instruments of Dalit human rights monitoring and legal support, public hearings and jury panels linked to national and international human rights bodies (the latter having the objective of bringing international pressure on the Indian state on the question of caste discrimination) – all part of the internationally linked network function.

This brings me to the second effect of the Dalitization of development under an international civil society human rights frame, namely the selectivity of attention to Dalit experience it involved. There are again different aspects to this. For one thing, within this frame Dalits are positioned as 'specific victims of discrimination and violence' (Steur 2012: 65–6). The horrific cases of violence, rape and murder have, not surprisingly, been most prominent in construing Dalit experience as the abuse of human rights. This brings a legal framing and recourse to special criminal legislation (the Scheduled Castes (Prevention of Atrocities) Act 1989), with the inevitable consequence that everyday actions of anti-Dalit violence and humiliation are 'recontextualized' into crimes that individualize and arguably exceptionalize caste discrimination (Rao 2009). This leads Steur to ask whether the human rights focus might 'detract from examination of structural socio-economic relations' (2012: 66). This question applies equally to manifestations of untouchability beyond the most extreme atrocities, especially the routine indignities including exclusion from teashops, streets, burial grounds, temples or worship prioritized within Dalit human rights action. Might attention again be drawn to untouchability as a ritual relationship isolated from a wider set of relationships of exploitation, exclusion and restricted opportunity?

Dalit NGO-backed claims to, and conflicts over, village resources have indeed been construed as action against untouchability. Particular focus is placed on the *commons* such as water, fish, trees or grazing land through which caste hierarchy was (and is) symbolically and ritually enacted. NGOs have also organized action for the repossession of lands allocated by British district administrators to Dalits but alienated by 'upper' castes (the *panchami* land). Not only does such action recall histories of caste injury and involve acts of Dalit political assertions, signified for example by erecting statues of Dr Ambedkar, using slogans, drumming, cooking beef and other reversed symbols of Dalit humiliation (Mosse 2012: 222–4), but it also frames action against caste abuse in a way that allows appeal to anti-untouchability law.

This is strategically important action, but, because of the way in which the discourse on caste has been historically constituted and internationally articulated, Dalit experience tends to be selectively construed in ways that import distinctions (caste/non-caste) which reproduced rather than break from the inherited conceptual divide between the religious-cultural and the political-economic, caste and class, caste and gender, and analogous distinctions. The Dalit rights agenda tends to be conceptualized in ways that take the village as the quintessential site of struggle; if not over ritual exclusion and the humiliations of untouchability, it is in the form of struggles over land, the commons or village-level power. This can be problematic because it is not always possible to localize the Dalit rights agenda into collective caste struggles, since today caste is active in shaping opportunity in new and invisible ways through the connections and capital necessary for entry into higher education or employment in public or private sectors, or through 'non-traditional' forms of discrimination in hiring or renting, or in the weakness of Dalit caste networks (or the lack of capital) in securing education, skills or employment, crucial structural processes that are not easily made visible as Dalit rights abuse. Many of the concerns of Dalit villagers themselves (access to credit, education, jobs in towns, and migrant labour), especially among young women and men, may not articulate well with the anti-untouchability or caste-culture framing of development. In this vein Anandhi (2012) explains how the Dalit rights discourses of national or international networks into which local NGOs are linked can hinder their ability to respond to complex forms of local gender-and-caste oppression, including persisting patriarchy and domestic violence.

NGO workers are not unaware of these dilemmas. While framed in the language of Dalit human rights, their interventions are understood and acted upon locally in different and more meaningful terms. So, for example, grassroots women's groups reinterpret networked Dalit rights activism to address gender-specific local issues such as obtaining house sites in women's names (Anandhi 2012, 2013); or, in another case, anti-untouchability criminal law is deliberately used to back land reoccupation, not to underline the caste basis of the claim but because the legal procedure allows the infringement of Dalit rights to be *individualized* to particular non-Dalit occupiers of *panchami* land, thereby avoiding broader conflict between Dalits and caste Hindus (Sundara Babu 2012).

Nonetheless, it is the case that caste/class and other distinctions through which action is represented become increasingly rigid as the discourse of Dalit rights travels 'outward' to national campaigns, UN advocacy or debates on caste discrimination in other legal jurisdictions (e.g. the UK) wherein the specific injuries of inherited status, ritual impurity, pollution and stigma are re-centred.[11] The critical question is whether a 'culturalization' of caste inherited from the earlier missionary 'spiritualization' of caste-poverty threatens to diminish the capacity of development actors (state, NGO, Church) to address the reality of Dalit poverty by obstructing the under-standing of complex and changing local realities requiring varied approaches. At the very least, work is needed by development's varied brokers and translators (Lewis and Mosse 2006) to mediate the disjunctures between NGO discourse shaped by its own political logic (as was the missionaries') and the realities of local problems and actions.

The third effect of rights approaches, more broadly, concerns the way these are changing the local articulation of demand. In this regard, Krishnan (2011: 1) observes among Dalit villagers 'a tendency to move from cultural-political emancipatory approaches to those of right-based approaches'. Rather than engage in agonistic relationships with dominant castes in struggles over resources and respect, Dalits 'characterise the grievances suffered as a failure of the state in implementing statutory measures of welfare and compensation', conceived as the abrogation of their rights – right to work, right to education, right to health, etc. – even though at one level a history of caste domination lies behind such state failure.

The discourse of rights and of discrimination in development comes with the deeper politi-cization of Dalit identity in relation to demand from the state. The struggles for land or employ-ment are for *Dalit* land and *Dalit* jobs or *Dalit* enterprises. At the micro-level, as Krishnan notes (personal communication), when Dalits are excluded for example from a water source installed by the state in the main village (the *ur*), the conflict that arises is resolved by provision of another water facility in the Dalit 'colony' (the *ceri*). The absence of collective action to break down the residential segregations produced historically through mechanisms of power, labour control, and denial of property which divide Tamil villages into the dominant *ur* and the Dalit *ceri* is strik-ing.[12] At the macro-level, Dalit organizations campaign for a proportionally allocated budget for the Dalit population, known as the Special Component Plan, under the slogan 'Where is *our* money?',[13] that is, for a share of resources generated by capitalist growth, but not necessarily against the structural inequalities produced by that model of growth (Steur 2012). Thus, while NGO networks have significantly increased the effectiveness of mobilization of Dalits against discrimination and for rights to development through politicized identities, it may be asked whether these demands for welfare parity leave unchallenged the structural relations of power and political economy (Steur forthcoming). Does the tactical focus on Dalit rights involve a merely *political* reversal in face of political-economic transformations (here neoliberal ones) that impoverish or dispossess (to use terms from Steur's (forthcoming) engagement with Partha Chatterjee and Eric Wolf)? Might structural power even push tactical struggles in the direc-tion of 'mere' identity politics which reproduce the divisions of caste among those with shared interests as exploited groups, perhaps through the agency of Dalit NGOs themselves (ibid.)? This is not the place to further debate these issues. But what can be noted is the way in which caste continues as a means for the articulation of 'old antinomies of materialism and idealism' (Roseberry in Steur forthcoming).

Summary and conclusions

My purpose in this chapter, as a contribution to contentious debate on 'religion' and 'develop-ment', has been to trace connections and continuities in a long trajectory of the artefactual and institutionally driven bifurcation of religion and economy, culture and development, caste and class, identity politics and political economy, idealism and materialism and the related processes of disembedding and abstraction, whether in Christian mission, development or Dalit human rights activism. We started with the fact that drawing a distinction between the religious and the political-economic, or between caste and class, misunderstands the condition of Dalits for whom caste is a political-economic-ritual relationship, and whose labour was (and is) organized and controlled through ritual relations. This reality of caste is independent of religious affiliation (Hindu, Muslim, Christian). This is significant because a long history of 'development' interventions on behalf of Dalits – missionary, state and NGO, colonial and postcolonial – had a double effect: first 'culturalizing' caste (Natrajan 2012) to produce the modern Dalit as a religious identity subject to ritual humiliation and ideological challenge (for example through religious conversion) and institutionalized into a denial of state protections and privileges to Christian or Muslim Dalits; and second producing the modern category of 'labour' separate from caste, or 'shorn of heathenish caste characteristics' (Viswanath 2014a: 8). The categorical distinctions between the religious and the economic, and caste and class, served the particular interests of outsiders and their political and administrative exigencies (Viswanath 2014a: 3). Beginning with Christian missionaries, these categorizations shaped the field of development for the state and NGOs, and provide a mould for contemporary forms of activism and advocacy on Dalit human rights and development.

While the disembedding of particularistic caste into the universals of religion or rights constantly reintroduces misleading categorical distinctions, it should not be ignored that this may also be important, even necessary, as well as constraining. The Protestant Christian rendering of caste as 'spiritual slavery' vastly increased the attention to untouchability (as an extreme form of subordination) and widened the potential networks of support and solidarity in the late nineteenth and early twentieth centuries. The human rights (rather than religious) framing of untouchability achieves even wider reach for Dalits today. It has enabled the problem of caste to be explained in ways that can be communicated to an international audience (for example, as a form of racism, Indian apartheid or religious persecution) and inserted within global forums such as the WCAR or the World Social Forum. The idea of Dalit rights has facilitated the mobilization of financial support for Dalit NGO work in the expectation that this framing empowers local claims for resources or justice (Steur 2012).

But we also know that what works well for 'upward' channelling within a Dalit human rights chain, or outward transmission to national and global forums, does not best serve the need for horizontal connections between different identities (Dalit, tribal [*adivasi*], labour, migrant) in relation to some particular and urgent livelihood threats or impoverishing processes. As Luisa Steur (2012) puts it, the question is what sort of solidarity is possible or desirable: a compassion-based response to Dalit suffering or a solidarity-based response to dispossession? In practice these imply different kinds of networks, on the one hand networks of professionalized NGOs and churches, on the other labour movements and unions.

Several NGO donors have themselves now begun to disfavour building development strategies on caste identities or Dalit dignity separate from class, investing not in 'caste-communitarian' development but in wider coalitions of interest around exploitation, livelihood threats, or land and employment rights in the context of India's rapid capitalist growth, reconnecting the politics of recognition to the politics of redistribution (see Mosse 2011). In this connection, Steur (forthcoming) shows how building alliances to challenge a 'land grab' from multinational corporate investments near Chennai produced new practices of Dalit identity reconnected to land and economy. This involved different horizontal and international connections, while facing off co-opting 'corporate social responsibility' discourses and the state criminalization of local protest.

Meanwhile, Indian Dalit activism itself turns from claims about injury to claims *for* development, from universal human rights to specific economic rights in the form of national budgeting and the Special Component Plan, which is itself a challenge to the in-built assumption that Dalits derive entitlements as compensation for religiously defined disadvantage suffered historically (or even on-going discrimination within the social and economic system), but insists instead on Dalits' common entitlement (as Hindus, Muslims or Christians) to a share of the national wealth. Both the NGO 'de-Dalitization' of development in favour of solidarity, and the demands for state budget allocations involve different ways to secularize caste and to dismantle the inherited categories of religion and development through which responses to Dalit impoverishment continue to be structured.

Notes

1 The research for this chapter was undertaken with support from an Economic and Social Research Council (ESRC) grant 'Caste out of Development: Civil Society Activism and Transnational Advocacy on Dalit Rights and Development' (RES-062-23-2227).
2 For the extensive literature on this see the bibliography in Frykenberg (2008).
3 Honed into a theoretical position in the work of Louis Dumont (1980).
4 Such cross-cultural mission encounters played a significant part in the early modern separation of the religious and the secular in Europe (and the establishment of a secular framework within which the current debate on religion and development is possible).
5 Even a Hindu Dalit faces the fact that, in the public and legal terms which give her certain rights as a member of a Scheduled Caste, her identity is fixed as a matter of lineage and historical injustice rather than present aspiration, and so this does not 'relieve her from the burden of bearing the injured identity in her inner domain' (Krishnan 2011).
6 This itself proved controversial, since some castes among Dalits were and some were not associated with the Christian churches, and in an increasingly caste-divided Dalit social field contests arise over who defines 'Dalit culture' or 'Dalit religion' or 'Dalit arts'.
7 Krishnan (2011) has traced these developments across the discourses of government and political actors through a detailed reading of vernacular and ideological literature.
8 This is further underlined by Hindu nationalist trends in Indian politics that entrenched a conceptual fault line between Dalits and 'caste Hindus'.
9 For example, the World Bank's recent India Poverty Assessment, negotiated with the government, deftly combines institutionalism and cultural reification, asserting that: 'The rules of the game in the caste system – to borrow a formulation of North (1990) – are rooted in a religiously sanctioned ordering of occupations described in ancient Hindu texts such as the *Manusmriti*' (World Bank 2011: 15).
10 Throughout the 1990s, Church-based NGO donors had been especially willing to reframe their development objectives in Dalit terms because of the nature of their home and Indian constituencies and the mediated links between them. And in the other direction, for Dalits (and NGO leaders), being Christian and participating in the universalist language of Christianity allowed a collaboration with other universalist languages in development or human rights within which caste discrimination could be understood and acted upon (Mosse 2012: 278).
11 Thus the debates on legislation against caste discrimination in the UK mobilized religious groups (Hindu, Sikh) as stakeholders alongside Dalit ones (see Dhanda *et al.* 2014).
12 For an exceptional break with the social geography of the 'caste street' see Mosse (2012: 244).
13 The increase in state revenues and a dramatic reduction in, and greater state surveillance of, foreign funding for NGOs are also in part responsible for this focused attention on state-backed Dalit development to ensure that Dalits are part of India's 'inclusive growth' (Steur 2012).

References

Anandhi, S. (2012) 'Discrimination and Development: A Case Study of Dalit Women's Activism in Tamilnadu', paper for Panel on 'The Development Turn in Dalit Activism: Disquieting Caste and Capitalism in Contemporary India', EASA Conference, Paris, 9–12 July.
Anandhi, S. (2013) 'The Mathammas: Gender, Caste and the Politics of Intersectionality in Rural Tamil Nadu', *Economic and Political Weekly*, XLVIII (18), 64–71.
Appadurai, Arjun (2004) 'The Capacity to Aspire: Culture and the Terms of Recognition', in V. Rao and M. Walton (eds), *Culture and Public Action*, Stanford, CA: Stanford University Press, pp. 59–84.

Chatterjee, Partha (1999) 'The Nation and Its Fragments', in *The Partha Chatterjee Omnibus: Comprising Nationalist Thought and the Colonial World, The Nation and Its Fragments, and a Possible India*, Delhi: Oxford University Press.

Deshpande, Ashwini (2011) *The Grammar of Caste: Economic Discrimination in Contemporary India*, Delhi: Oxford University Press.

Dhanda, M., Mosse, D., Waughray, A., Keane, D., Green, R., Iafrati, S. and Mundy, J. K. (2014) *Caste in Britain: Experts' Seminar and Stakeholders' Workshop*, Research Report no. 92, Manchester: Equality and Human Rights Commission.

Dumont, Louis (1980) *Homo Hierarchicus: The Caste System and Its Implications*, trans. M. Sainsbury, Chicago: University of Chicago Press, and London: Paladin.

Escobar, Arturo (2012) *Encountering Development: The Making and Unmaking of the Third World*, 2nd edn, Princeton, NJ: Princeton University Press.

Fountain, Philip (2013) 'The Myth of Religious NGOs: Development Studies and the Return of Religion', in Gilles Carbonnier (ed.), *International Development Policy: Religion and Development*, London: Palgrave Macmillan, pp. 9–20.

Frykenberg, Robert Eric (2008) *Christianity in India: From Beginnings to the Present*, Oxford: Oxford University Press.

Gorringe, Hugo (2005) *Untouchable Citizens: Dalit Movements and Democratisation in Tamil Nadu*, Delhi: Sage.

Gow, David (2008) *Countering Development: Indigenous Modernity and the Moral Imagination*, Durham, NC: Duke University Press.

Gowthaman, Raj (2002) *Siluvairaj Sarithram* [Chronicles of Siluvairaj], Chennai: Tamil-Ini.

HRW (Human Rights Watch) (1999) *Broken People: Caste Violence against India's 'Untouchables'*, New York: HRW.

Jones, Ben and Juul Petersen, Marie (2011) 'Instrumental, Narrow, Normative? Reviewing Recent Work on Religion and Development', *Third World Quarterly*, 32 (7), 1291–1306.

Knox, Hannah, Savage, Mike and Harvey, Penny (2006) 'Social Networks and the Study of Relations: Networks as Method, Metaphor and Form', *Economy and Society*, 35 (1), 113–40.

Krishnan, Rajan Kurai (2010) 'Development, Dalits and Christianity: A Few Ethnographic and Conceptual Notes', paper for Caste Out of Development: Mid-Term Review Workshop, Chennai, December.

Krishnan, Rajan Kurai (2011) 'Caste and Religion in the Age of the Nation-State: Certain Polemical Blinders and Dalit Situations', conference paper for Caste Out of Development Conference, Chennai, 15 December.

Lewis, David and Mosse, D. (eds) (2006) *Development Brokers and Translators*, Bloomfield, CT: Kumarian Press.

Mosse, David (2010) 'A Relational Approach to Durable Poverty, Inequality and Power', *Journal of Development Studies*, 46 (7), 1156–78.

Mosse, David (2011) 'Uncertain Networks: NGOs, Dalit Rights and the Development Agenda in South India', background paper for ESRC Caste Out of Development Project Conference, Chennai, December.

Mosse, David (2012) *The Saint in the Banyan Tree: Christianity and Caste Society in India*, Berkeley: University of California Press.

Natrajan, Balmurli (2012) *The Culturalization of Caste in India: Identity and Inequality in a Multicultural Age*, London: Routledge.

Nirmal, Arvind P. (1990) 'Towards a Christian Dalit Theology', in Xavier Irudayaraj (ed.), *Emerging Dalit Theology*, Madras: Jesuit Theological Secretariat, and Madurai: Tamilnadu Theological Seminary, pp. 123–42.

North, D. (1990) *Institutions, Institutional Change, and Economic Performance*, Cambridge: Cambridge University Press.

Peel, J. D. Y. (1978) '*Olaju*: A Yoruba Concept of Development', *Journal of Development Studies*, 14 (2), 139–65.

Pieris, Aloysius (1993) 'Does Christ Have a Place in Asia? A Panoramic View', in L. Boff and V. Elizondo (eds), *Any Room for Christ in Asia?*, London: SCM Press, pp. 33–47.

Rao, Anupama (2009) *The Caste Question: Dalits and the Politics of Modern India*, Berkeley: University of California Press.

Robbins, J. (2004) *Becoming Sinners: Christianity and Moral Torment in a Papua New Guinea Society*, Berkeley: University of California Press.

Roberts, Nathaniel (2012) 'Is Conversion a "Colonisation of Consciousness"?', *Anthropological Theory*, 12 (3), 271–98.

Salemink, O., Giri, A. and van Harskamp, A. (2004) *The Development of Religion/The Religion of Development*, Delft: Eburon.

Steur, Luisa (2012) 'Dalit Civil Society Activism', *Seminar*, 633, 63–7.

Steur, Luisa (forthcoming) 'Subaltern Studies, Marxian Anthropology and the Thervoy Land Struggle', in Alf Nilsen and Srila Roy (eds), *New Subaltern Politics: Reconceptualizing Hegemony and Resistance in Contemporary India*, New Delhi: Oxford University Press.

Still, Clarinda (2007) 'Gender, Education and Status in a Dalit Community in Andhra Pradesh, South India', Ph.D. thesis, London School of Economics and Political Science.

Sundara Babu, N. (2012) 'Assertion for Resources and Dignity: Dalit Civil Society Activism in Tamil Nadu', paper for Panel on 'The Development Turn in Dalit Activism: Disquieting Caste and Capitalism in Contemporary India', EASA Conference, Paris, 9–12 July.

Thorat, S. and Newman, K. (eds) (2010) *Blocked by Caste: Economic Discrimination in Modern India*, Delhi: Oxford University Press.

Viswanath, Rupa (2008) 'Religion, Secularism, Solicitude: Ways of Speaking about Pariah Conversion in Colonial Madras', paper presented at the London School of Economics, January.

Viswanath, Rupa (2010) 'Spiritual Slavery, Material Malaise: "Untouchables" and Religious Neutrality in Colonial South India', *Historical Research*, 83 (219), 124–45.

Viswanath, Rupa (2014a) 'Rethinking Caste and Class: "Labour", the "Depressed Classes", and the Politics of Distinctions, Madras 1918–1924', *International Review of Social History*, 59 (1), 1–37.

Viswanath, Rupa (2014b) *The Pariah Problem: Caste, Religion, and the Social in Modern India*, New York: Columbia University Press.

Washbrook, David (1993) 'Land and Labour in Late Eighteenth-Century South India: The Golden Age of the Pariah?', in P. Robb (ed.), *Dalit Movements and the Meanings of Labour in India*, New Delhi: Oxford University Press, pp. 68–86.

World Bank (2011) *Poverty and Social Exclusion in India*, Washington, DC: World Bank Publications.

15

RELIGION, GENDER AND DEVELOPMENT IN SOUTH ASIA

Tamsin Bradley and Nida Kirmani

Introduction

The achievement of gender equality, which has historically focused on improving the status of women but has recently been expanded by some international development organizations and donor agencies to include the rights of sexual minorities, has consistently been identified as a key development goal. In the context of the rights of women and sexual minorities, religion has generally been viewed as a conservative force – one that acts as a hindrance to the achievement of gender and sexual equality. This has been no less true in India and Pakistan, where conservative groups across religious traditions have emerged as opponents of movements for gender equality. At the same time, religion has at times also been used as a means of supporting arguments for gender or sexual equality by those advocating equal rights. This chapter will explore the interaction between religious discourses deployed by a variety of actors and movements for gender or sexual equality specifically in India and Pakistan (see also Tomalin, Chapter 13). Because South Asia is such a vast and diverse region, it is not possible to discuss it in its entirety, and therefore we have chosen to focus only on India and Pakistan. Both countries provide an interesting comparison, as the former is officially a secular state while the latter is officially religious. However, religion and politics have been closely intertwined in both countries, with similar detrimental effects on the rights of women and sexual minorities. In both settings the women's movements tend to be secular in the sense of viewing religion as something that should not influence politics (although private religious observance is acceptable) but may engage with religious values and actors strategically in order to achieve their goals.

Each section will include a brief discussion of the relationship between religion and the women's movement historically and then in contemporary settings in each country. In each location the focus is slightly different in order to reflect the particular issues and concerns that have come to the fore in each. Moreover, we focus on the majority religion in each setting – the section on India focuses on Hinduism but with some discussion also of Islam, and the section on Pakistan looks only at Islam. However, both sections draw out the ways in which the movements for gender equality have engaged with religious discourses and actors and how religion has been used to justify the denial of equal rights to women and sexual minorities. In particular, this chapter will focus on a series of issues where the nexus between religion and gender or sexual rights has been most clear. This includes the issues of women's rights within

215

marriage, violence against women, and the rights of sexual minorities including homosexuals and transgender communities. These issues will be discussed within the wider contexts of how movements and campaigns for gender or sexual equality in both countries have (or have not) engaged with religious discourses and actors as part of their struggles. Underlying this discussion is the notion that the achievement of gender equality, which includes the rights of women and sexual minorities, is a key development challenge for both India and Pakistan.

Religion, gender and development in India

Those advocating gender equality in India, who have typically tended to be secular in their outlook, have always had to confront the issue of religion as part of their campaigning efforts. While early women's rights activists and social reformers rarely challenged religious precepts outright, the contemporary women's movement has been more confrontational in its approach to religion, challenging religious conservative groups in particular. This has been most clear in the campaigns related to women's rights within marriage, including on the issues of Muslim personal law and dowry in particular. Furthermore, the issue of violence against women has exposed the underlying patriarchal logic of some interpretations of religion, which often justify violence against women if not explicitly then implicitly within their discourses and institutions. Finally, the rights of sexual minorities, which have become a matter of public debate only in the last ten years, have faced direct challenges from conservative religious groups across the spectrum. This next subsection will outline the changing contours of the relationship between religion and gender and sexual equality historically in India.

The women's movement and religion historically

The relationship between religion and the struggle for gender equality has shifted according to the changing social and political context across the subcontinent. While early social reformers in Colonial India used religious symbols and texts in support of their campaigns against practices such as *sati* and child marriage, which were associated with the Hindu tradition (Kirmani 2011), the contemporary women's movement,[1] which emerged during the 1970s, has either openly challenged religious traditions and precepts or at least avoided actively engaging with religion in its struggles. For example, the women's movement has campaigned against *sati* and dowry, which has brought the movement face to face with Hindu conservative groups. At the same time, some sections of the contemporary women's movement also attempted to engage positively with Hinduism. Sunder Rajan (2000: 36) points to the strategic co-optation of religious symbolism by some members of the women's movement who 'invoked "traditional" (read: Hindu) symbols in some cases as a means of diluting, if not countering, the Western bias of "feminism"'. The use of goddess imagery, exemplified by the naming of the first feminist publishing house Kali for Women, and the celebration of women's spirituality in the journal *Manushi* can be seen as attempts to broaden the appeal of the women's movement by 'indigenizing' feminism.[2]

In addition to the engagement between feminists and the Hindu tradition, Islamic beliefs and practices, as well as the way that tradition is structured in relation to the Indian legal system, have drawn attention from women's groups. A key example is what came to be known as the Shah Bano case. In 1978, an elderly Muslim woman claimed maintenance from her ex-husband through the court under the Indian Civil Code and attracted much critique from Muslim conservative groups which saw this as a violation of Muslim personal law.[3] The Supreme Court eventually ruled in Shah Bano's favour, sparking protests from Muslim conservative groups across the country. This case brought national attention to the conflict between Muslim women's rights and those of religious conservative groups to define the interests of 'the community'. Within these debates the women's movement first argued for a uniform Civil Code, which would abolish the system of religion-based personal laws, but later revised its position, arguing for reforms in the existing personal laws (Chhachhi 1991). This was partially a reaction to the growing influence of the Hindu Right, which was also calling for an abolition of Muslim personal laws as part of its agenda to impose a Hindu identity on the nation. In the end the Congress-led government conceded to the demands of Muslim conservative groups by passing the Muslim Women (Protection of Rights on Divorce) Act, 1986, which stated that Muslim family laws would not be dealt with under the Indian Civil Code and would be decided by local *waqf* boards, which are generally in charge of managing religious endowments and charity, instead.[4] This case sparked a wider national debate in which Muslim women became symbols for various political interest groups, with the voices of actual Muslim women remaining largely absent at this time (see Hasan 1994, 1998; Kumar 1994; Kishwar 1998).

Since the Shah Bano case, Muslim women's organizations and networks have emerged across India, which work within and outside the mainstream women's movement and utilize both Islamic feminist and secular, human rights-based strategies in their advocacy. Two such networks include the Muslim Women's Rights Network (MWRN) and the Bharatiya Muslim Mahila Andolan (BMMA), both of which diverge in their strategies vis-à-vis religion. The MWRN takes a secular, human rights-based approach, while the BMMA works from both a human rights framework and one that draws from 'Islamic feminism'. While neither group has been successful in enacting reforms related to Muslim personal laws, both have been successful in helping to widen the terms of the debate on Muslim women's rights and in challenging the authority of conservative religious bodies such as the All India Muslim Personal Law Board. Furthermore, both groups have engaged in similar strategies at the grassroots level in order to secure women's rights, for example inserting clauses that would protect women's rights into the *nikahnama*, or Muslim marriage contract, as a means of protecting women's rights within marriage without challenging Muslim personal laws. These networks disturb the secular/religious binary through their advocacy, which must necessarily straddle both sets of discourses in order to manoeuvre effectively within a context in which the Muslim minority is increasingly under attack both physically and symbolically by the Hindu Right (see Kirmani 2010, 2011, 2013; Kirmani and Phillips 2011).

Contemporary women's rights advocacy

Much of the campaigning undertaken by the women's movement in India since the 1970s has been related to eradicating violence against women in its multiple forms. While violence against women continues to be a persistent problem, various groups have emerged that are campaigning against conservative, patriarchal and homophobic ideologies. Success can be seen in the passage of new anti-rape legislation following the release of the Verma report in 2013,[5] but understandings of the root of this violence and oppression are still limited. As in most contexts, competing tensions between a web of diverse standpoints – secular, religious, liberal and conservative – are often played out through and on women's bodies and by governing sexual relationships in general.

Violence against women often emerges through tight controls placed over women's lives through practices such as dowry and son-preference as well as through the general legitimization of male control over women, which sanctions violence as a means of ensuring women do not transgress their domestic–mothering role. Feminists actively involved in the women's movement since the 1970s have raised concerns over the increasing rather than decreasing influence of religious conservatism on the lives of women. This, they claim, feeds into and perpetuates the oppression of women within a narrow domestic–mothering role. For example, the prominent feminist activist and publisher Ritu Menon of Women Unlimited stated:

> We have seen a shift to the right both nationally in India but also globally that has given rise to more and more religious groups who pursue an ideology which sees women's role as purely domestic and will go to any lengths to ensure they remain locked into the private sphere.
>
> (Interview, July 2013)

Some activists express concern that the focus has shifted away from issues of marriage and dowry and on to other forms of violence that are receiving global attention and campaign money, for example trafficking and prostitution. Yet, for feminist activists and scholars such as Professor Rajni Palriwala, the 'old' issues are still at the foundations of the systematic abuse of women, namely marriage and related practices such as dowry, which act to ensure continued violence against women and marginalization. This reality has not shifted despite women's gains in other areas such as employment and education:

> Women are the target for many forms of violence especially if they are at home; this has not changed. I think that we can see it is a backlash because more women are speaking out; for someone like me I really have to be jolted to see how things have changed.
>
> (Interview, January 2014)

In trying to explain the continuing prevalence of violence against women, it is important to highlight the increased prominence and influence of conservative religious groups. As already acknowledged in the interview with Ritu Menon, religious teachings are heavily gendered and often project images of femininity that link women to the domestic sphere.

Many religious leaders in India (and indeed across the globe) refuse to acknowledge the ways in which religion can legitimize practices that are in themselves violent or lead to violence. They often employ the artificial division between religion and culture to argue that religion does not endorse the use of violence against women; abusive practices are identified as culture so as to exonerate religion. This reading however ignores the ways in which religious teachings promote male dominance, rendering women passive and subservient and ultimately vulnerable to violence (see Bradley 2010, 2011). Religious leaders often promote patriarchal discourse, which, although challenged in different ways by groups of religious women as well as secular feminist groups, still prevails in shaping and weaving the fabric of the social, cultural and political environment. In the case of Hinduism, religious leaders who promote women's subservience to their husbands often present Sita as an ideal role model (neatly avoiding interpretations of the *Ramayana* that highlight Sita's suffering at the hands of a cruel husband) and in doing so endorse female inferiority and male dominance as the norm. Patriarchy is then further enforced by and through specific practices such as dowry (Bradley 2011). In turn these practices depend on the threat or actual use of violence in order for them to be maintained and to secure the continuation of the heterosexual model of marriage and motherhood. So whilst religion may not sanction violence against women directly it does so covertly by rigidly projecting a narrow and ultimately misogynistic system.

The link between certain interpretations of religion and violence against women is perhaps clearest with regards to the issue of dowry. Dowry exists because it functions to protect the heterosexual institution of marriage, which, many feminists argue, is at the root of women's oppression (Basu 2009; Palriwala 2009). When measuring progress, it is depressingly clear that the situation in some areas is in fact worsening. Kaur and Palriwala (2013) note that rates of both sex-selective abortions and female infanticide are on the increase.[6] The pressures on women to have sons therefore continues unabated, supported by the growth in dowry demands. Sons bring in money through dowry; girls are considered a financial drain.

Other instances of violence against women are either increasing or becoming more visible. The gang rape and murder of Nirbhaya[7] in Delhi in December 2012 sparked widespread anti-rape protests across the country. Analysis into the motivation of different groups who took part in the protests offers insights into the wide spectrum of views held on women's roles and reveals the liberal-conservative tensions bubbling across Indian society, which are being played out on women's bodies. In an interview in July 2013 with a feminist activist working in Himachal Pradesh, the interviewee commented that the main success of the anti-rape protests was the unity they achieved between vastly different ends of the political spectrum. Groups joined forces from secular liberal feminists through to the conservative Hindutva political parties. She went on to offer her views as to why this apparent unity was possible: Nirbhaya was viewed by the conservative Hindu Right as a woman who had done everything right. She was not out alone but accompanied by her partner; she was not returning late; she was dressed modestly. She had not, in the eyes of the Hindu Right, provoked the attack, and she had maintained her honour and conformed to what is expected of a 'good woman'. The Hindu Right has been behind numerous brutal attacks on women who challenge the oppressive and constraining parameters of womanhood prescribed by Hindutva ideology (e.g. Mondal 2012; Lanikesh 2013). These attacks have targeted women who transgress the conservative religious codes of female modesty and subservience, including women who drink alcohol in pubs and bars or go to nightclubs, wear Western clothes, and have numerous sexual partners. Nirbhaya did none of these things, and so the use of brutal violence against her was, in the eyes of the Hindutva movement, illegitimate.

The outcries from the left of the political spectrum, largely secular feminist organizations, were motivated by very different reasons; they saw this rape as yet another sign of the misogyny lying at the foundations of Indian society. The brutality of the rape was merely a sign of how little progress has really been made in reconstructing dominant images of female sexuality in a more liberal frame. The realization that so little has changed seemed to act as the catalyst for many others who were not part of the women's movement to take to the streets and demand change. Ritu Menon described the anti-rape outcries as follows: 'What was very different this time is the general outrage; it wasn't just women's groups, it wasn't just activists, not just people who have been talking and agitating about it for a long time but a huge swathe of society that I think was just galvanized into being vocal' (interview, July 2013).

Further motivation for the protests comes from how uncomfortably this violence sits against a backdrop of the country's apparent economic success. The world's media have not been slow in picking up on this ironic contradiction – economic success considered the result of a liberalizing agenda hides what has been termed 'a dark underbelly' (e.g. Adler 2012).

The recent anti-rape protests reveal once again the way in which women's bodies remain the battleground for competing discourses on gender and sexuality in India. For example, Sarkar and Butalia (1995) and Sarkar (2002) have written extensively about the gendered thread running through Hindutva ideology and Bradley (2010) examines the implications for women's rights of a Hindutva organization that seeks to educate women 'in the right image' as a way of ensuring India remains true to its golden age of the Vedic era. Hindu role models such as Sita are used by religious leaders to enforce the image of a good, subservient woman. Clear examples of this can be seen in the teachings of one such Hindutva religious leader – Dada Vaswani:[8]

> Now woman gets her chance. She is called upon to build a New World. She is a symbol of *shakti* in the Hindu scriptures. And *shakti* is not a force. *Shakti* is integration. This includes intelligence. Education, more education, is needed. But it must be education of the right character.
>
> (Vaswani 2007: 84)

> Educate women and you educate the whole country.
>
> (Sadhu Vaswani Mission teaching, www.sadhuvaswanimission.org)

Such discourses demonstrate how control over female sexuality is crucial in ensuring women conform to their role as procreators and nurturers of the next generation. Female sexuality is associated with maintaining the status of the imagined nation.

Feminist campaigning in recent decades has focused on improving women's lives in a holistic sense, creating employment and educational opportunities for women in the hope that, with greater independence, women would challenge the structural constraints that limited their choices. Research presented here highlights that these shifts have not entirely taken place, and patriarchal values and beliefs projecting rigid gender roles continue to hold firm. It is not a coincidence but directly linked that, as conservative religious groups increasingly assert their presence through strict gender codes, practices such as dowry and related violence have become further embedded into the fabric of Indian society.

Sexual minorities

A growing network of organizations is emerging across India who work for the rights of lesbian, gay, bisexual, transgender and intersex people. These organizations have been successful in opening the space for discussion around alternative sexualities. However, apart from small gains for the transgender or *hijra* community in terms of the legal recognition of a third gender in some (though not all) government schemes,[9] little legal progress has been made.

The major legal stumbling block for gay, lesbian, bisexual, transgender and intersex communities in India has been section 377 of the Indian Penal Code, which was established during the colonial period, and which makes non-peno-vaginal sex 'against the order of nature' and thus illegal. Section 377 was declared unconstitutional by the Delhi High Court in July 2009 after a sustained campaign led by rights activists. However, on 11 December 2013, a judgment of the Supreme Court was passed overturning the decision of the Delhi High Court and reinstating section 377 (see Banerjee 2013). The petition to overturn the High Court judgment was led by several conservative groups, including Hindu, Muslim and Christian organizations. Representatives of some of these organizations issued a joint statement welcoming the decision, which stated:

> Our India is a religious country whose overwhelming majority believes in religion and upholds traditions of the east. All religions emphasize on construction of a family through marital relation between men and women, on which depend not only the existence of human race and lasting peace and tranquillity in the society but it also establishes the respected and central position of woman in the society.
>
> ('Joint Statement' 2013)

This statement, which is a rare instance of interreligious cooperation, places heterosexual marriage at the centre of both religious and national identity. A notion of nature emerges in this discourse as a symbol of a normative order that is used to evidence and justify the dominance of the heterosexual model of marriage. Protests against the Supreme Court verdict were widespread and included lesbian, gay, bisexual, transgender and intersex individuals and organizations in cities across India.

The battleground over sexuality will probably become more visible in the future as conservative religious groups defensively cling to their worldview and as the coherence and global visibility of the feminist, gay and transgendered movements drive the push for radical change. The movement for the rights of sexual minorities can be viewed as part of wider struggles related to the achievement of gender equality in India – a struggle in which religious discourses and organizations have for the most part stood in the way of progress. The following section outlines a similarly fraught relationship between religion, gender and development across the border in Pakistan, where religion is more explicitly intertwined with the state.

Religion, gender and development in Pakistan

The relationship between religion and the rights of women and sexual minorities in Pakistan has been a contentious one. For the women's movement in particular, opposition to women's rights from religious conservative groups, who are increasingly patronized by the state and who place women's bodies and the regulation of sexuality at the centre of their constructions of the community and hence the nation–state, has been one of the greatest hurdles they have had to face, particularly since the 1980s. The 2012 attack by the Taliban on the young activist Malala Yusufzai brought this tension dramatically to the fore in the eyes of the national and international media. At the same time, it was the imposition of religious-based laws such as the Hudood Ordinances under the dictatorship of Zia-ul-Haq that helped actually consolidate the contemporary women's movement. Since the 1980s, women's rights activists have vacillated between taking a 'secular', human rights-based approach – one that does not explicitly engage with religion – and adopting a strategy of engaging with religious discourses in their struggles for gender equality. This section will focus largely on the relationship between women's rights advocacy and Islam,[10] but it will also touch briefly upon the rights of sexual minorities, including members of the third gender, or the *Khwaja Sira* community as they have come to be known in Pakistan, as well as people who engage in same-sex sexual practices. In particular, the section will explore how the increasing intertwinement of conservative and patriarchal interpretations of religion with the state has placed constraints on activism related to gender equality.

The women's movement and religion historically

During Pakistan's early years of existence, women's rights advocates did not openly confront religious precepts in their activism but rather worked within the existing cultural and political system in order to push for reforms. Early women's rights activists used Islam as a means of securing their rights, both within the family and in the economic sphere. Passed soon after Pakistan was created, the Muslim Personal Law of Shariat (1948) recognized women's right to inherit property, including agricultural property (Mumtaz and Shaheed 1987: 55–6). The next major law affecting women's rights was the Muslim Family Laws Ordinance (MFLO), which was introduced by Ayub Khan as part of his drive to modernize the Pakistani legal system. The passage of the MFLO in 1961 was the result of years of struggle waged by women's rights activists and progressive elements during the 1950s. The main aim of the MFLO was to regulate the procedure for divorce and to discourage polygamy. The MFLO also raised the minimum age of marriage from 14 to 16 for girls and from 18 to 21 for boys.[11] Despite the fact that the MFLO does not openly challenge religious precepts and works from within an Islamic framework, it has continually been challenged by certain members of the *ulama* (religious scholars) in Pakistan, and many of its stipulations, such as the requirement that a man must seek permission of the first wife before marrying a second wife, are deemed to be 'un-Islamic' by conservative elements (Ansari 2009). Therefore, although women's rights activists have always faced opposition from conservative *ulama*, women's rights activists were able to use Islamic and secular[12] arguments to secure increased rights and representation during Pakistan's first three decades.

The contemporary movement for gender equality emerged in the 1980s, which witnessed a dramatic shift in the Pakistani political and cultural landscape as a result of the military dictator Zia-ul-Haq's Islamization programme, which focused to a great extent on the control and regulation of issues related to gender and sexuality. This included the passage of the Hudood Ordinances, which introduced punishments such as amputations, public whippings, and stoning to death. It also criminalized consensual sex (*zina*) between unmarried women and men, and made it necessary for a woman to produce four male witnesses in order to prove that she had been raped; if she was unable to do so, she could be charged with committing the crime of *zina*, the maximum punishment for which is death by stoning (Shaheed 2010).[13] Zia-ul-Haq also introduced the Qanun-e-Shahadat (Law of Evidence), which made the testimony of two women or two non-Muslim men equal to that of one Muslim man. Apart from the passage of retrogressive laws, Zia's Islamization programme included a range of measures which aimed to control women's mobility and dress, such as introducing mandatory headscarves for all women working in government offices or appearing on television, as well as banning women's participation in certain public events such as spectator sports (Mumtaz and Shaheed 1987). The overall aim of such measures was to push women back into the confines of the *chador* and *chardiwari* (the veil and the four walls of the home), thus marking women's bodies as the symbols of the Islamic nation.

The Women's Action Forum (WAF), which spearheaded the women's movement at the time, was established in 1981 and was a platform for individual women and women's organizations to organize against Zia's Islamization programme. While they intentionally maintained a publicly ambiguous position vis-à-vis religion throughout the 1980s, for the most part WAF chose to work within a universalistic human rights framework in their campaigns to repeal these laws. In her narrative of WAF's experiences during the 1980s, Hina Jilani, a prominent lawyer and member of WAF, says:

> We did go to the universal and international human rights framework because for us that was a necessity. We wanted an anchor, a sound anchor to work for women's rights so that the national political environment of the country could not dislodge the concept that we were trying to get accepted, so religion did not figure as a point of reference.
>
> (Interview, 12 March 2012)

In an article published during that period, Jilani (1986) argued that engaging with Islam was futile, as it contains many schools of thought and it would inevitably be the school favoured by the government that would dominate. Similarly, Rubina Saigol argues that women's rights activists would never win if they were playing on the 'mullah's wicket' and hence needed to create a wicket of their own (interview, 15 April 2011). This concurs with Jamal's (2005) contention that Pakistani women's rights activists tend to invoke universal human rights as a means of challenging patriarchal nationalism, which very often appears in a religious guise.

However, WAF did not operate as a monolithic entity, and there were important differences that emerged amongst its members throughout the 1980s over whether or not to work within a religious framework. Khawar Mumtaz, who is one of the leading members of WAF, argues that it was impossible *not* to engage with Islam at the time:

> We thought the best way of responding was to get progressive interpretations of Islam given that context, given the nature of the law, and given at the time it was an Islamic, very conservative religious government and military government that had imposed the law. The parameters were in a sense defined.
>
> (Interview, 11 May 2011)

Therefore, according to Mumtaz, engaging with Islam was not a choice for women's rights activists but a necessity, as the issues were being framed in a religious manner by the state itself. For this reason, WAF periodically engaged with religious scholars and texts in order to prove that measures such as the Hudood Ordinances, the law of *Qisas* and *Diyat*,[14] and the Law of Evidence were in fact fundamentally un-Islamic rather than simply against the norms put in place by the international human rights framework (see Mumtaz and Shaheed 1987). While differences of opinion over the strategic use of religion remained within WAF throughout the 1980s and were left unresolved, WAF finally declared that it supported a separation between religion and the state during its 1991 convention, long after Zia's demise (Shaheed 1998). However, even this did not mean an end to debates around religion, and differences of opinion continue to exist amongst women's rights activists on the issue of religious engagement (see Zia 2009).

Contemporary women's rights advocacy

Since the 1990s, women's rights activists in Pakistan have for the most part utilized a universalist human rights framework as the foundation for their organizing efforts. At the same time, they continue to engage periodically with religious texts and scholars in order to defend against religious-based justifications for the denial of women's rights. For example, women's rights activists provided legislators with religious-based arguments against the Hudood Ordinances during the Musharraf regime in order to aid them in legislative debates (interview, Khawar Mumtaz, 11 May 2011). These arguments may have been helpful in the eventual passage of the Women's Protection Act (2006), which effectively took the teeth out of the Hudood Ordinances by placing rape within the jurisdiction of civil law and making it illegal for a woman to be convicted of adultery on the basis of her own complaint. The passage of the Women's Protection Act was aided by the favourable political opportunity structure provided by the Musharraf regime in its agenda to promote 'enlightened moderation' in relation to Islam (Jamal 2011: 205).

Beginning with the Musharraf regime (2001–08) and continuing in the democratically elected Pakistan People's Party-led government (2008–13), several progressive pieces of legislation were passed in favour of women's rights. In 2002, Musharraf revived and increased the number of reserved seats for women in the national and local assemblies – a move which may have contributed to facilitating the passage of women-friendly pieces of legislation in subsequent years. In the seven years between 2004 and 2011, seven pro-women pieces of legislation were passed, including laws related to honour killings, acid attacks and harmful customary practices. Furthermore, as stated earlier, the controversial Hudood Ordinances were amended in 2006 with the passage of the Women's Protection Act. In interviews conducted with women's rights activists lobbying for legislative change throughout this period, they stated that they generally preferred to frame their arguments in the language of universal human rights. At the same time, an analysis of debates taking place in the media reveals a sustained effort by some writers, activists and politicians to deploy a more 'progressive', woman-friendly interpretation of Islam in the public sphere.[15] Hence, while some women's rights activists continue to hold the stance that engaging with religion proactively is futile, others have argued for women's equality through Islam, and these religiously framed opinions occupy relatively more space in the public discourse. It is, in fact, rare to find public statements supporting a separation of religion from the state, even from those who hold this position privately, as the space for such positions has continuously shrunk since the Zia era.[16]

At the same time, moves to protect and promote women's rights continue to be met with consistent opposition from conservative religious groups. For example, the Women's Protection Act was challenged by the Federal Shariat Court in 2010 and later by the Council of Islamic Ideology, which argued that the amendments to the Hudood Ordinances were unconstitutional, with the National Commission on the Status of Women immediately issuing a statement protesting against this ruling ('Shariat Court' 2010). Furthermore, the Domestic Violence Bill, which was in the National Assembly in 2009, was met with opposition by the Council of Islamic Ideology for being discriminatory against men and for giving the police too great a role in 'family affairs' ('Domestic Violence Bill' 2009). In 2012, when the government moved to have the bill passed as an act, stiff opposition was raised by the Islamic party, the Jamiat Ulema-e-Islam-Fazl (JUI-F) and the Deobandi seminary, Wafaq-ul-Madaris-Al-Arabia, for undermining Islamic values and traditions (Gishkori 2012). More recently, the Council of Islamic Ideology ruled that DNA evidence was not permissible in court as evidence of rape after an 18-year-old was gang-raped in Karachi ('CII Rules Out DNA' 2013). Hence, the debate over the relationship between the law and religion continues, and women's rights activists continue to fight a defensive battle against the proponents of conservative and retrogressive interpretations of Islam.

Apart from legal advocacy, women's rights activists have been working at the community level in order raise awareness about existing rights and to have an impact on social attitudes. NGOs working for women's rights also engage with Islam periodically in their efforts to advocate gender equality. For example, one of the leading women's rights organizations in Pakistan, Shirkat Gah, has put together a handbook outlining women's rights within Islam as well as occasionally working with progressive religious scholars at the community level on issues such as marital rights and family planning. Shirkat Gah has long worked on raising awareness at the community level of women's legal rights, which in the context of Pakistan also means their rights within Islam. This includes informing women about the importance of Islamic injunctions such as *haq mehr*, which is a gift given by a husband to his wife at the time of marriage, and the concept of *talaq-e-tafwid*, which gives a woman the right to divorce her husband if it is specified in the *nikahnama* (marriage contract). Other NGOs, such as the Aurat Foundation, have conducted workshops for members of civil society in which the notion that Islam does not discriminate against women was stressed ('Workshop Stresses Gender Equality' 2011). However, such approaches continue to draw criticism from within and outside the movement for limiting the terms of the debate, for being ideologically vague, for playing into the hands of right-wing Islamist groups, and for being exclusionary in nature (see Sumar 2002; Zia 2009).

Sexual minorities

Organizing publicly for the rights of sexual minorities, which include transgenders and those engaged in same-sex sexual practices, has only begun in Pakistan in the last five years. While the presence of the third gender, or *Khwaja Siras* as they have been come to be known in Pakistan, has deep historical roots, the rights of *Khwaja Siras* have only emerged as an issue in public debates over the past five years. One of the reasons for the increased organization amongst *Khwaja Siras* might be the increase in funding for HIV/AIDS-related projects, which has benefited organizing amongst sexual minorities across the developing world (see Fried and Kowalski-Morton 2008). The first major victory for *Khwaja Siras* was the addition of a third gender category in the national identity cards in 2011 (Khan 2011). This landmark decision, which meant the formal recognition that there are more than two genders, paved the way for the struggle for other rights such as the right to education, healthcare and a 2 per cent reservation for members of the third gender in government jobs (Sikander 2013).

However, Bindya Rana, one of the leading *Khwaja Sira* activists in Pakistan, said that transgender activists mainly argued for their rights through the universal human rights discourse. While she noted that transgenders were creations of God and hence deserving of the same rights as women and men, she did not point to an engagement with specific religious texts or scholars as part of their campaigning strategies. While *Khwaja Siras* face discrimination and harassment on a daily basis, Bindya Rana did not cite any major opposition from conservative religious groups, apart from a few statements made on television. She also said that some religious scholars had issued statements in support of the laws passed for transgender rights, stating that there was a place for people of the third gender in Islam (interview, 23 January 2014). Hence, religion has posed neither as a major hurdle for transgender activists nor as a source of support, and like women's rights activists, they have found it most effective to utilize the language of universal human rights in their campaigning efforts.

While efforts to claim rights for transgenders have only just begun, even less public action has been taken in the realm of lesbian, gay and bisexual rights. While homosexual practices are widespread in Pakistani society, particularly amongst men,[17] homosexuality has only recently begun to be discussed in the public sphere and claimed as a separate identity category, and that too by a relatively small number of largely urban middle-class and elite people (see Ladly 2012; Azher 2013).[18] While engaging in same-sex sexual activities has arguably been made easier with the spread of information technology, any attempt formally to organize for rights and recognition has been met with staunch opposition, particularly from religious conservative groups. For example, in 2011 the US embassy in Islamabad organized a meeting in support of lesbian, gay, bisexual and transgender rights, which sparked protests across the country. At a public rally in Karachi, Mohammad Hussain Mehnati, the city's chief of Jamaat-e-Islami, the largest Islamic political party in Pakistan, stated that this was an act of 'cultural terrorism' being unleashed against Pakistan by the United States.[19] Furthermore, Pakistan along with 57 countries of the Organisation for Islamic Cooperation declared opposition to the UN's discussions on violence based on sexual orientation ('Pakistan Opposes' 2012). Hence, any moves to publicly claim homosexuality as an identity or to claim rights for people engaged in homosexual practices has been firmly opposed both by the state and by religious conservative groups.

Overall, the relationship between those struggling for gender and sexual equality and religion has been contentious in the Pakistani context, with religious conservative groups posing as the greatest obstacles to progress. At the same time, small victories have been won by women's rights activists in particular through the strategic engagement with religious discourses in their lobbying vis-à-vis the state as well as at the community level. Therefore, it is not fair to argue simply that there is an adversarial relationship between religion and movements for gender or sexual equality. However, it is fair to say that there is a clear opposition to the rights of women and sexual minorities posed by religious conservative groups, and particularly Wahhabi-inspired

Islamist groups, which have increased in size and influence since the 1980s. It is their influence on the state in particular that is cause for concern amongst activists mobilizing for women and sexual minorities.

Conclusion

In this chapter we have given an overview of movements for gender and sexual equality in both India and Pakistan. We have focused on how, within these movements, different groups have engaged or not with religion and the implications this has for furthering the rights of women and sexual minority groups. In both contexts we can see in recent years a strengthening of the threat posed by conservative religious groups and have argued that their agendas are most visibly played out through control over women's lives and suppression of diverse sexual identities.

Gender-based violence, which includes violence against members of sexual minorities, is a critical stumbling block for the achievement of equality and social justice worldwide, which have consistently been identified as key development-related goals. Conservative ideologies, which often use religion as a means of justifying their agendas, have played a persistent role in perpetuating and promoting different forms of violence, both physical and symbolic, against women and sexual minorities. In both contexts legal changes to improve the justice for female victims of violence have been made, although this has not necessarily been translated into a reduction in actual instances of abuse. The same cannot be said for sexual minorities, although limited victories have been won for the transgender community in both India and Pakistan.

At the same time, in relation to an opening up of women's role beyond the domestic sphere and in respect of sexual minorities, we see a consistent and violent backlash on the part of right-wing religious groups. Movements for gender equality in India and Pakistan, therefore, face a serious challenge from the religious right and, in particular, from the growing influence of such groups within the state. While at times advocates of gender equality have attempted to engage strategically with religious discourses in support of their arguments, for the most part activists on both sides of the border have chosen to work within a secular, human rights-based framework. The question remains as to whether the avoidance of engaging proactively with religion on the part of gender rights activists has allowed the religious right, whether Hindu or Muslim, to hijack religious discourses in support of their own regressive agendas or whether this has, in fact, been the most effective and least exclusionary means of achieving social change for gender equality.

Notes

1 This subsection focuses on the mainstream women's movement – what is often called the 'autonomous women's movement' – with the understanding that these are contentious terms representing what are fluid and loosely organized networks, which are constantly shifting (see Katzenstein 1989; Butalia 2002). This does not deny the presence of multiple women's movements across India that may not have termed themselves as such, but that have nevertheless been struggling to protect the rights of women as members of their communities.

2 However, the co-optation of Hindu symbols also contributed to the alienation of non-upper-caste Hindu women, particularly Muslims, Christians and Dalit women, from the movement (Agnes 1995; Sunder Rajan 2000).

3 In India, in addition to the Indian Civil Code, there exist different systems of personal law that reflect the religious background of the individual involved in any case. It is typical that issues around marriage are dealt with by the relevant religious system of personal law and not the (secular) Civil Code.

4 This meant that Muslim women would technically not be able to appeal to the civil courts in matters related to marriage and family laws. However, in practice many Muslim women continued to approach the courts in order to claim for maintenance, and often the courts have managed to secure handsome settlements for divorced women through liberal interpretations of the Muslim Women (Protection of Rights on Divorce) Act, 1986 (see Vatuk 2014).

5 Justice Verma was tasked with chairing a commission to review the legislative and referral processes for victims of violence. The final report was critical of the slow process of justice and highlighted police failings in ensuring justice to victims of violent abuse. In order to rectify these failings the report recommended significant changes to criminal laws.

6 Globalization, they argue, and the emergence of a richer middle class have enabled India to develop better technologies, which can now be afforded in a way they could not before. These technologies mean that families can determine the sex of the unborn foetus and abort if it is a girl.

7 The honorary name 'Nirbhaya', which means 'courageous one', was given to the victim of the brutal rape and murder in Delhi in December 2012. The name was awarded to her by members of the protest movement as a way of acknowledging the brutality she endured and as a sign of respect. The December 2012 case, although one of many reported each day, triggered widespread protests and forced the government to commission a review of the legislative framework, policies and protection afforded to rape victims.

8 Dada Vaswani is the nephew of Sadhu Vaswani, who founded an organization focused on the education of girls. The Sadhu Vaswani movement originated in Sindh, which then became partitioned, leaving many Hindus displaced. The ideology of the organization is shaped by a nationalist view emanating from the experiences of partition.

9 The category 'transgender' was recognized by the government's Aadhar programme, which helped marginalized communities gain access to services such as opening a bank account, getting a mobile phone, or receiving assistance from some government programmes. However, *hijras* are still barred from getting driving licences, ration cards or PAN cards by the government ('India's "Third Gender"' 2011).

10 While I do not intend to overlook the rights of religious minorities, of which Christians and Hindus make up the largest groups, as Pakistan is 97 per cent Muslim, and as most laws related to gender or sexuality are made in accordance with particular interpretations of Islam, this discussion will also focus largely on the relationship between struggles for gender equality and Islam.

11 Women's organizations are currently campaigning to raise the age of marriage for women from 16 to 18 years of age.

12 I use the term 'secular' with caution, particularly in the Pakistani context, where it has been translated as *ladiniyat* ('without religion') and associated with atheism (see Iqtidar 2011: 7). For the purposes of my research, 'secular' refers to those discourses and strategies that do not explicitly engage with religion.

13 While no woman has ever been stoned to death for adultery, thousands were imprisoned under these laws, including scores of women who had been raped but were unable to produce the necessary witnesses to prove their case.

14 This law relates to retaliation and settlement of criminal offences and legalized the concept of blood money as compensation for a murder, bodily harm and abortion, and valued the lives of women and non-Muslim men at half the value of the lives of Muslim men.

15 One of the most prominent such writers is Asma Barlas, who takes an 'Islamic feminist' approach and wrote a series of articles in 2002–03 arguing that Islam had been subject to centuries of patriarchal misinterpretation, which obscured the egalitarian nature of its original message (see Barlas 2002, 2003a, 2003b, 2003c).

16 Some would argue that the process of Islamization began much earlier than Zia's regime with the incorporation of the Objectives Resolution in 1951 in the Constitution, which declared Pakistan to be an Islamic state. This process was further accelerated under Zulfiqar Ali Bhutto, who gave in to Islamic conservative groups by banning the sale of alcohol, prohibiting gambling and closing down nightclubs.

17 The space for lesbians is even narrower than it is for gay men, which must be understood within a wider context in which any expression of female sexuality is considered against social, cultural and religious norms (see Azher 2013).

18 Homosexual acts are still considered to be illegal in Pakistan under section 377 of the Pakistan Penal Code, which was established in 1860 under British rule.

19 At the same time, this issue cannot be separated from the wider political context, in which the US has been widely condemned for the 'War on Terror' being waged in Pakistan, and particularly for the drone attacks.

References

Adler, W. (2012) 'The Dark Underbelly of Modern India', http://www.huffingtonpost.com/warren-adler/katherine-boo-india_b_1382122.html (accessed 10 February 2014).

Agnes, F. (1995) 'Redefining the Agenda of the Women's Movement within a Secular Framework', in T. Sarkar and U. Butalia (eds), *Women and Right-Wing Movements: Indian Experiences*, New Delhi: Kali for Women, pp. 136–57.

Ansari, Sarah (2009) 'Polygamy, Purdah and Political Representation: Engendering Citizenship in 1950s Pakistan', *Modern Asian Studies*, 43 (6), 1421–61.

Azher, M. (2013) 'Gay Pakistan: Where Sex Is Available and Relationships Are Difficult', http://www.bbc.co.uk/news/23811826 (accessed 19 January 2014).

Banerjee, P. (2013) 'Decoding Section 377: How the Verdict Erased Basic Human Rights', *Hindustan Times*, http://www.hindustantimes.com/india-news/decoding-section-377-how-the-verdict-erased-basic-human-rights/article1-1165215.aspx (accessed 8 February 2014).

Barlas, A. (2002) 'Religious Authorities in Islam', 31 December, http://archives.dailytimes.com.pk/editorial/31-Dec-2002/religious-authorities-in-islam (accessed 19 January 2014).

Barlas, A. (2003a) 'Islam, Women and Equality', 6 May, http://archives.dailytimes.com.pk/editorial/06-May-2003/islam-women-and-equality (accessed 20 January 2014).

Barlas, A. (2003b) 'Islam, Women, and Equality II', 20 May, http://archives.dailytimes.com.pk/editorial/20-May-2003/islam-women-and-equality-ii (accessed 20 January 2014).

Barlas, A. (2003c) 'Islam, Women, and Equality III', 3 June, http://archives.dailytimes.com.pk/editorial/03-Jun-2003/islam-women-and-equality-iii (accessed 20 January 2014).

Basu, S. (2009) 'Legacies of the Dowry Prohibition Act in India: Marriage Practices and Feminist Discourse', in T. Bradley and E. Tomalin (eds), *Dowry: Bridging the Gap between Theory and Practice*, Delhi: Women Unlimited and Zed Books.

Bradley, T. (2010) *Religion and Gender in the Developing World: Faith-Based Organisations and Feminism in India*, London: I. B. Tauris.

Bradley, T. (2011) *Women, Violence and Tradition*, London: Zed Books.

Butalia, U. (2002) 'Confrontation and Negotiation: The Women's Movement's Response to Violence against Women', in K. Kapadia (ed.), *The Violence of Development: The Politics of Identity, Gender and Social Inequalities in India*, New Delhi: Kali for Women and Zubaan, pp. 207–34.

Chhachhi, A. (1991) 'Forced Identities: The State, Communalism, Fundamentalism and Women in India', in D. Kandiyoti (ed.) *Women, Islam and the State*, New Delhi: Macmillan, pp. 144–75.

'CII Rules Out DNA as Primary Evidence in Rape Cases' (2013) 23 September, http://www.dawn.com/news/1044879/cii-rules-out-dna-as-primary-evidence-in-rape-cases (accessed 16 January 2014).

'Domestic Violence Bill to Push Up Divorce Rate: CII' (2009) 25 August, http://www.dawn.com/news/855084/domestic-violence-bill-to-push-up-divorce-rate-cii (accessed 1 February 2014).

Fried, S. and Kowalski-Morton, S. (2008) 'Sex and the Global Fund: How Sex Workers, Lesbians, Gays, Bisexuals, Transgender People, and Men Who Have Sex with Men Are Benefiting from the Global Fund, or Not', *Health and Human Rights*, 10 (2), 127–36.

Gishkori, Z. (2012) 'Citing "Controversial" Clauses: Clerics Vow to Resist Passage of Domestic Violence Bill', 17 April, http://tribune.com.pk/story/365842/citing-controversial-clauses-clerics-vow-to-resist-passage-of-domestic-violence-bill/ (accessed 1 February 2014).

Hasan, Z. (1994) 'Minority Identity, State Policy and the Political Process', in Z. Hasan (ed.), *Forging Identities: Gender, Communities and the State*, New Delhi: Kali for Women, pp. 202–17.

Hasan, Z. (1998) 'Gender Politics, Legal Reform, and the Muslim Community in India', in P. Jeffrey and B. Amrita (eds), *Appropriating Gender: Women's Activism and Politicized Religion in South Asia*, New York: Routledge, pp. 71–88.

'India's "Third Gender": A Marginalized Social Class' (2011) http://stream.aljazeera.com/story/201310170000-0023115 (accessed 10 February 2014).

Iqtidar, H. (2011) *Secularizing Islamists?*, Chicago: University of Chicago Press.

Jamal, A. (2005) 'Transnational Feminism as Critical Practice: A Reading of Feminist Discourses in Pakistan', *Meridians: Feminism, Race, Transnationalism*, 5 (2), 57–82.

Jamal, A. (2011) 'Just between Us: Identity and Representation amongst Muslim Women', *Inter-Asia Cultural Studies*, 12 (2), 202–12.

Jilani, H. (1986) 'The Pakistan Women's Action Forum: Struggling against Fundamentalism', *Canadian Women's Studies*, 7 (1–2), 107–10.

'Joint Statement of Religious Leaders on "Supreme Court Order on Section 377"' (2013) http://jamaateislamihind.org/eng/joint-statement-of-religious-leaders-on-supreme-court-order-on-article-377/ (accessed 8 February 2014).

Katzenstein, M. (1989) 'Organizing against Violence: Strategies of the Indian Women's Movement', *Pacific Affairs*, 62 (1), 53–71.

Kaur, R. and Palriwala, R. (2013) *Marrying in South Asia: Shifting Concepts, Changing Practices in a Globalising World*, Hyderabad: Orient Blackswan.

Khan, A. (2011) 'Transgender Rights: SC Tells NADRA to Amend Gender Verification Process', http://tribune.com.pk/story/156256/sc-directs-nadra-to-include-eunuchs-in-gender-column/ (accessed 17 January 2014).

Kirmani, N. (2010) 'Claiming Their Space: Muslim Women-Led Networks and the Women's Movement in India', *Journal of International Women's Studies*, Special Issue on Muslim Women's Movements, 11 (1), 72–85.

Kirmani, N. (2011) 'Beyond the Impasse: "Muslim Feminism(s)" and the Indian Women's Movement', *Contributions to Indian Sociology*, 45 (1), 1–26.

Kirmani, N. (2013) 'Strategic Engagements: Analyzing the Relationships of Indian and Pakistani Women's Movements to Islam', *Asien: The German Journal on Contemporary Asia*, 126, 10–25.

Kirmani, N. and Phillips, I. (2011) 'Engaging with Islam to Promote Women's Rights: Exploring Opportunities and Challenging Assumptions', *Progress in Development Studies*, 11 (2), 87–99.

Kishwar, M. (1998) 'Who Am I? Living Identities vs Acquired Ones', *Manushi*, May–June.

Kumar, R. (1994) 'Feminism Faces Fundamentalism in India', *Agenda*, 21, 81–92.

Ladly, M. (2012) 'Gay Pakistanis, Still in Shadows, Seek Acceptance', 3 November, http://www.nytimes.com/2012/11/04/world/asia/gays-in-pakistan-move-cautiously-to-gain-acceptance.html?_r=1& (accessed 18 January 2014).

Lanikesh, G. (2013) 'The Sene Patis Lose Their Marbles', http://www.outlookindia.com/printarticle.aspx?285356 (accessed 10 February 2014).

Mondal, S. (2012) 'The Rise and Fall of a Hindutva Hitman', http://www.thehindu.com/news/cities/Mangalore/the-rise-and-rise-of-a-hindutva-hitman/article3704704.ece (accessed 10 February 2014).

Mumtaz, K. and Shaheed, F. (1987) *Women of Pakistan*, Lahore: Vanguard.

'Pakistan Opposes UN Discussion on Violence against LGBT' (2012) 6 March, http://tribune.com.pk/story/346244/pakistan-opposes-un-discussion-on-violence-against-lgbt/ (accessed 13 January 2014).

Palriwala, R. (2009) 'The Spider's Web: Seeing Dowry, Fighting Dowry', in T. Bradley and E. Tomalin (eds), *Dowry: Bridging the Gap between Theory and Practice*, Delhi: Women Unlimited and Zed Press.

Sarkar, T. (2002) *Hindu Wife, Hindu Nation: Community, Religion and Cultural Nationalism*, New Delhi: Permanent Black.

Sarkar, T. and Butalia, U. (1995) *Women and Right-Wing Movements: Indian Experiences*, London: Zed Press.

Shaheed, F. (1998) 'The Other Side of Discourse: Women's Experiences of Identity, Religion and Activism in Pakistan', in P. Jeffery and A. Basu (eds), *Appropriating Gender: Women's Activism and Politicized Religion in South Asia*, New York: Routledge, pp. 143–64.

Shaheed, F. (2010) 'The Women's Movement in Pakistan: Challenges and Achievements', in A. Basu (ed.), *Women's Movements in the Global Era: The Power of Local Feminisms*, Boulder, CO: Westview Press, pp. 110–66.

'Shariat Court Knocks Out 3 Sections of Women's Protection Act' (2010) 22 December, http://www.dawn.com/news/592972/shariat-court-knocks-out-3-sections-of-womens-protection-act (accessed 16 January 2014).

Sikander, M. (2013) 'Unwillingness to Tap into Immense Potential: What the Transgender Community Can Contribute to Pakistan', *Blue Chip*, http://bluechipmag.com/unwillingness-to-tap-into-immense-potential-what-the-transgender-community-can-contribute-to-pakistan/ (accessed 26 January 2014).

Sumar, S. (2002) 'Women's Movement in Pakistan: Problems and Prospects', in S. Naseem and K. Nadvi (eds), *The Post-Colonial State and Social Transformation in India and Pakistan*, Oxford: Oxford University Press, pp. 413–46.

Sunder Rajan, R. (2000) 'Is the Hindu Goddess a Feminist?', in A. Hiltebeitel and K. M. Erndl (eds), *Is the Goddess a Feminist? The Politics of South Asian Goddesses*, New York: University of New York Press.

Vaswani, J. P. (2007) *Peace or Perish: There Is No Other Choice*, Pune: Gita Publishing House.

Vatuk, S. (2014) 'The Application of Muslim Personal Law in India: A System of Legal Pluralism in Action', in E. Giunchi (ed.), *Adjudicating Family Law in Muslim Courts*, Abingdon: Routledge, pp. 48–69.

'Workshop Stresses Gender Equality in Islam' (2011) http://archives.dailytimes.com.pk/national/14–Oct-2011/workshop-stresses-gender-equality-in-islam (accessed 20 January 2014).

World Bank (2012) *Gender Equality Report 2012*, Washington, DC: World Bank.

Zia, A. (2009) 'The Reinvention of Feminism in Pakistan', *Feminist Review*, 91 (1), 29–46.

PART 5

East and South-East Asia

16

RELIGION AND DEVELOPMENT IN CHINA[1]

André Laliberté

Introduction

Understanding the role of religion for the development of China requires first a distinction between China as a civilization and China as a polity. Looking at China as a civilization allows us to look at a material culture and a cultural tradition that have unfolded over millennia and extended their influence over a number of other societies in East Asia, such as Japan, Korea, and Vietnam. This approach allows us to look at different strands in a tradition that includes communal religions, Taoism, Confucianism, Buddhism, and other forms of religiosities embedded with the state and other social systems such as the economy, education, health, and the family. It also allows us to include Islam and Christianity as religions from other parts of the world that gradually integrated into the fabric of Chinese civilization.[2] China *qua* civilization includes the long line of dynasties followed by Republican and Socialist successor regimes, as well as the overseas Chinese communities dispersed throughout all continents, which count over 30 million people. For reasons of space, this chapter will not address the complexities of the overseas communities.

Limiting ourselves to looking at China as a single polity, i.e., the People's Republic of China (PRC), which claims an undivided authority in international society over the territory it governs, plus Taiwan, would mean excluding Taiwan, which has exercised effective sovereignty independently from the PRC since 1949, as well as Hong Kong before 1997 and Macau before 1999, when both city-states were colonies of European powers.[3] Looking at China *qua* the PRC, the discussion of religion's role in development shows that, for the first three decades of the Socialist regime, the Communist Party of China (CPC) looked at religion as an obstacle to development. This approach changed in the 1980s, and by 2000 the CPC, in the shape of Ye Xiaowen, director of the State Administration for Religious Affairs (SARA), proclaimed that religion plays a positive role in a socialist society (Ye 2000). In so doing, the PRC has moved closer to the other polities of Taiwan, Hong Kong, and Macau, which have never looked at religion as an obstacle. In these three societies, religions have been partners to the state in development, albeit a partnership that was at times enforced rather than voluntary, as we will see later.

The distinction between the PRC and the other three polities is important on one crucial issue that matters for the ability of religions to affect development: the autonomy of religious institutions from state control. The PRC's corporatist system imposes many legal limitations on this autonomy: it recognizes only five religions (Buddhism, Taoism, Islam, Protestantism, and Catholicism) and imposes on them an institutional framework regulating their activities, comprising the SARA, which supervises the activities of these five national religions, as well as the 'patriotic' associations for each of them.[4] This structure of control contrasts with the case of the other three polities, where no institution comparable to SARA exists. Although recent scholarship has shown that the structure of control for religion in the PRC is changing dramatically, it is important to keep in mind that the CPC under Mao left an institutional legacy that religious actors must take into account in their social actions, strategies, doctrines, and theologies.

Besides political differences, however, these four polities share an important characteristic: the pluralism of China *qua* civilization inherent in its variety of religiosities. We need to appreciate this diversity in the discussion of religions' role in development. Taking into account this religious diversity immediately brings to the fore the fact that the term 'religion' in the context of China, and East Asia more generally, is a contested one, and its use requires some clarification. Scholars have struggled to find a term that reflects more accurately the reality of Chinese religiosity while ensuring that the terminology used could allow for comparative studies with other regions of the world. In this chapter, I adopt C. K. Yang's inclusive definition of religion, premised on a belief in the supernatural (C. K. Yang 1994: 2). This definition embraces a wide variety of social and cultural practices, alongside institutional religions. These practices range from the worldviews and rituals that people label 'superstitions' (*mixin*) or 'popular beliefs' (*minjian xinyang*) to the organized belief systems taught by groups that many denounce as 'sects' (*paibie zongjiao*) and 'cults' (*xiejiao, yijiao*).

Although this definition is very inclusive, it is important to keep in mind the inter-cultural dynamics that have made so difficult the acceptance of the term 'religion' in this broader sense and the implementation of this acceptance in the legal sphere of the PRC today, and in Taiwan until the 1980s, when the government decides what counts as a religion and what does not. The 'foreignness' of the term 'religion', influenced by Western Christians and the critiques of religion in the West, has no doubt shaped ideas about what constitutes a proper religion. For many intellectuals in China since the nineteenth century, the term 'religion' was reserved to a specific category of social activities and institutions that must include belief in a supreme being, along with specific scriptures, rituals, professionals, and space to transmit that belief, in contrast to other categories such as 'superstitions', science, and healing. Although the CPC officially maintains in its institutions that categorical division, many intellectuals in the PRC have moved beyond that, like their counterparts in Taiwan and Hong Kong.[5]

This chapter takes into account the diversity of societies influenced by Chinese culture by distinguishing between the influence of religion in development in the PRC and other societies with a Chinese cultural heritage such as Taiwan, Hong Kong, and Macau. Having already outlined some terminological considerations about China as a polity *and* a civilization, as well as the need to define religion in an appropriate way, the chapter starts with a discussion about the importance of religion in general and in the development of China in particular, before 1949. The chapter then discusses in turn the plural reality of religion in the PRC, the importance of thinking within the CPC to our understanding of the place of religion in development and, conversely, some important changes in CPC thinking about the place of religion in development. A short section on Taiwan and Hong Kong will remind us that there are many approaches Chinese governments can adopt in the inclusion of religion in development. Finally, the chapter looks at religious views on development in the PRC, Taiwan, and Hong Kong, and presents some of the specific achievements of religious people in poverty alleviation.

Religion and development in Chinese history

It may constitute a form of anachronism to write about religion and development before the 1960s, but once we consider acceptance of the broader and more inclusive notion of religion adopted by C. K. Yang (1994) outlined above, and take into account categories such as cultivation and healing as predecessors to the modern notions of education and medicine – two of the central components of development – we can appreciate the relevance of religious institutions, rituals, and practices to development more clearly. Education before the 1898 reform, notes Schipper, transmitted a Confucian canon, and in schools that often depended on Buddhist monasteries and Taoist temples (Schipper 2008: 385).[6] Since the Sui–Tang period (581–907), in fact, Buddhist monastic orders have played an important role in charitable works, including building bridges and planting trees, operating dispensaries in times of natural disasters and epidemics, and running free hospitals (Wright 1959: 75). Yet religious institutions became victims of their success when their close association with the state exposed them to the attacks of political and social reformers, as the Chinese government in the late Qing Dynasty (1644–1911) appeared unable to respond adequately to the military and political challenges from the West. To understand his, we need to appreciate the links between religion and politics in China.

In many societies, religions can influence the shaping of political institutions and laws, collective views on a nation's future, and the responses to the development strategies of international agencies and foreign governments (Rakodi, Chapter 2), but China's long history reminds us of another reality when the state and religion are mutually constitutive. From ancient times, the Chinese state political authority was a religious authority (C. K. Yang 1994: 111–12). From this perspective, we can understand the project of the neo-Confucian government elite,[7] who wanted to get rid of Taoist and Buddhist rituals and shamans from the Ming Dynasty (1368–1644) not so much as a state exercise of political authority over religion but rather as the enforcement of a religious state orthodoxy (Lagerwey 2010: 3–4). After the failed One Hundred Days Reform of 1898,[8] the Republican Revolution of 1911 tried to put an end to this sacralization of power.

The turmoil experienced by China after 1839 had heralded a new era that fundamentally altered the traditional landscape of religious life. The defeat in the Opium War (1839–42)[9] and the disaster of the Taiping Rebellion (1850–64)[10] convinced many reformers that traditional religion stood as an impediment to China's quest for wealth and power. The Opium War exposed the weakness of China in military and strategic terms, and many members of its educated elite laid the blame on Confucian education for its backwardness relative to European powers.[11] The Taiping Rebellion, which included elements of Christian eschatology in its guiding ideology, represented a dramatic attack against the Chinese religious traditions from which the Qing Dynasty never fully recovered (Platt 2012). The Taiping Rebellion and the Boxer Rebellion (1899–1900),[12] by weakening the Chinese state, not only led to Western military intervention and aggravated political interference, but also offered Christian missionaries opportunities to increase their influence under the protection of foreign powers (Bays 2012: 58–61). Although the influence of Christian missions was positive in higher education and philanthropy (Bays 2012: 99–104), many Chinese patriots felt that the protections enjoyed by Christians represented a violation of national sovereignty. These anti-Christian sentiments, however, were not so much anti-religious as traditionalist or nationalist (Goossaert and Palmer 2011).

Redefining the religious landscape

Reformers – such as Liang Qichao (1873–1929), who believed that it was better to establish a distinction between 'superstitions' and 'religions' (*zongjiao*) – adopted a similar approach to cultural renewal. Their categorization, which gave a superior status to Christian churches by virtue of their association with wealth and power, also included Buddhism, a religion of importance in Japan and Thailand, two Asian societies that had resisted the encroachment of Western powers on their soil. Nationalist politicians of the Guomindang (GMD, the Nationalist Party)[13] adopted his distinction between 'real' religions and 'superstitions'.[14] In doing so, they represented a religious reform movement rather than an atheist movement (Goossaert and Palmer 2011: 51). Their perspective remains influential today.

The more radical views adopted, among others, by the CPC, and that criticized religion per se, emerged in the 1920s. Many of the patriots and modernizers who had prevailed over the old regime with the establishment of the ROC in 1911 held to a view that was generally hostile to religion. They launched campaigns that targeted not only communal religions[15] but also 'world religions' such as Buddhism and Christianity (Duara 1991). These views received encouragement from afar, in a Zeitgeist that saw the outbreak of secular revolutions in Turkey, Iran, Mexico, and Russia. The dramatic political changes following the Republican Revolution of 1911, which ended 2,000 years of the imperial regime, and the Sino-Japanese War (1937–45) changed further the religious ecology of China. Among the most remarkable changes, the emergence of 'redemptive societies' – new religious movements and new religious associations that emerged as alternatives to Christianity, Buddhism, and other established religions – such as the Red Swastika Society and the Yiguandao provided support to the poor and refugees from war and natural disasters (Duara 2003; Goossaert and Palmer 2011: 90–108). These religions are still thriving in Taiwan and among the overseas communities today.

At the conclusion of the Chinese Civil War (1947–49) between the CPC and the GMD over the control of China, the CPC faced an already weakened religious establishment in Mainland China. The anti-religious currents, embraced by young radicals and abandoned by the GMD in the 1930s, resurfaced and culminated with the Cultural Revolution. After the launch of the Opening and Reform Policy in 1978, however, CPC leaders realized that in the end they had failed to eradicate religious life completely. In fact, religion is experiencing a resurgence in the PRC despite the CPC's attempt to limit its growth, thereby questioning the validity of theories about secularization (Marsh 2011; F. Yang 2012). The changes in the recent religious landscape include a dramatic expansion of Christianity, a major Buddhist revival, new forms of religiosity associated with qigong, and a rehabilitation of communal religions as 'intangible heritage' (M. M.-H. Yang 2008; Ashiwa and Wank 2009). As the CPC has come to accept this reality and adopted approaches more tolerant of religion, however, it mostly sees religious associations as actors that should obey and follow its directives, not as legitimate sources of critique that could influence independently public debates. The GMD and the authorities in other Chinese societies outside the PRC, on the other hand, appear more open to let religious institutions propose new approaches to development.

The place of religion in the PRC

We need to approach the sphere of the religious in the PRC in the plural: we find many religions, some that have grown from within China and some that have come from abroad and acclimatized themselves over centuries if not millennia, and new ones that are emerging. Historians and anthropologists consider the communal religions as the fundamental form of Chinese religion as well as the most ancient: a discussion of Chinese religions today must start with them (C. K. Yang 1994; Schipper 2008; Lagerwey 2010). Communal religions at the village levels were the primary actors involved in the provisions of social services. Since the end of the nineteenth century, however, modernizers perceived the practices of communal religions as too parochial, and blamed them as defenders of local interests, at the expense of the nation that the GMD wanted to build, or the new society that the CPC later on sought to establish. During the Land Reform of 1950,[16] the CPC saw communal religions as a major source of resistance to its policies and sought systematically to suppress their activities (Perry 2002: 277–87). They targeted communal religions as 'feudal superstitions' or 'reactionary sects', and depicted them as standing in the way of development and modernization. This was the dominant form of religious practice in the countryside, where the vast majority of the population lived until the 1970s. After 1978, when the policy of reform and opening kick-started a massive rural exodus and accelerated urbanization, this aspect of religiosity appeared condemned to oblivion in the wake of social change. Yet three mutually reinforcing factors have led to a dramatic revival of communal religions since the late 1970s: the relaxation of state control has allowed for the rebuilding of temples, transnational networks have helped reconstitute local memories and identities, and increasing prosperity has provided the wealth necessary for rebuilding (Goossaert and Palmer 2011: 242). This revival varies across regions, but it is nonetheless significant (Dean 2003). As the basic form of religious life embraced by a majority of the population, communal religions in the PRC matter: the government has elevated their status as part of 'intangible heritage'.[17] But this celebration of an important dimension of social life in the PRC does not mean that it benefits from a legal recognition as a religion.

Since 1949, the CPC has recognized only five religions: Buddhism, Taoism, Islam, Protestantism, and Catholicism. The patriotic associations, mentioned earlier, and their branches at the provincial, municipal, and/or district level represent each of these religions. The leaders of these associations, working with the bureaucracy of religious affairs bureaus at all levels of government and CPC cadres, ensure, theoretically at least, that their associations maintain orthodox practices and root out 'superstitions'. According to recent surveys, Buddhism counts over 200 million followers, and the most optimistic surveys about the number of Christians in the PRC claim 150 million believers (F. Yang 2012: 92–7). The totals for believers in these five religions, which do not include people who practise communal religions, suggest that a majority of the population is either atheist or non-religious. The CPC's recent policies, which the following section discusses, suggest that it is through these associations that the government may be willing to include religion in its development policies.

An unknown number of individuals in the PRC practise forms of religiosity that are not recognized as legitimate by the five official religions, and do not benefit from the ambiguous status of intangible heritage granted to communal religions. Hence, it is difficult to assess the number of redemptive societies such as Yiguandao, which can register as Buddhist or Taoist associations, but always remain vulnerable to a clampdown following a hardening of government policy. The campaign of the central government against Falungong since 1999 illustrates the challenges that non-recognized organized religion can face (Ownby 2008). Confucianism enjoys an increasingly ambiguous status in the PRC: not recognized as a religion, but often a component of communal religions, it has found a number of enthusiastic propagandists who proclaim its value as a secular civil religion (Bell 2008). It is too early to say if they will be successful at convincing the authorities that they should recognize Confucianism as a sixth religion, if not *the* Chinese religion. In its ambition to determine what religion is acceptable and legal, the CPC still acts in many ways as a religious actor. A consideration of the religious dimension of the CPC *Weltanschauung* can shed light on this paradox.

The dynamics just described have been in flux since the founding of the PRC. They show that the definition of what is a 'normal' religious practice or an 'acceptable' form of religiosity has been negotiated constantly, and it is difficult to predict where this process will lead. The practice of qigong that flourished during the Jiang Zemin administration offered a good example of this competition for legitimacy and authority between state and religious actors. Qigong was supported by the regime as a uniquely Chinese form of healing and self-cultivation, and as a helpful complement to public health, as long as its religious dimension was not affirmed too openly (Palmer 2007; Ownby 2008). And yet, while the regime launched persecution against qigong groups it denounced as 'evil cults' (*xiejiao*), it celebrated ostensibly the worship of the Yellow Emperor, the mythic ancestor of the Chinese people (Billeter 2007). These events suggest that, although new forms of religiosity can emerge from below, the CPC's ability to shape this evolution is not unlimited, especially when religious views can challenge its authority on the issue of development.

The CPC view of development and religion

To the extent that we can discern a 'Chinese' model of development, the approach used by the CPC is central. The influence of religion to the CPC's own view is indirect at best. The CPC approach rests on an adaptation to Chinese conditions of a philosophy of history that celebrates progress, and which resembles elements of a messianic ideology. Hence, the idea of an unjust world capitalist order that collapses under the weight of its own contradictions because of class struggle and imperialist wars seems not too far removed from the theme of the apocalypse and the end of days found within Christian traditions. The idea of an ideal world without contradiction and plenty of material abundance is the closest thing to a secular analogy of paradise. More provocatively, the sociologist of religion Ninian Smart had noted of Maoism that it contained the doctrine, the mythology, the social and ethical belief, the ritual, the experience of conversion, and the institution that constituted the six dimensions of his definition of religion (1974: 84–6). Smart's views, accurate in his observation that Marxism–Leninism and Maoism share some of the features of an institutionalized religion but without its numinous dimension, missed the important point that most religious practices in the PRC, such as those of communal religions, are not institutionalized rigidly like the Abrahamic religions, Buddhism, or some of the new religions that seek such institutionalization. Yet the CPC remains central to our understanding of the religious influence on Chinese models of development, because the Party's view on development until very recently rested on its opposition to organized religion.

Nominally, the 'Chinese model' of development refers to the historical materialism of Marxist-Leninist ideology, and references to 'Chinese characteristics' such as 'Mao Zedong's thought'[18] and 'Deng Xiaoping's theory'[19] served to offset the fact that Marxism-Leninism is a foreign import. Since the beginning of the reform policy in 1978, the PRC's model has adopted many features of the Western-based neo-liberal approach to development, including the recent acceptance of religious NGOs in the provision of some social services. The enormous cognitive dissonance between the ambition to implement socialism and the realities of increasing social inequities and privileges expose many to a crisis of faith towards the official ideology and, for some sociologists and historians, may explain the religious fervour seen in the PRC since 1978 (Bays 2012; F. Yang 2012).

Despite this major malaise, the Party still holds on to this ambition of directing development because of its self-perception as a vanguard organization, armed with a superior form of scientific knowledge that supersedes all religious values. In this perspective, religions should serve the Party. The CPC has adopted a variety of policies on religious affairs over the nine decades since its creation in 1921, always premised on the disappearance of religion as a social fact when society has reached the development goal of socialism (Potter 2003). For the last two decades, however, the CPC has accepted the fact that religion remains alive in contemporary societies where productive forces have reached advanced stages of development, such as the United States and Japan. It also agrees that the fact of this religious resilience is compatible with the goals of socialism and stability it cherishes (Ye 2000). For that purpose, the Party discussed in February 2012 a policy and legal 'opinion' issued by a number of Party and state organs,[20] about the desirability for religious organizations to deliver social services and serve the public interest (*CDB* 2012). Only the religious organizations that the state recognizes can perform these kinds of activities, however. Moreover, the CPC does not invite religious leaders to express their views on development as possible alternatives to the Party's perspectives on the matter.

Religious influence on Chinese models of development

Besides the vague analogy between Judaeo-Christian teleology and the foundations of Chinese communism just mentioned, there is little that these two types of worldview share, and they were bound to enter into conflict when the issue of development emerged. The same is true for the CPC worldview and that of traditional Chinese religions. The concepts of filial piety in Confucianism, compassion and impermanence in Buddhism, and the central principle of non-action in Taoism could hardly be reconciled with the ideas of class struggle that were promoted under Mao. Yet, in the last two decades, some convergence appears to have evolved. The references to 'harmonious society' by CPC General-Secretary Hu Jintao – between 2004 and 2012 – have led many to see a reappropriation of Confucianism by the CPC, and therefore the introduction of traditional worldviews, if not religions, in the thinking of the PRC's leaders (Bell 2008). It is too early to tell if Xi Jinping, who took over in 2012 as CPC General-Secretary, will continue along the path opened by Hu or change course. However, keeping in mind the importance of communal religions and organized religions discussed above, it is relevant to discuss religious perspectives and their potential influence on development in the PRC.

One could understand why a significant proportion of the population in the early stages of the CPC regime embraced its campaigns against religion and its social influence. The historical memory of the enormous human costs of the Taiping and Boxer rebellions, and the detrimental consequences both events had on China's prosperity and sovereignty could explain why religiously inspired solutions to the problems of development appeared problematic (Cohen 1997; Platt 2012).[21] The disasters of the Great Leap Forward (1957–61) and the anarchy of the Cultural Revolution, however, have ranked on a comparable scale to these earlier events in terms of loss of life and destruction. There is little research possible to address candidly to what extent Chinese today still embrace the earlier CPC views on the destructive potential of religion. Emerging evidence from fieldwork, however, suggests that an increasing number of people have a different view and trust a variety of religious actors as agents for development.

Recent research on communal religions by Adam Chau in the Shanbei region in North-West China and Lily Tsai in villages across the country consists of detailed surveys of village life and provides important information about the relations between political authorities and religious leaders (Chau 2005; Tsai 2007). However, this field of research is relatively recent, and the available evidence suggests that the role of communal religions in local development varies considerably from one location to another. Ethnographies by Chau and Tsai suggest that this variation between places depends on the nature of relations between communal religious leaders and local governments, and does not correspond to a systematic approach by the central government (Chau 2005; Tsai 2007).

Some of the fundamental concepts and beliefs of communal religions, however, can have some damaging consequences for development. For example, the requirement that only male descendants can perform the rituals of ancestral worship condoned by communal religions, combined with the government's one-child policy, has led for the last 30 years to an increase in sex-selective abortions that have targeted disproportionally female foetuses. As a result of this bias, the PRC's population registers one of the world's worst cases of a skewed sex ratio, whereby men largely outnumber women in the overall population (Attané 2010).[22] It is not entirely clear to what extent this skewed sex ratio results from beliefs held by communal religions on masculine spiritual superiority, but this discrimination bodes ill for sustainable and equitable development. We need more research to understand to what extent communal religions are subscribing to the old views on patriarchy responsible for a skewed sex ratio, or to what extent the rural exodus has changed the family structure and the religious values that sustain it. Some limited evidence suggests that the situation is changing. Hence, Kang Xiaofei's ethnography of temple management in rural Sichuan by elderly women suggests that communal religions can also empower women by offering them new forms of socialization, spiritual comfort, and moral capital outside the networks of markets and state (Kang 2009). In relation to the above, the specific contribution of Taoism to development remains unclear. The strategy used by redemptive societies and communal religions to register as members of the Taoist Association of China (Goossaert and Palmer 2011: 347) makes it even more difficult to obtain a clear picture of Taoist involvement in the provision of social services.

The contribution of Buddhist institutions to development presents its own set of contradictions. Most Buddhists in China claim an affiliation to the trend of 'Buddhism for the human realm' (*renjian fojiao*). This approach represents a conservative variant of a major doctrinal innovation by an early twentieth-century Chinese monk, Venerable Taixu, known as 'humanistic Buddhism' (*rensheng fojiao*), which espoused an activist approach to Buddhism that gave more importance to the role of the laity, and encouraged social engagement (Pittman 2001).[23] Taixu's approach, which was somewhat politicized and sympathetic to both nationalism and socialism, was reinterpreted by Venerable Yinshun,[24] a monastic ordained in Beijing in 1930 and exiled to Taiwan after 1952. He and others, such as Xingyun and Zhengyan, inspired most Buddhists in the PRC and Taiwan to adopt 'Buddhism for the human realm', a more conservative variant that, in particular, looked down on participation in politics. That variant of Buddhism is noticeable for its engagement in society with the practice of philanthropy and charity, and its absence of advocacy. The CPC has observed this development with great interest over the years thanks to academic and cultural exchanges across the Taiwan Strait. Increasingly, it has looked positively at this approach, and in recent years its United Front Work Departments (UFWD)[25] at different levels of governments have instructed bureaus for religious affairs and Buddhist associations to approve the institutionalization of Buddhist charities (*cishan*), foundations (*jijinhui*), and merit societies (*gongdehui*), which distribute relief to victims of natural disasters and run a limited number of social services (Laliberté 2012). The evidence available suggests that the extent of Buddhist devotees' contribution to development, as is the case with communal religious associations, depends on local governments' relations with local Buddhist associations, more than a general directive from the national Buddhist Association.

Christianity, both Protestant and Catholic, has experienced a contradiction between its positive association with modernity and China's progress, on the one hand, and its role as an instrument to advance the interests of foreign powers, on the other. Historically, Christian missions have contributed to the development of communities, but their reliance on foreign powers for protection had tainted their contributions in the eyes of patriotic Chinese. This guilt by association, which overlooked the positive contributions of Christians in the development of higher education, orphanages, and health care, made them vulnerable to persecution after 1949 by the CPC, which expelled foreign missionaries and forced Chinese Christians to join the state-sponsored Christian associations.[26] Their previous contributions to development served them well, however, as they were looked upon as important elements of the United Front policy, important allies in nurturing good relations with third world countries where Christians are important in numbers (Bays 2012: 202–05). With respect to Islamic influence on development thinking in the PRC, it remains under-researched, in contrast to studies about ethnic identity and issues of security relevant to the Hui and Uyghur people, as well as other Muslim minorities in the PRC.

Along with the 'rehabilitation' of communal religions evoked above, the revisionist appreciation of Confucianism runs against the tide of the late century that blamed China's ills on this teaching and, in doing so, follows the views of scholars who advocated the centrality of that tradition in accounting for development in societies influenced by Chinese traditions (Tu 1996). The role of Confucianism as an inspiration for development has not convinced everyone, however, and critics have noted that it is more a legitimating device used by governments than an explanation (Chan 1996). At best, apologists for Confucianism's contribution to development claim that the respect for authority and hierarchy that this promotes serves to discipline the workforce. The patriarchal dimension of Confucianism, moreover, remains a blind spot for its proponents, as will be discussed below. Before concluding on that issue, it is important to keep in mind the different institutional legacies in Taiwan and Hong Kong that can give religious actors a greater influence on development policies.

The views on religion and development outside the PRC

The CPC approach to development since 1978 is indebted in part to approaches developed in Taiwan, Hong Kong, and Macau. These states have adopted strategies of export-led economic growth, and a political system that discipline the workforce by using tight control of labour. Similarities between the PRC after 1978 and Taiwan under martial law are even greater if we consider the strategy of state-led development wherein the state controls key industries and the reliance on special economic zones. In Taiwan and Hong Kong, governments have welcomed religious institutions as providers of social services, including the delivery of health care and education. One of the most important trends of the last two decades has been the gradual acceptance of organizations from Taiwan and Hong Kong in the PRC to deliver humanitarian relief, and fund schools in impoverished areas, as well as encouragement from authorities for Chinese religious organizations to learn from the practices of their Taiwanese and Hong Kong counterparts.

It is too early to see in these developments a sign that the PRC is about to adopt liberal policies on religious affairs that compare to those of Taiwan and Hong Kong, but it is important to recall that, a few decades ago, the GMD had also subjected Taiwan to a rather rigid regime of control over religious affairs that shared many characteristics with the one that is enforced now by the CPC. For a brief period at the beginning of the Republican era, many radical members of the GMD had adopted a radical attitude towards religion, and only after Chiang Kai-shek took control of the Party in 1926 did the GMD repudiate that policy and let a variety of religious institutions support the governments in areas as diverse as humanitarian relief, education, and health care. Humanitarian organizations such as the Buddhist Red Swastika Society and different Protestant churches were active during the Sino-Japanese War (1937–45) to provide support to the civilian population. The GMD carried on this policy of cooperation with religious institutions in Taiwan after 1949: it allowed Christian churches to run hospitals, clinics, schools, and universities, and encouraged the Buddhist Ciji Foundation to establish its own network of hospitals.[27] Different government agencies organized sessions with religious institutions to discuss their contributions to social services and approve their accreditations to establish universities (Clart and Jones 2003). In other words, the opening to religion happened before the process of democratization unfolded in Taiwan: there are signs that authorities in the PRC want to adopt a similar approach, directing religious institutions to address social issues on behalf of the state. In Hong Kong, colonial authorities and then the government of the special administrative region[28] have supported the initiatives of Christians and Buddhists to run their own hospitals, schools, and institutes of higher education. In both Taiwan and Hong Kong, government authorities have adopted a laissez-faire attitude that let churches and religious associations intervene in the public sphere.

This attitude of governments in Taiwan and Hong Kong was probably facilitated by the fact that in both cases a vibrant civil society existed, and religious institutions could successfully mobilize their adherents to defend their interests. Such mobilization, in particular for Christians, was greatly facilitated by the fact that political leaders were themselves members of Christian churches and that they, in turn, depended for the survival of their regime on the support of foreign countries where Christians represented important and powerful constituencies, such as the United States, for Taiwan, and the United Kingdom, for Hong Kong before 1997. This connection between Western Christianity and Christian elites in Taiwan and Hong Kong, however, is exceptional, and could hardly serve as a model for the PRC.

The ambiguous relationship of religion to development in the PRC

As we have seen above, the CPC and many intellectuals have long believed that religion cannot be a positive force for development. In that respect, their perspective mirrored the view held by many in mainstream social science in the West, which includes the Soviet variant of Marxist perspectives, and saw, at best, religion as an opiate of the masses or, worse, as an institutional obstacle that the state needed to remove to achieve modernity. The Western influence in China, while not as pervasive there as it was in Africa and South Asia, added a layer of complexity: the support of the colonial powers to Catholic and Protestant missionaries left behind a legacy of ill will towards Christianity for many Chinese patriots. The fact that many of the exiled opponents of the regime are recent Christian converts does not help to assuage that perception.

The contribution to development of communal religions is less obvious than the obstacles it presents to development. As discussed earlier, some of these values can have a devastating effect on development and in particular on the dimension of gender, because of their adverse effects on fertility and demographic imbalances. Economic explanations for the PRC's skewed sex ratio and the traditional preference for boys have often pointed to the expectation from parents that sons are more likely to take care of their parents, but recent evidence suggests that girls are more likely to fulfil their filial duties (Attané 2010). This recent finding gives even more weight to cultural factors than was previously assumed: the Confucian tradition, prevalent in popular beliefs, that only males can perform the rituals of ancestor worship influences many couples' preferences for having a son, despite the fact that daughters are more likely than sons to care for their parents. The allegiance of many Chinese to Buddhism and Taoism, moreover, does not necessarily attenuate this influence of Confucian values: the success of some Buddhist spiritual leaders rests on their embrace of Confucian family ethics (Dutournier and Ji 2009). However, until reliable surveys can be done, it will remain difficult to measure how widespread such beliefs, and the social practices they condone, are.

Chinese Buddhists can also hold very ambiguous views on development. As discussed above with reference to the reformist monk Taixu, many Buddhist clerics and lay people have embraced development to ensure the survival of their tradition. As Ji Zhe has documented, Buddhist monasteries early on sought to break with the traditional approach of living on lay people's alms by encouraging self-sufficiency, for example by getting involved in local economic activity through pilgrimage tourism (Ji 2004). This growing prosperity of Buddhism has made them important actors in local programmes of poverty alleviation and led to the development of an important philanthropic sector in which Buddhist charities deliver help to children of impoverished areas and assist local authorities following natural disasters (Laliberté 2012). Protests by Buddhist devotees, however, have revealed tensions between them and local state agencies because of the latter's support for development brought by pilgrimages, which many see as a negative influence on temples (Fisher 2008).

Among the areas of contention between the churches and the state in relation to development, different denominations hold a variety of perspectives. Traditional Christian views on contraception, abortion, and sexuality can hardly be reconciled with those of the government on family planning. Beyond this, however, we find too much diversity of views to make generalizations. While the theology of the Three-Selves Churches[29] recognized by the government espouses 'liberal' interpretations of the scriptures that do not oppose the state, house churches, evangelical movements, and sects such as Eastern Lightning have views that range from the mainstream to millenarian (Bays 2012).[30] Western Christian theology has supported a wide variety of views on gender relations, but most of them have not sacralized gender hierarchies the way Confucian patriarchy does. We need to do more research to know how much the indigenized breakaway churches, which often incorporate elements of Chinese religious traditions, have adopted the cosmology that sees sons as necessary for ancestor worship.

In recent years, the visibility of religious life in the PRC has increased significantly, and one way to legitimize this presence is through the performance of philanthropy, through religious non-government organizations (RNGOs). Tolerated since the 1990s, these organizations have received significant official support with the February 2012 'opinion' already mentioned above. Whether these RNGOs are established through the support of local officials from the state or the Party, or through grassroots initiatives, they are made possible because of a certain degree of connivance between political and religious leaders that was inconceivable when the provision of social services was the responsibility of the people's communes. The growth of these associations reveals how far the situation of religion has evolved. While not excluding the reality of contestation and repression for people who join a religious organization of which the regime still disapproves, there is an important reconstruction of religious life in the PRC, and where this process will lead the country is hard to predict.

Chinese believers working in RNGOs face both opportunities and tremendous challenges, in relation to their religious beliefs and practice, and in relation to their ideas and actions in favour of development. The century-long strife between modernist and secular reformers and religious people, who were often equally committed to the renewal of their country, casts a long shadow on their activities. There is no iron-clad guarantee that the regime will continue to implement the current, relatively lenient, if not positively supportive, policy towards institutionalized and legally recognized religions. This heavy legacy from the past includes lack of agreement about the activities that RNGOs can and should undertake, in education, health care, or disaster relief. Another source of tension between RNGOs and outsiders, whether it is the state or non-religious people in Chinese society, is how far RNGOs can conceal their religious identity *qua* religious organizations. Should they openly advertise their religious identities as they register, or should they avoid disclosure of their religious identity to avoid the charge from government that they mix proselytizing with their work on development? The contrast between Ciji, which is registered in the PRC and in Taiwan as non-religious philanthropy, despite the Buddhist identity of its organization and core membership, and the Hebei Province Buddhist Foundation, which does not shy away from displaying its identity, demonstrates that, even within one religious tradition, many approaches are used to address this issue. This diversity reveals that divisions within religions, among clerics and among lay people, make the involvement of RNGOs in development even more complex. Even outside the PRC, followers of any religion can be divided within their own congregation or community over the extent to which the teachings of their spiritual leaders and the traditions they follow can justify their actions in favour of development.

Religions and strategies for liberating the poor

The nature of the regime in the PRC makes it difficult for religious institutions to articulate strategies for liberating the poor: they risk the enmity of the regime if they do so too openly. The CPC has invested much of its legitimacy in its ability to achieve poverty alleviation thanks to its approach to 'scientific development', and the suggestion that religious institutions could provide better solutions to social problems such as inadequate health facilities can attract the wrath of the regime. Followers of Falungong, whose public practice of breathing exercises was interpreted by the CPC and others as embodying a critique of the PRC's health care institutions, have learned this reality the hard way as victims of a massive persecution (Shue 2002; Thornton 2002). The genuine achievements of the government between the beginnings of the reform policy in 1978 and the 1990s undoubtedly give credence to the official claim that the Chinese government has developed the best strategies to liberate the poor. However, the growth of social and economic inequalities, corruption, and collusion between wealth and power, during the last two decades, raises questions about the CPC's approach to poverty alleviation (Pei 2006; Shirk 2007). Many analysts have pointed to the rise of religious activities in the PRC as a rebuttal of the CPC's mode of governance in that regard (M. M.-H. Yang 2008; Ashiwa and Wank 2009; Marsh 2011; F. Yang 2012).

For the three decades after 1949 it was difficult for religious institutions in the PRC to devise strategies to liberate the poor independently of the directives issued by the CPC, while religious hierarchies in Taiwan and Hong Kong had to tread carefully, out of fear of being accused of communist sympathy. While Catholic Liberation Theology in Latin America and, up to a point, engaged Buddhism in South-East Asia (Queen and King 1996) have included development as a central concern of their respective religious teachings, it was difficult for fellow Buddhists and fellow Christians in the PRC, Taiwan, and Hong Kong and Macau to adopt such approaches in these societies. For adherents of Taoism, communal religions, and new religious movements, we need more research to evaluate the extent to which these religious practices and beliefs have been successful at nurturing approaches to development that are sustainable, widespread, and effective. These traditions do not have the level of international support that Christians, and to a certain extent Buddhists and Muslims, can obtain from fellow believers abroad, especially those who are from Taiwan and Hong Kong.

After decades of tribulations, Catholics have found ways to act in accordance with the Church's social doctrine. The Catholic clergy in the PRC, mostly cut off from their co-religionists abroad during the three decades after 1949, experienced bitter divisions between priests who remained loyal to Rome and others who preferred to reach some accommodation with the regime (Madsen 1998: 49). Numerous events have contributed to change this situation, as younger Catholics are more exposed to international models of development and benefit from increasing transnational links and exchanges. The 'patriotic' and unregistered churches have moved closer following the 'open letter to China' from Pope Benedict XVI in 2007, which asked all Catholics to consider themselves as 'one church' in 'two communities'. Despite the remaining difficulties they experience, as shown by the house arrest of the new Bishop of Shanghai after his consecration, or the remaining disagreement over appointments of bishops, Catholics are increasingly active in social service, for activities ranging from disaster relief to rural development and poverty alleviation. They also get involved in advocacy work, for victims of HIV/Aids and for palliative care. They have established large, church–run social service centres in places such as Shijiazhuang (which has the only nationally registered centre), Xi'an, Shenyang, and Shanghai.[31]

The evolution of the Catholic Church in Taiwan, Hong Kong, and Macau followed a very different path. Liberation Theology was problematic in that part of the world because of its links to Marxism in Latin America: for most of the four decades after 1949, the governments of these three polities were staunchly anti-communist and did not hesitate to harass people whom they suspected of being close to the CPC. The hierarchies of most religious associations in these three polities did not need much convincing from the authorities to support these anti-communist policies, since many priests, monks, pastors, and other religious personnel were themselves victims of persecution by the CPC (Madsen 1998: 143–6). Recent evolutions in the PRC, however, are erasing these differences between the Catholic community, as they do for other religions.

Non-Catholic Christians, active in many churches, have developed a variety of approaches and varying degrees of commitment to the 'social gospel'. Like their Catholic counterparts, they have been very active in social service despite the obstacles. Protestantism, albeit led in the PRC by a single patriotic association like Buddhism, Taoism, and Catholicism, experiences doctrinal divisions likely to reverberate in the Chinese world, if not in the PRC, where every Protestant church has to join the official Three-Selves patriotic association. Despite this regulation, however, large numbers of Protestant Christians worship in 'domestic churches'. This division between a community of legalized and state-sanctioned churches and a community that does not benefit from state support mirrors divisions within the Catholic Church. Similar divisions exist within the state administration, as revealed by the variety of policies adopted by officials towards churches, ranging from support to churches in both Protestant and Catholic communities to the occasional harassment of congregations, such as the Beijing Shouwang Church, and the few cases of church demolition, as seen in 2014 in the city of Wenzhou, Zhejiang. The expansion of Protestant Christianity in China is remarkable, and the involvement of many churches in social services reflects confidence about its growth. A growing area of research among Chinese scholars in social science focuses on this involvement, but only a fraction of that research can be accessed in English.

Where the denominational pluralism of Protestant Christianity does not face legal-political obstacles, and a variety of churches can exist, the diversity of approaches to development and strategies adopted to alleviate poverty reflects this pluralism. In Taiwan, for example, conservative denominations co-exist with progressive ones, such as the Presbyterian Church, which early on spoke out in favour of the aboriginal people's right to dignity and development (Rubinstein 1991). Being a missionary religion introduced in the island from abroad, the social gospel promoted by that church became an integral part of the island's social and political life, following a long period of indigenization.

Discussions on 'engaged Buddhism' have emphasized the role of individuals such as the Dalai Lama, Sulak Sivaraksa, Thich Nath Hanh, and Dr Ambedkar in a variety of causes ranging from pacifism to empowerment of the downtrodden and the necessity to find an alternative to capitalist development (Queen and King 1996). 'Engaged Buddhism', however, has eluded the PRC. As we have seen above, the trend of 'Buddhism for the human realm', despite its remarkable achievements in the provision of health care and education, has moved away from the critical thinking present in the views of Taixu, and tended to be supportive of established regimes. Most of those who adopt the approach of 'Buddhism for the human realm' are willing to work under the restrictive conditions imposed by repressive regimes, whether Taiwan during the period of martial law (1949–87) or the PRC under the current regime (Laliberté 2012). Official Buddhist institutions formally recognized by the CPC belong to that trend, and so do many of those who follow the teachings of spiritual masters living abroad, such as Venerable Jingkong, a monk living in the West but popular in the PRC and outside, known for conservative views that are even more removed from the limited ideas of development held by the mainstream associations the PRC regime supports (Dutournier and Ji 2009). In the long run, however, this doctrinal prudence may help the expansion of Buddhist philanthropy in the PRC. The state does not see in Buddhist institutions an actor supported by foreign powers, and it sees in 'Buddhism for the human realm' a doctrinal approach that can be compatible with modernity, including socialism. The CPC had the opportunity to observe across the Taiwan Strait what Buddhists could achieve in Taiwan when the island was under martial law and has no reason to believe it could not achieve similar results, within certain limits.

Conclusion

We must understand the relation of religion to development in Chinese societies in the plural. There is a diversity of political regimes with different approaches to religion: paternalistic in the PRC, and increasingly laissez-faire in Taiwan and Hong Kong, which welcome the activities of religious institutions in development. It is not too far-fetched to think that the CPC regime considers adopting the approach of the latter two polities, as it embraces many other aspects of their social and economic policies. We must also understand the plural in the sense of religious diversity, which compares to that of other modern societies, despite the efforts of the CPC to maintain a rigid structure of limited recognition over the complex religious landscape of society. In that aspect as well, it is hard to tell how long the PRC will avoid implementing legal and regulatory structures that reflect better society's situation on the ground, as Taiwanese and Hong Kong institutions do.

All of the above discussion suggests that the relations between the Chinese government and the different religions are complex and evolving. Among the many scenarios envisaged about the role of religion and development in the Chinese world, the recent evolutions suggest that the previous attitude of excluding religion is less likely, notwithstanding occasional cases of persecution against clerics or believers. The slogan of 'harmonious society' by ex-president Hu Jintao, a barely veiled reference to Confucianism, had suggested that the CPC was willing to reconsider its previous stance on traditional culture and thereby revealed the depth of popular aspirations for better public morality. In that context, religions, as providers of moral values, matter to the regime. As the governments of the PRC, Taiwan, Hong Kong, and Macau look at religious institutions as partners in development, will they also rely on them as tools for the display of soft power, or persuasion without coercion on international affairs? But other scenarios are possible, as the boundaries of who is 'Chinese', or what is 'religious' or not, continue to change.

Notes

1 I would like to thank the Social Science and Humanities Research Council of Canada for its financial support allowing time and research assistance. I am also grateful to the anonymous reviewers for their very helpful comments and suggestions. All omissions and errors are mine.
2 China as a cultural tradition remains influential in the following polities: the PRC, established in 1949 after the CPC defeated the GMD (Nationalist Party) in the Chinese Civil War (1947–49); Taiwan, controlled since 1945 by the Republic of China (ROC), a state established in 1911 in the territory of what is today the PRC and Mongolia, whose de facto sovereignty was limited to the island after 1949; Hong Kong; and Macau. This tradition also remains important in Singapore and among overseas Chinese communities around the world, but the issue of Chinese sovereignty and the contentions it raises are limited to the first four polities.

246

3 It also excludes, obviously, all the other communities where Chinese tradition matters but on which the PRC does not assert claims of sovereignty.

4 The Buddhist Association of China; the Chinese Association of Taoism; the Patriotic Catholic Association of China; the Chinese Islamic Association; and, for Protestants, the China Christian Council and the Committee for the Three Autonomies of the Patriotic Protestant Church of China.

5 For an extensive discussion of these issues, see Goossaert and Palmer (2011), as well as Ashiwa and Wank (2009).

6 The 1898 reform failed, but the goals of the reformists were vindicated in 1905, when the Confucian exams were abolished.

7 Confucianism had been important as an intellectual tradition since the Han Dynasty, but it was eclipsed for centuries by Buddhism and Taoism, which received government support. It re-emerged under the Song Dynasty, transformed by the influences of these two religions, and became the curriculum that aspiring state officials needed to master, described by scholars as neo-Confucianism.

8 Led by the young emperor Guangxu (1871–1908), the reform sought, among other things, to replace the neo-Confucian examination system, which was seen by reformers as responsible for China's weakness relative to Western powers, but a coup led by conservative factions in the court put an end to the attempt.

9 The Opium War opposed Great Britain and China over the issue of China's refusal to allow opium trade in the country.

10 The Taiping Rebellion caused an estimated 30 million deaths. It had multiple causes: poverty in rural South-West China, dissatisfaction of the Hakka people vis-à-vis the central government, and lack of good governance.

11 The view that the Confucian tradition was a hindrance to economic growth found an echo in the West, when Max Weber asserted at the beginning of the twentieth century that this tradition had deprived China of the impulse to develop. The rise of Japan, the 'four dragons', or new industrialized economies, of South Korea, Taiwan, Hong Kong, and Singapore in the 1970s, and then the PRC in the 1990s have led to a new and equally simplistic axiom that sees Confucianism as the source of development in East Asia (Tu 1996).

12 Another rebellion with an aetiology comparable to that of the Taiping Rebellion, but in the North China plain it had the added dimension of feuds between villages.

13 The GMD was founded after 1911 and controlled most of China between 1927 and 1936, when the Eastern part of the country was invaded by the Japanese imperial army, the North-West fell under CPC control, and the North-East was under the 'puppet governments' of Manzhouguo, controlled by Japan. It nominally recovered control of China after the Second World War but lost the Civil War to the CPC in 1949 and relocated its government to Taiwan, which it ruled for 38 years under a regime of martial law.

14 It is only when Taiwan entered into a phase of democratic consolidation that the GMD abandoned this view. The CPC, however, still maintains this distinction.

15 The variety of religious practices and rituals adopted in villages throughout China, which may or may not include elements of Confucian, Taoist, and Buddhist rituals and beliefs, along with mythologies and worship of local deities, village ancestors, and ghosts.

16 The landlords targeted by the Land Reform often headed the temple managing committee of communal religious temples, or the communal religious temples themselves owned land that the CPC wanted to expropriate.

17 This does not mean that the state recognizes communal religion *qua* religion, but at least it does not condemn the practice as 'feudal superstition'.

18 Mao, *inter alia*, believed that the peasantry was central for the success of the Chinese Revolution, in contrast to the classical Marxist tenet that saw the urban proletariat as the vanguard of communist revolutions. Mao, however, also believed that the traditional culture and the religions of China's peasants were contributing to the country's backwardness.

19 Deng sought to correct Mao's most extreme policies against Chinese traditions and religions, believing that this would encourage Chinese living overseas who had remained attached to China's cultural heritage and hitherto repelled by Mao's policies to invest in China.

20 They were the State Administration for Religious Affairs, the United Front Department of the Communist Party of China, the State Council's National Development and Reform Commission, the Ministry of Civil Affairs, the Ministry of Finance, and the State Administration of Taxation.

21 The leader of the Taiping Rebellion believed that he was the younger brother of Jesus, and many of his followers shared that belief; the Boxers adhered to an ancient belief system according to which the practice of some physical exercises would render them invulnerable to bullets.

22 Globally, the average sex ratio at birth is estimated at 106 boys born for 100 girls. However, the PRC stands out, with India, as a country where this 'natural number' is skewed because of sex-selective abortions. The World Bank estimates that in 2012 the PRC sex ratio at birth was 119 boys born for 100 girls.

23 This form of 'humanistic Buddhism' should not be confused with 'engaged Buddhism', the object of a growing literature about the role of Buddhism in development, because this movement has little impact in China. The only connections with China are the fact that its founder, exiled Vietnamese monk Thich Nath Hanh, asserts that Taixu inspired his approach, and the fact that the Dalai Lama is a major figure of the movement.

24 Yinshun is also the spiritual master for Zhengyan, the nun who established the Ciji Foundation in Taiwan. See also Fountain, Chapter 6.

25 The UFWD is a Party organ that communicates to non-Party associations and individuals instructions about its policies, and ensures that they comply, through persuasion.

26 The Committee for the Three Autonomies of the Patriotic Protestant Church of China and the Patriotic Catholic Association of China.

27 Ciji is better known as Tzu chi, following the Taiwanese usage.

28 Hong Kong's official status after the end of British colonial rule in 1997: it recognizes China's sovereignty over Hong Kong, but Hong Kong maintains its own political institutions.

29 The expression means 'self-governance (no control from overseas churches)', 'self-support (no outside funding)', 'self-propagation (no foreign missionaries)'.

30 Many do not consider that Eastern Lightning qualifies as a Christian organization.

31 I would like to thank the anonymous reviewer for this information.

References

Ashiwa, Y. and Wank, D. L. (eds) (2009) *Making Religion, Making the State: The Politics of Religion in Modern China*, Stanford, CA: Stanford University Press.

Attané, I. (2010) *En espérant un fils: La masculinisation de la population chinoise*, Paris: Les éditions de l'Ined.

Bays, D. H. (2012) *A New History of Christianity in China*, Chichester: Wiley-Blackwell.

Bell, D. A. (2008) *China's New Confucianism: Politics and Everyday Life in a Changing Society*, Princeton, NJ: Princeton University Press.

Billeter, T. (2007) *L'empereur jaune*, Paris: Les Indes savantes.

CDB (*China Development Brief*) (2012) 'Religious Organizations Can Establish Foundations, Social Welfare Organizations, and Nonprofit Hospitals in Accordance with the Law', Caixin, February, http://www.chinadevelopmentbrief.cn/?p=637 (accessed 13 June 2013).

Chan, A. (1996) 'Confucianism and Development in East Asia', *Journal of Contemporary Asia*, 26 (1), 28–45.

Chau, A. (2005) *Miraculous Response: Doing Popular Religion in Contemporary China*, Stanford, CA: Stanford University Press.

Clart, P. and Jones, C. B. (2003) *Religion in Modern Taiwan: Tradition and Innovation in a Changing Society*, Honolulu: University of Hawai'i Press.

Cohen, P. (1997) *History in Three Keys: The Boxers as Event, Experience, and Myth*, New York: Columbia University Press.

Dean, K. (2003) 'Local Communal Religion in Southeast China', in D. Overmyer (ed.), *Religion in China Today*, Cambridge: Cambridge University Press, pp. 338–58.

Duara, P. (1991) 'Knowledge and Power in the Discourse of Modernity: The Campaigns against Popular Religion in Early Twentieth-Century China', *Journal of Asian Studies*, 50 (1) (February), 67–83.

Duara, P. (2003) *Sovereignty and Authenticity: Manchukuo and the East Asian Modern*, Lanham, MD: Rowman & Littlefield.

Dutournier, G. and Ji, Z. (2009) 'Expérimentation sociale et "confucianisme populaire": Le cas du Centre d'éducation culturelle de Lujiang', *Perspectives chinoises*, 109 (4), 71–86.

Fisher, G. (2008) 'The Spiritual Land Rush: Merit and Morality in New Chinese Buddhist Temple Construction', *Journal of Asian Studies*, 67 (1), 143–70.

Goossaert, V. and Palmer, D. (2011) *The Religious Question in Modern China*, Chicago: University of Chicago Press.

Ji, Z. (2004) 'La nouvelle relation Etat–bouddhisme', *Perspectives chinoises*, 84 (1), 2–10.

Kang, X. (2009) 'Femmes en milieu rural, vieillesse et activités dans les temples: Une étude de cas dans le nord-ouest du Sichuan', *Perspectives chinoises*, 109 (4), 44–55.

Lagerwey, J. (2010) *China: A Religious State*, Hong Kong: Hong Kong University Press.

Laliberté, A. (2012) 'Buddhist Charities and China's Social Policy: An Opportunity for Alternate Civility?', *Archives de sciences sociales des religions*, 158 (April–June), 95–117.

Madsen, R. (1998) *China's Catholics: Tragedy and Hope in an Emerging Civil Society*, Berkeley: University of California Press.

Marsh, C. (2011) *Religion and the State in Russia and China: Suppression, Survival, and Revival*, New York: Continuum.

Ownby, D. (2008) *Falungong and the Future of China*, New York: Oxford University Press.

Palmer, D. (2007) *Qigong Fever: Body, Science, and Utopia in China*, New York: Columbia University Press.

Pei, M. (2006) *China's Trapped Transition*, Cambridge, MA: Harvard University Press.

Perry, E. J. (2002) *Challenging the Mandate of Heaven: Social Protest and State Power in China*, Armonk, NY: M. E. Sharpe.

Pittman, D. A. (2001) *Towards a Modern Chinese Buddhism: Taixu's Reforms*, Honolulu: University of Hawai'i Press.

Platt, S. R. (2012) *Autumn in the Heavenly Kingdom: China, the West, and the Epic Story of the Taiping Civil War*, New York: Vintage Books.

Potter, P. (2003) 'Belief in Control: Regulation of Religion in China', *China Quarterly*, 174 (June), 317–37.

Queen, C. S. and King, S. B. (eds) (1996) *Engaged Buddhism: Buddhist Liberation Movements in Asia*, Albany: State University of New York Press.

Rubinstein, M. (1991) *The Protestant Community on Modern Taiwan: Mission, Seminary, and Church*, Armonk, NY: M. E. Sharpe.

Schipper, K. (2008) *La religion de la Chine: La tradition vivante*, Paris: Fayard.

Shirk, S. (2007) *China: Fragile Superpower*, New York: Oxford University Press.

Shue, V. (2002) 'Global Imaginings, the State's Quest for Hegemony, and the Pursuit of Phantom Freedom in China: From Heshang to Falungong', in C. Kinnvall and K. Jonsson (eds), *Globalization and Democratization in Asia: The Construction of Identity*, London: Routledge, pp. 210–29.

Smart, N. (1974) *Mao*, Glasgow: Williams Collins.

Thornton, P. (2002) 'Framing Dissent in Contemporary China: Irony, Ambiguity and Metonymy', *China Quarterly*, 171 (September), 661–81.

Tsai, L. (2007) *Accountability without Democracy: Solidary Groups and Public Goods Provision in Rural China*, Cambridge: Cambridge University Press.

Tu, W.-M. (ed.) (1996) *Confucian Traditions in East Asian Modernity: Moral Education and Economic Culture in Japan and the Four Mini-Dragons*, Cambridge, MA: Harvard University Press.

Wright, A. (1959) *Buddhism in Chinese History*, Stanford, CA: Stanford University Press.

Yang, C.-K. (1994) *Religion in Chinese Society: A Study of Contemporary Social Functions of Religion and Some of their Historical Factors*, Taipei: SMC Publishing.

Yang, F. (2012) *Religion in China: Survival and Revival under Communist Rule*, New York: Oxford University Press.

Yang, M. M.-H. (ed.) (2008) *Chinese Religiosities: Afflictions of Modernity and State Formation*, Berkeley: University of California Press.

Ye, X. (2000) 'Recalling and Thinking over Religious Work at the Turn of the Century', *Tripod*, 118.

17

CRITICAL PERSPECTIVES ON RELIGIONS – ESPECIALLY CHRISTIANITY – IN THE DEVELOPMENT OF SOUTH KOREA POST-1945

Kirsteen Kim

Introduction

Under Japanese colonial oppression from 1910, Communism and Christianity emerged among Koreans as offering alternative, and mutually antagonistic, ideals for nationalists and for post-colonial development. Broadly speaking, after the liberation from Japan in 1945, Kim Il-sung and his regime developed the North as a type of Communist state, and Syngman Rhee, and a series of dictatorial successors, developed the South as a right-leaning capitalist state oriented to the West. Soon after it began, this process was interrupted by the devastating Korean War (1950–53), which left both Koreas among the poorest nations in the world. But today South Korea is a member of the G20, produces some of the world's most high-tech goods and exports its popular culture through music and film. This chapter contributes to understanding the relationship between religions and global development by showing how Christianity in particular played a highly significant role in the development of South Korea. It will offer some additional reasons why Korea's other religions have had less impact on development over this period.

In this unique historical context of South Korea, the religions – including also Confucianism, Buddhism and indigenous religions – had been disempowered by Japanese colonialism. But now national survival depended on strong ties with the West, Korean Christianity was in an advantageous position compared to other religions, and moreover it strongly articulated visions of modernization and development. However, in the context of religious freedom, many different Christian churches, actors and movements were involved, so the Christian impact was felt in a variety of ways, which are treated here: inspiring visions of a modern, independent nation; community development; presenting a political alternative to Communism; post-war relief and development; legitimizing and encouraging wealth creation; struggling for labour and civil rights; world mission; peacemaking and humanitarian initiatives; and activism on justice, peace and life issues. I will argue that Christianity's impact was due to the resources and models of development it offered and also because leaders in South Korea selectively appropriated particularly those aspects of the faith that they believed would aid national recovery and well-being. Christian initiatives in modernization and development were not nationally or governmentally coordinated; indeed they sometimes worked against each other. Nevertheless, taken together they played a highly significant role in both the nation's economic success and its democratization.

Nineteenth-century Korean visions for a modern, independent nation

The period covered in this chapter is only the most recent of a long Korean history stretching over two millennia, during which a series of different religions were dominant (Grayson 2002). The Korean kingdoms which were unified in the tenth century patronized Buddhism for the protection it was believed to offer them, but after a change of dynasty in 1392 an alliance of scholars and dynastic rulers re-modelled and transformed Korean society according to Confucian ideology (Deuchler 1992). As part of this process, Buddhism was suppressed; Buddhist monks were excluded from cities, and their temples survived only in remote rural areas. There monasteries were a refuge for the disenfranchised and the weak, and a source of relief in times of famine and flood, but there was little possibility of engagement with wider society (KBRI 1993: 169–218). However, by the nineteenth century, Confucian Korea (Joseon) faced serious challenges from natural disasters, social unrest, the weakening of China, loss of its protection and patronage, and encroachment by other foreign powers (Eckert *et al.* 1990: 178–98). The authorities responded to this crisis by sealing off the country and fiercely suppressing the main group with foreign links: the embryonic Catholic Church, which had been founded in 1784 by Korean scholars who had studied Christian literature from China (Choi Jai-keun 2006).

From the 1860s Japan, which had a head-start in technological development, signalled its ambition to annex Korea, an intention it justified by representing Korean society as without the capacity to develop itself (Miller 2010). Korea was forced to conclude a treaty with Japan in 1876 by which it declared its independence from China, but in so doing it laid itself open to aggression by Japan and other powers, such as Russia, France and Britain. A policy of modernization was adopted to help the country resist, and many Korean progressives looked to Japan as a model. Some also regarded a renewal and reform of Buddhism, which flourished in Japan, as a pre-requisite for modernization (Jin Y. Park 2010: 2), but others preferred to develop indigenous Korean religions such as Cheondogyo (Grayson 2002: 198–202). Many looked beyond Japan and regarded the West as the real source of modernity. They also saw the USA as a possible ally, believing it would not seek territorial power on the peninsula (Chung-shin Park 2003: 25). They did not distinguish Western culture from Christian faith, regarding the latter as the ideological foundation for Western power and economic success. Some of this elite became Protestants and invited missionaries to Korea along with Western mining, railway, communications and other companies. From the 1880s missionaries were admitted on the understanding that they would not proselytize but contribute to modernization, primarily through medical and educational work. As the government increasingly lost ideological control of the country, Koreans and missionaries became engaged in proselytizing, religious freedom was acknowledged, and Protestant congregations were established alongside the revived Catholic ones (Paik 1970 [1929]). The stronghold of Korean Protestantism was the Pyongyang area, and the educational advantages and training in Western organizational patterns this gave some of the population were among the reasons why the region saw the birth of Korean industry (Michael D. Shin 2011). Seeking to sever Korea from domination by the traditional Confucian worldview that they regarded as anti-modern as well as anti-Christian, Christians campaigned for social reforms such as the abolition of the caste system and remarriage of widows (Chandra 1988). However, in the event these and other reforms were forced on Korea by the Japanese, who dismantled the Confucian system in 1895 after defeating China. After victory against Russia a decade later, Japan declared a protectorate over the peninsula and formally annexed Korea in 1910.

Christian churches as self-help communities

In the deteriorating economic conditions, increasing social chaos and military conflicts of the late nineteenth and early twentieth centuries, Christian congregations formed strong communities offering mutual support and protection. Owing to earlier persecution, Catholics were already living mainly in close-knit, self-sufficient village communities in remote regions but were marginalized economically and politically (Choi Jai-keun 2006: 143). Meanwhile Protestant Christians worked hard at spreading their new faith, and the Protestant missionaries, mostly Evangelicals from the USA, encouraged the 'three-self' missionary method: that is, that each congregation should become self-supporting, self-propagating and eventually self-governing (Charles Allen Clark 1930). When a village became Christian, the people built themselves a church, which became the social centre, and also established a village school. The missionaries managed secondary schools, hospitals, literature work and theological education (Paik 1970 [1929]; Allen D. Clark 1971). Owing to the harsh conditions, some Christian villages migrated together to Manchuria or the Maritime Provinces of Siberia, and even Hawai'i, in search of livelihood, and after 1905 to resist colonial rule. The mutual support offered and nationalist role of the Protestant churches encouraged many to identify as Christians in exile, and this resulted in a predominantly Protestant diaspora that supported the churches inside Korea (Schmid 2002: 224–52).

Colonial rule brought modernization, but according to a Japanese model in which there was little place for Korean leadership (Lee Hong Yung *et al.* 2013; cf. Gi-wook Shin and Robinson 1999). Korean language and culture were suppressed; the resources of the country were appropriated for Japanese interests and the Korean people impoverished (Eckert *et al.* 1990: 263; Kang Man-gil 2005: 98–100). After annexation, the Japanese moved to control the religions, because they were the only remaining Korean national organizations. Some of the Confucian elite committed suicide, but most were co-opted to support the Japanese, and only a small minority maintained strict Confucian practice. Korean indigenous religions, having no outside support, were mostly suppressed (Wi-jo Kang 1987). Buddhists had tried to re-establish and reform their faith to play a role in modernization. They even adopted Christian practices, including social service activities such as modern education and medical work (Grayson 2001), but they were gradually subsumed under Japanese Buddhism (KBRI 1993: 221–41). The Cheondogyo (an indigenous religion) leadership had initially supported the protectorate but now turned against Japanese rule. In the period to 1920 the Protestant churches and Cheondogyo formed the main political resistance. Together, and with some Buddhist support, they organized an independence demonstration on 1 March 1919 at the same time as seeking representation for their cause of self-determination at the Paris Peace Conference. The March 1st Movement was brutally put down (Wells 1990: 82–97). Cheondogyo was crushed but Christianity, having Western links and a network of exiles, was hard to suppress while the Japanese were concerned about international opinion.

After about 1920, Korean Socialists also began to resist the Japanese, while at the same time criticizing Christians and religion in general, but successive Communist parties were rooted out by the Japanese (Kang Man-gil 2005: 52–60). Meanwhile Protestant villages were noticeably more advanced than others, and Korean and Western organizations were active in rural mission (Brunner 1928). However, as Japanese rule wore on, Christian schools became harder to maintain, and many leading Protestants argued that cooperation with the Japanese was the best way to develop Korea until such time as it achieved independence (Wells 1990). Meanwhile the Catholic Church continued an apolitical stance that in practice meant acquiescence and a concordat that was eventually signed with the Japanese government in 1936. By the late 1930s, the Korean-led Protestant churches had become the only public bodies using, promoting and educating in the Korean language (Kwan-sik Kim 1947). They resisted joining Japanese Christian denominations and, when the Japanese authorities imposed worship at Shinto shrines as part of civic duty, some Protestants mounted ongoing resistance, arguing that the rites were idolatrous and claiming religious freedom. In the late 1930s and early 1940s the church institutions were forcibly taken over by the Japanese. But Christian communities – Protestant and Catholic – being self-supporting, they maintained their faith and congregational life in the mountains and islands of the peninsula or in exile (Allen D. Clark 1971: 221–32).

Post-liberation Christian political engagement against Communism

As a result of their experiences of persecution, both Catholic and Protestant churches which re-emerged after the liberation from Japanese rule in 1945 at the end of the Second World War were organized at a local level, self-sufficient and largely lay-led. Both Christian bodies had reputations nationally and internationally as resistance movements. (Catholic martyrs under Confucianism were beatified in 1925.) Moreover, they formed the strongest and most educated nationwide networks. The Japanese government approached a Protestant, Yeo Un-hyeong, to lead a provisional government. He brought together leading nationalists – mostly Christians, Socialists or both – and encouraged the organization of local 'people's committees', of which most local chairmen were Protestant ministers or lay Christian leaders and many of which met in church premises. After Japanese troops had withdrawn, Yeo declared the Korean People's Republic (KPR; late August to early September 1945), a left-leaning coalition (Eckert *et al.* 1990: 331–2; Armstrong 2004).

In anticipation of elections being called, Protestant leaders formed political parties and articulated a vision for an independent nation based on Christian values and with US-style democracy and a free-market economy. The leading Protestant pastor in the second half of the twentieth century was Han Kyung-chik, whose sermons of that period express this vision (Kim Eun-seop 2010: 383–508). However, the Soviets had moved into the North in 1945 to disarm the Japanese after their surrender, and to occupy it according to the four-party trusteeship (between the Soviet Union, the United States, China and Britain) agreed with the Allied powers at the end of the Second World War. Christian-led parties there, which initially recruited much more strongly than the Soviet-backed Korean Workers' Party, were forcibly disbanded. Their leaders disappeared or fled to the South, where they were followed in the next few years by many other Christians who feared for their life or livelihood under Communism (Allen D. Clark 1971: 239–47). In the South, the US military government, which took power there in 1945, saw the newly declared Korean People's Republic as a Communist front and moved to suppress it. But Socialism had widespread support among the Korean people across the country, because it offered much-needed land reform and policies to benefit the poor (Eckert *et al.* 1990). The actions against it made the occupying army in the South very unpopular, and the US military suppressed widespread unrest. However, since the US military was supportive of the re-establishment of Christian churches, brought in a Christianized culture and appeared committed to democracy, it won qualified support from Christian leaders. As the situation polarized and Soviet Communism emerged as a threat to Christian existence on the peninsula, national security and anti-Communism became paramount for Christian leaders. This was one of the main reasons why they eventually gave their support to the right-wing party backed by the US which in 1945 had called as its leader long-term political exile Syngman Rhee (Donald N. Clark 2007).

Rhee was a Protestant married to an Austrian Catholic. He advocated a US-style political and economic system and believed its values of freedom and equality were founded on Christianity. Like many Christian leaders, he combined his faith with strong ethnic nationalism, and he had no qualms about linking religion with politics (Chung-shin Park 2003: 173–8; Gi-wook Shin 2006: 100–103). It gradually became apparent that the Soviet and American regimes would not be able to agree to form a joint administration in Korea, owing to their ideological differences. By 1947, Kim Il-sung and the Communist Workers' Party in the Northern zone of occupation were carrying out land reform and other promised measures, marginalizing the Christian parties and then moving to suppress the churches and other religious groups. Kim refused to allow the United Nations access to the North to oversee elections there. Rhee pressed for separate elections in the South, and he established the Republic of Korea (ROK) (South Korea) in 1948, with strong encouragement from the global Catholic Church, which was vehemently anti-Communist in this period (Cumings 2005: 346–7). Less than a month afterward the declaration of the People's Republic of Korea was declared in the North.

In late 1948 both armies of occupation withdrew from the peninsula, leaving in place two separate nations, which had opposing ideologies. Both states claimed to be the legitimate Korea, and their governments each laid claim to the whole peninsula. Each rhetorically attacked the other, and war soon broke out between them, although this was precipitated by aggression from the North. The Korean War of 1950–53 escalated into the first proxy war of the Cold War. The North received support from the USSR and the PRC; the United Nations backed the South and sent troops under US command.

Christian leadership in post-Korean War relief and development

During the Korean War, the churches supported the United Nations Command, and Christian leaders who had international connections were active in organizing evacuations and help for refugees and the wounded. Immediately after hostilities subsided in the South, Korean Christians were active not only politically but also practically in cooperating with the UN Command and then the South Korean government to restructure and rebuild the nation with the help of various Western church and mission agencies. At the end of the war, the country was devastated and 3 million Koreans (roughly 10 per cent of the population) were killed, wounded or missing (Oberdorfer and Carlin 2014: 8). It was estimated that half of the nation was in need of relief. An estimated 2 million were homeless, packs of destitute children roamed the street, and 300,000 widows and their children had no means of support. Korean Christians offered shelter to refugees, started many orphanages and offered skills training for widows (Allen D. Clark 1971: 249–58; Kim Heung-soo 2003: 330–43).

As the initial effort to reconstruct Europe was over and the agenda of development was turned toward the rest of the (non-Communist) world, government and church agencies – especially from the USA – flooded into South Korea to offer relief (*IRM* 1953). In view of the Communist threat, US government aid was very generous (Cumings 2005: 299–309). The reputation of the Korean churches for fervent faith as well as their anti-Communism attracted strong support from church agencies in the USA, which mostly channelled their aid through two umbrella bodies: the Church World Service (Protestant) and Catholic Relief Services. In addition to the Catholic Church, Presbyterian and Methodist churches, which had a long-standing mission connection in Korea, were heavily involved, and newer Evangelical agencies were also attracted. Three new Evangelical development organizations were founded in the early 1950s specifically to address the plight of Korean orphans: World Vision, Compassion International and Holt International.

Christians tended to have an advantage over other Koreans in relating to the US authorities, because they were more likely to know English and have some familiarity with Western culture. The same advantages accrued in the case of the Western development agencies, which additionally appreciated the fact that their Christian contacts were connected into church networks which could be used for distribution and dissemination. So there were tangible benefits to the growth of Christianity during this period of development: a church member was in an advantageous position for employment in aid and also belonged to a network receiving and distributing foreign aid (Donald N. Clark 2007: 174–5). Although other religions also offered practical service, they did not have access to resources on anything like the same scale, and Rhee openly supported Christianity (Chung-shin Park 2003: 173–4). Furthermore the re-establishment of Buddhism, South Korea's largest organized religion, was hampered by the legacy of Japanese domination (KBRI 1993: 221–41).

Conservative Christians, church growth and prosperity theology, 1950s onward

Bolstered by Christian refugees from among what had been an emerging middle class in the industrialized areas around Pyongyang, for the next two decades the churches in the South for the most part supported Rhee's regime, including his belligerent stance during the Korean War. On balance, Christians considered the anti-Communism and national security doctrine of Rhee and the succeeding military dictatorships until the 1980s, their promotion of economic development and their tolerance of religious activity more important for national flourishing – or the realization of the kingdom of God – than civic freedoms and human rights (cf. Kang In-cheol 2004).

The Christian vision for Korea included the planting of strong and populous church communities as the means by which the Christian faith would become established locally without the need for further missionary presence. However, the struggle against Communism and the context of democratic elections gave particular importance to Christian numbers. From the 1950s, all churches began to hold mass events to encourage the faithful and attract more adherents, and also as a demonstration to North Korea of the strength of Christianity in the South (Timothy S. Lee 2010). Whether as a result of these, or for other reasons, the growth in numbers gave Christians a greater voice in society. Numbers also provided greater income – especially in Protestant churches, where tithing (giving a tenth of one's income) was the norm, and was used to develop their community life and also for their educational and charitable activities. Between 1950 and 1985, Protestants grew from an estimated 2.5 per cent of the population to 16 per cent. Catholics were less than 5 per cent (IHCK 2009: 116), and the well-supported Protestants dominated Korean Christianity. From the 1960s, increasing numbers of people identified as Buddhists as well – about 20 per cent in 1985 – and the overall number of people of no religion steadily declined (although in most cases this did not mean they had no religious practice; Baker 2006).

Their focus on economic development is shown by the fact that Christian leaders lent their support to the bold economic development programmes of President Park Chung-hee, a Buddhist, who took power by military coup in 1961. He intended to ensure that South Korea became prosperous and powerful so that it would not again be annexed or occupied. In the context of widespread poverty, church leaders backed wealth creation and encouraged their members to work hard to build businesses and demonstrate Christian ethics and commitment to the nation by outdoing others at work (Ogle 1977: 31). Government industrialization plans were mirrored in the setting of numerical church growth targets, ambitious church-building projects and entrepreneurial home and overseas missions (Timothy S. Lee 2010). Evangelical churches and the Pentecostal churches which emerged in the late 1950s developed theologies of prosperity which saw wealth as a sign of God's blessing and favour and legitimized its accumulation using biblical verses (e.g. Matthew 7: 7–11; 2 Corinthians 8: 9). Individual or family prosperity was welcomed as a blessing for the whole nation but usually on condition that it was shared with the church community. The metaphor of growth from within the economic sphere was identified also in the New Testament (e.g. Matthew 13: 31–3) and applied to church membership as the measure of faith (cf. Acts 2: 41). This mind-set encouraged the rise of 'mega-churches' with more than 10,000 members each. Such churches built empires of extensive charitable, educational, welfare and mission programmes. The most outstanding example is Yoido Full Gospel Church led by Cho Yonggi (see Ma *et al.* 2004). However, the first mega-church was Youngnak Presbyterian Church, pastored by Han Kyung-Chik.

Progressive Christians in the labour and democratization movements, 1970s and 1980s

While conservative Christians – Protestant and Catholic – largely accepted that military, or at least strong, government was necessary in view of the Communist threat and in order to create the conditions for growth, some Christians became increasingly alarmed by the cost that was being paid for industrialization in terms of workers' rights. The World Council of Churches sponsored the Urban Industrial Mission to work in factories. Together with the Catholic organization Young Christian Workers (JOC), it challenged employers and attended to the needs of exploited workers (Ogle 1977). The conscientizing work of these organizations contributed to strikes, particularly among young women in the textile industry, in which 15- to 18-year-old girls were trafficked from the countryside for work in sweatshops. The self-immolation of Methodist Sunday-school teacher Jeon Tae-il in November 1970 in protest at such conditions particularly stirred Protestant consciences into forming a progressive Christian movement for social justice (Koo 2007), and the arrest of Bishop Chi Hak-soon galvanized a Catholic Church hitherto reluctant to speak out against government abuses into action (Sohn 1989). The movement identified with the *minjung* or masses of Korean society and claimed the legacy of the 1919 Independence Movement and the symbols of nineteenth-century peasant uprisings. Inspired by German political theology and encouraged by the development of liberation theology in Latin America in a similar context of dictatorship and oppression, *minjung* theology emerged as the discourse of the movement. It was articulated by Protestant intellectuals but also had an artistic expression among Catholic artists and poets (Kim Yong-bock 1981).

Not only were workers' complaints inadequately addressed by President Park's regime but activists and protestors were routinely arrested and tortured by the Korean Central Intelligence Agency (KCIA), and some died in custody (T. K. 1976). Freedoms were further eroded by the regime of President Chun Doo-hwan in the 1980s. He was already notorious as the military general responsible for the brutal suppression of the democratization movement in the southern city of Gwangju in 1980 in which at least 165 people died. When he took power he sent 37,000 activists and intellectuals to 'purification camps' in remote mountain areas (Katsiaficas 2012). As a result of these excesses, Christian activists were able to build a wider coalition for human rights and democracy including Buddhist and other religious leaders, which eventually brought down Chun and ended military rule in 1988. Its success was in no small part due to the activism of about half of the Catholic priests and the outspoken denunciation of government actions by their leader in South Korea, Stephen Cardinal Kim Sou-hwan. Although the more conservative

Catholic hierarchy resisted political involvement, Myeongdong Cathedral in Seoul became the symbolic heart of the movement and a place of refuge for protestors. The *minjung* and democratization movements also gathered international support through Korean diaspora networks and global church links in the World Council of Churches and the Catholic Church. Sympathetic foreigners smuggled evidence out of Korea, and Christian groups in Japan, the USA, Canada and Germany lobbied for international support (Baker 2007).

Korean world mission, 1988 onward

Korean Christians of all kinds were aware that they were part of a worldwide movement and conscious that they had received the Christian gospel from overseas. Both Christian gratitude and Confucian custom demanded that this gift be reciprocated. Furthermore, Korean Protestants particularly understood that participation in world mission was the key mark of a mature church. So, when it was constituted in 1907, one of the first acts of the Presbyterian Church of Korea was to form a mission committee, and in 1913 it sent its first three missionaries to evangelize Shandong Province of China (Choi Young-woong 2002). Decades of poverty and restriction on travel and the movement of currency had inhibited the development of a full-scale overseas missionary movement, but Korean diaspora churches in China, Japan, Russia, the Pacific and the Americas provided bases for missionary outreach into the respective wider communities. With the integration of South Korea into the international community signalled by its hosting of the 1988 Olympics, restrictions on travel were lifted and South Korea's growing wealth and human resources enabled the sending of missionaries by all the main Protestant churches (Donald N. Clark 1997). The energy behind the rapid growth of Christianity inside Korea exploded into the second-largest worldwide Protestant missionary movement (Johnson and Ross 2009: 259), which in 2011 was sending more than 19,000 Korean Protestant missionaries to 177 countries (Steve Sang-cheol Moon 2012).

More than half of Korean missionaries are serving in other parts of Asia, including the Middle East – the main destinations being China, Japan and the Philippines. Russia, Thailand, Indonesia and India were also large fields, and there were several hundred Korean missionaries involved in campus ministries in the USA, Germany and Canada (Steve Sang-cheol Moon 2012). In 2006 nearly 40 per cent were extending the primary mission activity of Korean churches – planting church communities – and others were engaged primarily in education, social welfare and community development, including medical and IT services. Korean missions also build institutions, including theological seminaries, clinics and hospitals (Steve Sang-cheol Moon 2008). Korean Protestants tend to replicate overseas the evangelism and aid they themselves receive and to plant 'three-self' churches to continue that process. The Korean missionary movement is primarily a religious movement. It is not co-opted to secular or government development agendas because it uses almost entirely funds raised from Korean churches. However, it is linked with Korean business and is an expression of national expansion and soft power. The Korean Catholic Church also has a missionary movement, similarly motivated by gratitude, responsibility and compassion but better coordinated globally (see Sebastian C. H. Kim and Kim 2014). Similarly, Korean Buddhists too are increasingly found overseas. The JungTo Society of engaged Buddhists is networked with others globally and has outreach in India, North Korea and other parts of the world.

Christian initiatives toward North Korea, 1980s onward

For all their global missionary activity, the one country South Koreans found most difficult to penetrate was North Korea. Indeed the partition of the country into North and South was the overriding reality, and anti-Communism and anti-North Korean rhetoric was integral to sermons and public pronouncements by churches. At the same time, hope of unification pervaded their prayers and gave urgency and focus to their mission. The Evangelical and Pentecostal approach to the North was to try to penetrate it to preach the gospel in the hope of building up an underground church and bringing about regime change (Yi 2006). It is not inconceivable that a religious revival might play a part in regime change leading to peaceful reunification (cf. Kim Hyun-sik 2008). However, from a political point of view, the sudden collapse of the regime in the North is not a likely or, from an economic or military point of view, a desirable scenario (Samuel S. Kim 2006: 302–07). Meanwhile, the activists for democracy in South Korea had come to see the division of the peninsula as the flip side of the suppression of civil and human rights. So it was natural that, having ousted the military regime, they should turn their attention to unification and, unlike the conservatives, they were willing to have a dialogue with the North. In 1986 through the mediation of the World Council of Churches, the first ever non-governmental direct dialogue took place in Switzerland between South Korean Protestant leaders and the Chosŏn Christian Federation, a North Korean government-sponsored agency (Yi 2006). With the permission of the government in the North, which probably saw it as a way of gaining much-needed international respectability, South Korean churches – Protestant and Catholic – supported the construction of churches in Pyongyang in the 1980s and 1990s.

In 1988 the National Council of Churches of Korea (a Protestant body dominated by progressives) issued a declaration on reunification and peace. Despite strong criticism by the anti-Communist mainstream of the churches, the declaration resulted in a flurry of activity by student movements and civil society. Its call for national unity to be pursued by the two Koreas independently of other powers and by peaceful means was incorporated into the agreements adopted by both Koreas in 1991 and 1992 (Yi 2006; Sebastian C. H. Kim 2008). When Kim Dae-jung – a Catholic and supporter of the *minjung* movement – was elected president in 1997, he translated many of the ideas from the declaration into his Sunshine Policy toward North Korea. This rejected any military solution, or the absorption of one Korea by the other, proposing instead a period of peaceful coexistence of the two states in a federation before eventual reunification. The policy also strengthened economic links and encouraged reunions of separated families. It resulted in the first ever North–South summit, held in Pyongyang in June 2000, for which Kim Dae-jung received the Nobel Peace Prize (Chung-in Moon 1999; Cumings 2003). However, while George W. Bush was US president, international discussion of North Korea tended to focus on terror and weapons questions, and little progress could be made. What is more, the North Korean regime offered little in return, and the more dialogically minded Christians had difficulty convincing their more conservative co-religionists to engage with the North.

In addition to evangelism and peacemaking initiatives with regard to the North, and despite political and even denominational differences, South Korean Christians of all kinds took the lead in responding to news of food shortages in North Korea and mounted a huge aid effort. As early as 1989 and before government aid began, Han Kyung-chik and Youngnak Church initiated the nationwide Rice of Love campaign, which later expanded to become the South–North Sharing Campaign. It gained support from across the Protestant spectrum but, since the progressive churches were few in numbers, it was conservatives and Pentecostals who bankrolled most of the Protestant aid effort. The Reconciliation Committee of the South Korean Catholic Church's Help North Korea campaign also sent millions of dollars in aid to the North (Yi 2006). A series of natural calamities in 1995–97 led to a severe famine in the North in which 2–3 million people are estimated to have died (Cumings 2005: 442–3), and the aid effort intensified. By the mid-1990s many South Korean Christian churches and organizations were operating independently to aid the North. Some were accused of triumphalism, paternalism and misusing aid to pursue an 'aggressive' conversion agenda (Donald N. Clark 1997: 211–12 n. 32), but their generosity was not in doubt. They provided cows and goats for dairy production, seeds and fertilizers, and clothing. They also built hospitals and orphanages in North Korea (Yi 2006: 254–5). Other Christians and agencies sought more long-term engagement with the North through development work in agriculture, medicine, education and business enterprises (Hoare and Pares 2005: 46–83). As people began to cross into China to obtain necessities, some Evangelical agencies took advantage of the situation to proselytize, despite evidence that those who had had contact with religious groups were punished on return (Hoare and Pares 2005: 77). However, as conditions deteriorated further and North Koreans migrated into China, these and other agencies formed an underground network that shielded them from the Chinese authorities, whose policy it was to return them, and arranged their transfer to South Korea. There, churches helped North Korean refugees adjust to differences in the language, access information, enter business and education, address issues of physical and psychological health, and so on (Verdier 2014).

The South Korean Christian aid operation suffered constant setbacks owing to relations between North and South but continued for more than a decade. However, President Lee Myung-bak, a conservative Protestant who took office in 2008, initiated a more hard-line approach to the North, arguing that propping up the regime was simply delaying reunification and even increasing the threat to the South. Even relief workers were divided about whether or not aid should be conditional – on implementation of human rights, peace or regime change – and conservative Christians could not stomach the compromises with the atheistic regime that were necessary to work in the North (Flake and Snyder 2003; Schloms 2003). The change of policy, together with the first North Korean test-firing of a missile in 2009, led to all South Korean and other aid activities being scaled back severely. Raised tensions on the peninsula and between China, Japan, Russia and the USA, which still has troops in South Korea, make reunification seem a more distant possibility and the agenda of world peace even more important.

Religious activism on justice, peace and life issues, 1990s onward

The change from military government to popularly elected governments in the late 1980s and early 1990s in South Korea and the emergence of civil society significantly affected the role of religions in public life. Political influence was less dependent on access to government and social status. Secular and younger voices were increasingly heard, and this trend was considerably increased by the rapid development of the internet, which was part of the government response to the economic crisis, and made South Korea the most internet-penetrated country on earth by 2002 (Janelli and Janelli 2005). Christianity – especially Protestantism – came under particular criticism online for aggressive evangelism, religious domination, perceived privileges and alleged corruption (Lee Jin-gu 2004). Buddhists protested against what they saw as bias against them in the government of President Lee Myung-bak, and in 2008 monks led a demonstration in Seoul that was tens of thousands strong.

After the struggle for democratization was won, religious activism turned to peace movements and campaigns on economic, environmental and other life issues. The Catholic Church's pro-life agenda was strengthened in the 1990s, as Korean scientists rose to prominence in stem-cell research. After the revelation in 2005 that research results had been fabricated, the church's bioethics committee campaigned more strongly against stem-cell research and on other issues such as the high abortion and suicide rates and against the death penalty (RFKCH 2010: 169–70). More progressive Christians engaged in various peace movements linked to hope of reunification and to concern about peninsular security and environmental issues, many of which were intertwined with questions of ROK–USA relations (Chung 2011). The Catholic Priests' Association was especially active in campaigns against the presence of military bases and plans for new ones, against the annual joint exercises between the ROK and US militaries, in protest at President Bush's 'axis of evil' rhetoric against North Korea, and against the Free Trade Agreement with the USA in 2008 (Sunhyuk Kim 2007). Its leadership of the peace demonstrations is shown by the prominence of candle-lit vigils (cf. Cumings 2005: 401–02). In this context, the *minjung* Buddhist movement within the democratization coalition emerged as a significant social movement in its own right (Jorgensen 2010), particularly through the Buddhist Coalition for Economic Justice (BCEJ), which was founded in 1991 as a non-violent movement drawing on Buddhist doctrines of interdependence that aims to build one community in Korea through campaigns for justice and peace and humanitarian work (Tedesco 2002; Mitchell 2008: 273).

Environmental concerns resonated especially strongly in South Korea as the damage done by war and decades of rapid industrialization and urbanization began to tell, and from the 1990s the Green movement expanded rapidly (Sunhyuk Kim 2007). Both the Bishops' Conference and the Priests' Association supported campaigns against state-sponsored large-scale environmental projects on both environmental and human rights grounds (Park Moon-su 2012). Progressive Protestants also joined environmental campaigns and developed eco-theologies in line with the World Council of Churches agenda for justice, peace and the integrity of creation, which was launched in Seoul in 1990 (Yi 2006; Hwang 2007). Buddhist environmental organizations combine popular visions of the Pure Land, a place of respite from karmic transmigration in the Mahayana tradition, with communitarian ideals which develop the concept of *sangha* (Tedesco 2002).

The South Korean economy benefited from globalization and became one of the 'Asian tigers'. In 1996 it reached 11th in the world rankings and achieved a milestone of economic development when it joined the Organisation for Economic Co-operation and Development. But the seemingly inexorable economic growth went into reverse in 1997–98 when an economic crisis led to IMF intervention and programmes of restructuring (Cumings 2005: 331–4). Despite severe pressures on the weekly and other offerings on which they depended, churches took the lead in supporting government initiatives to economize, share, exchange and recycle. They also raised special collections for relief work and did practical service for unemployed and homeless people. Protestant and Catholic churches cooperated with NGOs to address structural problems in the economy, such as the power of the *chaebol* or conglomerates, and initiated actions by small shareholders and the monitoring of business corporations. Progressives campaigned against the sale and privatization of public utilities and started a movement for social and ethical investment (Chai 2003).

Although it might be thought the economic crisis would test faith in a gospel of prosperity, the immediate conservative Christian response was rather that it was a challenge to pray and work harder to defeat the IMF and other perceived enemies that would wreck what had been achieved (Cumings 2005: 398). However, as the income gap widened significantly and the South Korean economy became further entwined with the global economic system, reflection on the crisis raised basic questions about the nature of globalization and its role in global oppression. In this context, the simple and non-materialist lifestyle of the Seon tradition (the Korean precursor to the Japanese Zen) had renewed appeal, and Buddhist initiatives included a Back to the Farm movement which aimed to re-educate the unemployed in farming skills (now part of the IndraNet Life Community; Tedesco 2002). Korean progressive Christians, who were in dialogue with Buddhists, borrowed some of their philosophy in an international initiative calling for a restructuring of the global economy toward a 'sharing community' and supported an international coalition for alternative globalization (*IRM* 2008: 129–34).

Within two years, South Korea returned to growth, and in 2002–03 it briefly regained its former ranking before being overtaken by other emerging economies. But for conservative Protestants the faltering of economic growth coincided with a crisis in the church growth that had been in many respects modelled on it. From the early 1990s, Protestant churches began a gradual decline numerically. Many reasons have been suggested for this, but major factors included a loss of public credibility due to poor financial accountability, abuse of power by some leaders and the inability of older pastors to move with the times or relinquish their roles (Timothy S. Lee 2010: 146–51). However, Christian growth as a whole continued at least until the census in 2005 owing to remarkable Catholic growth in this same period. Surveys showed that, in contrast with Protestantism, the Catholic Church commanded a great deal of respect for its conservative moral values, solidarity with the poor, openness to other faiths and example of social service (Sebastian C. H. Kim 2013). After the economic crash, the Catholic Church was reportedly the most active religious denomination in providing social services and programmes for those who had lost their jobs. It now delivers about half of the government's social welfare facilities, although these projects are mostly reliant on the state for their funding (Yungseok Moon 2011; Park Moon-su 2012: 102–03). Buddhist educational and medical institutions are significantly fewer than Christian ones and, by their own admission, socially engaged Buddhists remain few (Tedesco 2002: 134–6). Buddhists also fared badly in the surveys of public trust. They continue to struggle mainly to reform their own organization, especially its mainstream, the Jogye Order, which is dominated by ordained male monks and has long been beset by power struggles and allegations of corruption. The Buddhist Society for Reform (BSR), founded in 1999, aims to address these issues from within the Order and re-orient it toward social service (cf. Tedesco 2002; Mitchell 2008: 273).

Conclusion

By 2005, according to the national census, Christians had reached 29 per cent of the population of South Korea – 18 per cent Protestants and 11 per cent Catholic – while Buddhists were only about 23 per cent. Other religious traditions were negligible in comparison to these traditions. In the late nineteenth century, Christians were a tiny minority. However, the selective appropriation of Christianity by Koreans had enabled self-development at a time when Korea was being developed – and exploited – by Japanese interests. Later the churches – first Protestant and later also Catholic – articulated a vision of a liberal-democratic society in the face of the Communist alternative, which the other religions of Korea were unable to do for various reasons. Furthermore, the churches themselves were communities in development, encouraging education, wealth creation and upward mobility. Local churches and indigenous Christian organizations offered emergency and social service as part of their agenda of evangelization. Korean church personnel and networks formed effective channels for the implementation of the substantial aid, relief and development by Western governments and global Christian organizations.

The Christian mission and development agendas were largely inseparable in Korea, for several reasons: first, most churches were nationalist; second, churches were often the most effective, or even the only, nationwide networks; third, development aid and mission enterprise overlapped because they came mostly from the common source of the USA. Although in 1945 Christians probably numbered less than 4 per cent of the population in the South, the close cooperation between mission and development gave Christians political and economic advantages in the reconstructed society of South Korea. On the one hand this was a factor encouraging church growth, and on the other it led to Christian, especially Protestant, dominance in public life.

This Christian hegemony was predominantly anti-Communist in ideology and right-wing in politics and tended to support the policies of successive Korean governments in these directions. However, a minority of Christians – progressives both Protestant and Catholic – also challenged these governments and other Christians to pay attention to human and civil rights and to reach out to North Korea. They played an important role in ending military rule and in South–North dialogue.

Since the end of the Cold War and the democratization of South Korea, civil society has flourished, and the churches are competing with many other voices in public life. Furthermore, as personal wealth and social welfare have increased, Christian communities are no longer so attractive as sources of social security. Nevertheless, Christianity continues to thrive, although the Catholic Church, which amounted to 40 per cent of Korean Christians in the last census, may soon overtake Protestants in numbers and influence on society. The current Korean social values, mass educational goals and welfare systems owe a great deal to the example set by Christian missions and churches from the nineteenth century onwards, which are also emulated by Buddhists and other smaller religions in Korea. This same model of development is now being exported globally through the Korean missionary movement with the support of nearly 14 million mostly middle- and upper-class Christians. It is having a global impact (Kim and Kim 2014), although research is needed to assess the extent and nature of this.

Until the economic crisis of 1997–98, the model of development to which most South Koreans aspired was a Euro-American one. Since the disillusionment with the international community caused by the IMF restructuring demands, and since South Korea is now a world leader in so many respects, its religious visions, values and achievements provide models for the countries which once sought to develop it. It is consciously exporting these. Korean Christianity especially in its various expressions provides models for Christians in other parts of Asia especially, particularly in China. At the same time South Korea is rediscovering its older traditions. Although Buddhism has been a lot less visible than Christianity in modern South Korea, traditional temple lifestyles and Buddhist thought on ecological and economic issues have had a significant influence on Christians, both directly through interreligious dialogue and collaborative activities and also more generally as part of their Korean heritage. Whereas once Buddhists copied Christian methods, the two traditions now enjoy a more mutual relationship. Although it hardly exists as an organized religion in South Korea, Confucianism is being reassessed as a foundation for Korean social values and a basis of future development (e.g. Bell and Hahm 2003). Furthermore, as part of the search for peace with the North, Korean indigenous religion, the basis of ethnic nationalism, may become a more significant factor.

The Korean case presents a unique historical example of the interrelationship between religions and development. In this instance Christianity has had a significant positive impact on economic, political and social development. But the example of neighbouring Japan, where Christians are less than 1 per cent of the population, shows that the adoption of Christianity is not a necessary pre-requisite for high levels of technological and social development, and there are many other examples to prove that it is not a guarantee either. What is significant about South Korea is that post-1945 Korean Christians had a vision for national development in the face of imminent Communist threat and a faith that resourced that vision both theologically and practically. Furthermore, Koreans benefited from the global networks of the world's largest religion through the Korean diaspora and Christians in the West, especially the USA, who shared their concern. It is to be hoped that an even wider coalition can be mobilized to solve the outstanding issue for Korean development – the ongoing crisis on the peninsula.

References

Armstrong, Charles K. (2004) *The North Korean Revolution, 1945–1950,* Ithaca, NY: Cornell University Press.

Baker, Don (2006) 'The Religious Revolution in Modern Korean History: From Ethics to Theology and from Ritual Hegemony to Religious Freedom', *Review of Korean Studies*, 9 (3), 249–75.

Baker, Don (2007) 'International Christian Network for Korea's Democratization', in *Democratic Movements and Korean Society: Historical Documents and Korean Studies*, Kim Dae-Jung Presidential Library and Museum, Seoul: Yonsei University, pp. 133–61.

Bell, Daniel A. and Hahm, Chaibong (2003) *Confucianism for the Modern World*, Cambridge: Cambridge University Press.

Brunner, Edmund de Schweinitz (1928) 'Rural Korea: A Preliminary Survey of Economic, Social and Religious Conditions', in International Missionary Council (ed.), *The Christian Mission in Relation to Rural Problems: Report of the Jerusalem Meeting of the IMC*, vol. VI, London: Oxford University Press, pp. 100–208.

Chai, Soo-il (2003) '*Missio Dei* – Its Development and Limitation in Korea', *International Review of Mission*, 92 (367), 538–49.

Chandra, Vipan (1988) *Imperialism, Resistance, and Reform in Late Nineteenth Century Korea: Enlightenment and the Independence Club*, Berkeley: University of California, Institute of East Asian Studies.

Choi, Jai-keun (2006) *The Origin of the Roman Catholic Church in Korea: An Examination of Popular and Governmental Responses to Catholic Missions in the Late Chosŏn Dynasty*, Cheltenham: Hermit Kingdom Press.

Choi, Young-woong (2002), 'The Mission of the Presbyterian Church of Korea in Shandong, North China, 1913–1957', in Klaus Koschorke (ed.), *Transcontinental Links in the History of Non-Western Christianity*, Wiesbaden: Harrassowitz Verlag, pp. 117–30.

Chung, Steve Lok-Wai (2011) 'Peace Movements in South Korea and Their Impacts on the Politics of the Korean Peninsula', *Journal of Comparative Asian Development*, 10 (2), 253–80.

Clark, Allen D. (1971) *A History of the Church in Korea*, Seoul: Christian Literature Society.

Clark, Charles Allen (1930) *The Korean Church and the Nevius Methods*, New York: Fleming H. Revell.

Clark, Donald N. (1997) 'History and Religion in Modern Korea: The Case of Protestant Christianity', in Lewis R. Lancaster and Richard K. Payne (eds), *Religion and Society in Contemporary Korea*, Berkeley: University of California, Institute of East Asian Studies, pp. 169–214.

Clark, Donald N. (2007) 'Protestant Christianity and the State: Religious Organizations as Civil Society', in Charles K. Armstrong (ed.), *Korean Society: Civil Society, Democracy and the State*, 2nd edn, Abingdon: Routledge, pp. 167–86.

Cumings, Bruce (2003) 'Cold War Structures and Korea's Regional and Global Security', in Jang Jip Choi (ed.), *Post-Cold War and Peace: Experiences, Conditions and Choices*, Seoul: Asiatic Research Centre, pp. 129–50.

Cumings, Bruce (2005) *Korea's Place in the Sun: A Modern History*, 2nd edn, New York: W. W. Norton.

Deuchler, Martina (1992) *The Confucian Transformation of Korea: A Study of Society and Ideology*, Cambridge, MA: Harvard University, Council on East Asian Studies.

Eckert, Carter J., Lee, K.-b., Lew, Y. I., Robinson, M. and Wagner, E. W. (eds) (1990) *Korea, Old and New: A History*, Seoul: Ilchokak.

Flake, L. Gordon and Snyder, Scott (eds) (2003) *Paved with Good Intentions: The NGO Experience in North Korea*, Westport, CT: Praeger.

Grayson, James H. (2001) 'Cultural Encounter: Korean Protestantism and Other Religious Traditions', *International Bulletin of Missionary Research*, 25 (2), 66–72.

Grayson, James H. (2002) *Korea: A Religious History*, rev. edn, Abingdon: RoutledgeCurzon.

Hoare, J. E. and Pares, Susan (2005) *North Korea in the 21st Century: An Interpretive Guide*, Folkestone: Global Oriental.

Hwang, Jae-buhm (2007) 'A New Confession of Faith with an Eco-Theology and a Father-Centred Trinitarianism', *International Review of Mission*, 96 (380–81), 128–41.

IHCK (Institute of the History of Christianity in Korea) (2009) *A History of the Korean Church*, Vol. III (in Korean), Seoul: Institute of Korean Church History Studies.

IRM (*International Review of Mission*) (1953) 'Survey of the Year 1952', *International Review of Mission*, 42 (1), 3–70.

IRM (*International Review of Mission*) (2008) 'Bringing Together Ubuntu and Sangsaeng: A Journey towards Life-Giving Civilization, Transforming Theology and the Ecumenism of the 21st Century', *International Review of Mission*, 97 (384–85), 129–34.

Janelli, Roger L. and Janelli, Dawnhee Yim (2005), 'The Cyberspace Frontier in Korean Studies', Biennial Conference Keynote Address, Association for Korean Studies in Europe.

Johnson, Todd M. and Ross, Kenneth R. (eds) (2009) *Atlas of Global Christianity*, Edinburgh: Edinburgh University Press.

Jorgensen, John (2010) 'Minjung Buddhism: A Buddhist Critique of the Status Quo – Its History, Philosophy and Critique', in Jin Y. Park (ed.), *Makers of Modern Korean Buddhism*, Albany: State University of New York, pp. 275–313.

Kang, In-cheol (2004) 'Protestant Church and Wolnamin: An Explanation of Protestant Conservatism in South Korea', *Korea Journal*, 44 (4) (Winter), 157–90.

Kang, Man-gil (2005) *A History of Contemporary Korea*, Folkestone: Global Oriental.

Kang, Wi-jo (1987) *Religion and Politics in Korea under the Japanese Rule*, Lewiston, NY: Edwin Mellen Press.

Katsiaficas, George (2012) *Asia's Unknown Uprisings*, Vol. 1: *South Korean Social Movements in the 20th Century*, Oakland, CA: PM Press.

KBRI (Korean Buddhist Research Institute) (ed.) (1993) *History and Culture of Buddhism in Korea*, Seoul: Dongguk University Press.

Kim, Eun-seop (ed.) (2010) *Kyong-Chik Han Collection*, Vol. 4: *Sermons 1*, Seoul: Kyung-Chik Han Foundation.

Kim, Heung-soo (2003) *Documents of the WCC Library: The Korean War*, Seoul: Institute for Korean Church History.

Kim, Hyun-sik (2008), 'Reflections on North Korea: The Psychological Foundation of the North Korean Regime', *International Bulletin of Missionary Research*, 32 (1), 22–6.

Kim, Kwan-sik (1947) 'The Christian Church in Korea', *International Review of Mission*, 36 (2), 125–40.

Kim, Samuel S. (2006), *The Two Koreas and the Great Powers*, Cambridge: Cambridge University Press.

Kim, Sebastian C. H. (2008) 'Reconciliation Possible? The Churches' Efforts toward the Peace and Reconciliation of North and South Korea', in Sebastian C. H. Kim, Pauline Kollontai and Greg Hoyland (eds), *Peace and Reconciliation: In Search of Shared Identity*, Aldershot: Ashgate, pp. 161–78.

Kim, Sebastian C. H. (2013) 'Contemporary Korean Christianity in Economics, Politics and Public Life: "Credit Crunch" of Korean Protestant Churches?', *Theologia Viatorum*, 37 (1), 26–49.

Kim, Sebastian C. H. and Kim, Kirsteen (2014), *A History of Korean Christianity*, Cambridge: Cambridge University Press.

Kim, Sunhyuk (2007) 'Civil Society and Democratization in South Korea', in Charles K. Armstrong (ed.), *Korean Society: Civil Society, Democracy and the State*, 2nd edn, London: Routledge, pp. 53–72.

Kim, Yong-bock (ed.) (1981) *Minjung Theology: People as the Subjects of History*, Maryknoll, NY: Orbis Books.

Koo, Hagen (2007) 'Emerging Civil Society: The Role of the Labor Movement', in Charles K. Armstrong (ed.), *Korean Society: Civil Society, Democracy and the State*, 2nd edn, London: Routledge, pp. 73–94.

Lee, Hong Yung, Ha, Yong-chool and Sorensen, Clark W. (eds) (2013) *Colonial Rule and Social Change in Korea, 1910–1945*, Seattle: University of Washington Press.

Lee, Jin-gu (2004), 'Korean Protestantism as Viewed by Netizens: A Focus on Recent Activities of Anti-Christian Sites', *Korea Journal*, 44 (Winter), 223–45.

Lee, Timothy S. (2010) *Born Again: Evangelicalism in Korea*, Honolulu: University of Hawai'i Press.

Ma, Won-suk, Menzies, William W. and Bae, Hyeon-sung (2004) *David Yonggi Cho: A Close Look at His Theology and Ministry*, Seoul: Hansei University Press.

Miller, Owen (2010) 'The Idea of Stagnation in Korean Historiography', *Korean Histories*, 2 (1), 3–12.

Mitchell, Donald W. (2008) *Buddhism*, 2nd edn, Oxford: Oxford University Press.

Moon, Chung-in (1999) 'Understanding the DJ Doctrine: The Sunshine Policy and the Korean Peninsula', in Chung-in Moon and David I. Steinberg (eds), *Kim Dae-jung Government and Sunshine Policy: Promises and Challenges*, Seoul: Yonsei University Press, pp. 35–56.

Moon, Steve Sang-Cheol (2008) 'The Protestant Missionary Movement in Korea: Current Growth and Development', *International Bulletin of Missionary Research*, 32 (2), 59–64.

Moon, Steve Sang-cheol (2012) 'Missions from Korea 2012: Slowdown and Maturation', *International Bulletin of Missionary Research*, 36 (2), 84–5.

Moon, Yungseok (2011) 'Sociological Implications of the Roman Catholic Conversion Boom in Korea', *Korea Journal*, 51 (1) (Spring), 143–75.

Oberdorfer, Don and Carlin, Robert (2014) *The Two Koreas: A Contemporary History*, 3rd edn, New York: Basic Books.

Ogle, George E. (1977) *Liberty to the Captives: The Struggle against Oppression in South Korea*, Atlanta, GA: John Knox Press.

Paik, Lak-geoon George (1970 [1929]) *The History of Protestant Missions in Korea 1832–1910*, 2nd edn, Seoul: Yonsei University Press.

Park, Chung-shin (2003) *Protestantism and Politics in Korea*, Seattle: University of Washington Press.

Park, Jin Y. (2010) 'Introduction: Buddhism and Modernity in Korea', in Jin Y. Park (ed.), *Makers of Modern Korean Buddhism*, Albany: State University of New York Press, pp. 1–15.

Park, Moon-su (2012), 'Urgent Issues Facing Modern Korean Catholicism and Their Subtext', *Korea Journal*, 52 (3) (Autumn), 91–118.

RFKCH (Research Foundation of Korean Church History) (2010) *Inside the Catholic Church of Korea*, Seoul: RFCKH.

Schloms, Michael (2003) *North Korea and the Timeless Dilemma of Aid: A Study of Humanitarian Action in Famines*, Münster: LIT.

Schmid, Andre (2002) *Korea between Empires, 1895–1919*, New York: Columbia University Press.

Shin, Gi-wook (2006) *Ethnic Nationalism in Korea: Genealogy, Politics, and Legacy*, Stanford, CA: Stanford University Press.

Shin, Gi-wook and Michael Robinson (eds) (1999) *Colonial Modernity in Korea*, Cambridge, MA: Harvard University Asian Centre.

Shin, Michael D. (2011), 'Pyeongan Province and the Origins of Modern Society', *Papers of the British Association for Korean Studies*, 23, 59–88.

Sohn, Hak-kyu (1989) *Authoritarianism and Opposition in South Korea*, London: Routledge.

Tedesco, Frank M. (2002) 'Socially Responsive Buddhism in Contemporary Korea', *Review of Korean Studies*, 5 (1), 133–57.

T. K. (Chi Myeong-gwan) (1976) *Letters from South Korea by T. K.*, trans. David L. Swain, Tokyo: Iwanami Shoten.

Verdier, Marie-Laure (2014) 'Contextualised Mission: The South Korean Evangelical Responses to the Humanitarian Crisis in North Korea (1995–2012)', Ph.D. thesis, University of London, School of Oriental and African Studies.

Wells, Kenneth M. (1990) *New God, New Nation: Protestants and Self-Reconstruction Nationalism in Korea, 1896–1937*, Honolulu: University of Hawai'i Press.

Yi, Mahn-yeol (2006) 'Korean Christianity and the Reunification Movement', in Robert E. Buswell Jr and Timothy S. Lee (eds), *Christianity in Korea*, Honolulu: University of Hawai'i Press, pp. 238–57.

18

RELIGION AND GENDER IN DEVELOPING SOUTH-EAST ASIA

Monica Lindberg Falk

Introduction

South-East Asia is described as one of the most culturally and religiously heterogeneous areas in the world (Steedly 1999; Adams and Gillogly 2011: 6–7) and in recent decades has undergone rapid economic growth, financial crises and social transformations that have influenced women and men's daily lives. In South-East Asia religious traditions are considered inseparable from the social and cultural fabric (Skidmore and Lawrence 2007: 5). Researchers have found that gender discourses in South-East Asia are both context dependent (Brenner 1995) and multiple (Meigs 1990; Burghoorn *et al.* 2008: 3–4). In spite of the region's tremendous complexity, one aim of this chapter is to capture recent trends concerning gender and family structures that are influenced by religious values and practices. Another aim is to explore gender and religion in crisis situations, through the HIV/AIDS emergency in Thailand.

It is often alleged that women in South-East Asia enjoy a higher status than those in neighbouring countries, particularly India, Pakistan and China (Errington 1990: 1). While Errington is cautious that there is often a tendency to overgeneralize these claims and to extend them across the entire region, typically without evidence, several features are highlighted in studies that note women's relative autonomy. While there are exceptions, attention is drawn to the existence of bilateral and matrilineal kinship systems as well as the fact that women are more likely to engage in economic activities and the control of money and family (Errington 1990: 3–4; Dube 1997: 6; Victor T. King and Wilder 2003: 263; Devasahayam 2009: 2). Moreover, in many areas of South-East Asia women inherit on equal terms to men, and financial exchanges at marriage flow in both directions, meaning that daughters are not perceived as a financial burden on the family as they are in South Asia and China (Errington 1990: 3–4; Alexander and Alexander 2001). However, politics and religion are male-dominated structures, and in those realms women face considerable gender inequality (Iwanaga 2008; Victor T. King 2008: 205–06).

In this chapter I draw on scholarship on contemporary South-East Asia from a variety of disciplines and on my own anthropological research carried out there since the mid-1990s, mainly in Thailand, in order to explore the impact of the relationships between gender and religion upon processes of social change. In what ways do religion and culture have an impact on family and kinship dynamics, and what are the implications for women's development and empowerment? What roles does religion play in crisis situations in the region, and in what ways are they gendered? The chapter is organized into three sections. First, I will discuss broad themes related to religion and gender in the region. Second, I will give an overview of how family and kinship are organized in South-East Asia. This also includes a discussion of changing marriage and divorce patterns, as well as a look at sexuality and the sex industry. The chapter ends with a case study (based on fieldwork carried out in Thailand between 2004 and 2006 with several follow-up visits) that deals with socially engaged Buddhist activities around HIV/AIDS and displays how family, faith and religious institutions are intertwined and interdependent.[1]

Religion and gender in South-East Asia

All world religions are present in South-East Asia, brought there by missionaries, by way of trade and personal contacts and incorporated with local traditions and beliefs. Today Theravada Buddhism is the dominant religion in Thailand, Lao PDR, Myanmar and Cambodia; and Islam is prevalent in Indonesia and is the state religion in Malaysia and Brunei. While Roman Catholicism is the dominant faith in Timor Leste and the Philippines, where the people were converted to Catholicism through the Spanish colonizers and not through trade and personal contacts, as was the case with the spread of Hinduism, Buddhism and Islam in South-East Asia (Adams and Gillogly 2011: 141), there are only small percentages of Christians in the other South-East Asian countries. Most people in Vietnam and Singapore adhere to the Chinese belief system. That system includes Confucianism, Daoism and Mahayana Buddhism, often practised simultaneously. Pure Land and Zen are the dominant forms of Mahayana Buddhism, which are practised in Vietnam as well as in Singapore. In Singapore about 20 per cent of the population belong to Islam and 10 per cent are Christians. The female Buddhist *bodhisattva* Kuan Yin (Goddess of Mercy), who is considered to belong to Mahayana Buddhism, is venerated throughout South-East Asia by Theravada Buddhist followers. South-East Asia is also the home of a large number of minority groups, some of whom have converted to one of the 'world religions', often to Christianity.

Across the region culture and religion have influenced social relations and gender orders in profound ways, which in turn have had significance for women's opportunities for development. Scholars have drawn attention to the ways in which colonialism and religious conversion to Christianity played a role in overturning the 'complementarity of men's and women's work and the relative lack of ritual or economic differentiation' that was traditionally pervasive in South-East Asia (Errington 1990: 1). As Ong and Peletz have emphasized, the Spaniards' arrival to the Philippines in the sixteenth century together with Catholicism altered gender orders in the country and illustrates how negatively that affected the spiritual influence women had previously enjoyed (1995: 2; Adams and Gillogly 2011: 13). It is also the case that masculinity and males are commonly more closely linked with divinity, spiritual powers and high ethical standards than are femininity and females, and this has implications for how males and females are understood and represented (Peletz 2007: 11). Females are more restricted than males with regard to accessing sacred objects and places, such as temples. This is partly explained by the bodily processes of menstruation and childbirth, which are considered polluting in a number of religions. These symbolic associations may legitimize gender inequalities that exist in households, families, economic domains, political arenas and other venues of everyday life. These religious factors also play a role in shaping moral paradigms for women and men in different ways. Within South-East Asian settings, women are supposed to be monogamous, and sexual contacts outside marriage are unacceptable. Moreover, in marriage women should ideally be innocent and passive, but it is possible for women to choose not to marry as long as they fulfil their filial piety, which makes the adoption of religious ordination a less viable option for women than men.

Islam is widespread across South-East Asia, and the majority of the populations of Brunei, Malaysia and Indonesia are Muslims. Peletz points out that in Malay communities the Islamic terms *nafsu* (passion) and *akal* (reason, rationality) are used in gendered ways (2007). All humans possess both *nafsu* and *akal*, but *nafsu* is more concentrated on women and *akal* with men (2007: 14). Another important concept for Indonesian people and Malay groups in South-East Asia is *adat* (derived from the Arabic *'adat* and meaning 'non-Islamic custom'). This is of significant importance for women and includes rules about proper conduct and their role within the family, which typically places them subordinate to men, as well as the injunction to wear a veil, which has become more widespread over recent decades (Adams and Gillogly 2011: 32). *Adat* is a complicated set of customary laws that covers, among other things, morality and appropriate behaviour. It is transmitted from the ancestors and is learned from childhood. However, *adat* is beyond what can be seen as daily life customs, to the point that an expert in *adat* (*tokoh adat*) is needed in order to state what is correct. Moreover, today *adat* is the object of specific articulation in Indonesia (e.g. in Aceh), where the establishment of Islamic law has meant that the Aceh government has to 'reconcile Sate law, adat law and sharia' (Safitri 2011: 130). All religious traditions regularly undergo reformation processes in order to recall a religious tradition to its normative ideals and to 'update' its institutions and teachings (Swearer 2010: 159). For instance, according to Nagata, in the 1980s the *dakwah* movement (meaning 'call to the faith' and derived from the Arabic term *da'wah*) began to influence Islam in Malaysia, and it developed in a more orthodox direction, implying that local elements were diminished (2011: 54). One of the visible changes was that Malay Muslims became stricter in how they dressed, and young women began wearing a fuller head covering (*tudung*) which leaves only the face visible. Nagata suggests that, in contrast to how it was before, Malayness today is almost exclusively expressed through Islam (2011: 57). In Muslim South-East Asia (Indonesia, Malaysia, Brunei, southern Thailand and the southern Philippines), for instance, women did not usually don veils or other Islamic headgear prior to the Islamic resurgence that began, in mostly urban areas, in the 1970s and 1980s (Peletz 2007: 28).

Nonetheless, while the main religions in South-East Asia are patriarchal and typically led by men, female goddesses and Buddhist women who have reached the final stage of enlightenment are also venerated (Murcott 1991; Holm and Bowker 2001; Ursula King and Beattie 2005). Moreover, most religions emphasize a gender divide based on notions of differences between the sexes, but Theravada Buddhism, for instance, teaches that gender is unimportant for reaching the ultimate goal of enlightenment (Gross 1993: 116). This notion was supported by interviews conducted in 1997 and 1998 with *mae chis*, who stated that their gender identity was not an impediment to spiritual progress (Falk 2007). However, there are contradictory attitudes toward women in the Buddhist texts. One example is that female rebirth is a result of negative karma. Another example is that a Buddha has to be male and, therefore, makes male rebirth necessary for women in order that they can be reborn as a Buddha. A third example is that gender is irrelevant for salvation in the sense that gender is one of the traits of the ego, which need to be transcended (Gross 1993: 115–17). The third example corresponds with the Buddhist notion that sex is simply another form of bodily attachment. Buddhist texts take a consistently negative stance towards all expressions of sexuality as being impediments to spiritual progress (Zwilling 1992: 210). Thus, the gender ideologies expressed within religious traditions in South-East Asia are not one-dimensional and can be seen to block as well as support equality between men and women.

Religion and family and kinship systems

Despite inequality within the realm of religion, South-East Asia is known for relative equality within its family and kinship systems. However, it is difficult to define equality and compare status between men and women, since groups and individuals might have high status in different social and cultural areas (Stoler 1977; Errington 1990: 9–10; Victor T. King and Wilder 2003: 262–86; Devasahayam 2009: 2; Winzeler 2011: 14). To avoid this problem, anthropologists often view men and woman as having complementary roles rather than being situated within a hierarchical relationship (Errington 1990: 1; Victor T. King and Wilder 2003: 263; Peletz 2009: 194). As already mentioned, the notion of relative gender equality in South-East Asia has been noted in terms of the positive attitude shown towards both daughters and sons, as well as cultural attitudes around the idea that women possess superior marketing expertise and skills in managing money, which is reflected in their typically being granted control over this domain of family activity (Li 1989; Errington 1990: 4; Sullivan 1994; Karim 1995: xiv; Klein-Hutheesing 1995: 75; Alexander and Alexander 2001; Van Esterik 2008: xxii). A further factor that anthropologists have argued contributes to women's higher social status is rice production, which involves both men and women. Food is an important principle of social organization, and in South-East Asia the production of rice is considered central, with those who eat together related through food (Van Esterik 2008: xxii). Moreover, as Janowski and Kerlogue explain, throughout rice-growing mainland South-East Asia rice is symbolically associated with a 'female principle' and is widely associated with female goddesses and deities, seen as a gift from a divine and ancestral female entity (2007: 9–10). Women, therefore, have a special position in rice cultivation, with respect to which they are almost always the main decision makers and also take responsibility for the religious and ritual aspects of rice growing (ibid.). As we will see in the next subsection, additional equality markers include the widespread existence of a bilateral kinship structure and sons and daughters having equal inheritance rights.

Kinship systems

In South-East Asia a bilateral or cognatic kinship form is most common, meaning that the lines of descent are from both the mother's and the father's side, with relatives on both sides belonging to the family. Moreover, matrilocality is widely practised, with the husband moving to the wife's household upon marriage. Besides the bilateral system, the patrilocal patrilineal descent system is also common and is predominant in Vietnam, where it is modelled on the Chinese kinship structure, which is supported by patriarchal Confucian ideals of order through ancestor worship as well as age and gender hierarchies (Adams and Gillogly 2011). Nonetheless, while the gender order in Vietnam is structured by the dominant patrilineal organization that subordinates women, as Nhung (2008) has demonstrated, in the local villages women find ways to create authority for themselves by being in control of the everyday life. Under certain circumstances widows, for instance, enjoy autonomy, but they are commonly not in charge of ancestor worship and maintaining the ancestor shrines (ibid.). Patrilineal and patrilocal organization is also prevalent among other groups, including the highlands people of mainland South-East Asia. In Thailand, patrilineality is the principal form among many of the urban affluent people and the Sino-Thai population, but the ideal Chinese family contrasts with the ideal Thai family in post-marital residence patterns and kinship systems. Traditionally, a Thai husband is expected to move into the family compound of his wife and to provide labour for her family.

By contrast, in the north and north-east regions of Thailand, matrilineal organization is present and is also practised by other groups in South-East Asia, for example the Minangkabau of Sumatra. In the matrilineal system, the descent is traced through women and land is passed from mother to daughter, with sons-in-law more loosely tied to their married family. In matrilineal and matrilocal systems, women live close to their natal family and relatives and that gives women greater autonomy and a stronger position than in the patrilineal organization where the husband and his family have the authority. However, the extent to which these matrilineal and matrilocal systems necessarily entail gender equality is not guaranteed. Instead the gender balance within the family and the position of the wife's brother and other male family members also play a role. According to Vignato (forthcoming), Laderman (1982) points out that, amongst the Negeri Sembilan Malays, very strict and defined patriarchy can be observed at all levels of society in spite of a strong element of matriliny. The fact that a generally spread bilateral system structurally allows a balance between men and women all over South-East Asia does not mean that in each specific sociocultural context the structures of power are gender-neutral (Vignato forthcoming).

Thus, other gender patterns interact with these kinship systems and with social relations more widely, as well as with age-related customs. For instance, in Buddhist societies in South-East Asia sons and daughters are expected to repay their lifelong debt to their parents in gender-specific ways. In Thailand, a son performs a highly meritorious act for his parents by becoming a Buddhist novice monk (typically temporarily), hence transferring merit to his parents, particularly to his mother. Thai women have thus traditionally been dependent on sons to achieve this merit, which they cannot attain on their own because women are excluded from receiving full ordination from the Thai Buddhist *sangha*. In Theravada Buddhist countries in South-East Asia daughters are therefore not expected to renounce the world but may be expected to be caretakers of their parents and younger siblings. Often that takes the form of financial support, with professional and wage-earning women sending money home to support their parents and siblings (Tantiwiramanond and Pandey 1987; Mills 1999; Falk 2007). Nonetheless, although a person's position is typically based on a combination of gender, age, class, rank, education and occupation, there are instances where gender appears to be less important than these other factors. For instance, there are many female political leaders in South-East Asia who are family members of past male political leaders, and while this should not be mistaken for women's prominence in politics more widely (which is typically weak across the region) it displays how family bonds and rank can outflank gender.

Asian values and the Asian family: the threat of divorce and non-marriage

In many parts of South-East Asia, from the beginnings of the 1990s we also begin to find the promotion of so-called 'Asian values' within 'some of the economically most vigorous East and South East Asian development states or newly industrialized economies . . . propagated by certain Asian state elites in think-tanks, academic institutions or the mass media' (Loh and Khoo 2013 [2002]: 2). As a reaction against Western liberal democracy, the concept of Asian values, traditionally oriented around the ideal Asian family, has been important for South-East Asian countries' development, integration and nation-building processes. As Hayami tells us, in Indonesia the idea of the family was prominent in nationalist ideology as a means of integrating the nation (2012: 9), and in Singapore and Malaysia Stivens's research demonstrates how the conservative Asian family ideology was advocated as a means of creating a distance from the Western family, considered to be in chaos (1998: 103–04).

Nonetheless, even the South-East Asian family is not so stable in reality, with smaller domestic units, an ageing population and a rapid decrease in fertility rates, which means a heavier burden on caregivers (Hayami 2012: 1). Compared to East and South Asia, the divorce rate in South-East Asia is high, and this has been ascribed to women's perceived relative autonomy, which means that divorce does not badly affect their livelihood or status (Reid 1988: 632; Dommaraju and Jones 2011: 734). However, in Malaysia, for instance, rates of divorce are higher for Malays than for Chinese and Indians (Dommaraju and Jones 2011), and divorce rates among the non-Muslim populations in Thailand and the Philippines have been low compared to Muslim divorce rates in these countries. Dommaraju and Jones suggest that in Muslim communities where (parent-arranged) marriages occur at a young age they are less likely to succeed (2011). However, a shift to love marriages as well as later marriage, in combination with increased education and economic development, has resulted in a decline in the divorce rate (Jones 1997). The decision not to marry is also increasingly acceptable (although this varies according to the status of individuals and their location and religion), but there is still widespread stigma to having children outside marriage (Dommaraju and Jones 2011: 745). For instance, in both Thailand and the Philippines it is socially accepted that couples live together and they are considered married without having formally registered their marriage (Knodel *et al.* 1987; Limanonda 1995; Kabamalan 2011). However, a number of single women have told me that the risk of men having more than one wife, combined with men's promiscuity, is a reason for not getting married. Although polygamy has officially been abolished in Thailand, for example, it is still widely practised there and in other settings across the region. There are protests against polygamy in Muslim societies (Rinaldo 2013: 96–100), and Buddhist women are critical of the practice of men having concubines and minor wives (Littleton 2000: 130–37).

Sexuality and the sex industry

Despite the traditionally strong emphasis upon the family in South-East Asia as well as conservative attitudes towards women's sexuality, it is significant that the Western binary gender construction of male and female has been considered unable to account for the fluidity of understandings of 'gender' in South-East Asia. Peletz, for instance, distinguishes five sets of cultural and institutional gendered categories in contemporary South-East Asia. They are in brief: females and femininity; males and masculinity; inter-sexed, who are partly male and partly female; transgendered, who are engaged in practices that transcend normative boundaries; and neutered or ungendered (Peletz 2007: 5–6). While others have criticized him for using an externally developed schema to label gender types, rather than capturing local subjectivities (Boellstorff 2005; Blackwood 2010), there is agreement that a greater sexual pluralism exists in South-East Asia, where ritual specialists are often expected to transgress gender and mediums are commonly transsexual persons (Sinnott 2004: 56; Peletz 2007: 12).

Thailand, for instance, has a rich indigenous history of complex patterns of sexuality and gender. Traditionally there have been three gender categories in Thailand, masculine men, feminine women and the *kathoey*. *Kathoeys* are visible in society and are described as a distinctive third sex, which occupies a middle ground between male/masculine and female/feminine (Jackson 1995b: 194). The contemporary *kathoeys* are transgender males, although historically *kathoeys* were both men and women. Today women who dress and behave like men are called *tom*, a word derived from the English word 'tomboy'. *Tom* or *tomboy* denotes a masculine-acting lesbian, while *dee*, from 'lady', denotes a feminine lesbian (Sinnott 2004: 29). Jackson tells us that the Buddhist Vinaya (monastic rules) identifies not two but 'four gender types: male, female, *ubhatobyanjanaka* [hermaphrodites] and *pandaka* [male transvestites and homosexuals]' and that the 'contemporary Thai stereotypes of *kathoeys* (transvestites and transsexuals) have precedents in descriptions of *pandaka* in Pali' (Jackson 1995a). While the *pandaka* of the Buddhist texts was not permitted to ordain, and neither are *kathoeys* today, the texts have mixed attitudes towards them. However, negative attitudes within Buddhism towards *kathoeys* did increase with the HIV/AIDS crisis in the 1980s (Jackson 1995a).

Kathoeys in Thailand are also prominent within the sex industry, because – as Tan writes – they 'have limited choices in the job market and are thus likely to end up in the sex and entertainment industry' (2014: 4). Moreover, *kathoey* sex workers have relatively high HIV infection rates.[2] Opportunities for sex work increased dramatically in the mid-1960s as a result of official agreements established between the Thai government and the United States that Thailand should serve as the main destination for 'rest and recreation' for American and other soldiers during the Vietnam War (Jeffrey 2002: xii). The existence of such a developed sex industry is also at the root of the HIV/AIDS epidemic in Thailand, where there is hardly a community that has not been affected in one way or another. The outbreak of HIV/AIDS in Thailand during the early 1990s caused alarm among many Thai people, with most of them ignorant about the disease and associating it only with promiscuity and homosexuality. Since the end of the 1990s I have followed work that Buddhist monks and nuns have carried out to help people infected with HIV/AIDS. In the next section of this chapter I will examine the role that religion can play in times of hardship and disasters, when it can become important even to people who usually do not pay much attention to it in their everyday life. However, the role of religion is complex and often ambiguous. While monks and nuns have played an important role in helping people with HIV/AIDS, breaking down stigma and raising awareness, it is also the case that others within the Buddhist community have strongly resisted this type of work, viewing it as un-Buddhist. Moreover, if prostitution is one of the primary causes of the spread of HIV/AIDS then studies that argue Buddhism plays a role in legitimizing the sex industry first require some attention.

Spiritual activism against HIV/AIDS in Thailand

The sex industry and Buddhism

The role that Buddhism has played in legitimating the sex industry in Thailand has attracted academic and activist attention. Simply put, Buddhism is viewed as providing a moral framework for men's hierarchical precedence over women (Khin Thitsa 1980: 7; Hantrakul 1988). Moreover, Khin Thitsa (1980: 7) argues that there is also a view within Buddhism of women as more connected to the material world, which can legitimate the idea that prostitution is an occupation where women can fulfil role expectations attached to worldly matters. There is a large literature on female prostitution in Thailand and the reasons for women's participation in sex work. The idea that Thai prostitutes are young girls dutifully sacrificing themselves for their rural families has become one of the widely accepted explanations among the Thai middle class and foreign commentators alike (Cook 1998: 264). Muecke (1992: 891) argues that there is a strong cultural continuity in northern Thai attitudes towards daughters supporting families by prostitution, where prostitution is the equivalent for today's daughters as selling food to supplement the family income was for their mothers' generation. However, not all poor parents allow their daughters to perform sex work, and in many cases prostitutes disguise their real occupation in fear of their families' disapproval. Also, many young women, like young men, migrate to urban areas against their families' wishes, and not all sex workers support their families (Cook 1998: 268). Prostitution provides a means of employment, and the economic gains make it appealing for those who are poor with a low level of education (Cook 1998: 259; Law 2000: 97; Victor T. King and Wilder 2003: 270; Ford and Lyons 2011: 295–302). Typically, Buddhism does not hold a judgemental attitude to matters in the secular realm, and hence it does not condemn prostitutes or refuse sex workers' donation to the *sangha*. For this reason, scholars have argued that Thai Buddhism in fact legitimates trafficking and prostitution (Muecke 1992; Satha-Anand 1999; Tomalin 2006). Moreover, some Thai Buddhist nuns have opened schools providing secular education for poor Thai girls, similar to the education that Buddhist temples offer to poor boys, as a strategy to prevent girls from ending up in sweat shops and in sex work (Falk 2000, 2007). Today the Thai government offers all children 12 years' education, but the costs of school still put the education of girls beyond the ability of poor families (e.g. in terms of uniforms, school books or travel) (Falk 2013; Tomalin and Starkey 2013), and the 'nunnery schools' also fill a much needed gap in providing safety for girls who live in remote areas and need a female boarding school to access education (Falk 2013).

Buddhist actors and HIV/AIDS

The HIV/AIDS epidemic has had considerable consequences for individuals, families and communities in terms of social stigmatization. Both male and female sex workers have been badly hit by HIV/AIDS, and the epidemic has spread to their clients and to the clients' wives. The response of civil society has been significant and continues through efforts by the government, non-government agencies, community self-help groups and Buddhist monks and nuns. During fieldwork in northern Thailand in 2004 and 2005 I accompanied small groups of monks and social workers visiting people who needed support, including people with HIV/AIDS. Some hospitals realized the potential of the monks' involvement and aimed to more formally involve them, including providing information about HIV transmission prevention and caring for people with AIDS. This placed the monks in a position to teach villagers about how to live alongside people with HIV/AIDS and how to protect themselves against the virus, as well as to assist at the hospitals and give consultation and advice on AIDS prevention and care. Buddhist monks' HIV/AIDS projects have been important in providing monastic-based hospices, meditation and counselling services for people living with HIV/AIDS, and income generation activities. Monks are also involved in HIV/AIDS prevention projects for lay people, and there are HIV/AIDS education projects for Buddhist monks and nuns (see Dane 2000). However, not all monks and villagers were positive towards these activities. Some senior monks prevented the establishment of hospices, and other activities were brought to an end because of villagers' protests.[3]

While Buddhist monasteries are a refuge for people in need and sometimes the last resort, HIV/AIDS is a highly stigmatized disease, and when people with AIDS came to the Buddhist temples only some monks were brave enough to help and risked losing lay support. Although there are almost 300,000 monks and novices in Thailand, who have had a traditional role as healers using herbal medicine, very few were initially involved in the AIDS issue.[4] There was a perception that the temples should not deal with AIDS, since it was related to sexuality and promiscuity (Vaddhanaputi 1999: 9). Those who did become involved worked to tackle stigma and discrimination, but also received a great deal of publicity, which was not always positive about their involvement (Jackson and Cook 1999: 220–21; Darlington 2012: 236–7).

One of the first monastic-based hospices in Thailand was established in 1992 by Phra Alongkot Dikkapanyo, the well-known abbot of the Buddhist temple Wat Phra Baht Nam Phu, in Lopburi province in central Thailand (120 kilometres north of Bangkok). Phra Alongkot turned a small up-country temple into a hospice to care for AIDS patients to help them die peacefully with as little pain as possible. It started with eight beds and has grown into a hospice with 400. Most of the patients are not from the temple's area, and many of them come from the north-east region of Thailand. In 2005, on average, three patients per day died at the hospice, and several thousand patients have died at the temple since it started. The temple grounds host a gas compressor crematorium, and after being cremated remains are sent to the family by registered mail. However, in most cases the family or relatives do not collect the ashes and they are returned to the temple (interviews and participant observation at Wat Phra Baht Nam Phu 2004, 2005 and 2007).

273

Another example is the work of Phra Phongthep, who lived in a large temple in northern Thailand, associated with the famous, socially engaged monk Buddhadhasa.[5] Phra Phongthep recognized how badly people with AIDS were treated and decided to open a hospice in 1994. His original plan was to teach Buddhism and provide a place where people with HIV/AIDS could learn meditation. However, he was advised by the abbot to relocate, since HIV/AIDS-related activities were not felt to be appropriate for the temple. Phra Phongthep established a *samnak song* (a small temple without an ordination hall) and a hospice. Most of the people he met with AIDS desperately needed medical and nursing care, but they were poor and had little knowledge about their illness. Moreover, their families were afraid to stay close to them and did not know how to handle the situation. Since it was almost impossible to have these patients admitted to hospitals, he pledged to take care of them. In contrast to the case at Wat Phra Baht Nam Phu, most of the patients who stayed at his hospice came from nearby urban areas.

Stigma has been a major obstacle for the monks to tackle. In some communities, there were fears that HIV/AIDS could spread when a person died, corpses were wrapped in plastic to mark that they were the corpses of people with AIDS, and villagers did not attend the funerals of people who had died from AIDS. In Phra Alongkot's village people were even afraid to come near the monks, including giving alms, and also feared that the HIV virus would contaminate the corn they grew in the fields near the temple. High levels of poverty in some regions, particularly the north-east of the country, have meant that remittances from migrant family members are of crucial importance for many families.[6] However, migrants who became infected with HIV/AIDS often did not return home for fear that their families would be discriminated against or that they would become a burden to them (Vaddhanaputi 1999: 28; about stigma see Fordham 2005: 106–08).

Gendered HIV/AIDS work

So far we have considered only the HIV/AIDS work undertaken by Buddhist monks, but also important within Thai Buddhism are the white-robed *mae chis* (nuns). Whereas in some Buddhist traditions women can ordain to the same level as men, receiving the *bhikkhuni/bhiksuni* ordination, in Thailand (as well as some other Buddhist settings) this option is not available to women (Findly 2000; Tsomo 2004; Mohr and Tsedroen 2010). Whereas a Theravada male monk, *bhikkhu*, receives 227 precepts and a Theravada female monk, *bhikkhuni*, receives 311 precepts, the *mae chi* usually receives eight precepts. The eight precepts that the *mae chis* follow are the same as those observed by lay people on special occasions. However, not only are *mae chis* ordained at a lower level than men, but they are not fully recognized as ordained persons, but as pious laity, and are excluded from benefits that monks enjoy. They do not receive support from the government on account of their official status as laity but at the same time are denied the right to vote in public elections on the basis of their renunciation of worldly matters (Falk 2007).

The ambiguous position of the *mae chis*, as simultaneously belonging to both the religious and the lay realm, has made them vulnerable as religious specialists. Working with HIV/AIDS would particularly risk undermining their religious role in the eyes of lay people, and in Thailand there are few *mae chis* who are explicitly involved in HIV/AIDS work. There were none working at Wat Phra Baht Nam Phu or at Phra Phongthep's hospice, and monks I interviewed in the Chiang Mai area considered that *mae chis* were unqualified for working with HIV/AIDS projects. Exceptions to this include a hospice in Bangkok that was established and run by the late Mae Chi Khunying Kanitha Wichiencharoen, a prominent, well-educated *mae chi* who was engaged in various social projects on women's rights issues. Another example is the work of Mae Chi Sansanee Sthirasuta, a socially engaged *mae chi*, who is also well known and well educated, and runs a Buddhist centre on the outskirts of Bangkok with various projects for people in vulnerable situations, including those with HIV/AIDS.

The small number of *mae chis* involved in HIV/AIDS-related work could be a consequence of the Buddhist *sangha's* lack of formal recognition of this institution and ambivalent social attitudes towards women who become *mae chis* in order to renounce the world and to live a monastic life. As Muecke (2004: 227) suggests, there are a variety of discourses on *mae chis* in contemporary Thailand, from portraying them as weak, lacking family support and even fallen women, to the notion that they are revered meditation teachers, admirable in their vocation and beneficial for society. Educated *mae chis*, of whom there are increasing numbers, are especially aware of their capacity to help lay people yet are sometimes unable to respond owing to a lack of infrastructure and support. This was also an issue in the wake of the 2004 Indian Ocean tsunami in Thailand, when Buddhist temples, monks and some nuns were crucial in the aftermath of the catastrophe and became a refuge for the survivors (Falk 2014). Despite this, most temples in Phang Nga province, the worst hit, do not host *mae chis*. That meant that *mae chis* in other parts of Thailand who wanted to help the survivors had nowhere to stay. I observed that female survivors especially appreciated talking with the few *mae chis* who visited the area. The *mae chis* explained to me that the women felt a closeness to them that they did not feel to the monks, because they were women. While there are many temples in Thailand that do not accept *mae chis*, others welcome them, considering them to be invaluable because they carry out practical chores as well as being important religious specialists. Thus, *mae chis* are valuable for lay people in their capacity as religious specialists, and a number have now established self-governed 'nunneries' (*samnak chis*) with support from the lay community (see Falk 2007).

Concluding remarks

During the last half-century opportunities for women and girls in South-East Asia have grown. Access to education is almost the same as for boys (Jones 2009: 12–13), and globalization and labour migration have given South-East Asian women and men the chance to earn more money than they could at home (albeit at the high price of leaving their families behind). However, the idea that women in South-East Asia have greater gender equality, for instance, than women in India and China is far older than this. The bilateral kinship system and widely practised matrilocality are believed to have influenced the relative autonomy that women in South-East Asia have enjoyed since pre-colonial times. While Errington (1990) and others have advised caution in overgeneralizing these claims, and that there are exceptions, women in South-East Asia are more likely to engage in economic activities and to control money and family, to inherit on equal terms to men, and not to be considered a financial burden on the family as they are in South Asia and China. However, this should not be mistaken for gender equality in all realms in society. The realms of politics and religion are examples of male strongholds in South-East Asian societies. Religion shapes family and gender orders in South-East Asia in ways that both support and block greater gender equality, seen not least in the ways in which Buddhist nuns (*mae chis*) are limited in the scope of the religious and social support they can provide for people owing to lack of recognition by the male-dominated *sangha*.

Social engagement, for instance with respect to HIV/AIDS or the tsunami aftermath, may threaten the Buddhist ascetic vows of both monks and nuns, because of the lay character of the social activities, thereby undermining their religious authority. I have suggested that this is a particularly precarious situation for nuns, who have lower levels of support and recognition than the monks do. However, religion has the capacity to install hope, create meaning and transform orders, especially in times of difficulties, and for centuries Buddhist temples have been centres of community activities and social engagement, and lay people have turned to the monks for support and advice. People with HIV/AIDS turned to the temples as a last resort, and monks and nuns became refuges in crisis situations. Engaged Buddhism can sometimes be seen as controversial simply because it challenges tradition by working in innovative ways.

Notes

1 I would like to acknowledge my informants in Thailand for generously sharing their knowledge and experiences with me. I am grateful for the constructive comments from the editor, Emma Tomalin, and from anonymous reviewers.
2 http://www.ncbi.nlm.nih.gov/pmc/articles/PMC3242825/ (accessed 8 June 2014); also, as Tan writes, most academic attention about the sex trade has focused upon women, and the 'role that male to female transgender bodies play in personifying Thailand as a (sex) tourism destination' has to date been largely neglected (Tan 2014: 1–2).
3 Interviews with monks in north-east Thailand in 2005.
4 Information about the numbers of monks is from 'Basic Religious Data', Data Statistics and Information Section Planning Division, Department of Religious Affairs, Ministry of Education, and includes novice monks.
5 Interviews in 2004.
6 http://unesdoc.unesco.org/images/0012/001262/126289e.pdf (accessed 8 June 2014).

References

Adams, Kathleen and Gillogly, Kathleen A. (eds) (2011) *Everyday Life in Southeast Asia*, Bloomington: Indiana University Press.
Alexander, Jennifer and Alexander, Paul (2001) 'Markets as Gendered Domains: The Javanese *Pasar*', in Linda J. Seligmann (ed.), *Women Traders in Cross-Cultural Perspective: Mediating Identities, Marketing Wares*, Stanford, CA: Stanford University Press.
Blackwood, Evelyn (2010) *Falling into the Lesbi World: Desire and Difference in Indonesia*, Honolulu: University of Hawai'i Press.
Boellstorff, Tom (2005) *The Gay Archipelago: Sexuality and Nation in Indonesia*, Princeton, NJ: Princeton University Press.
Brenner, Suzanne A. (1995) 'Why Women Rule the Roost', in Aihwa Ong and Michael G. Peletz (eds), *Bewitching Women, Pious Men: Gender and Body Politics in Southeast Asia*, Berkeley: University of California Press.
Burghoorn, Wil, Iwanaga, Kazuki, Milwertz, Cecilia and Wang, Qi (2008) *Gender Politics in Asia: Women Manoeuvring within Dominant Gender Orders*, Copenhagen: NIAS Press.
Cook, Nerida (1998) 'Dutiful Daughters, Estranged Sisters: Women in Thailand', in Krishna Sen and Maila Stivens (eds), *Gender and Power in Affluent Asia*, London: Routledge, pp. 250–90.
Dane, Barbara (2000) 'Thai Women: Meditation as a Way to Cope with AIDS', *Journal of Religion and Health*, 39 (1), pp. 5–21.
Darlington, Susan M. (2012) *The Ordination of a Tree: The Thai Buddhist Environmental Movement*, New York: SUNY Press.
Devasahayam, Theresa W. (ed.) (2009) *Gender Trends in Southeast Asia: Women Now, Women in the Future*, Singapore: ISEAS.
Dommaraju, Premchand and Jones, Gavin (2011) 'Divorce Trends in Asia', *Asian Journal of Social Science*, 39 (6), 725–50.
Dube, Leela (1997) *Women and Kinship: Comparative Perspectives on Gender in South and South-East Asia*, Tokyo: United Nations University Press.
Errington, Shelly (1990) 'Recasting Sex, Gender and Power: A Theoretical and Regional Overview', in Jane Monnig Atkinson and Shelly Errington (eds), *Power and Difference: Gender in Island Southeast Asia*, Stanford, CA: Stanford University Press, pp. 1–58.
Falk, Monica Lindberg (2000) 'Thammacarini Witthaya: The First Buddhist School for Girls in Thailand', in Karma Lekshe Tsomo (ed.), *Innovative Buddhist Women: Swimming against the Stream*, Richmond: Curzon Press.

Falk, Monica Lindberg (2007) *Making Fields of Merit: Buddhist Female Ascetics and Gendered Orders in Thailand*, Copenhagen: NIAS Press, and Seattle: University of Washington Press.

Falk, Monica Lindberg (2013) 'Buddhism as a Vehicle for Girls' Safety and Education in Thailand', in Vanessa R. Sasson (ed.), *Little Buddhas: Children and Childhoods in Buddhist Texts and Traditions*, Oxford: Oxford University Press.

Falk, Monica Lindberg (2014) *Post-Tsunami Recovery in Thailand: Socio-Cultural Responses*, London: Routledge.

Findly, Ellison Banks (ed.) (2000) *Women's Buddhism, Buddhism's Women: Tradition, Revision, Renewal*, Somerville, MA: Wisdom Publications.

Ford, Michele and Lyons, Leonore (2011) 'Narratives of Agency: Sex Work in Indonesia's Borderlands', in Kathleen M. Adams and Kathleen A. Gillogly (eds), *Everyday Life in Southeast Asia*, Bloomington: Indiana University Press.

Fordham, Graham (2005) *A New Look at Thai AIDS: Perspectives from the Margin*, Oxford: Berghahn Books.

Gross, Rita (1993) *Buddhism after Patriarchy: A Feminist History, Analyses, and Reconstruction of Buddhism*, Albany: State University of New York Press.

Hantrakul, Sukanya (1988) 'Prostitution in Thailand', in Glen Chandler, Norma Sullivan and Jan Branson (eds), *Development and Displacement: Women in Southeast Asia*, Monash Papers on Southeast Asia no. 18, Melbourne: Monash University, Centre of Southeast Asian Studies, pp. 115–36.

Hayami, Yoko (2012) 'Introduction: The Family in Flux in Southeast Asia', in Yoko Hayami, Junko Koizumi, Chalidaporn Songsamphan and Ratana Tosakul (eds), *The Family in Flux in Southeast Asia: Institution, Ideology, Practice*, Chiang Mai: Silkworm Press, and Kyoto: Kyoto University Press.

Holm, Jean and Bowker, John (eds) (2001) *Women in Religion*, London: Continuum.

Iwanaga, Kasuki (2008) *Women's Political Participation and Representation in Asia: Obstacles and Challenges*, Copenhagen: NIAS Press.

Jackson, Peter A. (1995a) 'Thai Buddhist Accounts of Male Homosexuality and AIDS in the 1980s (Thai Sexuality in the Age of AIDS: Essays in Memory of Robert Ariss)', *Australian Journal of Anthropology*, 6 (3), 140–53, http://ccbs.ntu.edu.tw/FULLTEXT/JR–EPT/anth.htm.

Jackson, Peter A. (1995b) *Dear Uncle Go: Male Homosexuality in Thailand*, Bangkok: Bua Luang.

Jackson, Peter A. and Cook, Nerida (eds) (1999) *Genders and Sexualities in Modern Thailand*, Chiang Mai: Silkworm Books.

Janowski, Monica and Kerlogue, Fiona (eds) (2007) *Kinship and Food in South East Asia*, Copenhagen: NIAS Press.

Jeffrey, Leslie Ann (2002) *Sex and the Borders: Gender, National Identity, and Prostitution Policy in Thailand*, Chiang Mai: Silkworm Press.

Jones, Gavin W. (1997) 'Modernization and Divorce: Contrasting Trends in Islamic South-East Asia and the West', *Population and Development Review*, 23 (1), 95–114.

Jones, Gavin W. (2009) 'Women, Marriage and Family in Southeast Asia', in Theresa W. Devasahayam (ed.), *Gender Trends in Southeast Asia: Women Now, Women in the Future*, Singapore: ISEAS.

Kabamalan, Maria Midea M. (2011) 'Cohabitation and Poverty in the Philippines', in Gavin W. Jones, Terence H. Hull and Maznah Mohamad (eds), *Changing Marriage Patterns in Southeast Asia: Economic and Socio-Cultural Dimensions*, London: Routledge.

Karim, Wazir Jahan (ed.) (1995) *'Male' and 'Female' in Developing Southeast Asia*, Oxford: Berg.

Khin Thitsa (1980) *Providence and Prostitution: Image and Reality for Women in Buddhist Thailand*, Change International Reports: Women and Society, London: Change International Reports.

King, Ursula and Beattie, Tina (eds) (2005) *Gender, Religion and Diversity: Cross-Cultural Perspectives*, London: Continuum.

King, Victor T. (2008) *The Sociology of Southeast Asia*, Copenhagen: NIAS Press.

King, Victor T. and Wilder, William D. (2003) *The Modern Anthropology of South-East Asia: An Introduction*, London: Routledge.

Klein–Hutheesing, Otome (1995) 'Gender at the Margins of Southeast Asia', in Wazir Jahan Karim (ed.), *'Male' and 'Female' in Developing Southeast Asia*, Oxford: Berg.

Knodel, John, Aphichat Chamratrithirong and Nibhon Debavalya (1987) *Thailand's Reproductive Revolution: Rapid Fertility Decline in a Third-World Setting*, Madison: University of Wisconsin Press.

Laderman, Carol (1982) 'Putting Malay Women in Their Place', in Penny Van Esterik (ed.), *Women of Southeast Asia*, Monograph Series on Southeast Asia Occasional Paper no. 17, Northern Illinois University, Center for Southeast Asian Studies.

Law, Lisa (2000) *Sex Work in Southeast Asia: The Place of Desire in a Time of AIDS*, London: Routledge.

Li, Tania (1989) *Malays in Singapore: Culture, Economy and Ideology*, New York: Oxford University Press.

Limanonda, Bhassorn (1995) 'Families in Thailand: Beliefs and Realities', *Journal of Comparative Family Studies*, 26 (1), 67–83.

Littleton, Chris (2000) *Endangered Relations: Negotiating Sex and AIDS in Thailand*, Amsterdam: Overseas Publishers Association.

Loh, Kok Wah Francis and Khoo, Boo Teik (eds) (2013 [2002]) *Democracy in Malaysia: Discourses and Practices*, New York: Routledge.

Meigs, Anna (1990) 'Multiple Gender Ideologies and Statuses', in Peggy Reeves Sanday and Ruth Goodenough (eds), *Beyond the Second Sex: New Directions in the Anthropology of Gender*, Philadelphia: University of Pennsylvania Press.

Mills, Mary Beth (1999) *Thai Women in the Global Labor Force: Consuming Desires, Contested Selves*, New Brunswick, NJ: Rutgers University Press.

Mohr, Thea and Tsedroen, Jampa (eds) (2010) *Dignity and Discipline: Reviving Full Ordination for Buddhist Nuns*, Somerville, MA: Wisdom Publications.

Muecke, Marjorie (1992) 'Mother Sold Food, Daughter Sells Her Body: The Cultural Continuity of Prostitution', *Social Science and Medicine*, 35 (7), 891–901.

Muecke, Marjorie (2004) 'Female Sexuality in Thai Discourses about *Maechii* ("Lay Nuns")', *Culture, Health and Sexuality*, 6 (3), 221–38.

Murcott, Susan (1991) *The First Buddhist Women: Translations and Commentaries on the Therigatha*, Berkeley, CA: Parallax Press.

Nagata, Judith (2011) 'Question of Identity: Different Ways of Being Malay and Muslim in Malaysia', in Kathleen Adams and Kathleen A. Gillogly (eds), *Everyday Life in Southeast Asia*, Bloomington: Indiana University Press.

Nhung, Tuyet Tran (2008) 'Gender, Property, and the "Autonomy Thesis" in Southeast Asia: The Endowment of Local Succession in Early Modern Vietnam', *Journal of Asian Studies*, 67 (1), 43–72.

Ong, Aihwa and Peletz, Michael G. (eds) (1995) *Bewitching Women, Pious Men: Gender and Body Politics in Southeast Asia*, Berkeley: University of California Press.

Peletz, Michael G. (2007) *Gender, Sexuality and Body Politics in Modern Asia*, Ann Arbor, MI: Association for Asian Studies.

Peletz, Michael G. (2009) *Gender Pluralism: Southeast Asia since Early Modern Times*, New York: Routledge.

Reid, Anthony (1988) 'Female Roles in Pre-Colonial Southeast Asia', *Modern Asian Studies*, 22 (3), 629–45.

Rinaldo, Rachel (2013) *Mobilizing Piety: Islam and Feminism in Indonesia*, New York: Oxford University Press.

Safitri, Myrna A. (2011) 'Legal Pluralism in Indonesia's Land and Natural Resource Tenure: A Summary of Presentations', in Marcus Colchester and Sophie Chao (eds), *Divers Paths to Justice: Legal Pluralism and the Rights of Indigenous Peoples in South East Asia*, Moreton-in-Marsh: Forest Peoples Programme, and Chiang Mai: Asia Indigenous Peoples Pact, pp. 126–32.

Satha-Anand, Suwanna (1999) 'Looking to Buddhism to Turn Back Prostitution in Thailand', in J. R. Bauer and D. A. Bell (eds), *The East Asian Challenge for Human Rights*, Cambridge: Cambridge University Press.

Sinnott, Megan J. (2004) *Toms and Dees*, Honolulu: University of Hawai'i Press.

Skidmore, Monique and Lawrence, Patricia (2007) *Women and the Contested State: Religion, Violence, and Agency in South and Southeast Asia*, Notre Dame, IN: University of Notre Dame Press.

Steedly, Mary Margaret (1999) 'The State of Culture Theory in the Anthropology of Southeast Asia', *Annual Review of Anthropology*, 28, 431–54.

Stivens, Maila (1998) 'Sex, Gender and the Making of the New Malay Middle Classes', in K. Sen and M. Stivens (eds), *Gender and Power in Affluent Asia*, London: Routledge, pp. 87–126.

Stoler, Ann (1977) 'Class Structure and Female Autonomy in Rural Java', *Signs*, 3 (1), 74–89.

Sullivan, Norma M. (1994) *Masters and Managers: A Study of Gender Relations in Urban Java*, Sydney: Allen & Unwin.

Swearer, Donald K. (2010) *The Buddhist World of Southeast Asia*, New York: SUNY Press.

Tan, Qian Hui (2014) 'Orientalist Obsessions: Fabricating Hyper-Reality and Performing Hyper-Femininity in Thailand's Kathoey Tourism', *Annals of Leisure Research*, 17 (2), 145–60.

Tantiwiramanond, Darunee and Pandey, Shashi Ranjan (1987) 'The Status and Role of Thai Women in the Pre-Modern Period: A Historical and Cultural Perspective', *Sojourn*, 2 (1), 125–49.

Tomalin, Emma (2006) 'The Thai *Bhikkhuni* Movement and Women's Empowerment', *Gender and Development*, 14 (3), 385–97.

Tomalin, Emma and Starkey, Caroline (2013) *Gender, Buddhism and Education: Dhamma and Social Transformation within the Theravada Tradition*, in Z. Gross, L. Davies and A.-K. Diab (eds), *Gender, Religion and Education in a Chaotic Postmodern World*, Dordrecht: Springer.

Tsomo, Karma Lekshe (ed.) (2004) *Buddhist Women and Social Justice: Ideals, Challenges, and Achievement*, New York: SUNY Press.

Vaddhanaputi, Chayan (1999) 'A Cultural Approach to HIV/AIDS Prevention and Care', UNESCO/UNAIDS research project report.

Van Esterik, Penny (2008) *Food Culture in Southeast Asia*, Westport, CT: Greenwood Press.

Vignato, Silvia (forthcoming) 'Short Marriages with the Beloved Boys: Post-War Sexuality in Muslim Aceh (Indonesia)', in Laila Prager and Patrick Franke (eds), *Beyond the Patriarchal Family: Female Centered Forms of Life in Muslim Societies*, London: I. B. Tauris.

Winzeler, Robert L. (2011) *The Peoples of Southeast Asia Today: Ethnography, Ethnology, and Change in a Complex Region*, Lanham, MD: AltaMira Press.

Zwilling, Leonard (1992) 'Homosexuality as Seen in Indian Buddhist Texts', in José Ignacio Cabezon (ed.), *Buddhism, Sexuality, and Gender*, Albany: State University of New York Press.

PART 6

The Middle East and North Africa

19

RELIGION AND DEVELOPMENT IN THE MIDDLE EAST AND NORTH AFRICA (MENA)

Poverty relief or social transformation?

Rana Jawad

Introduction

The role of religious actors, values and institutions in shaping public policy interventions, in terms both of policy formulation processes and of outcomes for end users, has become much more prominent in development studies and social policy in the last decade. This flourishing academic literature has so far paid little attention to the Middle East and North African region, in part perhaps as a result of the hegemony of political science (a discipline that typically does not engage with religious topics except for their salience to security issues) in Middle Eastern studies and the dominant concerns with issues of international security and geo-politics. Yet the study of development, social welfare and social justice issues has never been more urgent in the MENA region as now, and no doubt made so by the civil unrest which has swept across MENA countries starting with Tunisia in 2011.

For clarity, the chapter is focused on the Arab countries of the MENA region but also makes reference to Turkey and Iran owing to the discussion of Islamic welfare and development practices which are prioritized in it. There is a long-standing presence of religious diversity in the MENA region, with Jewish, Christian, Zoroastrian and Baha'i (to name but a few) populations also residing there, but with varying degrees of political integration and social freedom. The region has the highest rate of adult and youth unemployment, 17 per cent of which is female unemployment. Though poverty levels are below the world average, they have remained consistent, with almost two-thirds of MENA populations not having any form of social security.

To a large extent therefore, the task ahead for scholars studying religion and development issues in the MENA region is not a small one. The line of argument followed in this chapter, which has been attempted in a very small number of academic works (for example Bonner 2003; Heyneman 2004; Karshenas and Moghadam 2006; Jawad 2009), is twofold: first, that a new generation of social scientists outside the discipline of political science need to consider the MENA region in their academic work and to explore the social and developmental issues which this region faces; and, second, that these social scientists should consider in more depth the intersection between religion and development in the MENA region. To this end, the chapter draws upon extensive research conducted by the author on the social and development policies in the MENA region.

The research on which this chapter is based covers public interventions by state agencies, international development agencies, and indigenous NGOs from Muslim (Shi'a and Sunni) and Christian (Catholic, Anglican and Orthodox) denominations. It begins with some basic conceptual discussion in order to set the scene for critically evaluating the relationship between religion and development in the MENA region. This entails a consideration of how modern international development policies and practices have been shaped in the MENA region and what, in comparison, the history of religious interventions in the public sphere has entailed. In some respects, we may say that these are parallel universes. Today, the region is described as being 'richer than it is developed' (UNDP 2002: 99). To a large extent, this is reflected in the trajectory of development initiatives in the MENA region, which have been couched in terms of uneven processes of nation building, continued conflicts over identity politics and a lack of effective engagement with processes of economic globalization. Thus, the MENA region is marked by 'exceptionalism' not only because it has not successfully integrated into the world economy, but also because it is the home of 'political Islam'.

Thus, the influence of religion on processes of social change and development action in the MENA region can be partly understood in relation to the relative success or failure in the countries of the MENA to establish legitimate modern secular states that are responsive to the needs of their citizens. Instead, this is a region plagued since the time of independence of its nation states by a disjuncture between state and society, a situation which has been both reinforced and exacerbated by the rise of political Islam and the entry of Islamic movements into the political epicentre following the uprisings in Tunisia in 2011. Against this backdrop of political upheaval at the macro-level, the MENA region boasts a vibrant non-state sector where religiously inspired philanthropic, charitable and civic actors engage in a vast array of both development and humanitarian relief work, depending on whether there is war or peace. The chapter will categorize the different types of religiously inspired social welfare and development action offered by the non-state sector in the MENA region in order to make two key arguments:

1 Religion has played a historical role in the development of the public sphere in MENA. Institutions such as the *waqf* and the *zakat* have been instrumental in developing notions of the common good and public services from health to education to economic development. Today, most religiously motivated development and social welfare organizations operate as non-governmental or civil society organizations drawing upon religious precepts of fellowship and responding to human need. However, religiously informed social and development policies also operate through the state apparatus in many MENA countries, as in Iran and Saudi Arabia (Saeidi 2004). Indeed, most Arab countries, particularly in the Gulf region, and even after the Arab Spring uprisings, declare allegiance to Islam in their constitutions (Jawad 2009). Thus, the chapter explores the varieties of institutional mechanisms through which religion interacts with social welfare and development by discussing a typology of religious development action developed by the author (Jawad 2009). Five types are discussed.

2 The research evidence on the extent to which religion is a force for transformative social change in the MENA region is not conclusive. The ethos of charity continues to prevail, and civil conflict interrupts development work as religious organizations respond to emergency humanitarian needs. Thus, the extent to which religion can promote a substantive discourse of development in the MENA region has yet to be realized. In the meantime, most MENA states work closely with international development institutions to implement socio-economic policies or social safety net programmes which, at best, produce piecemeal solutions to the critical social challenges the region faces.

Social welfare and development policy in MENA: historical developments

Global forces have played a key role in the shaping of the modern Middle East, the definition of its social problems and avenues to their policy solutions: from European economic domination in the seventeenth century to colonization and mandate rule to modern-day global economic integration (El-Ghonemy 1998). Since the 1980s, the region has also been subjected to the pressures of economic reform in the context of a globalizing economic world order and structural adjustment programmes led mainly by international development agencies such as the International Monetary Fund (IMF) and World Bank. These factors have resulted in public policy becoming dominated by the interests of elites made up of tribal, religious or ethnic leaders and wealthy merchants whose privileged status during mandate rule and afterwards marginalized the interest of a primarily rural agricultural population (El-Ghonemy 1998). The increasing market orientation of Arab economies and the privatization programmes they underwent under the influence of globalization and international development actors have further diminished the role of the state as main provider of social services and employer in the public sector.

El-Ghonemy (1998), Henry and Springborg (2001), Clark (2004) and Karshenas and Moghadam (2006) argue that states in Arab countries have failed or are failing to develop effective democratic institutions that can ensure representative government and political participation for all citizens. Whether over-sized and coercive (such as Egypt and Saudi Arabia) or weak and dysfunctional (such as Sudan and Lebanon), states are prevented from functioning effectively by corruption. State social provisioning is especially affected because of several factors, namely: (1) the misallocation of resources and the prioritization of military spending over other important social policy sectors such as health and education; (2) the narrow economic focus of public policy, which links social progress to economic prosperity; (3) the dominance of minority factions in Arab countries dating back to the colonial era; (4) political insecurity and military conflict, including the Arab–Israeli conflict; (5) high levels of state indebtedness, which have taken away funds from social welfare services; and (6) the introduction of structural adjustment programmes in the 1980s and the subsequent push towards economic privatization which have reduced the role of the state further as provider of social services and public sector jobs (El-Ghonemy 1998; Bayat 2006; Karshenas and Moghadam 2006). The resulting social ills of unemployment, wealth polarization and even undernourishment need to be addressed through the reform of public policy and state legislation.

The most comprehensive employment-based social security schemes are enjoyed by urban public sector workers, with the best forms of protection going to the army and security forces. At the heart of this minimalist state approach to social policy lies an emphasis on economic development in public policy and a corresponding lack of importance accorded to the social sphere. A significant example of this 'residual approach' (where social welfare services are provided only as a last resort and as a short-term measure) can be found across the MENA region today, where states rely on employment-based formal social security or encourage philanthropy and charity, as well as family-based support.

Yet MENA populations are calling for the continuation of state intervention in the public sphere, no matter how meagre this role may be. In Egypt for example, Bayat (2006) shows how, since the 1990s, the state has not been able to cut back on key consumer subsidies (such as on cooking oil, fuel and bread) owing to the outbreak of violent public protest. Ironically, this is one social right accorded to Arab citizens which has proved difficult to retract. Related to this is the characterization of Arab states as 'rentier', meaning states where the main source of government revenue is from natural resources such as oil or gas and not the productive domestic economy (Beblawi 1990). The oil windfall in the region which occurred in the mid-twentieth century is depicted as a curse by El-Ghonemy (1998), since it has weakened the structures of social citizenship and the need to develop the productive capacity of the local population, because of the over-reliance on foreign labour.

The uprisings of the Arab Spring have made these issues much more urgent. If issues of social justice and social welfare were not a concern for governments and development agencies in the region a few years ago, they are now. Momentum has grown among international development agencies to begin to engage with issues of social protection in the MENA countries and what suitable social policy responses might look like.

The United Nations Economic and Social Council for Western Asia (UN-ESCWA), for example, has published five reports over the course of the last few years which seek to define social policy in a suitable way for the MENA countries and explore options for future action. In this view, development policy is not only about the enhancement of state social protection systems but, for some countries, it may be the case that a mixed-economy welfare model is being proposed (UN-ESCWA 2014) whereby the state is no longer the sole provider of social and development services but civil society actors too are called upon by government or in partnership with multi-lateral agencies to play a role. In accordance with this new trend, governments in the region have also been seeking to draw up 'social vision statements' which reflect the rights and obligations of their citizens towards their states. But to a large extent these remain vision statements. In Lebanon, for example, a National Social Strategy was produced in 2011 as a product of collaboration between private research organizations, the UNDP and the Ministry of Social Affairs. However, the local lay population is unaware of this endeavour even though local NGOs were consulted. In some ways, this inconsistent governmental engagement with issues of social welfare is historically rooted (Jawad 2009).

It is partly explained by the dominance of religious actors and institutions in the social welfare sphere since the pre-colonial period. Islamic and Christian forms of social welfare action have dominated the Arab region for centuries. Before the emergence of the modern nation states when the region was still ruled by the Islamic Khalifat system, religious institutions such as the *waqfs* (religious endowments) flourished and were seen to contribute in fundamental ways to public life and economic development. For example, the city of Istanbul is particularly noted in this regard (Jawad 2009). *Waqf* institutions were also means by which women could own property and invest capital in the public sphere. *Waqfs* included capital such as land, buildings or livestock which were put to use for public good, for instance by being used as schools or hospitals or to feed the poor. Often wealthy families would endow their personal wealth for public use. Since wealthy families could endow their assets, a tactic often employed to keep wealth in a family was for female members of such families to inherit property, which they later put to the use of local deprived populations (Richardson 2004). Dallal (2004) and Singer (2008) discuss in depth the range of economic, social, political and cultural impacts which the *waqf* institution has produced, though this changed with the growth of modern forms of governance, as explained above. During colonization, many of the *waqf* institutions and practices were destroyed by European colonizers who sought to seize land and assets that were profitable. Public life and political institutions gradually became overtaken by more modern forms of government which reflected the tendencies and interests of urban elites.

Public policies aimed at social development outcomes increasingly became politicized and used instrumentally by the state to gain power and political legitimacy (Jawad 2009). Some authors argue that this is a historical factor; for example, the introduction of social benefits to workers and employment guarantees to university graduates in Iran and Egypt in the 1950s and 1960s were motivated by the need to win the support of the working classes in the post-colonial states, and were not based on the policy objectives of expanding social citizenship (Bayat 2006). Today, social benefits are channelled through clientelist networks, which link ruling governments to their supporters. Hence, the long-running social policy challenges facing the Arab countries in terms of social welfare provisioning are less about the long-term structures of democratic participation and a share in decision making by society, and more about the urgent measures of wealth redistribution, income transfers, provision of basic needs and ensuring the basic support systems of survival (Karshenas and Moghadam 2006).

Today, the region demonstrates diverse socio-economic profiles, with per capita income levels ranging from over US$25,000 to below US$1,000. The first Arab Human Development Report (AHDR) (UNDP 2002: 99) described the Arab region in particular as being 'richer than it is developed', with its oil-driven economic policies resulting in substantial social and economic volatility. There is also limited availability of poverty statistics. The region has made some progress in reducing absolute poverty levels in the last two decades. Extreme poverty is especially acute in the low-income Arab countries, affecting around a third of the population. A distinctive demographic feature with important development policy implications is the region's 'youth bulge', with around 60 per cent of the population under the age of 25 years. But poverty is a multi-dimensional phenomenon (UNDP 2009). There are, therefore, a variety of social problems which Arab countries today are grappling with, namely unemployment (particularly among the youth), population growth, adult illiteracy, high school drop-out rates, lack of access to universal health care, and social, income and gender disparities (UNDP 2009).

The key characterization of the Arab region has, therefore, been one of a detachment between state and society (Henry and Springborg 2001), and this has come to a head with the current uprisings. The sense of social unrest is exacerbated further by the common notion within the different societies that the state should take more responsibility for the welfare of citizens and that the latter have the right to be provided with state social services. Discord between state and societal groups over the public sphere is most acutely expressed in the rise of Islamic groups in the Arab countries, which are providing vital public and social services, and thus challenging the state not only as a provider of welfare but as a modern secular institution of government (Jawad 2009). Some of these groups are well-known political groups such as the Muslim Brotherhood (Egypt) and Hezbollah (Lebanon), but others are more local and less political, such as the Islah Charitable Society in Yemen or the Mustafa Mahmood Health Clinic in Egypt (Clark 2004).

There are a variety of ways in which countries of the MENA region accommodate religious belief and practices. These in effect amount to various systems of governance, since in essence all political regimes in the MENA region, and particularly the Arab ones, extend their powers over religious leaders. Religious and political elites promote each other's legitimacy. From Saudi Arabia to Jordan to Turkey to Algeria, the state is able to control religious sermons in order to influence public political opinion. In countries where military rule has been long-standing, such as in Egypt, the state has entered into direct conflict with religious movements, where the latter have historically felt disenfranchised from mainstream political power (Clark 2004). This reflects the broader tradition of social struggle and protest which Muslim social movements have occupied in the MENA region as vehicles of democratic protest again dictatorial rulers (Jawad 2009).

Principles of social justice in Islam

Islam (like Judaism and Christianity) exercises tremendous influence on social and political institutions in the Arab world and even makes its way directly into government social vision statements, as in the cases of Qatar and Saudi Arabia. Islamic values and traditions also have a direct influence on social welfare programmes and inheritance laws, as well as family planning. In this sense, Islam is sometimes considered to perpetuate wealth and gender inequalities, although perspectives differ, with researchers arguing women do have rights to property and to work or do have a say in family planning (Bowen 2004).

Islamic doctrine makes specific provisions for welfare through a variety of practices and institutions. Bonner (2003: 13) discusses in historical terms the principles of 'return of wealth' (*radd* or *ruju'*) to the poor and *masala 'amma* (public welfare) through obligatory Islamic practices such as the *waqf* (religious endowments) and *zakat* (an obligatory 2.5 per cent tax levied on assets). *Zakat* has acted as an important source of poverty alleviation for the poor, and *waqf* played a key role in the socio-economic development of the Middle East in the last few centuries prior to colonization (Heyneman 2004). Islamic principles have also entered particular public policy areas such as health, finance and the economy, and human rights legislation (ibid.). In the health sector, for example, some countries such as Iran have been able to improve primary care thanks to the influence of Islamic principles in Iran after the revolution, which allowed them to focus more on direct care to local families (Underwood 2004). In contrast to *zakat*, which may be seen more as a tool of social assistance and wealth redistribution, *waqf* has played a much more important role in the development of MENA societies, as discussed above.

The relevance of religion to development in the MENA region

Today, governments and international development agencies are becoming more interested in social justice and social welfare issues (which clearly overlap with development issues) in the MENA region (particularly in the Arab and Muslim-populated countries). Ten years ago, this was a very different story. No one spoke of the need to protect citizens in the MENA region (except perhaps for some of the UN Arab Human Development Reports), and government officials did not really know what social policies aimed at enhancing development social welfare would look like. But, since the mid-2000s, we have had an explosion of new terms such as 'social protection', 'social security', 'social assistance', 'social solidarity', 'social integration' and 'new welfare mix' which headline reports and conference events in the region. But are we any closer to understanding how social policy systems work in the MENA region and, crucially, what the way forward might be now that the Arab Spring has brought issues of social justice and social welfare in MENA to the fore?

A decade ago, religious organizations in the MENA region offered a much more welcoming environment to researchers. They were much less suspicious because few people paid attention to them. Even groups of a political nature with well-established welfare wings such as Hezbollah or the Muslim Brotherhood were much more open to outside researchers coming to see what they did. Iran was also a country to which Western researchers could gain an entry visa in reasonable time and through standard application processes. Today, the situation is very different: the doors to researchers have been shut as Muslim organizations undertaking social welfare work come under heavy scrutiny by Western governments and international bodies (Juul Petersen 2011). Increasingly, the suspicion has grown that Muslim international aid agencies are a cover for Islamic fundamentalist groups. However, this chapter focuses primarily on how religious development groups operate within their own countries in the MENA region, since they are little researched and yet form a pillar of local forms of development and social welfare. In any case, dealing with the change in circumstances which has led to increased scrutiny is crucial for finding a way forward, because:

1   Muslim groups, no matter how linked they are to armed military struggle, have extensive social welfare networks in the countries in which they operate, which are well organized and successfully solve the daily social and economic problems that everyday people face;

2   it is impossible to devise policies that can support social integration and social security in the MENA region without taking into account the place and role of religious groups in society there.

Here is the important point: when we compare the types of services that are provided by religious NGOs in the MENA region, regardless of what political affiliation that organization might have, we find that all of these organizations have a similar social welfare ethos which prioritizes vulnerable groups such as orphans, the elderly and female-headed households. Indeed, they all operate on a social assistance basis, be this of an in-kind or in-cash nature. Take the case of Emdad and Caritas in Lebanon, for example. Emdad is part of the family of Hezbollah-led welfare associations, but it offers social assistance to some of the poorest segments of society, which tend to be of the Shi'a denomination (Jawad 2009). Caritas is also a very prominent welfare and development organization with a Catholic orientation – it provides the same kinds of social assistance and family support services as Emdad (Jawad 2009). These types of services are the most wide-spread and underpin the social assistance ethos which dominates much of the work that religious NGOs do in the MENA region.

Another key area of activity of religious NGOs in the MENA region is micro-credit and small enterprise loans. All religious groups operate with the ethos of fostering autonomy among their service users, though the extent to which they achieve this is not always proven. Many NGOs set up credit unions or offer direct loans to their beneficiaries, in an attempt to keep families together and, in cases where the father is absent, to support the mother in finding a new source of income. Some of the larger Islamic groups such as the Jihad Al Binaa, which is affiliated to Hezbollah, invest in major rural development projects supporting farmers and subsidizing them in remote, rural parts of Lebanon. So to what extent would Islamic welfare initiatives be viewed with suspicion?

Religion is a force that is here to stay, in both the Eastern and Western hemispheres. Alexis de Toqueville, in his famous travels around America, remarked that the roots of Western democracy lay in the hundreds of voluntary religious associations that undertook a whole array of neighbourhood and community work in the eighteenth and nineteenth centuries (Skocpol 2000). Those early forms of spontaneous social organization laid the foundations for the more complex modern systems of governance that we have today. Could mainstream academic and policy observers both in the West and in the MENA region consider Islamic welfare groups in the MENA region today as helping to develop civic associations and social solidarity instead of simply seeking to manipulate local populations for their political or fundamentalist motives?

In the Western world, academic and policy observers are largely in agreement about the due credit that is to be given to the churches and religious groups in public life. In the UK, for example, it is accepted that the welfare state could not have come about without the cooperation of the Church of England in the aftermath of the Second World War and the vision of the senior clergy of the time for a state administration to take charge of the reconstruction effort. Prominent sociologists in North America and Europe such as Jurgen Habermas, Robert Bellah, Robert Putnam and even at one time Anthony Giddens have been ready to pay homage to religion as a civic force which helps to promote community ties and social support networks. Yet, with respect to Islamic welfare practices in the MENA region, some academic, media and policy observers both in the West and in MENA more readily associate Muslim welfare practices with regressive, conservative forces. Why is this so, and how can social science research add insights?

The research on which this chapter is based has helped to develop a typology of religious action in the social welfare and development spheres (Jawad 2009): it illustrates various forms in which religion influences state and non-state structures in development activity in the MENA region. There are five 'types', some of which overlap. The make-up of these types depends on the circumstances that led to the establishment of the particular religious NGOs.

The first type of religious development organization is entirely clergy-led, for example Caritas in Lebanon. We may call this type 'the religious order'. This organization is part and parcel of a religious body, such as the Catholic Church or a religious order. It may employ lay individuals, but the managerial cadre is reserved for clerics, who carry out the social services themselves. This is in line with Christian social activism around the world and is characterized by the monastic character of some Christian traditions where the clergy decide to leave the seclusion of the church to engage in social life and help those less fortunate. There are various degrees of 'monasticism' – some clergy-led social welfare groups are staffed only by clergy, whereas others do employ lay members of their religious communities.

A second type, 'the elite family', is directly linked to the elite families of particular communities, such as the case of Dar Al-Aytam in Lebanon, which was set up by prominent Beirut families, or Al-Maadi Community Foundation in Cairo, Egypt (Lethem-Ibrahim and Sherif 2008). In the case of Dar Al-Aytam, the Beirut families established an Islamic orphanage to care for orphans and widows living in the capital city and its suburbs. Some organizations are a joint endeavour between religious and political elites. The charitable activities of upper-class families in the Middle East have a long history and are closely linked to public action (Lethem-Ibrahim and Sherif 2008). In Egypt, in 1882, the first feminist movement mobilized in this way under the name of the Women's Educational Society. The 1940s and 1950s, which witnessed waves of anti-colonial movements in the region, often involved aristocratic families. In Turkey today, it is common for prominent families to set up charitable public institutions such as schools and universities, otherwise translated from the Islamic concept of *waqf* (religious endowment) into English as 'social foundations'.

The third type, 'the popular political movement', is perhaps the most revolutionary and indeed the most politicized. It is the one under which Hezbollah in Lebanon falls. This type can also be found in Egypt, Morocco and the Palestinian Territories in the example of movements with a clear Islamic ideology, such as the Muslim Brotherhood, Justice and Development Charity Movement and Hamas. It is important to pause here and consider the literature on Islamic social movements. Sutton and Vertigans (2005) and Makris (2007) make a distinction between 'radical Islamic movements' such as al-Qaida and 'mass organizations' such as Hamas, the Muslim Brotherhood and Hezbollah. This chapter goes some way to demonstrating how a consideration of the developmental role of religious groups in the MENA region helps to enhance understanding of the role of 'mass organizations'.

As argued in Jawad (2009), this chapter uses the term 'popular political movement' (type 3) to denote the 'mass organizations' referred to above, since a key facet of their identity is their populist character expressed through their discourses on anti-imperialism (usually American), social justice and active involvement in development action. Salamey and Pearson (2007), in analysing the particular case of Hezbollah, speak of a populist proletarian movement which is part of an anti-imperialist international alliance. This, they argue, takes better account of the particular political discourse adopted by Hezbollah. Here, the populist pro-poor discourse feeds into one of resistance, not just against neo-colonial dominance but also against poverty and ignorance.

A fourth type of religious development organization exists and is particularly prominent in Iran and Turkey as a result of the penetration of religious allegiances into the state apparatus. This type is 'the international humanitarian relief organization'. Organizations such as Insani Yardim Vakfi and Deniz Feneri in Turkey have become well known for their international relief efforts to emergency situations around the world. They also provide aid within Turkey. It is noteworthy that the religious NGOs that were researched for this chapter can sometimes work with each other in practice. As part of its international relief efforts, Deniz Feneri, for example, has offered financial aid to Emdad of Lebanon. This links more broadly to an international Islamic identity that these organizations adhere to. Emdad of Iran is also beginning to cross international borders, though it primarily denotes a fifth type of Islamic development organization, particular to a theocratic state (see below).

This fifth type we may call 'the para-state organization', following Saeidi's (2004) classification, based on the *boniyad* (the Persian name for welfare institutions). The general public perception in Iran is that Emdad is the welfare arm of the state. This view differs from that of the organization itself, since its staff members see it as a 'holy organization' set up by Imam Khomeini to serve the people. Indeed, the populist association emerges again here, with staff members arguing that the local population are more likely to donate to and support a non-governmental organization which they trust (Jawad 2009). As Saeidi (2004) argues, Emdad is part of a large array of development and social welfare institutions in Iran which offer a variety of services. He argues that, since 1979, development policy in Iran has in some cases increasingly been used as a tool of social control and political legitimization. In this sense, the formal apparatus of government in Iran is an administrative structure, since development organizations such as Emdad respond directly to the supreme leaders.

Conclusion

The chapter has provided an overview of the role of religion in social welfare and development in the MENA region. This a region which has long been considered as lagging behind on social and economic indicators and one which has occupied political and academic debate more for concerns with terrorism and political Islam than social welfare and development. This makes the argument presented in this chapter, that religion in the MENA region and Islam in particular can be a force for development and civic flourishing, an important departure from conventional scholarship.

MENA states continue to prioritize economic growth as their main development strategy, but the greater visibility which issues of poverty and social justice now have has meant that government policy can no longer turn a blind eye to social development and welfare concerns. NGOs that have a religious character are also striving to bring about long-term social and economic development through for example rural development projects and micro-credit programmes, but these programmes are outweighed by social assistance services focused on family allowances and emergency relief to families who have lost their main breadwinner. This social safety net approach helps to bring strong bonds of solidarity with the poor but also dependency.

It may also be argued that for many religious NGOs in the Middle East and North Africa, there is an overriding moral concern to protect destitute families from criminal or sexually deviant behaviour. Hence, these NGOs give a lot of emphasis to moral and spiritual education among their service users, in whom they try to foster a spirit of independence. There is therefore a difficult balancing act which religious NGOs perform. They are more likely be involved in poverty relief activities than they are in economic and social transformation. Having said this, religious NGOs have a strong sense of civic duty and service, and in some cases their beneficiaries later become volunteers. They are also able to work at grassroots level in a way which many MENA governments are unable to do as a result of weak institutional and governance capacities.

Governments and global development agencies will do well in the formulation of new development policies if they take serious account of the experience of religious NGOs in social action. But, beyond this, religion informs the salient moral values which underpin particular conceptualizations of the good society in the MENA region. An example discussed in this chapter is how the family remains central in religious thinking on well-being – what we find in MENA countries is that both state agencies and religious organizations target services to vulnerable groups such as orphans or female-headed households because they have no male breadwinner. So for policy purposes we can only understand patterns of development and social welfare organization in the MENA region by making the link to religion – for better or worse, this is a force of which the MENA region should not be ashamed but with which it should enter into dialogue.

References

Bayat, A. (2006) 'The Political Economy of Social Policy in Egypt', in M. Karshenas and V. Moghadam (eds), *Social Policy in the Middle East*, UNRISD Social Policy in a Development Context Series, New York: Palgrave Macmillan, pp. 135–55.

Beblawi, H. (1990) 'The Rentier State in the Arab World', in G. Luciani (ed.), *The Arab State*, London: Routledge, pp. 85–98.

Bonner, Michael (2003) 'Poverty and Charity in the Rise of Islam', in M. Bonner, M. Ener and A. Singer (eds), *Poverty and Charity in Middle Eastern Contexts*, New York: SUNY Press, pp. 13–30.

Bowen, Donna Lee (2004) 'Islamic Law and Family Planning', in S. P. Heyneman (ed.), *Islam and Social Policy*, Nashville, TN: Vanderbilt University Press, pp. 118–55.

Clark, J. A. (2004) *Islam, Charity and Activism: Middle Class Networks and Social Welfare in Egypt, Jordan and Yemen*, Bloomington: Indiana University Press.

Dallal, Ahmed (2004) 'The Islamic Institution of Waqf: A Historical Overview', in S. P. Heyneman (ed.), *Islam and Social Policy*, Nashville, TN: Vanderbilt University Press, pp 13–43.

El-Ghonemy, R. (1998) *Affluence and Poverty in the Middle East*, London: Routledge.

Henry, C. M. and Springborg, R. (2001) *Globalization and the Politics of Development in the Middle East*, Cambridge: Cambridge University Press.

Heyneman, S. (2004) 'Introduction', in S. P. Heyneman (ed.), *Islam and Social Policy*, Nashville, TN: Vanderbilt University Press, pp. 1–12.

Jawad, R. (2009) *Social Welfare and Religion in the Middle East*, Bristol: Policy Press.

Juul Petersen, Marie (2011) *Islamizing Aid: Transnational Muslim NGOs after 9.11*, Baltimore, MD: International Society for Third-Sector Research and Johns Hopkins University.

Karshenas, M. and Moghadam, V. (2006) 'Social Policy in the Middle East: Introduction and Overview', in M. Karshenas and V. Moghadam (eds), *Social Policy in the Middle East*, UNRISD Social Policy in a Development Context Series, New York: Palgrave Macmillan, pp. 1–30.

Lethem-Ibrahim, B. and Sherif, H. D. (eds) (2008) *From Charity to Social Change: Trends in Arab Philanthropy*, Cairo: American University in Cairo Press.

Makris, G. P. (2007) *Islam in the Middle East: A Living Tradition*, Oxford: Blackwell.

Richardson, Gail (2004) 'Islamic Law and Zakat: Waqf Resources in Pakistan', in S. P. Heyneman (ed.), *Islam and Social Policy*, Nashville, TN: Vanderbilt University Press, pp. 156–80.

Saeidi, A. (2004) 'The Accountability of Para-Governmental Organizations (Bonyads): The Case of Iranian Foundations', *Iranian Studies*, 37 (3), 479–98.

Salamey, I. and Pearson, F. (2007) 'Hezbollah: A Proletarian Party with an Islamic Manifesto – a Sociopolitical Analysis of Islamist Populism in Lebanon and the Middle East', *Small Wars and Insurgencies*, 18 (3), 416–38.

Singer, Amy (2008) *Charity in Islamic Societies*, Cambridge: Cambridge University Press.

Skocpol, T. (2000) 'Religion, Civil Society and Social Provision in the US', in M. J. Bane, B. Coffin and R. Thiemann (eds), *Who Will Provide? The Changing Role of Religion in American Social Welfare*, Boulder, CO: Westview Press, pp. 21–50.

Sutton, P. W. and Vertigans, S. (2005) *Resurgent Islam: A Sociological Approach*, Cambridge: Polity Press.

Underwood, Carol (2004) 'Islam and Health Policy: A Study of the Islamic Republic of Iran', in S. P. Heyneman (ed.), *Islam and Social Policy*, Nashville, TN: Vanderbilt University Press, pp. 181–206.

UNDP (United Nations Development Programme) (2002) *Arab Human Development Report 2002: Creating Opportunities for Future Generations*, New York: UNDP.

UNDP (United Nations Development Programme) (2009) *Arab Human Development Report 2009: Challenges to Human Security in the Arab Countries*, New York: UNDP.

UN-ESCWA (United Nations – Economic and Social Council for Western Asia) (2014), *Integrated Social Policy Report V: Towards a New Welfare Mix? Rethinking the Role of the State, the Market and Civil Society in the Provision of Social Protection and Social Services*, Beirut: UN-ESCWA.

20

ISLAMIC FINANCE, FINANCIAL INCLUSION AND POVERTY REDUCTION IN MENA

Amin Mohseni-Cheraghlou

Introduction

Over the past decade, financial inclusion – the proportion of individuals, households and firms using any kind of financial services – has entered the centre stage of many national and global policy debates. For example, the leaders of the G20 endorsed a Financial Inclusion Action Plan in the G20 Summit in Seoul in November 2010, which has resulted, among other things, in the collection and dissemination of data on the G20 Basic Set of Financial Inclusion Indicators through Global Partnership for Financial Inclusion (GPFI; Global Partnership for Financial Inclusion n.d.). Also, financial inclusion was the focus of the World Bank's second series of the *Global Financial Development Report*, which was released in November 2013 (World Bank 2013a). Finally, enhancing financial inclusion is now part of the mandate of about two-thirds of regulatory and supervisory bodies around the world, and many countries now have clearly defined targets for financial inclusion (World Bank 2013a). This increased interest is in turn due to recent theoretical and empirical findings that show access to a variety of complementary financial services has positive impacts on economic development and growth, and if done in an equitable and responsible manner it can also reduce poverty and inequality and boost shared prosperity (Beck *et al.* 2004; Levine 2005; World Bank 2007; Beck and Demirgüç-Kunt 2008; World Bank 2013a).

However, half of the world's adult population, about 2.5 billion adults, are without an account at a formal financial institution (Figure 20.1), with the Arab MENA region recording the lowest rate, at 18 per cent. While lacking an account at a formal financial institution is not always tantamount to lacking access to financial services, it is nevertheless a good proxy for financial inclusion (or exclusion), because most if not all forms of formal financial activities are often linked to formal accounts. Individuals or firms without a formal account are often forced to address their financial needs through the informal financial markets, which are often associated with higher costs and risks and little to no legal protections against frauds or breaches in the contract.

Another important caveat that needs to be heeded is that having an account at a formal financial institution is not equivalent to its usage. According to the Global Financial Inclusion (Global Findex) Dataset, about 8 per cent of adults with formal accounts do not use them and about 65 and 27 per cent of them use their accounts one to two times and three times or more

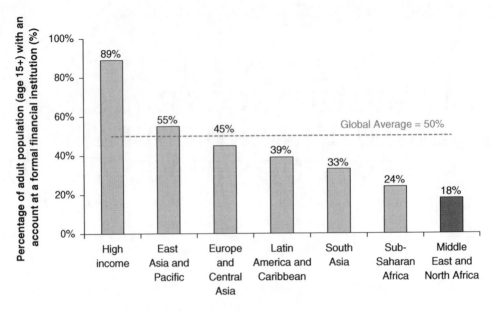

Figure 20.1 Account penetration rates by region, 2011

Source: World Bank (2011); author's calculation.

in a typical month, respectively (World Bank Data Bank 2014). The Global Findex also reports that in 2011 only 22 and 9 per cent of adults saved at and borrowed from formal financial institutions, respectively. However, it is clear that having an account is a necessary but not sufficient condition for its usage. As a result, account penetration rate measured as the percentage of adults (age 15 or over) with an account at a formal financial institution is a good starting point for measuring financial inclusion.

The high prevalence of financial exclusion alongside high adherence to Islam in the Arab MENA region (see Gallup World 2010) might lead us to examine whether the two are related, making it crucial to analyse the link between religiosity and financial exclusion in this region. Global Findex data reveal that, amongst the reasons given by individuals for not having a bank account, religious factors were the third-highest reason for not having an account in the MENA region, amounting to 12 per cent of unbanked individuals and around 17 million people in total. Therefore, it is imperative to examine the potential role of Islamic finance in increasing financial inclusion and therefore reducing poverty and boosting shared prosperity in this part of the world, which is plagued with below-average economic development and is home to more than 190 million poor people, which translates to more than half of its population.[1]

The rest of the chapter is organized as follows. The next section briefly highlights the potential benefits of enhanced financial inclusion for equitable growth, shared prosperity and poverty reduction. The chapter then discusses very briefly the various reasons for financial exclusion and briefly introduces the Global Findex Dataset. It then provides some preliminary findings on religious reasons for financial exclusion in predominantly Muslim countries in general and in the Arab MENA region (referred to as MENA region hereafter) specifically. The chapter goes on to address the role of Islamic finance in reducing religiously motivated financial exclusion. The final section concludes the discussion.

Financial inclusion, equitable growth and poverty reduction

Financial inclusion, if promoted responsibly, can be associated with significant benefits in terms of inclusive and equitable growth and poverty reduction. A 2013 World Bank report entitled *Financial Inclusion* provides a rich and comprehensive synthesis of the existing literature as well as the World Bank's own detailed research on this topic (World Bank 2013a). The report concludes that:

- There is a notable level of inequality in access to financial services. 'The poor, women, youth, and rural residents tend to face greater barriers to access financial services. Among firms, the younger and smaller ones are confronted by more binding constraints. For instance, in developing economies, 35 percent of small firms report that access to finance is a major obstacle to their operations, compared with 25 percent of large firms in developing economies and 8 percent of large firms in developed economies' (World Bank 2013b).
- Financial inclusion is important for equitable growth and poverty reduction. 'Considerable evidence indicates that the poor benefit enormously from basic payments, savings, and insurance services. For firms, particularly the small and young ones that are subject to greater constraints, access to finance is associated with innovation, job creation, and growth' (World Bank 2013b).
- Financial inclusion must be done responsibly to benefit the targeted population. This does not mean finance for all at all costs. 'Some individuals and firms have no material demand or business need for financial services. Efforts to subsidize these services are counterproductive and, in the case of credit, can lead to overindebtedness and financial instability' (World Bank 2013b).

Therefore it should not come as a surprise that access to financial services is strongly correlated with productivity, income and wealth, both within a country and across countries.

Reasons for financial exclusion

The reasons for financial exclusion, defined here as not having an account at a formal financial institution or being unbanked, are rooted in a complex set of economic, legal, social, political, cultural and personal factors but can be classified into two main categories: voluntary and involuntary reasons (Figure 20.2). As shown in Figure 20.2, some adults are financially excluded and voluntarily so because of religious considerations.

A new survey, the Global Findex Dataset,[2] is the first international database that makes it possible to get a first glimpse at the various aspects of financial exclusion at the individual level. In addition to many other questions, this survey asks the unbanked respondents (i.e. adults lacking a formal account) about the reason(s) as to why they do not have an account at a bank, credit union or other financial institution. The respondents in turn could choose one or more of the following reasons:

1   They are too far away.
2   They are too expensive.
3   You don't have the necessary documentation (ID, wage slip).
4   You don't trust them.
5   You don't have enough money to use them.
6   Because of religious reasons.
7   Because someone else in the family already has an account.

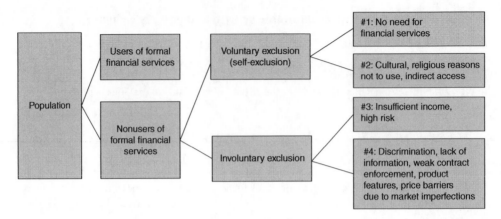

Figure 20.2 Financial exclusion

Source: World Bank (2013a)

Two notes are in order here. First, one can think of many more reasons for an individual not to have an account that are not part of the above seven reasons. For example, one can think of concerns with government taxes and identification of wealth, no need, preferences in using informal financial services, being illiterate and not knowing how to open an account as some other valid reasons for not having an account. Second, while allowing the selection of multiple reasons provides a more complete picture of the reasons behind an individual's lack of an account, this makes it impossible to identify the ultimate binding constraint facing the unbanked individuals who have provided more than one reason. For example, if a person has pointed to distance and costs (options 1 and 2 above) as her reasons for being unbanked, then we would have no way of knowing if she will remain unbanked if one of the obstacles (either distance or cost) is removed, presenting policy makers with a certain level of uncertainty.

Acknowledging these two caveats, this question nevertheless provides a valuable entry point for analysing the reasons why 2.5 billion adults around the globe are unbanked. According to this question, not having enough money is the most cited reason for being unbanked, followed by cost, another family member having an account, and distance (Figure 20.3), while exclusion for religious reasons is the least cited reason.

Reasons for exclusion vary across regions (Figure 20.4). While lack of sufficient funds was by far the most frequently cited reason for not having an account for unbanked adults in all regions, there was no other common similarity in reasons for exclusion among all regions. For example, lack of trust was the second most frequently cited reason for being unbanked in Europe and Central Asia (ECA), while being too expensive occupied the second position in Latin America and the Caribbean (LAC), the Middle East and North Africa (MENA) and Sub-Saharan Africa (SSA). Also, while religious factors were the third-highest reason for not having an account in MENA (12 per cent), this reason was cited least frequently by the unbanked adults in other regions.

The complex combination of social, economic, political, demographic, historical, security and legal factors in countries would make reasons for exclusion also vary widely across countries. A look at Table 20.1 highlights the stark differences between different countries even when they are in the same income group or region. For example, one can point to Afghanistan and Bangladesh, two South Asian low-income economies that have widely different account penetration rates and differ widely on reasons for exclusion. As an example, 32 per cent of unbanked

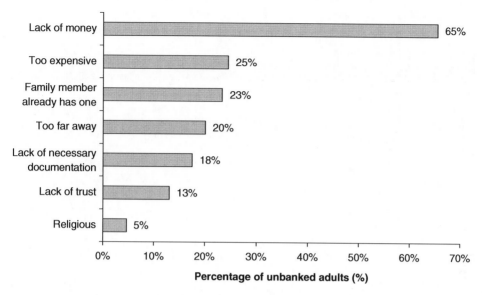

Figure 20.3 Reasons for financial exclusion, 2011

Source: World Bank (2011); author's calculation.

Note: Respondents could choose more than one reason.

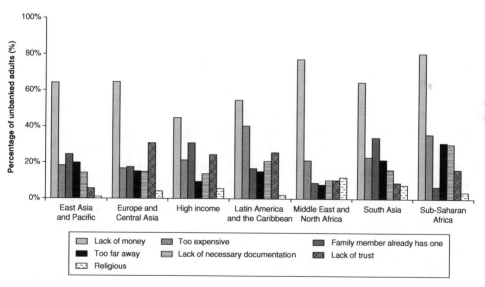

Figure 20.4 Reasons for financial exclusion by region, 2011

Source: World Bank (2011); author's calculation.

adults in Afghanistan reported religious reasons for not having an account, while this figure was only 4 per cent in Bangladesh. This is despite the fact that both countries have comparable ratios of Muslim population (98 per cent and 90 per cent in Afghanistan and Bangladesh, respectively) and religiosity levels[3] (97 per cent and 99 per cent in Afghanistan and Bangladesh, respectively).

Table 20.1 Reasons for financial exclusion by country, 2011

Country	Adults with no account (% age 15+)	Too far away (% unbanked adults)	Too expensive (% unbanked adults)	Lack of necessary documentation (% unbanked adults)	Lack of trust (% unbanked adults)	Lack of money (% unbanked adults)	Religious (% unbanked adults)	Family member already has one (% unbanked adults)
Afghanistan	91%	39%	37%	37%	37%	40%	32%	13%
Albania	72%	11%	14%	14%	12%	49%	7%	17%
Angola	60%	18%	30%	37%	21%	48%	11%	15%
Argentina	67%	5%	36%	20%	27%	62%	1%	13%
Armenia	83%	8%	23%	17%	24%	74%	0%	5%
Australia	1%	0%	0%	0%	0%	34%	0%	24%
Austria	1%	0%	4%	1%	3%	20%	0%	8%
Azerbaijan	85%	5%	16%	22%	20%	68%	5%	6%
Bangladesh	60%	13%	30%	10%	9%	71%	4%	23%
Belarus	41%	20%	14%	13%	28%	65%	3%	24%
Belgium	2%	0%	3%	5%	1%	0%	0%	34%
Benin	90%	23%	26%	37%	24%	91%	2%	5%
Bolivia	72%	35%	41%	15%	34%	52%	2%	14%
Bosnia and Herzegovina	43%	14%	35%	46%	19%	53%	1%	36%
Botswana	70%	36%	35%	46%	19%	89%	5%	9%
Brazil	44%	15%	42%	25%	19%	62%	1%	29%
Bulgaria	47%	10%	12%	11%	25%	83%	0%	20%
Burkina Faso	87%	30%	28%	21%	9%	90%	1%	2%
Burundi	93%	15%	39%	9%	7%	87%	2%	1%
Cambodia	96%	15%	10%	10%	15%	87%	4%	2%
Cameroon	85%	24%	27%	11%	29%	79%	1%	1%
Canada	4%	20%	30%	1%	11%	16%	0%	44%
Chad	91%	40%	37%	42%	23%	60%	9%	13%
Chile	58%	10%	45%	23%	37%	65%	2%	11%
China	36%	13%	8%	7%	3%	57%	0%	31%
Colombia	70%	10%	47%	17%	30%	61%	2%	15%
Comoros	78%	9%	15%	22%	10%	82%	6%	6%
Congo, Democratic Republic	96%	34%	26%	22%	23%	71%	2%	1%

Congo, Republic	91%	11%	13%	26%	9%	81%	0%	2%
Costa Rica	50%	9%	19%	16%	20%	33%	2%	21%
Croatia	11%	10%	11%	20%	13%	53%	0%	36%
Cyprus	15%	3%	7%	1%	8%	34%	1%	29%
Czech Republic	19%	11%	45%	10%	41%	69%	3%	46%
Denmark	0%	0%	0%	30%	0%	30%	0%	30%
Djibouti	**87%**	**20%**	**31%**	**24%**	**18%**	**69%**	**22%**	**13%**
Dominican Republic	62%	4%	15%	14%	11%	73%	1%	6%
Ecuador	63%	18%	38%	21%	29%	53%	4%	14%
Egypt, Arab Republic	**90%**	**1%**	**13%**	**5%**	**2%**	**95%**	**3%**	**2%**
El Salvador	86%	16%	29%	24%	19%	38%	3%	7%
Estonia	3%	16%	14%	6%	8%	36%	2%	40%
Finland	0%	9%	9%	0%	0%	0%	0%	9%
France	2%	17%	3%	21%	0%	21%	5%	51%
Gabon	81%	20%	32%	30%	15%	84%	1%	2%
Georgia	67%	7%	18%	17%	12%	80%	1%	9%
Germany	1%	4%	4%	20%	16%	17%	0%	28%
Ghana	71%	28%	21%	22%	17%	83%	2%	5%
Greece	22%	7%	10%	4%	21%	73%	2%	44%
Guatemala	78%	18%	31%	28%	24%	61%	5%	14%
Guinea	96%	22%	22%	26%	7%	89%	5%	2%
Haiti	78%	25%	35%	34%	31%	67%	9%	8%
Honduras	79%	20%	24%	19%	21%	52%	4%	13%
Hong Kong SAR, China	11%	31%	37%	46%	27%	77%	14%	57%
Hungary	27%	10%	39%	6%	29%	70%	0%	27%
India	65%	23%	24%	17%	8%	63%	8%	41%
Indonesia	80%	37%	43%	27%	9%	83%	1%	9%
Iraq	**89%**	**15%**	**17%**	**13%**	**32%**	**66%**	**24%**	**10%**
Ireland	6%	16%	31%	10%	9%	35%	4%	53%
Israel	9%	6%	26%	28%	21%	60%	3%	37%
Italy	25%	0%	19%	5%	9%	32%	0%	29%
Jamaica	27%	3%	12%	20%	12%	51%	3%	9%
Japan	2%	6%	0%	26%	0%	7%	0%	39%
Jordan	**75%**	**3%**	**23%**	**4%**	**1%**	**70%**	**10%**	**27%**
Kazakhstan	57%	12%	13%	16%	20%	58%	2%	22%

(continued)

Table 20.1 (continued)

Country	Adults with no account (% age 15+)	Too far away (% unbanked adults)	Too expensive (% unbanked adults)	Lack of necessary documentation (% unbanked adults)	Lack of trust (% unbanked adults)	Lack of money (% unbanked adults)	Religious (% unbanked adults)	Family member already has one (% unbanked adults)
Kenya	58%	35%	43%	25%	12%	88%	4%	5%
Korea, Republic	7%	13%	9%	14%	7%	30%	0%	45%
Kosovo	55%	12%	17%	12%	12%	40%	10%	33%
Kuwait	**13%**	**2%**	**15%**	**32%**	**3%**	**32%**	**2%**	**81%**
Kyrgyz Republic	96%	32%	18%	11%	21%	73%	7%	3%
Lao PDR	73%	21%	13%	8%	7%	85%	1%	8%
Latvia	10%	11%	4%	4%	13%	64%	0%	38%
Lebanon	**63%**	**2%**	**27%**	**1%**	**7%**	**82%**	**7%**	**19%**
Lesotho	82%	49%	51%	33%	14%	84%	3%	11%
Liberia	81%	36%	29%	43%	30%	71%	6%	12%
Lithuania	26%	6%	12%	11%	28%	71%	0%	40%
Luxembourg	4%	2%	5%	4%	5%	32%	2%	59%
Macedonia, FYR	26%	15%	19%	25%	22%	58%	7%	43%
Malawi	83%	13%	25%	17%	10%	89%	1%	2%
Malaysia	33%	27%	16%	35%	3%	56%	0%	26%
Mali	92%	35%	21%	23%	8%	87%	3%	2%
Malta	5%	1%	5%	2%	9%	38%	0%	32%
Mauritania	83%	31%	29%	23%	24%	66%	16%	13%
Mauritius	20%	7%	8%	19%	8%	66%	2%	31%
Mexico	71%	19%	47%	21%	29%	35%	2%	12%
Moldova	82%	12%	29%	12%	28%	87%	2%	7%
Mongolia	22%	18%	5%	8%	7%	61%	0%	49%
Montenegro	49%	5%	13%	18%	19%	65%	5%	32%
Morocco	**61%**	**18%**	**49%**	**36%**	**22%**	**60%**	**25%**	**32%**
Mozambique	60%	13%	18%	27%	10%	78%	2%	10%
Nepal	74%	25%	25%	9%	6%	71%	1%	18%
Netherlands	0%	0%	8%	0%	0%	8%	0%	26%
New Zealand	0%	13%	0%	0%	75%	13%	0%	75%
Nicaragua	86%	17%	25%	27%	18%	36%	10%	11%

Niger	98%	68%	54%	59%	37%	92%	23%	4%
Nigeria	70%	30%	37%	40%	13%	83%	3%	8%
Oman	**26%**	**13%**	**17%**	**21%**	**19%**	**56%**	**15%**	**54%**
Pakistan	89%	14%	13%	14%	8%	71%	7%	9%
Panama	75%	20%	28%	40%	34%	33%	10%	22%
Paraguay	78%	9%	11%	8%	20%	72%	5%	14%
Peru	79%	24%	55%	16%	37%	54%	2%	11%
Philippines	73%	34%	51%	42%	14%	78%	7%	26%
Poland	29%	11%	24%	15%	24%	68%	1%	27%
Portugal	15%	1%	9%	2%	10%	23%	1%	11%
Romania	55%	11%	19%	12%	23%	69%	0%	13%
Russian Federation	51%	12%	15%	13%	38%	69%	4%	22%
Rwanda	67%	24%	38%	19%	6%	88%	1%	7%
Saudi Arabia	**53%**	**5%**	**12%**	**13%**	**10%**	**45%**	**23%**	**51%**
Senegal	94%	28%	37%	34%	13%	84%	6%	5%
Serbia	37%	10%	18%	22%	17%	58%	1%	35%
Sierra Leone	85%	37%	44%	42%	20%	82%	9%	7%
Singapore	2%	0%	16%	0%	6%	71%	0%	28%
Slovak Republic	20%	15%	44%	11%	29%	75%	0%	41%
Slovenia	3%	5%	24%	21%	6%	63%	0%	66%
South Africa	46%	34%	40%	23%	18%	73%	3%	12%
Spain	7%	19%	30%	19%	32%	52%	9%	42%
Sri Lanka	31%	26%	17%	13%	12%	67%	2%	27%
Sudan	93%	23%	45%	27%	13%	82%	4%	15%
Swaziland	71%	30%	34%	38%	13%	72%	6%	10%
Sweden	1%	0%	19%	39%	10%	10%	0%	0%
Syrian Arab Republic	**77%**	**9%**	**33%**	**0%**	**4%**	**27%**	**15%**	**2%**
Taiwan, China	12%	7%	9%	10%	7%	43%	6%	44%
Tajikistan	97%	28%	18%	22%	21%	78%	8%	4%
Tanzania	83%	48%	46%	35%	13%	78%	4%	8%
Thailand	27%	13%	9%	4%	3%	57%	1%	47%
Togo	90%	27%	20%	32%	17%	91%	1%	2%
Trinidad and Tobago	21%	4%	35%	38%	13%	67%	1%	10%
Tunisia	**68%**	**15%**	**25%**	**17%**	**18%**	**73%**	**26%**	**20%**
Turkey	42%	13%	26%	21%	26%	48%	7%	20%

(continued)

Table 20.1 (continued)

Country	Adults with no account (% age 15+)	Too far away (% unbanked adults)	Too expensive (% unbanked adults)	Lack of necessary documentation (% unbanked adults)	Lack of trust (% unbanked adults)	Lack of money (% unbanked adults)	Religious (% unbanked adults)	Family member already has one (% unbanked adults)
Turkmenistan	100%	36%	12%	21%	10%	52%	10%	3%
Uganda	80%	42%	54%	38%	23%	85%	3%	7%
Ukraine	59%	24%	19%	11%	55%	67%	4%	18%
United Kingdom	2%	20%	29%	10%	32%	21%	6%	13%
United States	11%	14%	28%	17%	46%	49%	7%	19%
Uruguay	76%	7%	26%	8%	19%	70%	0%	5%
Uzbekistan	77%	19%	7%	16%	15%	60%	6%	9%
Venezuela, RB	55%	8%	16%	3%	16%	75%	0%	15%
Vietnam	78%	13%	8%	13%	9%	50%	1%	12%
West Bank and Gaza	**81%**	**3%**	**23%**	**5%**	**12%**	**67%**	**24%**	**18%**
Yemen, Republic	**96%**	**13%**	**17%**	**9%**	**8%**	**86%**	**9%**	**3%**
Zambia	79%	21%	50%	32%	9%	85%	1%	6%
Zimbabwe	60%	14%	39%	27%	20%	82%	1%	8%

Source: World Bank (2011); author's calculation.

Note: MENA countries are in bold.

Financially excluded for religious reasons: who and where?

As seen earlier about 5 per cent (or 125 million) of the unbanked adults around the world reported religious reasons for not having an account. But who are these adults, to which religion do they adhere, and in which region and countries do they reside? As the following examples seem to demonstrate, all three Abrahamic religions (Judaism, Christianity and Islam) appear to prohibit interest-based financial transactions, also termed 'usury'. However, it can sometimes be unclear whether usury refers to the excessive charging of interest or the charging of any interest at all. The following examples are from the Old Testament, which is a key text both for Jews and for Christians, and the Qur'an, which are among many that prohibit interest or usury (in Arabic *riba*):[4]

> Deuteronomy 23/19: Thou shalt not lend upon interest to thy brother: interest of money, interest of victuals, interest of anything that is lent upon interest.
>
> *(Webster Bible* n.d.)

> Qur'an 2/275: Those who charge usury are in the same position as those controlled by Satan's influence. This is because they claim that usury is the same as commerce. However, God permits commerce, and prohibits usury. Thus, whoever heeds this commandment from his Lord, and refrains from usury, he may keep his past earnings, and his judgment rests with God. As for those who persist in usury, they incur Hell, wherein they abide forever.[5]

> Furthermore, one can find demeaning references to usurers in the sacred texts of Hinduism and Buddhism:

> For example, Vasishtha, a well-known Hindu law-maker of that time, made a special law which forbade the higher castes of Brahmanas (priests) and Kshatriyas (warriors) from being usurers or lenders at interest. Also, in the Jatakas, usury is referred to in a demeaning manner: 'hypocritical ascetics are accused of practicing it'.
>
> (Visser and McIntosh 1998: 176)

Therefore, the original teachings of world religions (having 84 per cent of the world's religious adults as followers; CIA 2012) certainly problematize and question usury and in some instances also seem to forbid it altogether, considering it a grave sin or a demeaning practice unfitting for honourable and dignified individuals. However, in the current times, Muslims and especially those in MENA seem to be more conscious of this prohibition than the followers of other religions.

A review of Table 20.1 shows that the unbanked adults in Muslim majority countries tend to have a higher likelihood of citing religious reasons for not having an account. This information in summarized in Figure 20.5. As evident from this figure, 28 out of 47 countries where religious reasons are chosen by at least 4 per cent of the unbanked adults are those countries where Muslims constitute a majority of the total population (highlighted in green and red bars). From these 28 countries, 11 are located in the MENA region (highlighted in red bars). It important here to realize that, while about 5 per cent of adults worldwide cited religious reasons for not having an account, financial exclusion rates because of religious reasons are above 20 per cent for only eight countries, six of which are located in the MENA region. Furthermore nine MENA countries have financial exclusion rates because of religious reasons at 10 per cent or more. Overall, an estimated 13 per cent of the unbanked adults in the MENA region cited religious reasons for being financially excluded. This translates to about 17 million of MENA's adult population.[6]

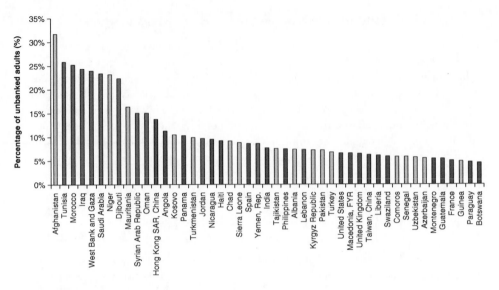

Figure 20.5 Financially excluded for religious reasons, 2011

Source: World Bank (2011); author's calculation.

Note: Light grey and *mid-grey* bars refer to countries where followers of Islam constitute 60 per cent or more of the population. *Mid-grey* bars refer to countries in the MENA region.

Moreover, Figure 20.6 confirms that self-identified non–Muslims are about twice as likely to have an account as their Muslim counterparts (44 per cent versus 24 per cent). This gap is about 13 percentage points in the MENA region.

Cross-country regression results in Table 20.2[7] also show that residing in the MENA region is the most important determining factor for being financially excluded because of religious reasons, followed by share of Muslim population in a given country.

Overall then, the above findings suggest that financial exclusion for religious reasons is a phenomenon that is predominantly associated with the MENA region, followed by other Muslim majority countries. About 10 per cent of all adults (or 13 per cent of the unbanked adults) in the MENA region try completely to avoid formal financial institutions that are not Shari'ah-compliant (i.e. are not in accordance with the Islamic legal system) by not even opening an account in such institutions, therefore voluntarily excluding themselves from the many potential benefits of financial services that were highlighted earlier in this chapter.

Islamic finance and financial inclusion

Based on the evidence presented thus far it could be argued that enhancing the size of and access to Shari'ah-compliant Islamic financial products can reduce voluntary financial exclusion for religious reasons. In other words, if the earlier findings are true, one should expect to see a negative correlation between the density of Shari'ah-compliant financial services and the percentage of adults who are unbanked for religious reasons. Table 20.3 provides some evidence supporting this hypothesis. The negative and statistically significant coefficients for two different measures of density of Shari'ah compliance show that, after controlling for other relevant factors, the percentages of people who report religious reasons for not having an account are lower in countries where Islamic finance has a stronger presence.

304

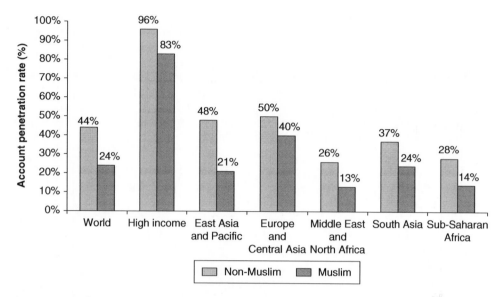

Figure 20.6 Differences in financial inclusion between Muslims and non-Muslims, 2011

Source: Demirgüç-Kunt *et al.* (2013).

Note: The difference between Muslims and non-Muslim is statistically significant at the 1 per cent level. Analysis is based on 64 countries. Countries with less than 1 per cent and more than 99 per cent Muslim population are excluded from the analysis.

This suggests that increasing the presence of formal Shari'ah-compliant financial services in countries with a considerable Muslim population could reduce the level of voluntary exclusion from financial markets for religious reasons. At the very minimum, this is certainly true for at least 13 million adults who, according to Global Findex Dataset, cited only religious reasons for not having an account, more than 11 million of whom are residing in countries with 90 per cent or more Muslim population.

Furthermore, Table 20.4 provides some anecdotal evidence that increasing the share of Shari'ah-compliant assets vis-à-vis total banking assets in a country can help reduce the percentage of small firms that cite access to finance as a major obstacle in their operations. This is in line with the fact that small firms are often managed and operated by members of a family, where religious considerations are more likely to enter their financing decisions than for larger firms, which are often operated by professional executives.

Several recent case studies from other regions have also highlighted the potential role of Islamic finance in reducing voluntary financial exclusion among the Muslim population in both Muslim majority and Muslim minority countries. For example, Adeyemi *et al.* (2012) show that Islamic microfinance can in fact provide financial services to a considerable segment of Nigerian society who for religious reasons avoid dealings with conventional financial institutions. Also, according to the 2006 Sachar Committee Report on the social, economic and educational status of the Muslim community of India (Government of India 2006), the share of Muslims in amount outstanding is about 4.6 per cent, while that of other minorities is about 6.5 per cent, which is disproportionate to their share in India's population (13.4 per cent for Muslims and 5.6 per cent for other minorities). Therefore in a joint report prepared by Infinity Consultants and Ethica Institute of Islamic Finance, it is proposed that only through increasing the presence of Islamic finance in India's financial fabric can the Indian government increase the use of financial

Table 20.2 Determinants of financial exclusion for religious reasons

	Model 1	Model 2	Model 3	Model 4	Model 5	Model 6	Model 7	Model 8	Model 9
GDP (2005 $ billion)	0.000061	0.000255	0.000091	0.00028*	0.00034*	0.00158	0.00032*	0.00054***	0.00036*
GDP per capita, PPP (2005 $ international thousand)	-0.0694*	-0.0110	0.0152	0.0236	-0.0416	-0.0892	-0.0256	-0.123	-0.0666
Muslim population (% total population)		0.0927***		0.0914***	0.0762***	0.0512***	0.0755***	0.0624***	0.0626***
Religiosity (% adults)			0.0745***	0.0258	-0.0160	-0.00866	-0.0172	-0.0209	-0.0190
East Asia and Pacific dummy					-1.480	-1.907	-1.953	-1.674	-1.802
Europe and Central Asia dummy					-1.476	-0.233	-2.071	-1.487	-1.695
Latin America and the Caribbean dummy					1.291	0.499	0.978	0.915	0.646
Middle East and North Africa dummy					6.493*	7.997**	5.906*	9.447**	8.926**
South Asia dummy					3.018	-3.642	2.044	2.789	2.982
Sub-Saharan Africa dummy					-0.224	-2.991	-2.382	-1.318	-1.322
Literacy rate (% people 15+)						-0.0964			
Life expectancy at birth							-0.116		
Commercial bank branches per 100,000 adults								-0.00142	
Commercial bank branches per 1,000 km²									0.00791***
Observations	133	133	102	102	102	83	102	86	86
R-squared	0.024	0.361	0.071	0.364	0.455	0.536	0.459	0.500	0.546

Note: OLS regression with robust standard errors. *p<0.10, **p<0.05, ***p<0.01. Dependent variable is the percentage of adults reporting religious reasons for not having an account, which is taken from World Bank (2011).

Table 20.3 Density of Shari'ah-compliant assets and financial exclusion for religious reasons

	Model 1	Model 2
GDP (2005 $ billion)	0.000527★★★	0.000420★★★
GDP per capita, PPP (2005 $ international thousand)	−0.0791★	−0.0405
Religiosity (% adults)	0.00559	0.0102
Muslim population (% total)	0.0718★★★	0.0623★★
Middle East and North Africa dummy	11.97★★★	11.31★★★
Commercial bank branches per 1,000 km²	0.00748★★	0.00636★
Ratio of Shari'ah-compliant assets to total assets (%)	−0.296★★★	
Shari'ah-compliant assets per adult ($ 000s)		−0.563★★★
Observations	85	86
R-squared	0.588	0.557

Source: Shari'ah-compliant (Islamic) assets and total assets from Bankscope.

Note: OLS regression with robust standard errors. ★p<0.10, ★★p<0.05, ★★★p<0.01. Dependent variable is the percentage of adults reporting religious reasons for not having an account, which is taken from World Bank (2011). Only those variables that were significant in at least one of the models in Table 20.2 were included in these regressions.

Table 20.4 Density of Shari'ah-compliant assets and financial obstacles for firms

	All firms	Small firms	Medium firms	Large firms
GDP (2005 $ billion)	0.00527	0.00256	0.00437	0.0117
GDP per capita, PPP (2005 $ international thousand)	−0.648★	−0.670★★	−0.466	−0.578
Religiosity (% adults)	0.0449	0.0903	−0.0282	0.0311
Muslim population (% total)	−0.0107	−0.0219	0.00266	0.00703
East Asia and Pacific dummy	−7.151	−4.761	−0.674	−14.36
Europe and Central Asia dummy	6.191	8.228	6.648	4.250
Latin America and the Caribbean dummy	2.243	3.251	5.120	−6.898
Middle East and North Africa dummy	14.63	21.39★★★	22.01	38.76
South Asia dummy	−2.692	−1.287	3.233	−7.182
Sub-Saharan Africa dummy	17.36★	20.30★★	19.21★	0.186
Commercial bank branches per 1,000 km²	0.0419	0.169	−0.0225	−0.214
Ratio of Shari'ah-compliant assets to total assets (%)	−0.0723	−0.157★★★	−0.389	−0.744
Observations	68	68	68	68
R-squared	0.475	0.482	0.375	0.384

Source: Shari'ah-compliant (Islamic) assets and total assets from Bankscope.

Note: OLS regression with robust standard errors. ★p<0.10, ★★p<0.05, ★★★p<0.01. Dependent variable is the percentage of firms reporting access to finance as a major obstacle in their operations, which is taken from World Bank (2014). Only those variables that were significant in at least one of the models in Table 20.2 were included in these regressions.

services by its largest minority group, the 180 million Muslims residing in India (Ahmed 2012), adding to the economic growth of India while at the same time increasing the well-being of and reducing poverty among its poverty-ridden Muslim population.

Over the past few years an increasing number of Muslim and non-Muslim policy makers, bank governors and politicians have also shown growing interest for a more pronounced presence of Islamic finance in the global financial architecture because of its potentially important role in enhancing financial inclusion. In her Islamic Development Bank (IDB) Prize Lecture in November 2013, Zeti Akhtar Aziz, governor of the Central Bank of Malaysia (Bank Negara Malaysia), referred to the potential role of Islamic financing models in enhancing financial inclusion (Aziz 2013). Again, in November 2013, the governor of the Central Bank of Nigeria, Lamido Sanusi, identified Islamic finance as having the capacity to increase financial inclusion among a large segment of the population in Nigeria (*BusinessNews* 2013). In September 2013, Nestor Espenilla, deputy governor of the Bangko Sentral Pilipinas (BSP), the Philippines' central bank, laid out one of the most ambitious efforts in the world in introducing Islamic finance in a Muslim minority country, in an endeavour to enhance financial inclusion among the Muslim population of the Philippines (Lema and Vizcaino 2013). Finally, in December 2013, the IMF director of the Middle East and Central Asia Department, Masood Ahmed, highlighted the fact that, if properly regulated, faster expansion of Islamic finance in MENA can lead to higher levels of financial inclusion among the religiously minded population (IMF 2013).

Based on the above, it is therefore safe to suggest that Islamic (i.e. Shari'ah-compliant) finance can play a non-trivial role in enhancing financial inclusion among the unbanked adults in MENA. For example, risk-sharing contracts (such as *murabaha*, *musharaka* and *mudaraba*) and wealth redistribution instruments in the Islamic financial system (such as *zakat*, *sadaqa* and *qard hassan*) are the two main mechanisms through which Islamic finance could promote financial inclusion, boost shared prosperity and reduce poverty and inequality.

Shari'ah-compliant risk-sharing contracts can provide access to finance and insurance (*takaful*) for micro, small and medium enterprises (MSMEs). This is crucial because, as pointed out by the World Bank's (2014) *Enterprise Survey*, somewhere between 30 and 40 per cent of all small and medium-sized firms in MENA countries identify access to finance as a major constraint in their operations. Furthermore, built into the Islamic law and code of ethics are mandatory almsgiving and voluntary almsgiving, known as *zakat* and *sadaqa* respectively, with *qard hassan*[8] falling between the two. Through analysing the available data for nine MENA countries, Mohieldin *et al.* (2011) find that, if implemented effectively, *zakat* funds in all these countries are more than sufficient to eliminate the extreme poverty, measured as having an income of less than \$1.25 a day.[9]

It must however be pointed out here that, while increasing the availability of Islamic finance is a necessary ingredient for increasing access to finance and insurance for the poor households and MSMEs, other supporting factors such as adequate physical, legal, financial, regulatory and educational infrastructure must also be in place for Islamic finance to operate effectively and efficiently. It is a reality that most MENA countries lack many of these necessary pre-requisites, creating extra hurdles for the efficient operation of Shari'ah-compliant financial institutions in MENA. As a result, community-based local formal institutions providing Islamic financing schemes seem to be the most appropriate avenue for boosting financial inclusion among the estimated 54 million extremely poor[10] or the 190 million poor[11] residing in the MENA region. *Murabaha* (cost plus mark-up sale contract) and *qard hassan* (benevolent interest-free loan) are examples of such community-based Islamic financing programmes, which are the most popular forms of Islamic microfinance schemes in the MENA region and other Muslim majority countries such as Indonesia, Pakistan and Bangladesh (Figure 20.7). These schemes are practically risk-free financial instruments suitable for the vulnerable and the poor who would otherwise have no form of access to financial services, increasing their chance of moving out of poverty by providing a temporary financial breathing space, increasing financial literacy and capability, and building credit history.

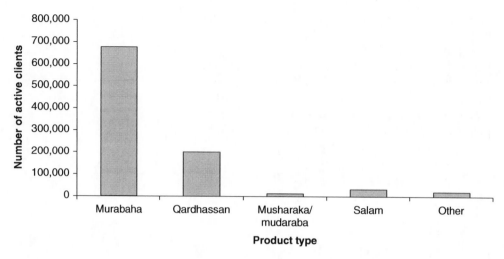

Figure 20.7 Islamic microfinance schemes, number of active clients, by product type

Source: El-Zoghbi and Tarazi (2013).

Note: Countries included are Afghanistan, Bangladesh, Burkina Faso, Cambodia, Cameroon, Côte d'Ivoire, Egypt, Indonesia, Iraq, Jordan, Kosovo, Lebanon, Pakistan, Palestine (West Bank and Gaza), Saudi Arabia, Sri Lanka, Sudan, Syria and Yemen.

In addition to *murabaha, qard hassan, zakat* and *sadaqa*, there are many other financing schemes that are in compliance with Islamic Shari'ah (i.e. the Islamic legal system). Table 20.5 provides a brief overview of these financing instruments, most of which are suitable for the poor and the vulnerable. Clearly, the availability of these financial instruments to the Muslim population of MENA would increase the participation of religiously minded individuals and firms (especially the poor and the vulnerable) in the financial sector of the economy, therefore leading to more stable, equitable, inclusive and robust growth rates in the MENA economies.

It is also interesting, from a policy perspective, to note that, in comparison to those who did not cite religious reasons, the unbanked adults who cited religious reasons are significantly more likely also to cite other reasons, except lack of money. This differentiation is more evident in the case of lack of trust, where the gap between the two groups is about 30 percentage points, followed closely by lack of necessary documentation (Figure 20.8). In other words, those who cite religious reasons are much more likely also to report lack of trust and lack of documentation as reasons for not having an account, followed by other reasons. In the case of lack of money the two groups behave more or less similarly.

This alongside the earlier findings suggests that, in addition to increasing and deepening the presence of Shari'ah-compliant financial institutions in their countries, financial inclusion policies in the MENA and other Muslim majority countries must pay close attention to increasing the trust in these institutions (and the banking sector in general) and reducing bureaucratic hurdles for opening an account. The development of transparent and internationally and nationally recognized standardization and accreditation processes can play a significant role in increasing trust in the compliance of the Islamic banks with Shari'ah rules. Other necessary, but relatively less important, factors are reducing cost and addressing the distance barrier, by increasing the number of physical branches in remote areas, establishing branches in densely populated areas and/or developing correspondent and mobile banking platforms.

Table 20.5 Overview of main Islamic financial instruments

Financing scheme	Brief description	Most appropriate population target
Mudaraba	The supplier of capital contracts (the lender) and a working partner (the borrower) on the basis of sharing the resulting profits. Losses, if any, are considered loss of capital and borne by the owner of capital. The working partner, in that case, goes unrewarded for its efforts. This is the 'loss' borne by the working partner, a feature of mudaraba which has led some to characterize it as 'profit and loss sharing' (PLS). The sharing contract when applied to farming is called muzara'ah or share-cropping.	Poor or non-poor who lack capital but have skills to carry out or manage a specific business operation.
Musharaka	Two or more parties supply capital as well as work/effort. They share the resulting profits according to agreed proportions, but losses are to be borne in proportion to the respective capitals.	Non-poor.
Murabaha	A sale agreement under which a seller purchases goods desired by a buyer and sells it to him/her at an agreed marked-up price, but with a deferral of payment as agreed in the contract.	Poor or non-poor who are able to pay for an item they need (either for small business or household use) in installments.
Takaful	An Islamic insurance concept based on pooling risks through cooperative and mutual insurance schemes where risks are spread across members. In this system members contribute certain sums to a common pool. In this scheme the objective is not to make profit.	Poor or non-poor.
Muzara'ah	An agreement between two parties in which one agrees to allow a portion of his/her land to be used by the other in return for a part of the produce of the land.	Poor or non-poor who lack capital but have skills to carry out agricultural operations.
Salam	Payment is made now for agricultural products to be delivered at a specified time in the future with the price being agreed now.	Poor or non-poor.
Istisna'	Salam applied to manufactured goods, with the possibility of payment in installments as the goods are delivered.	Poor or non-poor.
Ijara	The leasing of a property, capital good or any other good.	Poor or non-poor.
Sukuk	Bonds that are in compliance with Shari'ah, which are based on partial ownership of the debt, asset, investment or business. The issuer of a sukuk sells the certificate to an investor, who then rents it back to the issuer for a predetermined rental fee. The issuer also makes a contractual promise to buy back the bonds at a future date at face value.	Non-poor.
Qard	Interest-free loan.	Poor or non-poor.
Qard hassan	A charitable type of loan which, in addition to being a qard (interest-free loan), also contains elements of good will, benevolence and generosity whereby the lender, depending on circumstance, is willing to relax some or all of the terms of the loan contract, including the agreed-upon repayment schedule.	Poor and also non-poor who are at risk of poverty if not financially supported.
Zakat	Mandatory transfer of a small percentage of one's surplus income or capital to the poor.	Poor.
Sadaqa	Voluntary transfer of money or any form of capital to the poor.	Poor.

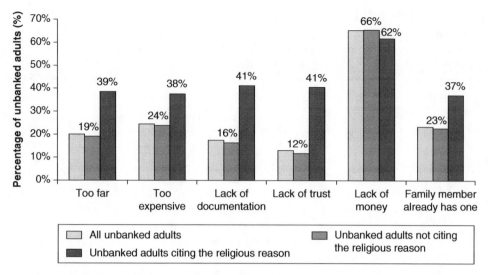

Figure 20.8 Religious reasons and other reasons for not having an account
Source: World Bank (2011); author's calculation.

Conclusion

According to the 2011 Global Findex Dataset, more than 125 million adults around the world avoid interactions with formal financial institutions for religious reasons. This chapter and Demirgüç-Kunt *et al.* (2013) have shown that Muslims, and especially those residing in MENA, are more likely to be financially excluded for religious reasons. This chapter suggests that the percentage of unbanked adults for religious reasons is positively correlated with being situated in the MENA region and with the share of Muslim population in a given country and negatively correlated with the density of Shari'ah-compliant financial assets in an economy. These findings point to the potential role of Islamic finance in enhancing financial inclusion and its many benefits for reducing poverty and inequality among Muslim communities around the world and especially in some of the MENA countries, where financial exclusion for religious reasons is among the highest in the world.

The presence of this relatively large population that has opted out of currently available financial services provides a great business opportunity for Islamic financial institutions (IFIs) to service their financial needs. However, several obstacles have hindered the growth of this industry, the most important of which has been the lack of transparency and the absence of a broadly accepted standardized process for assessing the compliance of financial institutions with Shari'ah guidelines. This has made it difficult for many individuals to distinguish between financial institutions that are genuinely operating based on Shari'ah specifications and those institutions that are not. The establishment of the Islamic Financial Service Board (IFSB) in 2003, as an internationally recognized body of regulators and supervisors for developing and disseminating Shari'ah-compliant standards in Islamic finance, has been a significant positive step in this regard.

Another main difficulty has been the lack of information and training on Islamic finance. For example, only about 48 per cent of adults in five MENA countries (i.e. Algeria, Egypt, Morocco, Tunisia and Yemen) have heard about Islamic banks (Demirgüç-Kunt *et al.* 2013). Here the recent opening of the Global Centre for Islamic Finance housed in the Borsa Istanbul (or Istanbul Stock Exchange), which is envisioned to act as a global knowledge and research hub for the development of Islamic finance, can prove to be beneficial (World Bank 2013c). The growing number of higher education institutions offering certification as well as undergraduate and graduate degrees in Islamic economics, banking, finance, insurance and investment will also increase awareness and understanding of the Islamic financial industry around the globe. One such newly established but highly promising institution that has become globally recognized for the quality of its programme and its famed faculty is the International Centre for Education in Islamic Finance (see INCEIF n.d.).

Finally and partly because of the lack of a standardized process and shortage of human resources in the field of Islamic finance, it is usually the case that Islamic financial products are more expensive than their conventional counterparts, reducing their competitiveness among the faithful Muslims despite their clear religious appeal. In this regard, while improvement in standardized processes and training can help reduce costs facing IFIs, the issue of scale must certainly be addressed in order for the relatively newly established IFIs to have the capacity and breathing space to compete with their conventional counterparts. Supportive government policies and regulations towards the promotion of Islamic finance and its competitiveness in the financial industry are necessary. Here, the World Bank's recent growing interest in the potential of Islamic finance in promoting financial inclusion and shared prosperity is promising. With the signing of memoranda of understanding with the Islamic Development Bank (IDB) and INCEIF, the recent opening of the Global Centre for Islamic Finance, which is a common project between the Turkish government and the World Bank, and an increasing volume of World Bank publications on topics related to Islamic finance, the World Bank has formally entered Islamic finance policy and research circles. Therefore, the World Bank could act as a key conduit for knowledge and expertise and provide technical assistance for countries interested in the role of Islamic finance for enhancing financial inclusion and shared prosperity.

In the end, as with their conventional counterparts, Shari'ah-compliant financial institutions and markets do not operate in a vacuum, and their performances are affected by the economic, political, legal, educational and social contexts within which they operate. Therefore, increasing the presence of Islamic finance is only a necessary but not a sufficient factor in boosting financial inclusion among religiously minded Muslims in the MENA region.

Notes

1 Measured at $4 a day international poverty line. See Vishwanath and Serajuddin (2012).
2 See World Bank (2011). The 11 out of 18 MENA countries included in this survey are Algeria, Djibouti, Egypt, Iraq, Jordan, Lebanon, Morocco, Syria, Tunisia, West Bank and Gaza, and Yemen.
3 Religiosity level represents the percentage of adults in a given country who responded affirmatively to the question 'Is religion an important part of your daily life?' in a 2010 Gallup poll (Gallup World 2010).
4 With respect to charging interest on monetary loans, some Islamic scholars have argued that interest rates indexed to inflation are not *riba* and therefore are sanctioned in Islam. Using the famous concept of *Laa Dharara wa Laa Dheraar* ('one should not be harmed and should not harm') in the Islamic legal system, it has been argued that money is solely a measure of account and medium of exchange, the value of which is not fixed. Therefore, if interest is not paid to the lender on money loaned in line with the rate of inflation, the lender would be harmed, as the lender's purchasing power would be diminished over time, and ever more so in a high-inflation environment. Others, though, have looked at money as a commodity and have banned the collecting of interest altogether, no matter what the inflation rates.
5 Author's own translation.
6 The 17 million estimate is on the conservative side, as it does not include countries such as Algeria, Bahrain, Iran, Qatar, Somalia and the United Arab Emirates which are home to about 140 million Muslim (about 10 per cent of the global Muslim population).

7   All models include GDP and GDP per capita to control for different levels of development on the economic, legal, social and governance fronts. This is based on the fact that legal, social and political development are often strongly correlated with levels of economic development and the size of an economy.

8   *Zakat* is mandatory charity where a certain percentage (usually 2.5 per cent) of one's accumulated annual wealth beyond a certain limit (usually equivalent to three ounces of gold) is allocated to the needy. *Sadaqa* is a charity extended to the poor on a voluntary basis. So, if one is not required to pay *zakat*, one can pay *sadaqa*, or if one has paid the required *zakat* one can also pay *sadaqa*. *Qard hassan* is a charitable and benevolent interest-free loan extended to the needy. In this type of loan the lender is willing to relax the terms of the loan and duration of the repayment in an act of benevolence towards the poor.

9   These countries are Algeria, Djibouti, Egypt, Iran, Iraq, Jordan, Morocco, Syria and Yemen.

10 Measured at $2 a day international poverty line. See Vishwanath and Serajuddin (2012).

11 Measured at $4 a day international poverty line. See Vishwanath and Serajuddin (2012).

References

Adeyemi, Adewale Abideen, Pramanik, Ataul Huq and Meera, Ahamed Kameel Mydin (2012) 'A Measurement Model of the Determinants of Financial Exclusion among Muslim Micro-Entrepreneurs in Ilorin, Nigeria', *Journal of Islamic Finance*, 1 (1), 30–43.

Ahmed, Saif (2012) *Achieving Financial Inclusion for Muslims in India: How Can Islamic Finance Help?*, http://www.ethicainstitute.com/webinar/Achieving_Financial_Inclusion_For_Indian_Muslims.pdf (accessed 2 July 2014).

Aziz, Zeti Akhtar (2013) 'Islamic Finance: Financial Stability, Economic Growth and Development', http://www.bis.org/review/r131129b.htm (accessed 2 July 2014).

Beck, Thorsten and Demirgüç-Kunt, Asli (2008) 'Access to Finance: An Unfinished Agenda', *World Bank Economic Review*, 22 (3) (November), 383–96.

Beck, Thorsten, Demirgüç-Kunt, Asli and Levine, Ross (2004) *Finance, Inequality, and Poverty: Cross-Country Evidence*, Policy Research Working Paper Series no. 3338, Washington, DC: World Bank.

BusinessNews (2013) 'Islamic Finance Has Potential for Financial Inclusion – Sanusi', http://businessnews.com.ng/2013/11/05/islamic-finance-potential-financial-inclusion-sanusi/ (accessed 2 July 2014).

CIA (Central Intelligence Agency) (2012) *People and Society: The World Factbook*, Washington, DC: CIA.

Demirgüç-Kunt, Asli, Klapper, Leora and Randall, Douglas (2013) *Islamic Finance and Financial Inclusion: Measuring Use of and Demand for Formal Financial Services among Muslim Adults*, Policy Research Working Paper no. 6642, Washington, DC: World Bank.

El-Zoghbi, Mayada and Tarazi, Michael (2013) *Trends in Shari'a-Compliant Financial Inclusion*, CGAP Focus Note no. 84, Washington, DC: Consultative Group to Assist the Poor.

Gallup World (2010) *Religiosity Highest in World's Poorest Nations*, http://www.gallup.com/poll/142727/religiosity-highest-world-poorest-nations.aspx (accessed 2 July 2014).

Global Partnership for Financial Inclusion (n.d.) *The G20 Basic Set of Financial Inclusion Indicators*, http://www.gpfi.org/featured/g20-basic-set-financial-inclusion-indicators (accessed 2 July 2014).

Government of India, Cabinet Secretariat, Prime Minister's High Level Committee (2006) *Social, Economic and Educational Status of the Muslim Community of India: A Report*, New Delhi: Government of India.

IMF (International Monetary Fund) (2013) 'Keynote Speech: 5th Annual Arab Policy Forum on Financial Inclusion', http://www.imf.org/external/mmedia/view.aspx?vid=2916041477001 (accessed 2 July 2014).

INCEIF (n.d.) Home page, http://www.inceif.org/ (accessed 2 July 2014).

Lema, Karen and Vizcaino, Bernardo (2013) 'Bangko Sentral's Islamic Banking Bid to Boost Financial Inclusion of Muslims', http://www.gmanetwork.com/news/story/328419/economy/moneyandbanking/bangko-sentral-s-islamic-banking-bid-to-boost-financial-inclusion-of-muslims (accessed 2 July 2014).

Levine, Ross (2005) 'Finance and Growth: Theory and Evidence', in Philippe Aghion and Steven Durlauf (eds), *Handbook of Economic Growth*, Vol. 1, Amsterdam: North-Holland Elsevier, pp. 865–934.

Mohieldin, Mahmoud, Iqbal, Zamir, Rostom, Ahmed and Fu, Xiaochen (2011) *The Role of Islamic Finance in Enhancing Financial Inclusion in Organization of Islamic Cooperation Countries*, Policy Research Working Paper no. 4435, Washington, DC: World Bank.

Vishwanath, Tara and Serajuddin, Umar (2012) 'Poverty in MENA – Advances and Challenges', MENA Knowledge and Learning Quick Note Series no. 64, https://openknowledge.worldbank.org/bitstream/handle/10986/10841/682720BRI0Box367908B00PUBLIC00QN64.pdf?sequence=1 (accessed 2 July 2014).

Visser, Wayne A. M. and McIntosh, Alastair (1998) 'A Short Review of the Historical Critique of Usury', *Accounting, Business and Financial History*, 8 (2), 175–89.

Webster Bible (n.d.) Deuteronomy 23, http://www.biblestudytools.com/wbt/deuteronomy/23.html (accessed 2 July 2014).

World Bank (2007) *Finance for All? Policies and Pitfalls in Expanding Access*, Washington, DC: World Bank.

World Bank (2011) *Global Financial Inclusion (Global Findex) Dataset*, Washington, DC: World Bank, http://datatopics.worldbank.org/financialinclusion/.

World Bank (2013a) *Global Financial Development Report 2014: Financial Inclusion*, Washington, DC: World Bank.

World Bank (2013b) *Global Financial Development Report 2014: Financial Inclusion: The Report: Main Messages*, http://go.worldbank.org/GWESKFYMY0 (accessed 3 July 2014).

World Bank (2013c) 'Press Release: Turkey and World Bank Group Reinforce Cooperation on Improving Islamic Finance and the Country's Investment Climate', http://www.worldbank.org/en/news/press-release/2013/10/30/turkey-and-world-bank-group-reinforce-cooperation-on-improving-islamic-finance-and-the-country-investment-climate (accessed 2 July 2014).

World Bank (2014) *Enterprise Survey*, Washington, DC: World Bank, http://www.enterprisesurveys.org/.

World Bank Data Bank (2014) *Global Findex (Global Financial Inclusion Database)*, http://databank.worldbank.org/data/views/variableselection/selectvariables.aspx?source=global-findex-(global-financial-inclusion-database) (accessed 2 July 2014).

21

SEXUALITY, DEVELOPMENT AND ISLAMOPHILIA IN THE ARAB UPRISINGS

The missing links

Mariz Tadros

Introduction

The revolutionary aspirations of bread, freedom and dignity or social justice that inspired millions to take to the streets of Tunisia, Egypt, Yemen and Libya did not produce the kind of governance and development outcomes that people hoped for, at least up to the end of 2013. Many countries witnessed political chaos and breakdowns in the rule of law and extreme security laxity leading to unsafe streets (and homes too). The absence of safety had a spillover into every aspect of women's lives: it undermined mobility, increased vulnerability to violence, hampered economic opportunities for them and their families, reduced leisure activities (such as visiting family and parents) and threatened to stall girls' access to schools. This chapter argues that, in addition to the impact of security breakdown and severe economic hardships, women's situations were particularly worsened as a consequence of a backlash spearheaded by various Islamist groups, movements and parties, who sought to exercise an epistemic power over not only lived realities but also the normative values underpinning the kind of society and politics post-ruptures. The Islamists' role was inimical to development conceived of as positive social change in that they were actively involved in voicing and publicizing a rhetoric that advocated greater control over women's bodies, mobility and voices, mobilized to strip women of legislative rights, and policed women's presence in public spaces. The chapter argues that their impact on women's realities was omitted from Western analysis of the unfolding political situation in the Middle East because of Islamophilia. Islamophilia is conceived in terms of censoring oneself or others from criticizing anything associated with Islam or Islamists in order to avoid seeming Islamophobic (seeming to hate anything that is Islamic) (Tibi 2013: 435).

The chapter first presents the vignette of an important, perhaps the most important, debate on sexuality in the Arab world in the aftermath of the uprising, which was spurred by an article by Mona Eltahawy (2012) to highlight ways in which fears of neo-orientalism and Islamophobia have been deployed in the study of sexuality. I discuss how Tibi's (2013) discussion of Islamophilia provides a constructive critical lens to engage with some of the underlying power dynamics. The 'Islamophilia lens' provides the conceptual framing behind discussing changing dynamics of sexuality in the rest of the chapter, albeit with some revisions. The chapter then discusses the disjunctures between the positive role played by women in the revolutions and the

315

backlash against them that ensued. This is followed by a discussion of the role of the Islamists in seeking to narrow women's rights on a policy level and their increasing encroachment on women's bodily integrity, spaces and freedoms at a community level. Finally, it examines struggles of resistance against the increasing assault on women's sexual freedom, and the emergence of counter-hegemonic forms of masculinity and their expression through mobilized activism.

The methodological approach informing this chapter is qualitative, based on the collection of primary and secondary data in the period from 2011 to 2013. The primary data collected included the undertaking of in-depth interviews from women and men in Tunisia, Libya and Egypt from different political orientations, and in different capacities (governmental, non-governmental, media, revolutionary activists), in February and March 2012.[1] This approach was complemented by an analysis of media reports, relevant documents, grey literature and a thorough literature review on women and the Arab uprisings.

The red lines around debating sexuality in the Arab uprisings

In April 2012, Mona Eltahawy, a columnist and political activist, wrote an article in *Foreign Policy* which became one of the most controversial and widely debated pieces to be written about women in the aftermath of the Arab revolts (as of March 2014 it had more than 76,000 hits and the number of downloads was probably considerably higher). Her article, titled 'Why Do They Hate Us?', argued that misogyny is insidious, prevails widely and affects all spaces and relations whether in the bedroom or in the corners of presidential offices. She argued that the revolution will not be complete until the sexual oppression of women, which permeates every aspect of political, economic and social life in public and private space, is defeated. Eltahawy makes a number of key arguments in her article, summarized below.

First, poverty and sexual oppression do not necessarily go hand in hand: none of the Middle East countries have made it on to the Gender Empowerment Measurement (GEM) Report irrespective of the level of economic development. She compares wealthy Saudi Arabia with Yemen, which is one of the poorest countries, as both suffering from poor women's human rights. Her second argument is that the sexual regulation of women has been buttressed by those who are authoritative figures of Islamic teaching, including popular mainstream clerics (such as the Egyptian cleric based in Qatar Yusuf Al Qaradawy) who have propagated ideas and values that are premised on the sexual control of women. Her third observation is that the revolution has removed the lid on the worst facets of misogyny which have been given voice and direction by the Islamists who have come to power in all of the countries that have experienced regime ruptures.

The intense debates that her article generated brought to the fore the complex historical, political and ideological conundrums related to the study of sexuality in the Middle East. The study of sexuality in the Middle East has always been entangled in deeply politicized power struggles of a historic and contemporary nature. The historical construction of sexuality by Western colonialist powers, as pointed out by Edward Said (1978) in his pioneering work *Orientalism*, has been premised on the demasculinized male and the sexually repressed female. Said's thesis demonstrates how sexuality was at the core of the narrative of the inferiority of the East to the West in orientalist literature and was used to justify imperialist and colonialist projects (1978). Orientalism, in its new forms (neo-orientalism), many have argued, is at the heart of a lingering Western narrative regarding the sexual oppression of women in the Middle East, in an era when military interventions in the region are legitimated in the name of saving women (Abu Lughod 2002): hence the name 'neo-orientalism'.

Monica Marks, an academic and researcher of women in the Middle East, argued that Eltahawy's article plays into the political aims of imperialists and colonialists. Marks reminds readers that 'History is rife with examples of seemingly women-friendly arguments hijacked in the service of imperialistic and aggressive ends' (2012). Marks's argument is premised on a critique of Western historical use of arguments about the sexual oppression of women in the Middle East as part and parcel of the political project of justifying military aggression: 'Ms. Eltahawy's work [is] within a growing trend of "native informants" whose personal testimonies of oppression under Islam have generated significant support for military aggression against Muslim-majority countries in recent years' (2012). A very important dimension of the critique of Eltahawy's article on the basis of its neo-orientalist underpinnings is that the author is an Arab residing in the West and speaking to a Western audience. Critiques argued that it is Eltahawy's positionality, being an Arab living in the West, that makes her poorly qualified to speak on behalf of Arab women.

Eltahawy's argument that the oppression of women lies in men's hatred of women may be critiqued for failing to take into account the historic, political and economic factors contributing to women's predicament such as global economic policies, absence of human security or poor governance. It is also true that misogyny as an explanation has limited explanatory powers as to the variation in women's predicament across different parts of the Middle East and among women in the same country. In other words, Eltahawy's article may be critiqued along the same lines that more contemporary expressions of feminist scholarship have flagged with respect to radical feminism's focus on patriarchy as a universal system of oppression that may take different forms, but in essence targets women in their capacity as women.

However, the scale, intensity and personal nature of the assault on Eltahawy's article was symptomatic of a crisis in the study of Middle East politics and culture that once again was being played out on women's bodies. Bassam Tibi's (2013) analysis of the tensions between Islamophobia and Islamophilia, their origins and their implications for debates on current affairs in the region is particularly relevant with respect to understanding not only the contours of the debate on sexuality that Eltahawy's article generated, but the broader study of sexuality in the Arab uprisings, as will be shown below.

Tibi's case rests on the idea that the rejection of Islamophobia has led the pendulum to swing to the other side, such that we have Islamophobia in reverse or Islamophilia, a phenomenon in which legitimate fears about the demonization of Muslims block possibilities for critical debate on actors, agendas and power configurations on the ground if they happen to be Muslim (Tibi 2013: 435).

This state of Islamophobia in reverse has influenced the state of debate in a number of ways. First, it has meant that there has been a confluence of Islam and Islamism, akin to the same pitfalls afflicting the Islamophobes. Islamism is an ideological movement whose followers subscribe to the idea that Islam is not only a religion but a system of governance, which operationally means the implementation of the Shari'a. The concept he argues was coined by the founder of the Muslim Brotherhood Hassan el Banna and became adapted by other Islamist movements that emerged thereafter. The conflation of Islam with Islamism has produced a number of unhelpful power dynamics. Islamophilia has meant that 'the earlier censorship practiced in the name of political correctness is replaced with a reference to "Muslim sensibilities" as a pretext and legitimation for forbidding critical thinking about Islamism' (Tibi 2013: 443–4). This has become a global phenomenon, particularly salient in Western scholarship, policy-making circles and certain parts of the media. Hence, any critiques on the political thinking and practices of Islamist movements are dubbed 'Islamophobia' because there is no distinction made between Islam and the movements that claim to speak in its name. This became manifestly overt in the case of the critiques of Eltahawy's article in which critics argue that her attack on Islamist movements' stance on gender issues stemmed from Islamophobia. Maya Mikdashi, the co-founder of *Jadaliyya*[2] and an academic, suggests that Eltahawy demonstrates a selective fear of Islamists which has more to do with Islamophobia than a genuine concern with gender justice (2012). However, the labelling of any criticism of Islamist movements as Islamophobic obstructs any possibilities of holding accountable political parties and forces that exercise any power in politics or society simply because they claim to derive from Islam. This confluence between critiquing the Islamists and Islam can only serve to increase the powers of Islamist political movements in ways that allow them to exploit the sacred for political ends.

There is another danger to the confluence of Islam and Islamism, namely the negation of the diversity in perspectives, standpoints and intellectual engagements that exist among Muslims on questions of governance, rule and politics and society. When the narrative about Islamists' credentials becomes hegemonic, it sidelines and downplays the role and agency of Muslims who have adopted alternative positions (Tibi 2013: 435). This became very clear in the debates that ensued following the publication of Eltahawy's article. The voices of Muslim women activists who have collectively organized to challenge and contest the growing powers of Islamist movements in their own countries hardly featured in the written or electronic platforms in which the article was being discussed. While there is no definitive evidence, we cannot rule out the possibilities that such voices were muted or censored or too scared to speak openly for fear of being labelled Islamophobic. However, even if such voices were not subjected to any exclusion, it is revealing that hardly any of the platforms that debated her article featured perspectives that differed from the most popular one of lambasting her.

By sidelining critiques of Islamism, even those pursued by Muslims themselves (such as Eltahawy), Western academia, the policy arena and the media are strengthening the Islamists' own marginalization and condemnation of voices of dissent in their own communities – this time not as neo-orientalists, but as *kufar* (apostates). The digression from the mainstream position taken by Islamists on religious matters has often been addressed by Islamist movements as a deviation from Islam itself, rather than a presentation of diverse viewpoints (Tibi 2013: 442). Just as Islamophobia was characterized by a prejudice of the Muslim as the religious 'other', so too Islamophilia manifests an intolerance towards those who challenge the moratorium on criticizing all that is Muslim (Tibi 2013). Instead of engaging with issues at hand, there is a lashing of others in a 'violence of rhetoric' (Tibi 2013: 443), akin to the reaction to Eltahawy's article.

It is also regrettable that, when Islamophobia is replaced with Islamophilia, what emerges is apologist stances that are not conducive to protecting, let along advancing, women's rights. In effect, it means letting off the political actors in a way that suggests that a fear of perpetuating Islamophobia or neo-orientalism overrides the defence of women's rights. This has manifested itself in two ways in the debate regarding Eltahawy's article. First is a stance that defends Islamists on the basis that many of the women who belong to these movements have progressive stances on women's equality (Marks 2012). However, Marks does not reflect on the way in which her own positionality as a Westerner may have affected the discourses of these Islamist women in engaging with her, namely that they would adopt a progressive discourse in order to speak to what they believe she would like to hear. Second, she does not explain why these progressive voices are so marginal in these movements and their influence on policy so marginal, and that the general political will of many of these parties has been to encroach on women's rights.

Another apologist argument is that Islamists are no worse than their non-Islamist counterparts. As Maya Mikdashi writes, 'Unfortunately, Islamists do not have an exclusive license to practice patriarchy and gender discrimination/oppression in the region. The secular state has been doing it fairly adequately for the last half a century' (2012). She makes a number of convincing arguments in her article, namely that there is a danger of disentangling gender justice 'from the struggles for economic and political justice' (2012). It is also true that non-Islamist political actors have sometimes displayed the worst traits of misogyny and been the most conservative advocates of patriarchy. However, to claim that the state that has been in place in the region is secular is highly problematic. The family law in most countries of the Middle East has been regulated by Shari'a law, and Shari'a law is inscribed as a source of legislation in several countries. Further, the idea of the secular state needs to be weighed with the political reality on the ground in many of these countries in which there has been an Islamization from below. Islamist political forces have supported the religionization of the public sphere in a way which rendered the idea of a secular order disconnected from the ground a reality well before the uprisings. Moreover, what is particularly serious about Mikdashi's stance is that, by equalizing the level of patriarchy across all political forces, it fails to recognize the fact that there has been an intense backlash against women's rights since the uprisings and, while not the only actors, Islamists have played a key contributing role in that (as will be discussed below).

The conceptual discussion of sexuality in terms of the debates that followed Eltahawy's article and their analysis through the lens of Tibi's framing of the study of Middle East politics more widely is informed by the critical juncture which this chapter investigates: how Islamists' vision of post-rupture society rested on a control of women's sexuality, which in turn had a ripple effect on many aspects of their well-being and prospects for eliciting development in the sense of positive social and political change. The chapter refrains from pursuing an approach that analyses the Islamist actors' gender agenda independently, and is cautious about examining their agency in relation to other actors according to changing power configurations locally and regionally in order to acquire a nuanced picture.

A people's revolution is no sexual revolution

Women played a central role in the uprisings that shook Tunisia, Egypt, Yemen and Libya. They took to the streets, encouraged others to do so, and made significant personal sacrifices. In all four countries, women broke ranks with conventional expectations of how women 'should' behave as circumscribed in each society. In Egypt, women spent the nights in tents in Tahrir Square in a context where social norms dictate that women should not spend the night outside their families' homes (except when travelling) and they should certainly be indoors. While this was not the first time social norms have been broken in this manner (women factory workers occupied factories to press employers to respond to their demands), it was the first time that tents were set up in Tahrir Square in such a manner. In Tunisia, one of the most salient images was that of women being carried on the shoulders of men, while shouting revolutionary slogans, again breaking the social precept of avoiding bodily contact in public. In Yemen, where gender segregation is the norm, women marched side by side with men, often assuming a leading role in mobilizing the masses. In Benghazi, Libya, women defied their families and went out on the streets to join the revolutionaries. Interestingly, in most accounts across all four countries, many women who took part in the protests insisted that they participated first as *citizens*, not as women. They insisted if there was any identifier to the uprisings, it was that it was youth-led. Similarly, when asked whether women assumed leadership positions in the uprisings, there is an insistence that there were no leaders, since in each country the revolutions, as they are near-universally locally called, were leaderless.

The predominant narrative of women and men side by side in a liberation struggle against dictatorship very quickly dissipated after the ousting of President Zein el Abbedin in Tunisia and President Mubarak in Egypt. The youth movements that had praised the role of women in the revolutionary struggles did not envisage social transformation in gender relations as central to the national project of establishing new democratic regimes. In Egypt, for example, Sally Toma,

319

a psychiatrist, founding member of the Egyptian Social Democratic Party and spokesperson for the Coalition of Revolutionary Youth,[3] was one of the few women activists to assume a leadership position in the newly emergent political forces. She argued that, even among the most progressive political forces from the uprisings, few recognized women's roles in the uprisings by giving them leadership positions. Many of the new youth coalitions – unintentionally, presumably – reproduced the old patriarchal division of labour by relegating women to 'mobilizing' roles or 'administrative coordination', while 'leadership' became the domain of men. Similarly, in Tunisia, many activists noted that, when references to women were made, they were in relation to their roles as extensions of men – as the wife or daughter of a particular man – or women were simply referred to as part of the crowds, the women in the shadows, in the background. Samira Shouwashy, the official spokesperson for Al Moubadra al Hokukiyya Party in Tunisia, said in an interview: 'What really hurts me is that women were there [in the revolution] at the forefront . . . and yet when men talk about the revolution they refer to them as "wife of so-and-so".'[4] These counter-narratives expose the patriarchal underpinnings of ways of thinking and engaging which were untransformed by the experience of participating in revolutionary uprising. They remained in stark contrast with the more formal and 'official' narratives locally and in the West which continued to recognize women's full political agency.

Whereas, within the youth revolutionary force, disjuncture between the formal and informal rhetoric is reflective of deep-seated patriarchal values rather than an overt political agenda of marginalizing women, the same cannot be said of the narrative of some of the Islamist groups regarding the revolution. The narratives of some of the Salafi groups and other Islamist groups featured women's political agency as morally and socially deviant. They began to circulate among their followers stories of dishonourable and sexually promiscuous behaviour on the part of the women activists who participated in the revolution, specifically the women of 'secular' political orientation. The narrative of denigrating secular women's political agency in the revolution served two ends that converged. The first is ideological, namely women mingling with men in public protests was anathema to the sexual order in which women's natural place is in the home, and in which women are to be segregated from men in public space. The concept of *fitna* (strife or unrest) is key to understanding the demarcation between the public and the private in many of these discourses, since in radical Islamist discourse women are a source of *fitna*, provoking men to lose their peace and become aroused. The second goal intended to be achieved in the condemnation of women in revolt is political: to undermine the secular forces contending for political power.

The newly opened political spaces in Tunisia, Egypt, Yemen and Libya meant that different political forces competed for leadership in state and society. The competition was to be found between and among secular and Islamist groups, and mobilization was to be found along political agendas and different leaderships. However, in all four countries, what began to emerge was a very clear ideological demarcation between the Islamist and non-Islamist political forces. While there was competition within groups in each camp, nevertheless, while non-Islamist political forces were by and large fragmented and suffered from rivalry among different leaders, Islamist groups succeeded at critical junctures in creating strong alliances and coalitions. For example, in Egypt, at the constitutional referendum of 2011 and at the presidential election of 2012, strong Islamist coalitions were forged (though they dissipated afterwards). In Yemen, the Islah Party was in and of itself a strong coalition of different Islamist groups. In Tunisia, too, there were critical points where the Nahda Party coalesced – at least informally – with the Salafis. If such political alliances were often of a transitory nature, there was a more permanent and binding ideological project of defeating the secularists. Secularism was represented as the enemy of Islam. Political polarization along 'Islamist' versus secularist lines became sharp and deep-seated, in particular in Egypt and Tunisia. In such a context, the rejection of the women revolutionaries was also a political statement of rejecting the 'secular other'.

Sexual politics of the pulpits and parliaments

During and in the aftermath of the period when Islamist political parties were vying for office, spokespersons from these movements were keen to assure the public that rights, including those of women, would not be encroached upon should they come to power. The Muslim Brotherhood in Libya made public statements that citizenship rights would be assured for all, irrespective of gender. In Egypt and Tunisia the Muslim Brotherhood made frequent public statements in a context where vocal feminist groups were pressing them to give concrete assurances that women's rights would be assured should they ascend to power. This was the golden opportunity for the Islamists of different shades and across the ideological spectrum to show that the long-established image of their enmity towards women's rights is a misnomer and their version of a society and political order premised on Islamist principles is not inimical to the idea of choice and tolerance of differences.

Proponents of moderate Islam (with reference to Islamists who have rejected violence as a pathway to rule and who believe in participation in the political system of a country by way of elections and other democratic procedures) have long argued that once moderate Islamist political groups were liberated from the shackles of authoritarian regimes they would pursue a more reformist agenda compatible with democratic freedoms and citizenship rights, including those relating to women's equality. However, the experience of having Islamist groups participate in the political life of the nation following the uprisings challenged the myths of a moderate Islamism's democratic and inclusive model of governance, in particular with respect to the question of management of difference and diversity. Two qualifiers need to be made regarding Islamists' engagement with women's citizenship rights. First, not all Islamist groups that were labelled as moderate (such as El Nahda in Tunisia and the Muslim Brotherhood in Egypt) espoused or propagated the same discourse and policy vis-à-vis women's equality; there were different shades of varying nuances. Second, not all Islamist groups of different shades and ideological orientations in the same country necessarily practised or advocated the same gender agenda. For example, in Egypt, while the Muslim Brotherhood's political arm, the Freedom and Justice Party, endorsed women's political representation and leadership in parliament, the Salafi political wing, the El Nour Party, did not (at least in the 2011 parliamentary elections). Third, during those two years after the revolutions (2011–13) the political situation was very dynamic, and accordingly political actors adapted to the volatility by changing their stance. A case in point is that of El Nahda, which abandoned its Islamization of the constitution plans vis-à-vis gender matters after the ousting of the Muslim Brotherhood in Egypt (H. Saleh and Daragahi 2014). For example, in the period prior to the ousting of President Morsi in Egypt, El Nahda had insisted that the constitution should state that women and men complement each other, thereby entrenching the principle of division of labour premised on biology. Non-Islamist groups, in particular feminists, strongly rejected the complementary clause and insisted that the constitution should stress equality between men and women, in order to ensure equal citizenship.

However, across each and every context, irrespective of the variation between and across Islamist groups, their political ascendancy to power in the period from 2011 carried a threat to women's legally recognized rights, in particular with respect to sexuality and gender hierarchies, and an increased regulation of sexual freedoms in public space. Each will be tackled separately below.

In contrast to well-meaning assumptions by many Western analysts that the Islamists who assumed political office would de-prioritize matters of sexuality, the unfolding events in Tunisia and Egypt suggested that the regulation of women's sexuality was placed very high on the agenda. Historically, political battles for power have often been fought over women's bodies because, in countries such as Egypt and Tunisia, Shari'a law was mostly not implemented except in the case of personal status law – legislation pertaining to the regulation of marriage, divorce, inheritance and custody matters. The personal status laws are critical because they play a central role in regulating women's private, and by default public, lives. Tunisia's leading Islamist Al-Nahda Party has promised not to seek to change the country's personal status law, widely viewed as among the most progressive in the Arab world. But a statement, later withdrawn by the minister of women (Sihem Badi), raised alarms among women's rights activists when she publicly defended the practice of informal, *urfi* marriage, a Muslim marriage that may, under certain circumstances, be seen as religiously binding but which is not registered with the state. Being informal, *urfi* marriages fail to secure women's conjugal or divorce rights.

In Egypt, Azza Garaf, a female member of parliament representing the Freedom and Justice Party (the political wing of the Muslim Brotherhood), and other MPs belonging to the Muslim Brotherhood, lobbied when in office to amend Egypt's divorce law to cancel *khul'* divorces whereby women can divorce their husbands without having to prove a reason in exchange for forfeiting some of their financial rights.[5]

Moreover, after almost two decades of local activists' efforts to transform social values regarding the practice of female genital mutilation (locally referred to as female circumcision), activists found themselves in 2011 faced with a counter-campaign led by the Islamists encouraging people to 'say yes to female circumcision'. Garaf called for the revision of the child law in order to de-criminalize female genital mutilation, claiming that the practice protects women's chastity. In the non-formal political arena, the Muslim Brotherhood's Freedom and Justice Party's mobile health clinics were offering female circumcision 'surgeries' for a fee in Upper Egypt (Tadros 2012a). This however did not seem to raise alarm bells except among some circles of concerned feminist activists in Egypt.

In Libya, president of the National Transitional Council Moustafa Abd al-Jalil's first triumphant speech to the nation after the success of that revolution declared that all laws in violation of Shari'a law are null and void, restrictions on polygamy would be removed, and women's access to divorce, in all but a few limited circumstances, would be prohibited.

On a grassroots level, in all four countries, the mosque became increasingly what one Egyptian female activist called 'a pulpit for politics'. In Egypt, Libya and Tunisia in particular, the lifting of authoritarian surveillance over places of worship and the take-over of mosques by different Islamist groups led to their transformation into platforms for propagating political agendas inimical to progressive notions of the rights of women and minorities. In the months following Egypt's uprising, worshippers across the country reported seeing their old, government-appointed preacher forcibly removed from the premises and replaced with a more conservative scholar.[6] Mosques increasingly became the medium through which Salafis and other ultra-conservative groups disseminated messages regarding 'appropriate' gender behaviour, mores and roles. The regulation of women's sexuality became a priority concern. Unveiled women on the street in Tunisia and Egypt increasingly reported being subjected to what they see as verbal abuse at the hands of emboldened Islamists. Twenty-two-year-old Samah Koraishah, an activist with Sawti ('my voice'), an organization formed after the revolution by youth with the aim of deepening democratic values and citizenship in Tunisian society, argued that the level of verbal and physical violence against women increased with the rising influence of Salafi forces. She recounted that close to where she lives is a mosque where Salafi forces are dominant, and as she left her home, though fully covered, she often received remarks such as 'Isteghfar Allah'.[7] 'I am made to feel as if I am an *'awra'*,[8] she said.

Female activists from Tunisia spoke about the alarming increase in vulnerability to both verbal and physical forms of assault on the streets at the hands of Islamists who believed that they were not dressed in sufficiently modest attire. Women from Libya told similar stories of being subjected to verbal abuse as they walked in the street, or in university campuses – with the effect that they were now staying at home. Yemeni women tell stories of girls being subjected to acid attacks as a way to discourage parents from sending them to school.[9] While the lax security situation bears the greater proportion of blame for girls' obstructed access to schools, what is suggested here is that attempts to enforce new controls on women's bodies represent added pressures on families to fear for the well-being of their girls in sending them to school. This represents a denial of one of the fundamental dimensions of development, the right to education.

Tunisian, Egyptian, Libyan and Yemeni women's rights activists say that emboldened Islamists in some instances organized into bands of zealots roaming the streets to enforce their conceptions of what constitutes vice and good behaviour. Samah Krichah, a Tunisian activist and board member of the Tunisian think tank The Democratic Lab, noted how new groups, such as the ultra-radical Islamist Salafis, became very active in public spaces after 2012. She noted that they assumed the authority to verbally (and sometimes physically) 'chastise' unveiled women for their attire, with the police doing nothing to restrain them or hold them in check. However, this is not only on the streets, but also in the universities and schools. As one interviewee told me: 'My sister who is 14 years old was reproached by the school guard for wearing a half-sleeved shirt. My father went to school to tell him not to talk to her' (Tadros 2013). Anecdotal evidence from Shubra and Shubra el Kheima[10] in Egypt in 2012 indicated that, while groups formed and assumed the right to intimidate those they saw as inappropriately dressed, this has backfired severely against them, as people resisted them, telling them to mind their own business and to go away. However, throughout the phase from 2011 to mid-June 2013 in Egypt, there were several instances in which women were assaulted on the streets by supporters or members of Islamist groups on account of not being seen to be dressed modestly enough. While the increased sexual assault of women after the Egyptian revolution of 2011 is a multi-pronged phenomenon driven by a complex set of varying factors including a breakdown in security, when the Islamists assumed a policing role in the streets, it led to the increased encroachment on women's agency, and an increased focus on their bodies as sites of *fitna* for men.

Resistance and defiance

One of the most promising outcomes of the revolutionary rupture in Egypt was the transformation of political culture, such that youth became particularly involved in public life and street politics. In reaction to the growing sexual assaults on women in public space, men and women mobilized into vigilante groups that created new initiatives intended to stop assaults, raise awareness through campaigns and provide authoritative accounts of the situation on the ground. The participation and leadership of men in these groups represents an alternative to the hegemonic concepts of masculinity prevalent in Egyptian society. This is not to suggest that the bulk of men in Egypt support assaults on women. However, it is to say that mobilization of these men in defence of women's bodily integrity is a divergence from what men would conventionally mobilize around. While hegemonic concepts of masculinity consider it macho and fun to assault women, these men propagated a message that 'real men do not harass'.

In spite of the differences in backgrounds, political orientation or objectives of the initiatives, the men in these initiatives all shared an unqualified belief in a woman's right to be in a harassment-free public space irrespective of what she was wearing, whom she was with, and her whereabouts (Tadros 2014). While these men did not speak explicitly of sexual liberation or sexual rights (some were religiously conservative too), their awareness campaigns and their peer-to-peer engagement with other men in the streets and in public transport suggested a belief in women's rights to bodily integrity. They also led and participated in protests decrying Egyptian women's exposure to sexual assault. Men involved in these newly formed initiatives to combat sexual assault of women on the street were of different political orientations (or none), yet they rejected discourses by Islamist political leaders and the Freedom and Justice Party that assign women the responsibility for assault (see for example Opantish, Fouada Watch and Basma) (Tadros 2013). They also rejected any attempt by liberal political forces to make political gains from women's assault. These initiatives were the offspring of the revolution and reached the apex of their activism from mid-June 2011 to mid-June 2013. It is unclear whether they will sustain their activism in the years to come. However, they represented an important rupture in hegemonic masculinity, and their alliances with women's groups, some political parties and broad-based youth movements to mobilize against gender-based violence in public space represent an important testament to the emergence of counter-hegemonic masculinities in times of crisis and the dissent against the sexual intimidation of women.

Voices of dissent against the increasing engagement with women as sources of *fitna* were emerging from several quarters of Egypt. Women who were not veiled (or not sufficiently veiled to accommodate the new demands for the adoption of more conservative forms of veiling) often resisted calls to change their attire. Open defiance took many forms, most notably protests. In two instances non-Muslim women in Egypt led protests to express their anger at being assaulted because they were not veiled (see Tadros 2012b).

Whereas in the Egyptian revolution of 2011 feminists and women activists assumed a gender-blind stance in terms of negating how being women affected how they were engaged with, intensity of the backlash in its aftermath generated mass mobilization of women to demand that their rights be protected and their roles in the revolutionary struggle be rewarded through their active participation in the new structures of power. In 2011, the protests in Tahrir Square to champion women's rights were aimed at acquiring recognition for women's rights in the post-Mubarak Egypt. However, by 2013 women's mobilization had taken the form of a counter-offensive to the authorities, with huge banners bearing hard-core messages. One banner prophetically said 'Shura Council, we will oust you like we ousted Mubarak' (see N. Saleh 2013). The Shura Council was the acting legislative authority at the time and had convened its human rights committee to discuss the wave of acts of sexual assault in Tahrir Square on 25 January 2013. During the discussions, Reda Al-Hefnawy, a Freedom and Justice Party (FJP) member, blamed women for going to protest spaces in the first place. 'Women should not mingle with men during protests', he said, adding: 'How can the Ministry of Interior be tasked with protecting a lady who stands among a group of men?' (Taha 2013). Other voices also blamed women for the assaults. This in turn prompted another wave of assaults organized by various coalitions and alliances to condemn gender-based violence against women.

In May 2013, a youth-based group, Tamarod (meaning 'Rebel'), called upon the Egyptian people to mark President Morsi's year in office by taking to the streets in mass demonstrations to press him either to call early presidential elections or to step down.

Tibi spoke of how upgrading Islamism (via the workings of Islamophilia) led to the non-recognition of the voices of liberal-progressive Muslims who have alternative visions and ideas of religion in their societies (2013). He believed it is these voices that reject Islamists that form the corps of the resistance against upgrading Islamism. However, in the case of Egypt, dissent against the Islamist rule came from the non-intelligentsia. Ordinary citizens rose en masse against the Muslim Brotherhood regime in June 2013 catalysed by poor governance, and unmet aspirations for jobs, livelihoods and safer streets. It is important to note that their uprising was one premised not on a rejection of Islam, but on a rejection of the very political forces that Western academia, several think tanks and the media had convinced us were representative of the mainstream (see Lynch 2012 as an example).

Mohamed Bamyiah, a sociology professor, thought that the people who rose against the regime in June 2013 rejected the Brothers' reign in a particular socio-cultural engagement with religion:

> we are speaking of a country characterized by pervasive but pragmatic social conserva-
> tism, coupled with preference for informality and results rather than rigid, formal rules.
> The fact that a large number of traditional religious individuals joined the June rebel-
> lion against an Islamic party in power shows not their 'liberalism', but something more
> basic. It shows their resistance to the idea that religion should be transformed from
> a voluntary ethical system that is controlled and interpreted by the pious individual
> situationally and as needed, into a rigid structure of laws imposed by a government,
> and thus outside of the control of the pious individual. If the latter were to happen,
> religion would be transformed from a source of freedom from other human authori-
> ties and of self-discipline, into its exact opposite: a system of control and discipline by
> other human authorities.
>
> (Bamyiah 2013)

Bamyiah's point that the citizens who rose in June 2013 were conservative and did not consti-
tute a liberal, progressive crowd is pertinent in its confirmation of Tibi's contention that Islam and Islamism need to be disentangled; one is not the other. The crowds did not reject Islam; they rejected the Muslim Brotherhood's version of governance and the idea that they were the representatives of Islam.

It is noteworthy that women rose up in far greater numbers in 2013 than they did in 2011, both in terms of numbers and as a proportion of the overall citizenry. It is difficult to determine the extent to which the Islamists' informal measures to control women's sexuality were a driver of the protests, since the women who rose in June 2013 were not a monolithic group, and were differentiated by geographic location, class, political orientation and religion. However, the broader implications for well-being were tangibly felt in the workforce, education, gender relations at home, and public space.

Moreover, what is clear is that, unlike the case in the revolution of 2011 where women did not raise any banners associated with gender matters, in 2013 some of the banners and chants to be heard in Tahrir Square and its vicinity represented a conspicuous dissent against women's sexuality as conceived by some Islamists. The overthrow of the Islamists' sexual order may not have been the main driver of dissent on 30 June. However, it cannot be dismissed as one of the drivers, at least for some of the demonstrators. The most popular of such banners or slogans is perhaps '*Sawt al mar'a thawra mish 'awra*' (The voice of a woman is a revolution not a depravity). The slogan, which rhymes in Arabic, is a subversion of the radical Islamist discourse which con-
ceives of a woman's voice as an *'awra*, something that is supposed to be hidden, covered from the public eye because of its sexual nature. It was in effect reclamation of voice, in an expression of rejection of the Islamist regulation of women's sexuality and disciplining of their bodies. Yet, in line with Tibi's contention of a cautious refraining from criticizing all that is of an Islamist nature and the marginalization of the voices of other Muslims, women's activism in June 2013 hardly featured in the Western media and policy circles. In contrast with the January 25th

Revolution of 2011, where women's numbers and visibility were strikingly less than those of June 2013, there was no celebration of women's agency. The contentious discourse of women demonstrators was not aligned to the Western engagement with Islamists as representing the mainstream in Muslim countries.

Conclusion

This chapter examined how the changing power configurations in Arab transition contexts affected and were affected by sexual politics. It showed how power struggles between different political factions, in particular between the Islamists and non-Islamists, were literally played out on women's bodies. As the political scene in Tunisia, Egypt, Libya and to a much lesser extent Yemen became one characterized by the polarization between the Islamists and the non-Islamists, the struggle increasingly became one being played on women's bodies. For some of the Islamists, the regulation and disciplining came to embody notions of propriety, authenticity, religious piety and even patriotism. For some of the non-Islamists, women's increasing subjection to sexual oppression was at times deployed to make political gains against their opponents. In some instances, because of changing shifts in political configurations, the El Nahda Party chose to forge alliances with the non-Islamist bloc and not with the ultra-radical Salafis. Parts of the party endorsed the non-Islamist bloc in the assembly in their bid to secure women's rights gained in the previous constitution, which was successful. This represented a change of political strategy by El Nahda at a critical juncture. The ousting of Muslim Brotherhood President Morsi in 2013 convinced El Nahda that a change of strategic engagement was necessary if they were to avoid encountering a similar political trajectory. In such an instance, alliances securing political interests (not being ejected from power) trumped ideological inclinations (a firm belief in the complementarity rather than equality of gender roles). The outcome was Al Nahda and other political parties' ability to arrive at a consensus around a constitution that firmly secures women's rights.

This chapter sought to present an alternative narrative on women's realities in the immediate aftermath of the revolutionary ruptures in Tunisia, Egypt, Yemen and Libya (2011–12), highlighting how Islamist movements, though varying in agenda and across time and space, spearheaded processes of regulating women's sexuality. Certainly the Islamists were not the only actors to have been involved in the backlash against women, nor is it possible to understand the threats to women's well-being without taking into account the far-reaching impact of the security breakdown. However, based on empirical data, this chapter makes three contentions. The first, the Islamists' impact on the encroachment on women's agency was not only in terms of daily experiences but on a normative level, in terms of conceptions of gender hierarchies and relations in post-rupture societies. The second argument is that Islamists' engagement with women's sexuality had a far-reaching impact on not only bodily integrity but broader dimensions of social well-being and development. Third, the failure of Western academia, policy spaces and parts of the media fully to recognize the role of Islamists in the backlash and their impact on women's well-being is suggestive of Islamophilia. Finally, while there was resistance in many outsider circles to engaging with the dynamics of Islamists' projection of their political project, there was substantial resistance on the ground, which took the form both of individual acts of subversion and of overt forms of organized activism.

Notes

1 Interviews in Egypt were conducted by Mohammed Hussein, in Libya by Alaa Murabit and in Tunisia by Mabrouka Gasmi and Fadhila Bergaoui.
2 An electronic platform offering analysis of Middle Eastern affairs (http://www.jadaliyya.com/).

3 The Coalition of Revolutionary Youth was an early attempt to organize the young people who had participated in protests into a group that could speak for them politically once sustained protests subsided with the overthrow of former president Hosni Mubarak.

4 Interview with Samira Shouwashy, Tunis, 2012.

5 Interview with Azza Garaf, Cairo, May 2012.

6 ECFR interviews, Muslim congregants, Cairo, Minya, Mansoura, Qena and Alexandria, February–April 2011.

7 Denoting that she is evil, and a source of causing others to sin.

8 *'Awra* is a term used in Islam to denote the intimate parts of the body for both women and men which should be covered. Exposing an *'awra* is considered a sin. However, within the different Islamic schools, the specific definition of *'awra* varies from one school of Islamic thought to another.

9 ECFR interview, Basma al-Qubati, Tunis, 19 April 2012.

10 Two densely populated urban suburbs in Egypt, the former mostly middle-class, the latter mostly working-class.

References

Abu Lughod, L. (2002) 'Do Muslim Women Really Need Saving? Anthropological Reflections on Cultural Relativism and Its Others', *American Anthropologist*, 104 (3) (September), 783–90.

Bamyiah, M. (2013) 'The June Rebellion in Egypt', *Jadaliyya*, 11 July, http://www.jadaliyya.com/pages/index/12876/the-june-rebellion-in-egypt.

Eltahawy, M. (2012) 'Why Do They Hate Us? The Real War on Women Is in the Middle East', *Foreign Policy*, 23 April, http://www.foreignpolicy.com/articles/2012/04/23/why_do_they_hate_us.

Lynch, M. (2012) 'Reflections on Egypt's Latest Crisis', *Foreign Policy*, 29 December, http://lynch.foreignpolicy.com/posts/2012/12/29/reflections_on_egypts_latest_crisis?wp_login_redirect=0 (accessed 7 May 2013).

Marks, M. (2012) 'Do Arabs Really Hate Women? The Problem with Native Informants', *Huffington Post*, 25 April, http://www.huffingtonpost.com/monica-l-marks/do-arabs-really-hate-wome_b_1453147.html.

Mikdashi, Maya (2012) 'The Uprisings Will Be Gendered', *Jadaliyya*, 28 February, http://www.jadaliyya.com/pages/index/4506/the-uprisings-will-be-gendered.

Said, Edward (1978) *Orientalism*, Harmondsworth: Penguin Books.

Saleh, H. and Daragahi, B. (2014) 'Tunisia's Assembly Passes New Law', *Financial Times*, 27 January, http://www.ft.com/cms/s/0/eca21fa6-8734-11e3-ba87-00144feab7de.html#axzz2wDSpIt32.

Saleh, N. (2013) 'In the Cradle of the Revolution, Women Will Not Be Silenced', *Egyptian Streets*, 28 March, http://egyptianstreets.com/2013/03/28/rights-of-women-not-forgotten/.

Tadros, M. (2012a) 'Mutilating Bodies: The Muslim Brotherhood's Gift to Egyptian Women', *OpenDemocracy*, 12 May, http://www.opendemocracy.net/5050/mariz-tadros/mutilating-bodies-muslim-brotherhood%E2%80%99s-gift-to-egyptian-women.

Tadros, M. (2012b) 'Egyptian Women Have Had Enough of Being Told to Cover Up', *Guardian*, 29 May, http://www.guardian.co.uk/commentisfree/2012/may/29/egypt-women-cover-up-coptic.

Tadros, M. (2013) 'Women's Human Security Rights in the Arab World: On Nobody's Agenda', *OpenDemocracy*, 2 December, http://www.opendemocracy.net/5050/mariz-tadros/women%E2%80%8099s-human-security-rights-in-arab-world-on-nobodys-agenda.

Tadros, M. (2014) 'Reclaiming the Streets for Women's Dignity', Evidence Report no. 48, Institute of Development Studies, University of Sussex, http://www.ids.ac.uk/publication/reclaiming-the-streets-for-women-s-dignity-effective-initiatives-in-the-struggle-against-gender-based-violence-in-between-egypt-s-two-revolutions.

Taha, N. (2013) 'Shura Council Members Blame Women for Harassment', Gender Information Network for South Caucus, 12 February, http://www.ginsc.net/home.php?option=article&id=25049&lang=en#.Uyb94oURe4ghttp://www.ginsc.net/home.php?option=article&id=25049&lang=en#.Uyb94oURe4g.

Tibi, B. (2013) 'The Islamist Venture of the Politicization of Islam to an Ideology of Islamism: A Critique of the Dominating Narrative in Western Islamic Studies', *Soundings: An Interdisciplinary Journal*, 96 (4), 431–49.

PART 7

Development policy and practice

22

FAITH-BASED ORGANIZATIONS AND DEVELOPMENT

Laurie A. Occhipinti

Introduction

What are often referred to as "faith-based organizations" (FBOs) make up a significant sector of non-profit organizations working in economic development and on other global issues. In recent years, donors, development professionals, and scholars have demonstrated a willingness to engage with religion, with a moral framework for development, and with religious organizations that have long been an important part of providing services to the poor. These FBOs draw on symbolic and material resources that appear to make them distinct in the world of NGOs and secular development, building on religious traditions of charity and justice, institutional networks that span global regions as well as social classes, and a position of moral legitimacy and authority. For most FBOs, faith is not an "add-on" to development work but an essential part of it, and often is the primary reason for engaging in such work at all. Yet the category "faith-based organization" is itself often taken for granted,[1] without clarification or definition, despite the enormous variation in organizations that could fall within this category. This could include places of worship that carry out welfare and development work, informal and local organizations that may be linked to places of worship or may have sprung up independently, and formally registered organizations that resemble NGOs and which may have an international reach. There is a diverse range of FBOs that are influenced by the faith tradition from which they come, not just in terms of their theology but in terms of their structure and scope; they vary in size, from one or two people working out of the back room of a church to international professional service providers; they vary in their approach to development and the ways in which they conceptualize what people need in order to live a dignified life. Moreover, is it really so easy always to distinguish between faith-based and non-faith-based organizations, particularly in settings where religion permeates all aspects of life?

In this chapter, I will examine the rise of FBOs in recent decades and how they have been viewed by both proponents and critics. Researchers have suggested various definitions and typologies that attempt to distinguish FBOs from other NGOs and to better describe and analyze the variations between organizations. I synthesize these typologies to offer a framework that encourages greater clarity in thinking about FBOs along three key dimensions: the different degrees to which organizations are faith-based, the work in which they engage, and their degree of formality and association with official religious structures. While such an approach may prove inadequate to capture the complexity of these organizations, it can be helpful to researchers as well as practitioners in thinking about critical elements to consider in describing and analyzing the roles of FBOs in development.

The rise of FBOs

Religious organizations of different types, including places of worship and their congregations, have a long history of providing charity, relief, and social services, a history that "long predates the concept of 'development'" (Lunn 2009: 943; see Deacon and Tomalin, Chapter 5). As noted in the introduction, today there are a wide variety of religious actors that engage with development processes, many working across the boundaries of religious tradition (indeed some are dedicated to interfaith activities) as well as engaging with secular organizations as part of an emergent global civil society. While there are no systematic data on the number of FBOs or their contribution to providing services (partly because there is a lack of clarity about what constitutes an FBO), like other NGOs they became more prevalent in the 1980s, as "pressure to downsize the state . . . led to renewed reliance on non-state providers in service delivery" (Deneulin and Rakodi 2010: 48). Since that time, their role has grown, even as the distinction between "religious" and "secular" non-governmental organizations has often become increasingly blurry.

In the 1990s, both the US and Great Britain engaged in major policy shifts towards supporting FBOs. In the US, changes in policies associated with the "Charitable Choice" initiatives of George W. Bush[2] made increased funding available to FBOs, both domestically and internationally (Adkins *et al.* 2010; Cooper 2014). US government funding to FBOs nearly doubled from 2001 to 2005, from 10.5 percent of aid to 19.9 percent (James 2009), with much of this increase going to evangelical Christian organizations (Hackworth 2012). In Britain, the Department for International Development (DFID) "began to think more seriously about relationships with faith communities and with FBOs" (Clarke 2007: 85), a shift from treating FBOs like any other non-profit and expecting them to behave as though they were essentially secular, to engaging more deeply with religion as an element of development itself.[3] Other governments, including those in Switzerland, the Netherlands, Denmark, and Sweden, as well as the World Bank, also channeled both attention and funding to FBOs (see Marshall 2001; Jones and Juul Petersen 2011: 1294–5; Clarke 2013; Haynes 2013; also see Deacon and Tomalin, Chapter 5).

As part of this shift and perhaps also underpinning it, FBOs were widely seen as having two latent strengths in terms of development (Lunn 2009: 944). One is organizational. They have strong links to the grassroots, and often are already located in relatively remote rural areas. Many FBOs have already established a long-term presence in communities, giving them a knowledge of local circumstances and contexts, local networks, and often a level of trust that lends them the ability to be perceived as a legitimate moral voice (Rivlin 2002: 157; Bradley 2005; Occhipinti 2013). Many FBOs enjoy good domestic and international networks, drawing on the structures and networks of the religious community to which they pertain. They may also be able to tap into this network for funding and fundraising, making them less donor dependent than other NGOs (Pereira *et al.* 2009; Leurs 2012). These organizational strengths mean that FBOs can often be uniquely effective on the ground. The second frequently touted advantage of FBOs is motivational: religious organizations are seen to have a commitment to and enthusiasm for serving people and communities. Donors may believe that they are more responsive to local needs, more flexible, and more honest, and promote the development of social capital.[4] FBOs are seen by scholars and donors as distinctive in being able to draw on spiritual and moral values and influence institutions that instill values, such as schools and families (Peters 2009; Leurs 2012).

They are able to mobilize adherents, including those who may feel estranged from secular development programs.

Even as there has been this burst of enthusiasm for FBOs, some researchers have sounded a cautionary note (for example, Tomalin 2012). Some criticisms have been rooted in pragmatic concerns. For example, like any small or grassroots organizations, some FBOs are unprepared to "scale up," lacking infrastructure, experience, and staff to deliver services on a broader scale (Alvaré 2009). Moreover, FBOs can come with baggage around issues such as gender equality (Pearson and Tomalin 2008; Tadros 2010), patriarchy (DeTemple *et al.* 2009), and an intolerance of traditional religions (Hovland 2008). Some FBOs continue to focus programs on adherents of their own faith traditions, and may have exclusionary policies that make some donors uneasy. Additionally, FBOs are often viewed suspiciously by donors and funding agencies because their development activities may disguise or legitimize evangelism and conversion, and in particular there are concerns that they may apply pressure to convert on those who are most economically vulnerable (Bradley 2005; de Kadt 2009; Lunn 2009; see Fountain, Chapter 6). Some critiques (for example, de Kadt 2009), however, also fail to recognize the heterogeneity of the organizations categorized as FBOS. As Rakodi (2012a: 623) cautions, researchers should analyze FBOs rather than endorse them, and need to avoid essentializing religion, either positively or negatively.

An additional critique of the newfound enthusiasm for FBOs is that donors have tended to favor particular kinds of religious organizations over others. It has been argued that they are more likely to engage with those that express their faith passively (Clarke 2008: 33) and which resemble formal NGOs, rather than the innumerable places of worship, congregations, and local informal faith-based initiatives which may find it more difficult to separate their development activities from their core religious business and which may not have the structures to deliver or carry out "development" in the way dictated by the development industry. Moreover, funding agencies and secular development agencies have often engaged selectively with religious bodies, usually on issues seen to be relevant to religion or to the work that FBOs have already been involved in, such as education (Deneulin and Bano 2009: 24). As donors have moved towards increasing partnerships, as well as towards a greater embrace of the idea of religion as part of development, they have tended to build relationships with FBOs that most resemble secular NGOs (Deneulin and Bano 2009: 25). The religious nature of these FBOs becomes non-threatening to secular development organizations, nearly "invisible," since they tend to share the same cultural background and perspectives on development work. Gerard Clarke (2006: 836) also voices concern that donors tend to favor liberal and moderate organizations that are tied to Catholic or liberal (mainline) Protestant religions, failing to engage with FBOs from other faith traditions. This favoritism may stem from concerns about proselytizing as well as from a lack of familiarity with other, particularly non-Christian, faith traditions, and happens even though, as Clarke points out, there are numerous FBOs within those other traditions (see also Fountain 2013). Carole Rakodi (2012b) suggests that the new interest in FBOs has been shadowed by a failure of Western actors to recognize their own, at least cultural, Christian faith background and a tendency of donors to support Christian organizations. Liberal Christian FBOs have a long presence in development work, and have adapted to become similar to secular NGOs in their policies and programs, even as some scholars find that they mobilize a distinct discourse of development (Bornstein 2005; Halvorson 2013). Kartas and Silva suggest that such FBOs have taken a role not only as providers of development projects but often in contesting the neoliberal discourse of poverty and inequality itself (2013: 218), offering alternative visions of morality and what it means to live a good life.

Moreover, while FBOs have been perceived by donors and some scholars as having advantages over secular NGOs, this has not been empirically established; evidence that would allow a systematic comparison of performance is simply not available. There has been little systematic research that compares the results of secular versus religious service programs, and Carole Rakodi (2012b) argues that this comparison cannot really be made for several reasons. First is the very complexity of the category of FBO, which includes a wide array of religious traditions and organizations; this will be addressed further below. Moreover, the contexts of development projects vary tremendously, creating an array of methodological obstacles to making this assessment. Because of these and other methodological obstacles of searching for comparative advantages, Rakodi suggests that it would be better to ask "whether and how religious organisations make *distinctive* contributions to development and service delivery, with respect to the inputs they use, their ways of operating and the outcomes and impacts of their activities" (2012b: 642). A hermeneutic, interpretive approach may yield more useful information than a positivist approach (Deneulin and Rakodi 2010: 52).

Defining faith-based organizations

Despite the apparent ubiquity of faith-based organizations and their long history in providing various social services – or perhaps because of these factors – arriving at a definition of faith-based organizations is challenging. In important ways the term itself is relatively recent, traceable as Tomalin has argued to:

> a rise in awareness of the resurgence of religious activity in public life globally . . . the era of the Republican government of George W. Bush in the USA (2001–2009), during which there was an increased desire to draw religious organisations into public life around the agendas of social cohesion and service delivery.
>
> (Tomalin 2012: 692)

And, as we have seen, the term can be used to apply to an enormous range and variety of entities, from informal groups based in religious communities to international NGOs. Moreover, the term FBO itself is not used consistently, either co-existing with other terms, such as religious NGOs (RNGOs) or faith-based initiatives (FBIs), which are equally subject to interpretation, or not being used in self-designation by organizations themselves. For example, in Pakistan Kirmani and Zaidi found that Islamic charities in Karachi did not identify themselves as "FBOs" (2010; Kirmani 2012) for complex reasons that reflected the lack of relevance in that setting of distinguishing "faith-based" from "non-faith-based" organizations as well as the desire to avoid the political sensitivity of issues of faith and religion. This notwithstanding, the category of faith-based organization is widely recognized in development circles, but not least because, as Thomas Jeavons wryly suggested, it seems as though we "know one when we see one" (Jeavons 2004). He notes that "the current catch-all term *faith-based organizations* confuses and divides because no clear definition exists of what it means to be faith-based" (2004: 109–10), advocating a typology for understanding FBOs, rather than a definition. I agree that a typology is a useful approach in order to gain a more nuanced understanding of what an FBO is, and I will explore a typological approach in the next section of this chapter. A definition, however, is a worthwhile starting point, in helping to clarify what is meant – and perhaps equally importantly what is excluded – by *faith-based organization*. Several definitions offered by researchers and practitioners offer a starting point, as well as an indication of why a single definition continues to be elusive.

The first issue to consider, in defining what an FBO is, is what to include and what to leave out. While some commentators take a broad definition of FBO, and include within that category the wide range of organizations involved in religiously engaged development and welfare activity (e.g. Clarke 2008: 6; see below), others take a narrower view. Julia Berger (2003), for instance, takes a narrow definition, writing about NGOs represented at the UN, and defines what she calls *religious NGOs*, rather than FBOs, as "formal organizations whose identity and mission are self-consciously derived from the teachings of one or more religious or spiritual traditions and which operates on a nonprofit, independent, voluntary basis to promote and realize collectively articulated ideas about the public good at the national or international level" (2003: 16). This definition differentiates religious NGOs from congregational and denominational structures, which tend to focus more narrowly on their own membership. While this difference between the terms *religious NGO* and *faith-based organization* may be fairly minimal, a question of usage and style rather than a specific technical difference, Boehle (2010) suggests that the term RNGO is more common at the UN, while FBO seems to be more widely used by scholars, practitioners, and policy makers, particularly in the US.

To restrict the definition of the term FBO to organizations which are focused on development, charity, or service provision rather religious institutions themselves (such as congregations) is arguably more common in the US context with its emphasis on the separation of church and state (Tomalin 2012: 693). Jeavons, writing from the US domestic setting, for instance, emphatically argues that "congregations should not be described as FBOs under any circumstances" (2004: 144) in order to preserve the church–state distinction fundamental to the US constitution. Particularly since the last decade has seen an increasing willingness on the part of many governments to partner with FBOs to provide social services (for example, Mourier 2013), to focus on FBOs that are like NGOs may be helpful in distinguishing between organizations whose primary mission, as it were, is to engage in development practice rather than other kinds of religious organizations such as congregations or administrative bodies.[5]

Gerard Clarke and Michael Jennings, by contrast, ask "What exactly can, or cannot, be labelled as a faith-based organization? Do we, for instance, exclude Sunday schools, basic Christian Communities, or informal temple committees?," and they offer a broader definition of an FBO as "any organization that derives inspiration and guidance for its activities from the teachings and principles of the faith or from a particular interpretation or school of thought within the faith" (2008: 6). Clarke and Jennings's definition opens the possibility that an organization can be considered an FBO if it considers itself as such – if it is founded with the idea of a spiritual attachment or goals, rather than whether it is structurally connected, through shared members or formal ties, with a faith community or tradition. This definition can include places of worship and congregations themselves, as well as numerous organizations that are not affiliated with a larger faith community and are not formally registered like NGOs, encompassing many small, evangelical Christian organizations as well as non-Christian organizations in faiths where there may not be a centralized religious institutional structure; this approach to self-definition, however, does not address the question of how to categorize an organization that is unfamiliar with the term or chooses not to use it.

The ways in which FBOs are defined and understood has clear policy implications, as donors embrace partnership with organizations that fall into this (somewhat indeterminate) category rather than another, and as organizations themselves maneuver to be considered more, or sometimes less, faith-based (Tomalin 2012). But, even as donors and academics may seek definitional clarity about the category of FBO, it is crucial to recognize that there is not a clear line between religious and secular, that organizations take many forms, and that organizations classified by donors and policy makers as FBOs may have wildly various interests and goals.

Typologies

Because of the complexity of the category, it may be more useful to think of FBOs in terms of a typology rather than just a simple definition. A number of different typologies have been suggested for classifying FBOs (Berger 2003; Sider and Unruh 2004; Clarke 2006, 2008; Bradley 2009; Hefferan *et al.* 2009; Noy 2009). Boehle, for instance, argues that a typology that distinguishes between types of organizations in terms of how they use faith can be important in collaborations. He suggests that, "when an organization deploys faith in an exclusive and mandatory way, it is difficult to see how secular government agencies can justify giving public funds to an organization that may use those funds according to discriminatory, faith-based priorities" (Boehle 2010: 281). That said, a typology itself, much like a definition, cannot be applied over-schematically, attempting to create clearly differentiated "types" when these may not exist (Rakodi 2012b: 648). Any typology can conceal as much as it reveals by privileging some dimensions over others. With this caution in mind, I suggest characterizing FBOs along three dimensions which can assist development donors, policy makers, and practitioners in better understanding the terrain of FBOs globally and deciding which ones to partner with and in what ways: (1) the ways in which they are faith-based; (2) their activities (or the kinds of work in which they are engaged); and (3) the way they are organized in terms of their degree of formality and relationships with other faith and non-faith structures.

Thinking about FBOs according to the ways in which they are "faith-based"

While organizations may identify themselves as faith-based or not, faith can be manifest in different ways and to different degrees. The "faith" component of "faith-based" is not merely a set of institutional ties, but an expression of underlying principles, principles that then shape (at least potentially) the organization's work and the ways in which it understands that work from a larger perspective. To the extent that FBOs do, or can, represent a different approach to development than that of their secular peers, it must surely be embedded in this distinctive perspective. Michael Taylor comments wryly on this difference: "At most, I have heard it said, [faith] is like dressing on the salad, adding a bit of flavour but not greatly affecting the substance" (1995: 101). On the contrary, he continues, organizations such as the World Council of Churches see theology as both deeply embedded in and expressed by the service work of the organization itself, not just "Oxfam with hymns" but a fundamentally different approach to development (Taylor 1995).

Taylor's comments notwithstanding, it is not always as obvious as it may seem to distinguish between secular and religious organizations, a binary that is not always clear in either theory or practice (Fountain 2013). A survey that asked organizations to self-identify as religious or not found that categorization can be problematic, with highly variable terms, including words like "non-secular," being used by organizations to explain their orientation (Berger 2003). In addition to how an organization categorizes itself, the staff of both faith-based and secular organizations may be motivated in varying degrees by a personal sense of "faith" (Hovland 2008; Noy 2009). A simple, dichotomous secular/religious categorization is inadequate. Opening up the question of what it means, then, to be "faith-based" is one of the reasons that a typology can offer additional analytical clarity, allowing a more nuanced view than a binary of "secular" or "faith-based" can capture and recognizing that the ways in which an organization is "faith-based" can vary tremendously.

For some organizations and individuals, development work is a part of how one's own faith is lived out, as a good person in the world (Deneulin and Bano 2009). For others, development work is about righting injustices. And for others it is a pathway to, or form of, creating conditions for religious conversion. For many religious communities, engagement in development essentially represents an attempt to live a good life, in accordance with religious precepts, within a given social, political, and economic context (Deneulin and Bano 2009: 74). Yet FBOs incorporate and manifest their faith in widely varying ways; even within a single organization, the role of faith can be understood and expressed in multiple ways (de Wet 2013, for example). Thus, what it means for an organization to be "faith-based" can vary tremendously, with some organizations merely nodding in the direction of religiously inspired values, while others may be deeply and structurally connected to a faith community. FBOs are varied in the way that they deploy faith in mobilizing their own staff and supporters, in working with beneficiaries and partners, and in appealing to donors and funding sources (Clarke 2008: 32). Clarke offers a typology that suggests four ways in which FBOs deploy faith through social and political engagement or in links to their development objectives. The categories he suggests are (2008: 32–3):

- passive – reliance on broad ethical principles rather than specific religious teachings;
- active – faith is used explicitly to motivate staff and supporters and to identify or work with beneficiaries, but in a context of religious tolerance;
- persuasive – as with active, but also aims at proselytizing or promoting the religion;
- exclusive – faith is the chief consideration in service provision, identifying beneficiaries, and engaging in social and/or political action.

This typology and the resulting patterns of engagement, Clarke notes, present four problems (2008: 33–4). First, the categories are not always clear or exclusive. An organization can be passive in one regard and exclusive in another. Second, FBOs are highly networked, and may have different arms or branches that, while structurally separate, are closely coordinated, with affiliated organizations strategically taking different approaches. Third, the distinction between active and persuasive is nuanced and may be culturally specific or contextualized. Fourth, FBOs that are persuasive or exclusive – approaches which may be less acceptable to some donors – may help large numbers of poor people, who may thus have a high degree of confidence in them, in part because of shared religion.

An alternative typology, which avoids characterizing FBOs as located within one or other fixed category, was developed by Sider and Unruh (2004) to capture the ways in which faith orientation can be understood as a spectrum across different dimensions of an organization's structure, mission, and activities. This typology was developed to reflect the domestic setting in the USA and was refined by Hefferan *et al.* (2009: 20–25) to suit a development context; I have further adapted it here. This typology does two things. First, it allows organizations to be categorized on a scale from "faith-permeated" to "secular," conceptualizing an organization's expression of religion along a spectrum, and, second, we are then able to assess the degree of expression of faith across a number of different aspects of the organization. Such a typology allows researchers as well as practitioners to use the notion of "faith-based" with a more nuanced awareness of what this can mean, applying this spectrum to different aspects of the organization rather than to an organization as a whole. This spectrum includes the following general types (Hefferan *et al.* 2009: 20–25):

- faith-permeated – faith is an integral component and is openly and explicitly expressed;
- faith-centered – faith is important and taken for granted, but may be implicit rather than explicit;
- faith-affiliated – a faith background is important, and the organization draws on a faith community for some aspects of its support, but this may be more implicit or structural than explicit or embedded in discourses;

- faith background – more loosely tied to a faith tradition, whether this is through historical ties or faith-based values, but with few overt references to faith otherwise;
- faith–secular partnership – few references to faith, an attitude of respect and tolerance towards varying faith perspectives, or a completely secular perspective;
- secular – no faith content or overt faith references.

This spectrum of the ways in which faith can be expressed can then be applied to any dimension of an organization, ranging from its hiring practices and expectations of its personnel and their own affiliations, to the ways in which its programs are conceived and described to various stakeholders. Such dimensions can include:

- self-identification – mission statements, organizational ties, organized faith practices, use of faith symbols;
- staff and leadership – including founders, paid staff, volunteers, board members;
- financial support – degree of reliance on religious or secular funding sources; discourses that are used to raise money or obtain funding;
- programming – how faith is integrated into services and programs, expectations of beneficiaries, connections between faith and expected outcomes of programs.

In this way, the links between religion and development in any particular case study can be better understood, and more meaningful comparisons can be made between different organizations.

Thinking about FBOs according to their activities

A second dimension that characterizes FBOs is the kind of work in which they are engaged, or their activities. Importantly, Boehle, who is writing about religious NGOs at the UN, points out that not all are focused primarily on development issues; some focus on themes of peace and justice, environmental issues, or fostering dialogue on religion, in addition to those that provide social, humanitarian, and other assistance (2010: 282). In order to capture this diversity of types of organization, which may be involved in development work yet not have it as their primary or only activity, Clarke developed the following widely cited typology of FBOs (2006: 840). In particular, this draws attention to FBOs other than specific "development organizations":

- faith-based representative organizations or apex bodies – these are core religious organizations that rule on doctrine, govern the faithful, and represent the faith;
- faith-based charitable or development organizations – these mobilize the faithful in support of the poor or other marginalized groups;
- faith-based socio-political organizations – these interpret and deploy faith as a political construct and mobilize social groups based on a shared faith identity;
- faith-based missionary organizations – these are primarily engaged in recruitment and proselytizing;
- faith-based illegal or terrorist organizations – these engage in illegal activities on the grounds of faith.

In his discussion of this typology,[6] Clarke makes a number of additional comments on these categories. Some organization types are more common in some faith traditions but less common or nonexistent in others; apex organizations, for example, are more evident in religions that have an internal hierarchy, such as Christianity. Other faiths, such as Islam or Hinduism, lack this centralized administrative structure, which can make it more difficult for donors to identify interlocutors or representatives for key issues. Socio-political organizations are the most diverse of his categories, including political parties, social movements, professional associations, and secret societies. They differ from apex organizations in that they do not dictate doctrine. They do have a particularly important role where religious identity is central to identity politics, and often provide various social services, sometimes just to their members. Importantly, although just one of these categories refers specifically to development organizations, which have drawn the most recent attention from both donors and researchers, Clarke suggests that all of these kinds of organizations play a role in development in many contexts. In part, this may be because development – in the sense of social justice and creating a better world, in the sense of a world which is more in line with a sacred vision – is part of what a religious community understands itself to be (Deneulin and Bano 2009: 73).

Clarke calls mission organizations "invisible NGOs" (2006: 843; also Hearn 2002), invisible because their role in development has been ignored by both development studies and religious studies. An example of a mission organization engaged in development work is examined in a case study by Abbink (2004), who looks at Presbyterian missionaries among Suri pastoralists in southern Ethiopia. In this case, the Suri, who had been hostile to earlier Christian mission efforts, gradually came to accept the presence of these "new" missionaries, because the focus of the mission was on development work, with a low-key mission strategy that did not press for conversion. Abbink recognizes that the term "missionary" has many connotations, and he calls the group he studies "development workers with a religious inspiration" (2004: 137). The Presbyterians, in this case, focus on improving living conditions and, while they do desire the formation of a religious community, they wait for locals to take the initiative towards conversion. Clarke recognizes that mission groups are very active in the context of development, especially Pentecostal, evangelical Christian, and Muslim organizations, which have come to eclipse more traditional Protestant missions, spending large sums of money annually.[7]

The final type, "faith-based illegal or terrorist organizations," is significant also, yet frequently overlooked or dismissed. While the labels "illegal" or "terrorist" are highly subjective and can vary according to local, international, and national political and legal preferences, this category highlights the important and significant work that many organizations that are viewed as illegal or terrorist by the West carry out in developing contexts. For instance, in Pakistan after the earthquake in 2005 radical Islamic groups, banned elsewhere, were amongst the first on the scene providing humanitarian aid.

One shortcoming of classifying organizations by typology is that there may be considerable overlap between any of the categories. This is certainly true of Clarke's typology, as any single organization may operate in multiple capacities. While FBOs often conceive of their role as holistic, the above typology could make it seem as though they are taking on roles outside of some kind of "primary function." Given the complexity and diversity of the various roles of different organizations and the ways in which they overlap, I suggest that, rather than categorizing FBOs in terms of particular types of organization, we instead shift the emphasis from the type of organization to the activities that are performed by a particular organization. This recognizes that a single organization may have a "complex mix of attributes" (Kartas and Silva 2013: 210) and may see itself as having multiple functions or activities. Instead, a typology can be constructed that is similar to Clarke's but takes as its categories the *activities* of any particular organization, rather than the *type of organization* it represents:

- Religious policy, networking, and cooperation – this constitutes providing rulings on doctrine, governance of the faithful, and representing the faith. I include here ecumenical work, or networking and outreach between faiths, as well as representing a faith and its members to other organizations (such as the UN).
- Charitable and development work – this includes a range of activities that provide services to the poor or other marginalized groups, which can include health care, education, economic development, community development, and so on.
- Political activism and lobbying – this involves the political mobilization of social groups based on a shared faith identity. While Clarke's typology separates out terrorist organizations as a separate category, I would include illegal acts that are intended to serve a political agenda in this category, although it clearly represents an extreme and unusual variation; the political activities of most FBOs are undertaken with great consideration of ethical and legal means.
- Proselytizing and recruitment.

While both typologies aim to draw attention away from the fact that "development" is a discrete activity, which takes place only in particular settings, the function of my typology is somewhat different to that of Clarke's. Whereas the aim of Clarke's typology is to classify all the relevant religious actors that engage in development work, either explicitly or as a by-product, by the type of organization they represent, the purpose of my proposed typology is to draw attention to the different activities that may be found within any particular FBO. While some organizations may undertake only work that falls into one of these categories, many more have several, often overlapping, goals, activities, and functions. Particularly in the contemporary context, in which donors are increasingly seeking partnerships with such organizations and government agencies have been ever more willing to fund the work of FBOs, organizations see themselves as having a range of functions and activities. The degree to which a *donor* stresses the need to separate out "development" and "religious" activities may be the impetus for FBOs themselves to make this distinction, which otherwise may be understood holistically within the organization itself. By recognizing that an organization may engage in multiple kinds of work, this typology allows a more nuanced consideration of the roles of FBOs.

A study by Julie Hearn (2002) of FBOs in Kenya demonstrates the usefulness of thinking about the role of FBOs in terms of their multiple activities. Hearn documents that, as the number of missionaries in Africa has grown in recent years, US evangelical mission organizations have become among the most important groups of NGOs in Kenya, in an environment in which NGOs are heavily promoted and financed. Missionary organizations have benefited from a policy environment which favors "partnerships" between government agencies and NGOs, and have thus become instrumental in implementing US policy objectives, including the privatization of health care, increased family planning, controlling the spread of HIV/AIDS, and the provision of food aid. The article gives a brief case study of five FBOs, showing that organizations for which individual conversion is the primary goal have taken on an important new role as service-providing NGOs. A focus on activities, rather than "type" of organization, allows a more thorough consideration of various actors engaged in development or charity work.

Conceptualizing the work of FBOs according to their activities, rather than shoe-horning them into particular organizational "types," may better capture the perspective of many FBOs themselves, which tend to see the various kinds of work that they do as holistically connected (Hogue 2009). As a Christian missionary working in the Dominican Republic told me, for example, "You can't talk to someone about Jesus if they are hungry, or don't have a roof over their head" (field notes, April 2013). He clearly saw the development work that he was engaged in as prerequisite to proselytizing. For FBO staff and organizations, faith underlies and connects all of their activities.

Thinking about FBOs according to the degree of formality and relationships with other faith and non-faith structures

As we have already seen, while some FBOs resemble NGOs in having a formal structure, other FBOs may resemble grassroots organizations or movements, or may be identical to places of worship and congregations. At times a distinct "FBO" may not even be evident, where, for example, social services that are provided on a consistent basis over time may be "hidden" as part of the activity of a religious congregation or community, without separate legal status or even a separate formal structure. As Clarke (2006) indicates, however, researchers and donors have tended to focus on FBOs that function like other NGOs, with a limited understanding of, or interaction with, the other diverse kinds of FBOs that are present in the life of the poor. When considering FBOs, an important consideration is the way in which an organization is related to a religious tradition or to a specific religious community. As with approaching the issue of what "faith-based" means, a spectrum rather than a fixed set of types may begin to offer a sense of the range of kinds of organizational structures of FBOs, in terms of degree of formality and relationships with other faith and non-faith structures:

- initiatives within a larger faith organization that are volunteer-based, informal, and directed at members of the faith community;
- an organization that has formal structure within a denomination or faith that is oriented towards service provision, but is still subsidiary to a parent religious organization in terms of legal status, membership, and/or financing;
- a formal, independent NGO with ties to a particular religious community, such as a congregation, but with an independent organizational structure and identity;
- a formal NGO with loose ties to a parent faith, with ties to multiple faith communities, or autonomous from any particular faith.

This classificatory scheme can be even more complex in practice, considering that organizations can shift their position on the spectrum over time and for strategic reasons. For example, I did research with a small Catholic FBO in Argentina that originated as an outreach program of the church. Clergy and a few church leaders sought ways to improve the standard of living of people in the area where the church was located, combining development work with religious outreach in a rural region (Occhipinti 2005). The program operated for over a decade on this basis, run by volunteers and clergy. Only much later did it become a formal organization, when it became advantageous to do so in order to apply for government funding for some of its programs. This example illustrates how FBOs, to a much greater degree than secular NGOs, may be able to rely on the organizational structure of the parent faith, making them more likely to be hidden or invisible, operating under the auspices of a sponsoring religious organization or congregation. Religious organizations are also more likely than secular NGOs to be able to draw on these "parent" structures for funding, making them more independent from other donor organizations. They also are often able to mobilize horizontal and vertical networks that are associated with the religious tradition or communities to which they belong.

Thus, applying even this kind of a spectrum to actual case studies may be challenging, and this is further complicated by the multiple ties that organizations can have. Janine

Clark's (2008) case study of the Islamic Center Charity Society (ICCS) in Jordan, for example, illustrates the complex interrelationships between an FBO and other organizations. The ICCS is the social service "wing" of the Muslim Brotherhood, and part of a network of Brotherhood-affiliated aid organizations. The ICCS is structurally separate, in terms of decision making and funding, from both other aid organizations and from the political wing of the Muslim Brotherhood, thus placing it on the typology/spectrum above as a formal, independent NGO, but it is still clearly subsidiary to the larger Brotherhood organization, with significant overlaps in terms of membership and support, meaning that functionally it could be placed in the second category above. As it is an FBO embedded within larger networks, its actions have implications for relationships with the population, with the state, and for the internal politics of the larger movement, in which "the act of giving aid and support is itself the expression of faith" (Clark 2008: 151). In order to understand the work of such an FBO, it has to be seen in the context of its role as part of a larger socio-political movement.

Conclusion

As Tomalin (2012) and others have indicated, claims that FBOs have a comparative advantage over secular NGOs, or even that they are truly distinctive, need to be treated skeptically. The recent wave of enthusiasm for FBOs may be founded more in changing global political realities and an implicit recognition of the ongoing – not new – role of religious organizations in development discourse and practice than it is on any empirical evidence. The very complexity of the work of development organizations, including FBOs, may make such empirical evidence impossible to obtain. The increasing array of scholarly case studies that have been produced in recent years serves to illustrate the range and diversity of FBOs, and the need to be cautious in generalizing – or overgeneralizing – FBOs as a category of analysis and, even more, policy making.

As we have seen, definitions and typologies of FBOs can work to include or exclude organizations from this category, based on criteria like organizational structure and the ways in which faith is expressed and enacted. The degree of inclusiveness or exclusiveness may have profound policy implications. A donor, for example, may require a clear separation of religious and charitable functions, which can lead a religious community to create an administratively independent unit in order to be eligible for funding (as has been the case in the USA). From a theoretical perspective, however, a broader definition such as that offered by Clarke and Jennings (2008) allows a fuller consideration of FBOs as a category of actors in international economic development. While an inclusive definition such as that offered by Clarke and Jennings (2008) provides a useful point of reference, a typology allows a more nuanced perspective on what is a complex and heterogeneous category of organizations.

I have explored three typologies that allow us to better understand: the ways in which FBOs are faith-based; their activities (or the work in which they are engaged); and the way they are organized in terms of their degree of formality and relationships with other faith and non-faith structures. Taken together, I argue, these provide a framework for approaching the study of FBOs in terms of understanding what they do and how the religion impacts upon their work. In constructing this framework, I have avoided creating a set of categories or a rubric, however complex, into which organizations could simply be slotted. Instead, it encourages examining FBOs, and their internally constituent parts, through a number of lenses, along a number of spectra. Again this is important not only for academic interest but because it has implications for policy and funding, where the tendency to use the term FBO as though it is a singular and obvious category can obscure more than it illuminates. Instead, more complex and nuanced frameworks are necessary for increasing our knowledge about the nature and activities of the nebulous "FBO."

Notes

1 In fact different terms have been used to describe what we are calling here "FBOs," including "religious NGOs" (RNGOs) or "faith-based development organizations" (FBDOs).
2 The "Charitable Choice" provision in the 1996 Welfare Reform Act allowed "religious organizations" to compete for government contracts to provide welfare services, creating an environment that made it easier for faith-based organizations to receive federal funding. Prior to this only religiously affiliated organizations could apply for money, whereas congregations and/or places of worship could not. When George W. Bush came to power, as Chaves (2003) writes, "he signed two executive orders in the opening days of his administration – one establishing a White House Office of Faith-Based and Community Initiatives (OFBCI) and another establishing centers for Faith-Based and Community Initiatives in five federal departments. The White House office is charged with identifying and eliminating funding barriers faced by faith-based programs."
3 However, the religious contexts in the US and the UK are quite different; in the US, the Charitable Choice initiatives enjoyed the support of conservative and evangelical religious organizations and blurred the line between religious and development activities, while the UK did not have similar conservative religious growth, and the largest FBOs in the UK were "quasi-secular" in their policies and outlook (Clarke 2007: 84).
4 Many of these assertions echo those made about NGOs more generally in the 1980s.
5 This focus on activities of organizations will be addressed in the typology below.
6 It is notable that, despite the inclusive definition of FBO outlined above (Clarke and Jennings 2008), in this typology Clarke does not refer specifically to actual places of worship or congregations, which may engage in an array of welfare and development activities in addition to worship.
7 Mission-oriented FBOs are less common in other faith traditions which do not have an emphasis on proselytizing.

References

Abbink, J. (2004) 'Converting Pastoralists: Reflections on Missionary Work and Development in Southern Ethiopia', in Oscar Salemink, Anton van Hargkamp and Ananta Kumar Giri (eds), *The Development of Religion/The Religion of Development*, Delft: Eburon Academic Publishers, pp. 133–41.

Adkins, Julie, Hefferan, Tara and Occhipinti, Laurie (eds) (2010) *Not by Faith Alone: Social Services, Social Justice, and Faith-Based Organizations in the United States*, Lanham, MD: Lexington Books.

Alvaré, Bretton (2009) 'Fighting for "Livity": Rastafari Politics in a Neoliberal State', in Tara Hefferan, Julie Adkins and Laurie Occhipinti (eds), *Bridging the Gaps: Faith-Based Organizations, Neoliberalism, and Development in Latin America and the Caribbean*, Lanham, MD: Lexington Books, pp. 51–68.

Berger, Julia (2003) 'Religious Nongovernmental Organizations: An Exploratory Analysis', *Voluntas: International Journal of Voluntary and Nonprofit Organizations*, 14 (1), 15–39.

Boehle, Josef (2010) 'Religious NGOs at the UN and the Millennium Development Goals: An Introduction', *Global Change, Peace and Security*, 22 (3), 275–96.

Bornstein, Erica (2005) *The Spirit of Development: Protestant NGOs, Morality, and Economics in Zimbabwe*, Stanford, CA: Stanford University Press.

Bradley, Tamsin (2005) 'Does Compassion Bring Results? A Critical Perspective on Faith and Development', *Culture and Religion*, 6 (3), 337–51.

Bradley, Tamsin (2009) 'A Call for Clarification and Critical Analysis of the Work of Faith-Based Development Organizations (FBDO)', *Progress in Development Studies*, 9 (2), 101–14.

Chaves, Mark (2003) 'Debunking Charitable Choice', *Stanford Social Innovation Review*, http://www.ssireview.org/articles/entry/debunking_charitable_choice.

Clark, Janine (2008) 'FBOs and Change in the Context of Authoritarianism: The Islamic Center Charity Society in Jordan', in Gerard Clarke and Michael Jennings (eds), *Development, Civil Society and Faith-Based Organizations: Bridging the Sacred and the Secular*, New York: Palgrave Macmillan, pp. 145–70.

Clarke, Gerard (2006) 'Faith Matters: Faith-Based Organisations, Civil Society and International Development', *Journal of International Development*, 18, 835–48.

Clarke, Gerard (2007) 'Agents of Transformation? Donors, Faith-Based Organisations and International Development', *Third World Quarterly*, 28 (1), 77–96.

Clarke, Gerard (2008) 'Faith-Based Organizations and International Development: An Overview', in Gerard Clarke and Michael Jennings (eds), *Development, Civil Society and Faith-Based Organizations: Bridging the Sacred and the Secular*, New York: Palgrave Macmillan, pp. 17–45.

Clarke, Gerard (2013) 'The Perils of Entanglement: Bilateral Donors, Faith-Based Organisations and International Development', in Giles Carbonnier (ed.), *International Development Policy: Religion and Development*, Basingstoke: Palgrave Macmillan, pp. 65–78.

Clarke, Gerard and Jennings, Michael (2008) 'Introduction', in Gerard Clarke and Michael Jennings (eds), *Development, Civil Society, and Faith-Based Organizations*, New York: Palgrave Macmillan, pp. 1–16.

Cooper, Melinda (2014) 'The Theology of Emergency: Welfare Reform, US Foreign Aid and the Faith-Based Initiative', *Theory, Culture and Society*, January, Doi:10.1177/0263276413508448.

de Kadt, Emanuel (2009) 'Should God Play a Role in Development?', *Journal of International Development*, 21, 781–6.

Deneulin, Séverine and Bano, Masooda (2009) *Religion in Development: Rewriting the Secular Script*, New York: Zed Books.

Deneulin, Séverine and Rakodi, Carole (2010) 'Revisiting Religion: Development Studies Thirty Years On', *World Development*, 39 (1), 45–54.

DeTemple, Jill, Eidenshank, Erin and Josephson, Katrina (2009) 'How Is Your Life since Then? Gender, Doctrine, and Development in Bolivia', in Tara Hefferan, Julie Adkins and Laurie Occhipinti (eds), *Bridging the Gaps: Faith-Based Organizations, Neoliberalism, and Development in Latin America and the Caribbean*, Lanham, MD: Lexington Books, pp. 119–32.

de Wet, Hannah Lindiwe (2013) 'Transformational Development: World Vision South Africa's Response to Poverty', in Giles Carbonnier (ed.), *International Development Policy: Religion and Development*, Basingstoke: Palgrave Macmillan, pp. 95–114.

Fountain, Philip (2013) 'The Myth of Religious NGOs: Development Studies and the Return of Religion', in Giles Carbonnier (ed.), *International Development Policy: Religion and Development*, Basingstoke: Palgrave Macmillan, pp. 9–30.

Hackworth, Jason R. (2012) *Faith Based: Religious Neoliberalism and the Politics of Welfare in the United States*, Athens: University of Georgia Press.

Halvorson, Britt (2013) 'Woven Worlds: Material Things, Bureaucratization, and Dilemmas of Caregiving in Lutheran Humanitarianism', *American Ethnologist*, 39 (1), 122–37.

Haynes, Jeffrey (2013) 'Faith-Based Organizations, Development, and the World Bank', in Giles Carbonnier (ed.), *International Development Policy: Religion and Development*, Basingstoke: Palgrave Macmillan, pp. 49–64.

Hearn, Julie (2002) 'The "Invisible" NGO: US Evangelical Missions in Kenya', *Journal of Religion in Africa*, 32 (1), 32–60.

Hefferan, Tara, Adkins, Julie and Occhipinti, Laurie (2009) 'Faith-Based Organizations, Neoliberalism, and Development: An Introduction', in Tara Hefferan, Julie Adkins and Laurie Occhipinti (eds), *Bridging the Gaps: Faith-Based Organizations, Neoliberalism, and Development in Latin America and the Caribbean*, Lanham, MD: Lexington Books, pp. 1–34.

Hogue, Emily (2009) '"God Wants Us to Have a Life That Is Sustainable": Faith-Based Development and Economic Change in Andean Peasant Communities', in Tara Hefferan, Julie Adkins and Laurie Occhipinti (eds), *Bridging the Gaps: Faith-Based Organizations, Neoliberalism, and Development in Latin America and the Caribbean*, Lanham, MD: Lexington Books, pp. 133–50.

Hovland, Ingie (2008) 'Who's Afraid of Religion? Tensions between "Mission" and "Development" in the Norwegian Mission Society', in Gerard Clarke and Michael Jennings (eds), *Development, Civil Society and Faith-Based Organizations: Bridging the Sacred and the Secular*, New York: Palgrave Macmillan, pp. 171–86.

James, R. (2009) *What Is Distinctive about FBOs?*, Praxis Paper no. 22, Oxford: INTRAC.

Jeavons, Thomas H. (2004) 'Religious and Faith-Based Organizations: Do We Know One When We See One?', *Nonprofit and Volunteer Sector Quarterly*, 33 (1), 140–45.

Jones, Ben and Juul Petersen, Marie (2011) 'Instrumental, Narrow, Normative? Reviewing Recent Work on Religion and Development', *Third World Quarterly*, 32 (7), 1291–1306.

Kartas, Moncef and Silva, Kalinga Tudor (2013) 'Reflections on the Role of Religion and Faith in Development Discourse and Practice', in Giles Carbonnier (ed.), *International Development Policy: Religion and Development*, Basingstoke: Palgrave Macmillan, pp. 209–20.

Kirmani, Nida (2012) 'The Role of Religious Values and Beliefs in Charitable and Development Organisations in Karachi and Sindh, Pakistan', *Development in Practice*, 22 (5–6), 735–48.

Kirmani, Nida and Zaidi, Sarah (2010) *The Role of Faith in the Charity and Development Sector in Karachi and Sindh, Pakistan*, Religions and Development Research Programme, Working Paper 50, Birmingham: Religions and Development.

Leurs, Robert (2012) 'Are Faith-Based Organisations Distinctive? Comparing Religious and Secular NGOs in Nigeria', *Development in Practice*, 22 (5–6), 704–20.

Lunn, Jenny (2009) 'The Role of Religion, Spirituality and Faith in Development: A Critical Theory Approach', *Third World Quarterly*, 30 (5), 937–51.

Marshall, Katherine (2001) 'Development and Religion: A Different Lens on Development Debates', *Peabody Journal of Education*, 76 (3–4), 339–75.

Mourier, Eliott (2013) 'Religion as a Social Substitute for the State: Faith-Based Social Action in Twenty-First Century Brazil', in Giles Carbonnier (ed.) *International Development Policy: Religion and Development*, Basingstoke: Palgrave Macmillan, pp. 79–94.

Noy, Darren (2009) 'Material and Spiritual Conceptions of Development: A Framework of Ideal Types', *Journal of Developing Societies*, 25, 275–307.

Occhipinti, Laurie (2005) *Acting on Faith: Economic Development in Indigenous Communities in Northern Argentina*, Lanham, MD: Lexington Books.

Occhipinti, Laurie (2013) 'Liberating Development: Religious Transformations of Development Discourse', *Perspectives on Global Development and Technology*, 12, 427–43.

Pearson, Ruth and Tomalin, Emma (2008) 'Intelligent Design? A Gender-Sensitive Interrogation of Religion and Development', in Gerard Clarke and Michael Jennings (eds), *Development, Civil Society, and Faith-Based Organizations: Bridging the Sacred and the Secular*, New York: Palgrave Macmillan, pp. 46–71.

Pereira, Javier, Angel, Ronald J. and Angel, Jacqueline L. (2009) 'A Chilean Faith-Based NGO's Social Service Mission in the Context of Neoliberal Reform', in Tara Hefferan, Julie Adkins and Laurie Occhipinti (eds), *Bridging the Gaps: Faith-Based Organizations, Neoliberalism, and Development in Latin America and the Caribbean*, Lanham, MD: Lexington Books, pp. 151–64.

Peters, Paul A. (2009) 'Faith-Related Education NGOs in Latin America: The Case of Fé y Alegria in Peru', in Tara Hefferan, Julie Adkins and Laurie Occhipinti (eds), *Bridging the Gaps: Faith-Based Organizations, Neoliberalism, and Development in Latin America and the Caribbean*, Lanham, MD: Lexington Books, pp. 165–80.

Rakodi, Carole (2012a) 'Religion and Development: Subjecting Religious Perceptions and Organisations to Scrutiny', *Development in Practice*, 22 (5–6), 621–33.

Rakodi, Carole (2012b) 'A Framework for Analyzing the Links between Religion and Development', *Development in Practice*, 22 (5–6), 634–50.

Rivlin, Benjamin (2002) 'Thoughts on Religious NGOs at the UN: A Component of Global Civil Society', in Peter Hajnal (ed.), *Civil Society in the Information Age: NGOs, Coalitions, Relationships*, Aldershot: Ashgate, pp. 155–73.

Sider, Ronald J. and Unruh, Heidi Rolland (2004) 'Typology of Religious Characteristics of Social Service and Educational Organizations and Programs', *Nonprofit and Voluntary Sector Quarterly*, 33 (1), 109–34.

Tadros, Mariz (2010) *Faith-Based Organizations and Service Delivery: Some Gender Conundrums*, UNRISD Gender and Development Programme Paper no. 11, Geneva: United Nations Institute for Social Development.

Taylor, Michael (1995) *Not Angels but Agencies: The Ecumenical Response to Poverty – a Primer*, Geneva: WCC Publications.

Tomalin, Emma (2012) 'Thinking about Faith-Based Organisations in Development: Where Have We Got To and What Next?', *Development in Practice*, 22 (5–6), 689–703.

23

RELIGION AT THE INTERSECTION OF DEVELOPMENT AND PUBLIC HEALTH IN DEVELOPMENT CONTEXTS

From advocacy about faith-based organizations to systems thinking

Jill Olivier

Introduction

In an unprecedented move in 2005, the World Health Organization (WHO) commissioned a consortium of university-based researchers to go out into the field to find and map any religious communities and institutions that were engaged in HIV/AIDS and healthcare more generally in Zambia and Lesotho (ARHAP 2006). What is most interesting about this small commission was that it originated from a realization within the WHO, the world's premier public health authority, that there was no currently available information on the presence or contribution of religion to healthcare in development contexts. Said differently, no one knew what religious healthcare entities were out there, what they were doing or even where they were. This was acerbated by the realization that the WHO's existing mapping and assessment system at the time, the Service Availability Mapping (SAM) system, did not have a category for religious institutions engaged in healthcare – so, in effect, could not 'see' them.

How had this happened? How had the world of public health and policy become blind to the presence and contribution of religious institutions in development contexts? All the world's main religions have health and healing as central tenets of their faith. This leads inevitably towards religious communities being engaged in health-related activities, and in many cases the formal provision of healthcare, as an expression of that faith (see Olivier and Paterson 2011). Islamic hospitals and Christian missionary facilities were often the first modern healthcare providers in development contexts, and established the first health systems in these countries (see Schmid *et al.* 2008). Religious bodies were also strongly involved in early public health advocacy, and in shaping global health policy – the most obvious example being the influence of religious-medical thinkers and the Christian Medical Commission in the shaping of the Alma

Ata Declaration of 1975 on primary healthcare and 'Health for All', which has remained a core ideal of global health (see Gunderson and Cochrane 2012).

As a result of more recent research work, we now know that religious healthcare providers continue to be a substantial presence in many development contexts, and their activities can be seen across the spectrum of local community initiatives up to tertiary-level and specialist hospitals (Olivier and Wodon 2012c). However, at the beginning of the twenty-first century, all that was visible was a massive informational black hole, so much so that the estimates of percentages of religious healthcare market share that are visible in the literature from around 1980 to 2005 were mainly based on a single rapid survey of a few countries conducted in the 1960s – the only figures that would be available for the next half-century (Olivier and Wodon 2012b).

In this chapter, we consider the nature of the intersection between religion and public health in development contexts. What we are most interested in are the forces that resulted in a general loss of awareness of the work and presence of religious institutions at the level of policy, international discussion and arguably resource allocation – and a resulting turn-around and refocusing of attention that occurred in the last decade. We first consider why religious healthcare institutions dropped off the international map, and then the significant advocacy efforts required to bring them back into view. Finally, we consider the emerging arena of health systems research and engagement and why getting religious institutions to that table is of particular relevance and importance. This chapter therefore seeks to provide important background for those seeking to understand the nature and influences at play in the space between religion, public health and development. This understanding is especially important for new actors and researchers seeking to engage and collaborate in that complex space.

Getting religious health institutions (back) onto the global health map

Lee and Newberg talk about the ancient relationship between religion and health as having 'cycled between cooperation and antagonism throughout history . . . physicians', scientists', and healthcare providers' views of religion have ranged from interest to disinterest to disdain' (Lee and Newberg 2005: 443–4). From around 1980 to 2000, the view from public health towards religion can only be described as a cycle of general disinterest. There are several key reasons for this perspective. Firstly, the effects of secularism and modernization thinking gave rise to the idea that, as societies developed and modernized, religion would increasingly be relegated to the back seat and lose its influence on public life as rational science and thinking gained strength. Modernization thinking held (and holds) an inherent bias towards religion, where religions were seen as obstacles to progress (see Melkote and Steeves 2001).

By the second half of the twentieth century, religion had been overtly removed from politics in most development contexts, as part of the separation of church and state (as religion became held to be something private). From a development perspective, religious organizations working in health became classified as a subset of non-governmental organizations within civil society. From a health systems perspective, religious health providers were reclassified as part of the private health sector. This latter change was particularly apparent in post-colonial contexts in the latter half of the twentieth century, where health systems were entirely reconfigured after independence, substantive new public sectors were established, and waves of health sector reforms were implemented. As a result, in many African countries, while at the time of independence religious health providers might have been the majority providers of modern healthcare, a few decades later most now held substantially smaller comparative slices of their reconfigured health systems (Wodon et al. 2014).

In academia, as secularization discourse began to dominate across the human and natural sciences, religion began to be written out of any kind of public health or medical curricular or research field (see (Melkote and Steeves 2001; Cochrane 2006b). This all worked to create an inherent bias against religion in many of these fields which lingers today, and resulted in a kind of 'blindness' towards religion (see Casanova 1994; Cochrane 2006b). In many disciplines, 'religion' was constructed as the binary opposite of 'science'. For example, O'Connor and Meakes (2005) speak of the influences of the scientific revolution, and that the relationship between religion and science has evolved into two forms, a relationship of either antagonism or separation. In fact, a number of powerful binary discourses emerged, with science–rationality–progress on the one side, and religion–irrationality–tradition on the other; and, in these discourses, public health emerged very much on the opposite side from religion, on the side of science–rationality–progress. It is not a surprise that public health evidences a strong modernist approach given that it emerged in a post-Enlightenment period (see Petersen and Lupton 1996). Linked to the scientific revolution and the emergence of biomedicine as the dominant force of the modern era, public health rose to become a dominant social, political and academic force. Some have labelled the twentieth century 'the century of public health', the era in which public health made significant advances in safe water, sanitation and immunization (Cochrane 2006a: 60–61). In the 1970s and 1980s public health's successes against the pandemics of infectious diseases, for example 'conquering' smallpox and polio, were applauded as 'grand monuments to the work of public health practitioners and policy makers' (Cochrane 2006a: 61; see Detels and Breslow 1997).

Therefore, as a result of this burgeoning dominance of modernist science, biomedicine and public health, the public health work of religious communities and organizations quietly disappeared from sight and importance at an international policy level. It is important to note that this does not mean that religious institutions and communities stopped being engaged in public health action, but rather that this activity disappeared from view at the level of international policy and from research priorities, and therefore also from publication. Coffman argues that this schism occurred at several levels (speaking of the global context in the nineteenth and twentieth centuries):

> in the midst of this flood of discovery and progress, a tragedy occurred. Many of the bridges between faith and health were washed out. In the excitement and thrill of the explosion of scientific knowledge, the church relinquished her position as the centre of healing for individuals and communities. The bridges that existed for centuries collapsed in a matter of a few decades. Faith and health were segregated. . . . We take our bodies to doctors, our souls to church, and our minds to school.
>
> (Coffman 2002: 2)

The (re-)emergence of religion into public life, academia and policy

Then, late in the twentieth century, something unexpected happened. Contrary to the predictions of modernist and secular theories, religion began to re-emerge into public life on a startling number of fronts. There was an undeniable flourishing of religious movements across the globe, for example Pentecostal and charismatic varieties of Christianity in Africa and a highly political Islam in North Africa, as well as religious revivals in Asia and the United States (see Derrida and Vattimo 1998; Ellis and ter Haar 2001). Religion also began to re-emerge as a valid topic in several public arenas of inquiry. The most obvious example of this was the reappearance of religion in the political sphere, challenging the secular–modernist conceptions of separation of religion and state, such as when newly elected President Chiluba officially declared Zambia to be a Christian nation in 1991 (see Berger 1999). Another obvious re-emergence of religion on to the political stage came after the 11 September 2001 attacks in America, which resulted in a rapid politicization of religion on a global scale, most often as a political liability, but nevertheless spurring an increase in interest, commentary and inquiry into the role of religion in public life.

Less public, but just as surprising, has been the re-emergence of religion in academia and scholarship. The most obvious sign was the emerging popularity of critique of the secularization and modernism theses, in particular the basic idea that development or modernization equals secularization. For example, Berger, earlier a key proponent of the secularization thesis, admitted bravely in 1999 that 'the assumption that we live in a secularised world is false. The world today . . . is as furiously religious as it ever was, and in some places more so than ever. This means that a whole body of literature by historians and social scientists loosely labelled "secularisation theory" is essentially mistaken' (Berger 1999: 2).

Interestingly, while religion was slowly regaining some lost ground as a valid area of inquiry, public health was cycling into a minor slump. Garrett describes what she terms the 'collapse' of global public health in the 1980s and 1990s, saying 'the past decade has witnessed a profound transformation in the challenges to global health; persistent problems have been joined by new scourges in a world that is ever more complex and interdependent' (Garrett 2000: 9). Garrett gives examples such as weakened health systems, increasing environmental loads, increased vulnerability and general failures in public health strategies. She describes the WHO, 'once the conscience of global health', as having 'lost its way in the 1990s' (Garrett 2000: 9). Even in the face of scientific and biomedical advances, public health found itself struggling for self-definition and clear 'wins' in the late twentieth century (see Farmer 1999; Garrett 2000). A significant factor in this was the emergence of HIV/AIDS in the 1980s, which seriously undermined previous confidence in public health (and that epidemic disease had been conquered) and emphasized failures of public health programmes and strategies as well as severe weaknesses in underlying health systems, particularly health systems in development contexts. In Africa, it became clear that a price was being paid for a history of inadequate health resources and poorly targeted interventions (see Farmer 1999; Kim *et al.* 2000). In an echoing of the failure of the secularization thesis, against all expectations, global public health (backed by modernization, scientific progress, development strategies and massive funding) had apparently not resulted in the improvement of health generally or the strengthening of health systems to the extent that had been expected.

It is in this context of a waxing of interest in religion and a waning of confidence in public health that religion re-emerged onto the radar of global development and public health agendas. In a rush of high-level advocacy and increased dialogue in the early twenty-first century, a few leaders of religious institutions were amazed to find themselves invited as representatives of the 'faith sector' to high-level strategy meetings and consultations. An early example is the much-quoted participation of the World Council of Churches and religious institutions in the UN Special General Assembly on HIV/AIDS, in June 2001. Religious representation at international health and development conferences and gatherings became more apparent; key international institutions published new reports on their partnership strategy with the so-called 'faith sector'; new collaborative networks and facilitating organizations were formed; and new academic programmes focusing on the interface between religion, development and public health were initiated (Olivier 2010). This re-emergence was rapid and significant, as a few religious institutions and leaders suddenly found themselves back in the international policy spotlight – for some, also resulting in significantly increased financial support (see Olivier and Wodon 2014). As Benn said in 2003, speaking about religious institutions engaged in healthcare, 'for decades they were at best tolerated but not actively supported. Now there is almost a competition among big secular donors to fund the best programmes' (Benn 2003: 9).

However, it is important to understand that this increased enthusiasm came with its own challenges, and did not automatically lead to widespread improved cooperation or increased support for all. There was a substantial lingering bias towards religious perspectives, individuals and institutions within the worlds of global public health and international development. In fact, 'religionophobia' in the form of doubt, suspicion and negative perceptions continues to linger today. In a 2009 meeting on mapping standards in Geneva, Canon Ted Karpf, then of the WHO, noted:

> There is a great deal moving in the international community on the global health stage. A parallel movement [is] going on among those administering faith health assets. . . . While it would appear that these separate movements are converging towards a common expression, I regret to tell you that they are not . . . there are several of us in the UN and intergovernmental system who have been successful in moving the door ajar . . . organisations such as UNAIDS, the Global Fund, World Bank, UNFPA, UNDP and WHO have increased their dialogue and begun to deepen their understanding of the faith communities and the health and social services they provide . . . the fact remains that religious health assets are a 'hard sell' for many who are not often the recipients of their services . . . simply put, the cultural environment is still hostile towards neutral, and only occasionally welcoming, usually when there are systemic failures or a global health emergency.
>
> (Karpf in WHO–CIFA 2009: 12–13)

Such negative and resistant perspectives remain strong in many circles – and are often based on substantial concerns and experiences, such as the fear that development aid or public resources might be utilized towards proselytization or the promotion of religion.

However, even more significantly, engagement continues to be severely hampered by a lack of basic information about religion and religious entities engaged in health and development. In other words, the increased spotlight only highlighted the fact that the area of inquiry had been badly neglected for several decades prior to this, and showed up the resulting lack of basic empirical evidence of the presence, role, impact and characteristic differences of religious entities engaged in health and development at different levels. In response, a relatively small community of inquiry emerged at what was then seen as a new intersection of interests: between religion, public health and development. For the first few years (around 2000–2010), many researchers and practitioners focused primarily on arguing for the validity of a focus on religious institutions and communities (arguing why it was worth researching religiously influenced things), and provided many landscaping reviews and studies demonstrating the presence of religious institutions engaged in HIV/AIDS and health (see Olivier 2010). As a result, reviews show a massive bloom of publications (mainly grey literature and reports) at the intersection of religion, development and public health in the last decade (Olivier *et al.* 2014a, 2014b). However, this remains an area of significant informational gaps, and calls for increased research and more targeted attention continue to be made (see Olivier and Wodon 2012c; WFDD 2012).

Key features of an emerging field (2000–2010)

There are several key features of this emerging field that need to be understood by anyone seeking to engage in this space or seeking to translate research into action. It cannot be overestimated how strongly HIV/AIDS has influenced the agenda and shaping of this area of inquiry. As a demonstration, a comparison of a current database on religion and HIV/AIDS and another on religion and public health shows that almost two-thirds of all literature on religion and public health is focused on HIV/AIDS (see Olivier *et al.* 2014a, 2014b). The politics and priorities of the HIV/AIDS field have infused into the broader inquiry into religion and development and religion and public health. The influence of HIV/AIDS-driven inquiry also explains why it is so difficult to distinguish between inquiry on religion and development and that on religion and public health (as demonstrated in this chapter and this volume more broadly), since HIV/AIDS came to be understood as an epidemic of health and of development, so has influenced massive cross-over between these areas.

The emergence of HIV/AIDS as a complex social problem forced a greater engagement with complex social issues – for every solution, there was a confounding and unexpected problem. This opened the door to mainstream inquiry that addressed religion, since religion was raised as one of those confounding and often unaccounted-for factors in the lives of people living in the contexts most affected by HIV/AIDS (see Olivier and Wodon 2012a). When Peter Piot opened the Mexico AIDS Conference in 2008 he said, 'Let's never forget that the epidemic could still bring us new surprises – as it has done so many times already. If we are to get ahead of this epidemic, it is time to come to terms with complexity' (Piot 2008: 2). This necessity to grapple with complexity focused new international attention on religion in two main ways: firstly, on religion as a potentially important factor in individual health-related decision making; and, secondly, the idea that religious communities and institutions held untapped resources or assets that could be used by a global community against HIV/AIDS.

The first area of attention, on religion as an important factor affecting individual behaviour, tied in well with a parallel cluster of inquiry, namely research on 'spirituality and health'. There are several useful reviews of this body of literature (see Koenig *et al.* 2001), and it has been noted that, while before 1970 there was little research exploring the link between spiritual care and health, since then the amount of research by healthcare professionals on spiritual care and health has 'exploded' (O'Connor and Meakes 2005), with one review estimating a 600 per cent increase in publications on 'spirituality and health' during the period 1993 to 2002 (Stefanek *et al.* 2004: 450). Interest also grew significantly from around 2005 into how religion affects individual health and behaviours in development contexts. For example, researchers began to note that religion was often highly significant for Africans and other development contexts and that, for a majority of such people, their interpretations of life and health would be powerfully religious, and any public health strategy that did not recognize this would be likely to fail (see Benn 2002; de Gruchy 2006).

The other main area of attention can be seen in a strong discourse that emerged (and is still visible) in the policy and research documentation: that speaks of religion and religious assets as untapped resources available to be used for the broader goals of development and public health (Olivier 2010). For example, the World Bank says: 'the role of African faith-based organizations in combating HIV and AIDS is widely recognized as having growing significance but, at the same time, one which is not fully exploited, given the influence and reach of FBOs in African societies' (World Bank 2004: 1). The Zambian national HIV and AIDS strategy similarly states a primary objective as being 'to fully exploit the potential of faith-based organisations in the fight against HIV/AIDS' (Zambia Ministry of Health 2005: 22). This discourse has also caused significant discomfort among religious institutions, which have protested against being treated in an instrumental fashion by the international community (see Olivier and Paterson 2011). Paterson warns that religious organizations have begun to be seen as a bottomless pit of volunteers: 'FBOs have felt good about being drawn in, and are suddenly part of the solution, but do we want to be regarded in this instrumental way, and should we be thinking through the values we want to bring to the table?' (Paterson 2008: 1).

However, despite significantly increased attention, dialogue and publications, this area of inquiry has remained fairly inconclusive. A major challenge is that there continue to be broad generalizations made within the literature and commentary about the suspected generic strengths and weaknesses of all 'faith-based organizations', and these continue to be easily challenged from those operating at a policy level (see Olivier and Wodon 2012a). For example, as a result of these generalizations, based on the current literature 'any position or conclusion about religious entities and the religious response to HIV/AIDS can be defended' (Olivier and Wodon 2012a: 31). And this highlights one of the main challenges in this area of inquiry – the massive diversity and complexity of what has been termed the 'faith sector'. While advocacy efforts have sought solidarity by clustering 'things of faith' together, this has continued to challenge any empirical research or inquiry. For example, every study that assesses the religious response to HIV/AIDS in Africa (a common theme) tends to have a different unit of analysis. Said differently, for every study the term 'faith-based organization' means something different, and for many this is inclusive of any entity (whether local informal community initiative or tertiary hospital) that has some relation to religion and is in some way engaged in health or development. In some studies, mainstream religious groups are merged with indigenous cultures, while in other studies only one religious group is assessed. There is currently also no shared typology of what is a 'faith-based organization'. This makes cross-analysis difficult, and makes integration of this work with other development or public health evidence virtually impossible. This diversity also makes it difficult to make policy-level statements. For example, policy-level engagement strategies are rare, given that they would differ greatly if you were addressing Catholics or charismatics, informal women's groups or complex hospital systems – all of which are often called 'faith-based organizations' in the current literature (see Olivier 2011; Olivier and Wodon 2012a, 2012b).

This challenging complexity extends to the subgroup of religious healthcare providers. For example, in Africa, each country context has a different configuration of religious facilities engaged in healthcare, depending on history and health systems development. For example, in many Islamic-majority territories, especially those in Central and Northern Africa, there are comparatively few religious healthcare institutions (although Islamic facilities are growing in some areas); in Christian-majority and Anglophone countries, religious healthcare providers are still significant but play a secondary role to the public sector; and, in some post-conflict contexts, religious providers sometimes support most of the national health system. What this demonstrates is that any generalization about religious providers engaged in healthcare in Africa or internationally should be viewed with caution, as local context and diversity are massively relevant. In addition, within national health systems, different religious actors have different forms and structures (even if they are sometimes networked together), which means that complexity is unavoidable in relation to systems-level engagement (see Dimmock *et al.* 2012; Olivier and Wodon 2012a; Wodon *et al.* 2014).

Mismatching discourses hampering interdisciplinary and multisectoral collaboration

One of the most significant barriers to improved collaboration and engagement between religion, development and public health has been a hugely problematic mismatch of discourses. This may seem fairly innocuous, but is indicative of an underlying clash of knowledge paradigms. When religion began to emerge back on to the radar of public health in the early twenty-first century, even some of the first meetings noted this to be a major challenge. For example,

Marshall (then of the World Bank) noted that at a first meeting between leaders at Lambeth Palace in London in 1998:

> that meeting – exploratory and private – gave rise to two convictions. First, common interest in fighting poverty was a powerful impetus for collaboration; and second, major efforts to bridge gaps between secular and faith organisations in communication styles as well as practical perspectives were essential if the common interests were to go beyond words . . . the large gulf between faith and development worlds in developing countries: in particular, secular and religious organisations simply do not understand their respective vocabularies . . . they tend to expend energy in debates that too often pass like ships in the night.
>
> (Marshall and Van Saanen 2007: 7–10)

This communicative difficulty has been noted by many others. For example, the partnerships advisor for the Joint United Nations Programme on HIV/AIDS (UNAIDS), which has played a pivotal role in building a collaborative network between religious partners in the UNAIDS environment, has spoken of these challenges, saying 'UNAIDS has been working with FBOs to enhance communication skills to be able to bridge gaps created when agencies and FBOs speak two different languages' (Smith in WHO–CIFA 2009: 17). Benn, from the Global Fund to Fight AIDS, TB and Malaria, agrees, saying 'Sometimes the biggest challenge for forging collaboration around this theme between public health experts, representatives of international organizations, and the faith community is the lack of a common language and terminology, which often leads to misunderstandings and frustrations' (Benn 2009: 16).

This 'communication gap' is evident across the broad literature, and discourse analysis reveals that, despite explicit common ground and goals (such as the desire to end poverty or a social justice orientation), there are significant communicative challenges that remain present at multiple levels. Differences of language (of discipline and culture rather than linguistics), disciplinary perspectives and practices can be seen: of how truth is measured and described; of whether complexity is measured away or embraced; of clashes in terminology and units of analysis; and of differences in values and goals, discursive authority and power (Olivier 2010). What this means is that increased resourcing of dialogue does not necessarily mean improved communication or collaboration between religious, public health and development actors (Olivier 2010). It also means that this remains a diverse and complex field of engagement, with uneven data and often conflicting messages. This communicative gap continues to hamper dialogue: 'Even when common ground can be established, such as key HIV/AIDS problems requiring shared investigation, or a shared inclination towards justice and equity in health, differences in discursive styles can be significantly off-putting, and can hamper communication to the point that participants lose sight of more fundamental common ground' (Olivier 2010: 133).

Getting to the new table: religion in health policy and systems research

So far, this chapter has addressed the obstacles encountered during the period in which religion and religious institutions cautiously emerged back on to international policy agendas. However, one must ask where the new frontier for engagement, advocacy and inquiry is now? There are now many more institutions and individuals engaging at the intersection of religion, development and public health (see WFDD 2012; Smith and Kaybryn 2013). There is some lack of clarity at the moment on where the cutting edge is, and where we should be giving priority and energy. Some of those who have been active in these intersections of inquiry for the last decade are increasingly arguing that 'systems thinking' is the great new challenge and opportunity ahead of us (see Gunderson and Cochrane 2012; Olivier and Wodon 2012c; Olivier 2014b). In effect, this would mean turning away from generalizing statements about 'faith-based organizations' and large-scale advocacy about valuing the faith sector, and instead dealing directly with the complexity of real-world health and development problems, and diving into the challenging evidence-based arenas of community and health systems strengthening.

We would argue that there are a number of reasons that health policy and systems research (HPSR) is a particularly relevant area for this inquiry to shift its energy towards.[1] Firstly, HPSR is an emergent field itself, and so is fairly open to interdisciplinary engagement and views, which those at the intersection of religion and public health have long struggled with. Within HPSR there is a growing acceptance of different paradigms of knowledge, and a willingness to engage across communicative gaps, for example highlighting the role of social science in public health, or demonstrating the value of ethnography and mixed methods approaches to real-world problems (see Sheikh *et al.* 2011).

Secondly, HPSR embraces complexity and context – a challenge that has continued to confound much of the work at the interface of religion, public health and development. In addition, HPSR values the cross-over between 'development' and 'public health', since a systems perspective seeks to take into account all actors and entities that influence health. An example of this is the Tallinn Charter's definition of a health system as the 'ensemble of all public and private organizations, institutions and resources mandated to improve, maintain or restore health (which) encompass both personal and population services, as well as activities to influence the policies and actions of other sectors to address the social, environmental and economic determinants of health' (WHO European Ministerial Conference on Health Systems 2008). It has been argued elsewhere that religious institutions and activities often tend to cross the boundaries between health and development (for example, a religious hospital might often be engaged in broader development activities) and that a systems perspective might enable a better understanding of this (Olivier and Wodon 2012a). HPSR also has a strong focus on the connection between community, facility and system, which is a continued challenge and largely unexplored area of inquiry in relation to religious institutions, which tend to have complex ties at local, national and international levels.

Thirdly, the systems dimension is what has been most neglected in relation to inquiry into religion and public health, for example the ignored religious healthcare institutions that might have managed to continue providing quality healthcare services to the poor in rural areas despite increased constraints. It is concerning to note that key questions that were being asked in the 1970s by those engaged in the Christian Medical Commission remain unanswered, for example questions about the nature of religious healthcare institutions' engagement in health, their role in facilities-based versus primary or preventative care, what it means to be a religious provider, whether it is possible to continue to bear the costs of a 'pro-poor' mission, or whether financial sustainability is possible given new systems constraints (see McGilvray 1981). The fact that these critically important questions continue to go unanswered suggests that these angles of inquiry have not as yet been adequately focused or resourced – and that they are essentially systems issues.

Fourthly, while there has been a lot of necessary advocacy to highlight the role and presence of religious institutions and activities, this has also sometimes caused a separation of these from the real-world contexts in which they operate. Said differently, religious institutions are most commonly researched and discussed as a separate sector (with their comparative differences being highlighted), and as a result they are now rarely considered as part of or in comparison to the broader systems in which they operate. While there were early calls for 'integration' of religious health assets (see ARHAP 2006), this has not been recognized in any substantial way at a policy level. This suggests that understanding religious healthcare institutions from a systems perspective might be of particular importance. Consider the following simple example of how religious healthcare institutions are integrated into their national systems. In Ghana, most religious healthcare providers have a strict management rule and culture that do not allow health workers to strike. However, what this means is that, when a national public health sector strike is under way (which is common in Ghana), then the religious sector picks up a lot of the burden of care. At the same time, because of service-level agreements that are now in place between government and religious healthcare institutions, health workers in the religious sector still benefit from any wage negotiations that occur (see Olivier 2014a). This brief example demonstrates the complex way that religious institutions are part of their national systems – and need to be understood in this way, rather than as a separate sector.

Finally, a key reason to consider religious institutions from a systems perspective is because of a core area of common ground – and that is a rights- and equity-based perspective towards healthcare provision which underpins systems thinking and which is also often stated as a core value of religious healthcare. Several authors have noted that social justice is a potentially powerful cause for common ground between religion and public health (see Benn 2009; Cochrane 2009). However, this common ground has not as yet been adequately explored, and perhaps the discussions and research under way within HPSR (for example on universal health coverage or human rights for health) might provide a powerful platform for future engagement.

Conclusions and cosmologies

Every culture has its originating mythology or cosmology, and disciplines are no different. Every field of inquiry has its foundational myths and theories that shape it, that define what is a valid enterprise within that area and where the boundaries of inquiry are drawn. For those engaged at the intersection of religion and public health, it is often articulated simply as a shared belief that this is a sadly neglected area of inquiry that is deserving of more attention.

For public health, one of the key foundational myths is the story of John Snow and the Broad Street pump handle. Dr John Snow was an English physician in the 1800s, and is considered to be one of the fathers of modern epidemiology (the disciplinary backbone of public health) as a result of his work in tracing the source of a cholera outbreak in London in 1854 to the water system – one of the first stories of an individual 'looking upstream' to the originating source of the health problem through scientific deduction, rather than only dealing with the individual effects of the disease 'downstream'. Certainly, when John Snow removed the Broad Street pump handle, he could not have known that he was about to become the 'father of public health'. A lot has been written about Snow and that particular cholera outbreak over the last 150 years, but a recent account by Steven Johnson in a book called *The Ghost Map* raises some interesting insights. In this version, which details Snow's journey of scientific inquiry in 1854, an additional character is woven into the narrative of Snow's discovery – the previously unacknowledged assistant curate Henry Whitehead from the local St Luke's parish. In this version of events, while Dr Snow was conducting his scientific-rational investigation, Whitehead was making his own parallel inquiry into the cholera outbreak in the Broad Street community while he made his usual rounds among his parishioners. *The Ghost Map* tells the story of two separate streams of inquiry, Snow '[drawing] maps in his head, looking for patterns, looking for clues' (Johnson 2006: 149) and Whitehead 'grappling with the theological implications of the outbreak', as well as his personal experiences in the community (Johnson 2006: 170). Ultimately, according to this account, it was the dialectical engagement between Snow and Whitehead that eventually solved the mystery, a combination of Whitehead's 'firsthand knowledge of the neighbourhood' (Johnson 2006: 53) and Snow's biomedical experience and innovation.

This small additional embellishment on the cosmology of public health is in fact a fairly significant revisionist history for those operating in the complex space between religion, public health and development. Whitehead's participation, which according to this account provided key information about the community which led to Snow's epidemiological success, has not been visible until now. The addition of a religious character into this key narrative is strongly telling about the environment of inquiry we are now in, and perhaps indicates that the worlds of religion and public health are no longer as separate or antagonistic as they once seemed.

Note

1 This section is drawn from consideration of the broad literature on religion and public health, as well as from key health policy and systems research texts (see Gilson 2012).

References

ARHAP (African Religious Health Assets Programme) (2006) *Appreciating Assets: The Contribution of Religion to Universal Access in Africa*, Report for the World Health Organization, October, Cape Town: ARHAP.

Benn, C. (2002) *The Future Role of Church Related Hospitals and Health Services in Developing Countries*, Tübingen: DIFAEM: German Institute for Medical Mission.

Benn, C. (2003) 'Why Religious Health Assets Matter', African Religious Health Assets Programme (ARHAP): Assets and Agency Colloquium, Pietermaritzburg.

Benn, C. (2009) 'The Continued Paradigm Shift in Global Health and the Role of the Faith Community', African Religious Health Assets Programme (ARHAP) Conference: When Religion and Health Align – Mobilizing Religious Health Assets for Transformation, Cape Town.

Berger, P. L. (1999) 'The Desecularization of the World: A Global Overview', in P. L. Berger (ed.), *The Desecularization of the World: Resurgent Religion and World Politics*, Washington, DC: Ethics and Public Policy Centre.

Casanova, J. (1994) *Public Religions in the Modern World*, Chicago: University of Chicago Press.

Cochrane, J. R. (2006a) 'Religion, Public Health and a Church for the 21st Century', *International Review of Mission*, 95, 59–72.

Cochrane, J. R. (2006b) 'Understanding Religious Health Assets for Public Health Systems', in DIFAEM, *Religion, Faith and Public Health: Documentation on a Consultation*, February, Tübingen: DIFAEM: German Institute for Medical Mission, pp. 14–45.

Cochrane, J. R. (2009) 'The Potential of Religious Entities for Strengthening Public Health Systems in Crisis', *Maghreb Review*, 31, 41–60.

Coffman, D. B. (2002) 'Linking Faith and Health', http://www.union-psce.edu/news/Publications/archive/LinkingFaithAndHealth.html (accessed 14 November 2009).

de Gruchy, S. (2006) *Re-Learning Our Mother Tongue? Theology in Dialogue with Public Health*, Washington, DC: American Academy of Religion.

Derrida, J. and Vattimo, G. (1998) *Religion: Cultural Memory in the Present*, Cambridge: Polity Press.

Detels, R. and Breslow, L. (1997) 'Current Scope and Concerns in Public Health', in R. Detels, W. W. Holland, J. McEwen and G. S. Omenn (eds), *Oxford Textbook of Public Health: The Scope of Public Health*, 3rd edn, New York: Oxford University Press.

Dimmock, F., Olivier, J. and Wodon, Q. (2012) 'Half a Century Young: Challenges Facing Christian Health Associations in Africa', in J. Olivier and Q. Wodon (eds), *Strengthening Faith-Inspired Health Engagement*, Vol. 1: *The Role of Faith-Inspired Health Care Providers in Sub-Saharan Africa and Public–Private Partnerships*, HNP Discussion Papers, Washington, DC: World Bank.

Ellis, S. and ter Haar, G. (2001) *Worlds of Power: Religious Thought and Political Practice in Africa*, Johannesburg: Wits University Press.

Farmer, P. (1999) *Infections and Inequalities: The Modern Plagues*, Berkeley: University of California Press.

Garrett, L. (2000) *Betrayal of Trust: The Collapse of Global Public Health*, New York: Hyperion.

Gilson, L. (ed.) (2012) *Health Policy and Systems Research: A Methodology Reader*, Geneva: Alliance for Health Policy and Systems Research and World Health Organization.

Gunderson, G. and Cochrane, J. R. (2012) *Religion and the Health of the Public: Shifting the Paradigm*, New York: Palgrave Macmillan.

Johnson, S. (2006) *The Ghost Map*, New York: Riverhead Books.

Kim, J. Y., Millen, J. V., Irwin, A. and Gershman, J. (eds) (2000) *Dying for Growth: Global Inequality and the Health of the Poor*, Monroe, ME: Common Courage Press.

Koenig, H. G. M., Michael, E. and Larson, D. B. (2001) *Handbook of Religion and Health*, Oxford: Oxford University Press.

Lee, B. Y. and Newberg, A. B. (2005) 'Religion and Health: A Review and Critical Analysis', *Zygon*, 40, 443–68.

Marshall, K. and Van Saanen, M. (2007) *Development and Faith: Where Mind, Heart, and Soul Work Together*, Washington, DC: World Bank.

McGilvray, J. (1981) *The Quest for Health and Wholeness*, Tübingen: DIFAEM: German Institute for Medical Mission.

Melkote, S. R. and Steeves, H. L. (2001) *Communication for Development in the Third World: Theory and Practice for Empowerment*, London: Sage.

O'Connor, T. S. J. and Meakes, E. (2005) 'Towards a Joint Paradigm Reconciling Faith and Research', in A. Meier, T. S. J. O'Connor and vanKatwyk, P. (eds), *Spirituality and Health: Multidisciplinary Explorations*, Waterloo, ON: Wilfrid Laurier University Press.

Olivier, J. (2010) 'In Search of Common Ground for Interdisciplinary Collaboration and Communication: Mapping the Cultural Politics of Religion and HIV/AIDS in Sub-Saharan Africa', Ph.D. thesis, University of Cape Town.

Olivier, J. (2011) '"An FB-oh?": Mapping the Etymology of the Religious Entity Engaged in Health', in J. R. Cochrane, B. Schmid and T. Cutts (eds), *When Religion and Health Align: Mobilising Religious Health Assets for Transformation*, Pietermaritzburg: Cluster Publications.

Olivier, J. (2014a) *Hierarchical but Decentralized: Governance Practices among Catholic Health Providers in Ghana, Cameroon and Malawi*, report for CORDAID, Cape Town: University of Cape Town, International Religious Health Assets Programme.

Olivier, J. (2014b) *Local Faith Communities and Immunization for Systems Strengthening: Scoping Review and Companion Bibliography*, London: Report for the Joint Learning Initiative on Faith and Local Communities.

Olivier, J. and Paterson, G. M. (2011) 'Religion and Medicine in the Context of HIV and AIDS: A Landscaping Review', in B. Haddad (ed.), *Religion and HIV and AIDS: Charting the Terrain*, Scottsville: University of KwaZulu-Natal Press.

Olivier, J. and Wodon, Q. (2012a) 'Layers of Evidence: Discourses and Typologies of Faith-Inspired Community Responses to HIV/AIDS in Africa', in J. Olivier and Q. Wodon (eds), *Strengthening Faith-Inspired Health Engagement*, Vol. 3: *Mapping, Cost, and Reach to the Poor of Faith-Inspired Health Care Providers in Sub-Saharan Africa*, HNP Discussion Papers, Washington, DC: World Bank.

Olivier, J. and Wodon, Q. (2012b) 'Playing Broken Telephone: Assessing Faith-Inspired Health Care Provision in Africa', *Development in Practice*, 22, 819–34. Olivier, J. and Wodon, Q. (eds) (2012c) *Strengthening Faith-Inspired Health Engagement*, Vols 1–3, HNP Discussion Papers, Washington, DC: World Bank.

Olivier, J. and Wodon, Q. (2014) 'Increased Funding for AIDS-Engaged Faith-Based Organizations in Africa?', *Review of Faith and International Affairs*, 12, 53–71.

Olivier, J., Leonard, G. S. D. and Schmid, B. (2014a) *The Cartography of HIV and AIDS, Religion and Theology: A Partially Annotated Bibliography*, Pietermaritzburg: University of KwaZulu-Natal, School of Religion and Theology, Collaborative for HIV and AIDS, Religion and Theology (CHART).

Olivier, J., Schmid, B. and Cochrane, J. R. (2014b) *The 'Semi-Bounded' Field of Religion and Public Health: An Ongoing Review and Bibliography*, Cape Town: International Religious Health Assets Programme (IRHAP).

Paterson, G. (2008) 'Religion and Children: Consultation on the Cartography of HIV and AIDS, Religion and Theology (CHART)', University of KwaZulu-Natal, School of Religion and Theology.

Petersen, A. and Lupton, D. (1996) *The New Public Health: Health and Self in the Age of Risk*, London: Sage.

Piot, P. (2008) *Don't Give Up the Fight! XVIIth International AIDS Conference*, Mexico City: UNAIDS.

Schmid, B., Thomas, E., Olivier, J. and Cochrane, J. R. (2008) *The Contribution of Religious Entities to Health in Sub-Saharan Africa*, Study for the Bill and Melinda Gates Foundation, Cape Town: African Religious Health Assets Programme.

Sheikh, A., Gilson, L., Agyepong, I. A., Hanson, K., Ssengooba, F. and Bennett, S. (2011) 'Building the Field of Health Policy and Systems Research: Framing the Questions', *PLoS Med*, 8, e1001073.

Smith, A. and Kaybryn, J. (2013) *HIV and Maternal Health: Faith Groups' Activities, Contributions and Impact*, London: Joint Learning Initiative on Faith and Local Communities.

Stefanek, M., McDonald, P. G. and Hess, S. A. (2004) 'Religion, Spirituality and Cancer: Current Status and Methodological Challenges', *Psycho-Oncology*, 14, 450–63.

WFDD (World Faiths Development Dialogue) (2012) *Global Health and Africa: Assessing Faith Work and Research Priorities*, Washington, DC: WFDD for the Tony Blair Faith Foundation.

WHO–CIFA (2009) *Report on WHO–CIFA Consultation: NGO Mapping Standards Describing Religious Health Assets*, 10–12 November, Chateau de Bossey, Bogis-Bossey, Switzerland: WHO Programme on Partnerships and UN Reform.

WHO European Ministerial Conference on Health Systems (2008) *Tallinn Charter: Health Systems for Health and Wealth*, Resolution EUR/RC58/R4, Geneva: World Health Organization.

Wodon, Q., Olivier, J., Tsimpo, C. and Nguyen, M. C. (2014) 'Market Share of Faith-Inspired Health Care Providers in Africa', *Review of Faith and International Affairs*, 12, 8–20.

World Bank (2004) *Concept Note: HIV and AIDS Workshop for Faith-Based Organisations and National AIDS Councils*, Accra: World Bank.

Zambia Ministry of Health (2005) *National HIV/AIDS/STI/TB Policy*, Lusaka: Republic of Zambia, Ministry of Health.

24

CONFLICT OR COMPATIBILITY?

Reflections on the nexus between human rights, development and religion in Muslim aid organizations

Marie Juul Petersen

Introduction

Are human rights compatible with religion? And is religion compatible with human rights? The answer to these often posed questions has typically been a straightforward no or yes (Banchoff and Wuthnow 2011: 3f.). Some commentators point to what they consider to be irreconcilable differences between the values and principles of the two meaning systems, arguing for the inherent incompatibility between religion and human rights. As Witte and Green (2012: 17) note, the human rights system teaches liberty, equality and pluralism, while most religions teach authority, hierarchy and orthodoxy. Others argue that human rights do in fact have religious roots, and that religious traditions and texts can be read as justification of principles of liberty, equality and pluralism, facilitating their compatibility with modern human rights.[1]

Much of this literature on religion and human rights, whether sceptical or enthusiastic about the potential for compatibility, provides valuable insights, especially into legal, theological and historical aspects of the nexus between religion and human rights. However, it remains largely theoretical, focusing on religious texts and traditions and seeking broad generalizations about the relationship of these to human rights (An-Na'im and Abdel Halim 2006: 7; Banchoff and Wuthnow 2011: 10). Similarly, it tends to approach human rights as a fixed legal discourse rather than as shifting, contested social claims of actual individuals and institutions. Thus there is an explicit lack of focus on how concrete religious actors engage with specific human rights discourses, how they approach, adopt and challenge these discourses, and not least how they, in so doing, contribute to redefining human rights (Redhead and Turnbull 2011: 177; Hilhorst and Jansen 2012: 895).

The chapter first argues that a 'development perspective' on the study of religion and human rights can contribute to a more practice-oriented, empirical analysis of the nexus between the two, directing attention to the ambiguities, contradictions and multiple realities of religious actors and their human rights practices (Hilhorst and Jansen 2012: 893). In turn, the focus on religion and human rights can also contribute valuably to development theory and practice, broadening the analysis of rights-based approaches and contributing to conceptualizing their strengths and limitations (see also Tomalin 2006).[2]

The chapter then explores concrete instances of the nexus between human rights, religion and development. Examining how contemporary Muslim aid organizations relate – or do not relate – to human rights and rights-based approaches to development, the chapter argues that traditional Muslim aid provision and mainstream human rights discourses clash in a number of areas. The chapter goes on to discuss how some Muslim aid organizations seek to deal with these problems, providing examples of how universal human rights discourses are translated in practice and demonstrating that the question of compatibility between religion and human rights cannot be answered with a straightforward yes or no.

Bringing 'development' into studies of religion and human rights

A 'development lens' can contribute to the study of religion and human rights in different ways. Overall, such a perspective brings empirical attention to other kinds of actors than those normally included in studies of religion and human rights. The development arena is inhabited by a wide range of religious actors, from large international faith-based NGOs to local charities, schools and hospitals, all of them engaged in the provision of different kinds of aid to the world's poor, and many of them either directly or indirectly relating their work to global discourses of human rights.

This attention to concrete religious actors can also contribute to a more nuanced understanding of religion than is often the case in conventional studies of religion and human rights (Banchoff and Wuthnow 2011: 14). Human rights are not accepted or rejected by static and monolithic religious traditions and texts, but by concrete individuals, organizations and institutions, presenting a plurality of discourses and practices, not only of human rights but of religion. Even among organizations belonging to the same religion, there can be substantial differences in the ways in which they conceptualize religion and its role in human rights and development aid, and, as we shall see, some organizations may find themselves closer to secular development NGOs than to fellow religious aid organizations. Similarly, conceptions of religion are not 'fixed, rigid and unchanging' (Peach 2000: 74), but change over time, influenced by and adapted to the contexts in which they are presented. In this, global discourses of development and human rights may play a defining role, contributing to the transformation of religious discourses and practices.

Finally, development studies' attention to social actors, agency and practices (Long and Long 1992; Lewis and Mosse 2006) can contribute to thinking about human rights as something more and other than fixed legal and moral discourses, directing attention to what Wilson (2006: 77) has called 'the social life of human rights'. Human rights are not abstract and generalized global discourses; they are always shaped by and embedded in specific, local contexts and practices (Hefner 2011: 41; Hilhorst and Jansen 2012: 894). Thus studies of human rights should focus not only on the ontological status of human rights, but on the everyday meanings and uses of human rights. What sorts of practices are human rights discourses embedded in? How do actors understand and apply these discourses? And what do they hope to achieve in so doing (Wilson 2006: 78; see also Goodale 2006: 4)?[3] This also means bringing attention to what is outside the mainstream human rights discourse. Who does not employ human rights discourses, why do they not employ them and what are the alternatives they present?

Bringing 'religion' into studies of development and human rights

While a development perspective can contribute to the study of religion and human rights, a focus on religion can in turn contribute to the study of development and human rights.

Human rights discourses increasingly influence the ways in which mainstream development organizations approach their aid activities, often under the heading of a 'rights-based approach to development' (Miller 2010: 916). This approach emphasizes an understanding of development and human rights as closely interlinked and interdependent, and aims to incorporate principles of 'equality and equity, accountability, empowerment and participation' into development activities (Tomalin 2006: 93).

The rights-based approach to development has its roots in international human rights instruments such as the Covenant on Economic, Social and Cultural Rights from 1966 and the 1986 Declaration on the Right to Development, but it was not until the 1990s that it gained popularity among development actors, encouraged by a post-Cold War blurring of boundaries between different categories of human rights (Kindornay *et al.* 2012: 477). Put somewhat simply, Europe and the US had until then tended to prioritize civil and political rights over economic, cultural and social rights, promoted by the Soviet Union and others.[4] Epitomized in the 1993 World Conference on Human Rights, the principle of the indivisible, interdependent and non-hierarchical nature of rights has now become a mainstream mantra (Cornwall and Nyamu-Musembi 2004: 1422), facilitating the merger of human rights and development.[5]

Over the years, this new approach has 'swept through the websites, policy papers, and official rhetoric of multilateral development assistance agencies, bilateral donors, and nongovernmental organizations worldwide' (Kindornay *et al.* 2012: 473).[6] Despite heated discussions as to what constitutes a truly rights-based approach, there is general agreement among mainstream development actors on the so-called Stamford Common Understanding of a Human Rights-Based Approach to Development Cooperation, adopted by the UN Development Group in 2003, and stating that:

> 1) All programmes of development co-operation, policies and technical assistance should further the realization of human rights as laid down in the Universal Declaration of Human Rights and other international human rights instruments. 2) Human rights standards contained in, and principles derived from, the Universal Declaration of Human Rights and other international human rights instruments guide all development cooperation and programming in all sectors and in all phases of the programming process. 3) Development cooperation contributes to the development of the capacities of 'duty-bearers' to meet their obligations and/or of 'rights-holders' to claim their rights.[7]

Proponents of the rights-based approach claim that this approach carries a number of benefits, both normative and instrumental, compared to conventional approaches to development. Normatively, human rights are seen to offer a coherent framework, grounded in a consensual global legal regime which creates a normative legitimacy and consistency that may help guide development interventions (World Bank and OECD 2013: 69). More specifically, rights-based approaches have the potential to empower people as rights-holders rather than passive recipients of aid, as well as to identify duty-bearers and assist them in fulfilling their obligations, addressing structural inequalities. Instrumentally, supporters argue that rights-based approaches can improve development processes and outcomes, contributing to more effective poverty reduction, and improving the coherence, quality and effectiveness of aid (World Bank and OECD 2013: 11).

While not necessarily questioning the strengths of the rights-based approach, critics have argued that this approach – and human rights discourses in general – runs the risk of marginalizing people in the south, because they take no account of the ways in which social, cultural and religious traditions shape social ethics.[8] If human rights norms are to be successfully translated into concrete development programmes and projects, development practitioners and scholars need to pay attention to the contexts in which aid activities are to be implemented. In so far as religious organizations make up an important part of the context in which aid activities are implemented, a focus on these organizations is crucial for improving the rights-based approach. Analyses of the ways and indeed extent to which religious aid organizations understand and use a rights-based approach to development can tell us important things about the strengths and limitations of this approach, just as they may point us in new directions, directing attention to alternative ways of interpreting and implementing human rights and rights-based approaches to development. A recent study shows that the concept of human rights is 'hard for the average person to understand and use' and further that 'ordinary people often viewed "rights" as an elite term belonging to educated or Westernized urban residents, well paid NGO workers or the political and social upper classes' (Kindornay *et al.* 2012: 495). Here, religious organizations, often firmly rooted in local networks and structures, and enjoying strong popular support and moral credibility, can serve as agents of translation between global discourses of human rights and local religious discourses.

Muslim aid organizations and rights-based approaches

The rights-based discourse has historically been largely driven by secular development organizations and institutions (Kindornay *et al.* 2012: 482). Apart from some Western Christian NGOs, very few religious aid organizations have fully adopted the rights-based approach in their development activities.[9] Why is that? What is it about the contemporary human rights discourse that makes it so difficult for them to adapt? Focusing on the ways in which Muslim aid organizations relate – or do not relate – to human rights in their provision of aid, this section explores the nexus between human rights, religion and development, pointing to four potential areas of contention.[10]

Before we proceed, a few words are needed on my use of the term 'Muslim aid organization'. With this, I refer to those aid organizations that constitute themselves with reference to Muslim discourses, that is, organizations that define themselves as Muslim, either by simply referring to Islam in their name or by explicitly referring to Islamic authorities, traditions, figures or concepts in their practices or structure (see Benedetti 2006 for a similar definition). This group includes a wide variety of organizations, spanning from large, international NGOs with programmes in several countries and funding from international donors, to small, local charities and *zakat* committees run from the basement of a mosque and depending on donations from the community. The present analysis is based on organizational material and interviews with representatives from more than 50 Muslim aid organizations, international as well as local, in Bangladesh, Britain, Jordan, Kuwait, Lebanon and Saudi Arabia.[11]

Islam is the solution

First, the difficulties that many Muslim organizations have in adopting a rights-based approach can be at least partly explained as a result of a particular interpretation of Islam, popular among many contemporary Muslim actors. Since the advent of what has been referred to as the Islamic resurgence in the early twentieth century, a particular interpretation of Islam has gained ground, epitomized in the Muslim Brotherhood's slogan 'Islam is the solution.' Underlying this slogan is an understanding of religion as an all-encompassing solution not only to moral and ethical problems, but also to economical, political and – not least – legal ones (Messick 1993; cf. Hefner 2011: 41). As the director of a Jordanian community organization proclaims: 'Islam is a comprehensive system – it is about politics, law, economy, social systems, culture, everything. You cannot just take a small part of it and leave everything else aside.'[12]

In this perspective, there is no need for additional legal systems such as the international human rights system, in so far as Islamic law already provides a comprehensive set of rights. 'You can derive human rights from Islam', says a woman from a Jordanian charity. One of the earliest proponents of this idea was the Pakistani scholar, Abul A'la Mawdudi who, in the 1970s, argued for an Islamic conception of human rights based on the Qur'an and the sunna (Bielefeldt 2000: 91). Examples of how these rights look can be found in the Organisation of Islamic Cooperation's 1991 Cairo Declaration on Human Rights in Islam, including, for instance, the right to marriage and family (article 6a), the right to 'both religious and worldly education' (article 9b) and the right to medical and social care (article 17b). These and all other rights in the Declaration are 'subject to the Islamic Shari'ah' (article 24) and '[t]he Islamic Shari'ah is the only source of reference for the explanation or clarification of any of the articles of this declaration' (article 25).[13]

At the same time, some Muslim organizations do not see human rights primarily as a legal system, but as a normative Western ideology. As Banchoff and Wuthnow (2011) note, in North America and Western Europe the association with human rights is generally positive, in so far as the turn to human rights coincided historically with the transition to democracy. However, in the Muslim world (and elsewhere, for that matter), 'the idea of human rights is often associated with the era of colonialism, when human rights discourse was used both to denigrate non-Western cultures and to obscure the self-serving domination of colonial rule' (Banchoff and Wuthnow 2011: 17). Thus, many Muslims see Western attempts at furthering human rights as a continuation of a colonial past (An-Na'im and Abdel Halim 2006: 17), a sort of moral imperialism (Hernández-Truyol 2002; cf. Goodale 2006: 2). This criticism has only been strengthened with the 'global war on terror', showing what Morris (2010) has called 'the other face' of human rights, in so far as the wars in Afghanistan and Iraq were both, at least in part, legitimated by the US and its allies with reference to human rights (Hilhorst and Jansen 2012: 898) and yet they still resulted in destruction and the deaths of thousands of civilians, most of them Muslims, prompting many people to interpret them as an ideological war against Islam.

Solidarity with the umma

Another reason for the reluctance of many Muslim aid organizations to adopt a rights-based approach lies in the underlying rationale of solidarity shaping much Muslim aid provision. According to this rationale, Muslims are obliged to show solidarity and to support one another because they belong to the same community, the *umma*. To turn one's back on a needy person in the community is to pretend there is no community – it is to break the bond of solidarity. Likewise, to give – and to receive – is to acknowledge and thereby strengthen the community (Kochuyt 2009: 110). Thus rich Muslims should engage in the provision of aid to poor Muslims, not because each individual poor person has a right to this aid, but because the poor and the rich are part of the same religious community and, as such, have a duty to help one another, thereby strengthening the community. Contrary to the rationale of human rights, then, the solidarity rationale prioritizes the community over the individual (Hefner 2011: 51). A statement from the Kuwaiti NGO International Islamic Charitable Organization (ICCO)'s website illustrates this:

> [Charity] is one of the faith's most effective tools for spreading the values of solidarity and support between the sons of the Ummah. It encourages them to remain united like one body, when one part of it suffers a complaint, all other parts join in, sharing in the sleeplessness and fever.[14]

Similarly, ideals of solidarity clash with the rights-based approach's emphasis on non-discrimination and equal treatment, in so far as they encourage a particularistic focus on fellow Muslim brothers and sisters rather than a universalist focus on humanity. As the IICO notes, it works primarily in 'impoverished Muslim countries and communities' to 'keep the Muslims safe and rescue them from hunger'.[15] Representatives from other Muslim aid organizations state that they help Christians once in a while, but their main focus is on Muslims. A staff member in a Saudi organization explains: 'In general, to be honest, they help Muslims first, but if there are non-Muslims in the area they will also help them, and in disasters they help everybody.'

A gift to a fellow Muslim brother or sister

A third area of contention between Muslim aid organizations and the rights-based approach to development has to do with the ways in which relations between the giver and recipient of aid are conceived. In a rights-based perspective, aid is the right of individual recipients, regardless of their gender, class, religion or other collective identity, and thus the relation between giver and recipient is conceived in terms of a contract between equal parties. In a religious perspective, however, aid is not necessarily conceived as a right, but as a gift given from a generous donor, obliged by a religious duty towards God.

Contrary to the rights-based approach's emphasis on accountability and institutionalization, the notion of aid as a gift encourages a personal and intimate relationship between recipients and givers. Emphasizing 'ties of interdependence, compassion and tender sympathy'[16] between givers and recipients, some staff in Muslim aid organizations point out that their aid is distinct from that of many other (non-Muslim, Christian or Western) organizations. 'We have a different way of dealing with people', says a staff member in the Saudi Arabian International Islamic Relief Organization: 'They don't have the same feeling of family as we have, that the orphans are a part of our family. . . . For them, it's routine. It's just a job they need to do. It's about finishing work to get home to your own family.' Another staff member from the same organization says: 'I feel responsible for these people [the recipients]. I cannot leave them. It's like a big family.' According to them, personal care and compassion are more important qualities in aid provision than accountability and professionalism; in fact, such qualities may even be counterproductive to the sense of solidarity between recipient and giver.

While predicated on notions of personalized care and compassion, at the same time this relationship carries inherent risks of hierarchy and inequality. A letter from an orphan to a sponsor in one of IIROSA's programmes illustrates this point, coined in a language of gratitude and submission:

> My dear sponsor. May Allah reward your goodness because you sponsor me and support me, together with Allah, so that I can make my hopes and ambitions come true and be of use to my religion and my community and my family, and I pray that Allah will save you on the Day of Judgement and that you will be saved from the torment of Allah, since you helped me.[17]

In the personalized relation of solidarity and gift giving, the reward is gratitude as much as religious rewards. Gratitude relies on the social logic of the gift between unequal parties. The gift without reciprocation binds the grateful recipient into a nexus of obligations and duties towards the generous donor, making him or her a perpetual object of the donor's generosity (Chouliaraki 2010: 113).

Women's rights in Islam

Finally, disagreements as to concrete human rights constitute a fourth area of contention and conflict between rights-based approaches to development and the approaches of Muslim aid organizations. From the perspective of some organizations, a number of human rights are controversial and either partially or wholly incompatible with Islamic traditions and practices. Most obviously, many of the women's rights specified in international human rights conventions may clash with traditional Muslim gender practices and values, especially in areas of family life, divorce and inheritance (Bielefeldt 2000: 103).

For many Muslim aid organizations, the problem is not the concept of women's rights as such, but the underlying assumption of sameness. 'We are equal but we have different rights and responsibilities' is a phrase often heard when raising the issue of women's rights with Muslim aid organizations. As a representative from a Jordanian charity notes: 'We benefit from the Western approach, but we only take the good things. For instance, women's empowerment – we adjust this to an Islamic context. From an Islamic view empowerment of women is totally acceptable. The problem is equality in all aspects. This is not what we are looking for.'

In many organizations, conservative Muslim gender practices are upheld, and female recipients are (often strongly) encouraged to dress according to religious prescripts. The director of a local Jordanian charity says:

> Of course the women should wear the veil. That's a condition [for participation in the organization's activities]. One time there was a lecture here and we had invited a number of women, also one without the veil, and there was a riot. All the women asked, why did you invite her? And I said, this is precisely why we should invite her – so we can convince her to wear the veil.

Similarly, there are restrictions on the kinds of activities that female recipients can take part in. Typical activities for women include health and child care education, cooking and other activities deemed suitable for a Muslim woman. 'We teach the women to make soap, how to make perfume from plants, how to keep vegetables in the kitchen', staff from Anwar al-Huda tell me. A representative from another Jordanian organization, Al Hussein, says: 'There are some restrictions regarding where women can work, from religion and from traditions. Women should work in jobs where they can maintain their dignity.'

This insistence on conservative, Islamic traditions, conflicting with international women's rights, not only is evident in relation to recipients, but also shows internally in most organizations. Compared to secular NGOs, Muslim aid organizations often have lower numbers of women employed. Few trustees are women, and very few management positions are occupied by women. Instead, women are employed in bottom- and mid-level positions as secretaries, teachers, nurses and project coordinators. This is even the case in otherwise liberal organizations such as Islamic Relief and Muslim Aid. 'We perform gender equality training, but we don't follow this ourselves', says one person. Some staff report 'massive pressure' on women to comply with religious requirements and wear hijab. Others report of more explicit demands for a 'modest dress code'. In one of the country offices, for instance, a young man tells me about an episode in which a visiting trustee from the UK asked the receptionist to put on a headscarf.

Integrating religion and human rights in aid provision

Despite these difficulties, many Muslim NGOs are finding ways to integrate human rights into their aid provision, whether as part of a deliberate strategy or not. Rather than a straightforward adoption of human rights, these strategies are perhaps better conceptualized in terms of a continuum, spanning from rejection to replication of global human rights discourses (Merry 2006: 44), with different kinds and degrees of integration or translation in between. In this section of the chapter, I outline four such strategies, distinguishing between implicit alignment with human rights, pragmatic and partial adoption of certain human rights, reinterpretation of Islamic traditions to accommodate human rights, and finally the full integration of human rights.[18] These strategies are not necessarily mutually excluding; in fact many organizations and even individual staff members seem to make use of several strategies at the same time, or shift from one strategy to another and then back again, depending on the context.[19]

Implicit alignment with human rights

Several organizations present Islamic interpretations of aid that correspond well with those of a rights-based approach even though these organizations and their staff members never explicitly apply a human rights discourse. This is the case with the understanding of religious almsgiving, or *zakat*, that some staff members in Muslim aid organizations promote, emphasizing an understanding of *zakat* as a duty imposed by God upon the wealthy, and a right endowed by God to the poor. 'God orders people to take from the rich and give to the poor. This is a basic thing in Islam. God also said that it is the right of the poor to receive this money', one person tells me. Others quote a verse from the Qur'an: '"And those in whose wealth there is a recognized right for the beggar who asks and for the unlucky who has lost his property and wealth."'

Contradicting traditional Muslim rationales for aid provision, this understanding of *zakat* presents aid as a right that the poor person can claim rather than a gift he or she must accept from a benevolent donor. A hungry person has the right to receive a share of the meal of the well-fed person and is allowed to use force if he or she is denied this right (Benthall 1999: 36). This perspective also emphasizes the duty of the giver, not only towards God, but also towards the poor, encouraging a contractual relation between equals. This understanding of *zakat* echoes that of the Islamic scholar and activist Sayyed Qutb, who argued that *zakat* was 'the outstanding social pillar of Islam', ensuring an equal relationship between giver and recipient by enabling individuals' efforts to be steered towards a common goal (cf. Benthall and Bellion-Jourdan 2003: 16). But it also, albeit unintendedly and perhaps unwillingly, echoes the rights-based approach's emphasis on contractual relations between equals.

Pragmatic and partial adoption of human rights

Other approaches do explicitly adopt human rights discourses, but they do so partially and pragmatically, incorporating only those rights that do not conflict with Islamic principles and practices. Despite all the talk of inherent incompatibilities between Islam and human rights, even the most conservative interpretations of Islam present substantial overlaps with international human rights standards. Children's rights, for instance, are much less controversial than, say, women's rights or the right to non-discrimination and, as such, they can, at least in part, be easily integrated into an Islamic aid framework.

Most Muslim aid organizations support children's rights, and many cooperate with local religious institutions on raising awareness of these rights in the population. In a partnership with UNICEF, the Islamic Center Charity Society in Jordan has worked with imams in local mosques to spread information on violence against children. The director explains:

We got the idea that the mosque would be a good place to reach people, so we convinced the imam to help us. Some imams rejected the idea until we gave an example from the Quran: the Prophet Mohammad actually played with his children and treated them well. There was one imam, he used to hit his children and never play with them; then he heard this story and participated in our course and he actually apologized to his child.

Also, even the most conservative organizations seem to agree on the right to education, not only for boys but also for girls. In a Muslim Brotherhood charity in Jordan, for instance, programmes for girls' education make up a large part of the organization's activities. 'We try to teach them to know themselves, to know their families, to know about life and society, through this project', a teacher told me. 'We don't only teach the basics of religion; we talk about protection from abuse, we talk about hygiene, and we talk about their rights – all from the point of view of religion.'

Reinterpreting Islamic aid traditions

A third strategy presents more radical reinterpretations of Islamic aid traditions and principles, facilitating the integration of human rights and rights-based approaches. In some larger Muslim organizations, especially in Western countries, common Islamic values of solidarity have been replaced by values of universalism and inclusion, justified with reference to Islamic sayings and stories, but almost indistinguishable from the values of mainstream human rights and development discourses and presented in the same language. The provision of aid is no longer restricted to fellow Muslim brothers and sisters, but extended to 'disadvantaged people across the globe, irrespective of their faith, colour and race'.[20] In the words of an Islamic Relief staff member in Bangladesh: 'We care about humanity. We don't care about their faith.' This emphasis on universalism and non-discrimination over religious solidarity is legitimated by reference to Islamic principles: 'If you look at it from the side of Islam, most instructions from the Prophet Muhammad and the Holy Qur'an are about motivating people to help others, to support and help especially the poor', says the country director in Islamic Relief's Bangladesh office. 'And they don't mention what kinds of poor – they don't say what gender, what race, what religion.' Similarly, Muslim Aid declares: 'Islam teaches the equality of *all* humanity and actively promotes individual rights such as the right to life and freedom, the right to justice, the right to freedom of thought and religion and the right to education.'[21]

The integration of Islamic aid principles and practices with international human rights is not only found among large, Western NGOs such as Islamic Relief and Muslim Aid, but also appears in the discourses and practices of some smaller Islamic charities. In Jordan, for instance, the organization Al Aqsa provides training and education for women on human rights. Nawal al-Faouri, the director and a famous Muslim women's activist, rejects traditional Islamic views on women's rights, arguing instead that Islam can accommodate and actually promotes women's rights as laid out in international human rights conventions: 'We are serious and honest about our attempts to promote women's rights in Islam. We know the international and the national conventions [on human rights] but we also know the local context and culture.' Finding her examples from the Qur'an and the sunna, al-Faouri argues for an Islamic justification of international human rights standards:

In Islam, there is nothing that prevents the woman from working any kind of job. Islam allows women to be free. The prophet's wife, Um Salama, was his political advisor and he listened to her and did not think any less of her opinion. Another wife, Aisha, memorized the Qu'ran and she was given a high status among Muslim scientists. The daughter of the prophet's friend was his secret intelligence agent.

Introducing a minimalist religiosity

Finally, towards the other end of the continuum, we find a fourth strategy for including human rights in Muslim aid provision. Presenting a radical reinterpretation not only of selected Islamic traditions and principles, but of religion and its role in aid provision as such, this strategy potentially allows for a full inclusion of human rights and a rights-based approach to development. So far, very few – if any – Muslim aid organizations seem to have adopted this approach, but in certain Western Muslim NGOs it can be found among individual staff members, most of them young and with a professional development background.

Turning away from an all-encompassing, 'maximalist' religiosity (Lincoln 2003: 59), influencing all aspects of human life, these staff members promote a more 'minimalist' understanding of religion, by and large relegated to the private sphere. In this perspective, religion is acceptable as the source of individual values, underlying principles and motivation, but not as public rituals and collective practices influencing the ways in which aid is provided and to whom it is given. This conception of religion is reflected in the frequent use of airy terms such as 'Islamic flavour', 'Islamic charitable values' and 'the humanitarian spirit of Islam', denoting an interpretation of Islam as an invisible, 'ethical reference' (Benedetti 2006: 855) rather than an orthodox, visible religiosity. A person from an international Muslim NGO says: 'We don't want to distinguish ourselves as Islamic. The humanitarian principles that we base our work on are universal. We don't need to raise the Islamic flag when we do humanitarian work. We don't need to say that we are more humanitarian because we are Islamic.' Another person says: 'Our main objective is to provide an input to beneficiaries – what they are doing in relation to Allah, to their God, that's their own business, that's not really our business.'

Such a quasi-secular religiosity, concerned with private values and morals rather than public law, allows for the full inclusion of international human rights principles and a rights-based approach to development. Bielefeldt (2000: 109) notes that 'the principles of human rights and democracy can be connected meaningfully with the spirit of the shariah, provided that the shariah is primarily understood as an ethical and a religious concept rather than as a legalistic one'. And this is precisely the case among certain staff members in organizations such as Islamic Relief and Muslim Aid. Their 'Islamic values' are underlying personal values that support and align with rather than define human rights.

Conclusions

This chapter has pointed to four areas of potential conflict and contention between discourses of human rights and Islam in contemporary Muslim aid organizations. First, and overall, the widespread notion of Islam as an all-encompassing religion, including its own comprehensive set of Islamic rights, sees international human rights as at best superfluous and at worst as expressions of Western superiority and hypocrisy. Second, the underlying rationale of solidarity found among many Muslim aid organizations may clash with human rights principles of non-discrimination and universalism. Third, notions of gift giving and duties are not easily combined with the rights-based approach's contractual focus on rights and equality. Fourth, specific human rights, in particular in the area of women's rights, may conflict with conservative Muslim ideals and principles.

However, parallel to these conflicts, the discourses and practices of many Muslim aid organizations also point to the existence of diverse strategies for overcoming such conflicts. The chapter has outlined four such strategies, best conceived not in terms of straightforward rejection or replication of international human rights, but as points on a continuum in between these two poles, representing different, albeit sometimes overlapping, kinds and degrees of translation. One is the implicit alignment with human rights while maintaining an Islamic aid discourse; another is the pragmatic and partial inclusion of certain human rights, compatible with conservative Islamic traditions; a third is the reinterpretation of certain Islamic traditions and principles; and a fourth is a more radical reinterpretation of the role of religion as such, facilitating the full inclusion of human rights.

Through different strategies of translation, then, Muslim aid organizations find practical ways to incorporate notions of rights without entirely abandoning their faith, showing that 'genuine tensions (between Islam and human rights) are more likely to be mediated through practice than definitely 'resolved' in purely theoretical terms' (An-Na'im and Abdel Halim 2006: 6). Thus this chapter has demonstrated the plurality and change that exist among contemporary Muslim aid organizations, pointing to the fact that, in discussions of Islam and human rights, religion is best understood not as a fixed and static concept, but as the living, flexible and ever changing discourses and practices of concrete actors.

Furthermore, in focusing on these actors, the chapter has directed attention to the necessity of including religion in the study and practice of rights-based approaches to development. If rights-based approaches are to be successful, they must take religion into consideration, reflecting the realities of the contexts in which these approaches are to be implemented. The integration of religion and human rights requires not only that religious actors reinterpret their own traditions and principles, as has been shown above, but also that human rights and development actors make room for religion. This might also mean moving away from an understanding of human rights as a normative and moral system towards a more legalistic one. As Bielefeldt (2000: 116) notes, the normative scope of human rights is limited, and thus they do not – and should not – constitute an all-encompassing 'global ethics' or 'civil religion', attempting to compete with the world's religious traditions. Instead, human rights are best conceived in terms of international legal and political standards, whose normative justification may come from a myriad of different sources, including both secular and religious ones, facilitating the broad popular support they deserve.

Notes

1 See for instance Witte and Green (2012) and Witte and van der Vyver (1996) for theological discussions of the compatibility of different religious traditions with human rights.

2 With Tomalin's (2006) and Miller's (2010) analyses as exceptions, there seems to be very little research exploring the nexus between religious organizations, development and human rights.

3 There is already an emerging anthropological literature on how human rights are interpreted locally through processes of translation and vernacularization (e.g. Goodale 2009). However, not much of this literature focuses on the role of religion and religious actors in this.

4 For a more accurate historical account of this schism, see Whelan and Donnelly (2007), Kirkup and Evans (2009) and Jensen (2013).

5 For a historical account of the notion of indivisibility, see Whelan (2010). For a general history of human rights, see Normand and Zaidi (2008) or Jensen (2013).

6 For more in-depth analyses of the rights-based approach, see Marks (2003), Cornwall and Nyamu-Musembi (2004) or Gready and Ensor (2005).

7 Statement on a Common Understanding of a Human Rights-Based Approach to Development Cooperation, available at http://www.hrea.org/index.php?base_id=104&language_id=1&erc_doc_id=3107&category_id=44&category_type=3&group (accessed 4 October 2013).

8 See Gready and Ensor (2005) for case studies of the practical implementation of rights-based approaches. However, none of these studies focus explicitly on religion and religious actors.

9 A group of Western Christian NGOs, including Catholic Relief Services, Christian Aid, the Church of Sweden and DanChurchAid, have outlined their conception of rights-based development in the paper 'Rights-Based Development from a Faith-Based Perspective', http://www.icco.nl/nl/linkservid/39FF5998-B5DD-797D-AD23DA65417D995B/showMeta/0/ (accessed 7 October 2013).

10 While this analysis focuses specifically on Muslim aid organizations, many of the same dilemmas and conflicts can arguably be found in many other religious organizations. See Tomalin (2006) for an analysis of Hindu organizations, and Miller (2010) for an analysis of Christian NGOs.

11 The interviews and data collection were carried out in the period 2007 to 2011, mainly as part of a larger research project on Muslim NGOs and aid provision. See Juul Petersen (2012a, 2012b, forthcoming) as well as Sparre and Juul Petersen (2007) for more in-depth analyses of these organizations. While the organizations studied here do present a broad variety of Muslim aid organizations, they do not necessarily make up a strictly representative sample of the group of Muslim aid organizations as such. Thus the following analysis should primarily be read as an overview of important trends and characteristics, rather than an exhaustive study of this group of organizations, something which would require larger, quantitative surveys and mappings.

12 See Mayer (2013) for a broad introduction to contemporary Islam and human rights. For theological discussions of the compatibility of Islam and human rights, see for example Sachedina (2009) or An-Na'im (2010). Several Muslim feminists have also contributed to the discussion of Islam and human rights, including Asma Barlas, Amina Wadud, Nimat Hafiz Barazangi, Riffat Hassan, Haifaa Jawad and Mona Siddiqi (Haddad 2011: 76).

13 The Cairo Declaration on Human Rights in Islam is available at http://www1.umn.edu/humanrts/instree/cairodeclaration.html (accessed 4 October 2013).

14 IICO website, http://www.iico.net/home-page-eng/News-08/aug_08/iico-eng-6.htm (accessed 23 April 2011).

15 IICO (n.d.) 'Pioneering in Charity', pamphlet, p. 2; and IICO (n.d.) 'Special Publication: Introduction to the International Islamic Charitable Organization', p. 5.

16 IIROSA Magazine (n.d.).

17 IIROSA (n.d.) 'Sponsor an Orphan', pamphlet.

18 See Bielefeldt (2000) for a similar categorization of approaches to Islam and human rights more generally.

19 Interestingly, the different strategies do not seem to correspond with geographic categories of Western and non-Western Muslim aid organizations, nor with size- or scope-based categories of local and international organizations. Instead, the degree to which Muslim aid organizations adopt and integrate human rights discourses seems to depend primarily on their relationship (or lack thereof) with mainstream human rights and development actors such as DFID, ECHO and large secular NGOs (Juul Petersen 2012a, 2012b), with organizations that receive funding from and cooperate with these actors tending towards more explicit use of human rights discourses in their aid work.

20 Muslim Aid, 'Trustees' Report and Financial Statements 2008', p. 11, http://www.muslimaid.org/images/stories/pdfs/financial_summary_2008.pdf (accessed 7 October 2013). Notably, this universalism does not include sexual orientation.

21 Muslim Aid, 'Strategic Framework 2007–2010', p. 15f., emphasis added, http://www.muslimaid.org/images/stories/pdfs/strategic_framework_2007_2010_final.pdf (accessed 7 October 2013).

References

An-Na'im, Abdullahi (2010) *Islam and Human Rights*, ed. Mashood Baderin, Farnham: Ashgate.

An-Na'im, Abdullahi and Abdel Halim, Asma Mohamed (2006) *Rights-Based Approach to Philanthropy for Social Justice in Islamic Societies*, Cairo: American University in Cairo, John D. Gerhart Center for Philanthropy and Civic Engagement.

Banchoff, Thomas and Wuthnow, Robert (eds) (2011) *Religion and the Global Politics of Human Rights*, Oxford: Oxford University Press.

Benedetti, Carlo (2006) 'Islamic and Christian Inspired Relief NGOs: Between Tactical Collaboration and Strategic Diffidence', *Journal of International Development*, 18 (6), 849–59.

Benthall, Jonathan (1999) 'Financial Worship: The Quranic Injunction to Almsgiving', *Journal of the Royal Anthropological Institute*, 5, 27–42.

Benthall, Jonathan and Bellion-Jourdan, Jerome (2003) *The Charitable Crescent: Politics of Aid in the Muslim World*, London: I. B. Tauris.

Bielefeldt, Heiner (2000) '"Western" versus "Islamic" Human Rights Conceptions? A Critique of Cultural Essentialism in the Discussion on Human Rights', *Political Theory*, 28 (1), 90–121.

Chouliaraki, Lilie (2010) 'Post-Humanitarianism: Humanitarian Communication beyond a Politics of Pity', *International Journal of Cultural Studies*, 13 (2), 107–26.

Cornwall, Andrea and Nyamu-Musembi, Celestine (2004) 'Putting the "Rights-Based Approach" to Development into Perspective', *Third World Quarterly*, 25 (8), 1415–37.

Goodale, Mark (2006) 'Introduction to "Anthropology and Human Rights in a New Key"', *American Anthropologist*, 108 (1), 1–8.

Goodale, Mark (ed.) (2009) *Human Rights: An Anthropological Reader*, Chichester: Wiley-Blackwell.

Gready, Paul and Ensor, Jonathan (eds) (2005) *Reinventing Development? Translating Rights-Based Approaches from Theory into Practice*, London: Zed Books.

Haddad, Yvonne (2011) 'Muslims, Human Rights and Women's Rights', in Thomas Banchoff and Robert Wuthnow (eds), *Religion and the Global Politics of Human Rights*, Oxford: Oxford University Press.

Hefner, Robert W. (2011) 'Human Rights and Democracy in Islam: The Indonesian Case in Global Perspective', in Thomas Banchoff and Robert Wuthnow (eds), *Religion and the Global Politics of Human Rights*, Oxford: Oxford University Press, pp. 39–69.

Hernández-Truyol, Berta Esperanza (ed.) (2002) *Moral Imperialism: A Critical Anthology*, New York: New York University Press.

Hilhorst, Dorothea and Jansen, Bram J. (2012) 'Constructing Rights and Wrongs in Humanitarian Action: Contributions from a Sociology of Praxis', *Sociology*, 46 (5), 891–905.

Jensen, Steven L. B. (2013) 'Negotiating Universality: The Making of International Human Rights, 1945–1993', unpublished Ph.D. dissertation, University of Copenhagen.

Juul Petersen, Marie (2012a) 'Islamizing Aid: Transnational Muslim NGOs after 9.11', *Voluntas: International Journal of Voluntary and Nonprofit Organizations*, 23 (1), 126–55.

Juul Petersen, Marie (2012b) 'Trajectories of Transnational Muslim NGOs', *Development in Practice*, 22 (5–6), 763–78.

Juul Petersen, Marie (forthcoming) *Aid and Islam: Transnational Muslim NGOs and Their Ideologies of Aid*, London: Hurst & Co.

Kindornay, Shannon, Ron, James and Carpenter, Charli (2012) 'Rights-Based Approaches to Development: Implications for NGOs', *Human Rights Quarterly*, 34 (2), 472–506.

Kirkup, Alex and Evans, Tony (2009) 'The Myth of Western Opposition to Economic, Social, and Cultural Rights? A Reply to Whelan and Donnelly', *Human Rights Quarterly*, 31 (1), 221–37.

Kochuyt, Thierry (2009) 'God, Gifts and Poor People: On Charity in Islam', *Social Compass*, 56 (1), 98–116.

Lewis, David and Mosse, David (eds) (2006) *Development Brokers and Translators: The Ethnography of Aid and Agencies*, Bloomfield, CT: Kumarian Press.

Lincoln, Bruce (2003) *Holy Terrors: Thinking about Religion after September 11*, Chicago: University of Chicago Press.

Long, Norman and Long, Ann (eds) (1992) *Battlefields of Knowledge: The Interlocking of Theory and Practice in Social Research and Development*, London: Routledge.

Marks, Stephen P. (2003) 'The Human Rights Framework for Development: Seven Approaches', Working Paper no. 18, Harvard University, François-Xavier Bagnoud Center for Health and Human Rights.

Mayer, Ann Elizabeth (2013) *Islam and Human Rights: Tradition and Politics*, Boulder, CO: Westview Press.

Merry, Sally Engle (2006) 'Transnational Human Rights and Local Activism: Mapping the Middle', *American Anthropologist*, 108 (1), 38–51.

Messick, Brinkley (1993) *The Calligraphic State: Textual Domination and History in a Muslim Society*, Berkeley: University of California Press.

Miller, Hannah (2010) 'From "Rights-Based" to "Rights-Framed" Approaches: A Social Constructionist View of Human Rights Practice', *International Journal of Human Rights*, 14 (6), 915–31.

Morris, Lydia (2010) 'Sociology and the Two Faces of Human Rights', *Sociology Compass*, 4 (5), 322–33.

Normand, Roger and Zaidi, Sarah (2008) *Human Rights at the UN: The Political History of Universal Justice*, Bloomington: Indiana University Press.

Peach, L. J. (2000) 'Human Rights, Religion and (Sexual) Slavery', *Annual of the Society of Christian Ethics*, 20, 65–87.

371

Redhead, Robin and Turnbull, Nick (2011) 'Towards a Study of Human Rights Practitioners', *Human Rights Review*, 12, 173–89.

Sachedina, Abdulaziz (2009) *Islam and the Challenge of Human Rights*, Oxford: Oxford University Press.

Sparre, Sara Lei and Juul Petersen, Marie (2007) *Islam and Civil Society: Case Studies from Jordan and Egypt*, DIIS Report, Copenhagen: Danish Institute for International Studies.

Tomalin, Emma (2006) 'Religion and a Rights-Based Approach to Development', *Progress in Development Studies*, 6 (2), 93–108.

Whelan, Daniel J. (2010) *Indivisible Human Rights: A History*, Philadelphia: University of Pennsylvania Press.

Whelan, Daniel J. and Donnelly, Jack (2007) 'The West, Economic and Social Rights, and the Global Human Rights Regime: Setting the Record Straight', *Human Rights Quarterly*, 29 (4), 908–49.

Wilson, Richard Ashby (2006) 'Afterword to "Anthropology and Human Rights in a New Key": The Social Life of Human Rights', *American Anthropologist*, 108 (1), 77–83.

Witte, John, Jr and Green, M. Christian (eds) (2012) *Religion and Human Rights: An Introduction*, Oxford: Oxford University Press.

Witte, John, Jr and van der Vyver, Johan (1996) *Religious Human Rights in Global Perspective: Religious Perspectives*, The Hague: Martinus Nijhoff.

World Bank and OECD (Organisation for Economic Co-operation and Development) (2013) *Integrating Human Rights into Development: Donor Approaches, Experiences, and Challenges*, Washington, DC: World Bank and OECD.

25

COMPLEX GLOBAL INSTITUTIONS

Religious engagement in development

Katherine Marshall

Introduction

This chapter focuses on the institutional dimensions of the principal global religious traditions and on the ways in which religious engagement with development approaches, policies, and programs can and does take place. Religious actors are involved in many aspects of what is understood as development (whether the changes of modernization or explicit development strategies or programs), and they may be directly engaged partners in formal, multilateral, or national development strategies. However, where the agendas and visions of development held by religious actors are at odds with those of state or development institutions, they may act independently, either contributing to deliberate social and economic change or working against it. There are instances where religious actors are pillars of and advocates for development strategies and others where they stand in active opposition to more conventional development work. In order to understand these complex relationships it is important to appreciate the varying institutional manifestations of religious traditions, which take different forms in different traditions and regions. This complexity and diversity mean that there is no single accepted "taxonomy" of religious institutions in either academic or policy usage.

My aim in this chapter is to introduce a framework that can help in understanding the variety of actors, with select illustrations of how various institutions relate in practice to development policies and programs. The framework underscores the wide variety of religiously linked institutions, with their frequent overlap and fuzzy boundaries. The chapter then highlights various live issues, viewed through an institutional lens, that are of particular interest to development practitioners (whether religious or secular); these issues emerged in a series of "mapping" overviews of religion and development.[1] Issues include, for example, approaches to gender relations, the boundaries of proselytizing and evangelizing in conjunction with service delivery, challenges of coordination and harmonization, and relationships between religion and politics as they relate to development. Finally, the chapter reflects on how various development organizations have sought to engage religious actors,[2] to illustrate both potential and pitfalls.[3]

The global religious landscape: political and social parameters that relate to development work

The political character and legal and social position of the variety of religious institutions are a starting point in understanding how they might link to development strategies and policies. National laws, their implementation, and broader cultural traits define the institutional context in which religious institutions operate, as do some elements of international law (notably in humanitarian situations). Each nation sets out (often in its constitution) how religious institutions and the state are to interact, either permitting or prohibiting direct religious engagement in various dimensions of national politics. These positions and arrangements vary widely and in a number of countries are undergoing significant change and contestation. The core relationship between religious and other institutions (often framed as a question of the degree of secular principles that underlie a nation's governance approach) colors discussions of religion and development in each country (see for example Casanova 1994, Berger 1999, and Thomas 2005 for context on secular versus religious approaches). In some settings a secular ethos and expectation that "church and state" are separate suggest limited religious engagement on topics related to national development. In others (for example where there is an established religion), religious engagement is defined and expected. In still others, the question is contested or ambiguous.

It is important to emphasize, as this discussion of development focuses on material, "worldly" dimensions, that religious institutions tend to define their central and core functions in different terms, as related to religious practice and spiritual welfare. However, they also have a large physical presence, with a deep footprint. Looked at globally and in many if not most local communities, they are among the most pervasive and active organizations. They employ millions of people, own extensive amounts of land and facilities, and manage large financial resources.[4] They run large health care (Aylward and Marshall 2012) and education networks and in most regions operate entities that provide social services such as orphan care, support to displaced people, and comfort to prisoners. Religious organizations can be big business, as for example in Sweden, where the Church of Sweden manages large tracts of forests, and Senegal, where Sufi orders long dominated the peanut and charcoal enterprises (Copans 1989). Religious communities are a critical element in the notion of social capital, notably as set out by Harvard scholar Robert Putnam (1993).

Several features of this wide and deep physical presence of religious entities are especially significant for development practice. First, the infrastructure of the religious institutions outlined below plays a large part in social cohesion, in part because of its ubiquity but also arising from its depth of penetration and long duration. Second, the presence varies widely, by region and denomination. In some places religious institutions are primary actors in governance and most aspects of life, while in others their roles are more at the margin. Broad generalizations are risky for this reason and each situation needs to be examined case by case.

Third, because of its diversity and the fact that its role is often contested, this religious presence has not been mapped in any methodical way. This explains why much religiously linked activity and many facilities are essentially ignored in traditional development planning. A material example is the difficulty in agreeing within global health circles on appropriate statistical measures related to religiously linked health care, even in physical inventories of health services. Similar comments apply for education. This complexity and the lack of meaningful mapping are one reason why much religiously linked activity and many facilities are essentially ignored in traditional development planning. Equally important, social surveys and other statistical measures that serve as common reference points often exclude part of or even all religious elements so that much religiously managed work on, for example, health and education is only partially captured. This may be inadvertence or it may reflect deliberate efforts to separate the religious from the secular.

Fourth, the geographic boundaries used by religious institutions often differ from secular boundaries and spatial definitions. There may thus be a distinctive religious geography with implications for development management. At one level this is relatively straightforward, as for example where boundaries of a parish or diocese differ from local government jurisdictions. However, transnational links may be more complex to discern. Religious institutions are described aptly as the first globalizers, and often have extensive transnational links and presence. The religious aspects of diaspora populations are increasingly recognized as important for development (notably for financial remittances but also for emergency and other support). These cross-boundary links can result in positive social exchange, though they can also at times work against national civic identity.

Fifth, a wide range of surveys (see for example Narayan 2000 but also various regional "barometer" surveys) indicate that trust levels for religious leaders and institutions are higher than for many if not most other categories of institutions and leaders. This trust together with their wide and longstanding presence explains why religious institutions are often first responders in emergencies and crises, including natural disasters and during and after wars. They are also a sustained, reliable presence in good times. Religious institutions are an important part of the resilience that is a focus of attention today in response to crisis and lasting development impact.

Exploring development roles of the major categories of religious institutions

Against this backdrop of the main ways in which the variety of religious institutions globally are significant for development practice, I now provide a broad institutional "map" to help in understanding and analyzing religious roles in development. It focuses on five types of institutions: religious structures; faith-inspired organizations; religiously inspired movements; community non-formal entities; and interfaith and intrafaith organizations (Marshall 2013).

Religious structures

In this chapter I am using the term "religious structures" to include a number of different sorts of entities that play a role in formally governing religious communities and which carry the responsibility for religious and spiritual matters, often embodying the understandings of religious authority. Included are the principal organizational mechanisms through which formal religious communities are governed (e.g. the Catholic Church, Buddhist Sangha, or a formal Muslim body like Al-Azhar University), religious entities like the many Catholic religious orders that are considered part of the Church hierarchy through formal governance arrangements (e.g. the Jesuits or Benedictines) as well as the vast *congregational* organizations (e.g. churches, mosques and temples) where the daily life of religious believers plays out. Large formal education and health networks run directly by religious authorities fit in this category. In the Christian and some other traditions, these organizations often take an explicit and often distinctly hierarchical form. In others they are highly decentralized. Leadership may be clearly defined, literally anointed, with explicit selection criteria and extensive formal training. However, it may also be informal and self-designated; as an example, in some Muslim countries, imams are selected by the community, while in others they are approved by national authorities. A common feature of formal religious hierarchies in many traditions is that formal leadership positions are held exclusively by men (a final glass ceiling that explicitly excludes women), and in many traditions these positions are associated with age. This is changing rapidly in some traditions, but by no means everywhere, as women and younger people assume larger roles. The representative character of religious organizations varies widely, but a democratic character, in a modern political sense, is rare.

These formal religious structures (and the leaders who tend to personify them) engage on development issues in many different ways. Action on development can be viewed as consisting of linked parts that include policy and socio-political mobilization, program planning and design, and local action, including community engagement and, in important areas, changes in behavior. In terms of policy and mobilization, Catholic social teaching and the advocacy work of different Christian denominations touch on most development topics (e.g. religious leaders played a vital role during the Jubilee Debt Campaign). However, religious structures from all traditions are increasingly involved on issues of climate change, as well as cooperation on the Millennium Development Goals (MDGs). Less positively, tensions around human rights are clouding relationships with a number of national governments and international institutions, as are religiously linked conflicts in several world regions. In terms of program design and management, many religious entities run social services, notably hospitals, schools, universities, orphanages, old age homes, and so forth. And at the community, congregational level communities play vital roles across the board; whether on energy access, water, family planning, HIV and AIDS, and virtually any other topic, religious structures have roles to play. Thus, the first and in many senses core institutional actors, looked at from the development perspective, are these religious structures.

Christian religious structures

Christian religious structures govern the religious affairs of some 2.18 billion people worldwide (see Pew Forum 2011 for some basic statistics). The Catholic Church, with an estimated 1.2 billion Catholics worldwide, is in some senses the quintessential religious structure, as both the largest single religious institution today and in many senses the best known. But Christian religious structures also include a wide variety of forms, ranging from those that are highly structured to others that are decentralized, although often still hierarchical (e.g. evangelical and Pentecostal denominations).

The Catholic Church merits special consideration both for its size and its influence. It functions as both a religious body and a sovereign state (the Holy See), where the Holy See is represented formally at the United Nations and in other transnational organizations (with a voice, though as an observer). It has a diplomatic service, with *nuncios*, as the equivalent of ambassadors are known, in many capitals. Moreover, many observers, including individuals involved in development work, tend to view the full gamut of religious institutions through a lens colored by the Catholic Church. This lens can be positive, taking into account the selfless service of many nuns and priests and the depth of Catholic social teaching, or negative, especially vis-à-vis approaches to reproductive health. Further, the Church engages actively and explicitly in development work and debates, the former through its extensive global networks of schools, hospitals, and other social bodies, the latter notably through Catholic social teaching (see Calderisi 2013). Formal teachings include encyclicals and documents like *Evangelii Gaudium* (Francis, Pope 2013), the first formal statement of Pope Francis in November 2013, which treats a wide range of development issues. Also highly influential is Liberation Theology, less formal but expounding a "preferential option for the poor" that colors development thinking well beyond the Church. In contrast, the voice of a more conservative arm of the Catholic Church, Opus Dei, also influences approaches to development issues like the role of the private sector in many situations.

The Catholic Church exemplifies the highly centralized organization and patriarchal character that is a common perception in many quarters about the nature of religious institutions. However, with some 2,800 dioceses worldwide (Buckley *et al.* 2010), there are in practice wide local variations. The Pope – who is held up as infallible – is the highest authority, and his many directives and social teachings cover not just religion, but topics such as just war, gender relations, labor practices, and environmental protection. The Roman Curia constitutes the formal administrative structure of the Vatican, and nine central bodies known as congregations have administrative oversight of various bodies, such as the Catholic education system. A network of territorial jurisdictions, or dioceses, forms the backbone of the web of Catholics worldwide. Working through separate hierarchies which depend also on the Curia are many religious orders and organizations, which may function with a high level of autonomy (e.g. the Jesuit Order). Women religious include 713,000 nuns today, who play leading roles in running schools, hospitals, and other organizations (Allen 2004; Linden 2009).

Also illustrating the complexity of Christian religious structures are the Eastern Catholic churches, a set of autonomous and self-governing churches that play important social and often political roles. They are considered to be "in communion" with the Roman Catholic Church, in the sense that the churches share a common view of liturgy and authority. The Eastern rite follows many theological traditions of the Orthodox churches, but differs in some important beliefs. Eastern Catholic churches recognize the authority of the Pope. Historically, Eastern Catholic churches were concentrated in Eastern Europe, the Middle East, and North Africa but today are present all over the world.

The Orthodox churches are leading institutions in several world regions, again with significant development roles. They differ significantly from the Catholic Church not only in doctrine but in organization. The Orthodox churches consist of 15 separate hierarchical churches, each with its own leader, who is called a Patriarch or Metropolitan; the term "autocephalous" refers to the independent heads of the churches. While there is no one central figure such as the Roman Catholic Pope, the Patriarch of Constantinople, one of the separate churches, is considered the highest-ranking bishop. Today, he is often referred to as the "Green Pope" because of his strong voice on environmental issues.

The Ethiopian Orthodox Tewahedo Church, one of the 15, has a unique history and influence; given Ethiopia's important development challenges its role and approach to development have special significance. One of the few pre-colonial Christian churches in Sub-Saharan Africa, it claims 40–45 million members today. It exercises substantial influence in Ethiopian politics and daily life and offers an example of active church engagement in development issues. The Patriarch has promoted HIV and AIDS awareness, and the Church, notably through a "development bible" that links development "messages" to each theme and time in the church calendar, has cooperated with development organizations in promoting behavior change in areas like early marriage and ending female genital cutting (FGC), as well as reliance on clean water. In contrast, the basic conservatism of the Church's traditions and teachings explains in part Ethiopia's slow development progress over many decades.

In contrast to the Catholic and Orthodox churches, contemporary Protestantism – comprising 38,000 different Protestant denominations serving an estimated 800 million people – tends to be far more decentralized. The various denominations fall into five loose, overlapping categories: historic Protestant churches (for example, Anglican, Presbyterian, Baptist), peace churches (for example the Quakers), churches specific to different regions (like African independent churches), new charismatic churches (with many called Evangelical or Pentecostal), and non-Trinitarian churches (for example Unitarians). The governance structures vary widely, from tightly run hierarchies to essentially democratic and horizontal structures. Many Protestant churches are active in education and in health care. As advocates of social justice many have also become deeply involved in issues like human trafficking.[5] Protestant denominations are well known for their missionary work and their role in the colonial enterprise (see Deacon and Tomalin, Chapter 5). This resulted in close links forged among churches across national and continental boundaries, but it has also produced tensions, past, but which linger on today (Woodberry 2012). The transnational links among different church denominations are important forces in development, often explaining financing flows and advocacy as well as exchanges of personnel, for education and broader church purposes.

Several formal ecumenical entities have emerged that link Christian churches around the world. Several focus explicitly on topics relevant to development. Some exercise considerable influence both within Christian circles and beyond. The Anglican Communion, Lutheran World Federation, Baptist World Alliance, and World Evangelical Alliance all claim tens of millions of members in dozens of countries worldwide. Given the rapid growth of Pentecostal and other charismatic Protestant traditions in many regions, the roles of the global evangelical organizations are important in addressing contentious issues like proselytizing. The World Council of Churches, which includes most historic Protestant and Orthodox churches and claims to represent over 525 million church members, promotes peacemaking, social justice, and health care worldwide.

Religious structures in other traditions

The Muslim faith, as the second-largest global religious tradition, counts some 1.5 billion adherents worldwide. In terms of approaches to development, Muslim teachings, as expounded by both political leaders and scholars, can be highly influential. The core Muslim practice of *Zakat* (alms giving) and other calls to charitable priorities (especially the priority given to care for widows and orphans) and to principles of finance play important roles. However, there is no structure comparable to the Catholic Church hierarchy or other Christian structures. Muslims who follow the Sunni traditions explicitly eschew any formal religious hierarchy of authority. Shia Muslims, in contrast, recognize strong temporal and spiritual authority, notably in religious leaders termed ayatollahs. Some leaders (for example the King of Morocco and the Aga Khan, Imam of Ismaili Muslims) trace lineage to the Prophet Mohammad, and thus carry both religious and political authority. In practice, the organization of religious, political, and legal authority within the significant number of Muslim majority countries varies widely, essentially by country. Various nations define themselves explicitly as Muslim, with legal systems following Sharia. Others have explicitly espoused secular governance approaches, and treat Islam as one of various religions. In several countries (notably those affected by the Arab uprisings but also Turkey, Bangladesh, and Indonesia) the role of Islam vis-à-vis the state (and thus in development) is hotly contested. These issues spill over into development debates, for example in relation to education and banking systems (see Jawad, Chapter 19; Mohseni-Cheraghlou, Chapter 20; and Tadros, Chapter 21).

Notwithstanding the absence of a single overarching religious authority or common hierarchy, important organizations and supranational entities link Muslims across boundaries and often purport to represent Muslims worldwide. The Organisation of Islamic Cooperation (OIC) is a political body whose members are 57 nation states; it has no explicit religious authority or role. However, it presents itself as "the collective voice of the Muslim world," committed to "ensuring to safeguard and protect the interests of the Muslim world in the spirit of promoting international peace and harmony among various people of the world."[6] Al-Azhar University in Egypt is the most respected center of Islamic learning and literature, and scholars from the university issue fatwas that address disagreements in the Sunni Islamic world. For example, in 2011 an Al-Azhar fatwa declared that female genital cutting is not sanctioned or required by Islam. The OIC works closely with the UN. It has issued an Islamic Declaration of Human Rights that differs in important respects from global principles of human rights, but it also sees its role as promoting tolerance and moderation. Affiliated organizations include the Islamic Development Bank (which promotes Islamic finance and works to fight poverty in member countries) and ISESCO, a Muslim parallel to UNESCO.

In contrast to Islam and Christianity other religious traditions are more difficult to define, and their structures have tended to be at a greater remove from the intellectual and administrative currents that have driven what might be termed mainstream development thinking. Two notable exceptions are the Baha'i faith, which has taken a particularly active role, with positions, notably in the United Nations, on a wide range of development issues, and the Jewish tradition, with its traditions of *tikkun olam* (healing the earth) and strong charitable traditions linked to social progress (see Plant and Weiss, Chapter 4). However, Buddhism and Hinduism – two large and important world religious traditions which merit attention, given their size and the significance of development for their communities of believers – have institutional characteristics that are difficult to define and vary widely. Some question whether they should even be counted as "religions" (see the discussion in Tomalin, Chapter 1). Perhaps the least structured of the large global faith traditions is Hinduism, and, while there is no central Hindu organization, some spiritual authority is vested in regionally based religious leaders known as *acharyas*. Also Hinduism stands out from other "world religions" in that most Hindus live in India (about 85 percent) and, moreover, this large Hindu majority has become a major vehicle for political mobilization since the 1980s. The role of Hinduism in national identity and in core political, social, and development strategies has long been the subject of intense contestation (see Tomalin, Chapter 13).

The organizational structures of Buddhism are also decentralized, though in some countries, such as Thailand, a national Sangha has explicit links to the government and a clear hierarchy. However, there is no global Buddhist organization, and different traditions evidence quite distinct organizations. Carrying on a tradition of Buddhist leaders who exercised both spiritual and temporal authority and responsibility, the most notable example today is the Dalai Lama and his spiritual and temporal organization based in Dharmasala (India). In general the local temple or pagoda is a focal point for community organization, having the most direct influence on the way people live their lives (and thus relate to development ideas and programs).[7] In the past in most Buddhist societies temples served roles as schools, also providing care for vulnerable children, and in some settings these roles continue today. There are a number of examples of Buddhist actors educating populations about HIV and AIDS as well as promoting and providing hospice care (e.g. in Thailand and Cambodia; see Falk, Chapter 18). An important and creative International Network of Engaged Buddhists actively urges Buddhist structures and monks (and sometimes nuns) to play more active roles, in advocacy for various causes, notably environmental protection, and in development areas like education. Active organizations include the World Fellowship of Buddhists, dominated by Theravada Buddhists, and the World Buddhist Sangha Council. To date these organizations have not exercised a significant voice in global development debates, nor have they claimed a significant role as development actors.

Finally, an important (if difficult-to-define) part of the religious landscape is indigenous traditions. With approaches to development in indigenous communities sharply contested, their voice and role have taken on increasing importance (e.g. see Bergmann, Chapter 26 for a discussion of this with respect to the effects of climate change). By their nature they are scattered, each community with its own individual governance arrangements. At the United Nations level, the World Council of Indigenous Peoples was established with the goal of representing the voices of indigenous faiths, but it disintegrated in the mid-1990s.

In considering the roles of religious institutions and their representation at the various tables where development policy is debated, the question arises as to how to treat atheists or humanists. As with some other decentralized, hard-to-define traditions, determining which voices to hear and how to select representatives is problematic, the more so as atheists tend to be conflated in debates with secular approaches. Various organizations aim to unite and define humanists nationally and worldwide (e.g. the Council for Democratic and Secular Humanism, CODESH).

Faith-inspired organizations

The second type of religious institutions are so-called "faith-inspired" organizations (FIOs), a well-known group of large, transnational organizations that play important and respected roles in development work.[8] Some FIOs are among the largest of global development actors outside governments, and they operate across the world. World Vision, originally a Christian evangelical organization, now broader but clearly Christian in orientation, has some 44,000 employees and works in many sectors. Caritas Internationalis is the development arm of the Catholic Church, active worldwide through a network of nationally based organizations that include Catholic Relief Services and CAFOD. Islamic Relief was founded in Birmingham, UK, in response to the drought in the Horn of Africa in 1984, and has grown into a global institution working not only in emergency situations but on a wide range of development challenges. The Aga Khan Development Network, inspired by the faith leadership of the Aga Khan as Imam and by Ismaili beliefs, is a standout leader among development organizations. This is simply to name some of the leading transnational FIOs. Many bridge the full gamut of humanitarian work (defined as responses to emergencies) (Barnett and Stein 2013) and development engagement, while others tend to have more specialized mandates, including energy access, housing, care of vulnerable children, trafficking, and water.

These organizations have many similarities to their non-religious counterparts like CARE and Save the Children, with highly professionalized staff and well-articulated management systems, including project evaluation. Most receive significant funding from a range of development organizations, and they are often part of multilateral and national aid coordination mechanisms at both national and international levels. Relationships vary with the religious traditions to which they are linked and draw their inspiration, ranging from formal engagement in management structures of religious structures to a loose affiliation or none at all. They also vary as to whether staff and leadership must adhere to the faith tradition involved.

But these well-established organizations are only the tip of the iceberg of formal organizations with a faith inspiration that work directly on the wide range of activities that count as development. There are hundreds of thousands of faith-inspired organizations, and they operate with varying degrees of legal and organizational clarity and in the nature of their development activities. They are transnational, national, and local. Most FIOs pride themselves on their wide outreach and commitment to serve humankind and separate their religious work from what they consider as development. Some, however, argue that religious beliefs and development work are inseparable and that it is impractical to expect them to separate proselytizing and support for followers exclusively from their development mission.

Religious and spiritual movements

Also playing a role in development is a group of religious or spiritual actors that can be termed "movements." In general these are not formally linked to religious structures and hierarchies but may relate to their core beliefs (Paranjape 2005 and Tyndale 2006 give special importance to this group of institutions). A religious movement may describe itself as part of a specific religious tradition (e.g. the Sarvodaya Movement is linked to Buddhism), while others state that they are "spiritual," and thus inspired by a broad spirituality that cuts across religious boundaries (e.g. Sri Sri Ravi Shankar's Art of Living Movement and the Brahmakumaris).

The presence of a wide variety of religious and spiritual movements, often taking inspiration from a charismatic leader, is particularly prominent in the Indian sub-continent, where dozens attract millions of followers and engage in a range of activities.[9] They take many different forms, including those that are well structured and legally recognized, and others that are loosely organized and informal. They may have segments that have a formal organization that would fit the FIO category, but the intensity of commitment of followers and flexible organization sets them apart. In other parts of the world, some Muslim movements are also centered around a charismatic individual, for instance the transnational Gulen or Hizmet Movement. And within Christianity a variety of movements like the Sant'Egidio Community, Focolare Movement, and Opus Dei also mobilize large and deeply committed followers.

The links to development of these movements vary. Some, like Sarvodaya, have deliberate and well-articulated philosophies of development, in this instance a strong community focus and commitment to principles of self-help. Others approach social issues through a broad net of ideas, for example personal responsibility and spiritual commitment. The Community of Sant'Egidio began as a student effort to serve poor people in the outskirts of Rome, but grew organically as a global movement known for its peacemaking prowess and commitment but also for its determined and high-quality work on HIV and AIDS and on registration of marginal populations. The Gulen Movement, which is distinctly Turkish and Muslim, enjoys wide if not very transparent business support and is known for its large and growing network of excellent schools, as well as for its purported involvement in Turkish politics. In short, these often uncounted and uncharted but important and dynamic movements play creative roles in engaging populations in a broader vision of a different society and in mobilization of financial and human resources through volunteer participation. They tend to operate independently of "classic" religious or secular organizations, following their own spiritual and practical principles.

Community organizations

An important category of organizations, the hardest to count and describe because of their variety and general informality, are locally inspired and led. These can range from bible study groups to groups formed to respond to an emergency or another special purpose. Few have formal organizational structures, and they relate to more formal religious structures in widely different ways. Many communities, if probed, will exhibit a range of organizations, and many have a faith inspiration or link. Examples include women's and youth groups and groupings that arise in response to a crisis or specific issue. This category might also encompass informal structures like savings groups or Koranic study circles. Within male-led religious organizations, for example the Senegalese Sufi orders, women are almost entirely invisible within the formal hierarchy. At the community level, however, networks of women in informal groupings play important roles both within the religious institutions and undertaking specific projects. These organizations and networks are rarely mapped, nor are they well understood by local or national leaders, religious or secular, or international development actors. But they are vital to community resilience and sustainability.

These informal organizations and networks play a wide variety of pertinent development roles. At a broad level they are a factor in social cohesion and have important actual and potential roles in conflict prevention and peacebuilding (for example in trauma healing). They also respond to specific social needs. The widely varied responses of communities to the HIV and AIDS crisis, for example caring for orphans and organizing home-based care, are an example. Where behavior change is an explicit objective, for example in ending female genital cutting or child marriage or in promoting child spacing, the informal groupings that are inspired by religious beliefs and a sense of community can make the difference between success and failure.

Interfaith and intrafaith organizations

A number of intra- and interreligious organizations have emerged, most over the past 120 years, dating from the 1893 Chicago Parliament of the World's Religions. Some are global, some more local. Their varying objectives often link to those of development actors. Their sharpest focus to date has been on peacebuilding, and thus fragile and conflict states. However, there is increasing interest in more strictly development-related activities like malaria, HIV and AIDS, and environmental protection. Inter- and intrafaith organizations and those who support them see cooperation among religious traditions, especially through practical engagement, as a path to easing social and especially religious tensions. Working through interfaith organizations also offers a promise of neutrality for a secular partner, since no one religious group is favored.

Most of the transnational intra- and interfaith organizations face organizational and other challenges, as they seek to bridge religious differences and the varying leadership hierarchies and styles of different organizations. This is a period of significant change in both organizations and approach (for a recent exploration see Halafoff 2013). Representation poses thorny problems. Financing for this type of activity is also hard to come by. However, they play important roles in the broad effort to reach across religious divides by increasing understanding and awareness of the human face of different religious traditions. The largest global interfaith organizations are Religions for Peace (formerly World Conference of Religions for Peace), the Parliament of the World's Religions, and the United Religions Initiative. A newer actor is King Abdallah International Center for Interfaith and Intercultural Dialogue (KAICIID), a well-funded organization sponsored by the governments of Saudi Arabia, Austria, and Spain, and based in Vienna, Austria.

Religious engagement in development: forms and issues

Religious and development institutions interact in widely varying ways, which differ by region, sector, and topic. Stepping back, what is striking is the numerous disconnects and tensions and the absence of structured institutional mechanisms for cooperation. Mainstream development institutions (as noted above) have rarely developed a capacity to appreciate the complex array of religious institutions and their relevance for development work and vice versa. Notwithstanding notable exceptions, generally there is far to go.

Discussion of religious roles in development in practice often focuses on service delivery (especially education and health care), because important education and health networks are managed by religious structures and FIOs. Their relevance to the Millennium Development Goals has encouraged exploration of how religion and development are related. Service delivery brings different institutions into communication about both the programs and the strategies of the major international and national development organizations.

Religious organizations have long played important roles both nationally and internationally as advocates for funding for development aid and for specific issues. They can represent powerful voices for the poor and marginalized. Examples of specific activism include the Jubilee Debt Movement and 2005 global mobilizations to end poverty. There are countless other examples at regional and national levels. Community-level engagement can reshape attitudes towards social and economic change and associated behaviors, and here also there are important instances of religious institutions playing significant roles.

A commonly voiced concern, particularly by academic observers but also people from religious institutions, is that religious engagement in development work is far too instrumentalized. What that means, crudely, is that development institutions see religious actors as supporters of "their" approaches and as implementers of "their" projects. Not surprisingly the view of religious counterparts and their supporters is that an instrumental approach is inappropriate and demeaning. Religious institutions have a longer history of engagement on many development issues than their secular counterparts. They have direct experience to bring to bear on policy debates and offer distinctive approaches and perspectives. To a degree this is an issue of mindset and approach, but it also involves power differences, especially where large funding is at stake. The goal is to move beyond such simplistic approaches and understandings, towards a model based on robust and thoughtful partnerships grounded in mutual understanding and respect, strong accountability, and conscious efforts to address imbalances in power (see Tomalin, Chapter 1).

Within the context of these areas of engagement, five topics illustrate both common ground and differing perspectives. I will discuss these in turn.

First, concerns about flows of finance to organizations that support or are seen to support terrorist activities have created significant tensions in the post-September 11 era. The United States Patriot Act and equivalents in other countries have constrained particularly organizations inspired by Islamic values and teachings. There are several consequences. Good work by some institutions has been brought to a halt, and the measures generate resentment of the countries behind the controls, especially when they are seen as arbitrary or unjust. The often arbitrary application of regulations encourages unreported cash transfers, outside official channels, exacerbating already serious problems of corruption and misappropriation of funds. Solutions need to look to proper processes of identifying truly problematic flows, and broad-brush application of controls to any or virtually any organization with a Muslim character needs to be avoided. Various initiatives, in the UK and in Switzerland in particular, aim to bring more rationality into the system.

A second issue centers on women and gender, highlighting problems that have tended to surround religious development relationships. Religious institutions are virtually the last bastions of the glass ceilings preventing women from exercising public roles. Religious and cultural beliefs are one reason why practices like child marriage and female genital cutting persist. Many religious leaders still believe in and argue for a hierarchical relationship between men and women where the man is superior and entitled to leadership roles. Reproductive health rights remain a highly sensitive issue (Aylward and Friedman 2014). Important denominations have adapted their teachings and practice to the modern understanding of full male and female equality. Nonetheless, visible realities of gender inequality within religious institutions explain much of the unease among mainstream development leaders and institutions about respecting religion and according to religious institutions a recognized place. A flip side is that many religious figures are uneasy about what they describe as "western feminism," which they equate with denigration and challenges to traditional cultures and beliefs and especially to that institution which virtually everyone agrees is the basic social cell, upon which all is built: the family.

The complication is that many if not most religious actors believe that they indeed stand for a truer and deeper appreciation of the common dignity of all persons than their secular counterparts. The challenge, therefore, is to deepen understandings and dialogue about where the problems indeed reside. Are there misperceptions, and how far are the basic human rights norms of equality called into question by religious communities and how? At the level of families and individual lived realities, how do religious beliefs and teachings influence behavior? Are the perils of modern women's roles underestimated? Given the critical and growing importance of male–female relationships in international affairs, these issues need to be confronted.

A third issue concerns human rights. The Universal Declaration of Human Rights is described (only somewhat tongue in cheek) as the religion of the United Nations system. It represents a common set of beliefs, articulated in the late 1940s, admittedly led by American and European actors notwithstanding valiant efforts to reflect values that are truly universal. The fact that there were and still are very different values and ethical norms was acknowledged, famously in philosopher Jacques Maritain's comment that all could accept the human rights as set out in the declaration as long as no one questioned why. This underscores the importance of the human rights framework as a foundation for the international system, its progressive refinement over the past 65 years, and continuing, nagging questions about its universality (see Juul Petersen, Chapter 24). There is considerable evidence of a mounting questioning of human rights, especially in various religious circles. Some groups (some US evangelical groups, for example) go so far as to describe a United Nations conspiracy to undermine religious values. Efforts to broaden definitions of rights, for example to apply to LGBT groups and to the disabled, fuel these perceptions.

A fourth issue surrounds aid coordination and harmonization, a central pillar of the final, eighth MDG that calls for strategic focus in achieving goals and for partnerships. It is axiomatic within global development institutions that fragmented and overlapping development work poses serious problems, and a series of efforts have defined elaborate measures to improve coordination and harmonization, under the leadership of the governments concerned (the Busan agreement in 2012 is the latest example). With the important and often creative faith-linked service delivery networks and approaches, it is striking how little systematic effort has gone into engaging with them in the context of aid effectiveness and harmonization, at country and international levels. Knowledge gaps, weak networks, and negative preconceptions (going both ways) are the likely explanations. More nuanced and respectful approaches to partnership might better capture the complex contributions and assets of faith actors and enhance their contributions to what are common ends.

A fifth issue that arises in virtually every world region is how and whether religious organizations exercise their right to freedom of religion through efforts to convert others, thus proselytizing or (as many prefer to term it) evangelizing or sharing their faith. This relates to practical applications of religious freedom in different societies and how such activities relate to the humanitarian and development work. Within international humanitarian law, the rules of the game and codes of conduct are, at least in theory, quite well established. Anything that involves conditionality or a quid pro quo is counter to international norms of neutrality and treatment of people in vulnerable positions. However, questions linger about the proper extent to which development workers can bring their religious beliefs explicitly into their development work. Faith organizations differ in nuanced ways, but most argue that the effects of overt proselytizing, particularly by evangelizing organizations, can be profoundly alienating and exacerbate social tensions, with spillover effects that extend to all development work. The counter-argument is that spiritual and material dimensions of development work cannot and should not be separated in artificial ways. In this debate, tensions between Christian and Muslim communities are the primary concern, but in largely Buddhist Sri Lanka and in India this remains a highly contentious and explosive issue. Defining boundaries and agreeing on clear and meaningful codes of conduct are possible avenues towards solutions.

Global institutions approach religion

Until the late 1990s, few global institutions (with the exception of the OIC and other Islamic institutions) had articulated positions on how they understood their relationships with religious bodies.

This was especially true for development-related topics despite the fact that a wide gamut of religious bodies had varying involvement within international organizations. UNESCO was the organization within the United Nations system with a mandate to deal with culture and religion, but religion was (and remains) essentially subordinate to culture within UNESCO's approach and organization. Moreover, religiously inspired NGOs accredited to the United Nations and the special role of the Vatican and Holy See give a visibility, sometimes unwelcome, to religious perspectives; that is particularly true where LGBT issues are at stake but also on topics concerning women and reproductive health. In general a search for religious references within the United Nations system turns up very little.[10] The major exception was the experience during the Cairo 1994 Conference on Population and Development and the 1995 Beijing conference on women. Both highlighted the growing intellectual and policy consensus within international development communities on the vital importance of changing women's roles ("Women's rights are human rights," famously declared Hillary Clinton). They also brought home clearly the religious doubts about these changing roles especially where human rights involved reproductive health. The alliance of Vatican and Muslim nations and, later, evangelical groups for the first time made clear the challenges they presented on the human rights front.

This disregard for religion within global institutions was changed after the 1979 Iranian Revolution and the rise of terrorism in the late 1990s and early 2000s entrenched religion on global agendas, if primarily in a negative sense. In different ways and at differing tempos, various institutions of the United Nations system came to reflect on how they should engage with religious institutions and the implications of doing so. UNICEF and the United Nations Population Fund (UNFPA) were among the leaders at a practical, field level, because their programs addressing respectively the needs of children, including mounting vaccination campaigns in contested areas, and women's reproductive health brought them into direct and continuous contact with religious actors and institutions.

At the leadership level the stance of individual leaders in key institutions plays significant roles in shaping approaches to the particularly sensitive topic of religion. Thus it was significant that leaders of four Washington, DC international institutions were among those arguing explicitly for a more dynamic and active stance on religion. Michel Camdessus, managing director of the International Monetary Fund, and his successor, Horst Köhler, reached out to religious leaders, especially the Vatican and intellectuals like Hans Kung. Enrique Iglesias was convinced, from his position as president of the Inter-American Development Bank, that systematic relationships with different religious institutions and leaders were critical to making breakthroughs on economic development in Latin America. And James D. Wolfensohn, as president of the World Bank, took the most active stance on the topic, convinced that the criticism of development institutions coming from religious institutions needed to be confronted, because they shared such strong common interests in fighting poverty (Marshall and Van Saanen 2006). He saw religious bodies as the world's largest distribution system, key actors in every dimension of humanitarian and development fields. The current World Bank president Jim Yong Kim also argues that religious institutions are and must be treated as central partners in mobilizing global energies to end world poverty.

Wolfensohn's initiative, launched in 1998 jointly with the then Archbishop of Canterbury, George Carey, was in fact quite modest, involving high-level meetings centered on dialogue (with no meaningful financial commitment at stake). They envisaged a continuing dialogue around topics like the Millennium Development Goals and country strategic priorities for poverty alleviation. Yet, significantly, the effort encountered quite strong opposition. The World Bank's executive directors, representing, then, over 180 countries, put forward a host of objections. In sum, they perceived the dialogue effort as entering dangerous political waters and were concerned by the patriarchal approaches of religious institutions. And many still clove to the increasingly discredited assumption that religion's role in public matters was on an inevitable decline.

The dialogue process brought home doubts that also prevailed within different religious institutions about the motivations and approaches of global institutions, and especially the multilateral development and financial institutions. These included their perception that multinational corporations and powerful governments called the shots, concerns with effects of development like displacement of populations, the grip of certain economic approaches that were described as rigidly theological in nature, and the fact that institutions seemed so enigmatic. Ethical concerns in development work were seen as invisible or muted.

What the efforts of these Washington-based institutions brought home most clearly, however, was the perils and special sensitivities involved in engaging religion in international organizations. The very complexity of religious institutions and their complex ties both to political entities and to each other were seen as a source of potential distortion of international, global goals and institutional frameworks. Several European countries whose development agencies have sought to engage more systematically on religion have met similar experiences (the United Kingdom, Norway, and the Netherlands among them). The message then is clear: proceed, but exercise caution.

In the past decade, global and religious institutions have worked out some new sets of relationships. The Millennium Development Goals have provided some impetus and a useful organizing framework. So, at least to a degree, has the looming awareness of the dangers of climate change. Concerns about security have at least increased attention to religious actors. As active members of the civil society bodies that play growing roles on virtually every global issue, faith-inspired organizations are increasingly visible and they have developed a growing set of relationships with virtually every United Nations institution.

Conclusion

Limited understanding and poor communication among religious and secular actors are themes running through this discussion. Both contribute to important misperceptions and have blocked potentially productive avenues for dialogue and cooperation that could enhance the quality of development. The disconnects result in part from the stubborn belief that "church" and "state" must be separate, with religion relegated largely to private roles in society. This lends ambiguity to how active religious institutions can be where issues of governance (for example, corruption) arise. This notional ideal is far from universal, and in practice religion and governance are often tightly intertwined. This can have positive benefits, where a religious tradition is engaged in an agenda of social, economic, and political change and helps in defining humanistic values for a society that allows today's plural societies to function peacefully. It can be negative, as in various Communist regimes that, at least in the past, set out to banish or root out religious influences entirely, or where exclusive religious approaches marginalize or result in the persecution of segments of the population.

Surveying the institutional landscape in relation to development practice, what seems to prevail today is an uneasy and often unclear set of relationships. This is especially true where the complex issues around development are involved. Religious voices and beliefs are often influential in shaping many policies and ideas, but in a contested and often rather ambiguous manner. The combination of this ambiguity and opaque relationships with dynamic and changing patterns and norms has contributed to a "religious illiteracy" (Prothero 2007), as education about religion dwindled in many educational curricula and as many professions acted on the assumption that religion was no longer a force to be reckoned with. Understanding the institutional context within which religious actors are involved in development is a good place to start in clarifying relationships and moving in positive directions.

Notes

1 See the websites of the Berkley Center for Religion, Peace and World Affairs at Georgetown University (http://berkleycenter.georgetown.edu/programs/religion-and-global-development) and the World Faiths Development Dialogue (http://berkleycenter.georgetown.edu/wfdd).
2 The term "religious actors" is used inclusively to identify the wide variety of organizations and individuals whose primary identification is religious. For example, the term is to include informal women and youth leaders, who are often overlooked by the typical focus on formal (male) religious leaders. It also includes non-formal institutions that might not be recognized in formal governance structures.
3 For useful background on the context for this institutional discussion see ter Haar (2011) and Shah *et al.* (2012).
4 International Interfaith Investment Group (3iG) and Alliance of Religions for Conservation (ARC) have tried to quantify these different categories, presenting dramatic results. The data, however, are difficult to obtain and to verify. Suffice it to say the amounts are large.
5 For an example of religious engagement in a specific country see http://berkleycenter.georgetown.edu/wfdd/publications/human-trafficking-faith-in-action-in-cambodia.
6 http://www.oic-oci.org/oicv2/page/?p_id=52&p_ref=26&lan=en.
7 For an example of how Buddhist organizations and followers work at a national level, including their development approaches and roles, see WFDD (2012).
8 I prefer the term "faith-inspired organization," as it is more inclusive; "faith-inspired" implies less formal links with religious structures and thus a wider range of organizations. The two terms (FBOs and FIOs) generally refer to organizations specifically created to perform a wide range of functions; in many settings they are treated as part of civil society and as such are commonly seen as the "face" of religion in discussions about development actors.
9 An effort to highlight features of several of these movements is Paranjape (2005).
10 A fascinating exception is the International Labour Organization (ILO), which has had a senior religious officer reporting to the director-general since the early 1920s (see Peccoud 2011).

References

Allen, John (2004) *All the Pope's Men: The Inside Story of How the Vatican Really Thinks*, New York: Doubleday Religion.
Aylward, Lynn and Friedman, Nava (2014) *Faith and International Family Planning*, February, Washington, DC: World Faiths Development Dialogue.
Aylward, Lynn and Marshall, Katherine (2012) *Global Health and Africa: Assessing Faith Work and Research Priorities*, April, Washington, DC: World Faiths Development Dialogue and Tony Blair Faith Foundation.
Barnett, Michael and Stein, Janice Gross (eds) (2013) *Sacred Aid: Faith and Humanitarianism*, New York: Oxford University Press.
Berger, Peter (1999) *The Desecularization of the World: Resurgent Religion in World Politics*, Grand Rapids, MI: Eerdmans.
Buckley, James, Bauerschmidt, Frederick Christian and Pomplun, Trent (2010) *The Blackwell Companion to Catholicism*, Chichester: John Wiley & Sons.
Calderisi, Robert (2013) *Earthly Mission: The Catholic Church and World Development*, New Haven, CT: Yale University Press.
Casanova, J. (1994) *Public Religions in the Modern World*, Chicago: University of Chicago Press.
Copans, Jean (1989) *Les Marabouts de l'Arachide: La Confrérie mouride et les paysans du Sénégal*, Paris: L'Harmattan.
Francis, Pope (2013) *The Joy of the Gospel*, http://w2.vatican.va/content/francesco/en/apost_exhortations/documents/papa-francesco_esortazione-ap_20131124_evangelii-gaudium.html.
Halafoff, Anna (2013) *The Multifaith Movement: Global Risks and Cosmopolitan Solutions*, Dordrecht: Springer.

Linden, Ian (2009) *Global Catholicism: Diversity and Change since Vatican II*, New York: Columbia University Press.

Marshall, Katherine (2013) *Global Institutions of Religion: Ancient Movers, Modern Shakers*, Abingdon: Routledge.

Marshall, Katherine and Van Saanen, Marissa (2006) *Mind, Heart, and Soul in the Fight against Poverty*, Washington, DC: World Bank.

Narayan, Deepa, with Raj Patel, Kai Schafft, Anne Rademacher and Sarah Koch-Schulte (2000) *Voices of the Poor: Can Anyone Hear Us?*, New York: Oxford University Press for World Bank.

Paranjape, Makarand (2005) *Dharma and Development: The Future of Survival*, New Delhi: Samvad India Foundation.

Peccoud, Dominique (2011) 'A Discussion with Dominique Peccoud, SJ', http://berkleycenter.george-town.edu/interviews/a-discussion-with-dominique-peccoud-s-j.

Pew Forum (2011) *Global Christianity*, http://www.pewforum.org/2011/12/19/global-christianity-exec/.

Prothero, Stephen (2007) *Religious Literacy: What Every American Needs to Know – and Doesn't*, New York: HarperCollins.

Putnam, Robert with Robert Leonardi and Raffaella Nanetti (1993) *Making Democracy Work: Civic Traditions in Modern Italy*, Princeton, NJ: Princeton University Press.

Shah, Timothy, Toft, Monica and Stepan, Al (2012) *Rethinking Religion and World Affairs*, Oxford: Oxford University Press.

ter Haar, Gerrie (2011) *Religion and Development: Ways of Transforming the World*, London: Hurst & Co.

Thomas, S. M. (2005) *The Global Resurgence of Religion and the Transformation of International Relations: The Struggle for the Soul of the Twenty-First Century*, Basingstoke: Palgrave Macmillan.

Tyndale, Wendy (2006) *Visions of Development: Faith-Based Initiatives*, Farnham: Ashgate.

WFDD (World Faiths Development Dialogue) (2012) *Buddhism and Development: Communities in Cambodia Working as Partners*, http://berkleycenter.georgetown.edu/wfdd/publications/buddhism-and-development-communities-in-cambodia-working-as-partners.

Woodberry, Robert D. (2012) 'The Missionary Roots of Liberal Democracy', *American Political Science Review*, 106 (2) (May), 244–74.

Websites

Berkley Center for Religion, Peace and World Affairs at Georgetown University, http://berkleycenter.georgetown.edu/programs/religion-and-global-development.

World Faiths Development Dialogue, http://berkleycenter.georgetown.edu/wfdd.

26

SUSTAINABLE DEVELOPMENT, CLIMATE CHANGE AND RELIGION

Sigurd Bergmann

Introduction: religion and environmental change

Global and local environmental change not only transforms the 'conditions of life' but also radically changes culture, religion (understood here as a cultural system – cf. Geertz 1973) and the very 'conditions for faith'. As the scientific study of climate impact clearly and irrefutably demonstrates, anthropogenic climatic changes have an impact on all parts of the Earth's ecosystem, continually altering living conditions for all current and future beings, and these changes are rooted in the development of human socio-physical activities within the last 200 years, since the Industrial Revolution. Moreover, if environmental change in modern times is becoming increasingly anthropogenic – as the 'anthropocene theory'[1] has recently contended (Steffen *et al.* 2007) – it becomes even more necessary to explore the human and cultural dimensions of global environmental change, including the reciprocal interaction between religion and environmental and climatic change. As religious beliefs always include a narrative about the origin, meaning and future of life, dramatic changes in the natural environment may also have an impact on beliefs in a divine creator and/or life-giving forces, causing people to doubt or critique their religious beliefs. However, while 'conditions for faith' might be transformed in this way, religions have also been transformed as the close relationship that sometimes exists between religious beliefs and practices and nature (particularly within many 'indigenous communities') has been severed by climate change. Nonetheless, there are many examples of where religions have produced an active and critical response to environmental and climate change through applying religious teachings to support strategies to mitigate and prevent further damage. Religions are not static over time, and the impact of environmental and climate change is but one example of different factors that are shaping religious change and generating what Brunn has called 'a new global map of religions' (2014). Thus, one of the key questions to be addressed in this chapter is: how does climate change alter religion, and what can religions do to address climate change?

Although climate change will be the main focus of this chapter, it is important to remember that ecological challenges to find forms of 'sustainable development'[2] include more than mitigation of and adaptation to climate change. Themes such as landscape preservation and biodiversity, land degradation and land grabbing, water utilization and the lack of a (local and global) water ethos, species extinction and desertification, and unjust energy systems and patterns of production and consumption are also relevant, and all present challenges within the ongoing anthropogenic change of our global climate. However, demands not only for climate protection but also 'climate justice' are turning into central tools for achieving a just and sustainable form of development globally. While climate protection is concerned with the introduction of measures that are typically scientific and technical, climate justice emphasizes the ethical dimensions of climate change, linking 'human rights and development to achieve a human-centred approach, safeguarding the rights of the most vulnerable and sharing the burdens and benefits of climate change and its resolution equitably and fairly' (Mary Robinson Foundation n.d.).

The effect of climate change on humanitarian and development issues caused by poverty, the displacement of people and armed conflict is likely to rise over the coming decades. This is especially so in those vulnerable regions of the world that are affected most by global warming, which are mostly located around and below the equator, where development challenges are already most acute. Figure 26.1 presents a global map visualizing estimated deaths attributed to climate change. It clearly illustrates the unequal distribution of climate impact on different continents and regions, and raises serious questions about climate justice and the (in)equalities between global citizens.

In the sections that follow I have two main aims: first, as already noted, I am interested in the ways in which climate change alters religion and what religions can do to address climate change. I will argue that climate change is, amongst other things, a cultural and religious change but that this dimension tends to be ignored by mainstream technological and policy approaches, even though it offers insights into the ways in which some communities experience and adapt to climate change. My aim in this chapter is to argue that it is important for decision makers and social organizations involved in climate change policy and activism to regard religion as a significant dimension in any serious approach to climate change. Some large international organizations have made tentative steps in this direction (e.g. in December 2007 the UNDP launched a three-and-a-half-year project to work with the world's major religions to tackle

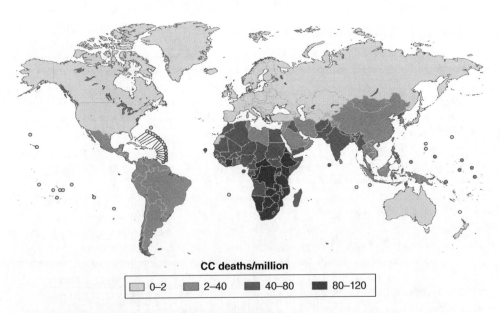

CC deaths/million

☐ 0–2 ▦ 2–40 ▪ 40–80 ▪ 80–120

Figure 26.1 Estimated deaths attributed to climate change

Source: Used with the permission of the Nelson Institute Center for Sustainability and the Global Environment, University of Wisconsin-Madison. Originally published in Patz *et al.* (2005: 313).

climate change, and UNEP and UNESCO have promoted religious dimensions to addressing environmental issues for many years also, but generally not much has yet been achieved).

I begin the discussion with an examination of the responses of faith communities to environmental and climate change since the 1980s, followed by a section that looks at the academic literature that has emerged around the topic of religion and environmental and climate change. Then I argue for the view that climate change is a form of cultural and religious change, outlining three reasons why religious practices should be explored in settings where climatic change is occurring and the need for further research in this area. In this chapter I view 'religion' as a cultural system (cf. Geertz 1973), and therefore if climate change affects culture it also has an impact on religious beliefs, traditions and practices. The thesis that climate change is 'ultimately about culture' not only focuses on the impacts of climate on culture but claims that climate change itself is part of a deeper cultural process that has transformed the conditions for the life of and on Earth (Crate and Nuttall 2009). In the penultimate section of the chapter I present three anthropological studies that support the argument that climate change is a form of religious and cultural change: Sakha belief and the effects of climate change in North-Eastern Siberia (Crate 2012); indigenous people and climate change in Indonesia (Frömming and Reichel 2012); and the impact of climate change on culture and religion in the Kilimanjaro region of North-East Tanzania (Bergmann 2014). Finally, the chapter discusses an alternative understanding of religion in this context – as a means for creative adaptation with respect to dangerous environmental change, providing the opportunity to 'make oneself at home' on Earth, our home, in general, and in places where survival is threatened in particular (Bergmann 2014).

Responses of faith communities to environmental and climate change

In addition to secular responses to climate change, some faith communities have responded to these challenges and mobilized in what we can call, for example, the *greening* of religion, the emergence of ecological spiritualities or religious environmentalism (Tomalin 2013). By the 1980s, the planetary scale of environmental change, coupled with processes of globalization that bind people, places and regions closer to each other, meant that other world religions also started to mobilize environmentally and to respond to issues around global warming and climate change (Globus Veldman *et al.* 2014). In the 1980s the term 'climate change' was not in such popular use (although it was current within scientific circles), and instead the public talked about 'global warming'. Concern about environmental destruction has steadily grown, and religious traditions were increasingly drawn into discussions about the causes of and solutions to what was now perceived to be an environmental crisis. In 1986 representatives of five of the world's major religions (Christianity, Buddhism, Islam, Hinduism and Judaism) met in Assisi, Italy, to make statements concerning the environmental nature of their religious traditions. This meeting was jointly organized by the World Wide Fund for Nature (WWF) and the International Consultancy on Religion, Education and Culture (ICOREC), an organization based in Manchester, UK. As the patron of WWF, Prince Philip, the Duke of Edinburgh, attended this event. The so-called Assisi Declarations constituted the first significant attempt by religious traditions to come together to discuss the relationship between their teachings and practices and the environment. Typically faith responses to ecological and climate change, including the Assisi Declarations, emphasize the ways in which the original teachings of the particular religious tradition strongly supported an ethical consideration of humanity's relationship to nature and suggested that there should be limits to human exploitation of natural resources. For instance, the Alliance of Religions and Conservation (ARC), founded in 1986 following the event in Assisi, describes itself as: 'a secular body that helps the world's major faiths develop environmental programmes based on their own core teachings, beliefs and practices. We help the religions link with key environmental organisations – creating powerful alliances between faith communities and conservation groups' (ARC n.d.).

With regard to Christianity, the development of ecotheology has not only contributed to environmental ethics and public environmental discourses, but also had a radical impact on Christian belief systems in general and led to the renewal of Christian doctrine.[3] In the ecumenical movement – where different confessions in the Christian family interact and where the majority of Christian believers living in the South are represented – a revisiting of the Christian belief in Creation began through the emergence of the awareness of the environmental crisis in the 1970s, and has functioned as a kind of ethical and ecclesiological locomotive, moving churches closer to each other.[4] It has produced the synthesis of feminist and ecological perspectives in ecofeminism (Eaton and Lorentzen 2003), challenged existing patriarchal power constellations and caused anthropocentric narrowness to be overcome.

In particular, the World Council of Churches was quick to provide a creative and constructive space in this arena for developing theoretical and practical ecological theology, and in the 1970s and 1980s ecumenical processes produced important outputs that influenced the political processes in the United Nations, which later resulted in the Rio assembly for 'Our Common Future', and put the term 'sustainable development' at its core. The notion of 'sustainable *and* just development' was coined in the ecumenical movement as early as 1974,[5] with the UN preparing the World Charter for Nature in 1982, ploughing the ground for the Rio assembly and convention in 1992. In Europe, an independent network on environmental issues was established in the wake of the break-through European ecumenical assembly in Basle in 1989 – the European Christian Environmental Network (ECEN) – where laypeople, scientists and committed church leaders shaped a forum for exchange and inter-confessional practices at administrative, economic, theological, liturgical and pastoral levels.

A similar process has also emerged within other religious traditions, including indigenous religions, in the global North as well as the global South. An ecotheology has started to develop in the Muslim spheres over the last ten years, with one of the key representatives of this approach being the Islamic Foundation for Ecology and Environmental Sciences,[6] even if, owing to an alternative structure of faith communities and organizations in Islam, the exchange between scientists, activists and religious leaders here has taken a different route, where believing scientists and not religious leaders have taken the lead.[7] While Christian environmental organizations are integrating religious and scientific approaches, Muslim scientists seek in a secular scientific context for a convergence of their practices as scientists with their religious belief systems and develop creative interpretations of Islam in the environmental context. Organizations such as the Bhumi Project (n.d.) support Hindu ecological action, and different organizations within the Engaged Buddhism movement (International Network of Engaged Buddhists n.d.) are prominent across Asian locations in linking Buddhist practice to environmental concern. Members of 'indigenous religions'[8] have also expressed concern over issues such as global warming and have engaged in environmental activism. In particular, the striving for ethnical identity, often in post-colonial settings, has merged with the emergence of an environmental commitment, where the specific human ecology of many indigenous people has worked as a critical contrast to large-scale industrialized colonization elsewhere. For instance, in 1990 the Indigenous Environmental Network was formed to represent North American indigenous people (Indigenous Environmental Network n.d.; Goldtooth 2005) and has taken part in local activism as well as participation in international conferences at Rio and Johannesburg. The discussion of the three case studies below will demonstrate that 'indigenous peoples' are amongst those who bear the brunt of the impact of climate change and whose religious traditions are most likely to be challenged. As Grim writes, 'Central to indigenous traditions is an awareness of the integral and whole relationship of symbolic and material life. Ritual practices and the cosmological ideas which undergird society cannot be separated out as an institutionalized religion from the daily round of subsistence practices' (Grim 1998).

However, it is not just the case that religious traditions have responded to environmental and climate change in terms of adapting their teachings and practices to transform the human interaction with the natural world. Religions as cultural systems are also fundamentally transformed by climate change. One of the functions of religion is to create meaning about the location and existential identification of the individual and collective amidst the surrounding reality and cosmos; dramatic changes in the surroundings offer serious and deep challenges to belief in a world of divinities, spirits and the Creator. Climate change, which threatens to culminate in disasters, offers a radical provocation of the spiritual order. This challenges the religious foundations of indigenous communities as well as Christian beliefs in a good Creator and Liberator. The scientific consensus about the anthropogenic contribution to climate change sharpens the theological and ethical dilemma even more, producing a 'spiritual earthquake' through questions such as: How can one make oneself at home as a human on Earth in a world that is shaken in its foundations by humans themselves? And how can one, in such a context, continue to believe in God as the Creator and Sustainer of all between Heaven and Earth? The Zambian theologian Rolita Machila took this dilemma to its extreme by asking: 'Why are Earth and God angry?' (Machila 2008; Bloomquist 2009). Her survey of Christian believers in different cultural and geographical contexts, conducted in the frame of the Lutheran World Federation, clearly showed how Christian belief affects the perception and interpretation of climate change, either as a God-given sign of the coming of the last days that can only be interpreted as fate, or as a consequence of human structural sin, which is the socialized violation of communities' welfare. Both perspectives lead to totally different cultural practices, and both are active in different contexts (Globus Veldman *et al.* 2014).

Responses of academic communities to the relationships between religion and environmental and climate change

This growth of religious environmentalism has also given rise to a dynamic academic field of study, often labelled under headings such as 'religion and ecology', 'religion and the environment', and 'religion, nature and culture', which are also the labels used by international research networks and organizations in this arena (Emerging Earth Community n.d.; European Forum for the Study of Religion and the Environment n.d.; Religion and Nature n.d.). In contrast to studies on religions and development, there exists a large body of literature on religions and the environment that has been developing since the 1980s. Currently, for instance, there are two peer-reviewed journals dedicated to this topic: *Worldviews: Environment, Culture, Religion*, published by Brill; and the *International Journal of Religion, Nature and Culture*, published by Equinox. A wealth of information mapping the greening of different religious denominations, and ecological spiritualities can be found in literature since the 1970s. A good sense of the diversity of literature published in this area globally can be gained from the bibliographies on the website of the Forum on Religion and Ecology at Yale. The forum arose from ten conferences that were held at Harvard University and which also resulted in the publication of ten volumes, published by Harvard University Press.[9] The forum itself is now based at Yale University, and its work includes a joint MA programme between the Yale School of Forestry and Environmental Studies (FES) and Yale Divinity School (YDS), publications, conferences, films and the website (Yale University n.d.).

While much of this literature has focused upon different types of environmental concern and change, relatively few have specifically taken religion and climate change as their focus. Globus Veldman *et al.* (2014) identify five types of literature that have emerged on the topic of religion and climate change, arguing that there has been a 'recent uptick in social scientific studies' in this area but that 'no comprehensive review of global religious responses to climate change exists at the time of this writing' (2014: 10). First, there is literature linking the 'theologies and ethics of particular faith traditions to the climate crisis (e.g. McFague 2008; Northcott 2007; Primavesi 2009; Skrimshire 2010; Xia and Schonfeld 2011)' (2014: 9); second, there are studies maintaining that religions 'will be productive in the fight to mobilize' against climate change (e.g. Tucker and Grim 2001; Gardner 2003; Posas 2007; Wolf and Gjerris 2009; Schipper 2010); third, there is a body of literature to communicate 'the issue of climate change to members of a particular faith' (e.g. Atkinson 2008; Hayhoe and Farley 2009; Merritt 2010); fourth, there are the findings of polls and surveys that link religiosity to climate change attitudes (e.g. Pew Research Center 2007, 2009; Barna Group 2008; Public Religion Research Institute 2011); and finally there are studies that include 'some empirical social scientific contributions about religion and climate change' (2014: 9). Texts in this final category include Crate and Nuttall (2009), Bergmann and Gerten (2010), Leduc (2010), Gerten and Bergmann (2012) and Wilkinson (2012) and will be further discussed in the case studies below. Before we do this, however, it is necessary to look more closely at the reasons why cultural and religious practices should be explored in settings where climatic change is occurring, the need for further research in this area and the particular role that humanities disciplines, such as theology, religious studies and anthropology, could play in research on climate change.

Why climate change *is* cultural and religious change

Climate change represents one of the most demanding contemporary challenges to humanity. While climate impact science is one of the most important developments of the last few decades, current scientific, political and public discussions about how to mitigate and adapt to the impacts of global climate change are dominated by propositions for technological and economic solutions, with decision makers usually underestimating the human, cultural and religious dimensions of global change. In the following paragraphs, I outline three reasons why religious practices should be explored in settings where climatic change is occurring and argue for the need for further research in this area, particularly involving the participation of theology, religious studies and anthropology. Climate change is not just a matter of science and technology, but the causes are underpinned by human action and values. Moreover the impact of climate change can change those actions, values and rituals. Worldviews matter when thinking about climate change.

The first reason relates to demographics and the fact that the majority of the world's inhabitants are practising religious believers. Climate change is not just a matter of science and technology, but its causes are shaped by social and cultural processes that influence human action and values, within which religion plays a role. Thus, a socio-cultural analysis of practices, values and worldviews relating to climate change must include the religious dimension, with all its ethical, aesthetic and political ambiguities. As the majority of the planet's inhabitants are affected by climate change, and as the majority identify themselves as believers, the question of what religion means for climate change mitigation and adaptation is raised.

A second reason relates to the ambivalence of ethics and religious teachings, in the sense that religions can be interpreted to support divergent courses of action regarding climate change. As we have seen above, faith communities in different religions and different regions of the planet have mobilized their adherents to engage actively against global warming (Globus Veldman *et al.* 2014). The public discourse about climate change provokes believers of all kinds to respond and intervene with individual and collective perspectives, values and suggestions. However, it is also the case that (the politically right-wing) Evangelical Christians in the USA, for instance, have split into two irreconcilable camps – one arguing for the urgent moral challenge presented by climatic change, and the other (the climate change deniers) claiming that the fear of climate change is promoting a new pagan religion similar to the medieval fear of hell (Oreskes and Conway 2010). The fact that we cannot make assumptions about the impact of religious ethics upon how people think about and understand climate change points towards the need for more studies that examine the way in which such values are lived out in practice and which consider the intermingling of religion, politics and climate change. Such examples show how climate change alters religious belief systems, provoking believers to respond in new ways, and further illustrates how the notion of religion – in a well-known modernist code – is used as a concept in opposition to rationality and science. We also see this use of 'religion' in climate change discourse in a 'denunciatory mode', involving the criticism of climate scientists by self-described sceptics (both academic and non-academic), who see climatologists as nothing more than religious missionaries threatening the identity of true objectivist science.

The third reason involves religious institutions and their intervention in the discourse on the 'moral climate' (Northcott 2007). Churches and other religious bodies intervene in the public sphere with declarations about the spiritual dimensions of a civilizational crisis. These groups have strikingly increased and intensified their contributions to the public sphere and climate discourse in recent years. For instance, the Archbishop of Uppsala's gathering of representatives from different international religions and spiritual traditions in 2008 and indigenous peoples' participation in a forum in Cancun (the International Indigenous Peoples' Forum on Climate Change, IIPFCC) show the emergence of an interreligious and intercultural process of fabricating meaning about the existential and moral challenges posed by climate change. As the 2009 United Nations Climate Change Conference (also known as the Copenhagen Summit), and discussions during the following years, failed to elicit agreements between nations about global CO_2 emissions beyond the Kyoto Protocol, one can only expect an even more intensified process in committed social movements, including faith communities. A core message, often emphasized in faith-based and NGO statements, consists of the need to fully include and acknowledge local skills and knowledge in order to attain environmental justice, where both the intrinsic value of species and ecosystems and the dignity of the world's poor are protected.

Humanities disciplines, such as theology, religious studies and anthropology, have a particular contribution to make to research on climate change, and there is a need to involve them more deeply. Environmental and climate change affects human beings across their entire bodily and cultural lives, which means that environmental problems should be approached in a multifaceted way, as 'integral theory' contends (O'Brien and Hochachka 2010). Anthropologists, who have rapidly and strikingly increased their research on climate change in recent years, correctly postulate that climate change is not simply a physical process but is ultimately rooted in culture. This imbalance in research approaches to climate change results in an imbalance in the perception of what it involves in popular science, media and public discourses. The Intergovernmental Panel on Climate Change (IPCC) has rightly been criticized as presenting climate change 'without a human face' (Finan 2009: 175). While there has been a tendency for mainstream approaches to climate change to ignore or marginalize the contributions of these areas of study, it is also the case that they themselves have not significantly taken up this challenge. Over the last five decades the humanities and social sciences have engaged with environmental science and environmentalism as social phenomena leading to significant new research fields. However, the agenda of climate science specifically has only been adopted in these fields to a limited degree. Overall social scientists are at the forefront of research on the so-called 'human dimension' of climate change, but this research usually neglects the subjective, cultural, aesthetic, ethical and spiritual dimensions of being human.

Climate science is moving towards an even more complex 'earth system analysis', which connects a wide variety of analytically different empirical phenomena including the 'anthroposphere', although this type of research mostly adopts a physical and biological perspective. There are only a few pioneers who acknowledge that earth system analysis needs to consider an immaterial 'global subject', i.e. the collective action of humanity as a self-conscious force, now able to oversee the global dimensions of environmental change and thus with the potential to avert them (Pitt and Samson 1999). Earth system analysis mostly reduces humans to 'the physiological-metabolic contribution of global civilization to planetary operation . . . qualitatively not dissimilar to the role played by the sheep of the world' (Schellnhuber 1999), which neglects the fact that humans are both predictable and unpredictable, can act both rationally and 'irrationally', and can mobilize liberating as well as destructive forces that cannot easily be quantified. Thus, the outcome of scientific research about the human in climatic change is to a large degree dependent on the scientist's concept of humans.

The exciting challenge of climate science within environmental humanities therefore lies in the spatial complexity of the climate scientist's scenic descriptions of the earth system, requiring complementation by equally sophisticated analyses of the spatial and temporal patterns of environmentally relevant features of human culture, including religion. A promising track for the study of religion in climatic change might hereby be to continue along the lines of the spatial turn, also seen in religious studies, and to connect concepts of lived space and lived religion (cf. Bergmann 2014). The human-ecological complexity of environmental space might then be better understood as a lived space of entanglement between humans and other beings in a common earth system, and to involve complex reciprocal interconnections.

Furthermore, climate change scientists sometimes move very quickly from research results to political conclusions and suggestions, which enhances the fear among citizens that the interests of those affected are overruled by socio-economic considerations adopting technical solutions that are imposed on them by elites from 'above' and 'abroad', whom they see as representing the interests of political bodies and business corporations rather than aiming for the common good (for human and other beings). As environmental problems are anthropogenic, with human beings featuring as both the producers and the subjects of these problems, solutions to such problems require research that integrates physical, human and socio-cultural dimensions. This is especially clear for climate impact science, where increasing climate changes will affect more of the world's population in a way where risks, burdens and suffering are distributed in an unjust way, breeding contempt. Climate change further sharpens security conflicts all over the planet, and it has the greatest disintegrating impact on economically vulnerable nations.

Case studies on climate change as cultural and religious change

In this section of the chapter I provide three short case studies that highlight the ways in which climate change has an impact upon religion and culture in different settings. The first is from Siberia and examines the effects of climate change on the beliefs of the Viliui Sakha; the second is from coastal Indonesia, and the third from the Kilimanjaro region in Tanzania. Each case study is focused upon indigenous people as, 'for many indigenous societies, the impact of climate change is not a problem of the future; it is already being felt' (Frömming and Reichel 2012: 215).

Sakha belief and the effects of climate change in North-Eastern Siberia

Environmental anthropologist Susan Crate is a pioneer in the study of the range of impacts that climate change has had on local populations over time (Crate 2012). She demonstrates clearly how the livelihoods, worldviews and belief systems of indigenous people are being adversely affected by climate change, which has a dramatic impact upon their relationship to the land. Her field research since 1991 has explored the native Viliui Sakha, who are agropastoralist horse and cattle breeders living in North-Eastern Siberia, a region experiencing a trend towards milder winters and wetter land surfaces as a likely consequence of climate change. The region is sub-arctic with continuous permafrost and annual temperature fluctuations of 100 degrees Celsius (from −60 to +40). They have adapted a horse and cattle breeding economy to this climate, keeping their cows inside for nine months and harvesting fodder in the summer.

While Crate has been working within this community since 1991, it was only in 2003 that she began to realize how 'climate change is affecting not only their physical but also their cultural and cosmological worlds' (2012: 175). Their belief system is animistic and 'recognized all aspects of the natural world as sentient . . . [and] their adaptation to the subarctic ecosystem is highly dependent on maintaining proper relationships with the spirit world' (2012: 171). She explains how the Viliui Sakha personify winter as a white bull (Jyl Oghuha) 'with blue spots, huge horns and frosty breath' (2012: 175), whose presence keeps the winter cold. Arriving from the Arctic Ocean in early December the bull keeps the temperature low in December and January. At the end of January he loses his first horn and the temperature warms up; then the second horn melts at the end of February. By the end of March his head falls off and spring arrives (2012: 175). However, in 2003 she heard the story retold but with an unexpected ending: as one of her informants told her, 'It seems that now with the warming, perhaps the bull of winter will no longer be' (2012: 175).

Since 2003 she has been working with these communities to understand how they 'perceive and understand the local effects of climate change' (2012: 175). One of the most pressing issues for people is the presence of increasing water on the land, which threatens their ability to continue with their practice of horse and cattle breeding. Moreover, cows are central to 'Sakha belief and sacred cosmology . . . essential to maintaining the social cohesion of rural village communities in a period of continued socio-economic and moral decline' (2012: 176). These environmental changes represent a challenge not only to the livelihoods of the local people but also to the related mythologies and beliefs. Crate emphasizes that 'if we are interested in gaining a comprehensive understanding of how place-based peoples are adapting and will be able to continue to adapt' it is important to develop 'means and methods to investigate the cultural and cosmological, as well as the physical, implications of global climate change' (2012: 176). Adaptation measures can probably only be successful if the local populations and their worldviews become an intrinsic part of decision making. Crate and other anthropologists have started to experiment with bringing local representatives together to share their personal observations of the changes and to 'enrich the scientists' understanding of how climate change is affecting local places and peoples' (2012: 189).

Indigenous people and climate change in Indonesia

A similar scenario appears in the Coral Triangle coastal zones of Indonesia, where the local population combine either Islam or Christianity with older indigenous religion. Environmental anthropologists Undine Frömming and Christian Reichel ask 'what kind of local knowledge exists both for predicting, and for adapting to, climate-related events . . . [and] what are the perceptions of current environmental change and in what sociocultural and/or cosmological ideas are they rooted' (2012: 215). While these communities have done much less to trigger these problems than people living in the global North, they are facing the consequences of 'poverty marginalisation and discrimination' (2012: 216). Frömming and Reichel argue that traditional beliefs have helped people cope with and mitigate environmental change and view 'all natural locations . . . to be inhabited by gods and spirits; therefore these locations are also invested with a series of taboos' (2012: 220). Taboos exist again 'trespassing' in spaces inhabited by gods and spirits, and 'natural disasters are seen as warnings of punishments from the Gods, in response to social misconduct' (2012: 221). Religious restrictions, like taboo areas or calendar systems, can play an ambiguous role here, as some seem inefficient while others 'bear a striking resemblance to modern strategies which seem innovative because they draw upon the latest research' (2012: 229). However, these indigenous systems are under threat from the missionary activities of certain forms of Islam and Christianity and also from environmental change. The Coral Triangle of Indonesia is a region that, owing to its high biodiversity and productivity, is home to some of the world's most valuable natural resources (from mangrove swamps to coral reefs). Nevertheless, the region is now experiencing the impacts of climate change (more frequent and stronger typhoons, rising sea levels and continued coral bleaching), which together with the overuse of (marine) resources put the habitat at risk of large-scale destabilization (2012: 216).

Frömming and Reichel's (2012) investigation focuses on different areas within this region. One, the area of Taka Bonerate, an atoll in the Flores Sea within this region, is composed mostly of two ethnic groups, the Bajau and the Bugis, who are differentiated by both language and culture and mostly work as fishers and traders. These peoples have various rules of conduct, as well as restrictions on when and where the exploitation of natural resources is allowed, in order to avoid damaging relations with the supernatural spirits of the sea. The Bajau, for instance, nominally declare themselves to be Muslims, but their religious worldview is still marked by a parallel belief that the sea is inhabited by 'gods' or 'sea spirits', as well as 'demons', who exist in a specific hierarchy and possess different powers. At the top of this hierarchy is a supreme divinity that lives in the sea and possesses more power than all the other supernatural beings, controlling the outcome of all activities taking place at sea. Fishing should be avoided in areas where this divinity is at work, in order not to disturb the god, a failure that might cause his anger and lead to natural catastrophes.

In contrast the Bugis practise a very orthodox style of Islam. Admittedly many are also convinced of the existence of supernatural beings such as angels (*mala'ika*), demons (*jinn*) and ancestral spirits, but these are integral parts of their Sunni Islam cosmology. According to most of them, 'there is no God except Allah, whose will is absolute and who determines all that happens'. The supernatural beings therefore take a mediator role between God and the humans, but they are not adored and not, as among the Bajau, celebrated and comforted in responsive rituals. Such a strongly orthodox interpretation of Islam without the belief in an animated nature entails that natural resources are intensely used, often destructively, without restrictions in time and place.

Many other beliefs, ritual practices, and religious norms and taboos regarding human ecology are seen on the atoll. For example, the Bajau believe that, 'under the multiplicity of things, there exists a cosmic order that influences all aspects of life, connecting everything together' (Frömming and Reichel 2012: 228). According to the Bajau, excessive or single-minded fishing activities could destabilize this order. To avoid this, the people of the atoll utilize a fishery system that precisely delineates permissible seasons for all market-oriented fishing activities, while conforming to the life cycles of these maritime species. During the fishing season, for example, only fish can be sold at market, while clams and sea cucumbers are harvested purely at subsistence levels. To disobey these regulations would be a violation of the accepted moral order and can be punished socially.

From this short depiction, it is clear that the religious belief systems of the local populations in this coastal zone provide them with power and knowledge that have deep significance for the environment and their human ecology. In a rapidly changing climate, such practical wisdom represents an important source and tool for seeking and finding alternative strategies for creative adaptation to environmental change. Environmental anthropologists therefore demand that local knowledge and religiously based belief systems must be included in negotiations about climate adaptation and sustainable development in the future.

The impact of climate change on culture and religion in the Kilimanjaro region of North-East Tanzania

Another region where the impact of climate change on culture and religion is of interest is the Kilimanjaro region of North-East Tanzania. Over the past decade, Mount Kilimanjaro has emerged as the best-known and most visible icon of climate change in Africa, with attention focused on the retreat of its high-altitude glaciers and studies documenting a decline in precipitation from twentieth-century records. The geography of Northern Tanzania is dominated by the contrast between semi-arid plains and the mountainous 'water towers'. These mountain areas are important, as they are the source areas of water for the lowlands and the Pangani River, because they capture orographic precipitation (when moist air is lifted as it moves over a mountain range) and because they are home to considerable population concentrations and economic activities. Religiously people in this region practise Christianity or Islam, typically combined with indigenous Bantu religion. This type of hybridization of indigenous and world-religious (Christian and Islam) belief systems is common across many parts of Africa.

The slopes of Mount Kilimanjaro have an extensive farming history, and intensive agricultural systems developed as a result, and during recent centuries the region developed the largest cluster of indigenous irrigation schemes in Sub-Saharan Africa, with more than 2,000 schemes based on a technology called 'hill furrow irrigation'. The current practice represents a continued development of technologies, institutions and cultures of water that have evolved over several centuries among several Bantu- and Nilotic-speaking ethnic groups in Eastern Africa. While these indigenous models remain relevant to resource management, despite changes relating to colonialism, socialism and Islam and Christianity they are also subject to multiple stresses from globalization, environmental and socio-economic change. Communities of smallholders managing their own irrigation schemes may find that their access to water becomes insecure through the double exposure of climate change and globalization. Globalization changes access to water, not only by causing increased demands for water to harvest sugar, starches and vegetable oils (which are preferred as a result of a decline in the coffee-based economy), but also through international environmental governance policies, management and entitlements (Tagseth 2009).

In this context, the ways in which farming communities interpret and respond to environmental and socio-economic changes and uncertainties, including the use of religious rituals, could usefully inform future research. Preliminary results from fieldwork suggest that local actors in the Kilimanjaro region draw on Bantu mythological narratives to explain these changes through discourses about aridity and marginalization, and recollect how ritual was used to bring about conditions of peace, fertility and rain in the past. In more practical terms, vulnerability depends on the agronomic and economic strategies available to farmers for reducing risks from climate variability, and related to this are issues of indigenous technical and agricultural knowledge, innovations and technical advice. Farming systems in the region tend to vary between agro-ecological zones, with differences in flexibility and drought risk existing between the main agricultural uses of land.

In this setting, religious discourses link environmental and climate change to the spiritual world and also contribute (with cultural wisdom) to local political negotiations amongst farmers about water usage, farming and the distribution of goods (even as conflicts between more or less traditional versus modern views run through these politics, as elsewhere in the post-colonial regions of the planet). While Christian churches act on an institutional level, by running tourist hotels, schools and health care units, and through providing moralities and liturgical and educational practices at local levels in the region, the influence of indigenous religion is stronger at the higher parts of the mountain region, where for example rituals of spiritual purification are practised in order to guarantee the welfare of human ecology by way of the spirits ruling over the water systems.

A discussion of the case studies and implications for a more holistic approach to climate science and policy making

While the problem that North-East Siberia faces is a warming of the climate, which has altered patterns of cold in the winter, the Kilimanjaro region faces a decreasing water supply (as the glaciers melt) and irregular precipitation, which affect all parts of the water system. Climate change in coastal Indonesia has affected both the sea (with regard to fishing ecology) and the patterns of wind and storms (whose damaging impact on the already vulnerable local population and environment has increased as a result). In all three cases, it is important to see how my initial hypothesis is manifested – that climate change affects religious belief systems. How religion, in such contexts, can be turned into a constructive tool for creating environmental adaptation is a crucial question that must be put at the top of agendas regarding sustainable development and climate mitigation and adaptation discourses, scholarly as well as political.

While conventional climate science almost exclusively investigates technological and scientific strategies for mitigation and adaptation, anthropological, cultural and religious studies such as those discussed above can contribute through insights into local strategies and knowledge, thereby enabling the design of more effective prevention and protection measures. This could significantly increase the potential to find paths and practices to facilitate a more sustainable form of development despite the threat of significant environmental change. A central issue here concerns whether indigenous societies are powerlessly indifferent to local climate change or whether, through religious interpretations and other forms of local knowledge, they are capable of confronting climate-related threats before a long-term impairment to their everyday life is produced. Such a conclusion seems, according to my view, highly relevant and also valid for many other world regions where local subsistence and spiritual identity are closely related. There is, however, an obvious tension here between the localized impact and relevance of the worldviews of indigenous communities and the fact that the causes of climate change are beyond the control of such communities. So, while adaptation is the key concern here, we might also want to examine the extent to which the gap between the local and the global might be bridged. And how can local dynamics develop both creative adaptation to accelerating environmental change *and* produce a critical force for mitigation at other places? Do we need some kind of translocalizing intercultural exchange that can break through the present state of an unequal and unjust distribution of climate-based risks, damages and emission-based wealth?

Not yet discussed is the way in which in all three regions, which resemble other environments affected by climate change, the destabilization of local habitats results in increases in so-called 'climate refugees' as natural resources shrink and livelihoods become threatened. This leads to existing conflicts being sharpened further by the refugees who are produced as the result of climate changes. Pressures on populations increase, with respect both to those who are pushed to migrate and to those who receive immigrants and must work out how to build a common future together. Thus, patterns of migration affected by climate change have a destructive impact on regions – an impact that adds to the other negative consequences of global warming.

Environmental and climate changes involve rises in temperature, sea water levels and CO_2 emissions, as well as changes in water systems, land usage and biodiversity. Thus, every nation and every section of the societies in each nation are affected by these changes in our environment, though in different ways. The scale and depth of this challenge at the global and local levels are clearly seen in Figure 26.2, which shows the migration waves that are expected as a result of increasing droughts and a lack of water (cf. Figure 26.1).

Many increasingly question what we can expect from a world community that is still incapable of achieving a political consensus about limiting emissions that might work to address successfully the problems of climate change if implemented today, and a world community that dismisses the suffering of vulnerable victims in bowing to the self-interest of the rich in preserving their power and the further quick development (with huge energy usage) of large, so-called developing countries such as China and India. What about the justice of the proportional

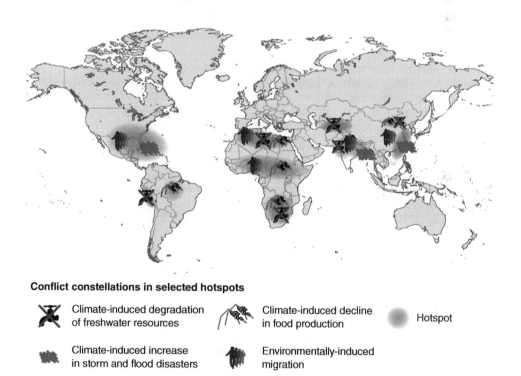

Conflict constellations in selected hotspots

- Climate-induced degradation of freshwater resources
- Climate-induced decline in food production
- Hotspot
- Climate-induced increase in storm and flood disasters
- Environmentally-induced migration

Security risks associated with climate change: Selected hotspots. The map only shows the regions which are dealt with in this report and which could develop into crisis hotspots.

Figure 26.2 Conflict constellations in selected hotspots

Source: WBGU (2007). Permission granted by the WBGU.

Note: Areas where drought, desertification and other forms of water scarcity are estimated are expected to worsen and could contribute to people migrating away from these areas to secure their livelihoods.

redistribution of costs for extensive processes of allocation in such a way that those who produce most CO_2 emissions should share the largest costs for the poor?

Conclusion

Climatic anthropogenic change represents a severe challenge to religious belief, as it radically questions the created goodness of the world and life in general, whether in the lens of theistic, animistic or other religious traditions. The experience of dangerous climate change raises questions for believers' essential faith in the surrounding and carrying world as good and choice-worthy to live in. Such an experience creates an earthquake in both religious and secular belief systems, where for example neither radical mammonism nor the creed of the eternal accumulation of financial capital can any longer be seen as plausible. Environmental and climatic change challenges and changes belief systems of all kinds. However, as I have argued elsewhere, one of the functions of religion is to contribute towards the process of *Beheimatung* (making oneself at home) (Bergmann 2014). Thus, religion should be regarded as a skill to 'make oneself at home' on Earth in general and, in particular, in places where survival is threatened by dangerous environmental and climatic changes that are experiencing unsustainable forms of development. Politically, such a perspective makes it necessary to include populations and their local, regional and global belief systems in the negotiations about what counts as good, sustainable development.

Notes

1 'Anthropocene' is a word used to denote 'in which humans and our societies have become a global geophysical force. The Anthropocene began around 1800 with the onset of industrialization, the central feature of which was the enormous expansion in the use of fossil fuels' (Steffen *et al.* 2007: 614).
2 The report of the Brundtland Commission, *Our Common Future*, by the World Commission on Environment and Development (WCED) in 1987, defined sustainable development as 'development that meets the needs of the present without compromising the ability of future generations to meet their own needs' and 'called for international strategies combining both environmental protection and development' (UN Documents n.d.).
3 Ecotheology emerged as a distinct field of theological disciplines of different kinds (biblical studies, ethics, systematic theology and practical theology) in the 1970s in the 'North' and has deepened and widened its activities since then. Since the 1980s it has also been developed in the 'South'.
4 For example in the European Christian Environmental Network (ECEN n.d.).
5 Search for a Just and Sustainable Society: WCC Conference on Science and Technology for Human Development, Bucharest, Romania, 24 June – 2 July 1974.
6 The Islamic Foundation for Ecology and Environmental Sciences was founded in the mid-1980s in the UK, with Fazlun Khalid as a central driving force (Islamic Foundation for Ecology and Environmental Sciences n.d.).
7 Ibid.
8 As Grim writes, 'The term "indigenous" is a generalized reference to the thousands of small scale societies who have distinct languages, kinship systems, mythologies, ancestral memories, and homelands.... Since these societies are extremely diverse, any general remarks are suspect of imposing ideas and concepts on them. Indigenous religions do not constitute a "world religion" in the same way as, for example, Buddhism or Christianity' (1998).
9 See, for example, the Religions of the World and Ecology Book Series, ed. Mary E. Tucker and John Grim (Forum on Religion and Ecology at Yale n.d.), and the *Encyclopedia of Religion and Nature*, ed. Bron Taylor (Religion and Nature n.d.).

References

ARC (Alliance of Religions and Conservation) (n.d.) Home page, http://arcworld.org (accessed 2 July 2014).

Atkinson, David (2008) *Renewing the Face of the Earth: A Theological and Pastoral Response to Climate Change*, Norwich: Canterbury Press.

Barna Group (2008) 'Evangelicals Go "Green" with Caution', 22 September, https://www.barna.org/barna-update/article/13-culture/23-evangelicals-go-qgreenq-with-caution#.U4Rd915mu24 (accessed 2 July 2014).

Bergmann, S. (2014) *Religion, Space and the Environment*, New Brunswick, NJ: Transaction Publishers.

Bergmann, S. and Gerten, D. (eds) (2010) *Religion and Dangerous Environmental Change: Transdisciplinary Perspectives on the Ethics of Climate and Sustainability*, Studies in Religion and the Environment 2, Berlin: LIT.

Bhumi Project (n.d.) Home page, www.bhumiproject.org (accessed 2 July 2014).

Bloomquist, K. with R. Machila (2009) *God, Creation and Climate Change: A Resource for Reflection and Discussion*, Geneva: Lutheran World Federation, http://www.e-alliance.ch/fileadmin/user_upload/docs/God__Creation_and_Climate_Change.pdf.

Brunn, S. D. (ed.) (2014) *The Changing World Religion Map*, New York: Springer.

Crate, S. A. (2012) 'Climate and Cosmology: Exploring Sakha Belief and the Local Effects of Unprecedented Change in North-Eastern Siberia, Russia', in D. Gerten and S. Bergmann (eds), *Religion in Environmental and Climate Change: Suffering, Values, Lifestyles*, London: Continuum, pp. 175–99.

Crate, S. A. and Nuttall, M. (eds) (2009) *Anthropology and Climate Change: From Encounters to Actions*, Walnut Creek, CA: Left Coast Press.

Eaton, H. and Lorentzen, L. A. (eds) (2003) *Ecofeminism and Globalization: Exploring, Culture, Context, and Religion*, Lanham, MD: Rowman & Littlefield.

ECEN (European Christian Environmental Network) (n.d.) Home page, http://ecen.org (accessed 2 July 2014).

Emerging Earth Community (n.d.) 'Forum on Religion and Ecology at Yale', http://emergingearthcommunity.org/forum-on-religion-and-ecology(accessed 2 July 2014).

European Forum for the Study of Religion and the Environment (n.d.) Home page, http://www.hf.ntnu.no/relnateur/ (accessed 2 July 2014).

Finan, T. (2009) 'Storm Warnings: The Role of Anthropology in Adapting to Sea-Level Rise in Southwestern Bangladesh', in S. A. Crate and M. Nuttall (eds), *Anthropology and Climate Change: From Encounters to Actions*, Walnut Creek, CA: Left Coast Press, pp. 175–85.

Forum on Religion and Ecology at Yale (n.d.) 'Religions of the World and Ecology Book Series', http://fore.research.yale.edu/publications/books/cswr/ (accessed 2 July 2014).

Frömming, U. U. and Reichel, C. (2012) 'Vulnerable Coastal Regions: Indigenous People under Climate Change in Indonesia', in D. Gerten and S. Bergmann (eds), *Religion in Environmental and Climate Change: Suffering, Values, Lifestyles*, London: Continuum, pp. 215–35.

Gardner, Gary (2003) 'Engaging Religion in the Quest for a Sustainable World', in L. Starke (ed.), *State of the World 2003*, New York: W. W. Norton, pp. 152–75.

Geertz, C. (1973) 'Religion as a Cultural System,' in *The Interpretation of Cultures*, New York: Basic Books, pp. 87–125.

Gerten, D. and S. Bergmann (eds) (2012), *Religion in Environmental and Climate Change: Suffering, Values, Lifestyles*, London: Continuum.

Globus Veldman, R., Szasz, A. and Haluza-DeLay, R. (eds) (2014) *How the World's Religions Are Responding to Climate Change*, London: Routledge.

Goldtooth, Tom (2005) 'Indigenous Environmental Network', in Bron Taylor (ed.), *Encyclopedia of Religion and Nature*, London: Continuum, pp. 838–45.

Grim, John A. (1998) *Indigenous Traditions and Ecology*, http://fore.research.yale.edu/religion/indigenous/ (accessed 2 July 2014).

Hayhoe, Katharine and Farley, Andrew (2009) *A Climate for Change: Global Warming Facts for Faith-Based Decisions*, New York: FaithWorlds.

Indigenous Environmental Network (n.d.) Home page, http://www.ienearth.org/about/ (accessed 2 July 2014).

International Network of Engaged Buddhists (n.d.) Home page, www.inebnetwork.org (accessed 2 July 2014).

Islamic Foundation for Ecology and Environmental Sciences (n.d.) Home page, www.ifees.org.uk/ (accessed 2 July 2014).

Leduc, Timothy (2010) *Climate, Culture, Change: Inuit and Western Dialogues with a Warming North*, Ottawa, ON: University of Ottawa Press.

Machila, R. (2008) 'Why Are Earth and God Angry?', *Thinking It Over* (Lutheran World Federation), 20 (August).

Mary Robinson Foundation (n.d.) *Our Common Future, Chapter 2: Towards Sustainable Development*, http:// www.mrfcj.org/about/principles.html (accessed 2 July 2014).

McFague, Sallie (2008) *A New Climate for Theology: God, the World, and Global Warming*, Minneapolis, MN: Fortress Press.

Merritt, Jonathan (2010) *Green like God: Unlocking the Divine Plan for Our Planet*, New York: FaithWorlds.

Northcott, Michael (2007) *A Moral Climate: The Ethics of Global Warming*, London: Darton, Longman & Todd, and New York: Orbis Books.

O'Brien, K. and Hochachka, G. (2010) 'Integral Adaptation to Climate Change', *Journal of Integral Theory and Practice*, 5 (1), 89–102.

Oreskes, Naomi and Conway, Erik M. (2010) *Merchants of Doubt: How a Handful of Scientists Obscured the Truth on Issues from Tobacco Smoke to Global Warming*, New York: Bloomsbury Press.

Patz, Jonathan A., Campbell-Lendrum, Diarmid, Holloway, Tracey and Foley, Jonathan A. (2005) 'Impact of Regional Climate Change on Human Health', *Nature*, 438, 313–17, http://www.ifu.ethz.ch/ESD/ education/master/AESEA/Patz_et_al_2005.pdf (accessed 28 September 2014).

Pew Research Center (2007) *Science in America: Religious Belief and Public Attitudes*, http://www.pewforum. org/2007/12/18/science-in-america-religious-belief-and-public-attitudes/ (accessed 2 July 2014).

Pew Research Center (2009) *Fewer Americans See Solid Evidence of Global Warming*, http://www.pewresearch. org/2009/10/22/fewer-americans-see-solid-evidence-of-global-warming/ (accessed 2 July 2014).

Pitt, D. and Samson, P. R. (eds) (1999) *The Biosphere and Noosphere Reader: Global Environment, Society and Change*, London: Routledge.

Posas, Paula J. (2007) 'Roles of Religion and Ethics in Addressing Climate Change', *Ethics in Science and Environmental Politics*, 2007, 31–49.

Primavesi, Anne (2009) *Gaia and Climate Change: A Theology of Gift Events*, Oxford: Routledge.

Public Religion Research Institute (2011) *Climate Change and Evolution in the 2012 Elections*, http://pub-licreligion.org/research/2011/09/climate-change-evolution-2012/ (accessed 2 July 2014).

Religion and Nature (n.d.) *The Encyclopedia of Religion and Nature*, http://www.religionandnature.com/ ern/index.htm (accessed 2 July 2014).

Schellnhuber, H. J. (1999) '"Earth System" Analysis and the Second Copernican Revolution', *Nature*, 402, Supp., C19–C23.

Schipper, Lisa E. (2010) 'Religion as an Integral Part of Determining and Reducing Climate Change and Disaster Risk: An Agenda for Research', in M. Voss (ed.), *Der Klimawandel: Socialwissenschaftliche Perspektiven*, Wiesbaden: VS Verlag, pp. 377–93.

Skrimshire, Stefan (2010) *Future Ethics: Climate Change and the Apocalyptic Imagination*, London: Continuum.

Steffen, W., Crutzen, P. J. and McNeill, J. R. (2007) 'The Anthropocene: Are Humans Now Over-whelming the Great Forces of Nature?', *Ambio*, 36 (8), 614–21.

Tagseth, M. (2009) 'Social and Cultural Dimensions of Irrigation Management in Kilimanjaro', in T. A. R. Clack (ed.), *Culture, History and Identity: Landscapes of Inhabitation in the Mount Kilimanjaro Area, Tanzania*, Oxford: BAR, pp. 89–105.

Tomalin, Emma (2013) *Religions and Development*, London: Routledge.

Tuan, Y.-F. (1968) *The Hydrological Cycle and the Wisdom of God: A Theme in Geoteleology*, Toronto: University of Toronto Press.

Tucker, Mary Evelyn and Grim, John A. (2001) 'Introduction: The Emerging Alliance of World Religions and Ecology', *Daedalus*, 130 (4), 1–22.

UN Documents (n.d.) *Our Common Future, Chapter 2: Towards Sustainable Development*, www.un-docu-ments.net/ocf-02.htm (accessed 2 July 2014).

WBGU (German Advisory Council on Global Change) (2007) *World in Transition: Climate Change as a Security Risk: Summary for Policy-Makers*, Berlin: WBGU.

Wilkinson, Katherine K. (2012) *Between God and Green: How Evangelicals Are Cultivating a Middle Ground on Climate Change*, New York: Oxford University Press.

Wolf, Jakob and Gjerris, Mickey (2009) 'A Religious Perspective on Climate Change', *Studia Theologica: Nordic Journal of Theology*, 63 (2), 119–39.

Xia, Chen and Schonfeld, Martin (2011) 'A Daoist Response to Climate Change', *Journal of Global Ethics*, 7 (2), 195–203.

Yale University (n.d.) 'Interdisciplinary Centre for Bioethics, Forum on Religion and Ecology', http:// www.yale.edu/bioethics/FORE.htm (accessed 2 July 2014).

27

RELIGION AND ECONOMIC DEVELOPMENT

Daromir Rudnyckyj

Introduction

The relationship between religion and economic development is evident both historically and in the present at multiple sites around the world. However, the precise contours of this relationship vary according to local histories and politics. As this chapter illustrates, there is no necessary or causal relationship between these two domains for apprehending and representing human action and relationships. In some parts of Africa, the failure of economic development and the retreat of the state's ability to guarantee social welfare have led religion to prove a refuge from the dislocations of development gone astray. Elsewhere in Africa and in Latin America, the retreat of the state and neoliberal economic restructuring have opened spaces for faith-based organizations and religious NGOs to take an increasingly active role in economic development. In Southeast Asia, prosperity religions, which preach that wealth will be granted to those who demonstrate exaggerated faith, flourish in countries which have experienced economic stagnation (e.g., the Philippines) or crisis (e.g., Thailand). In East Asia, economic development has spurred the development of new religious practices as well as the resuscitation of old ones. Contrary to common media and even scholarly representations of Islam as looking to the past and embracing outmoded institutions (Kuran 2011), across the Muslim world there is evidence of creative attempts to redeploy religion to address past economic failures and create new developmental paradigms. This chapter sheds light on these phenomena, as it illustrates the myriad articulations of religion and economic development.

This chapter argues that economic development cannot be fully understood without attention to religion. It begins by contrasting early classical social scientific accounts of the relationship between religion and development in the work of Marx and Weber. It then considers the secularization thesis, the recently contested notion that modernization would inexorably lead to the demise of religious authority and a general decline of religious practice. The chapter then considers contemporary approaches to religion and economic development, focusing on neo-Marxist approaches, the emergence of faith-based NGOs, and analyses that foreground the ways in which religious practice is motivated for economic development. Elements of these approaches form a platform upon which to contrast two empirical examples: in one configuration, religious practice is incited and enhanced for greater economic development; in the other, a zone of action demarcated as religious is mobilized as part of state development strategy.

Classical approaches to religion and economic development

The relationship between economic development and religion is of longstanding concern in the human sciences. Karl Marx and Max Weber are commonly viewed as having come to opposing conclusions regarding this relationship. Marx's historical materialism emphasized how material conditions determined social and cultural forms (including religion). In contrast, Weber sought to show how religious ideas exercised a formative influence on production.

Marx argued that humankind had progressed through stages of economic development with its own characteristic mode of production: from tribal society, through ancient society based on slave labor, to feudalism, and eventually capitalism. Thus, for Marx, the capitalist mode of production defined a particular historical epoch. It is related to the mode of production that precedes it (feudalism) but is distinct. This historically specific mode of production is characterized by wage labor, private property, class division, social relations mediated through things instead of people, and "the production and the circulation of commodities" (Marx 1977: 473). Marx's method of analyzing stages of economic development is both material and historical. Marx's material focus meant that religion was, for the most part, epiphenomenal to the fundamental processes that undergirded social life. Thus, he wrote that "religious estrangement as such occurs only in the realm of consciousness, of man's inner life, but economic estrangement is that of real life" (Marx 1978: 85). The organization of material production was key in creating the social and cultural relationships and religious practices of particular developmental stages. Although Marx sees religion as peripheral to the material economic processes that characterize each developmental stage and mode of production, he did view religion as useful in understanding the process of commoditization in the capitalist mode of production. Indeed, in a classic passage Marx remarks on the "mysterious character of the commodity-form" (Marx 1977: 164). In the capitalist mode of production, Marx wrote that:

> the definite social relation between men themselves . . . assumes . . . the fantastic form of a relation between things. In order, therefore, to find an analogy we must take flight into the misty realm of religion. There the products of the human brain appear as autonomous figures endowed with a life of their own, which enter into relations both with each other and with the human race.
>
> (Marx 1977: 165)

Marx deplores how, in a capitalist system of exchange, relations between things take on the characteristics of social relations. The result is what Marx saw as an inverted, unnatural relationship in which humans and human labors were objectified and objects assumed the position of subjects, insofar as the qualities of things come to stand in for the qualities of people. In this sense capitalism operates similarly to religion, as it creates an unnatural fetishism in which objects are endowed with characteristics proper only to living beings.

Weber's account opened up a fundamentally different approach to understanding the relationship between religion and economic development, seeking instead to show how "ideas become effective forces in history" and understand how "religious forces have taken part in the qualitative formation and the quantitative expansion of" the spirit of capitalism "over the world" (Weber 2001: 48). Beginning with the curious ethnographic fact that a greater number of Protestants than Catholics were "business leaders and owners of capital" (Weber 2001: 3) in *fin de siècle* Germany, Weber posits that something intrinsic to Protestantism precipitated the ethical dispositions characteristic of the spirit of capitalism.

Weber identifies two key Protestant innovations, the doctrines of the calling and predestination, as central to this process. The notion of a calling, formulated by Martin Luther as "a life-task, a definite field in which to work" (2001: 39), meant that "the fulfillment of duty in vocational callings became viewed as the highest expression that moral activity could assume. Precisely this new notion of the moral worth of devoting oneself to a calling was the unavoidable result of the idea of attaching religious significance to daily work" (2001: 39). This fundamentally new orientation toward work evaporated the Catholic distinction between spiritual and lay action and meant that the pious could fulfill moral duty through worldly action.

The doctrine of predestination, which Weber calls "the most characteristic dogma" of Calvinism, was perhaps even more pivotal to eliciting the subjective dispositions of the spirit of capitalism (Weber 2001: 56). According to this doctrine, God had determined prior to the creation of the world who would be saved and who would be damned. All creation exists for the sake of God, and has meaning only as a means to the glory and majesty of God. Human merit or guilt plays no part in the possession of grace, as that would make God's decrees subject to human influence. According to Weber, this would have precipitated "a feeling of unimaginable inner loneliness of the solitary individual" (Weber 2001: 60). Because salvation is fundamentally uncertain, individual believers must constantly be vigilant in its pursuit, which leads to a "systematic self-control which at every moment stands before the inexorable alternative, chosen or damned" (Weber 2001: 69–70). Whereas Catholics could live a segmented life, atoning for each sin in a piecemeal fashion, Puritans had no such escape and had to rationalize their lives and subject them to "a consistent method for conduct as a whole" (Weber 2001: 71). The combination of the two doctrines precipitated an ethic of worldly asceticism characterized by the "idea of the necessity of proving one's faith in worldly activity" (Weber 2001: 74). The spirit of capitalism is an expression of the ethical position of "faithful labor . . . through the conception of this labor as a calling, as the best, often in the last analysis the only means of attaining certainty of grace" (Weber 2001: 121).

Marx looked to religion to explain the way in which material objects were endowed with strange qualities. Thus, capitalist economic development was characterized by a set of unnatural substitutions in which commodity appeared to stand in for social relationships and the mystical religious practices associated with fetishes offered insight into how inanimate objects were treated as living subjects. Weber, in contrast, looked to religion not for insight into the mystical practices associated with economic development, but rather to understand its ascetic routines.

Weber is sometimes mistakenly understood to see Western economic development as the causal outcome of Christianity in general and Protestantism in particular. That is to say, some readers of Weber's work have interpreted him as arguing that Protestantism caused capitalist development. However, Weber cautioned against causal analysis in trying to understand history (Weber 1949: 33). Thus, he did not see the spirit of capitalism as the necessary outcome of the Protestant Reformation, but rather the contingent outcome of various efforts to reform religious practices and institutions. Indeed, Weber makes it clear that neither Luther nor Calvin had any interest in economic affairs – their entire preoccupation was the problem of the salvation of themselves and their followers. Weber emphasizes the contingency of the relationship between Protestant ethics and the spirit of capitalism. It just so happened that the doctrines by which Protestants lived, particularly those of the calling and predestination, created an ethic of worldly asceticism. In turn, worldly asceticism just happened to be conducive to economic accumulation, because Protestants did not purchase luxuries, donations to churches were limited, and giving money to the poor was generally frowned upon because a lack of worldly success was seen as the result of divine disfavor. Without any other outlet for their surplus capital, Protestants reinvested their money, which created a cycle in which they would accumulate more capital (Weber 2001: 116). Thus, according to Weber, religion did not cause the tremendous economic development of the West, but rather development was a contingent outcome of the religious ethics that gained popularity in Northern and Western Europe following the Reformation. The accounts of Marx and Weber exerted a formative influence on those who approached the problem of religion and economic growth during the post-World War II hey-day of development.

A manifesto of modernization

The dismantling of colonial empires that took place following the end of World War II brought about the era of high developmentalism. The world's advanced economies sought to counter the prospective influence of communism by raising living standards in formerly colonized countries. Although there was a precedent for such intervention in the name of reducing poverty and increasing living standards during late colonialism (Furnivall 1948), beginning in the 1950s development was accorded new prominence in the overseas policies of former colonial powers. Walt Rostow's *Stages of Economic Growth* served as a self-proclaimed manifesto for the logic of developmentalism. Perhaps surprisingly, given Weber's generative insights regarding the religious context of economic growth in Europe, economic development was seen as a completely secular process. Indeed, in Rostow's account there is scant reference to the role of religion in any of the developmental stages outlined, and he is generally dismissive of the role that religion may play in economic growth (Rostow 1960: 51). The guiding logic of development during the heyday of what came to be known as modernization theory was secular. The logic that guided much of the way in which the West engaged with the non-West presumed a split between the secular and spiritual in which religious action was properly consigned to the private and domestic spheres, whereas the public was designated as the space of economy and politics, from which religion was notably absent (Asad 2003).

Clifford Geertz offered a sustained response to modernization theory's latent assumptions regarding religion, addressing in part Rostow's arguments about a uniform structure for economic growth. Geertz pointed out that Rostow's focus on individual nation-states as homogeneous developmental units missed the diversity within these units; he persuasively argued for the key role that religion played in fostering economic ethics among local populations. In *Peddlers and Princes*, Geertz contrasts towns in two different parts of Indonesia, each with the inverse problem of the other. In predominantly Hindu Tabanan, cultural values of reciprocity inhibit the emergence of individual initiative. In mostly Muslim Modjokuto, the individualist ethics of Muslim market traders prevent the emergence of any kind of collective organizations or institutions (Geertz 1963: 127). Heavily influenced by Weber's work, Geertz successfully showed the important role that religious values played in facilitating economic action. In so doing, he questioned the secularizing thrust of Rostow's account of the process of economic development.

The neoliberal turn: religion, development and the problem of rationality

Economic crises following the oil shocks of the 1970s called into question many of the presumptions of modernization that took economic development as a progressive process (Ferguson 1999). Marxian approaches to the relationship between religion and economic development have emphasized religion as a realm of refuge from or means of resistance against the dislocations and disturbances precipitated by economic development. Especially notable was Michael Taussig's study of tin miners and plantation workers in South America (Taussig 1980). Taussig argued that workers on the periphery created their own critique of economic development by likening capitalism to the devil. Thus, the devil worship rites practiced by workers served as a critique of abstract exchange values by those newly exposed to a market economy.

The turn to religion and the occult to explain and critique the disruptive effects of economic development was also adopted by subsequent approaches. For example, describing what they call "millennial capitalism," Jean and John Comaroff identify a "culture of neoliberalism" that precipitates disorder and irrationality (2000). Drawing on Marx's work, the Comaroffs' claims are part of a larger body of work that has tended to see both religion and capitalism in terms of fetishization and mysticism. This work has analyzed how evangelical religions preaching prosperity enlist their flocks in the conviction that the creation of wealth is a matter of faith and prayer. Followers of prosperity movements believe that enhanced religious devotion will net them economic success through divine intervention (Coleman 2000). Several scholars have noted the popularity of so-called "prosperity religions" in areas where fast-paced economic development was followed by financial crisis and economic collapse (Jackson 1999; Haynes 2012). Especially popular in these movements is the seed-faith principle, in which adherents are encouraged to "invest in miracles" by making donations to religious groups as a means of "eliciting miracles from God" (Wiegele 2005: 21). Indeed, economic development has also created new religious practices. Taiwan has been the site of reconfigurations of Buddhism and Daoism, both heavily intermingled with Confucian moral discourse, as well as new forms of ancestor worship (Weller 2000; Pazderic 2004). Similarly, economic growth has spurred new religious practices in sites as diverse as China (Chu 2010), Thailand (Scott 2009), India (Froystad 2009), Mali (Soares 2005), Indonesia (George 2009), Russia (Luehrmann 2011), and Pakistan (Marsden 2007).

Religion has played a particularly important role in development's neoliberal turn, given the increasing prominence of NGOs in the wake of the so-called "retreat of the state" (Muehlebach 2012). Erica Bornstein shows how religious Western NGOs active in Zimbabwe adopted the welfare commitments that had otherwise been the purview of the state. In so doing, she reveals how the discursive practices of economic development, especially its commitment to progress and material well-being, were inflected by Christian religious principles (Bornstein 2005). Along similar lines, others have illustrated how Christian affect animates volunteer work for economic development in the global South (Richard and Rudnyckyj 2009; James 2010; O'Neill 2013). These accounts resonate with the growing awareness of the implicitly Christian eschatology of much development practice (Giri *et al.* 2004).

Another analysis of the articulation of economic development and religion has focused on how religious ethics and practices are mobilized to introduce economic rationality into human life. Scholars pursuing this line of inquiry have examined the ways in which both religion and economic development serve as domains for the formation of agentive subjects. This line of analysis has sought to demonstrate how religious practices are mobilized to elicit populations conducive to economic growth. For example, in a classic study of state-led economic development in Malaysia, Aihwa Ong examined how the moral discourses of Islamist political groups resulted in the increased discipline of female factory workers (Ong 1990).

Along similar lines, Johan Fischer has shown how the Malaysian state has deployed halal food certification standards to achieve what Nikolas Rose has called "government at a distance" (Rose 1999). Fischer showed how the Malaysian state sought to create an urban, educated, entrepreneurial and shareholding Malay middle class, known as "New Malays" (*Melayu Baru*) (Fischer 2008). Aihwa Ong had also earlier argued that the promotion of Islamic piety has been central to this project (Ong 1999: 204). In the process, self-discipline, the accumulation of wealth, and modern corporate skills are represented as outcomes of devout Islamic practice that are fully commensurable with the state's aims of economic development. Similarly Carla Jones has shown how Islamic fashion serves as a means through which middle-class laboring and consuming subjects are produced in Indonesia (Jones 2010).

Kevin O'Neill has shown how Protestant practices are motivated for economic development in the aftermath of Guatemala's decades-long civil war. Guatemala call centers promote Christian virtues among employees, who in some cases are deported former members of notoriously violent Los Angeles street gangs (O'Neill 2012). In a similar register, Mona Atia has described how faith-based development organizations link volunteerism, self-help discourses, and management science to Islamic piety (Atia 2012). This is part of an increasingly visible tendency among Muslim entrepreneurs to "promote economic development while also embedding economic practices within a framework of ethics and moral responsibilities deemed to be 'Islamic'" (Osella and Osella 2009: 202).

Empirical configurations of economic development and religion

These approaches to the articulation of the relationships between economic development and religion have provided a foundation for two research projects I have conducted on Islam in Southeast Asia. The first analyzed "spiritual reform" initiatives in Indonesia that sought to inculcate Islamic ethics among corporate employees, many of whom worked at state-owned enterprises, to make their firms more globally competitive (Rudnyckyj 2010). The second examined the globalization of Islamic banking and finance by documenting efforts to make Malaysia's capital, Kuala Lumpur, the central hub in an Islamic financial alternative to the conventional banking and finance system centered in New York, London, and Hong Kong (Rudnyckyj 2013, 2014). In both projects, religion was mobilized toward a broader project of economic development (albeit in significantly different ways). In both examples, practitioners, policy makers, and other experts sought to represent an economy and then shape the practices of market actors in an attempt to elicit practices commensurate with their definitions.

Ethical transformation for economic development

Efforts in Indonesia to inculcate Islamic ethics among company employees at state-owned enterprises, many of which were planned for privatization, were directed toward enhancing productivity and transnational competitiveness, thereby eliminating widespread corruption. Self-styled spiritual reformers sought to develop employees' Islamic faith to resolve Indonesia's late-1990s development crisis and economic downturn. In so doing, such reformers posed a question that has long been asked by scholars of religion and economic development: how do religious norms inflect economic action? They asked the question in order to better equip Indonesian companies to compete in an increasingly integrated global economy, given declining investment by the Indonesian state. They promoted a set of ethics they identified as intrinsic to Islamic practice and conducive to a new development regime.

Based on research primarily conducted at Krakatau Steel, a massive state-owned steel factory in western Java, I showed how corporate managers and human resources trainers found their company confronted by increasing international economic integration and in response introduced a training program grounded in moderate Islam. Long insulated from international competition by protective tariffs on steel and generous government subsidies conferred under a program of nationalist developmentalism, this company and others like it were confronted by the twin challenges of a massive economic crisis that swept across Southeast Asia in the late 1990s and increasing pressure to compete with firms outside Indonesia. Their response, intended to precipitate what proponents referred to as "spiritual reform," construed religious ethics as conducive to a new regime of economic development absent of state guarantees and characterized by increasing transnational competition.

The manner in which religion was mobilized to resolve the impasse of economic development was striking. Elaborate spiritual training programs, called Emotional and Spiritual Quotient training (ESQ), mixed the latest human resources management theory with collective prayers and lessons in Islamic history. The founder of the program, Ary Ginanjar, asserted that a work ethic conducive to business success was present in the five pillars of Islam. For example, the fourth pillar, the duty to fast during Ramadan, was recast as a directive for self-control and individual accountability. A charismatic former businessman, Ginanjar represented the prophet Muhammad as the model for a successful corporate executive, and participants were encouraged to emulate his example in business and trade. The gripping climax of ESQ included a simulation of events that take place during the annual *hajj* pilgrimage to Mecca. Most compelling for participants was a recreation of the circulation around the *kaaba*, the central shrine in the main mosque in Mecca. A replica of the *kaaba* the size of an SUV was placed in the center of the room and participants proceeded in rotation around it chanting, in Arabic, "There is no God but Allah." Participants also reenacted the stoning of *jamrat al-aqabah*, in which pilgrims hurl rocks at three representations of the devil, by launching small wads of paper at three demonic images elaborately illustrated on flip charts. These reenactments were designed to intensify the Islamic piety of corporate employees and, by so doing, to increase both their own motivation and ultimately corporate productivity and profitability.

These engaging, interactive ESQ sessions began in 2001 and had attracted a total of over 1 million participants by early 2011. Ginanjar used the latest high-tech media centered on a Microsoft PowerPoint presentation. His presentations featured graphs, charts, tables, and a steady stream of bullet points, as well as entertaining film clips, vivid photographs, and popular music with a driving bass line and catchy lyrics. He used a diverse array of popular media, websites, and academic journals, drawing as much on Hollywood blockbusters as the sage scholarship of the Harvard Business School.

Spiritual reform programs in Indonesia revealed how economic development and the threat posed by globalization were not conceived as abstract problems but rather as challenges that could be addressed through personal cultivation of religious practice. This involved developing and conveying empirical techniques for the rationalization of corporate conduct. Thus, participants were instructed in dispositions conducive to corporate success, which were likewise represented as central tenets of Islamic comportment. For example, participants in spiritual training programs were instructed in the value of time in the workplace and encouraged to be hardworking and disciplined. Corruption was represented as immoral and the kind of behavior that would lead to the bankruptcy of the company. Employees were lectured on the importance of individual accountability and to take care of problems as they arose, rather than waiting to be ordered to do so by a superior. Economic development was rescaled from a national problem to be addressed by the state to a personal problem to be addressed by individuals in their everyday practices.

Reframing economic development as an individual challenge involved explicit reflection on the practices of corporate employees and citizens of the nation more broadly. Participants were enjoined to diagnose the failures in both their specific workplaces and the nation at large and devise specific, practical solutions to address these issues as they saw them. In this sense, the economy and the economic crisis were not viewed as something outside the experience and intervention of employees. Instead they were seen as something in which the employees were directly implicated, but in which they could also intervene. Thus, the economy was something that could be affected through individual action. By adjusting their everyday practices in the workplace, employees could address the challenges that the company and the nation faced. Thus, programmatic efforts to enhance the Islamic ethics of corporate employees represented the economy not as a theoretical model legible only as an abstraction, but as something that could be influenced in practice.

Demarcating a religious economy: Islamic finance and Malaysia's development project

Efforts by state planners to make Malaysia the central global hub for Islamic finance are a state strategy to sustain the nation's impressive record of economic growth. In part, these efforts are a product of the way in which religion has been integrated into what Aihwa Ong has referred to as "postdevelopmentalism" in Malaysia (Ong 2006: 77). As in Indonesia and other newly independent countries, early leaders had pursued a post-colonial economic development strategy that largely presumed a secular separation between religion and economic action. As noted above, this was broadly commensurable with the presumption elsewhere in the world that economic development, together with secularization and democratization, were intrinsic to modernization (Rostow 1960). Thus, analysts of Malaysia have observed that, until the state-backed Islamic resurgence of the 1980s, economic modernization "had always been based on the secular Western model" (Mauzy and Milne 1984: 636).

Malaysia's initial economic development success stemmed from its position as a global center for high-tech assembly and offshore industrialization in the 1970s and 1980s (Ong 1987). With the active encouragement of the developmentalist state, Japanese, American, and European firms set up shop in extensive industrial zones and hired a vast number of new workers to provide the labor for export-oriented growth. Islam was deployed by corporations and the state as a means of disciplining especially the young, female laboring population involved in high-tech assembly (Ong 1990). Subsequently, in the 1990s the state embarked on a series of ambitious economic development projects, such as the Multimedia Super Corridor (MSC), which was conceived as a hub for the development of information and multimedia technology. The MSC included sites like Cyberjaya, which was intended to become the Silicon Valley of Southeast Asia, but has languished as the state's focus has shifted to other economic strategies (Bunnell 2004; Smeltzer 2008).

As the state developed industrial and service sectors that require more highly educated and skilled workers, religion has played a pivotal role in state development strategies and its efforts to create so-called New Malays equipped with characteristics favored by transnational corporations (e.g., diligence, accountability, and education). Furthermore, "government policies seek to bring Islam in line with capitalism" by promoting a form of Islam that is fully compatible with the state's development objectives (Ong 1999: 204). Thus, the New Malay is represented as "self-disciplined, able, and wealth accumulating, but in a way that is cast within the precepts of Islam rather than of capitalism" (Ong 1999: 204). Thus, the state has promoted a style of Islamic practice that is fully commensurable with capitalism and the state's efforts to reconcile Islamic piety and action with modernization (Sloane 1999).

Recently, rising income levels and the emergence of other, lower-wage sites for high-tech assembly in East and Southeast Asia (most notably China, Vietnam, and Indonesia) have created anxiety regarding Malaysia's export-oriented development paradigm and precipitated a turn toward the provision of professional services. Indeed, as income and education levels in Malaysia have increased, the state has sought to develop sectors to which its "knowledge-based society" can add value (Evers 2003: 355). Malaysia hopes to isolate a particular niche in providing services labeled Islamic, including making the country a global halal food certification center (Fischer 2011). The state's most aggressive endeavor in developing a service-oriented sector has been to make the country a global center of Islamic financial services. The state has sought to construct the infrastructure necessary for Islamic finance to function both domestically and transnationally, promoting research and innovation in Islamic financial instruments, and creating some of the premier global institutions for higher education in Islamic finance.

In the oil-rich countries of the Arabian Gulf, such as Saudi Arabia, Qatar, and the United Arab Emirates (see Jawad, Chapter 19), states took a mostly hands-off approach to Islamic finance. Most of these states were content to allow the industry to develop its own norms and standards, with little direction from the central government. In contrast, Islamic finance in Malaysia has been carefully fostered by the state. A particular concern of Malaysia's financial governance institutions, Bank Negara Malaysia (BNM, the Central Bank) and the Securities Commission of Malaysia (SCM), has been to provide clear and transparent regulatory guidance to industry players. Bank Negara, for example, has a dedicated Islamic Banking and Takaful[1] Department that sets policy for Islamic banking, maintains close ties with the industry, and regularly updates practitioners about policy changes. BNM issues directives in the form of guidance notes, circulars, standards, and other guidelines about the proper practice of Islamic banks.

Another step that Malaysia has taken to facilitate the growth of Islamic financial services as an engine for national economic growth has been to provide legal clarity and a well-organized legal infrastructure for resolving disputes in Islamic finance. Indeed, the Islamic financial system in Malaysia was initiated by the Islamic Banking Act, passed by the country's parliament in 1983. Thirty years later the governing legal system was updated with the Islamic Financial Services Act (2013), which clarified many of the vague provisions in the original law. For example, the new law actually defined "Islamic banking business" and clarified a number of operational procedures for Islamic banks, such as a clear distinction between investment and deposit accounts.

By laying down the most comprehensive global legal and regulatory infrastructure for Islamic finance, Malaysia has sought to be a key player in the Islamic finance business. The country was especially aggressive in becoming the leading site for the issuance of sukuk, accounting for about 65 percent of issues globally (Boey 2011: 32). Sukuk are debt certificates which resemble bonds and enable corporations or sovereign states to raise large volumes of capital in a shariah-compliant manner. Unlike bonds, sukuk rarely rely on loan contracts, owing to the Qur'anic prohibition against interest. Rather sukuk are based on shariah-compliant contracts that use an underlying asset as a basis to generate returns to the sukuk holders. The returns distributed to the sukuk holders are generated based on sales contracts, leasing contracts, or "the profit-sharing mechanism" in a "partnership contract" (Dusuki 2012: 16). To make Malaysia the leading global center for sukuk issuances, the state passed a number of tax deductions and exemptions which provided economic incentives for banks, corporations, and law firms to conduct sukuk business in Kuala Lumpur.[2]

Religious ethics and identities in development

Both of these projects analyzed the relationships between religion and economic development. However, the form that this articulation took differed in each configuration. This was particularly notable along three key axes: the scale of each project, whether religion was represented as an ethics or an identity, and the specific content of the religion. In terms of scale, spiritual reform in Indonesia made economic development a matter of personal religious piety. Thus, spirituality tied the project of development to individual efforts. Proponents of spiritual reform sought to address broad structural changes through the reform of individual practices. Thus enhanced religious piety was posed as the antidote for a reduction in state support, planned privatization of state-owned enterprises, and increasing economic competition from producers outside Indonesia.

In contrast, Malaysia's Islamic finance project focused much less on specific individual religious practices. Rather, it entailed incorporating religion into the state's economic development strategies. Thus, an entire domain of economic action was marked as Islamic and integrated into the broader project of state-led economic development. Religion was not mobilized to facilitate development through individual self-formation and subjectification, but rather Islam was applied to and assimilated in a discrete area of modern capitalism. The goal was to promote economic development by creating a sophisticated and well-regulated Islamic financial system. This entailed figuring out what Islamic finance is, how it might work, and how differences in interpretation between separate jurisdictions, most notably Malaysia and the Middle East, could be resolved. Thus, the difference is that, in spiritual reform, Islam is a practice, but in Islamic finance it denotes a domain for action.

A second difference was with the methods through which the articulation between religion and economic development was achieved. For spiritual reformers in Indonesia active at key sites of economic development, religion was ethical, in the sense that it was represented as a mode of embodied practice that could be enhanced for the benefit of economic development. In the ESQ training sessions, the five pillars of Islam were presented as directives for corporate success. For example, the second pillar of Islam, the duty of every Muslim to pray five times each day at specific times, was reinterpreted as a directive to be diligent and self-disciplined, by keeping attention to time and not reporting late for obligations.

The project of invoking Islam to make Malaysia a global hub for Islamic finance was not so much ethical as it was moral. Rather than focusing on transformation of embodied practices, it consisted mainly of elucidating and implementing rules regarding monetary transactions by classifying what was permissible and what was not. In other words, instead of extracting principles of economic action from the history and rituals of Islam, Islamic finance experts identified the formal rules of Islam and then created a system of financial action that conformed to those rules. Thus, those involved in designing Islamic financial systems examined texts, mainly the Qur'an and the hadiths,[3] and devised the contours of the system based on the rules articulated in those texts. Those involved in the operations of Islamic financial institutions are pragmatic in their approach and seek to devise systems and processes that work effectively. Thus, they tend to be more concerned with the letter of Islamic law, as opposed to its spirit. That is to say, technical and formal compliance with religious norms was of far more concern than trying to operationalize the norm in the sense of making it part of individual ethical practice.

Another difference lay in the way Islam itself was represented. In Indonesia, spiritual reformers insisted that Islam emphasized the same principles that were responsible for economic development in the West. ESQ founder Ary Ginanjar argued that the principles he identified in Islam that were conducive to business success were but one manifestation of universal "spiritual" principles. In this sense, asserting an Islamic identity was not a means of differentiation from Western capitalism, but rather an assertion that Islam offered a means to get to the same level of economic development as the West.

In contrast, in Malaysia's Islamic finance project, religion is an explicit mark of difference. In part, this is due to the fact that the addition of the modifier "Islamic" to the noun "finance" demands an assertion of difference. Indeed, the content of this difference was a recurrent subject of reflection among Islamic finance experts. While there were external critics, ESQ participants themselves did not call Islam into question or engage in debates over whether Islamic ethical principles were in fact being followed. However, in Islamic finance Islam was itself in question. There were recurrent debates over, as one Islamic finance expert said to me, "what the Islam in Islamic finance is." In workshops, classrooms, conferences, and conversations, experts asked each other whether replication of conventional finance in Islamic dress was sufficient or whether it had to fulfill Islamic principles explicitly. These debates often were framed in terms of whether Islamic finance achieved the goals or intentions (*maqassid*) of shariah and how it might better achieve these goals.

Furthermore, Islamic finance experts were not seeking to augment personal religious piety or achieve individual self-transformation among lapsed Muslims. Rather, they sought to enhance an already held sense of collective identity. Likewise, by realigning economic relationships under the banner of Islam, planners seek to facilitate access to certain markets to facilitate overall economic development. Given the massive amounts of surplus capital currently being generated in the Arabian Gulf region as a result of record high oil and gas prices, this may make wise development strategy. Islamic finance in Malaysia is heavy on Islamic symbolism as well as Arabic words. Islamic banks offer customers opening new accounts the opportunity to be entered in a raffle to win a *hajj* pilgrimage trip to Saudi Arabia. Advertisements for Islamic financial institutions often feature piously attired women in headscarves and men in dress suited for attending religious services in mosques. The contracts used by Islamic financial institutions are almost always referred to by their Arabic designations, such as *murabaha* (a cost–plus sale) or *mudarabah* (a profit-sharing contract; see also Mohseni-Cheraghlou, Chapter 20). These Arabic terms are often referred to in discussion of Islamic finance in Malaysia, even though most people do not speak Arabic. Islamic financial institutions often refer to these designations in the fine print in their client contracts. In addition, banking products are often given names that refer to Islamic history or society, such as Maybank Islamic's *Ikhwan* credit card. *Ikhwan* is an Arabic word that means "brethren" or "brothers" and evokes *al-Ikhwan al-Muslimun*, the Muslim Brotherhood, which was founded by Hassan al-Banna and has been an active political opposition movement in Egypt and other countries with large Muslim populations.

In Indonesia spiritual reformers made the articulation between religion and economic development by emphasizing religious similarity. Thus, they put a central emphasis on similarities of Islamic ethics to the ethics of Western capitalism. In contrast, Islamic finance experts in Malaysia go to great lengths to justify the appellation "Islamic." Islam is an explicit symbol of cultural difference and an assertion that Muslims can achieve economic development while maintaining their distinctiveness from the West.

Conclusion

This chapter demonstrates how religion inflects the thought and practice of economic development in myriad ways. For Marx, economic growth is accompanied by the fetishization of commodities that takes on a religious character. For Weber, economic development is in part explained by the ethical practices of the workers who fuel growth, and religion plays a key role in the production of subjects with specific dispositions. Even during the mid-twentieth century, at the apex of positivism and rational planning, when most development planners were wholeheartedly committed to secular knowledge, dissonant voices like Geertz's emphasized the important role that religious dispositions played in economic growth. Some recent scholarship has seen religion as a realm of refuge from the failures of development and charted the emergence of prosperity religions in response to crises of development. Rather than seeing these domains as opposed, other scholars have examined the convergence of religion and neoliberal economic development. Some have taken an institutional view, examining the role of faith-based organizations and other religious NGOs in promoting economic development in wake of the retreat of the state. Others have examined how new agents of development mobilize religious ethics for economic growth.

These varied approaches to the problem show that there is no necessary relationship between religion and economic development. The conjunctures and disjunctures that scholars have identified between these two domains of conceptualization are largely contingent on localized histories and political strategies. Ultimately, the empirical conditions in any given setting will determine how living subjects formulate relationships that straddle both domains.

Notes

1 Takaful is insurance that meets shariah restrictions on permissible economic action.
2 For a summary of the ten legal reforms implemented in Malaysia to provide incentives to make the country the leading site for sukuk issuance, see http://www.jkmifc.com/index.php?ch=ch_kc_framework&pg=pg_kcfm_incentives&ac=246.
3 The hadiths are textually recorded compilations of the words and actions of the prophet Muhammad. Following the Qur'an, they are the texts to which Islamic scholars refer most regarding matters of Islamic law and jurisprudence.

References

Asad, T. (2003) *Formations of the Secular: Christianity, Islam, Modernity*, Stanford, CA: Stanford University Press.
Atia, M. (2012) '"A Way to Paradise": Pious Neoliberalism, Islam, and Faith-Based Development', *Annals of the Association of American Geographers*, 102 (4), 808–27.
Boey, K. Y. (2011) 'Malaysia Woos Sukuk Trade', *International Financing Review*, 5 September, 32–3.
Bornstein, E. (2005) *The Spirit of Development: Protestant NGOs, Morality, and Economics in Zimbabwe*, Stanford, CA: Stanford University Press.
Bunnell, T. (2004) *Malaysia, Modernity and the Multimedia Super Corridor: A Critical Geography of Intelligent Landscapes*, London: RoutledgeCurzon.
Chu, J. Y. (2010) *Cosmologies of Credit: Transnational Mobility and the Politics of Destination in China*, Durham, NC: Duke University Press.
Coleman, S. (2000) *The Globalisation of Charismatic Christianity: Spreading the Gospel of Prosperity*, Cambridge: Cambridge University Press.
Comaroff, J. and Comaroff, J. (2000) 'Millennial Capitalism: First Thoughts on a Second Coming', *Public Culture*, 12 (2), 291–343.
Dusuki, A. W. (ed.) (2012) *Islamic Financial System: Principles and Operations*, Kuala Lumpur: International Shariah Research Academy for Islamic Finance.
Evers, H.-D. (2003) 'Transition towards a Knowledge Society: Malaysia and Indonesia in Comparative Perspective', *Comparative Sociology*, 2 (2), 355–73.
Ferguson, J. (1999) *Expectations of Modernity: Myths and Meanings of Urban Life on the Zambian Copperbelt*, Berkeley: University of California Press.
Fischer, J. (2008) *Proper Islamic Consumption: Shopping among the Malays in Modern Malaysia*, Copenhagen: NIAS.
Fischer, J. (2011) *The Halal Frontier: Muslim Consumers in a Globalized Market*, New York: Palgrave Macmillan.
Froystad, K. (2009) 'The Return Path: Anthropology of a Western Yogi', in T. Csordas (ed.), *Transnational Transcendence: Essays in Religion and Globalization*, Berkeley: University of California Press.
Furnivall, J. S. (1948) *Colonial Policy and Practice: A Comparative Study of Burma and Netherlands India*, Cambridge: Cambridge University Press.
Geertz, C. (1963) *Peddlers and Princes: Social Change and Economic Modernization in Two Indonesian Towns*, Chicago: University of Chicago Press.
George, K. (2009) 'Ethics, Iconoclasm, and Qur'anic Art in Indonesia', *Cultural Anthropology*, 24 (4), 589–621.
Giri, A. K., van Harskamp, A. and Salemink, O. (2004) *The Development of Religion/The Religion of Development*, Delft: Eburon.
Haynes, N. (2012) 'Pentecostalism and the Morality of Money: Prosperity, Inequality, and Religious Sociality on the Zambian Copperbelt', *Journal of the Royal Anthropological Institute*, 18 (1), 124–39.
Jackson, P. (1999) 'Royal Spirits, Chinese Gods and Magic Monks: Thailand's Boom-Time Religions of Prosperity', *Southeast Asia Research*, 7 (3), 245–320.
James, E. C. (2010) *Democratic Insecurities: Violence, Trauma, and Intervention in Haiti*, Berkeley: University of California Press.
Jones, C. (2010) 'Better Women: The Cultural Politics of Gendered Expertise in Indonesia', *American Anthropologist*, 112 (2), 270–82.

Kuran, T. (2011) *The Long Divergence: How Islamic Law Held Back the Middle East*, Princeton, NJ: Princeton University Press.

Luehrmann, S. (2011) *Secularism Soviet Style: Teaching Atheism and Religion in a Volga Republic*, Bloomington: Indiana University Press.

Marsden, M. (2007) 'All-Male Sonic Gatherings, Islamic Reform, and Masculinity in Northern Pakistan', *American Ethnologist*, 34 (3), 473–90.

Marx, K. (1977) *Capital: A Critique of Political Economy*, New York: Vintage Books.

Marx, K. (1978) 'Economic and Philosophic Manuscripts of 1844', in R. C. Tucker (ed.), *The Marx–Engels Reader*, 2nd edn, New York: Norton.

Mauzy, D. and Milne, R. S. (1984) 'The Mahathir Administration in Malaysia: Discipline through Islam', *Pacific Affairs*, 56 (4), 617–48.

Muehlebach, A. (2012) *The Moral Neoliberal: Welfare and Citizenship in Italy*, Chicago: University of Chicago Press.

O'Neill, K. L. (2012) 'The Soul of Security: Corporatism, Christianity, and Control in Postwar Guatemala', *Social Text*, 32 (2), 21–42.

O'Neill, K. L. (2013) 'Left Behind: Security, Salvation, and the Subject of Prevention', *Cultural Anthropology*, 28 (2), 204–26.

Ong, A. (1987) *Spirits of Resistance and Capitalist Discipline: Factory Women in Malaysia*, Albany: State University of New York Press.

Ong, A. (1990) 'State versus Islam: Malay Families, Women's Bodies, and the Body Politic in Malaysia', *American Ethnologist*, 17 (2), 258–76.

Ong, A. (1999) *Flexible Citizenship: The Cultural Logics of Transnationality*, Durham, NC: Duke University Press.

Ong, A. (2006) *Neoliberalism as Exception: Mutations in Citizenship and Sovereignty*, Durham, NC: Duke University Press.

Osella, F. and Osella, C. (2009) 'Business and Community between India and the Gulf: Muslim Entrepreneurs in Kerala, India', *Journal of the Royal Anthropological Institute (N.S.)*, 15 (s1), 202–21.

Pazderic, N. (2004) 'Recovering True Selves in the Electro-Spiritual Field of Universal Love', *Cultural Anthropology*, 19 (2), 196–225.

Richard, A. and Rudnyckyj, D. (2009) 'Economies of Affect', *Journal of the Royal Anthropological Institute (N.S.)*, 15 (1), 57–77.

Rose, N. S. (1999) *Powers of Freedom: Reframing Political Thought*, Cambridge: Cambridge University Press.

Rostow, W. W. (1960) *The Stages of Economic Growth: A Non-Communist Manifesto*, Cambridge: Cambridge University Press.

Rudnyckyj, D. (2010) *Spiritual Economies: Islam, Globalization, and the Afterlife of Development*, Ithaca, NY: Cornell University Press.

Rudnyckyj, D. (2013) 'From Wall Street to Halal Street: Malaysia and the Globalization of Islamic Finance', *Journal of Asian Studies*, 72 (4), 831–48.

Rudnyckyj, D. (2014) 'Economy in Practice: Islamic Finance and the Problem of Market Reason', *American Ethnologist*, 41 (1), 110–27.

Scott, R. M. (2009) *Nirvana for Sale? Buddhism, Wealth, and the Dhammakaya Temple in Contemporary Thailand*, Albany, NY: SUNY Press.

Sloane, P. (1999) *Islam, Modernity, and Entrepreneurship among the Malays*, New York: St Martin's Press.

Smeltzer, S. (2008) 'The Message Is the Market: Selling Biotechnology and Nation in Malaysia', in J. Nevins and N. L. Peluso (eds), *Taking Southeast Asia to Market: Commodities, Nature, and People in a Neoliberal Age*, Ithaca, NY: Cornell University Press.

Soares, B. F. (2005) *Islam and the Prayer Economy: History and Authority in a Malian Town*, Ann Arbor: University of Michigan Press.

Taussig, M. T. (1980) *The Devil and Commodity Fetishism in South America*, Chapel Hill: University of North Carolina Press.

Weber, M. (1949) *The Methodology of the Social Sciences*, New York: Free Press.

Weber, M. (2001) *The Protestant Ethic and the Spirit of Capitalism*, London: Routledge.

Weller, R. (2000) 'Living at the Edge: Religion, Capitalism, and the End of the Nation-State in Taiwan', *Public Culture*, 12 (2), 477–98.

Wiegele, K. L. (2005) *Investing in Miracles: El Shaddai and the Transformation of Popular Catholicism in the Philippines*, Honolulu: University of Hawai'i Press.

28

RELIGION, DEVELOPMENT, AND FRAGILE STATES

Seth D. Kaplan

Introduction

In recent years, state fragility has vaulted up the list of foreign-policy concerns as the United States and other developed countries respond to threats posed by well-organized extremist groups operating in weakly governed states. As Robert Rotberg wrote in *Foreign Affairs* following the September 11 terrorist attacks, "the threat of terrorism has given the problem of failed nation-states an immediacy and importance that transcends its previous humanitarian dimension" (Rotberg 2002: 127).

Rotberg's observation explains both the recent interest in state fragility by Western governments and why international efforts to stabilize fragile states often focus on regional or global security concerns at the expense of promoting development and state building. As development actors have long recognized, however, it is not coincidental that violence and poverty are both products of weak governance. The political instability and economic problems that typically plague fragile states create a cycle of dysfunction that holds these countries – and often their neighbors – behind. As a 2013 report from the Brookings Institution concluded, an increasing percentage of the world's poor live in fragile states, with the share "set to rise to half in 2018 and nearly two-thirds in 2030" (Chandy *et al.* 2013).

Religion's influence can be a blessing or a curse in such places. Sometimes it is both. Religious institutions, leaders, teachings, and groups impact the social and political environments of fragile states in myriad – and sometimes contradictory – ways. In its different manifestations, religion can be a mechanism to sow social divisions, undermine the effectiveness of government, systematically disadvantage certain groups, or catalyze extremist agendas. In Syria and across the Levant, for instance, the dynamism of religious extremists and longstanding divisions among religious groups have made prospects for peace dim. But shared religious values also can be a way to bridge differences, religious affiliation can promote social cohesion, and religious organizations can deliver much-needed public services (as occurs in many countries in Africa). As this chapter will explore, religion's impact can be quite varied even within the same country.

Local leaders and development organizations seeking to improve the welfare of people living in fragile states need to understand the variety of roles religious actors play in these places. Yet too often religion's crucial influence in fragile states is not sufficiently taken into account by the development community – especially when religion's claims clash with its own secular norms – with the result that religious leaders and teachings are underutilized when seeking to end conflict (as in Syria), religious organizations are underutilized when seeking to enhance service delivery (as in the Democratic Republic of the Congo), and religious values are underutilized when seeking to change social norms around things like corruption (as in Nigeria). Religion's impact is also underemphasized in analyses of state fragility (as in the numerous rankings of fragile states), leaving many actors unprepared for crises when they do erupt.

This chapter examines how religious elements both hamper and facilitate development in fragile states. It first introduces the concept of state fragility and how religion contributes to it. Later, it looks at how religion can help address the roots of fragility, focusing specifically on how formal religious organizations and informal religious networks can deliver services to the poor, enhance security, and promote development. Finally, the conclusion recommends avenues of further study to promote cooperation among development actors and religious leaders and organizations.

Fragile states: causes and consequences

Scholars and practitioners use terms such as "fragile states," "failed states," and "weak states" to describe countries unable to administer their territories effectively. While there is no set definition for these expressions, and therefore no consensus on which places qualify, most experts agree that any country where the government is unable to deliver even the most basic public services – such as territorial control and security – to a significant portion of the population is *failing*. A completely *failed* state – such as Somalia, Haiti, Liberia, and the Democratic Republic of the Congo (DRC) at one time or another – is one where the state has withered away in the face of violence, warlordism, or criminal activity.

The term "fragile" or "weak" encompasses those countries described above but also a much wider group of territories where the national government operates, but where institutions are so dysfunctional that they perform many of their tasks badly or not at all. Although many developing countries have flimsy institutional foundations, are plagued by corruption, are handicapped by ineffectual governing bodies, and suffer from weak rule of law, most scholars and practitioners agree that fragile states are only those where these problems have become so systemic that they threaten stability (Di John 2008). The state is so incapacitated that it cannot provide many essential services: public schools and hospitals barely operate in many places, police and judges are beholden to the rich and the powerful, and the black market trumps legitimate moneymaking activities. Depending on the degree of dysfunction, fragile states can be either close to collapse, as in Nepal, functioning at a bare-minimum level, as in Nigeria, or working haphazardly, as in Guatemala and Bolivia.

In a number of cases, the governing regime operates reasonably well but is unable to impose its rule throughout its territory. In Georgia, Colombia, and Pakistan, secessionists, drug gangs, and militants limit the national government's writ. Rebellious armies have carved out unrecognized mini-states in Azerbaijan, Georgia, and Mali. In other cases, such as Uzbekistan, pre-2003 Iraq, and pre-2011 Syria, the state may seem anything but weak; however, highly repressive policies hide a combustibility that can burst into flames if the regime loses control (Kaplan 2014). In all these cases, states suffer from weak capacity, an inability to enforce their authority, and limited legitimacy (OECD 2010). Interaction with forces beyond their borders exacerbates these problems (g7+ 2011).

The lack of a standard definition means that the line separating fragile countries from conflict countries has often blurred. In recent years, the term "fragile and conflict states" (FCAS) has gained currency as a result.

There are as many lists of fragile states as there are definitions. The most widely cited is *Foreign Policy*'s annual Failed States Index (FSI), produced in conjunction with the Fund for Peace. In 2012, Somalia topped the FSI's list of "failed or failing states," followed by the Democratic Republic of the Congo, Sudan, and Chad (Foreign Policy and Fund for Peace 2012). Other important lists include those produced by the Center for Systemic Peace, the Political Instability Task Force (originally the State Failure Task Force), the Institute for Economics and Peace (in conjunction with the Economist Intelligence Unit), the Brookings Institution, the World Bank, and the OECD (Rice and Patrick 2008; Marshall and Cole 2011; Institute for Economics and Peace 2013; OECD 2013; Political Instability Task Force 2013; World Bank 2013).

Virtually all the definitions take a functional approach, emphasizing the territorial, security, administrative, and economic aspects of statehood. The OECD, for instance, considers deficiencies in state capacity and authority as well as political will key drivers of illegitimacy and fragility (OECD 2011). Ashraf Ghani and Clare Lockhart, for instance, define "ten critical functions" that states must perform in the modern world (Ghani and Lockhart 2008). Stewart Patrick emphasizes the relative nature of a state's strength, based on how well it provides security, effective economic management, an environment conducive to social welfare, and legitimate institutions (Patrick 2011). Most of the lists are, as the Center for Systemic Peace describes its approach, based on "multi-dimensional schemes" that yield a "matrix of effectiveness and legitimacy dimensions as a method for assessing state fragility" (Marshall and Cole 2011: 28–9). The FSI, for instance, ranks countries according to 12 social, economic, political, and military indicators.

Religion does not play a large role in any of these lists. The lists tend to be heavily weighted towards measurements of government effectiveness, economic dynamism, demographics, and violence. But, to the extent that they take into account factionalization, group grievances, and discrimination, the lists do give a role to religion, albeit indirectly. For instance, of the 12 FSI indicators, five reflect to some extent pressures or measures that are related to religion. "Group grievances" (which encompasses religious discrimination and violence) and "human rights and rule of law" (which encompasses religious persecution) come closest. "Factionalized elites" (which could be the product of religious divisions), "uneven economic development" (which could highlight horizontal inequities), and "state legitimacy" (which encompasses government effectiveness and power struggles) are more indirectly related.

By not zeroing in more closely on religion (and identity-based divisions), these lists are missing or underweighting one of the most important factors determining the fragility of states. As a result, their assessments are often far off the mark, markedly reducing their capacity to predict crises even though this is one of their major aims. Pakistan deteriorated from 34th on the FSI in 2005 to 9th in 2006 (suggesting a marked increase in its fragility) when fatalities from terrorism began to rise. In 2010, just before its civil war began, Syria was placed 49th on the FSI. Bahrain, which now has its own simmering religious conflict, was placed 133rd. Clearly these states were not as stable as their ranking indicated.

My own research suggests that a better way to assess fragility is to examine the two most important factors determining a country's ability to navigate difficulties: the capacity of its population to cooperate (social cohesion) and the ability of its institutions (formal and informal) to channel this cooperation to meet national challenges (Kaplan 2008: 17–45). These two factors shape how a government interacts with its citizens, how officials, politicians, military officers, and businesspeople behave, and how effective foreign efforts to upgrade governance will be. In short, they determine both a society's capacity to overcome a shock or longstanding inadequacy that threatens its most basic institutions and its capacity to promote development over the long term.

Fragile states are deficient in both areas. Their populations have little capacity to cooperate in pursuit of public goods. A shortage of social cohesion (based on the relationship members of a group have with one another and with the group as a whole, levels of social cohesion determine the tendency for a group to unite in working towards a goal) plays a crucial role in the states' difficulties, something religious divisions contribute to but which religious actors may have a way to overcome. Put differently, populations in these contexts have severe ethnic, religious, clan, or ideological divisions that make cooperation among subnational (or supernational) identity groups to advance national goals problematic. When combined with weak (or dysfunctional) institutions, these structural divisions feed on each other in a vicious circle that severely undermines the legitimacy of the state, leading to political orders that are highly unstable and hard to reform. A strong national identity is crucial to the creation of state legitimacy, because a legitimate political order is usually built around a cohesive group – and it uses institutions that reflect that group's historical evolution (Hudson 1977). A cohesive identity depends on many factors. India and Indonesia have each had sufficient common history and culture, a long enough period of colonialism, a strong enough set of common institutions, and capable leadership at critical points – all of which accustomed their peoples to an overarching social cohesion despite religious and ethnic diversity.

Countries with strong social cohesion are more stable, better governed, more development oriented, and better able to deal with crises because common challenges trigger cooperation. Where social cohesion is lacking, political infighting and weak governing bodies undermine state legitimacy. This leads to greater conflict, poorer governance, poorer development outcomes, and greater instability. Divisions can make arduous the formation of apolitical state bodies capable of distributing public services and applying the law evenly, and the absence of these bodies further sharpens divisions. As William Easterly has written, diversity only dampens economic growth in the absence of effective institutions (Easterly 2000: 12).[1] As we'll see below, religion has a remarkable impact on cohesion.

How religion contributes to fragility

Religious belief and behavior play a crucial role in determining the prospects of many fragile states. However, the likelihood that faith will be used to promote or undermine stability depends significantly on the nature of the state and the context. The more effective governments are, and the less stark the social divisions, the less likely it is groups will mobilize along religious divides. As Timothy Sisk writes in *Between Terror and Tolerance*, "The interplay between religion, ethnicity, and state authority is central to an analysis of the prospects for conflict and the prospects for peace" (Sisk 2011: 229). Identity divisions play a large role in fragile states. Whereas successful countries are able to channel the affinitive power of identity and group allegiance into country development – yielding states that are more stable, faster growing, less corrupt, better governed, and more development oriented – the divided populations in fragile states possess neither a strong unifying identity nor the robust state institutions necessary to develop one. As a result, they often fall into a cycle of mistrust, zero-sum competition for power, exploitation, disorder, and stagnation, with dire consequences for economies and governance (Putnam 1993: 177).

Religion can function as a primary identity marker, but often it complements or exacerbates existing ethnic divisions and grievances (Little 2011: 9–28).[2] As the United States Institute of Peace's David Smock argues:

> While religion is an important factor in conflict, often marking identity differences, motivating conflict, and justifying violence, religion is not usually the sole or primary

cause of conflict. The reality is that religion becomes intertwined with a range of causal factors – economic, political, and social – that define, propel, and sustain conflict.

(Smock 2008: 3)

In countries such as Israel/Palestine, Nigeria, Bosnia, and Sri Lanka, for instance, ethnicity was far more important in the early stages of conflict; although religious affinity became more important as time went on, it was never the primary driver of conflict. In such cases, religion can become a tool for leaders or extremists seeking to advance an exclusionary agenda. Religious identity and belief – and calls to defend one's faith by religious leaders – mobilize fighters and populations in a way that ethnic sentiment may not. Practically speaking, however, theological or doctrinal differences are rarely the principal cause of conflict in what are very complex situations (Smock 2008: 2).

Religious conflict differs from ethnic conflict in a number of ways. Religious actors tend to draw on a deeper infrastructure and a more developed belief system than ethnic actors. They may be heavily influenced by what is happening elsewhere in the world (as in the Sunni–Shiite conflict discussed below) and have greater resources available if a conflict ignites (as the war in Syria attests). Religious identity may also make compromise harder at times (as in the Arab–Israeli conflict). Ethnic conflict, on the other hand, is much more localized – though diaspora can play a significant role (as in Northern Ireland). It may also be harder to end: there have been far more states created for the sake of ethnic nationalism than religious belief. This suggests that ethnic relationships are often more permanent than religious relationships, at least for larger populations. Smock concludes that "in many cases the lines between ethnic and religious identities have become so blurred that parsing them to assign blame for violence is difficult if not impossible" (Smock 2008: 2).

It should be noted that many conflicts that are called "religious" are actually multidimensional, with other elements playing prominent – often much more prominent – roles. As Frances Stewart has argued, horizontal inequalities between different identity groups (resulting from a combination of political, economic, and cultural marginalization) often play a significant role (Stewart 2010).

The state can either provide barriers to, or allow for, the use of religion to promote a sectarian agenda. Where the state is robust enough to act equitably and justly, ruling regimes will at least have the tools to promote political inclusion and encourage tolerance if they so desire. But the weak institutions in fragile states are especially susceptible to elite capture and favoritism. As such, they provide greater incentives for leaders opportunistically to use religion (and other identity markers) to gain, maintain, and project power. Nigeria and Sudan provide two examples of how religion became interwoven with longstanding grievances among identity groups (T. Barnard 2011).

In Nigeria, religion has increasingly become a factor in conflict, but it still plays a smaller role than ethnicity and the perceived unfairness of the economic and political systems. Nigeria's late 1960s civil war was rooted in ethnic divisions, and the longstanding conflict in the Niger Delta is based on local grievances regarding the division of economic spoils coming from the exploitation of oil. Disputes over political power, land, the placing of markets, the identity of officials, and the division of the country's enormous natural resource wealth – disputes which plague a much broader swathe of the country – occur often among migrants and indigenous populations, local populations and the central government, or two or more of the country's 250-plus ethnic groups. Religious differences exacerbate existing tensions, such as those between the north (which is mainly Islamic) and the south (which is mainly Christian and animist). The rise of Boko Haram, the Muslim fundamentalist sect that has become the biggest threat to the country's stability in recent years, reflects the growing salience of religion, but the roots of the insurgency can be traced to social exclusion and a lack of development that contributes to the impoverishment of the country's northeastern region (Johnson 2013).

The decades-long war between Sudan and South Sudan (they fought between 1955 and 1972 and again between 1983 and 2005) was often described as being religious in nature, but in reality the disputes were rooted in longstanding racial, ethnic, linguistic, and geographical divisions, with religion only coming into play towards the end. Northerners (actually northern-ers from a relatively small part of the north) controlled the central government and received a disproportionate share of its resources, enjoying a middle-income level of wealth, while those in the south (and in most outlying areas of the state) had little infrastructure, few public services, and great poverty. Northerners wanted Arabic to be the national language, whereas people in the south preferred English. Northerners identified with the Arab world, while southerners considered themselves African. Only later on, when an Islamic fundamentalist government came to power in Khartoum and southerners allied themselves more with Christian actors outside the country, did religion begin to play a major role. Meanwhile, Christians have fought Christians (from different ethnic groups) in the south over land and cattle, and Muslims have fought Muslims in places such as Darfur.[3]

Religion's influence is starkest in regions where affiliation plays a prominent or dominant role shaping identity. Such conditions are common in the Middle East where, as Bernard Lewis notes, "religion, or more precisely membership of a religious community, is the ultimate determinant of identity . . . the focus of loyalty and, not less important, the source of authority" (Lewis 1998: 15, 22). In places such as Lebanon, Syria, Iraq, and Northern Ireland, religion has been ethni-cized, making social divisions more permanent (Little 2011: 9–28). In such places, conflict may take on the attributes of both ethnic and religious conflict and prove very hard to end.

Syria's demographic mosaic has always made it highly vulnerable to conflict, especially given the artificial nature of the existing state (which was established by European colonists less than a century ago). Two of the country's three sharpest divisions are rooted in religion: that between Alawites (a sect of Shiite Islam with syncretistic elements) and Sunnis and between highly pious and secular Sunnis. (The third sharp division is between the Kurds and everyone else.) While religion has always played a role in the jockeying for power among the country's many groups, the civil war has accentuated its importance, turning the conflict into something akin to a religious war.[4] Shiite Iran and Hezbollah support the Alawite (which they consider an allied faith) government against the Sunni insurgents (which consider it heretical) backed by Sunni regimes in Qatar, Saudi Arabia, and Turkey. The country's 11 Christian sects (which make up roughly one-tenth of the population) are likely, as has been the case elsewhere in the region, to be among the biggest losers from the increasing importance of religion in political life. These groups have no state of their own and no significant backer within the international community (the West has long since ceased to support its co-religionists in the region).

Neighboring Lebanon is similarly divided into confessional groups that jockey for power, with Sunnis, Shiites, and various Christian groups playing major political roles. The constitution attempts to mediate among these by dividing up power among them. Seats in parliament are reserved for 11 different confessional groups, with Christians and Muslims receiving half each in total. Positions in the government bureaucracy are allocated on a similar basis. The top three public offices are distributed to a Maronite Christian (the president), a Shi'a Muslim (the speaker of the parliament), and a Sunni Muslim (prime minister), with smaller sects receiving smaller positions. But, despite such complicated efforts at maintaining stability, peace has always been fragile in the country; it suffered from a 15-year civil war and is highly vulnerable to spillover from Syria's conflict.

Although the Sunni–Shiite divide has its modern roots in an ethnic nationalist geopolitical conflict between Iranians and Arabs and was not driven by theological precepts or religious doctrine, but rather by political power calculations, this may be changing. Religious identity and belief are increasingly a vehicle for choosing sides in conflict, mobilizing support, formation of organizations, distribution of patronage, and forging political and geopolitical alliances. Even though the rise of religion as a force across the Middle East and wider Islamic world can be traced back at least to 1979 (with the antecedents slowly building since the 1960s) when religious groups claimed power in Tehran and religious extremists seized the Grand Mosque in Mecca (the holiest site in Islam), the Iraq War starting in 2003 and the forces unleashed by the Arab Awakening starting in 2011 have certainly brought religious divisions to the fore. The power vacuum that typically accompanies the collapse of authority in fragile states has made groups based on subnational (or supranational) identities the only safe refuge when the state is unable to ensure security. Conflict between Sunni and Shi'a groups now stretches from the Arabian Peninsula through Iraq and Syria and into Lebanon. Beyond the Middle East, extremist groups regularly target Shiites for attack in majority Sunni Pakistan.[5]

Where religion is a source of conflict, it is important to distinguish between religious nationalists and religious fundamentalists (Brahm 2005). Whereas the former are closely tied to a political identity or political unit (such as when Buddhists take a nationalist position supporting the Sinhalese in Sri Lanka's conflict), the latter are primarily driven by displeasure with modernity and often see people from their own faith as posing as much of a threat as those from other faiths. While many fundamentalists are willing to work peaceably towards their goals (such as the Salafis in Egypt, who have done surprisingly well at the country's post-Mubarak polls), the most notorious (such as al-Qaeda) have made terrorism a prime instrument. Such groups play highly destabilizing roles in fragile states because governments in such places lack the capacity to deal effectively with the threats they pose. They can hold back development by preventing the delivery of healthcare services (such as polio vaccines), education of women, and use of technologies such as the internet. In Pakistan, Somalia, and Nigeria, these fundamentalist groups undermine weak governments and prevent millions from receiving basic public services.

In all these cases, religion is most destructive when leaders are able to use religious affinity or beliefs to cloak or even encourage behavior that would normally be considered unlawful and immoral. In Rwanda, to give an especially stark example, some Catholic and Protestant churches encouraged the genocide by giving moral sanction to the killing. They had laid the groundwork through years of actively practicing ethnic discrimination and teaching obedience to government authority (Longman 1997, 2011).

How religion reduces fragility

Religion's ability to build social cohesion and social capital – both of which do not play prominent roles in most development programming[6] – gives it great potential to fill unmet needs in fragile states. Religion can reduce fragility in two ways. First, religious leaders can work to strengthen the bonds and common identity that tie people together (e.g., by appealing to common beliefs across faiths), reducing the possibility that social differences will lead to stark divisions or conflict. Second, religious individuals and organizations can play important roles in conflict resolution, peacemaking, and the enhancement of how government works.

Just as the sociopolitical context determines how divisive religion can be, it also determines how constructive a role it can play. Where a population shares a common faith, for instance, religious leaders and organizations can leverage the resulting social cohesion to resolve conflict. On the other hand, where religion has contributed to conflict, social and political conditions may make initiatives by these same actors much more difficult – though not less essential. After all, few religious leaders are going to challenge their confessional communities in the midst of a brutal sectarian war in which religion features prominently, such as the one in Syria.

Religious actors can promote stability or exacerbate fragility, depending on how their faith is understood and employed. Both violence-legitimating extremists and violence-renouncing peacemakers draw upon the same sources. As Scott Appleby writes:

> Tradition, in its fullness, encompasses the range of interpretations that have accumulated over time and achieved authoritative status because its supporters have probed, clarified, and developed the insights and teachings contained in their primary texts. To be traditional, then, is to take seriously not only the foundational sources of the religion, but also the various authoritative interpretations of these sources.
>
> (Appleby 2012: 249)

Religious leaders and organizations can reduce social fractures by appealing to religious tenets to frame political discourse in ways that promote respect, coexistence, compromise, forgiveness, and inclusiveness. They can also actively work to promote a stronger national identity (opposing parochial calls for putting one faith group above the needs of the state), build bridges with those from other religious groups, and develop institutions that work to promote a common agenda. In conflict zones, religious actors from outside may understand the issues better than a secular actor (Cox and Philpott 2012: 260) and may have a better chance at brokering a peace than anyone identified with one of the sides. Strong ties across social divides and a reputation for equitable and fair conduct are key in such places, but they take years if not decades to build up. In Mozambique, the Philippines, Guatemala, and Algeria, for instance, religious leaders have played a crucial role in brokering peace in conflict zones. In South Africa and Northern Ireland, they helped build and sustain processes to advance reconciliation in divided societies (Appleby *et al.* 2010).

According to Douglas Johnston, religious leaders and organizations can be very well placed to play critical roles in fragile states because of their high levels of credibility and trust, moral warrants to better society, leverage for advancing reconciliation between groups, ability to mobilize their communities, and a sense of calling that can inspire them to overcome obstacles that would deter others (Johnston n.d.: 3). To be sure, this depends on the context and role of religion in these places. In the case of individuals, David Little concludes that practitioners of religious peacemaking "have unique stature because of their religious identities . . . this gives them stature in the community and credibility to lead. It also gives them the standing to draw on religious resources in a call to forgive and to recognize the humanity of the 'other'" (Little 2007: 4–6). At the very highest levels political and development actors are now explicitly making statements about the constructive role that religious actors can play in bringing conflict to an end. In a somewhat broad – yet rhetorically powerful – statement UN Secretary-General Kofi Annan concluded in his 2002 report on the prevention of armed conflict that "religious organizations can play a role in preventing armed conflict because of the moral authority that they carry in many communities" (Little 2007: 4).

There are notable recent examples of how religious leaders and organizations can help resolve conflict. In South Africa, for instance, Anglican archbishop Desmond Tutu battled apartheid and then worked toward reconciliation between whites and blacks in South Africa after it was ended. As head of the country's Truth and Reconciliation Commission, he led efforts to heal the wounds from conflict through a process of restorative justice and truth seeking. The resulting social and political stability has been so widely admired that countries such as Sierra Leone, Guatemala, and Liberia have instituted similar commissions (Amnesty International n.d.).

In Nigeria, many interfaith religious organizations have worked to bring Muslims and Christians together, reduce violence, improve public services, and strengthen weak social bonds. Among these, two stand out. The Interfaith Mediation Centre, led by Reverend James Wuye and Imam Mohammed Ashafa, has trained young religious leaders in conflict resolution, sponsored a summit of religious leaders to combat violence during the 2007 election, and worked to reduce violence in places such as Kaduna and Plateau states (Interfaith Mediation Centre n.d.). The Nigerian Inter-Faith Action Association, co-chaired by the Sultan of Sokoto, Muhammadu Sa'ad Abubakar, president of the Nigerian Supreme Council of Islamic Affairs, and Pastor Ayo Oritsejafor, president of the Christian Association of Nigeria, has brought together Christian and Muslim leaders and communities to work together to combat poverty and disease (Center for Interfaith Action 2011). Prominent Muslim leaders, such as the Sultan of Sokoto, will have to make every effort to counter the extremist message of the religious fundamentalist group Boko Haram and to prevent those harboring deep grievances against the state from supporting the group if it is to be defeated (Zenn 2013).

In Sierra Leone, the Inter-Religious Council emerged as the most effective bridge builder between warring factions during the country's years of violence, partly because religion was never a driving factor in the conflict. Despite their spiritual differences, war brought Muslims and Christians closer together as they realized how much they needed each other to confront the country's challenges. Religious leaders preached against the barbaric nature of the violence and used their influence to work towards a peaceful resolution (Appleby 2000: 153–4; Turay 2000: 50–53).

The Community of Sant'Egidio, a Catholic lay association, played a prominent role facilitating the end of the 16-year war in Mozambique (which took over 1 million lives) because it had strong personal ties with the warring parties and special insight into their way of thinking. The organization's long experience working as a social service provider in the country and deep network of friendships gave it the credibility and relationships to act as mediator, influence the attitudes and actions of political leaders, and shape and monitor negotiations (Appleby 2012: 247; Cox and Philpott 2012: 257). It has worked on peace initiatives in Algeria, the Balkans, the Democratic Republic of the Congo, and other areas, in the belief that war is the "mother of every poverty."[7]

Religious organizations and networks: catalysts for development

As the preceding examples illustrate, religious actors have a remarkable role to play in resolving conflict and strengthening social cohesion in fragile states. The international development community can engage a variety of faith groups in pursuing development in such contexts. These groups include formal religious organizations (including institutions such as faith-based non-governmental organizations, schools, self-help associations, and places of worship) and informal faith networks (which are generally groupings of people with similar beliefs or backgrounds).

Religious groups of all kinds are often as strong as government is weak in fragile states: they shape values and develop skills; they are the primary means of association and of conflict management; and they offer a way to build social capital and to hold community leaders more accountable. As Gerrie ter Haar and Stephen Ellis explain:

> In many of Africa's poorest countries, effective, centralized bureaucracies hardly exist. . . . In countries of this type, power is, literally, dis-integrated. It becomes a matter of necessity rather than choice to consider how development could be enhanced

by using the resources in society at large. Many of the communities or social networks that carry the burden of development have a religious form or convey religious ideas in some sense.

(ter Haar and Ellis 2006: 362)

In the Middle East, the region with the second-highest proportion of states that are fragile after Africa, Islamic organizations have in many cases – and certainly in all the poorest communities – such legitimacy and constituency that it would be hard to effect substantial change without their participation. Indeed, various studies and symposia have concluded that there is enormous potential "in more purposeful efforts to associate development issues, practices, and organizations with Muslim traditions and actors" (Berkley Center and Center for International and Regional Studies 2007).

Whereas the government may barely exist outside a few main cities in some fragile states, closely knit religious groups (and traditional social groupings that have a strong religious component) often are deeply enmeshed in communities across a country, providing the most reliable form of security, justice, and support, especially for the poor. The more cohesive groups, such as the Mouride brotherhood (a large Islamic Sufi order found in parts of West Africa) and the Sikhs in India, have been able to leverage their spiritual networks to foster entrepreneurship, trade, and wealth creation in ways their host states cannot.

Religious organizations are often the only locally based groups working among the destitute, filling in for the state where it is too feeble to provide even basic schooling and healthcare. From the Congo to Pakistan, these more formal groups have a tangible and profound impact on the everyday activities of people underserved by their governments. They are essential providers of education, health, humanitarian relief, and microfinance to hundreds of millions of people. They range from large Western-based, faith-based development organizations such as Catholic Relief Services, World Vision, the American Jewish Joint Distribution Committee, and Islamic Relief to the much smaller locally based organizations typically centered on places of worship or on madrasas, seminaries, and other religious schools. Local religious organizations account for the bulk of organized group activity in many places, provide the primary means of relief for families in crises, and even play major roles in economic endeavors. The World Bank's 2000 *Voices of the Poor* study confirmed that, "in ratings of effectiveness in both urban and rural settings, religious organizations feature more prominently than any single type of state institution" (Narayan *et al.* 2000: 222).

The contribution of these groups is especially palpable in the education and health sectors. They deliver, for example, significant portions of all such services in many Sub-Saharan African countries, according to the World Bank (Wolfensohn 2004). In some places, such as parts of the DRC and Pakistan, churches and mosques have effectively replaced the state as the primary supplier of public goods. One study concluded that "the only significant reductions in HIV prevalence that have been recorded [in Uganda] are in contexts where the faith community took on a leadership role" (Berkley Center 2007: 20).

Religious organizations also attract and develop human capital. Given the loss of confidence in formal government institutions and the dearth of professional opportunities available in stagnant, unstable environments, many talented local people see religious organizations as one of the best outlets for their ambitions and energies, producing a noticeable shift of entrepreneurial skills from politics and business to religious entities. Groups such as Sri Lanka's Buddhist Sarvodaya Shramadana Movement (Sarvodaya), Turkey's Muslim Gülen movement, and Latin America's Jesuit-based Fe y Alegría all have used their reputation to attract highly capable people to contribute creatively to their societies.[8] Africa is full of burgeoning churches that provide a platform for people to improve their lives in a way no other institution can. Congregants gain access to a broad range of services and support groups while learning leadership skills. The most dynamic people in the least developed places often head up a church, mosque, or temple.

Working with religious organizations and networks

Faith often plays such an outsized role in the lives of people in fragile states that taking advantage of religion's values, organizations, and capacities to transform behavior and promote cooperation is one of the few ways to change the dynamics of development in fractured, dysfunctional countries. There are several avenues for international development organizations to partner with religious actors and groups as they serve populations in fragile states. These include developing management capacity, enhancing the ability to deliver services, expanding education, and leveraging networks' influence.

International mediators could help local religious leaders reach across social divides to work with organizations that represent other religious or ethnic groups, increasing the potential for conflict resolution. Similarly, training local spiritual and administrative leaders – everyone from ministers and imams to school principals and the heads of *waqf* foundations – on conflict resolution, management, economics, education, and social welfare would help their organizations take on larger projects, expand their services, and improve their operations. Measures that enhance the management of religious organizations would have a multiplier effect, as the better such institutions function the more likely they will be able to expand their services.

Development actors can assist religious organizations in expanding programs that deliver needed services to local communities. Assisting well-established institutions in introducing (in partnership, perhaps, with NGOs or private companies) savings and loans schemes, sanitation and garbage-collection systems, and housing development cooperatives could speed the spread of such programs throughout the developing world. Leveraging informal faith networks to promote services such as microlending and trade facilitation – services that require strong group-based social ties to ensure compliance with commitments – could open new opportunities for members of the networks to advance themselves.

Greater financial and material aid from the international community could enable mosques, churches, and temples to expand the numbers of poor children who benefit from the schooling they provide. The consequent boost in levels of literacy could, in turn, enable the poor to participate more fully in social, political, and economic life, give developing economies a better chance of meeting the challenges of globalization, and improve many other development indicators. An expansion of faith-based education might result in mixed outcomes in parts of the Muslim world, where local madrasas play a key role in delivering education but have been accused of spreading political fundamentalism. Since 9/11, many international development actors and local groups have encouraged madrasas to renounce extremism and introduce new subjects, including secular subjects, into their curricula. For instance, the International Center for Religion and Diplomacy (ICRD), based in Washington, DC, has trained leaders of Pakistani madrasas in "critical thinking skills, religious tolerance, and human rights" while reminding them of their religion's pioneering breakthroughs in the arts and sciences (Johnston 2009). Such efforts could usefully be expanded.

Finally, both religious organizations and informal religious networks offer opportunities to enhance government accountability and performance – but these opportunities usually depend on religious leaders to take the initiative. A partnership of the major religious organizations within a city or region could constitute a powerful lobby for bottom-up reform of state institutions and for greater accountability of officials. Such a partnership could gradually be extended to encompass other stakeholders with similar interests in government reform (such as compan tribal chiefs, and non-religious NGOs). Informal social networks shape values and behavior and could be used to persuade bureaucrats and businesspeople to eschew corruption (by, for instance, making such changes in behavior a prominent part of sermons).

To be sure, religious groups can cause problems. In addition to inspiring violence and acting as effective recruiting sergeants for terrorism (as discussed above), religious groups can also foster social exclusion in some contexts, and thereby contribute to poverty, disempowerment, and conflict. In some contexts, religious actors can discriminate against women and undermine attempts to improve human rights.[9] (In fact, local concepts of human rights may differ widely from international norms.) Proselytism (actual or perceived) in plural settings can foster mistrust and foment conflict, as has happened in places as diverse as Pakistan, Russia, and Nigeria (Dwarswaard 2010).

Any undertaking that engages religion in fragile states, and beyond, needs to be careful on a number of fronts. In particular, any activity that smacks of favoring one faith or denomination over another risks exacerbating, rather than healing, divisions. Outside assistance needs to be distributed in an evenhanded fashion, so that no religious community feels itself excluded from international largesse. The provision of assistance must also be handled very carefully when dealing with any organization that proselytizes, especially in a sectarian environment. The goal should be to ensure that aid is not used in any way to promote a specific religious or political viewpoint and that, where it is used to fund the delivery of services, those services are available without discrimination to everyone in a given area.

While care should also be taken to ensure that any monies distributed to local organizations do not end up with terrorists, in places such as Lebanon, Gaza, and Pakistan organizations such as Hezbollah and Hamas provide citizens with many of their most important public services in the absence of capable public authority. In Syria, millions of people may end up living in regions controlled by Jabhat al-Nusra, an al-Qaeda affiliate. Such situations are enormously complex and naturally produce moral dilemmas that are hard for any aid organization to tackle. A tradeoff between alleviating hardship and avoiding helping violent actors may not be avoidable.[10] In Somalia, Al-Shabaab, a terrorist organization, exploited the 2011 famine to collect "tax payments" from aid organizations seeking to help the millions suffering in the region they controlled (Tran 2013).

In order to take advantage of the human resources embedded in religious networks, Western development organizations, donors, multilateral organizations, and NGOs must seek a closer – and more evenhanded – partnership with local communities and the faith groups that play such prominent roles within those communities. This will require major changes in how these organizations operate. Besides reconsidering how development actually occurs – and how this might affect their programs – they will also have to reevaluate "the secular gospel underpinning the development enterprise" (Clarke 2005: 3) and begin "taking seriously people's worldviews and considering their potential for the development process as a whole" (ter Haar and Ellis 2006: 353). Western organizations that treat religion and development as separate and even incompatible fields not only undermine their program effectiveness but also risk offending and alienating the people of the communities they wish to serve (Deneulin and Bano 2009). This danger is especially acute in non-Christian environments, where local populations tend to equate "Western" with "Christian" and thus will regard any criticism of their religion (or indifference toward it) as a Christian slur.

International development organizations could be more effective dealing with the wide range of religious institutions and actors in fragile states if they stop emphasizing the amount of aid they disburse and focus instead on ensuring that financing complements and reinforces local capacities and institutions. Too often, they end up undermining or warping local arrangements by making local organizations dependent on foreign largess. While such organizations may gain prestige from the size of their budgets, community building based on a large number of small organizations – and most of the religious organizations that serve the poor are small – requires a delicate approach consisting of modest, carefully targeted investments that reinforce capacities without undermining internal coherence and accountability. Understanding the special needs of – and crafting the right strategy to partner with – the large number of small organizations in underdeveloped areas may even require the creation of a new, intermediary organization to work at "arm's length" to bridge the gulf between large donors and multinational NGOs and the many small grassroots entities that need support.[11]

Conclusion: conditions for cooperation

Many scholars and practitioners have pointed out the conditions under which international engagement with religious actors in fragile states can go wrong, but little thought has been done figuring out the conditions under which engagement with religious actors actually goes right. The field needs:

- a more careful empirical assessment and comparison of the types of approaches, programs, and projects through which external actors have sought to address conflict-inducing religious divisions through aid-funded projects;
- a better catalogue of lessons learned on the extent to which cooperative relationships between religious communities and governments may facilitate peace and development (lessen fragility);
- a better catalogue of the extent and quality of services offered by religious organizations in fragile states;
- a more careful empirical assessment and comparison of informal faith-based social networks and how they can be utilized to promote development and improve governance in states with weak institutions;
- a better understanding of how religious organizations work together and/or compete and how these dynamics affect fragility and development;
- a more careful empirical assessment and comparison of the types of approaches, programs, and projects with which secular donors and diplomats can successfully engage with religious organizations.

Religions comprise a vast and complex body of ideas, rituals, values, and wisdom accumulated over centuries. Their rich traditions have much to contribute to today's challenges. International development actors seeking to engage religion's potential in fragile states should foster a curiosity about local contexts and seek out opportunities for cooperation with people of faith.

Notes

1 "Ethnic diversity has a more adverse effect on economic policy and growth when institutions are poor. To put it another way, poor institutions have an even more adverse effect on growth and policy when ethnic diversity is high. Conversely, in countries with sufficiently good institutions, ethnic diversity does not lower growth or worsen economic policies" (Easterly 2000: 12).

2 For further understanding of the drivers of conflict, look at the larger "need, greed, creed" debate. See, for instance, Arnson and Zartman (2005).

3 For a good overview of the causes of conflict in Sudan, see de Waal (2007). For an overview of the identity issues, see Deng (1995).

4 See, for instance, A. Barnard and Saad (2013).

5 For more on the sectarian dimensions of the conflict, see Nasr (2006), Abdo (2013), and Wehrey (2013).

6 These have gained credence at the international policy level, but this attention has rarely translated into action at the programming level. See, for instance, Marc *et al.* (2012).

7 This quote is a maxim of the organization. See http://www.santegidio.org/en/pace/.

8 See websites for: Sarvodaya, http://www.sarvodaya.org; Fethullah Gülen, http://en.fgulen.com; and Fe y Alegría, http://www.feyalegria.org/en.

9 There are examples of this worldwide. See, for example, DeLong-Bas (2010) and Human Rights Watch (2013).

10 For a more in-depth analysis of this area, see Flannigan (2009).

11 I discuss this concept in more detail in Kaplan (2010). David Booth has suggested something similar to overcome the problems aid agencies have had trying to nurture governance reform. See Booth (2013).

References

Abdo, G. (2013) *The New Sectarianism: The Arab Uprisings and the Rebirth of the Shi'a–Sunni Divide*, Washington, DC: Saban Center for Middle East Policy at Brookings.

Amnesty International (n.d.) 'Truth Commissions', http://www.amnesty.org/en/international-justice/issues/truth-commissions.

Appleby, S. (2000) *The Ambivalence of the Sacred: Religion, Violence, and Reconciliation*, New York: Rowman & Littlefield.

Appleby, S. (2012) 'Religion and Global Affairs: Religious "Militants for Peace"', in D. Hoover and D. Johnston (eds), *Religion and Foreign Affairs: Essential Readings*, Waco, TX: Baylor University Press.

Appleby, S., Cizik, R. and Wright, T. (2010) *Engaging Religious Communities Abroad: A New Imperative for U.S. Foreign Policy*, Chicago: Chicago Council on Global Affairs Task Force on Religion and the Making of U.S. Foreign Policy.

Arnson, C. and Zartman, W. (eds) (2005) *Rethinking the Economics of War: The Intersection of Need, Creed, and Greed*, Baltimore, MD: Johns Hopkins University Press.

Barnard, A. and Saad, H. (2013) 'Sunni Cleric Issues Appeal for World's Muslims to Help Syrian Rebels', *New York Times*, 1 June, http://www.nytimes.com/2013/06/02/world/middleeast/syria-developments.html?hp&_r=0.

Barnard, T. (2011) 'The Role of Religion in African Conflicts: The Cases of Nigeria and Sudan', unpublished paper, https://www.academia.edu/715044/THE_ROLE_OF_RELIGION_IN_AFRICAN_CONFLICTS_THE_CASES_OF_NIGERIA_AND_SUDAN.

Berkley Center for Religion, Peace and World Affairs (2007) *Mapping the Role of Faith Communities in Development Policy: The US Case in International Perspective*, Washington, DC: Georgetown University.

Berkley Center for Religion, Peace and World Affairs and Center for International and Regional Studies (2007) 'Global Development and Faith-Inspired Organizations in the Muslim World', Symposium, Doha, Qatar, 17 December, http://cirs.georgetown.edu/research/program/101585.html.

Booth, D. (2013) *Facilitating Development: An Arm's Length Approach to Aid*, London: Overseas Development Institute, http://www.odi.org.uk/publications/7376-facilitating-development-arms-length-approach-aid.

Brahm, E. (2005) 'Religion and Conflict', in G. Burgess and H. Burgess (eds), *Beyond Intractability*, Boulder, CO: University of Colorado, Conflict Research Consortium, http://www.beyondintractability.org/bi-essay/religion-and-conflict.

Center for Interfaith Action (2011) 'Interfaith Action on Malaria: Nigeria Success Spurs Additional Investment', press release, http://www.cifa.org/images/stories/docs/interfaith_action_on_malaria_nigeria_results_september_2011.pdf.

Chandy, L., Ledlie, N. and Penciakova, V. (2013) *The Final Countdown: Prospects for Ending Extreme Poverty by 2030 (Interactive)*, Washington, DC: Brookings Institution, http://www.brookings.edu/research/interactives/2013/ending-extreme-poverty#fragile_states.

Clarke, G. (2005) 'Faith Matters: Development and the Complex World of Faith-Based Organisations', paper presented at the Development Studies Association annual conference, Milton Keynes, 7–9 September.

Cox, B. and Philpott, D. (2012) 'Faith-Based Diplomacy: An Ancient Idea Newly Emergent', in D. Hoover and D. Johnston (eds), *Religion and Foreign Affairs: Essential Readings*, Waco, TX: Baylor University Press.

DeLong-Bas, N. (2010) 'Women, Islam, and the Twenty-First Century', *Oxford Islamic Studies Online*, http://www.oxfordislamicstudies.com/Public/focus/essay1107_women.html.

Deneulin, S. and Bano, M. (2009) *Religion in Development: Rewriting the Secular Script*, London: Zed Books.

Deng, F. (1995) *War of Visions: Conflict of Identities in the Sudan*, Washington, DC: Brookings Institution Press.

de Waal, A. (2007) *Sudan: What Kind of State? What Kind of Crisis?*, Occasional Paper no. 2, London: Crisis States Research Centre.

Di John, J. (2008) *Conceptualising the Causes and Consequences of Failed States: A Critical Review of the Literature*, Working Paper no. 25, London: Crisis States Research Centre.

Dwarswaard, E. (2010) *Proselytism and Conversion Zeal*, Utrecht: Knowledge Centre for Religion and Development, http://www.religion-and-development.nl/documentation-centre/3411/proselytism-and-conversion-zeal#2114.

Easterly, W. (2000) *Can Institutions Resolve Ethnic Conflict?*, Policy Research Working Paper Series 2482, Washington, DC: World Bank.

Flannigan, S. (2009) *For the Love of God: NGOs and Religious Identity in a Violent World*, Boulder, CO: Kumarian Press.

Foreign Policy and Fund for Peace (2012) 'The 2012 Failed States Index', http://www.foreignpolicy.com/failed_states_index_2012_interactive.

g7+ (2011) 'The g7+ of Fragile and Conflict-Affected States', http://www.g7plus.org/.

Ghani, A. and Lockhart, C. (2008) *Fixing Failed States*, New York: Oxford University Press.

Hudson, M. (1977) *Arab Politics: The Search for Legitimacy*, New Haven, CT: Yale University Press.

Human Rights Watch (2013) *World Report 2013: Afghanistan*, http://www.hrw.org/world-report/2013/country-chapters/afghanistan.

Institute for Economics and Peace (2013) 'Global Peace Index 2013', http://www.visionofhumanity.org/#page/indexes/global-peace-index/2013.

Interfaith Mediation Centre (n.d.), Website, http://www.imcnigeria.org/.

Johnson, T. (2013) *Boko Haram*, Backgrounder, New York: Council on Foreign Relations, http://www.cfr.org/nigeria/boko-haram/p25739.

Johnston, D. (n.d.) 'The Religious Dimension', unpublished paper, based upon D. Johnston (ed.) (2003) *Trumping Realpolitik: Faith-Based Diplomacy*, New York: Oxford University Press.

Johnston, D. (2009) 'Madrassa Reform Key', *Washington Times*, 7 August, http://icrd.org/madrassa-reform-key.

Kaplan, S. (2008) *Fixing Fragile States: A New Paradigm for Development*, Westport, CT: Praeger Security International.

Kaplan, S. (2010) 'Inspiring Development in Fragile States', *Review of Faith and International Affairs*, 8 (4), 11–21.

Kaplan, S. (2014) 'How to Identify Truly Fragile States', *Washington Quarterly*, 37 (1), 49–63.

Lewis, B. (1998) *The Multiple Identities of the Middle East*, New York: Schocken Books.

Little, D. (2007) *Peacemakers in Action: Profiles of Religion in Conflict Resolution*, Cambridge: Cambridge University Press.

Little, D. (2011) 'Religion, Nationalism, and Intolerance', in T. Sisk (ed.), *Between Terror and Tolerance: Religious Leaders, Conflict, and Peacemaking*, Washington, DC: Georgetown University Press.

Longman, T. (1997) 'Christian Churches and Genocide in Rwanda', paper prepared for Conference on Genocide, Religion, and Modernity, United States Holocaust Memorial Museum, Washington, DC, 11–13 May, http://faculty.vassar.edu/tilongma/Church&Genocide.html.

Longman, T. (2011) *Christianity and Genocide in Rwanda*, Cambridge: Cambridge University Press.

Marc, A., Willman, A., Aslam, G. and Rebosio, M. (2012) *Societal Dynamics and Fragility: Engaging Societies in Responding to Fragile Situations*, Washington, DC: World Bank.

Marshall, M. and Cole, B. (2011) *Global Report 2011: Conflict, Governance, and State Fragility*, Vienna, VA: Center for Systemic Peace, http://www.systemicpeace.org/GlobalReport2011.pdf.

Narayan, D., Chambers, R., Shah, M. and Petesch, P. (2000) *Voices of the Poor: Crying Out for Change*, Washington, DC: World Bank.

Nasr, V. (2006) *The Shia Revival: How Conflicts within Islam Will Shape the Future*, New York: W. W. Norton.

OECD (Organisation for Economic Co-operation and Development) (2010) *The State's Legitimacy in Fragile Situations: Unpacking Complexity*, Paris: OECD, Development Assistance Committee (DAC) International Network on Conflict and Fragility (INCAF).

OECD (Organisation for Economic Co-operation and Development) (2011) *International Engagement in Fragile States: Can't We Do Better?*, Paris: OECD.

OECD (Organisation for Economic Co-operation and Development) (2013) 'Conflict and Fragility', Development Assistance Committee (DAC) International Network on Conflict and Fragility (INCAF) web page, http://www.oecd.org/dac/incaf/.

Patrick, S. (2011) *Weak Links: Fragile States, Global Threats, and International Security*, New York: Oxford University Press.

Political Instability Task Force (2013) Home page, http://globalpolicy.gmu.edu/political-instability-task-force-home/.

Putnam, R. (1993) *Making Democracy Work: Civic Traditions in Modern Italy*, Princeton, NJ: Princeton University Press.

Rice, S. and Patrick, S. (2008) *Index of State Weakness in the Developing World*, Washington, DC: Brookings Institution, http://www.brookings.edu/reports/2008/02_weak_states_index.aspx.

Rotberg, R. (2002) 'Failed States in a World of Terror', *Foreign Affairs*, 81 (2), 127–40.

Sisk, T. (2011) 'From Terror to Tolerance to Coexistence in Deeply Divided Societies', in T. Sisk (ed.), *Between Terror and Tolerance: Religious Leaders, Conflict, and Peacemaking*, Washington, DC: Georgetown University Press.

Smock, D. (2008) *Religion in World Affairs: Its Role in Conflict and Peace*, Special Report, Washington, DC: United States Institute of Peace, http://www.usip.org/files/resources/sr201.pdf.

Stewart, F. (ed.) (2010) *Horizontal Inequalities and Conflict: Understanding Group Violence in Multiethnic Societies*, London: Palgrave.

ter Haar, G. and Ellis, S. (2006) 'The Role of Religion in Development: Towards a New Relationship between the European Union and Africa', *European Journal of Development Research*, 18 (3), 351–67.

Tran, M. (2013) 'Al-Shabaab in Somalia Exploited Aid Agencies during 2011 Famine – Report', *theguardian.com*, December 8, http://www.theguardian.com/global-development/2013/dec/09/al-shabaab-somalia-exploited-aid-agencies-famine.

Turay, T. M. (2000) 'Civil Society and Peacebuilding: The Role of the Inter-Religious Council of Sierra Leone', *Accord* (Conciliation Resources), 9, http://www.c-r.org/sites/c-r.org/files/Accord%20 09_10Civil%20society%20and%20peacebuilding_2000_ENG.pdf.

Wehrey, F. (2013) *Sectarian Politics in the Gulf: From the Iraq War to the Arab Uprisings*, New York: Columbia University Press.

Wolfensohn, J. (2004) 'Millennium Challenges for Faith and Development: New Partnerships to Reduce Poverty and Strengthen Conservation', speech to the Interfaith Conference of Metropolitan Washington, Trinity College, Washington, DC, 30 March.

World Bank (2013) 'Harmonized List of Fragile Situations FY13', http://siteresources.worldbank.org/EXTLICUS/Resources/511777-1269623894864/FCSHarmonizedListFY13.pdf.

Zenn, J. (2013) 'Potential Role for Traditional Muslim Leaders to Counter Boko Haram', *Africa in Transition Blog*, 18 April, http://blogs.cfr.org/campbell/2013/04/18/potential-role-for-traditional-muslim-leaders-to-counter-boko-haram/.

29

DEVELOPMENT ORGANIZATIONS' SUPPORT FOR FAITH-BASED EDUCATION

Recent turns toward ethics and dialogue

Amy Stambach[1]

Introduction

The World Bank's World Faiths Development Dialogue (WFDD) was established in 1998. This relatively recent founding is remarkable in view of the fact that – notwithstanding conventional arguments to the contrary – western development policies have long been framed in and through Christianized forms of schooling.[2] Yet the year 1998 was approaching a pivotal time in roughly two decades' thinking about the place of religion in public life. During these decades, the World Bank and other post-World War II reconstructionist organizations sought to demonstrate greater social and community relevance: there was a "turn to religion," including channeling the energies of increasingly politicized religious groups into schools and voucher programs. UNESCO's Association for Interreligious Dialogue, founded in 1997, described itself as promoting discussion "among different religions, spiritual and humanistic traditions" (United Nations n.d.). The World Bank described its mission as alleviating poverty and combating social injustices by working with faith organizations, development institutions, philanthropists, and the private sector (UNESCO n.d.). Together these organizations and others reflected the charitable-religious spirit that – notwithstanding the mid-twentieth-century secularist turn toward thinking about religion as private – continued to inflect education development discourse.

Analysis of the WFDD's and other agencies' support for faith-based education – and discussion of what has come after yesterday's religious turn – provides a fertile field for examining the changing moral frameworks that underpin development agencies past and present. Accordingly, this chapter focuses on international agencies' support for faith-based education policies and programs, asking how religion in developmentalist discourse is gauged and where it is heading today. I argue that the "turn to religion" of the early twenty-first century is giving way to a more quiet use of religion to deliver educational programs and commodities, including through partnerships that faith groups are making with private companies and government agencies, and that this "quiet evangelism" works with new international partners including China and Brazil to develop new relationships of business investment, inspired by a "good works" philosophy.

Put concretely, I argue that religious organizations today work with governments to establish a moral basis for pursuing capitalist development. Thus the term "faith-based" that came to prominence in the 1990s is becoming a more secularized version of the same. Within developmentalist discourse, "ethics" and "dialogue" are key words now, and "faith-based" is moving to the sub-text of discussion. And the somewhat paradoxical language of "rallying the armies of compassion" as a way of privately funding basic education that was prominent in the early 2000s is turning to one of "lending a hand" to emerging economies in a world where China, India and Brazil are increasingly viewed by international development agencies as partners and platforms for delivering aid and education to the poor.

The fact that religion, within developmentalist discourse, has waxed and waned as an explicit "delivery" mechanism and topic of discussion raises the immediate question: in its current phase, how entrenched is religion within development programs involving education? Is religion integral to development policy? Is it a way of aligning international work to an image of international foreign policy, or possibly a means for leaders of economically poor countries to motivate and fund development? I argue here that it is a combination of these. I support my argument with reference to court cases and policies pertaining to religion and education, with regard to how certain national discussions and foreign policy interests (particularly of the US) work to align international programs with an ideology of economic growth at home, and finally with reference to how development discourses of charitable giving link with, for example, Chinese emphases on contractualism and neo-Confucianist ethics within education.

Is religion a public or private matter? From private schools to vouchers and beyond

From questions of evolution versus creationism in the United States to matters of veiling and secularism in Turkey or France, debates about religion and education often turn on the question of whether religion is a public or a private concern. This debate is typically framed in either–or terms within development studies and agencies, but in fact the distinction between public religion and private life – particularly when it comes to education – is not simple. To be sure, many governments restrict religious activity to a specialized, private sphere; however, some have argued that even this relegation of religion to the private is a manifestation of certain expressions of Protestant Christianity, whereby the individual is regarded as the self-responsible agent and the state is to interfere at most minimally with this form of personal liberty.

In the United States, the idea that religion is a private matter derives from the First Amendment to the US Constitution, which states that the federal government may neither endorse any religion nor prevent the expression thereof. Thus, the Constitution restricts religion to a specialized sphere of the socially discrete and private. Yet when it comes to education, the matter of religion is often polarized, as it was in a relatively recent case regarding the teaching of evolution versus intelligent design in a Pennsylvania public school. In 2005, a US District Court judge ruled against parents who required that teachers read aloud a statement about intelligent design to students in a ninth-grade science class. The ruling turned on the principle that intelligent design could not be taught as science. Yet parents saw this ruling as a threat to their community's faith and religious practice. Why? Because these parents did not feel that private religion could be separated from public life, any more than religion could be separated from science.

Such "maximalist" views of religion as all-encompassing informed popular support for US faith-based community initiatives enacted by President George W. Bush through executive order. In January 2001, President Bush signed an executive order establishing the White House Office of Faith-Based and Community Initiatives (OFBCI). Also in 2001, President

Bush requested, in a letter to the Senate Majority Leader, that Congress pass and sign into law a so-called Armies of Compassion bill that allowed charitable tax deductions for all income levels, protected faith groups from discrimination in access to federal funding, and supported faith groups' mentoring and assistance to populations in need, particularly children with parents in prison (in the UK, such assistance would be called "pastoral care"). The proposed Armies of Compassion bill gave rise to the Compassion Capital Fund and was signed into law in January 2002. In December 2002, President Bush used executive orders to grant "equal treatment" to religious groups applying for federal contracts (Baptist Joint Committee for Religious Liberty n.d.; US Government, n.d.a, n.d.b, n.d.c). By 2003, branch Offices of Faith-Based and Community Initiatives were established in eight offices of government: the Departments of Justice, Labor, Health and Human Services, Housing and Urban Development, Education, and Agriculture, the Agency for International Development (USAID) and the Corporation for National Community Services. On the face of it, such offices appeared to break the US constitutional requirement of separating church and state, but close reading of the public record suggests that the Offices of Faith-Based and Community Initiatives (OFBCI) since then through today require that religious activity remain separate "in time and place" from delivery of educational programs – including those located overseas – that are funded by the US government. Yet, as I have shown elsewhere, religious groups whose members deliver public education do not conceive of their faith as something they hold in private (Stambach 2010a, 2010b). Even if the law requires they segregate religion from secular activity, in practice these groups make no distinction: public life, many argue, is necessarily and thoroughly infused with the chance to demonstrate their firm belief in Christianity. Thus while many evangelizing educators may follow the law literally and hold classes in secular and not religious spaces, spiritually many make no public-secular/private-religious distinction.

Although a US model arguably dominates international policy because of the US government's disproportionate political and financial influence within international organizations, particularly the World Bank and UNESCO,[3] the relationship between public education and private faith takes many forms. In Commonwealth member countries, including Canada, legal frameworks allow a particular relation between government and faith groups working in public education that the US Constitution does not permit. In Canada, Parliament recognizes the Protestant United Church of Canada and permits provincial governments to fund some Catholic schools. Yet, in the 1980s and 1990s, questions about religious education in Canada also came to the fore. In 1996, non-Catholic parents (Jewish and evangelical Christian) asked the Ontario provincial government to fund their religious schools. When the Canadian Supreme Court denied their request but continued to support Catholic and Church of Canada schools, plaintiffs argued that the government discriminated on the basis of religious affiliation. The Canadian case is an interesting one in which arguments about religious neutrality reflect a historical legacy of support for some but not all religious schools.

The argument of Canadian evangelical and Jewish parents is not dissimilar to that of some Islamic groups I have studied in East Africa, who maintain that the post-colonial system of government-sponsored education – as well as development programs funded through North American and UK-dominated international organizations – bear a European colonial and Christian education legacy. These groups point to the religious affiliations of key personnel within systems of education administration and to the organization of the curricula and timetable, which are implicitly oriented toward Christian practices even though a broad-based religious education is included as a subject. Through the 1990s and through at least 2009, when the World Bank published *Emerging Evidence on Vouchers and Faith-Based Providers in Education: Case Studies from Africa, Latin America, and Asia*, such groups as the Islamic groups I studied lobbied for separate state-supported schools and, in some cases, for government vouchers. Instead of the state directly funding faith schools, vouchers were meant to offset the costs incurred by families who chose to send their children to private religious schools.

As in the US and Canada, where vouchers gained a degree of favor at this time on the grounds that they might help to offset economic inequalities between the socially marginalized religious and those more fully enfranchised, voucher programs also gained ground in the UK and other parts of Europe. Together with North American views, European perspectives influenced international development thinking. The Education Group in the Human Development Network at the World Bank, for example, largely composed of North American and EU-educated consultants and advisors, supported voucher programs – not in the sense of direct funding for vouchers but in commissioning and publishing research that at least in concept partly backed them. The language of the "potential" good "leading to efficiency gains and improved [educational] quality" (Barrera-Osorio *et al.* 2009: 1) that was predicted in policy programs and research, however, resulted in mixed and clearly context-based, case-by-case outcomes. In her introduction to the 2009 publication, Human Development Network Sector director of education Elizabeth King observes that the differences between various types of faith-based voucher programs and public schools are "not necessarily as large as one might think" (E. King 2009: xi).

As King points out, research shows that schools operated by faith-based organizations performed better in terms of student achievement and matriculation rates in two countries, the Bolivarian Republic of Venezuela and Sierra Leone, but not in the Democratic Republic of the Congo. She also notes that in Cameroon, "contrary to popular belief, faith-based schools are not necessarily more targeted toward the poor and are not necessarily cheaper than public schools" (E. King 2009: xii). While case studies covered in the World Bank report are detailed and empirically grounded, King nonetheless carefully notes that "their results are not necessarily of universal application, because context also matters" (2009: xii).

Also in the World Bank volume, Allcott and Ortega (2009) examine Jesuit mission schools targeting disadvantaged youth in Venezuela and suggest that students at such schools perform better on aptitude tests than students at other schools. However, they attribute their findings to relatively recent school decentralization policies rather than to a long history of Jesuit schooling in the region. They challenge the conventional argument that Jesuit schools' religious mission to serve the poor is well geared to addressing matters of inequality. They do so by suggesting that decentralized administrative structures, not religious orientation, correlate positively with students' test performance. Backiny-Yetna and Wodon's (2009) analysis, in the same volume, likewise points to the need to contextualize arguments about the benefits of faith-based schooling for the poor. Their own research, which compares the personal costs to parents (discounting school fees) at government-funded public and government-assisted faith-based schools in Cameroon, suggests that religious schools cost 40 percent more than public schools. As they put it, "data suggest that faith-based schools in Cameroon serve primarily better-off children" (2009: 167).

Approaching the topic from a different angle – that of comparing students' literacy and numeracy skills in faith-based versus government schools in Sierra Leone – Wodon and Ying (2009), also in the World Bank volume, suggest that poor students are better served in faith-based schools than they are in public, non-religious schools. The authors offer convincing contextual arguments for why this might be so: government and faith-based schools both "benefit from essentially the same government subsidies" but whereas public schools experience funding cuts and civil conflict, faith schools more easily link to "sister organizations in other countries" and "benefit from outside funding" (2009: 101). Wodon and Ying's analysis supports a case in favor of the academic benefits of religious schools. In contrast, in an examination of the performance of Islamic (madrasa) secondary schools in rural Bangladesh, Asadullah *et al.* (2009) document lower test scores for madrasa students – a finding the authors contrast to research conducted on madrasas in Indonesia (Beegle and Newhouse, 2005), which found no difference between students attending public madrasas and those attending public secular schools.

Of course, comparing and contrasting so many different systems – public, private, state-supported religious schools, state-supported secular schools, private religious, and private secular schools – and in contexts as diverse as Venezuela, Cameroon, and Bangladesh, render general statements about the benefit versus cost of faith-based versus secular schooling difficult to sustain. Instead, the most consistent observation researchers who published in this World Bank volume appear to make is that there is diversity in how religion and education go hand in hand. Such an observation, whether intentionally or not, keeps open a path for further policy innovation – and policy analysis – including consideration of how, in recent years, faith groups have been involved in policy not directly and solely as providers of aid, but more frequently as moral agents that public agencies can call upon as moral authorities to inspire and to influence governments.

How do religion and education link to economic development? From direct to indirect provisioning

Implicit within the questions about the place of religious education in public life that are at the core of debates about faith-based versus government schools is another concern: how religion and education link to economic development. In the realm of international educational policy, as well as within the larger field of development policy, I argue, enthusiasm for faith-based providers (e.g. of basic education) is waning. Elizabeth King's (2009) tepid introduction to the World Bank voucher study, introduced above, and, indeed, the mixed results reported in the World Bank publication, suggests evidence of a new landscape in which religion, education, and international development policy have been realigned. What we see just on this side of the horizon and gaining ground, I suggest, is a re-rationalization of religion within education policy as it is being crafted within certain old but key locations, including the World Bank, UNESCO, USAID and, increasingly, the OECD. Within these organizations, policy language has moved away from "Education for All" – which was to have been realized by 2015 – and increasingly toward a rationale that cedes responsibility for education to coalitions involving (1) governmental and international agencies, (2) private donors largely including those with industry connections to food and agriculture, biomedical technology, natural resources, and information technology, and (3) faith-based and community organizations that provide a moral rationale for providing education that generally complements and rarely critiques the idea that education stimulates social equity through the creation and growth of businesses.

Put another way, the war on terror that, during the Bush administration through the early 2000s, married faith with foreign policy has given way to a language of charitable giving in the form of public–private partnerships that stress technological literacy along with education that stimulates the growth of businesses. Such change entails a shift in the focus of education policy, from primary and secondary to tertiary schooling, and from education as a form of enlightenment to education as stimulation for the progress of industry. The education–religion–development triad today, in other words, has shifted its focus from basic to higher education, particularly in areas where university research and scientific development align with government policy and business interests. This is not to say that development agencies have entirely abandoned a focus on primary or basic education or that faith-based organizations are no longer direct providers of basic education, but that the thrust of policy discourse is on vocational, technical and higher education. This is particularly true of US and UK development programs that stress skills including adult literacy and health and HIV/AIDS education. But this shift from faith and belief to morals and ethics is also evident elsewhere, including in Fethullah Gülen's efforts to educate a generation of global business leaders equipped with what some regard as a secularized, depoliticized orientation to Islamic morals (Agai 2007), in an emerging Korean development discourse invoking Confucianism as a Korean "spiritual" force that might inspire educational development and business investment in Africa (ADEA Triennale 2011; Kim and Kim 2013), and in Brazilian state discourses of building businesses and education connections regionally through a common culture of Catholicism (Mourier 2013). Today's focus, in other words, is on advancing development multi-sectorally, and collaborating with international partners using a discourse of ethics and morality in preference to a language of faith to proffer aid.

Within this framework, religion is highly subsumed within a moral(izing) discourse, including within a rationale that focuses not primarily on salvation or pastoral care, as did US and UK development policies of recent years (Stambach 2010b; Kwayu 2012), but on developing a new moral outlook that is more ecumenical and wide-reaching. A brief look at recent changes within the USAID OFBCI will illustrate aspects of this argument.

USAID Office of Faith-Based and Community Initiatives

When President George W. Bush opened the branch Office of Faith-Based Initiatives within USAID by executive order on December 12, 2002, USAID used the language of needing to "work to level the playing field so that faith-based and community-based groups could compete for funding on a level playing field with other organizations" (USAID website, 2004). Federal funds were approved to support "start-up costs, operations or expansion of programs" to intermediary organizations that, in turn, would provide sub-awards "to programs that address homelessness, hunger, the needs of at-risk children, transition from welfare to work, and those in need of intensive rehabilitation such as addicts or prisoners" (US Health and Human Services 2002). The USAID OFBCI helped to advertise these Compassion Capital Funds (so named for reasons beyond the scope of this chapter). However, USAID also noted in 2004 that: "USAID has a long history of working with faith-based organizations. Since its inception in 1961, USAID has done extensive work with relief organizations affiliated with religious institutions. Today [in 2004], 25 percent of USAID's partners are faith-based organizations" (USAID website, 2004).

Fast-forward some seven years beyond this 2004 statement to 2011, when the USAID OFBCI was renamed the Center for Faith-Based and Community Initiatives (CFBCI), and observe two key changes in USAID CFBCI's self-representation. The first is that USAID now frames its mission as one that seeks to "increase collaboration among the people and organizations that are trying to address some of the greatest social service needs in our world today" (USAID 2014). Rather than emphasizing direct provision of USAID funds to faith groups and community organizations, as it had in 2002 and 2003, the office is now emphasizing its role as mediator and as a "bridge" between "groups with similar objectives and goals" (USAID 2014). Whether this change reflects a shift in presidential tone setting by which, within the Obama administration, the White House OFBCI became less overtly empowered as an aid provider, or whether the shift arose in response to concern that the Compassion Capital Fund breached the church–state divide, or both, the language of bridge building put forward by the early 2010s both reflected and helped further to facilitate new partnerships among public entities and private donors, including the Gates Foundation (see below), US universities and faith-based non-governmental organizations (NGOs).

Second, by the early 2010s, the USAID CFBCI began to reflect more on its service *within* government than on outreach to faith communities. "Over the last nine years," notes USAID on its History of the Center for Faith-Based and Community Initiatives web page:

> We have learned that educating USAID and Washington personnel and field staff about the role faith-based and community organizations can play in meeting develop-ment objectives is critical, that providing technical assistance for new and potential partners is important for a level playing field, and that communicating regularly with faith-based and community groups about conferences, funding opportunities, and reg-ulations regarding provision of US Government assistance is essential.
>
> (USAID 2014)

Changes within USAID toward this more pragmatic role of providing "technical assistance" and "educating USAID and Washington" (which also euphemistically may refer to informal forms of lobbying within Washington) were marked in part by the appointment of a new director of the CFBCI. Former director of the Church Relations Department at Bread for the World, a non-partisan, US-based Christian NGO, Mark Brinkmoeller moved into the posi-tion of USAID CFBCI director having had experience working with universities. Just prior to joining USAID in 2012, Brinkmoeller had been employed as an external advisor to ONE, a faith-based NGO that, among other projects, organized US university campus events involving popular musicians (e.g. U2 and Bono) to raise funds for charitable agencies. "Within this posi-tion," Brinkmoeller's current homepage reports, "Brinkmoeller developed high-level strategic partnerships within the faith, business and NGO communities to increase the effectiveness and reach of ONE's advocacy efforts" (USAID 2013).

Among these projects was a three-day Midwest summit held in 2011 consisting of presenta-tions, group discussions guided by university representatives seeking to coordinate participants' support for university-led funding proposals, and media events designed to generate pub-lic support for education-related development projects. The summit involved representatives from key US public research universities, the Gates Foundation, USAID (before Brinkmoeller took on the USAID CFBCI directorship), a senior professional staff member of the US Senate on the Committee on Agriculture (which at the time was seeking to pass a particular "farm bill," i.e. Congressional funding to US farmers to offset profit losses) and other private donors connected to the international food and agricultural industries. Gates's particular role at the summit was to inform universities about the Gates Foundation's African commitments and role in partnering with US universities and NGOs – particularly ONE – in advancing African development. Universities' roles were to provide scientific expertise for the proposals and, in serving as host for such events as this summit (other summits were held before and after), to provide a platform for educating the public about the value of spending public tax monies and working with for-profit corporations to support infrastructural development outside the United States. A director for agriculture at the Bill and Melinda Gates Foundation spoke on a panel with a Foods Resource Bank representative and a staff member of the Partnership to Cut Hunger and Poverty in Africa. All three speakers framed their goal as working with ONE to cut hunger and end poverty in Africa. And all collaborated to develop research capacity overseas while simultaneously funding faculty and researchers to generate new knowledge and potentially patentable technologies. In exchange, universities would gain research fund-ing, access to overseas locations for university students' internships as well as new sources of 'supply' for overseas students enrolling in US universities, and potential access to new patent-able technologies discovered or created through the partnerships. To render this rather large and seemingly nebulous project somewhat concrete for an otherwise welfare-wary American public, the summit included ONE advocacy workshops for public university students, remarks by Brinkmoeller representing ONE, a ONE training session for invited students on how to "conduct a U2 concert," and a U2 fundraising concert that drew thousands to the university football stadium for a Sunday evening Bono concert.[4]

From events such as this, Brinkmoeller carried ONE's language of providing relief for the poor into his work with USAID, and he adopted a language of "solidarity" and of the need to create "broad-based community coalitions" in his biographical self-presentation (USAID 2013). Regarding his international work, USAID reports that Brinkmoeller spent more than a dozen years with Catholic agencies:

> mobilizing diverse constituencies around a broad array of domestic and international issues. Core parts of this work included . . . establishing advocacy and education coalitions, direct lobbying of local, state and federal officials and a solidarity development project in Upper East Region of Ghana. He oversaw the building, operations, and programs of a new Catholic Multicultural Center in Madison, Wisconsin, that serves people from the US, Latin America, [and] Africa as well as Southeast Asia.
>
> (USAID 2013)

USAID's pro-poor language of using aid for development, highlighted in Brinkmoeller's work, may carry overtones of liberation theology, which in turn arguably informed the more liberal ideas of Vatican II. But only to a point. Although Brinkmoeller quotes Pope John XXIII in laying out an element of state relations that, to Brinkmoeller, represents the thinking of our time (USAID 2013), Brinkmoeller's language of solidarity and relief within the USAID CFBCI is necessarily limited by the agency's job of building partnerships with and through businesses. Consider, for instance, the concatenation of players and interests that are represented in the "News and Events" columns of recent USAID CFBCI newsletters. The newsletter content and list of organizations mirror those involved in the summit described above, including Bread for the World, the Gates Foundation, and Washington personnel and field staff.

For instance, in the article "Proposed Food Aid Reforms Will Feed 2–4 Million More People" (May 2, 2013), USAID reports that Bread for the World, along with Catholic Relief Services, American Jewish World Service, the Church World Service, and Maryknoll each supported USAID's major new food aid reforms. International food aid programs send US farmers' (government-funded, "farm aid") surplus overseas, thus in effect hiding development funding behind the guise of aid and calling on charitable groups to deliver it. In its January 31, 2013, newsletter, USAID CFBCI announced that it had joined together with the Bill and Melinda Gates Foundation as well as with the Norwegian Agency for Development Cooperation (NORAD), the UK Department for International Development (DFID), and Grand Challenges Canada to launch a Saving Lives at Birth new call for proposals that integrate "the latest scientific, technological, behavior change, and information communication advances into radical solutions for impact on maternal and newborn health." The link to Saving Lives at Birth offers a list of innovators "including non-profits, faith-based organizations, universities, and private enterprises" (USAID 2011). A click on any one of the three yearly lists reveals names of universities (particularly in the US and UK) and of university spin-off companies.

In my estimation, this turn toward technical assistance and solidarity development suggests a shift toward a less direct but no less involved approach to linking government funding with religious groups and educational institutions. Although my example here is US-focused, such linking also occurs within higher education institutions in Europe, Latin America, Africa, the Middle East and parts of Asia. UK DFID–ESRC research programs, for instance, stress the value of three-way partnership among businesses, researchers, and community and faith groups to prioritize research that enhances economic growth (ESRC n.d.). The Brazilian state partners with international universities, businesses and religious organizations to attract a Latin American population to its campuses (Tessler 2011). Private philanthropists in India (Bornstein 2012), Egypt (Starrett 1998) and Indonesia (Azra *et al.* 2007) also use a moralizing language to conjoin the interests of the business, religious and education sectors. A main difference regarding each of these countries today, compared with the early 2000s, is that religion comes into play in high-level partnerships, not simply as the direct provider of education to the world's poor, but as a moral force that cultivates public support for development work, which is itself now recast as helping the poor by providing communities with technical and vocational training to promote local and investors' business.

To say that religion has been relegated to an assisting rather than front-seat role in delivering education is not to say that faith groups' direct provisioning has ended. Hands-on work is still a part of faith-based groups' education-related development work; otherwise such groups would lose their role and purpose as charitable or welfare organizations. But the role of universities targeted by programs such as the 2011 Midwest summit is to provide meeting places, research capacity and data to support and provide a rationale for these new forms of engagement among government, private business and religion in return for financial support in an era of calls for greater efficiency of public spending on public education. Within such programs, religious groups are seen, not so much as direct providers, but as moral agents that public institutions call upon as a new resource base and for influencing governments and business. Under these new circumstances, corporate philanthropy is sometimes imbued with a positive moral ethos – as a sort of "business to the rescue" model that sees good work as evidence of faith and calling. Such may be the case regarding funds for research secured through, for instance, USAID programs that themselves are partly funded by the Gates Foundation or similar bodies. Acting charitably to help the poor (and eschewing corporate taxes as a means of doing), Gates itself might request some degree of price offset from, for instance, Pfizer to provide drugs at low cost that Gates then administers in its own global health campaign. If a university demonstrates partnership with such companies in the form of, for example, using company-patented equipment or corporate-owned laboratory techniques to test health campaign effects in exchange for company access to research results, that university may in turn qualify to bid on USAID funds that are themselves partly matched by, in this scenario, the Gates Foundation. In this way, that is, by offsetting restricted government funds with corporate gifts in exchange for research, and coupled with corporate philanthropy (by for example Gates), public funding for universities is cut, with some sort of market-oriented justification.

To sum up, I see this new mobilization of religion for education and development, particularly in the United States, as happening generally in at least three ways. One, it happens through generating popular support for the practices of NGOs such as ONE that rally support for "faith-inspired" but not direct-faith aid to the poor and hungry worldwide. As we saw in the example presented above, ONE and other faith NGO events have quietly created popular support for such programs as tax relief for US farmers ("farm aid"), which arguably help multinational agro-businesses but hurt independent, small-scale farmers. Two, this new mobilization of religion for education and development calls on the sentiments of private philanthropists who have industry connections to seed their own charitable monies in locations where they calculate private investment might seed-fund future markets. And, three, today's mobilization of religion for education and development is used to shore up what is also presented in public policies as the need for governments to down-size universities and public education.

Religion, in this new scenario, enters at the level of business relations that are highly moralized through shared if secularized religious sentiments of "doing good by doing well" (a cliché in American discourse). It also comes in through the very institutionalized structures of the Offices of Faith-Based and Community Initiatives that seek to "reach out" (as the language of today's corporate engagement goes) to groups and persons who have a mission – personal or otherwise – to invest in education. In brief, these three ways of mobilizing religion for education – as popular support, as moral rationale and as new funding source for education – constitute an emerging incarnation of what has long been the close interconnection of religion, education and development.

What other changes are emerging? Contractualism, ethics and education

If we are to understand religion, education and development more comprehensively, one final piece of the landscape requires sketching. This piece is related to how developmentalist discourses are currently broadening beyond seeing religion as either cause of or solution to poverty toward seeing religion as one of many elements within a multi-polar and multilateral world. Within this world, the relationships between religion and education are being reshaped and realigned in a manner that emphasizes a common ground, again not around faith and belief but around ethics and dialogue, where "dialogue" mainly refers to virtual networks and not necessarily to productive or innovative debate. Instead of framing religion as a matter of fighting for what is right and just, and instead of portraying education as a matter of morally and correctly inculcating young children who symbolize the next generation, contemporary development policies emphasize religion as ethics, and education as space for dialogue among researchers at different institutions (and, I warrant, the administratively choreographed summit above does not well illustrate US universities as sites of dialogue). Certainly, religious actors remain key players in delivering international development programs in education, but religion is increasingly framed as an ethical disposition rather than faith-based option or theological stance. Reasons for this turn, I suggest, have to do *not* with the failure of faith-based education programs in the scientific sense. After all, faith-based policies were neither systematically tested nor replicable, as the World Bank report amply illustrates. Instead, the current version of the "re-secularization of education" reflects a new alignment of key foreign policies with emerging markets and world powers. Specifically, as I see it, the re-secularization of education as space for dialogue reflects new Chinese and American bilateral relationships and these countries' collaboration within international agencies, although again I emphasize that my examples are largely from a US policy and western historical perspective. I will mention as examples higher education and social media programs within UNESCO.

Neo-Confucianist ideas advanced through contemporary Chinese state discourses seem to portray wisdom and authority as development motivators. Although more research is needed, work suggests that Chinese development policy, particularly in Africa, places a premium on contractual relationships and on the importance of respecting centralized authority (Lihua and Song 2011; K. King 2013). Whether such an appeal resonates favorably with Africanist cultural values underpinned by expressions of religion – particularly Islam and Christianity – remains to be seen. For now, ethically infused Chinese development policy in Africa seems to represent a growing bilateral developmentalist philosophy between the government of China and its aid and investment recipients. The nature of these ethics seems to be one of respect for authority and for principled relationships, not necessarily of open listening or the entertainment of diverse views. Thus the cultural bases of these relationships and principles are historically different from those at least theoretically embraced by the US or UK.

Differences in approaches between ethically infused and faith-based policies in Africa appear particularly evident in two UNESCO programs: higher education and ICT/social media. Within the UNESCO Section for Higher Education, Chinese Funds in Trust (CFIT) are used to foster "mutual understanding between China and African countries and the cultivation of top-level talents who can work effectively across borders" (presentation made by an unidentified UNESCO Education Program intern to visiting university delegates, 20 March 2014). Within UNESCO's ICT in Education program, Chinese Funds in Trust also support not necessarily education for all but education for top talent. CFIT fund ICT programs for teachers and adult students enrolled in Confucius Institutes located at selective African universities. According to a presentation made by UNESCO ICT representative Fenghun Miao (also 20 March 2014, to the same visiting delegates):

> Thanks to the newly established Chinese Funds in Trust, UNESCO is building the institutional capacity of teacher colleges in eight African countries. . . . The Chinese Funds in Trust Project to Enhance Teacher Education Institutes in Sub-Saharan Africa [will] increase the supply of qualified teachers particularly through open and distance training programmes, support teachers' continuous professional development via blended learning modalities [and] . . . reinforce networks of teacher education institutions for knowledge sharing.
>
> (Ibid.)

Here "knowledge sharing" constitutes a form of technology-mediated dialogue, albeit not necessarily one amenable to unmonitored or open debate.

The main theme of both the higher education and ICT/social media presentations was Chinese Funds for Development, but a trace of faith-based and corporate philanthropy provided by the west remained. Included within the presentation was reference to a US–UK university partnership involving ICT companies and a religious group, Catholic Relief Services in Niger: "Project AB – Mobiles 4 Literacy" uses "mobiles for basic literacy as a learning tool in Hausa and Zarma, with literacy classes targeting over 7,000 adults in 140 villages." However, the UNESCO presentation focused more on China's new role within UNESCO than on universities' and the faith group's partnership, suggesting that the direction within the ICT/social media program has moved or is moving away from the language of public–private partnerships and multilateral aid and relief that was typical of mid- to late-twentieth-century models of development to a new orientation that presents itself as neither charitable nor paternalistic but business-like and contractual.

As "faith-based policy" has shifted toward the kinds of program ONE represents in western settings, a Chinese state language of morality and of wisdom – "like Confucius" – arguably carries the potential for a growing partnership between western and Chinese governments, particularly because all of them (at least for the moment) operate uncritically within and according to a logic of market capitalism. Shared worldviews and articulation of goals and motivations associated with business opportunities now appear to be a part of US–China interactions. Today, western and Chinese governments seem more likely to work together through an idiom of respect and ethics, not religion. Certainly, different views of ethics are in play, particularly around copyright and intellectual property. However "western" and "eastern" countries' shared association of education with investment provides a common ground for mutual cooperation in funding education programs internationally.

Such new and complex entanglements not only of religious groups, educational institutions and development agencies but of the directionality of aid (from north to south, east to west, polarity to polarity) raise interesting new questions for researchers. Following on from the early 2000s, when religious groups made claims for greater access to government resources, to more recent years, when agencies appear to present religious groups more quietly as facilitators, researchers today have the opportunity to ask anew: What are the religious roots and sources of education and development? How is religion re-rationalized in ways that differ from the now classic models of Marx and Weber by which religion was seen, respectively, as false consciousness masking the bourgeois state (Marx) or as, relatedly, an idiom through which capital accumulation is rationalized (Weber)? To what extent does religion serve as an ancillary issue within education and development? And to what extent does it reflect a genuine concern for advancing and helping communities? Given the above discussion, it would seem that faith-based programs align domestic philosophies with international development policies, and that the turn from religion in recent years freshly re-secularizes religion without erasing a history of religion from development. After all, secularization is an inflection of religious sentiment; and religious sentiments are often secularized.

Conclusion

What, we might conclude, has been the legacy of the early-twentieth-century "turn to religion" on the global education and development program? Though it is difficult to summarize, one influence seems clear: discussion of religion is now fully permissible in policy circles and development discourses. The era of high modernization, in which religion was seen as an evolutionary vestige and as becoming obsolete, has given way to developmentalist policies that discuss religion explicitly. The question today is not whether but how religion is relevant to education policy.

This chapter, then, has explored past relationships among religion, education and development but with a focus on the present, and it has argued that yesterday's "turn to religion" as exemplified in the 1998 creation of the WFDD and in the 2002 creation of the USAID OFBCI is now beginning to shift toward a more quiet mobilization of faith groups for development. As many have illustrated, education was seen by western-educated scholars, state leaders and international agency representatives, through at least the 1980s, as a way to modernize and secularize underdeveloped communities and as a means, through at least the 2010s, to provide direct education services to the poor. However, today's mobilization of faith groups is beginning to shift from direct engagement to "technical assistance," where the latter refers to building relationships between and among private donors, with university researchers and with faith-based and community groups.

Notes

1 Acknowledgements: My thanks to the anonymous reviewers, to Emma Tomalin, and to pre-doctoral students in my Comparative and International Education course for insights on earlier versions of this chapter.
2 I develop this point and provide examples in Stambach (2010a).
3 Although see Andreescu's (2011) argument that the model dominates because it is intrinsically more equitable; and it should be recognized that the US *withholds* funds from UNESCO as a political measure.
4 For a fuller discussion of public–private partnerships in the US see Stambach (2014).

References

ADEA Triennale (2011) *Education and Training in Africa*, http://www.adeanet.org/triennale/press/macceuil.html.

Agai, Bekim (2007) 'Islam and Education in Secular Turkey: State Policies and the Emergence of the Fethullah Gulen Group', in R. W. Hefner and M. Q. Zaman (eds), *Schooling Islam: The Culture and Politics of Modern Muslim Education*, Princeton, NJ: Princeton University Press, pp. 149–71.

Allcott, Hunt and Ortega, Daniel E. (2009) 'The Performance of Decentralized School Systems: Evidence from Fe Y Alegria in Republica Bolivariana de Venezuela', in Felipe Barrera-Osorio, Harry Anthony Patrinos and Quentin Wodon (eds), *Emerging Evidence on Vouchers and Faith-Based Providers in Education: Case Studies from Africa, Latin America, and Asia*, Washington, DC: World Bank, pp. 81–98.

Andreescu, Liviu (2011) 'Education for a Secularist Citizenship', *Comparative Education Review*, 55 (1), 111–42.

Asadullah, Mohammad Niaz, Chaudhury, Nazmul and Dar, Amit (2009) 'Assessing the Performance of Madrasas in Rural Bangladesh', in Felipe Barrera-Osorio, Harry Anthony Patrinos and Quentin Wodon (eds), *Emerging Evidence on Vouchers and Faith-Based Providers in Education: Case Studies from Africa, Latin America, and Asia*, Washington, DC: World Bank, pp. 137–48.

Azra, A., Afrianty, D. and Hefner, R. W. (2007) 'Pesantren and Madrasa: Muslim Schools and National Ideals in Indonesia', in R. W. Hefner and M. Q. Zaman (eds), *Schooling Islam: The Culture and Politics of Modern Muslim Education*, Princeton, NJ: Princeton University Press, pp. 172–98.

Backiny-Yetna, Prospere and Wodon, Quentin (2009) 'Comparing the Private Cost of Education at Public, Private, and Faith-Based Schools in Cameroon', in Felipe Barrera-Osorio, Harry Anthony Patrinos and Quentin Wodon (eds), *Emerging Evidence on Vouchers and Faith-Based Providers in Education: Case Studies from Africa, Latin America, and Asia*, Washington, DC: World Bank, pp. 165–78.

Baptist Joint Committee for Religious Liberty (n.d.), http://www.bjcpa.org/Pages/Resources/RFTC%20PDF/April16.pdf (accessed 20 October 2003).

Barrera-Osorio, Felipe, Patrinos, Harry Anthony and Wodon, Quentin (2009) 'Public–Private Partnerships in Education: An Overview', in Felipe Barrera-Osorio, Harry Anthony Patrinos and Quentin Wodon (eds), *Emerging Evidence on Vouchers and Faith-Based Providers in Education: Case Studies from Africa, Latin America, and Asia*, Washington, DC: World Bank, pp. 1–15.

Beegle, Kathleen and Newhouse, David (2005) *The Effect of School Type on Academic Achievement: Evidence from Indonesia*, Policy Research Working Paper Series 3604, Washington, DC: World Bank.

Bornstein, Erica (2012) *Disquieting Gifts: Humanitarianism in New Delhi*, Stanford, CA: Stanford University Press.

ESRC (n.d.) http://www.esrc.ac.uk/funding-and-guidance/funding-opportunities/international-funding/esrc-dfid/guidance/poverty-alleviation-guidance.aspx, under 'Step 1, Read the Call Specification' (accessed 6 July 2014).

Kim, Ki-Seok and Kim, Sung S. (2013) 'A Historical Comparison of Intellectual Renaissance in the East and West', *Comparative Education*, 49 (1), 16–27.

King, E. (2009) 'Preface', in Felipe Barrera-Osorio, Harry Anthony Patrinos and Quentin Wodon (eds), *Emerging Evidence on Vouchers and Faith-Based Providers in Education: Case Studies from Africa, Latin America, and Asia*, Washington, DC: World Bank, pp. xi–xii.

King, K. (2013) *China's Aid and Soft Power in Africa: The Case of Education and Training*, Woodbridge: James Currey.

Kwayu, A. C. (2012) 'Faith Groups in British International Development Policies from 1992 to 2011', doctoral thesis, University of Nottingham, Department of Politics and International Relations.

Lihua, X. and Song, Z. (2011) 'Popularizing Chinese in Africa: Status Quo, Problems, and Solutions', *West Asia and Africa*, 3, 008.

Mourier, E. (2013) 'Religion as a Substitute for the State: Faith-Based Social Action in Twenty-First Century Brazil', *International Development Policy*, 4, 79–94.

Stambach, A. (2010a) 'Education, Religion, and Anthropology in Africa', *Annual Review of Anthropology*, 39, 361–79, http://www.annualreviews.org/doi/abs/10.1146/annurev.anthro.012809.105002.

Stambach, A. (2010b) *Faith in Schools: Religion, Education, and American Evangelicals in East Africa*, Stanford, CA: Stanford University Press.

Stambach, A. (2014) *Confucius and Crisis in American Universities: Culture, Capital and Diplomacy in U.S. Public Higher Education*, New York: Routledge.

Starrett, G. (1998) *Putting Islam to Work: Education, Politics and Religious Transformation*, Berkeley: University of California Press.

Tessler, L. R. (2011) 'The Pursuit of Equity in Brazilian Higher Education', *International Higher Education*, 63 (Spring), 23–5.

UNESCO (n.d.) 'Dialogue', http://portal.unesco.org/culture/en/ev.php-URL_ID=35270&URL_DO=DO_TOPIC&URL_SECTION=201.html (accessed 3 July 2014).

United Nations (n.d.) 'World Day for Cultural Diversity for Dialogue and Development', http://www.un.org/en/events/culturaldiversityday/background.shtml (accessed 3 July 2014).

USAID (2011) 'Saving Lives At Birth: A Grand Challenge for Development', http://savinglivesatbirth.net (accessed 3 July 2014).

USAID (2013) 'Who We Are: J. Mark Brinkmoeller', http://www.usaid.gov/who-we-are/organization/j-mark-brinkmoeller-0 (accessed 3 July 2014).

USAID (2014) 'Partnership Opportunities', http://www.usaid.gov/work-usaid/partnership-opportunities/faith-based-community-organizations/history (accessed 3 July 2014).

US Government (n.d.a) 'White House Office of Faith-Based and Community Initiatives', http://www.whitehouse.gov/government/fbci/index.html (accessed 20 October 2003).

US Government (n.d.b) 'Department of Health and Human Services', http://www.acf.hhs.gov/programs/region10/priorities/faith/background.html (accessed 20 October 2003).

US Government (n.d.c) 'White House Office of Faith-Based and Community Initiatives', http://www.whitehouse.gov/news/releases/2001/11/20011108-2.html (accessed 20 October 2003).

US Health and Human Services (2002) 'HHS Announces Availability of Funds to Assist Faith-Based and Community Organizations', News Release, 4 June (pdf available in Stambach's files).

Wodon, Quentin and Ying, Yvonne (2009) 'Literacy and Numeracy in Faith-Based and Government Schools in Sierra Leone', in Felipe Barrera-Osorio, Harry Anthony Patrinos and Quentin Wodon (eds), *Emerging Evidence on Vouchers and Faith-Based Providers in Education: Case Studies from Africa, Latin America, and Asia*, Washington, DC: World Bank, pp. 99–118.

INDEX

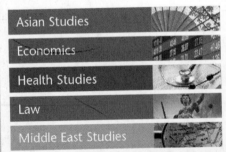